COVID-19

THE VIRUS THAT CHANGED AMERICA AND THE WORLD

from the author of **TREASON & BETRAYAL**

Kenneth Foard McCallion

ALSO BY KENNETH FOARD MCCALLION

Treason & Betrayal: The Rise and Fall of Individual - 1

The Essential Guide to Donald Trump

Shoreham and the Rise and Fall of the Nuclear Power Industry

COVID-19

THE VIRUS THAT CHANGED AMERICA AND THE WORLD

Bryant Park Press
An imprint of HHI Media, Inc.

from the author of **TREASON & BETRAYAL**

Kenneth Foard McCallion

Bryant Park Press
An imprint of HHI Media, Inc.

Copyright © 2020 by Kenneth Foard McCallion

Published by Bryant Park Press

All rights reserved, including the right to reproduce this book or portions thereof in any form whatsoever. For information about permisions, email permissions@hhimedia.net or submit request by facsimile to +1 (203) 724-0820.

Book Design by Christopher Klaich

Jacket Design by Danielle Allyssa

Jacket Photography from Adobe Stock
© vlad_g photo ID #27812917

Manufactured in the United States of America

ISBN: 978-0-9979292-8-7

TO THE ESSENTIAL WORKERS

This book is dedicated to Vepuka E. Kauari, RN, Katherine Kohari, MD, Ralph Cipriani, MD and all the other essential workers, including but not limited to doctors, physician's assistants, nurses, certified nursing assistants, pharmacists, home health care workers, and emergency medical technicians in the U.S. and around the globe who play critical roles and perform essential functions in the continuing battle against COVID-19. They do so each day at great risk to their own health and their own lives.

It is also for the other essential workers who make it possible for our society to continue to function during this time of crisis, providing us with the food and other necessities of life. These include all those who are part of the long food chain, from the farms to the grocery shelves to the checkout counters.

It is also for the mail carriers and other postal employees, UPS, FedEx and other delivery service providers, as well as the bus and truck drivers, railroad and subway workers and other personnel who keep America and the world moving.

It is for the domestic workers and janitorial service workers who help us maintain the high levels of hygiene and cleanliness that is more important than ever in this age of COVID.

It is for the rest of our fellow Americans and world citizens who perform essential functions so that the rest of us can continue to live, survive, and hopefully thrive.

All I can say is "thank you," and hope that this book will help America and the world more fully appreciate the value of your services, and to give you the honor and respect you so richly deserve.

ACKNOWLEDGMENTS

My heartfelt thanks to:
Damara L. Carousis, Peter Borisow, Christopher Klaich,
Aaron Jerome, Tom Holman, James Burchetta,
Emily Moriarty, Sharon Moriarty, Danielle Brown
and all the other researchers, fact checkers,
editors and friends who helped make this book possible.

COVID-19 TIMELINE

2004

A National Intelligence Council Report warns: "Some experts believe it is only a matter of time before a new pandemic appears, such as the 1918-1919 influenza virus that killed an estimated 20 million worldwide." It foresees that a pandemic would "put a halt to global travel and trade during an extended period, prompting governments to expend enormous resources on overwhelmed health sectors."

2017

A Pentagon Plan circulated to Trump administration officials identifies a "Novel Influenza Disease" as "National Threat #1. The plan specifically references coronavirus as a threat, saying that "coronavirus infections [are] common around the world," and that an "outbreak in a single community can quickly evolve into a multinational health crisis that causes millions to suffer, as well as spark major disruption to every facet of society." It anticipates a scarcity of medical equipment needed to combat the effects of the disease, including ventilators and personal protective equipment, such as face masks and gloves.

May 2018

The White House's National Security Council Directorate for Global Health Security and Biodefense is disbanded by Trump's NSA Director John Bolton. This global health unit of the National Security Council, which had been established in 2015 following the Ebola pandemic, was designed to mobilize the federal government's resources to prepare for the next pandemic. As a result, when the COVID-19 crisis arrives, there was no clear White House structure or plan in place to oversee this country's coronavirus response. Several critical weeks are squandered as the Trump White House breaks the cardinal rule in a public health security crisis, which is that speed is essential.

2019

January

The **Office of the Director of National Intelligence (DNI) Worldwide Threat Assessment** warns, "[t]he United States will remain vulnerable to the next flu pandemic or large-scale outbreak of a contagious disease that could lead to massive rates of death and disability, severely affect the world economy, strain international resources, and increase calls on the United States for support." Not only does the Trump administration ignore this warning, but it also holds up the release of the 2020 report in February 2020, which repeats the same dire warning.

September

The **U.S. Agency for International Development's PREDICT Program**, which was strongly backed by both the Bush and Obama administrations, is dismantled by the Trump White House. This program was an essential piece in an emerging global network for infectious-disease surveillance, giving scientists in the U.S. a head start in understanding pathogens that could eventually reach U.S. shores. If PREDICT's field teams had been active and detected the new coronavirus early, American scientists would have been able to begin work on tests, treatments, and cures much earlier. When it was in operation, PREDICT succeeded in collecting more than 100,000 samples and found nearly 1,000 new viruses, including a new Ebola virus.

October

The **Center for Strategic and International Studies** in Washington, D.C. runs a pandemic simulation involving a coronavirus virtually identical to the one that hit the U.S. a couple of months later. The purpose of the exercise was to advise U.S. Cabinet officials and other leaders on how to plan for a pandemic before it struck the country. This simulation predicts around a 3% mortality rate, a virus transmissible before symptoms showed, and highly contagious. One of the exercise's most important insights is that early and preventative actions are critical.

Ocotober (cont'd)

The **U.S. Dept. of Health and Human Services' (HHS's) "Crimson Contagion" Report** is based on a simulating of an influenza epidemic that spread to the U.S., eventually infecting 110 million Americans, leading to 7.7 million hospitalizations and 586,000 dead. According to this scenario, the hypothetical outbreak began in China and was quickly spread around the world by air travelers. Due to the delay and lack of preparation by the federal government regarding this pandemic, 110 million Americans are estimated to have become infected, leading to 7.7 million hospitalized and 586,000 dead. This HHS Report graphically details how underfunded, underprepared, and inept the federal government would be if confronted with a real life-and-death struggle with a virus for which no treatment existed.

November

The **National Center for Medical Intelligence (NCMI)**, which is part of the Defense Intelligence Agency (DIA), warns in an intelligence report that the spreading coronavirus disease in Wuhan could become a "cataclysmic event" and that the initial stages of a pandemic were already taking place. The Joint Chiefs of Staff at the Pentagon, the National Security Council, and the White House are briefed on these warnings. This report by U.S. intelligence concludes the Chinese leadership knew the epidemic was already widespread as of late November 2019, and that China was withholding crucial information about the true extent and danger of the crisis.

SARS-CoV-2 (also known as "2019 Novel Coronavirus"), which is the virus causing the disease "COVID-19," is first identified as spreading in Wuhan and the rest of the Hubei province in China.

December 31

The **U.S. Centers for Disease Control and Prevention (CDC)** first becomes aware of the virus outbreak in China and begins tracking it.

2020

January
Luciana Borio, the Director of the FDA's Office of Counterterrorism and Emerging Threats, who also had worked on President Trump's National Security Council, publicly urges the Trump White House to take immediate action to either avoid an American coronavirus epidemic or to prepare and mobilize the resources to fight it effectively. Borio's op-ed piece in The *Wall Street Journal* on January 28, 2020 outlines the simple steps that should be taken to ensure that the U.S. was ready for widespread testing and beefed up hospital preparedness.

January 3
CDC Director Robert Redfield is notified by a counterpart in China that a "mysterious respiratory illness was spreading in Wuhan [China]." Redfield notifies HHS Secretary Alex Azar shortly thereafter, who shared his report with the National Security Council (NSC).

The warnings about the virus are included in President Trump's President's Daily Brief (PDB) starting in early January. These PDBs traced the spread of the virus and the Chinese government's suppression of information about the transmissibility and lethality of the disease. They also raised alarms about the prospect of dire political and economic consequences for the U.S. Trump also received oral summaries of them two or three times per week.

Nevertheless, during the same time frame that he is receiving these dire warnings, Trump regularly downplays the coronavirus threat, minimizing the potential impact of the pandemic on the U.S. and comparing it to the common flu. No effort is made during this time frame to mobilize a coordinated federal response or to obtain the supplies and equipment that would be necessary for an effective response to the pandemic.

January 18
Trump receives his first substantial briefing about the coronavirus threat while he is at Mar-a-Lago, when he receives a call from HHS Secretary Azar. In this phone call, Trump tells Azar that he (Azar) is being an "alarmist."

January 21
The first recorded U.S. case of the new virus is an American citizen traveling from Wuhan, China to his home in Washington state.

January 22
Trump receives his first public question from a reporter regarding whether he was concerned about the coronavirus. Trump responds: "No, not at all. And we have it totally under control. It's one person coming in from China ... It's going to be just fine."

January 24
President Trump, in a tweet, praises China for its coronavirus efforts.

January 29
White House trade adviser Peter Navarro writes a memo saying that the coronavirus could cause as many as 500,000 deaths and trillions in economic damage. According to the *Washington Post*, Trump is informed about the contents of the Navarro memo.

January 31
The Trump administration declares a public health emergency and imposes a mandatory 14-day quarantine for any U.S. citizens who had visited Hubei Province in China within the preceding two weeks. However, 300,000 people already had traveled to the U.S. from China during the month prior to the ban.[1] Also, more than 40,000 people traveled from China to the U.S. after the January 31 partial ban, and around 430,000 total between December 31, 2019 and April 4.[2]

February 7
Trump says: "Nothing is easy, but [Chinese President Xi Jinping] ... will be successful, especially as the weather starts to warm & the virus hopefully becomes weaker, and then gone."

February 10
Trump continues to reassure the American public: "I think the virus is going to be — it's going to be fine." On the same day at a political rally in New Hampshire, Trump declared that "by April, you know, in theory, when it gets warmer, it miraculously goes away."

February 19
Trump announces: "I think it's going to work out fine. I think when we get into April, in the warmer weather, that has a very negative effect on that and that type of a virus. So let's see what happens, but I think it's going to work out fine."

February 24
Trump tweets: "The Coronavirus is very much under control in the USA. … Stock Market starting to look very good to me!" Trump also tweets: "CDC and [W.H.O.] have been working hard and very smart."[3]

February 25
Dr. Nancy Messonnier, Director of the CDC's National Center for Immunization and Respiratory Diseases, delivers a briefing warning that "disruption to everyday life might be severe." The New York Times reports that President Trump was "furious," and HHS Secretary Azar downplays her comments in a news conference later that day. Dr. Messonnier is never allowed to make another public statement about the pandemic.

February 28
Trump remains upbeat: "Only a very small number in U.S., & China numbers look to be going down. All countries working well together!" "I think it's really going well… "It's going to disappear. One day, it's like a miracle, it will disappear." Trump also lashes out at Democrats who question his handling of the virus threat, calling their criticism a "hoax" intended to undermine his leadership.

March 10
Trump reassures the country that "we're prepared, and we're doing a great job with it. And it will go away. Just stay calm. It will go away."

March 11
Trump gives an Oval Office address on the evening of March 11, announcing restrictions on travel from Europe, stating: "[For] the vast majority of Americans, the risk is very very low." Trump continues to resist calls for social distancing, school closures and any other steps that would imperil the economy.

March 12
In an email, Dr. James V. Lawler, an infectious disease specialist, tells Tom Bossart, Trump's former Homeland Security adviser, "We are making every misstep leaders initially made in table-tops [exercises] at the outset of pandemic planning in 2006… We have thrown 15 years of institutional learning out the window and are making decisions based on intuition."

March 12
The Trump administration postpones the Director of National Intelligence's (DNI's) annual US World-Wide Threat Assessment, warning the U.S. remains unprepared for a global pandemic.[4]

March 13
Trump declares a national emergency, but does not require or even recommend that American citizens engage in social distancing, wear masks or take any other steps to slow down the spread of the virus.

Despite Trump's attempts to downplay the crisis, he is made aware that an HHS report "not for public distribution" states that the COVID-19 "pandemic will last 18 months or longer and could include multiple waves of illness." The report also found that the "supply chain and transportation impacts" would "likely result in significant shortages."[5]

March 16
In a conference call with Michigan Governor Gretchen Whitmer and other governors, Trump essentially tells the governors that they are largely on their own in stocking up on equipment such as respirators and ventilators.

Los Angeles Mayor Eric Garcetti orders all bars, movie theaters, gyms and fitness centers closed, and directs all restaurants to only do take-out and delivery.

March 17
San Francisco, Santa Clara, Santa Cruz and the other Bay Area counties (combined population of 7 million) are placed under a mandatory "shelter in place" order.

March 19
Trump responds to criticism that his administration was not prepared for the crisis, saying: "I would view it as something that just surprised the whole world," adding later that it was "uncharted territory" and "Nobody knew there would be a pandemic or epidemic of this proportion." "So there's never been anything like this in history. There's never been," he said. "And nobody's ever seen anything like this."

March 20
Illinois and New York join California in ordering all residents to stay in their homes unless they have good reason to go out, restricting the movement of more than 70 million Americans.

The *Washington Post* reports that U.S. intelligence agencies were issuing classified warnings in January and February about the global danger posed by the coronavirus while President Trump played down the threat and failed to take action.[6]

New York Governor Andrew Cuomo, Illinois Governor J.B. Pritzker, and Los Angeles Mayor Eric Garcetti issue stay-at-home orders.

March 21
Trump tweets promote potential coronavirus treatments he likes, such as Hydroxychloroqine, which is later found to be of questionable efficacy and potentially dangerous.

March 24
Trump raises the possibility of undoing the virus restrictions by Easter Sunday, April 12th: "I would love to have the country opened up and just raring to go by Easter."

March 25
Senate Republicans and Democrats strike a deal on the passage of a huge $2.2 trillion CARES economic rescue package that provides relief aid to businesses, workers and health care systems. The bill provides for stimulus payments of $1200 to most adults, $600 a week in unemployment benefits (approximately $2400 per month) on top of state unemployment benefits, and $500 billion for businesses and municipalities.

April 7
President Trump threatens to withhold funding from the W.H.O.[7]

April 12
Dr. Anthony Fauci tells CNN's Jake Tapper that calls to implement social distancing measures "faced a lot of pushback" early in the U.S. coronavirus crisis, and that if "you started mitigation earlier, you could have saved lives."

April 14
The *Associated Press* reports Dr. Fauci as saying that "the U.S. does not yet have the critical testing and tracing procedures needed to begin reopening the nation's economy…"

April 15
A large scale rally called "Operation Gridlock" takes place in Lansing, Michigan to protest Governor Whitmer's stay-at-home orders.

April 16
The White House announces guidelines requiring that a state's number of cases should be declining for a period of 14 days, with a strong testing capability in place, before a state could start re-opening. Nevertheless, the Trump administration supports the decision of several Red State governors to open up their states even while their number of cases and deaths are still rising.

April 17
At a White House press conference, Trump rejects criticisms of the federal response efforts as "false and misleading" and reiterates his position that "the governors are responsible for testing." Earlier in the day, in a telephone call between Mr. Pence and Senate Democrats, Senator Angus King of Maine called the lack of national testing a "dereliction of duty."

In a series of all-caps tweets that started two minutes after a Fox News report on the protesters, the president declares, "LIBERATE MICHIGAN!" and "LIBERATE MINNESOTA!" — two states whose Democratic governors have imposed strict social distancing restrictions.

April 18
FDA investigators announce that the CDC's sloppy laboratory practices caused contamination that rendered the nation's first coronavirus tests ineffective.[8]

April 20
Georgia Governor Kemp announces that many businesses could reopen on April 24, including gyms, hair salons, bowling alleys and tattoo parlors, even though the number of cases and deaths is still rising in that state.

April 28
The US passes one million confirmed cases of the virus, according to Johns Hopkins.

May
By May 2020, the coronavirus crisis had already mutated into the worst economic crisis the country has faced since the Great Depression of the 1930s. More than 40 million people – one in four American workers - had filed for unemployment benefits since the coronavirus pandemic forced most of the U.S. economy to shut down in March.

May 1
Indiana Governor Eric Holcomb announces the end of the stay-at-home orders, even though Indiana is experiencing large case increases.

May 25
George Floyd - an unarmed, handcuffed Black man - is killed by a white police officer in Minneapolis after the officer refuses to take his knee off Floyd's neck for 8 minutes and 46 seconds, and despite Floyd's cries for help, saying "I can't breathe." This and other similar incidents around the country trigger several weeks of largely peaceful protests around the country.

May 27
Johns Hopkins University reports that the coronavirus has killed more than 100,000 people across the US, with an average of almost 900 Americans dying each day.

June 1
After spending part of the weekend in a bunker in the basement of the White House, Trump and Attorney General William Barr order federal troops to clear peaceful protesters demonstrating across from the White House in historic Lafayette Park, using tear gas, batons and mounted troop. Trump and assorted administration and military leaders then walk the short distance to St. John's Church, where he holds an upside down Bible above his head as part of a photo-op to show that he is not afraid to venture outside the White House.

June 4
Retired Marine Corps General James T. Mattis, who had resigned as Trump's Secretary of Defense, broke his silence and issued a public statement on June 4, excoriating Trump as "the first president in his lifetime who actively tries to divide the country" and suggesting Trump's actions "make a mockery of our Constitution."

June 8
New Zealand Prime Minister Jacinda Ardern announces that almost all coronavirus restrictions in New Zealand will be lifted after the country reported no active cases.

June 11
The US passes 2 million confirmed cases of the virus, according to Johns Hopkins.

June 20
Trump holds a rally in Tulsa, Oklahoma, even though the number of cases and deaths is sharply rising in that state. The Trump Campaign boasts that they got over 1 million RSVPs and expected 100,000 of the Trump faithful to attend the rally. Only 6200 Trump supporters show up, leaving vast empty spaces in the 19,000-seat arena.

June 30
There are 126,140 total deaths reported in the U.S. from the coronavirus, and 2.59 million confirmed cases.

July 1
The European Union bars travelers from the U.S. from entering, saying that it does not meet the criteria set by the EU for it to be considered a "safe country."

July 7
The Trump administration notifies Congress and the UN that the U.S. is formally withdrawing from the W.H.O.

July 27
A vaccine being developed by the NIH in partnership with the biotechnology company Moderna, enters Phase 3 testing to determine its safety and efficacy.

Late August
The U.S. passes the 5.7 million case mark, with more than 177,000 deaths.

TABLE OF CONTENTS

INTRODUCTION 1

1 THE PAST IS PROLOGUE 20

2 A BRIEF HISTORY OF PANDEMICS FROM PREHISTORIC TIMES TO THE 1500S 28

3 EARLY PANDEMICS IN THE U.S. 38

4 THE 1918 INFLUENZA PANDEMIC: IMPORTANT LESSONS LEARNED THAT ARE NOW BEING IGNORED 50

5 AMERICA AT ITS BEST 56

6 THE SARS AND SWINE FLU PANDEMICS 61

7 THE RAPID U.S. RESPONSE TO THE 2014 EBOLA CRISIS 71

8 THE TRUMP ADMINISTRATION IGNORES EARLY WARNING SIGNALS AND DISMANTLES PANDEMIC-PREPARATION PROGRAMS 76

9 WHAT IS COVID-19? 86

10 COVID-19 BREAKS OUT IN CHINA 99

11 THE TRUMP WHITE HOUSE DOWNPLAYS THE PANDEMIC AS IT HITS THE U.S. 110

12 TRUMP BLAMES CHINA, THE WORLD HEALTH ORGANIZATION, THE OBAMA ADMINISTRATION, THE GOVERNORS, ETC. 116

13 THE FAILURE TO CONDUCT ADEQUATE TESTING STALLS THE U.S. RESPONSE EFFORT 122

14 THE ANTIBODY TEST DEBACLE 137

15 CALIFORNIA AND OTHER WEST COAST STATES TAKE THE LEAD IN THE BATTLE AGAINST COVID-19 146

16 COVID-19 EXPOSES THE UGLY TRUTH ABOUT NURSING HOMES AND HOW AMERICA CARES FOR ITS ELDERLY 161

TABLE OF CONTENTS

17 THE PERSONAL PROTECTIVE EQUIPMENT CRISIS AND DARWINIAN FEDERALISM 179

18 A TALE OF TWO CITIES: SAN FRANCISCO QUICKLY DECLARES A STATE OF EMERGENCY WHILE NEW YORK CITY DAWDLES . . . 192

19 HOW THE FACE MASK ISSUE TURNED INTO A POLITICAL CULTURE WAR 209

20 CONSPIRACY THEORIES, SNAKE OIL SALESMEN AND THE HYDROXYCHLOROQUINE HYPE 225

21 HOW COVID-19 AND THE U.S. RESPONSE TARGETED MINORITIES. 241

22 TRUMP DECLARES "MISSION ACCOMPLISHED," AND THEN COVID-19 ATTACKS THE WHITE HOUSE. 253

23 COVID-19 AND THE ENVIRONMENT 259

24 HOW COVID-19 AND LAX HEALTH SAFETY STANDARDS ARE DEVASTATING WORKERS AT U.S. MEAT AND FOOD PROCESSING PLANTS 267

25 SACRIFICING HEALTH CARE AND OTHER ESSENTIAL WORKERS 279

26 THE FAILED LEADERSHIP OF BORIS JOHNSON OF THE U.K., DONALD TRUMP OF THE U.S., AND JAIR BOLSONARO OF BRAZIL. 296

27 TAIWAN, ICELAND, GERMANY, SOUTH KOREA, IRELAND, AND NEW ZEALAND RISE TO THE CHALLENGE 304

28 DID SWEDEN AND THE OTHER SCANDINAVIAN COUNTRIES TAKE THE RIGHT APPROACH? 317

29 COVID-19, RELIGIOUS FREEDOM AND THE STATES' RIGHTS TO RESTRICT RELIGIOUS SERVICES. 324

30 THE BACKLASH AGAINST CHINA AND THE WORLD HEALTH ORGANIZATION LEADS TO A NEW COLD WAR. 345

31 THE RACE FOR A VACCINE AND A CURE 356

32 THE COVID-19 CRISIS HIGHLIGHTS THE NEED FOR AN OVERHAUL IN THE U.S. HEALTH CARE SYSTEM 380

33 ANXIETY, STRESS AND PSYCHOLOGICAL TRAUMA IN THE AGE OF COVID 398

34 "LIVE AND LET DIE": SOME STATES RECKLESSLY TRY TO REOPEN WITHOUT MEETING FEDERAL GUIDELINES, WITH DISASTROUS RESULTS 410

35 AMERICA EXPLODES AS THE FEAR AND ANGER OF THE COVID-19 CRISIS IS FURTHER FUELED BY RACIST ACTS AND POLICE VIOLENCE 428

36 COVIDFEST 2020 440

37 THE WHITE HOUSE RAISES THE WHITE FLAG OF SURRENDER .449

38 EDUCATION IN THE AGE OF COVID 457

39 CORONAVIRUS AND THE COURTS 472

40 THE RICH GET EVEN RICHER AND THE POOR (YOU GUESSED IT) EVEN POORER 482

41 AMERICA'S UNLUCKIEST GENERATION: THE DOWNWARD MOBILITY OF MILLENNIALS 498

42 THE NEW NEW DEAL 507

43 LIFESTYLE CHANGES IN THE AGE OF COVID 517

44 LOVE IN THE TIME OF COVID 521

45 THE POST-COVID NEW WORLD ORDER 525

46 THE AWAKENING OF FAITH IN A TIME OF PANDEMIC 534

EPILOGUE THE STRUGGLE FOR THE SOUL OF AMERICA 550

IN MEMORIAM GEORGE PERRY FLOYD JR. 557

ENDNOTES 560

COVID-19

THE VIRUS THAT CHANGED AMERICA AND THE WORLD

INTRODUCTION

"In man's struggle against the world, bet on the world."
– Franz Kafka

Plagues, pestilence, and pandemics have always been an essential part of human existence since the dawn of recorded history. As we are now painfully aware, they are very much a part of modern life as well. Silent microbial killers have shaken and toppled civilizations in the past. Today, thanks to improvements in global transportation and technology, deadly viruses can spread faster than ever. Although humans have shown remarkable resilience in the face of adversity, these cataclysmic events have left a profound mark on every society and generation, including our own.

Epidemics force us to re-examine our relationship with each other, and - for those of us who are religiously inclined - our relationship with our Creator. Pandemics necessarily involve issues of life and death. They inevitably force us to come to grips with fundamental moral and existential questions. What is the good, the just, and the right thing to do in a global health crisis? What should we avoid doing? What sacrifices are we willing to make individually for the common good? How long are we prepared to make those sacrifices as the epidemic drags on from weeks into months, and possibly years? Are our leaders telling us the truth about these life-and-death matters? Are they interested in the health, safety, and survival of the maximum number of our fellow citizens, or are they acting in their own political and financial self-interest? In a pandemic, one person's actions or inactions – especially if they are in a leadership position - can have a profound effect on what happens to the rest of us. One infected person who does not abide by the rules of quarantine is jeopardizing countless others.

By now, we all know that the COVID-19 virus – unchecked by social distancing and other mitigation measures - can spread through an entire community like wildfire through dry brush. It has been said that a butterfly can bat its wings in one part of the world and create a ripple effect that becomes a hurricane on the other. Our fates are more interconnected than ever before. Yet, at the same time, we are so separated and isolated from one another.

In the pre-COVID-19 era, almost all of us were so wrapped up with the daily demands of family and our work that we had little time to reflect on the bigger picture. What are we doing here, and what is our place in the cosmos? Once we had to stay home, we had time to think about fundamental issues concerning the welfare and survival of our communities, our country, our way of life, and the planet.

Some of us who can't stand to have the TV on all of the time welcomed the silence. We took the time to read books (or even write them), take long walks, smell the flowers, or just let our minds wander to wherever they may take us. For me, the gnawing question that kept rising to the fore was: how did we get to this point? How can it be that we have been collectively brought to our knees by a single new virus? How did it happen with all the technological and scientific advances, with the "wonder drugs" and vaccines that have eliminated polio, measles, and smallpox?

Since the end of World War II, our society has faced several pandemics and public health emergencies. Still, none of them have closed down all of our businesses, our schools, and driven us in fear into our homes, knowing that there is no cure and no vaccine. In 1957, a vaccine for the Asian Flu was developed between the time that it was first reported in Hong Kong in April of that year and the time that American schools started opening up in the fall. U.S. government scientists and private industry saw that an epidemic was coming, mobilized their collective resources, and came up with a prompt solution. In 2003, during the first SARS pandemic, our federal government rose to the occasion. It minimized the potential impact of this deadly virus.

The U.S. government also responded admirably to the Ebola crisis of 2014. In the aftermath, critical government agencies were established as early warning systems against the next outbreak. We all expected that our country would be prepared to face the next challenge with equal efficiency and effectiveness. We were sorely mistaken in this assumption. We could not have foreseen that an accidental president would move into the White House, and then proceeded to dismantle the carefully crafted government plans designed to prepare for the next viral pandemic. The government's testing capabilities were woefully inadequate. The government stockpiles of necessary N95 and surgical masks, mechanical ventilators, and other essential medical supplies and equipment were depleted. There was no coherent federal response plan in place to deal with the crisis.

We now know the federal government knew as early as November of 2019 that a new and virulent virus was wreaking havoc in China. The White House and the rest of the federal government also knew from intelligence reports that it was likely this virus would spread to the U.S. within a matter of weeks. Nevertheless, the Trump Administration failed to heed the alarm bells that were ringing and the warning lights that were flashing, or simply ignoring them. Either way, the result was the same: critical weeks and months were squandered that should have been effectively used to prepare for the public health onslaught that was surely on its way.

As detailed in this book, U.S. officials knew about the virus outbreak in Wuhan, China as early as November and December 2019. By early January 2020, the U.S. Centers for Disease Control (CDC) was already in touch with its counterpart in China about this virus outbreak, and China provided the U.S. with the complete set of genetic material of the coronavirus. Also, in early January, the U.S. Department of Health and Hospital Services (HHS) had already started drawing up contingency plans for enforcing the Defense Production Act (DPA),[1] which enables the government to compel private companies to produce equipment or devices critical to the country's security. However, disputes within HHS and the White House prevented the government from implementing the DPA for many weeks. By January 18, Trump got a full briefing on the coronavirus threat to the U.S. from his HHS Secretary, Alex Azar. Trump's response was to discount the threat, telling Azar that he was "an alarmist."[2] Throughout January and thereafter, he was also being briefed on the risks of the pandemic spreading to the U.S. in the daily briefings that were compiled for him by U.S. intelligence agencies.

The U.S. reported its first confirmed coronavirus case on January 21, 2020, which was a U.S. citizen in Washington State who had recently returned from a trip to Wuhan, China. The U.S. thus knew by the second half of January that the virus was already in this country and that the prudent course of action would be to impose social distancing and other mitigation measures designed to slow the spread of the virus. Not only did the U.S. fail to take any steps to stop the virus's spread, but President Trump repeatedly downplayed the risk to the country. Indeed, on January 22, when asked while he was at the global economic forum in Davos, Switzerland whether he was worried about a potential pandemic, Trump responded: "No. Not at all. And we have it totally under control. It's one person coming in from China... It's going to be just fine."[3]

On January 29, President Trump and other senior White House officials were advised of a memo prepared by Senior White House Advisor Peter Navarro, warning that the coronavirus could cause as many as 500,000 deaths worldwide and trillions in economic damage, much of it in the U.S. The following day, January 30, HHS Secretary Azar again warned Trump about the "possibility of a pandemic."[4] Nevertheless, the U.S. failed to take any action in either January or February to restrict the spread of the virus that was already documented to be spreading in the U.S., although the Trump administration did declare a public health emergency and banned non-U.S. citizens from entering the country from Hubei Province in China. However, 300,000 people had already traveled to the U.S. from China during the month before the ban.[5] Also, more than 40,000 people traveled from China to the U.S. after the January 31 partial ban, and around 430,000 total between the December 31, 2019 disclosure of the outbreak by China and April 4.[6]

Throughout February 2020, the Trump administration continued its default policy of doing nothing to try to stop the spread of the virus in the U.S., while continuing to lull the American public into a false sense of security. On February 10, for example, Trump continued to reassure the American people: "I think the virus is going to be – it's going to be fine." On February 14, Trump reassuringly – and falsely – misrepresented the scope of the problem: "We have a very small number of people in the country, right now, with it. It's like around 12. Many of them are getting better. Some are fully recovered already. So we're in very good shape."

Behind the scenes, however, Trump and his senior officials continued to receive dire warnings that the pandemic spreading in the U.S. would have catastrophic results. On February 14, for example, a White House advisory group headed by Dr. Robert Kadlec, HHS Assistant Secretary for

Preparedness and Response (ASPR), circulated a memo in coordination with the National Security Council, entitled "U.S. Government Response to the 2019 Novel Coronavirus," documenting the drastic measures that were needed to combat the coronavirus' spread, including stay-at-home orders, bans on public gatherings and sporting events, school closures and social distancing. Nevertheless, Trump and his senior officials continued to ignore this rapidly growing crisis. They refused to make the hard decisions needed to stem the spread of the virus or to tell the American public the truth about the looming threat they were facing.

By late February, a leading Homeland Security medical officer and other experts concluded that the U.S. had already lost the fight to contain the virus and that the country needed to immediately switch to mitigation efforts such as social distancing and stay-at-home orders to stem the spread of the virus. Also, in late February, the White House coronavirus task force conducted a mock-up exercise of the pandemic, predicting that there would be 110 million infections, 7.7 million hospitalizations, and 586,000 deaths.[7] The White House task force also presented President Trump with a plan setting forth the "Four Steps to Mitigation," including recommendations for social distancing and other restrictions. President Trump, however, ignored all such warnings and recommendations. Instead, Trump continued with his optimistic happy-talk, saying, as he did on February 19: "I think it's going to work out fine. I think when we get into April, in the warmer weather, that has a very negative effect on that and that type of a virus."

In early March, the White House continued to refuse to warn the American public of the catastrophic pandemic descending on the U.S. or to urge the implementation of stay-at-home orders and other mitigation measures on a nationwide basis. The White House also ratcheted up its opposition to any vigorous pandemic response efforts by attacking the media and democratically elected representatives who were trying to sound the alarm about the spreading pandemic. For example, on March 9, Trump went into attack mode: "The Fake News Media and their partner, the Democrat Party, is doing everything within its semi-considerable power (it used to be greater!) to inflame the Coronavirus situation, far beyond what the facts would warrant. Surgeon General, 'The risk is low to the average American.'"

Trump also erroneously compared COVID-19 to the common flu: "So last year, 37,000 Americans died from the common flu. It averages between 27,000 and 70,000 per year. Nothing is shut down, life & the economy go on. At this moment, there are 546 confirmed cases of Coronavirus, with 22 deaths. Think about that!"

Similarly, on March 11, Trump gave an Oval Office address, stating: "[For] the vast majority of Americans, the risk is very very low." He also continued to resist calls for social distancing, school closures, and other necessary steps that he feared would have an undue impact on the stock markets. The following day, on March 12, the Trump administration postponed the Director of National Intelligence's (DNI's) annual U.S. World Wide Threat Assessment, warning that the U.S. was unprepared for the global pandemic.[8] On March 13, HHS completed a study "not for public distribution" that assumed the COVID-19 "pandemic will last 18 months or longer and could include multiple waves of illness." It also concluded that the "supply chain and transportation impacts" would "likely result in significant shortages." Still, the White House took no action. On March 16, in a conference call with Governor Gretchen Whitmer of Michigan and several other governors, Trump essentially washed his hands of any federal responsibility for the pandemic response efforts, telling the governors that they were basically on their own in securing vitally necessary equipment, such as respirators and ventilators.

In retrospect, the most critical time period for the U.S. to have taken action was the first two weeks of March. During the first week of March, from Sunday, March 1 to March 8, 2020, the number of coronavirus cases grew from only a handful to 500 coronavirus infections reported nationwide. However, the following Sunday, March 15, the number of confirmed cases had jumped to 2,000, with dozens of reported deaths.

During the first half of March, there was still a chance that public health officials might be able to contain the pandemic in this country through shutdown orders and other mitigation measures. But the federal government did nothing, and in fact, President Trump continued to downplay the seriousness of the pandemic. His soothing words tended to lull the American public into a false sense of security. The shutdown orders did not come until later in the coronavirus epicenters, such as New York, Illinois, and Ohio.

So, what would have happened if the federal government had acted with the degree of vigilance that we had come to expect from the Ebola crisis and other pandemic threats? What if those sweeping measures imposed on or after March 15 – a federal warning against large gatherings, health screenings at airports, states of emergency declared, etc. – had been announced one or two weeks earlier?

A group of Columbia University epidemiologists calculated that if social distancing and other mitigation measures had been put in place by March 1, then 54,000 Americans who subsequently died from the coronavirus would still be alive. And if those measures had been adopted one week later, on March 8, then 36,000 fewer American lives would have been lost, which would have meant that about 40% of the 93,000 COVID-related deaths in the U.S. reported as of the date of the study (May 20) would likely still be alive.

By May 2020, the coronavirus crisis had already mutated into the worst economic crisis this country has faced since the Great Depression of the 1930s. More than 40 million people – one in four American workers - had filed for unemployment benefits since the coronavirus pandemic forced most of the U.S. economy to shut down in March. This economic hardship fell the hardest – as it always had – on the poor, Native Americans, and people of color. The virus had descended on Black, brown, poor white, inner-city, rural and Native American communities like a heat-seeking missile, targeting the most vulnerable in our society which had already been beaten down by grinding poverty, chronic illness, diabetes, high blood pressure, opioid abuse, lack of educational and job opportunities, and hopelessness. A vast underclass in the country had been growing for decades, barely scraping by week after week and month after month, living from payday to payday until their jobs suddenly evaporated and they were unemployed.

Then the hopelessness and frustration caused by the public health crisis and the ensuing economic crisis collided with an even more toxic element that had been there all along, namely, the structural racism and brutality already ingrained in American life. These three elements – the virus, the economic meltdown, and racism – formed a combustible and toxic brew that exploded throughout the country. We learned to our horror that a young Black man in Georgia, Ahmaud Arbery, had been gunned down and murdered by three white men while he was out for a jog in broad daylight. Also, in Louisville, Kentucky, an unarmed Black woman, Breonna Taylor, was shot by police in her own apartment while they were executing a "no-knock" warrant. They ended up literally executing Ms. Taylor with multiple gunshot wounds.

The simmering rage in communities around the country finally boiled over into demonstrations and protests after George Floyd, another Black man, died while in police custody in Minneapolis on May 25. A video of the incident, which quickly went viral, showed Floyd handcuffed on the ground with a white police officer kneeling on his neck for 8 minutes and 46 seconds while he pleaded for his life, repeatedly saying, "I can't breathe." These were the same last words spoken by Eric Garner, yet another Black victim of police brutality, just before he too died on July 17, 2014 in New York City. It also turned out that George Floyd was infected with the coronavirus, but it was the systemic virus of racism that killed him.

The demonstrations that first erupted in Minneapolis were reasonably peaceful until a full four days after Floyd's murder, when former police officer Derek Chauvin – who had been fired along with three fellow officers immediately after the incident - still was not in police custody and not charged with a crime. After a night of violent protests, fires and looting ripped through Minneapolis and neighboring St. Paul on May 28, Chauvin was finally taken into custody on Friday, May 29.

Mostly peaceful demonstrations took place in almost every major city around the country, with some violence erupting, and the police over-reacting in several cities, including New York City. The demonstrators demanded that America acknowledge that Black Lives Matter and that the gratuitous killing of young Black men by the police and white vigilantes had to stop. The response to demonstrators demanding an end to police brutality of Black people was met, in many cases, with even more police brutality.

The demands of many demonstrators - many of whom were white, Hispanic, and Asian - expanded to include demands for the elimination of systemic racism in all aspects of American society, including employment, education, and housing. The issue of reparations to the African American community for 401 years of slavery, degradation, and discrimination also rose to the fore, and it seemed like a healthy debate was suddenly emerging as to long-needed reforms of the criminal justice system and policing in America. Confederate statues came down and, even more incredibly, NASCAR banned the confederate flag, which had been a mainstay at such events forever (or so it seemed).

Some of the demonstrations in Washington, D.C. took place in the historic Lafayette Park, immediately adjacent to the White House. Although generally peaceful, during a particularly boisterous Friday night demonstration that spilled over to an area close to the White House, the U.S. Secret Service moved President Trump and his family to a secure bunker in the basement of the White House. This bunker had last been used by Vice President Dick Cheney in the uncertain days following the September 11 terrorist attacks. When asked about it by reporters, Trump denied having hidden in the bunker, concocting a typically nonsensical story about having been down in the basement to "inspect" the bunker, as if bunker inspections were a previously undisclosed part of the president's job description.

Trump sat stewing in the White House all weekend, becoming increasingly irate over the press coverage characterizing him as having "hidden" in the basement bunker, making him look fearful and weak, the two adjectives that he most hated, except when used to describe anyone other than himself. And when he took a break and went to look out one of the White House windows, he became even more furious as he helplessly watched as Washington's mayor ordered the installation of a new street sign renaming the square across from the White House as "Black Lives Matter Plaza." To add insult to injury, the words "BLACK LIVES MATTER" were now written on the street in bright yellow giant block letters so they could be plainly seen from the White House.

Some bold, or even reckless, action had to be taken to prove that he was strong and tough. Trump feared that the public narrative was slipping away from him, and even his Secretary of Defense, Mark Esper, was starting to publicly express misgivings about ordering in federal troops to Washington, D.C. and creating a "Battlespace America" plan to confront the still growing demonstrations that were taking place now every night. Attorney General Bill Barr, however, had no such concerns about the potential for massive violations of the civil rights of peaceful demonstrators exercising their First Amendment rights of free speech and assembly. "General" Barr (as he liked to be called) took charge of the military-style response to the demonstrations outside the White House, calling in U.S. Bureau of Prisons riot police from as far away as Texas. These federal officers, who had a well-deserved reputation for quickly quelling prison riots through the use of "maximum lethality" if necessary, were part of the plan by Trump and Barr to "get tough" with the demonstrators and to "dominate" the D.C. battlefield. Other federal officers from multiple organizations flooded into Washington, but their names and affiliations were impossible to decipher since they were stripped of their insignias and other means of identification. These federal officers eerily resembled the unidentified Russian paratroopers sent by Putin to annex Crimea in 2014, who were referred to as "little green men," since their green uniforms had been stripped of all insignias.

On Monday afternoon, June 1, a snap decision was made by Trump that he would show America and the entire world that he was in total control of the situation and fearless enough to actually exit the White House on foot and then walk - with assorted military and non-military advisors - the short distance to St. John's Church on the other side of Lafayette Square.

But first Lafayette Square had to be cleared, in order to prevent any actual close physical contact between Trump and the American citizens peacefully assembled there. So, without warning, "General" Barr ordered the federal officers dressed in unmarked riot gear, backed by regular army units, to "clear" the park of peaceful protesters, which they did by assaulting the protesters with batons, pepper spray, shields and mounted horse units. What happened then was essentially an unprovoked police riot, resulting in the wanton and needless injury of numerous protesters, so that Trump could make a short triumphal walk with assorted officials to the front of historic St. John's Church.

Trump did not actually enter the Church to pray for peace and reconciliation of a grieving and divided nation. Nor did he, upon arrival at the front of the Church, say a few words of condolence to the family of George Floyd and the families of other vistims, promising a thorough federal investigation and proposing legislation to prevent such atrocities from continuing to occur on American streets. No. That was not his style. In fact, he said nothing, only awkwardly holding a bible upside down over his head. The bible had been brought along as a prop in by Ivanka in her expensive handbag. The bible was never opened during this "walk," and no biblical passages were read. Rather, the Holy Bible was merely a prop to be used as a signal to Trump's evangelical base that, yes, I too am a Christian soldier who will smite the nonbelievers who dare challenge the status quo and question the authority of the Chosen One to do whatever he wanted to do.

The inappropriate use of overwhelming and unwarranted force during the one-sided "Battle of Lafayette Square," and Trump's hastily organized photo op in front of St. John's Church was, to put it mildly, a bust. The photo of him awkwardly holding the bible drew derision from virtually every quarter, since even Trump's supporters knew that it was only being used as a prop, and that it was not in Trump's nature or temperament to actually open it up and read from it. To do so would run the risk of coming across one of the numerous references that were totally inconsistent with Trump's strategy of division, confusion, and belittlement. Passages such as "Blessed are the peacemakers" simply had no place in Trump's re-election playbook.

Trump's present and former generals found this photo op stunt to be a bridge too far. They convened what amounted to an informal "court martial" of the president, finding him not only to have violated his constitutional oath, but also to have failed to conduct himself as "an officer and a gentleman." Trump was also taken to task by the generals for dragging the U.S. military into disrepute. They were deeply concerned that the U.S. military was being drawn into what was mainly a political dispute, with military personnel being basically asked to suppress their fellow citizens' right to exercise their constitutionally protected First Amendment rights. Retired

Marine Corps General James T. Mattis, who had resigned as Trump's Secretary of Defense, broke his silence and issued a public statement on June 4 excoriating Trump as "the first president in his lifetime who actively tries to divide the country" and suggested Trump's actions "make a mockery of our Constitution." Other generals quickly followed suit, making a choice that all Americans will be called on to make sooner or later, which is to either declare your loyalty and fealty to the United States of America and the U.S. Constitution, or to Trump. Army Gen. Mark Milley, the nation's top military officer, said on June 11 that he was wrong to accompany Trump on the "walk" through Lafayette Square that ended in a photo op at a church. He said his presence, wearing combat fatigues like he was reviewing troops in a war zone, "created a perception of the military involved in domestic politics." The Chairman of the Joint Chiefs of Staff concluded his remarks at a National Defense University commencement ceremony: "I should not have been there."

As June wore on, Trump's mood and re-election prospects became increasingly dark and dim. He was trapped in the White House, pacing around the Oval Office, fearful of even going out for a short stroll after the June 1 fiasco in Lafayette Park. His advisors weren't letting him even go out for a round of golf or a weekend at Mar-A-Largo for fear of the "optics." They kept telling him that photos of him playing golf amidst the economic crisis and the growing number of coronavirus-related illnesses and deaths in red states such as Florida, Texas, Alabama and Oklahoma might be perceived as Nero fiddling while Rome burned.

From Trump's point of view, it was bad enough when it was the Blue States like New York and California were bearing the brunt of the virus's attack, but now it was hitting "Trump country" with a vengeance. Muttering to himself and snapping at his aides every five minutes, Trump's senior aides realized that they had to get him out of the White House to one of those old fashion MAGA rallies so that he could bask once again in the adulation of an adoring crowd. The caged animal in him had to be let loose, even if it meant going to an indoor arena in Tulsa on June 19, when the number of coronavirus cases was spiking, and where the Black community was getting ready to celebrate Juneteenth.

Juneteenth is the annual celebration of the reading of General Order No. 3 in Galveston, Texas, which freed the last slaves on June 19, 1865. It was also the 99th anniversary of the Tulsa Race Massacre of 1921, where a rioting mob of white men, including police and National Guard troops, wantonly killed 300 Black residents, incarcerated others for days, and burnt to the ground about 1200 homes and businesses in one of the most thriving Black communities and business centers in the U.S., known as Black Wall Street. Trump agreed to change the date of the rally to the following day, June 20, after a Black Secret Service agent (Trump was developing a bad habit of referring to them in shorthand as "S.S. agents") explained to him the significance of Juneteenth.

The Trump campaign hyped this "coming out" rally as having attracted up to a million Trump fans, with about 100,000 expected to attend. They could only cram 19,000 screaming Trump supporters into the closed arena, where they would be sitting and standing close together, most of them without face masks since the Great One had refused to wear a mask, and they did not want to be mistaken for some liberal Blue-State Democrat. It was also an inappropriate fashion statement to be wearing a MAGA shirt and hat and then to ruin the selfie with a face mask.

The rest of the Trump faithful were supposed to be in outdoor areas, with a stage being erected so Trump and V.P. Pence could address the crowd outside before making their way triumphantly into the arena to deafening applause. That was the plan anyway. State and local health officials described this as a classic "super spreader" event that would undoubtedly add further fuel to the still rapid spread of the virus across Oklahoma and the neighboring states where the Trump faithful would return. One commentator said that the event would be more appropriately named "Covidfest 2020."

So, what do you do when you throw a big party, get plenty of RSVPs, and practically no one shows up? Your worst nightmare, right? Especially if you have an enlarged ego and have staked a lot of political capital on this event as the "reset" for your re-election campaign. Shortly before 7 p.m. on the big night, the Trump campaign canceled the outdoor event and had the outdoor stage dismantled just as Trump was heading for the arena area.

Inside the arena, there were only about 6,200 people, leaving gaping empty holes in the arena's seating areas, which the media seemed to be fixated on more than Trump's rambling, incoherent two-hour rant. Trump filled his remarks with grievances against the Democrats, the media and especially the Chinese, referring to the virus by using the racist term, "Kung Flu." He also strangely felt it necessary to justify his recent slow and faltering walk down the steps from a stage at the West Point commencement address, and the need to use both hands to get a glass of water to his lips.

Trump even let it slip at one point that he had told his "people" to cut down on the coronavirus testing since when you take more tests, you find out that more people are infected with the virus, and this is bad for America's world image. Conversely, if you test less, there are fewer cases and infections identified, and the official numbers are lower. Get it? Only in Trumplandia does this make sense. One of his advisers said that this was a "joke," but Trump later confirmed that he was serious, doubling down on this by directing that federal assistance at several testing sites in Texas and elsewhere be terminated.

After the Tulsa Rally was a bust, Trump returned to the White House even further frustrated, with dark mutterings starting to emerge that maybe it wasn't such a good idea after all to hold an election this November. With the coronavirus crisis still out there, and the economic crisis looking to continue for at least the rest of the year, maybe America should just skip the presidential election until things settled down a bit. There was also the concern over the Antifa and Black Lives Matter movements, who no doubt were planning to cause more trouble. In addition, Trump also promoted the idea that that there would be "massive" voter fraud, especially if the Democrats got their way and people were allowed to freely mail in their ballots. If there was no election, then there would be no possibility of election fraud, right? Just as if there is no more testing, the number of positive coronavirus cases and deaths would be less, right?

Trump must have begun asking himself, "What would Putin do?" Or maybe he should just give his mentor a call and ask, "Vladimir, I got this little problem, and I was wondering if you could help me out ..."

Meanwhile, Trump and his administration had given up trying to deal with the coronavirus crisis, which refused to go away. The U.K., Italy and other countries that had severe coronavirus outbreaks had peaked, and their charts of cases and deaths looked like steep mountains, sharply rising and then sharply falling to negligible numbers. In contrast, the U.S. numbers had dramatically increased and then plateaued at a relatively high level, because while the number of cases had dropped in the Blue States on the East and West Coasts, the Red States in the South and the West were still spiking, with no end in sight. The Red States with Republican governors, such as in Florida, Arizona, and Texas, were not even requiring their citizens to wear face masks, even as the number of cases and deaths continued to climb.

Perhaps the chickens were now coming home to roost. The decades of displaying contempt for science and "fact-based" decision making had made the U.S. the leading "climate denier" country in the world, triggering well-deserved contempt and ridicule from our erstwhile allies as well as our geopolitical foes. It should not have been surprising that a dysfunctional Republican president and his virtual clones in various Red State governors' mansions would first deny the existence of the virus, and then make the refusal to promote the only effective public health measures available at the time – social distancing, the use of face masks, etc. – into a political and "civil liberties" issue. Only in America, sad to say.

We were once considered "exceptional" because we stood out among all other nations and were truly great. Now we are "exceptional" like a learning-disabled child who is still loved but able to function in the world only with the help of a large and dedicated support group.

Even more ominous is the apparent willingness of the Trump administration and the rest of their Republican enablers to fatalistically accept increasing numbers of serious coronavirus cases and deaths, even while knowing that many of these tragic outcomes could have been prevented if only they had followed the sound advice of the experts and made decisions based on facts and science, not politics and wishful thinking. Perhaps Americans have become calloused and oblivious to the tragic and unnecessary loss of life, after decades of mass shootings and ingrained gun culture.

Given his poor performance ratings and the persistence of reports of death and disease for so many months, Trump understandably wanted to change the subject. Many Americans were all too willing to let him do so, collectively shrugging their shoulders when they heard, for example, that as of late June, more than 120,000 of their fellow Americans had died so far as a result of this dreaded disease, and the number of U.S. dead broke the 150,000 barrier by late July. Have we become so morally and emotionally bankrupt that we are willing to accept the fact that thousands of our countrymen (and women) are dying unnecessarily?

As this book goes to press there is still no known effective cure or vaccine for COVID-19, and the number of infections and deaths is sure to rise in the coming months, if not for years. As the pandemic continues to unfold, however, a close look at the crisis to date shows beyond a doubt that the U.S. coronavirus response effort has been an unmitigated disaster, and that this disaster could have been avoided if the Trump administration and its federal agencies had followed the contingency plans already in place for a pandemic such as this one. If effective action had been taken when the first warning signs began flashing and the alarm bells started ringing, the pandemic could have been brought under control and the country could have been safely reopening, as is happening in countries that acted more prudently.

We know that one reason for the continued spread of the disease in parts of the South and in the West is that numerous states recklessly reopened their economies prematurely, even as their infection rates were still rising, and then were forced to close down once again when the number of cases and deaths inevitably spiked upwards. Many of these illnesses and deaths were avoidable, if only the country had adopted some of the sensible and effective measures implemented by other countries around the world, with positive results.

The U.S., which boasted the world's largest economy and led the world in almost every technological field, produced one of the worst records for its haphazard and ineffective coronavirus response effort. The U.S.'s reputation has been perhaps irreparably tarnished in the eyes of the world, and it has even suffered the humiliation of having the European Union, where the pandemic has been largely brought under control, ban travelers from the U.S. for fear that the U.S.'s mistakes and unnecessarily high infection rates might undermine the results of their own prudent efforts. As Fintan O'Toole wrote in The *Irish Times*, "The world has loved, hated and envied the U.S. Now, for the first time, we pity it."

How did this colossal tragedy come to pass? How did America - which not too long ago was the leader of the free world and beacon of liberty and hope for generations - fall so far so fast? Or maybe we just didn't notice it before, as almost every good and valuable quality that made America truly great gradually slipped away, bit by bit, drop by drop, until the country was little more than an empty shell of its former self. And where do we go from here? These are the simple – and complicated – questions that this book tries to answer. Someday in the future, when this is all over, the definitive history of this crisis will no doubt be written. But for now, there is more than enough information available to give some historical perspective to the unfolding disaster. How our country successfully dealt with past public health challenges, and how we failed so miserably in this instance to prepare and respond to the current crisis will be thoroughly examined.

This book also explores the profound impacts that the current crisis has already had - and will continue to have – on our communities, our country, and the entire world. Nothing will ever be quite the same again. As the Irish poet and writer W. B. Yeats would say, "A terrible beauty is born." There will be no going back to the old normal, and the "new normal" is still being shaped. Some of those changes will be for the better, and some of them will be for the worse. We don't know yet whether our democracy will be reinvigorated and the stronger for it in the end, following the maximum: "Whatever doesn't kill you makes you stronger." Or will the trauma of the crisis, and sense of powerlessness that it brings, lead us to collectively withdraw further into our own familiar political, social, and tribal camps? Will we come to distrust democracy and all of its inefficient "checks and balances"? Will there be an accelerated trend to become, like Hungary and other formerly democratic countries, a de facto authoritarian dictatorship with only vestiges of democratic window-dressing? Will the America that we thought we knew and loved – that shining city on a hill, beacon of hope, and defender of freedom and opportunity for all - become a distant memory?

Or will it mark the resurgence of an America more faithful to its roots, its core beliefs, and its mission?

Even if we survive as a species – as we undoubtedly will - the pandemic has and will continue to touch us profoundly. It has already brought out the best in some and exposed the worst in others. This paradox of human nature has played out with mixed results throughout history. Epidemics not only fatally weakened the political, social, and military pillars of the Roman Empire but also led to a crisis of the soul from which Rome never recovered. Will the same be said of Pax Americana? Will we overcome this challenge and emerge the stronger for it? We had faced dark days before, such as the Civil War, where the Union was torn apart. The devastating attack on Pearl Harbor on December 7, 1941 destroyed most of America's Pacific Fleet. The terrorist attack on September 11 sent the entire country reeling. And yet the United States of American survived the Civil War, defeated the forces of tyranny and oppression in World War II, dominated the world stage for decades after that, and has prevented any foreign terrorist attack on U.S. soil since 9/11. Can we overcome this challenge as well? Of course, we can (after all, we are "Ameri-cans," not "Ameri-cant's"). But we got off to a bad start, and the outcome is far from inevitable. We must collectively have the will and the resolve to do so, and we must have the leadership to show us the way.

A pandemic is both a public health crisis as well as a great morality play, with the end unknown until we get there. COVID-19 has been called "the great equalizer." But this is only partly true. Whether you are rich or poor, or somewhere in between, we all face the risk of infection, disease, and possible death. But some are more equal than others. The wealthy among us stand a better statistical chance of surviving since they have the financial ability to practice social distancing more rigorously in a larger house. They have the financial resources to stay at home and weather the storm. If they become ill, they are more likely to gain admission to a better-equipped hospital than us ordinary folk. For example, Mt. Sinai Hospital on the well-to-do East Side of Manhattan is in partnership with Elmhurst Hospital in a poorer section of Queens, New York. However, there can be little doubt that if you arrive by ambulance at Mt. Sinai Hospital, your chances of survival are higher. Elmhurst Hospital, which was at the epicenter of New York's coronavirus epidemic, was severely overstretched, and the staff was exhausted and overstressed. Some of the medical staff at Elmhurst Hospital were photographed wearing garbage bags as personal protective equipment. A lack of supplies led to protective masks being reused rather than discarded after exposure to COVID-19 patients.

We also must face the harsh reality that people of color, the poor and the elderly were – and still are - falling ill and dying in much higher numbers than the well-to-do. In this, the wealthiest country on earth, the poor are getting poorer, and the rich are getting richer at an increasingly alarming rate since the coronavirus struck. Nursing homes and extended care facilities throughout the country have been decimated by the deaths of elderly residents and their caregivers. There is little or no protective equipment used in many of these facilities, and the dead and dying are not necessarily accounted for in the grim statistics. At one nursing home, an anonymous tip about a body being stored in a shed led to the discovery of 17 bodies in a makeshift morgue in this overwhelmed facility. How many more horror stories will we hear?

Inequality of access to healthcare has been a reality in past pandemics, and history seems to be repeating itself. Is this who we are as people? Is this the new American reality? Will future generations of Americans view the Statue of Liberty as only some relic of the past? Are we still the same country that past generations fought and died for? If not, will we ever be able to reclaim that sense of inherent decency, goodness, and exceptionalism that bound us together? Time will tell.

In the meantime, let us take a closer look at where we have come from, what is currently happening, and what we need to do to get America back on track in our national work-in-progress towards true justice, equality, and opportunity for all.

August 15, 2020   Kenneth Foard McCallion

1

THE PAST IS PROLOGUE

During a White House press briefing on March 18, 2020, President Trump responded to criticism that his administration was unprepared for the coronavirus crisis, saying that the virus "snuck up on us."[1] The following day, Trump expressed the view that the virus was "something that just surprised the whole world,"[2] later adding that the crisis was "uncharted territory" and "there's never been anything like this in history."[3]

Trump's comments were wrong on several levels. First of all, plagues, epidemics, and pandemics have always been a part of human history, from ancient Greece and Rome to the Middle Ages, and well into the modern era. The Plague - or "Black Death" as it was called - killed at least 50 million people in the 14th century. That represented 60 percent of Europe's entire population, making it the worst natural catastrophe in human history – so far. The Spanish Flu swept the world in 1918, killing between 20 and 50 million people, with one-fifth of the world's population becoming infected by the deadly virus.

It is unlikely that the number of sick patients and fatalities arising from the COVID-19 pandemic will reach the deadly heights of the 1918 pandemic. However, the coronavirus has already infected and killed a large number of people in the U.S. and around the globe,[4] driven one-third of humanity into virtual lockdown,[5] and brought the economies of the United States and most of the rest of the world to their knees. This pandemic is destined to continue claiming more victims until there is an effective vaccine in place.[6]

Trump's claim that the deadly pandemic battering the U.S. was a big "surprise" is also false. Experts both in and out of the federal government have warned of the possibility of a significant pandemic for at least the past two decades. These warnings stressed the devastating consequences that would follow if the country was not adequately prepared. The National Intelligence Council (NIC) warned in its 2004 version of "Global Trends" that it was only a matter of time before the U.S. would experience a pandemic as deadly as the 1918 influenza.[7] It was projected that the virus would bring global travel and trade to a halt for an extended time, and would likely overwhelm health resources.

About ten years later, the Ebola crisis of 2014 led the Obama White House to form a global pandemic unit within the National Security Council. Its mission was to make sure that the federal government's extensive resources were ready to be fully mobilized when the next pandemic reached the U.S. The Trump White House later disbanded this unit after John Bolton took over as Trump's National Security Advisor in May 2018.

During President Trump's tenure in the White House, a 2017 Pentagon plan was circulated among senior officials in the Trump administration. The plan identified "a novel respiratory disease," such as influenza or coronavirus, as being "the most likely and significant threat" to the U.S.[8] If prior studies were not enough to trigger an emergency preparedness plan, the U.S. National Center for Medical Intelligence (NCMI)'s warning should have set off the alarms. NCMI issued a confidential report in November 2019, one month before the COVID-19 outbreak in Wuhan, China. The report warned the White House, Pentagon, and the National Security Council that the spreading coronavirus disease in China would be a "cataclysmic event."[9] NCMI stressed the outbreak in China was only the initial stage of a global pandemic.[10]

When the COVID-19 epidemic inevitably reached the U.S. in January 2020, the U.S. acted as if it was paralyzed and unprepared to mobilize the resources necessary to respond rapidly to this threat. The Trump White House squandered the first two critical months – from January through at least March 2020 – with a virtually incoherent stream of confusing public statements. These statements ranged from outright denials that the U.S. had any coronavirus problem to expressions of wishful thinking that the virus would quickly "wash" through the country and then disappear.[11] Most of these ill-conceived or intentionally false statements came directly from Trump. He and his closest advisors claimed media reports of the spread of the deadly virus were a "Democratic hoax" or "fake news." Trump claimed a liberal and hostile mainstream media perpetrated the hoax with the malign intent of damaging his presidency. Trump tried to both downplay the issue and to support his claim that the media was "over-reacting" by falsely commenting that the contagion was no more dangerous than the common flu.

The White House's dissemination of false information and blatant political opportunism amid the growing crisis was at odds with reliable details the White House had been receiving for several years. The country had conducted at least three "dry runs" on how to handle a pandemic over the past five decades. Based upon these studies and "tabletop" exercises, agencies within the federal government had in-depth institutional knowledge and a plan as to what needed to be done when the next virus-driven pandemic hit. The U.S.'s successful responses to previous epidemics and pandemics – including the reactions to the Asian Flu pandemic of 1957, the SARS epidemic of 2002-2004, the H1N1 Swine Flu pandemic of 2009, and the Ebola epidemic of 2014 - all left the federal government with a wealth of knowledge on how to respond to the next deadly virus.

Unfortunately, professional experts with institutional experience within federal agencies could not by themselves put an effective containment and response plan into place. Red flashing lights and sirens blaring their warnings could not be turned into a full-scale mobilization against this microbial attack until the White House gave the "go-ahead." Tragically, that signal never came until it was too late, and even then, the federal response was sluggish and poorly coordinated.

In short, a review of the Trump administration's handling of the coronavirus crisis amounted to a near "perfect storm" of errors, miscalculation, inattention, lack of political leadership, wishful thinking and sheer incompetence on the part of the White House and the relevant federal agencies, including the Centers for Disease Control and Prevention (CDC), the Health and Human Services Administration (HHS), the Food and Drug Administration (FDA), and the Federal Emergency Management Agency (FEMA). The CDC, for example, made the fateful, disastrous, and arrogant decision to develop its own coronavirus testing capability. In January and February 2020, the CDC shunned offers of assistance from the World Health Organization (W.H.O.), implying that the already-proven W.H.O. test was not good enough for America. The CDC also should have known that it did not have the in-house capability to mass produce the number of testing kits that would be necessary. The CDC then compounded this error by wasting critical weeks developing a test which, to everyone's horror, was flawed and required several weeks to correct.

The CDC also rebuffed offers of assistance from hundreds of public, private, and university laboratories. These formidable resources could have been enlisted early on in this extremely time-sensitive battle. The decision was particularly puzzling, considering the federal government had previously partnered with private labs, academic labs, and companies in developing effective responses to prior pandemics. For example, during the 1957 Asian Flu crisis, the U.S. recruited private testing companies and labs to develop an effective vaccine for the virus even before it reached U.S. shores.[12] This effort was spectacularly successful, in no small measure due to the public-private partnerships that were forged early on in the crisis. After a few months of research and development, the country had a vaccine ready to inoculate America's schoolchildren before they returned to school in the fall of 1957.

In contrast, the CDC held the private commercial lab companies and university labs at arm's length in responding to the coronavirus crisis. During the critical months of January and February 2020, the CDC and the FDA prevented these labs from developing their coronavirus tests by enforcing unnecessary regulatory roadblocks. Private and academic labs were required to go through a complex and agonizingly slow process of applying for their own "emergency use authorizations" (EUAs) from the FDA. Since the standard regulatory procedure to obtain a EUA can take weeks unless waived in the context of a national emergency, many of the best laboratories in the country were sidelined during this critical period.[13] Meanwhile, the academic laboratories that already developed tests were unable to conduct their testing. Nor could these labs help the local, city, and state public health officials with their urgent testing needs, since federal regulations did not allow them to do so.

Despite all the warnings that a major national emergency was unfolding, the federal agencies inexplicably failed to see any pressing need to waive the usual regulations. As late as January 28, CDC Director Robert Redfield was telling state public health directors that "the virus is not spreading in the U.S. at this time," because the CDC believed that the immediate health risk from COVID-19 to the general American public was relatively low.

As a result of the lack of any testing capability in the critical early weeks and months of the coronavirus crisis, the federal government, and most local, county, city, and state governments across the U.S., were left with insufficient and often misleading data as to the extent of the virus's spread at the local, regional and national level. Many virus carriers were "asymptomatic" and could have been spreading the virus to dozens or perhaps hundreds of people without even knowing that they were infected. There were few if any effective mitigation measures that were available other then blanket "stay-at-home" orders applicable to everyone. In other words, the U.S. was flying without a compass through the dense fog of the crisis without any reliable information or data that could only come from widespread and effective testing.

The U.S.'s utter failure to develop and deploy sufficient testing capability was in sharp contrast to South Korea's response, as well as that of several other countries. The South Korean government enlisted the support of private industry at an early stage in January 2020. They were able to engage in widespread and effective testing within weeks, making a significant difference in that country's ability to contain and respond to the crisis. Indeed, the U.S. government had to finally swallow its pride in mid-April and request 750,000 testing kits from South Korea, some of which started to be received almost immediately.[14] Still, by mid-April 2020, the critical early testing window was rapidly closing. The spread of the virus and the number of infections had already reached its peak in epicenters such as New York, New Jersey, Detroit (Michigan), and New Orleans (Louisiana).

The Trump administration also failed to take a leadership role in the implementation of any mitigation or "social distancing" rules. The administration left coronavirus response and mitigation to the cities, states, and counties, who were forced to make these critical decisions on their own. These age-old mitigation measures, such as "lockdowns" and quarantines, had proven to be effective in the past by slowing the spread of infectious diseases. Despite all of our scientific and technological advances, these traditional approaches - "social distancing," quarantines, and "stay-at-home" orders - appeared to be the *only* effective remedies at our disposal to "flatten the curve" of this pandemic.

Urgent efforts were undertaken to find an effective vaccine or treatment to combat coronavirus infections. Meantime, the country and the rest of the world were stuck with trying to live without them. But without a vaccine or effective treatment medications, it quickly became evident that even a partial reopening of the U.S. economy could only be safely managed if there were adequate testing capabilities in place. Without proper testing, it would be difficult, if not impossible, to determine, on any widespread basis, who was infected and who was not. And without sufficiently extensive antibody testing, it would also be impossible to identify all of those who had been previously infected and now could have immunity against the virus.

As a result of these lapses of federal leadership in the battle against COVID-19, thousands of Americans needlessly died. On April 9, 2020, New York Governor Andrew Cuomo announced that 799 people in New York had died from coronavirus in a single 24-hour period, more than 33 an hour.[15] As morgues became overwhelmed, filled to overflowing capacity, refrigeration trucks stood by at City hospitals to store the dead. New York City started burying unclaimed bodies and the bodies of the poor in New York City's Potter's Field on Hart Island, off the coast of the Bronx. As of April 10th, a long burial trench had been dug that was large enough to accommodate dozens of the dead.[16] These Hart Island burial grounds have been in operation since the mid-1800s. They were used to bury victims of the Spanish Flu in 1918 and 1919, and more recently, AIDS victims. The island was also used as a quarantine location for yellow fever and tuberculosis victims.

The inevitable changes to our way of life brought by this crisis will be undoubtedly profound. These changes are likely to accelerate trends already underway even before the coronavirus struck. Whether these changes are for better or worse (or a mixture of both) will depend to a large extent on what we do collectively in the coming years.

One thing for sure is that our democratic institutions will continue to suffer under the severe stress that has been placed on them for at least the past decade. These stress factors have become even more intense while Mr. Trump has occupied the White House. Meanwhile, Trump and his Republican enablers have used the current crisis to undermine and dismantle democratic norms. For example, on Tuesday, April 7, voters in Wisconsin were faced with a Hobson's choice: either risk their health and that of their neighbors by going out to vote in person, or opt to stay home and not vote.[17] Public health officials recommended that absentee mail-in ballots be used to keep people safe. Still, the Wisconsin Republican Party and gerrymandered Republican-dominated Assembly wanted none of it. The Republican legislature sued in federal court to defeat extended, mail-in ballot deadlines, and won in the U.S. Supreme Court, thanks to the Republican-appointed majority there. Republicans have also challenged state statutes calling for expanded absentee balloting in Michigan, Minnesota, Arizona, New Mexico, and elsewhere.[18]

Most Republican lawmakers couch their opposition to mail-in ballot initiatives as an effort to avoid or reduce voter fraud. However, as numerous objective studies have shown, voter fraud is mostly non-existent. Trump has been more candid than most when explaining why Republicans are so desperate to hold onto in-person voting requirements. He has complained that under Democratic plans for national expansion of early voting and voting by mail, "you'd never have a Republican elected in this country again."[19] Essentially, the easier the access to the ballot box, the higher the probability that the Republican Party will be facing an extinction event. Desperate people will do desperate things, especially when facing an existential political threat.

For better or worse (or both), the country is in the midst of a crisis that we will eventually emerge from, but with no clear idea of what that reality will be on the other side. To some extent, our society and way of life will be shaped by public health surveillance and testing procedures. We must learn to live with these new procedures since they are necessary to avoid a repeat of the current chaotic response effort. After 9/11, we had no choice but to accept enhanced security measures. The security in office buildings in New York and most other cities were "hardened" so that photo identification had to be shown at the front desk. The courthouses, airports, and other public facilities took security to an even higher level, with full-body scans and luggage searches. We willingly accepted those inconveniences to avoid a repeat of the 9/11 terrorist attacks. In other words, we were willing to give up some of our privacy and freedom of movement in the interests of greater security. We must be ever vigilant, though, that we do not cede any more of our privacy and liberty than absolutely necessary to meet the current emergency. Otherwise, we may wake up one day to find that the individual freedoms we thought we were protecting have vanished.

There can be no doubt that the post-COVID-19 world will be different, and I don't just mean that people won't be shaking your hand anymore. To enter a public place, you will have to submit to a temperature check, as they already are doing in China, Singapore, South Korea, and elsewhere.[20] Tens of millions of us will have to be tested on a daily or weekly basis, especially those of us working in the health care field, as first responders and essential service workers. We will have apps on our phones with GPS trackers so that we know where all of the COVID-19 infected people are located. This will allow us to keep our social distance from those still infected until they are declared healthy again. "Normal" social interactions between friends, as well as dating rituals, will become more of a challenge. And the list goes on.

While no one has a crystal ball to rely on, we already have enough information available at this point to confidently predict at least some of the future. In many (if not most) prior pandemics, there were no vaccines and no "wonder drugs" that could be taken to cure the deadly disease that had chosen us as its host. We had to rely on the same primitive "mitigation" tools of quarantine and isolation that we are relying on in the current crisis. Just think about it. Despite all the advancements in science, medicine, and technology, and billions of dollars spent on biological and chemical warfare research, our only defense now is to "shelter in place." We hide in homes for fear that a microscopic virus will target us, find us, and infect us. In other words, not much has changed since the Middle Ages.

We must learn the lessons of the past, as well as the hard lessons we are now learning in the present. Only when we are fully aware of what we have done right and what we have done wrong can we confidently sketch a road map that will bring us into a brighter and safer future.

2

A BRIEF HISTORY OF PANDEMICS FROM PREHISTORIC TIMES TO THE 1500S

A brief review of the great pandemics gives us some insights into how previous societies and civilizations successfully dealt with plagues, epidemics, and pandemics, and how others failed to do so.

Ancient Epidemics (Circa 3000 B.C.)

About 5,000 years ago, an epidemic wiped out a prehistoric village in China.[1] The bodies of the dead were stuffed inside a house that was burned down. No age group was spared, as the skeletons of juveniles, young adults, and middle-aged people were all found inside the home.[2] This archaeological site is named "Hamin Mangha," and it is one of the best-preserved prehistoric sites in northeastern China.[3] Archaeological and anthropological studies hypothesize the epidemic happened so quickly that there was no time to prepare for proper burials. Hamin Mangha was never inhabited again.

Before the discovery of Hamin Mangha in 2015, another prehistoric mass burial site, Miagozigou, was found in northeastern China. Experts believe the bodies and artifacts found at Miagozigou are dated roughly around the same time as those found at Hamin Mangha. Together, the discovery of these two sites suggests that an epidemic once ravaged the entire region.

The Athenian Plague

The first major reported epidemic was the Athenian Plague of 430-26 B.C. This epidemic occurred during the Peloponnesian War, which was fought from 431 to 404 B.C. between Athens and Sparta. The city of Athens was overcrowded because Pericles had arranged for the rural population to enter the city before the Spartan siege.[4] Because of these crowded wartime conditions in the city, the plague spread quickly, killing tens of thousands of people.[5]

Pericles, who himself became victim to the plague,[6] gave the funeral oration for the fallen at the end of the first year of the Spartan siege. By the late 5th century, it was an established Athenian practice to hold a public funeral in honor of all those who had died during the war.[7] After death, the bodies were cremated, and some of the bones were preserved for the annual funeral. The remains were left in a tent for three days so that offerings could be made.[8] After the three days, a funeral procession was held, including ten cypress coffins – one for each of the Athenian tribes – carrying the remains, and another for the remains of those who could not be identified ("the unknown"). Once the bodies were buried at Kerameikoz, a public grave, a prominent Athenian citizen concluded the ceremony with a speech.

The funeral oration of Pericles, amid war and plague, was a significant departure from other traditional Athenian wartime speeches. Pericles chose not to dwell on the great military achievements of Athens' past; instead, he focused on what he described as "the road by which we [the Athenians] reached our position, the form of government under which our greatness grew, and the national habits out of which it sprang."[9] Instead of glorifying the dead, he chose to praise his fellow citizens, and the city and the democracy for which they died. He emphasized attributes that made Athens exceptional, highlighting how the city stood out amongst its neighbors.

First and foremost, Athens was unique in that it was a democracy, thus placing the freedom of its citizens as a priority. Citizens – both as soldiers and as civilians – had put aside their personal desires and wishes for the greater cause. He described Athenian citizens as being open-minded and tolerant but also disciplined. Athenians would fight to the death because they had a voice in their democratic system, fighting for the cause of their own freedom and that of their fellow citizens.

Much like President Abraham Lincoln later did in his Gettysburg Address, Pericles' speech then turned to what is referred to as an "Exhortation to the Living." Pericles urged his fellow citizens: "You, their survivors, must determine to have an unfaltering a resolution in the field, though you may pray that it may have a happier outcome."[10]

It was a rather novel concept to praise civilian victims of a plague brought on by wartime conditions, in addition to the more traditional appreciation for the soldiers who had fallen in battle. Before this time, plagues were conventionally explained as mere punishment for those who might have angered the gods. Writings of Herodotus and Homer's *Iliad* hold the gods responsible for all the calamities to face humankind, including plagues.[11] The Book of Exodus in the Old Testament also followed along in this tradition. However, in his *History of the Peloponnesian War*, the Athenian general Thucydides focused more on the plague's impact on the social, political, and military life of the community. The work of Thucydides began a historiographical tradition that would become the model for many future historians.

Having suffered from the plague himself, Thucydides presented a very systematic account of the symptoms. His aim was merely to "describe what it was like, and set down the symptoms, knowledge of which will enable it to be recognized if it should ever break out again."[12] Thucydides wrote that "people in good health were all of a sudden attacked by violent heats in the head, and redness and inflammation in the eyes, the inward parts, such as the throat or tongue, becoming bloody and emitting an unnatural and fetid breath."[13]

The Athenian Plague originated in Ethiopia, and from there spread throughout Egypt and Greece.[14] Thucydides, however, remarked that the people of Athens suffered the highest toll from the disease.[15] Initial symptoms of the plague included headaches, conjunctivitis, fever, and a rash that covered the body. The victims then coughed up blood, and suffered from excruciating stomach cramping, followed by vomiting and attacks of "ineffectual retching."[16] Many people also experienced insomnia and restlessness. Thucydides also related that victims had such an unquenchable thirst that it drove them to throw themselves into the wells. Generally, infected individuals died by the seventh or eighth day. However, if anyone managed to survive past this time, they were stricken by uncontrollable diarrhea, which frequently caused death. Many of those who survived this stage suffered from partial paralysis, amnesia, or blindness for the rest of their lives.[17] Fortunately, infection of the plague provided immunity; when someone caught the disease twice, the second attack was never fatal.[18]

Thucydides also detailed the social consequences of the Athenian Plague. Noting that – just as the modern COVID-19 plague - doctors and other caregivers frequently caught the disease and died alongside those whom they had been attempting to heal.[19] Surprisingly, the Spartans besieging the city were not affected by the virus spreading through Athens.[20] If it were not for the war between the two city-states, both populations would likely have become infected, since airborne droplets probably carried it from one person to the next.

Thucydides believed the plague contributed to the defeat of Athens since it eventually broke the will of the people to endure suffering for an indefinite period for the public good. The despair caused by the plague within the city led the people to be "indifferent to the laws of men and gods."[21] Many immersed themselves in self-indulgence, rather than continuing to commit themselves to the common good.[22] In particular, Thucydides mentioned that no one observed the customary funerary rites, reflecting a general breakdown in culture, teachings, traditions, and the "old oracles."[23] With the decline in civic duty and religion, superstition and rumors took precedence.[24]

During the first century B.C., Lucretius would use this section of Thucydides' account of the Athenian Plague to support the teachings of Epicurus. Epicurus believed that the highest good is to seek modest pleasures to attain a state of tranquility, freedom from fear ("ataraxia"), and absence from bodily pain ("aponia").[25] To Lucretius, the plague illustrated not only human vulnerability but also the futility of religion and belief in the gods.

The Plague that Brought Down the Roman Empire

The Antonine Plague (165 to 180 A.D.), also known as the Plague of Galen after the Greek physician living in the Roman Empire who described it, was a severe pandemic. The virus most likely was brought to the Roman Empire by troops returning from campaigns in the Near East. Although the cause was never definitively determined, it is suspected that the plague was either smallpox or measles.[26] In fact, the epidemic may have claimed the life of a

Roman emperor Lucius Verus, the co-regent of Marcus Aurelius, who died in 169 A.D. Nine years later, the disease broke out again. According to the Roman historian Dio Cassius (155–235), the plague caused 2,000 deaths a day in Rome, about one-quarter of those who were affected, giving the disease a mortality rate of about 25%.[27] It is estimated the total death toll amounted to roughly 5 million.[28] The disease killed as much as one-third of the population in some areas and devastated the entire Roman army.[29]

The epidemic first appeared during the Roman siege of Seleucia in the winter of 165–166.[30] Ammianus Marcellinus reports that the plague spread to Gaul and the legions along the Rhine.[31] Eutropius asserts that a large percentage of the population died throughout the Roman Empire.[32] The epidemic had drastic social and political consequences. The historian Barthold Georg Niebuhr (1776–1831) concluded that the plague undoubtedly precipitated the crisis during the reign of Marcus Aurelius and that the ancient world never recovered from the blow inflicted by it.[33] During the Marcomannic Wars against the Germanic tribes along the northern Italian frontier in the early 170s A.D., Marcus Aurelius wrote his philosophical work *Meditations*. In his work, he laments that the pestilence around him was accompanied by the equally destructive tendency of his fellow Romans to engage in "falsehood, evil behavior, and lack of true understanding."[34] As he lay dying, Marcus Aurelius uttered the words, "Weep not for me; think rather of the pestilence and the deaths of so many others."[35]

The pestilence is reported to have severely degraded the Roman army's ability to both defend portions of the Roman Empire and to expand it. The Roman defenses were hampered when large numbers of troops succumbed to the disease when forces of Vologases IV of Parthia attacked Armenia, one of the eastern territories of the Roman Empire. According to the 5th-century Spanish writer Paulus Orosiu, many towns and villages in the Italian peninsula lost all their inhabitants. As the epidemic swept north towards the Rhine, in what is now Germany, the plague infected Germanic and Gallic peoples outside the Empire's borders. For several years, those northern Germanic and Gallic groups had pressed south in search of more lands to sustain their growing populations. With their ranks depleted by the epidemic, Roman armies could not push the tribes back north. From

167 A.D. to his death, Marcus Aurelius personally commanded legions near the Danube River, trying to control the advance of Germanic peoples across the river. A major offensive against the Marcomanni was postponed until 169 A.D. because of a shortage of Roman imperial troops.

The Antonine Plague contributed substantially to the decline and eventual fall of the Roman Empire in the 5th century. But the plague also led to a renewal of spirituality, creating conditions for the spread of Christianity.

The Plague of Justinian

Constantinople, the capital of the Byzantine Empire, was decimated by the plague in 541 B.C. when the bacterium Yersinia pestis was carried by ships sailing across the Mediterranean from Egypt to Constantinople.[36] Egypt was a vassal state in the Empire. It paid tribute to the Emperor Justinian in grain, which was riddled with plague-carrying fleas on the black rats that came along with the grain shipments. After decimating Constantinople, the plague quickly spread across Europe, Asia, North Africa, and Arabia, killing an estimated 30 to 50 million people. These deaths are thought to be about one-half of the world's population at the time.

The Black Death

About 800 years after Constantinople's decimation, the plague bacterium returned to Europe in 1347 A.D. as "The Black Death," or "the Plague," becoming one of the most devastating pandemics ever. Over just four years, the Plague killed 200 million people.

At the time, officials had no idea as to the Plague's cause. But they did have some understanding that its spreading had to do with proximity between people, leading to the first attempts at quarantines and "social distancing."[37] In the Venetian controlled port-city of Ragusa, newly arriving sailors were kept in forced isolation on their ships for 30 days, known in Venetian law as "Trentino."[38] The forced isolation period was increased to 40 days, or "quarantino," from which the term "quarantine" derives.[39] Quarantining became a useful public health tool for combatting the Plague. It is still the most powerful tool in the public health arsenal in the face of a runaway pandemic. Chinese officials recently used this age-old technique to combat the COVID-19 outbreak when they imposed a heavy-handed but effective quarantine on Wuhan and the rest of the province, encompassing up to 70 million people.

The Great Plagues of London

Between 1348 to 1665, the Plague resurfaced about every twenty years in London, causing an astonishing 40 outbreaks in 300 years.[40] Each of these resurfaced outbreaks killed 20% of the men, women, and children living in the city.[41] By the early 1500s, England imposed stringent laws intended to identify and isolate those who were sickened. Homes with plague victims inside were marked with a bale of hay strung from a pole outside. When any family member in that house went out, they had to carry the pole wherever they went.

The Great Plague of 1665 was the last crescendo of the plague era in London, killing 100,000 of London's inhabitants in just seven months. The wealthy and well-to-do – including most doctors, lawyers, and royalty – fled London for the countryside. They left the poor to die in the tens of thousands with little in the way of medical care or other assistance. The dead were buried in mass graves. All public entertainment was banned, and victims were forced to remain in their homes. It was a partially successful campaign to restrict the spread of disease. Red crosses were painted on their doors of the stricken, along with a plea for forgiveness: "Lord have mercy upon us."

While some of the techniques used to control the spread of disease were draconian – such as shuttering the sick in their homes until they died – the practice of "social distancing" came into vogue. It is now being implemented, several centuries later, as the most effective tool to stop or slow down the spread of an infectious disease. Social distancing is especially valuable where there is no known cure or vaccine. Those who implemented "social distancing" measures early on in the 1665-1666 plague cycle fared much better than those who did not.

Isaac Newton, a student in his 20s at Trinity College, Cambridge, was among those in England who survived the Great Plague in 1665 by merely isolating himself. Scientists and academics at the time did not know that the spread of bacteria was continuing to cause the Plague. In fact, scientists would not figure this out for another 200 years – but they strongly suspected that the crowded conditions in London, and other towns and cities, contributed to the spread of the deadly disease.[42] As a result, Cambridge University temporarily shut down, and the students, including Newton, were sent home to continue their studies there while trying to avoid contracting the spreading illness.[43] Cambridge's decision was the 1665 version of "social distancing." Unfettered by the typical restrictions of college, Newton thrived, later referring to this year away from formal schooling as his "annus mirabilis," his "year of wonders,"[44] during which he discovered gravity by watching an apple fall from a tree in his yard.

London had a quarter of its population die off in the Plague of 1665 to 1666. Newton and others who had wealth or family connections were able to self-isolate and lead reasonably productive lives during their self-imposed social distancing periods – even without the internet or social media! Given the lack of technological advances, the concept of "distance learning" was not very highly developed.

Smallpox and The American Plagues of the 1500s

The American Plagues are a cluster of Eurasian diseases, including smallpox, brought to the Americas by European explorers.[45] For many centuries, smallpox was a virtually continuous epidemic in Europe, Asia, and Arabia, killing off 30% of the population and leaving countless survivors with unsightly scars.[46] European explorers carrying the smallpox virus to the New World in the 1500s devastated the native people in the Americas.

Smallpox and other viruses brought to the Americas by the Europeans contributed to the collapse of the Inca and Aztec civilizations. Some estimates suggest that 90% of the indigenous population in the Western Hemisphere was killed off by smallpox and other epidemics alone.[47] The diseases helped Spanish forces conquer the Aztec capital of Tenochtitlán in 1519. Another Spanish force led by Francisco Pizarro conquered the Incas in 1532. Because the Aztec and Incan armies were ravaged by disease, they were unable to effectively defend against the Spanish troops. These diseases also helped other colonial powers such as Great Britain, France,

Portugal, and the Netherlands explore, conquer, and settle different parts of the Western Hemisphere. Diseases first introduced by Europeans vastly reduced the size of the indigenous peoples that opposed them.

The indigenous populations of the Americas had no natural immunity to smallpox, leading to the death of tens of millions of native peoples over one century. What is now modern-day Mexico had its population reduced from about 11 million people to only one million.[48]

When smallpox arrived in North America in the 1600s, it wiped out large numbers of Native American tribes, killing over 70% of the Native American population in the region.[49] Smallpox was also a scourge for the colonial community. In 1721, for example, 844 of the 5,889 Bostonians who had smallpox died from it.[50]

Smallpox has the distinction of being the first virus epidemic to be ended by a vaccine. In 1770, British doctor Edward Jenner deduced that the cowpox milkmaids contracted could be used to create a vaccine that immunized against smallpox.[51] It took nearly two centuries to eradicate this dreadful disease, and in 1972, a vaccination initiative led to the elimination of the disease in the U.S.[52] By the 1980s, the W.H.O. announced that smallpox – after having killed hundreds of millions of people – had finally been eradicated throughout the globe.[53]

Or so it was thought. However, in July 2014, a half-dozen forgotten vials of the smallpox virus were discovered while cleaning out a storage area on the campus of the National Institutes of Health (NIH) in Bethesda, Maryland.[54] The six vials of freeze-dried virus, apparently dating from the 1950s, were found by a scientist from the FDA in a cold storage room that was originally part of an NIH laboratory but was transferred to the FDA in the early 1970s. The vials labeled as containing variola (smallpox) were packed in a cardboard box along with ten other vials with unclear labels.[55]

Recently, the U.S. has been highly critical of the safety levels of Chinese labs, even going so far as to suggest that the COVID-19 virus may have been released from a Wuhan lab. Yet, the CDC and other relevant U.S. agencies should first make sure that their own house is in order before pointing their fingers at foreign entities. They should ensure that there are no U.S. labs from which deadly viruses, such as smallpox, can escape.

Although there is a smallpox vaccine, any party with malicious intent that succeeds in obtaining a smallpox sample, or that of another deadly virus, could possibly modify or "weaponize" it so that it is impervious to existing vaccines. This is the essence of Biological Warfare, or "Biowarfare," and we must be extremely careful that no modified or "enhanced" infectious diseases are accidentally or intentionally released, for if so, the current COVID-19 pandemic may seem more like a Sunday picnic.

3

EARLY PANDEMICS IN THE U.S.

FROM SMALLPOX, MALARIA, CHOLERA AND YELLOW FEVER TO THE POLIO EPIDEMIC OF 1916

Infectious diseases such as smallpox,[1] malaria, and yellow fever[2] were the most dangerous threats to life in colonial America. Obsession with the spread of disease was a familiar experience for early settlers of the country. Notably, Native Americans were decimated by European scourges that the new arrivals brought with them. Other infectious diseases like cholera that arrived in the 1800s brought even more misery and death. Epidemics of infectious diseases have plagued every generation of Americans from colonial times to the present, where we are still in the throes of the COVID-19 pandemic. Indeed, the history of the U.S. cannot be fully understood without understanding the history of its epidemics and their profound impact on its people.

Smallpox

Smallpox, which we now know is caused by the variola virus, is extremely contagious and can easily be spread by physical contact, affecting children and adults alike. Smallpox epidemics were frequent reoccurrences in Colonial America. The illness was deadly and usually left survivors disfigured one way or another.[3] In fact, it may have killed more of General Washington's troops in the Continental Army than British soldiers did.[4] Given its highly contagious nature, the utterance of the threatening epithet: "A pox on both your houses" was considered much more than a mere idle threat.

A particularly virulent sequence of smallpox outbreaks took place in Boston, Massachusetts, from 1636 to 1698, when Boston endured six epidemics. In 1721, when the most severe epidemic occurred, virtually the entire population fled the city, bringing the virus to the rest of the Thirteen Colonies.[5]

Colonists tried to prevent the spread of smallpox by isolation (quarantine) and vaccination, which caused a mild form of the disease and could often be as fatal as the disease itself. The vaccine was introduced in 1721 by Zabdiel Boylston and Cotton Mather, the leading Puritan minister in Boston.[6] The procedure involved injecting the infection into the patient, which resulted in a mild form of the disease. If the vaccine went according to plan, a person would have the smallpox for a shorter period of time than if it was contracted naturally.[7]

When the 1721 smallpox epidemic paralyzed much of New England, Cotton Mather's promotion of the use of vaccinations was embraced by many of his fellow colonials, particularly the well-educated and wealthy Puritan families in the Boston area.[8] Harvard College and the entire town of Cambridge successfully combined broad-based inoculation programs with inspection and isolation efforts. These efforts provided a model followed by other New England communities, which increasingly adopted immunization and quarantine policies by 1800.[9]

Malaria

Malaria is such an old disease that there are references to it in Chinese inscriptions on bones, tortoise shells, and bronzeware dating back more than 3500 years.[10] The cyclical nature of the disease, from human to mosquito and back to human, and the ability of the parasites to form resistance to treatments and the mosquitoes to insecticides, make malaria a difficult disease to eliminate, even today.

Malaria was deadly to many of the American colonists, especially in the Southern colonies. Of newly arrived healthy young men, over one-fourth died within five years of their arrival in the Carolinas.[11] Until the late 19th century, the cause of malaria was unknown. Colonial physicians attributed it to "miasma" or bad air.[12] In actuality, the disease is a parasite found in certain species of mosquitoes that breed rapidly, particularly in the Carolinas, where the lowlands flooded for rice cultivation.[13] The infection quickly spread as mosquito-bitten slaves working in the fields became hosts for the virus. Mosquitos then transmitted the parasite to other slaves and the white population, rapidly spreading to entire communities in the South and Northwest. People who newly arrived from Europe were especially vulnerable to the deadly disease. After the second generation, colonists typically suffered non-fatal cases, characterized by a "fever season" for a few weeks every year.[14]

Mortality rates from malaria were extremely high for infants and small children, as was also true for diphtheria, smallpox,[15] and yellow fever. Without many trained physicians, colonials relied on faith healers, minister-physicians, barbers, and apothecaries.[16] One of the standard treatments was bloodletting, with often fatal results due to the lack of knowledge of infections and disease at the time.[17] By the 18th century, however, colonial physicians introduced modern medicine to the cities based on models developed in England and Scotland, making significant advances in vaccination, pathology, anatomy, and pharmacology.[18]

The scourge of malaria is still very much with us today. More than 400,000 people are killed by malaria each year, most of them children under the age of five. About 1,700 cases of malaria are diagnosed in the U.S. each year.[19] The vast majority of cases in the U.S. are travelers and immigrants returning from countries where malaria transmissions still occur, such as sub-Saharan Africa and South Asia.

Enormous progress has been made in recent decades to combat malaria through the use of bed nets and insecticides. However, these efforts have stalled in recent years, even in countries that report the most cases. After a near-steady decline for about a decade, the estimated number of malaria cases across 91 countries increased from 211 million in 2015 to 216 million in 2016, according to the World Health Organization's annual World Malaria Report.[20]

In 2016, the W.H.O. identified 21 malaria-endemic countries that could feasibly eliminate the disease by 2020. Together, these countries formed the "E-2020 initiative" and were part of a concerted effort to drive indigenous malaria cases to zero within the 2020 timeline.[21] China and El Salvador brought their number of malaria cases to zero by 2017, and by 2019, Paraguay and Algeria were also certified as malaria-free.[22] Three other countries – Iran, Malaysia, and Timor-Leste – also achieved zero indigenous cases of malaria.

In a breakthrough just this year (2020), scientists in Kenya and the U.K. discovered a microbe that completely protects mosquitoes from being infected with malaria.[23] This malaria-blocking microbe, Microsporidia MB, was discovered in mosquitoes found on the shores of Lake Victoria. The researchers could not find a single mosquito carrying Microsporidia that was harboring the malaria parasite. According to Dr. Jeremy Herren from the International Centre of Insect Physiology and Ecology in Kenya, "The data we have so far suggest it is 100% blockage ... of malaria."[24]

This discovery has enormous potential to control the disease. People in at-risk areas will be protected from contracting malaria if the mosquitoes themselves are also protected from the disease. Researchers are now investigating whether they can release mosquitoes with this malaria-resistant microbe into the wild or use spores to suppress the disease. Male mosquitoes (which do not bite) could be infected in the lab and released into the wild to infect the females. This approach to the control of malaria would also reap environmental benefits since it would not involve the mass killing of mosquitoes that certain species depend on as a food source. A similar approach is being studied for the control of Dengue Fever. A type of bacteria called Wolbachia has been shown to make it harder for mosquitoes to spread dengue fever in real-world trials.[25]

However, the 2020 arrival of COVID-19 in African countries and elsewhere with malaria has stalled much of the progress in recent years. Due to the worldwide lockdowns in countries with malaria, the suspension of pesticide spraying to kill mosquitoes has led to a resurgence of malaria cases. Especially where pesticide spraying has been suspended, pregnant women, in particular, are more vulnerable to contracting COVID-19 in malaria-prone areas.[26]

This is because women's immune systems are lowered so as not to reject the fetus during pregnancy, in turn putting them at risk of contracting both malaria and COVID-19.[27] This problem is compounded by the fact that malaria and COVID-19 may have similar symptoms, which has led to confusion in diagnoses without widespread availability of coronavirus testing kits. The countries with the highest number of malaria cases, mainly in Africa, are also affected by conflict, population displacement, malnutrition, and stress. When COVID-19 is added to the mix, vulnerable populations – particularly pregnant women and older people – are put at extreme risk. The W.H.O. has urged countries not to lose focus on other health issues during the pandemic, warning that disruptions to malaria prevention and treatment could double the year's deaths in sub-Saharan Africa to more than 700,000.[28]

Typhoid

Typhoid fever, which causes a prolonged burning fever, is extremely debilitating and, if left untreated, has a mortality rate of up to 30%.[29] While typhoid can flare up at any time, it typically occurs in the hot summer months.[30] Shortly after the establishment of the colonial establishment of Jamestown, Reverend Robert Hunt reported the first typhoid epidemic in 1607 in what is now Virginia.[31] Typhoid fever was a significant factor in colonial military operations, causing a shortage of soldiers when large numbers of them became afflicted with the disease.[32] More men died from typhoid than in battle or from wounds.[33]

The most famous typhoid carrier in U.S. history was Mary Mallon, or "Typhoid Mary," who is believed to have infected 51 people with the disease, three of whom died. Mary was born in 1869 in Ireland and emigrated to the U.S. in 1884. She worked in a variety of domestic positions before settling into a career as a cook. Mary gained her notoriety by being the first otherwise healthy and known asymptomatic carrier of the bacterium Salmonella typhi, which was not isolated until later in 1880. Although she consistently denied being ill, the disease was traced back to her from numerous victims. Once identified, she was forced into quarantine on North Brother Island in the East River off Manhattan. She was quarantined for a total of 26 years. Her case has similarities to the COVID-19 epidemic. Both diseases were initially (and mistakenly) thought to be impossible to spread from person-to-person unless the infected person was exhibiting a fever or flu-like symptoms. The gravity of COVID-19, like typhoid, only became fully known after learning that there were asymptomatic carriers of the diseases like Typhoid Mary, who could still transmit the deadly virus to others. Each year there are about 350 typhoid cases in the U.S. The CDC reports these cases yearly, proving that poor sanitation and contaminated water remain an unfortunate reality in this country.

Yellow Fever Epidemics: 1668-1793

Between 1668 and 1693, Yellow Fever appeared in America, arriving first in Philadelphia and then in New York. It later appeared in Boston. In most instances, Yellow Fever was brought to those cities by ship from Barbados and other Caribbean islands.[34] Throughout the Colonial period, there were several epidemics in these three cities, as well as Texas, New Hampshire, Florida, and as far up the Mississippi River as St. Louis, Missouri.[35] During these outbreaks, residents who chose to stay in the area were advised to avoid contact with others by shutting themselves in their houses away from friends and jobs.[36] This "hiding away" is the same kind of "social distancing" practiced across America during the COVID-19 outbreak. It is evident that not much has changed since there are currently no known therapeutic medications that can "cure" coronavirus, and no vaccine has yet been developed. We now have sophisticated medical equipment available in emergency rooms and Intensive Care Units (ICUs), such as ventilators, to help with breathing, but even these modern medical devices may be of limited efficacy. In the early stages of the COVID-19 outbreak in New York City and elsewhere, the death rates were disturbingly high even for patients who were intubated and put on ventilators.

Just as COVID-19 has driven the U.S. economy into a tailspin, colonial epidemics caused widespread unemployment and business closings in early American cities hit with yellow fever. The death rate was so high that a large percentage of the still-healthy male members of the population had to work around the clock to bury the dead.[37] Of course, we now have refrigerated morgue trucks to help ease the burden. Still, even today, the reality of mass deaths is a frightening experience for entire communities. The number of dead and dying in the COVID-19 pandemic has taken a heavy toll. The burden was not just on those who were sick and dying, but also on the still healthy. This toll was disproportionately borne by medical professionals, those already ill with other ailments, and by the elderly. Since family members cannot be present, hospital health care workers have been far too often the last witnesses to those who die in emergency rooms and ICUs.

The most massive and best recorded Yellow Fever epidemic in America hit Philadelphia in 1793. With a population of approximately 55,000, Philadelphia was America's largest city, its capital, and its busiest port. The summer of that year was unusually dry and hot. The water levels of streams and wells were dangerously reduced, providing an excellent breeding ground for insects. By July, the city's inhabitants were remarking on the extraordinary number of flies and mosquitoes that swarmed around the dock area.

July of 1793 also brought refugees escaping political turmoil in the Caribbean Islands, particularly from Barbados. What started as a trickle became a torrent of thousands, as ship after ship unloaded its human cargo on the Philadelphia wharves. They brought with them Yellow Fever, a disease easily and quickly transmitted from the sick to healthy people by mosquitoes. Yellow Fever tended to come on very suddenly, beginning first with a headache, backache, and fever, making the patient extremely ill from the very start.[38] The disease gets its name from the yellow color of the skin that develops the third day of the illness. At the end of one week, the afflicted person was either dead or on the way to recovery.[39]

As the number of dead rapidly mounted in Philadelphia, the local physicians, having been taken entirely by surprise and having no idea how to treat this illness, were terrified. The afflicted initially experienced pains in the head, back, and limbs, accompanied by high fever. Symptoms would often disappear after a few days, leaving a false sense of security. The disease would shortly return with a more severe fever and turn the victim's skin a ghastly yellow, with the victim vomiting black clots of blood. Death soon followed as the victim slipped into a helpless stupor. Nothing could be done to alleviate the suffering of the victims, other than to try to find enough coffins to bury the dead and men to bury them.

Unaware of the link between mosquitos and the disease, Philadelphia's medical community was dumbfounded. Dr. Benjamin Rush, the city's leading physician and a signer of the Declaration of Independence, advised citizens to flee the city. He worked tirelessly to comfort the hapless victims, but, just as in the case of COVID-19, there was no known medical treatment available. The course of the disease was often swift, with a victim considered to be in good health one day but buried the next. Burning fever sometimes led to paroxysms of rage, driving some patients from their beds into the streets. In some instances, they ran to the river where they drowned. Insanity was often the last horrible stage of the disease.[40]

At least 17,000 of the residents of Philadelphia abandoned the city, including most of its well-to-do population, along with members of Congress, President Washington, and his Cabinet. The epidemic may have hastened the move of the nation's capital from Philadelphia to a new city to be called Washington, D.C. However, the poor and the already sick in Philadelphia had nowhere to flee, which left them completely vulnerable and exposed to the spreading disease. The epidemic subsided and finally disappeared with the arrival of cold weather in November of 1793. Still, five thousand people died before it was over.

A vaccine for Yellow Fever was later developed in 1935 and licensed in 1954.[41] There is no known cure, but one vaccine is enough for lifetime immunity.

Cholera

Cholera is a highly contagious disease that occurs in settings without clean water and proper sanitation, such as poor, remote villages to overcrowded cities, refugee camps, and conflict zones.[42] It is a bacterial infection that causes cells lining the intestine to produce large amounts of fluid. It spreads when someone ingests contaminated food or water, which can rapidly cause massive outbreaks. It causes profuse diarrhea and vomiting, which can lead to death by intense dehydration, sometimes within hours. An English physician, John Snow, was the first to link the disease to contaminated water in 1854.[43]

Since its spread in the 19th century, cholera has killed tens of millions of people.[44] Between 1847 and 1851, more than one million people perished from the disease in Russia alone.[45] During the second of seven cholera pandemics during the 1800s, the disease killed 150,000 Americans.[46] There were three large cholera outbreaks in the U.S. in the 1800s, and it is believed to have spread primarily through interior waterways such as the Erie Canal in upstate New York, and routes along the Eastern Seaboard.[47] The rapid spread of cholera also resulted from other advancements in transportation and global trade, as well as from increased immigration into the U.S. from Europe.[48]

The most severe cholera epidemic in the U.S. lasted from 1826 to 1837. New York City and other U.S. cities did not have the effective sanitation systems, water purification, and treatment facilities as exist today. Thus, cholera spread rapidly through the water systems and sewers.[49]

In Washington, D.C., Michael Shiner, an enslaved laborer at the Washington Navy Yard, recorded the following: "The time the [cholera] broke out in about June and July, August and September 1832. [I]t Raged in the City of Washington and every day [there were] twelve or 13 carried out to [their] graves a day."[50] By late July 1832, cholera had spread to Virginia, and on August 7, 1832, Commodore Lewis Warrington confirmed to the Secretary of the Navy, Levi Woodbury, that cholera was at the Gosport Navy Yard: "Between noon of that day, [August 1] and the morning of Friday [August 3], when all work on board her USS Fairfield stopped, several deaths by cholera occurred, and fifteen or sixteen cases (of less violence) were reported."[51]

Cholera is no longer considered a pressing health threat in Europe and North America due to the filtration and chlorination of water. Yet, cholera still heavily affects populations in developing countries, particularly those with poor water and sewer treatment systems.[52] In fact, cholera affects an estimated 3 to 5 million people worldwide, causing roughly 58,000 to 130,000 deaths a year, in addition to the many unreported cases.[53] In the early 1980s, death rates were believed to have been greater than three million a year.[54] A cholera outbreak began in war-ravaged Yemen in October of 2016, returning in 2017, with approximately 200,000 cases resulting in 1,300 deaths.[55] In 2017, an outbreak in Somalia resulted in 50,000 cases and 880 deaths.[56] In August 2018, there were cholera cases reported in Algeria, and in September 2018, there was a cholera outbreak reported in Zimbabwe.

Now that we are in the age of coronavirus, it is important to remember that it is not the only ongoing plague that the world is facing. Since cholera first spread across the globe two centuries ago, it has killed about 50 million people.[57] And it is not done yet. It will continue to kill people in developing countries that are mostly ignored by the West.

Although we are understandably obsessed with coronavirus right now, cholera claimed as many or more lives than COVID-19 during the period from January 1 to March 25, 2020.[58] But you are unlikely to hear much (or anything) about the scourge of cholera, since it has no significant presence in the U.S., Europe or the rest of the developed world. Westerners can easily get their hands on the most effective vaccine, Dukoral, to stave off cholera.[59] Cholera vaccines are not as accessible where they are needed the most: where poor sanitation and contaminated water provide fertile ground for the disease to prosper.

1889-1900 Flu Pandemic (the "Russian Flu")

With the coming of the modern industrial age, new transport links made it easier for influenza and other viruses to spread and develop into epidemics, and even pandemics. Better known as the "Russian flu," this deadly influenza pandemic killed about one million people worldwide. It was the last major pandemic of the 19th century, spreading across the globe in just a few short months. The virus strain responsible is believed to be an influenza A virus (subtype H2N2), and it took only five weeks for the epidemic to reach its peak.

The earliest cases were reported in Russia, where the virus spread rapidly throughout St. Petersburg. The virus quickly made its way throughout Europe and the rest of the world, even though air travel did not yet exist. In 1889, Russian influenza posed little cause for concern for America; after all, there was a vast ocean between Europe and America to protect it from foreign invasions, whether they be of a military or microbial nature. However, before very long, this first modern pandemic spread across the globe and reached the East Coast of the U.S. by steamship. Thousands of Americans were hit with sudden chills and headaches, followed by a sore throat, laryngitis, and bronchitis.

Public health officials at the time (late 1889 and early 1890) tended to downplay the danger of the Russian flu, reassuring the public that it represented a mild strain of the flu. Similarly, the Trump administration's first reaction to the COVID-19 pandemic was to downplay the severity of the disease, as Trump himself compared it to the common flu.

The newspapers in 1889 also downplayed the epidemic: "It is not deadly, not even necessarily dangerous," The *Evening World* in New York announced, "but it will afford a grand opportunity for the dealers to work off their surplus of bandanas."[60] However, on December 28, 1889, after newspapers reported the first death in the U.S. – that of 25-year-old Thomas Smith of Canton, Massachusetts – and the rising death toll, Americans began to take the threat seriously. For the first week of January 1890, New York reported a wintertime death record of 1,202 people.[61] While only 19 of those cases were attributed to influenza alone, the numbers revealed a startling spike in deaths from related diseases: "Persons with weak lungs and those suffering from heart disease or kidney troubles are most seriously affected, and in many cases, the influenza leads quickly to pneumonia," the *New York Tribune* reported.[62] Meanwhile, with the help of America's vast network of railroads, the disease spread inland, as it did in Europe. Reports of the disease came in from Chicago, Detroit, Denver, Kansas City, Los Angeles, San Francisco, and other U.S. cities.

One Los Angeles victim gave a particularly vivid description of the experience: "I felt as if I had been beaten with clubs for about an hour and then plunged into a bath of ice," he told a reporter, "My teeth chattered like castanets, and I consider myself lucky now to have gotten off with a whole tongue."[63] People coped as best they could, but those sick with the Russian flu seemed to be everywhere. "On a Sixth Avenue elevated train this morning fully one-half of the passengers were coughing, sneezing, and applying handkerchiefs to noses and eyes, and many of them had their heads bundled up in scarves and mufflers," The *Evening World* reported, "They were a dejected and forlorn appearing crowd."[64]

Pharmacists throughout the country noted an unusually high demand for quinine, which some health authorities had suggested as a possible remedy. However, medical journals warned against the dangers of self-medicating, urging people to let the disease run its course.

According to contemporary accounts, influenza had disappeared mainly in the United States by early February 1890. At the peak of the Russian flu epidemic, New York City recorded the highest number of deaths, at 2,503. However, Boston, with a smaller population, was harder hit on a per-capita basis. The total U.S. death toll was about 13,000, according to the U.S. Census Office, with nearly 1 million deaths worldwide. The Russian flu returned every several years after that. Still, fortunately, a large portion of the U.S. population was immune by then, having been exposed to it during its first visit.

Today, the Russian influenza is mostly forgotten, overshadowed by the far more devastating Spanish flu of 1918. But it did give Americans a preview of life—and death—in an increasingly interconnected world where pandemics could be expected to arrive on a fairly regular basis.

American Polio Epidemic: 1916

A polio epidemic that started in New York City in 1916 caused 27,000 cases and 6,000 deaths in the U.S.[65] The disease mainly affected children and sometimes left survivors with permanent disabilities. Franklin D. Roosevelt, who went on to be a four-term president of the U.S., was diagnosed with polio in 1921 and partially crippled by the age of 39.

Polio epidemics occurred sporadically in the U.S. until Jonas Salk developed a vaccine in 1954.[66] As the vaccine became widely available, cases in the U.S. declined. The last polio case in the U.S. was reported in 1979. Worldwide vaccination efforts have significantly reduced the disease, although it is not yet wholly eradicated.

4

THE 1918 INFLUENZA PANDEMIC: IMPORTANT LESSONS LEARNED THAT ARE NOW BEING IGNORED

The 1918 flu pandemic (also known as The Spanish Flu) was an unusually deadly influenza pandemic.[1] Lasting from January 1918 to December 1920, it infected 500 million people – about a quarter of the world's population at the time.[2] The death toll is estimated to have been anywhere from 17 million to 50 million, and possibly as high as 100 million, making it one of the deadliest pandemics in human history.[3] The death toll in the U.S. was 675,000.[4]

To maintain morale, World War I censors minimized early reports of illness and mortality in Germany, the U.K, France, and the U.S.[5] However, newspapers were free to report the epidemic's effects in neutral Spain. Reports such as the grave illness of King Alfonso XIII and other stories created a false impression that Spain was especially hard hit.[6] This gave rise to the name "Spanish Flu."

From September through November of 1918, the death rate from the Spanish Flu skyrocketed. In the U.S. alone, 195,000 Americans died from the Spanish Flu in just the month of October.[7] Unlike a typical seasonal flu, which claims victims among the very young and very old, the second wave of the Spanish Flu exhibited a so-called "W curve." In a "W Curve," there are high numbers of deaths among young and old, and a significant spike in the middle.[8] This spike is composed of otherwise healthy 25- to 35-year-olds in the prime of their life. This curve was especially shocking to doctors and the American public. They had never before experienced a disease that killed so many otherwise healthy young men and women in such a painful and gruesome fashion. These victims were being struck with blistering fevers, nasal hemorrhaging, and pneumonia, with the patient drowning in their own fluid-filled lungs.

Only decades later were scientists able to explain this phenomenon now known as "cytokine explosion." When a virus is attacking the human body, the immune system sends messenger proteins called cytokines to promote helpful inflammation.[9] But some strains of the flu, particularly the H1N1 strain responsible for the Spanish Flu outbreak, can trigger a dangerous immune overreaction. In those cases, the body is overloaded with cytokines, leading to severe damage to healthy cells and the fatal buildup of fluid in the lungs.[10] British military doctors conducting autopsies on soldiers killed by this second wave of the Spanish Flu described the substantial damage to the lungs as akin to the effects of chemical warfare.

The rapid spread of Spanish Flu in the fall of 1918 can be at least partially blamed on public health officials who were unwilling to impose quarantines during wartime. In Britain, for example, government officials knew full well that a strict civilian lockdown was the best way to fight the spread of the highly contagious disease. However, British authorities decided that they could not risk crippling the war effort by keeping munitions factory workers and other civilians at home. British civilians were encouraged to simply "carry on" as usual during the pandemic, leading to a greater spread of the infection. This spread led to resulting illness and death far more than would have otherwise occurred if a quarantine had been imposed.

Similarly, most of the civilian leadership in the U.S. was reluctant to dampen the high level of patriotism and support for the U.S. war effort with any "alarmist" measures to restrict the rapid spread of the virus throughout the country. A severe nursing shortage further hampered the public health response to the Spanish Flu crisis in the U.S. Thousands of nurses had been deployed to military camps and the front lines. The shortfall was worsened by the American Red Cross's refusal to use trained African American nurses until the worst of the pandemic had already passed.

Medical professionals in the U.S. thought that aspirin might be a cure for the Spanish Flu; however, the overuse of aspirin only made the situation worse, not better. This "wonder drug" had been trademarked by Bayer in 1899. When the patent expired in 1917, other companies started to manufacture it during the pandemic.[11] At the time, medical professionals were recommending up to 30 grams of aspirin daily.[12] We now know that this dosage can be toxic since doses above four grams are now considered to be unsafe.[13] Aspirin poisoning symptoms include hyperventilation and pulmonary edema, also known as "fluid in the lungs." These symptoms were two of the most commonly noticed among Spanish Flu patients who were taking "aspirin treatments" before they died.

However, perhaps the primary reason that the Spanish Flu claimed so many lives in 1918 was that science simply didn't have the tools yet to develop a vaccine for the virus. Microscopes couldn't even see something as small as a virus until the 1930s. Top medical professionals in 1918 were erroneously convinced that a bacterium caused the Flu.[14] Doctors spent much time, money, and resources fruitlessly trying to find a cure for this imaginary bacillus. The first flu vaccine to be licensed in the U.S. came about in the 1940s.

Another reason the Spanish Flu was so lethal was there were no antibiotics to treat secondary bacterial infections. Control efforts around the globe were limited to nonpharmaceutical responses like isolation, quarantine, disinfectants, and limitations on public gatherings. For the most part, the federal government refused to consider the 1918 influenza epidemic as a national problem. The lack of national leadership led to an often inconsistent patchwork of approaches by cities and states across the county. The results were disastrous, similar to what we have experienced during the coronavirus crisis.

During the current pandemic, the Trump administration has refused to formally impose a uniform quarantine and stay-at-home restrictions applicable in all 50 states. This national quarantine could have been done relatively quickly and effectively if only the federal government had the foresight and political will to do it. But this did not happen. What we have today concerning the response to the COVID-19 pandemic is much the same as what happened in 1918. The leadership in the fight to limit the spread of the virus in the U.S. came from Governors of the states, mayors of the major cities, and other local officials.

Back in 1918, New York City health officials took a proactive approach to the influenza epidemic by issuing regulations distancing healthy New Yorkers from those infected. New York officials increased disease surveillance capacities, including physician reportings and health inspections. New York also mounted a large-scale health education campaign about the dangers of coughing and sneezing in public, while also regulating public spaces such as schools and theaters. A broad spectrum of mandatory and voluntary public health control measures was implemented. There was a prohibition against spitting in public, and a full spectrum of compulsory and optional measures.[15]

Most of New York City's public health responses to the 1918 influenza epidemic were adapted from its previous campaigns against tuberculosis.[16] The most important strategies to control the spread of influenza were changes in New York City and State laws. They mandated staggered business hours to avoid rush-hour crowding.[17] New York also established more than 150 emergency health districts and centers to coordinate home care and case reporting. The sick were cared for in hospitals, at home, in gymnasia, and armories throughout New York City. Careful records and statistics were taken to document the course of the pandemic and the treatment of each patient.[18]

State health officials also used a modified maritime quarantine for New York City-bound ship traffic. The harbor's naval quarantine was in place for at least a month before the press reported the first confirmed cases of influenza in New York City on August 14, 1918.[19] At the ports, traditional maritime quarantines usually carried out by New York State officials were abandoned in favor of a more flexible land-based quarantine strategy.[20]

New York fared comparatively well during the 1918 pandemic. New York City's excess death rate per 1,000 was reportedly 4.7, compared with 6.5 in Boston and 7.3 in Philadelphia.[21] New York City emerged from the three waves of the influenza pandemic (September 1918 to February 1919), officially recording approximately 30,000 deaths out of a population of roughly 5.6 million.[22]

Philadelphia suffered its first fatality from influenza on September 17, 1918, and city officials launched a campaign against coughing, spitting and sneezing in public the very next day.[23] However, Philadelphia waited eight days after their death rate began rising before banning gatherings and closing schools.[24] The city then held a massive parade viewed by 200,000 people supporting the war effort ten days after the virus was first detected in the City.[25] Primarily due to this erratic approach to social distancing, Philadelphia endured the highest peak death rate of all the U.S. cities that have been studied.[26]

In general, cities such as St. Louis and New York that had strong social distancing measures had lower total death rates.[27] These restrictions also succeeded in "bending the curve" by delaying their peaks in reported deaths. Conversely, these cities faced sharp increases in reported illnesses and deaths when restrictions were temporarily relaxed. The deaths due to the virus were about 385 people per 100,000 in St. Louis, compared to 807 per 100,000 in Philadelphia during the first six months—the deadliest period—of the pandemic.[28]

In 2007, the National Institute of Health (NIH) conducted an in-depth study of varying cities' responses to the 1918 pandemic, finding: "Cities where public health officials imposed multiple social containment measures within a few days after the first local cases were recorded cut peak weekly death rates by up to half compared with cities that waited just a few weeks to respond."[29]

In the 2007 study, Dr. Anthony S. Fauci, director of NIH's National Institute of Allergy and Infectious Diseases (NIAID), and a prominent advisor to the Trump administration's efforts to respond to the current COVID-19 crisis, is quoted as saying that "a primary lesson of the 1918 influenza pandemic is that it is critical to intervene early."[30] He added: "While researchers are working very hard to develop pandemic influenza vaccines and increase the speed with which they can be made, nonpharmaceutical interventions may buy valuable time at the beginning of a pandemic while a targeted vaccine is being produced."[31]

If the Trump administration had taken Dr. Fauci's 2007 advice, it would have imposed national social distancing and stay-at-home orders when the national emergency was declared in February 2020. If this had been done, then based on the statistical differences in death rates between the various cities in 1918, thousands of lives would have been spared. But those who do not learn the lessons of history are doomed to repeat their mistakes.

In short, the concept of social distancing is not a new or controversial topic, or at least it should not be after its proven success during the 1918 Spanish Flu. Even a week or two delay in the implementation of social distancing mandates and quarantines can make a huge difference in outcomes and can save thousands of lives. More than 100 years after these lessons were learned, the failure of the federal government, as well as some governors and mayors, to implement social distancing and stay-at-home orders at the very start of the crisis was inexcusable. These delays have led to avoidable increased rates of infection, illness, and death, and these adverse consequences will continue to haunt us for the foreseeable future.

5

AMERICA AT ITS BEST:

THE ASIAN FLU (1957-1958) AND DR. MAURICE HILLEMAN

In 1957, America successfully stopped the Asian Flu from overwhelming the country.[1] This fact is a little known story outside the relatively small world of vaccines and virology. Still, it is worth retelling now since it is highly relevant to our current predicament. It is a reminder of what this country is capable of achieving within a relatively short time frame when a virus attacks America.

A deadly Asian Flu was beginning to wreak havoc on Asia in February and March of 1957.[2] American scientists knew the flu would come to the U.S., and they realized they only had a few months to develop a vaccine. They took up the challenge, mobilized the necessary resources to accomplish their mission, and succeeded. They were able to create a vaccine before the Asian Flu was estimated to hit the U.S. in the fall of 1957.[3] This ingenuity is how America gets things done (or used to anyway).

Dr. Maurice Hilleman led the effort. As a government scientist at Walter Reed Hospital in Bethesda, Maryland, Hilleman first learned there was a large outbreak of a new strain of influenza in Hong Kong in April 1957.[4] He immediately mobilized federal government resources to ensure that the U.S. would have a vaccine against this new virus by the time it got here.[5]

Although Dr. Hilleman is to vaccines and microbiology what Babe Ruth is to baseball, he was an extremely modest man of humble origins. He never named any of the 40 vaccines he discovered after himself.[6] There are no statues or monuments of him in Washington, D.C., and yet he profoundly touched the lives of every American at the time, and for all times to come.

Hilleman was born in the town of Miles City, Montana, which is in Custer County, named after General George Armstrong Custer. His family were farmers, and he was the youngest child of Anna and Gustav Hilleman. He had been born a twin, but his twin sister died at birth, and a few days later, his mother also died. He spent his youth working on his uncle's chicken farm. He didn't know it at the time, but learning about chickens would prove very helpful later in life. From the 1930s, fertile chicken eggs were used to grow viruses for vaccines.[7]

Hilleman graduated with honors from Custer County High School, but his family lacked the funds to send him to college. It was assumed that he would remain on the farm. Fortunately for the young man, and luckily for the rest of us, his eldest brother managed to scrape together enough funds for Maurice to register at Montana State University. Hilleman graduated first in his class from MSU. After graduation, the University of Chicago offered Hilleman a fellowship and full scholarship, which he accepted. In 1944, the University of Chicago awarded him a Ph.D. in microbiology.[8]

Dr. Hilleman's first job was with E.R. Squibb & Sons (now Bristol-Myers Squibb), the pharmaceutical giant.[9] While working at Squibb, he developed a vaccine against Japanese B encephalitis, which had threatened American troops in the Pacific during World War II.[10]

Hilleman then took on the position of Chief of the Department of Respiratory Diseases at the Army Medical Center.[11] Before the 1957 flu crisis, Hilleman had discovered that genetic changes occur when influenza viruses mutate. This mutation, known as "shift and drift," helped him anticipate that the flu in Hong Kong in 1957 could become a massive pandemic.

On April 17, 1957, The *New York Times* reported that women with babies tied to their backs were waiting in long lines at Hong Kong clinics. The babies were described as "glassy-eyed."[12] According to the *Times*, there were an estimated 250,000 Hong Kong residents – 10 percent of the region's population – that were being treated for the disease.[13] Since the first reported cases were in February 1957, this meant that the flu epidemic was already spreading widely in China. With reports like this, it was clear that the flu in China was fast spreading and could quickly invade the rest of the globe.

The World Health Organization was primarily tasked with keeping tabs on new virus outbreaks in Asia and Africa, where most of the epidemics seemed to originate. Unfortunately, the W.H.O. had not sounded any alarms as of April 17, when Hilleman sat down for breakfast and read his copy of the *Times*.[14] U.S. Army Intelligence in the Far East also failed to pick up on the growing public health crisis.

When Hilleman read the news account, it struck him that this flu virus might be a particularly virulent strain and that it might be targeting children. He realized that he and his colleagues in the government now had an urgent mission to stop the spread of the virus, if possible before it reached the U.S. At least they could develop a vaccine before the U.S. schools opened in the fall. Hilleman quickly sounded the alarm to his fellow government researchers that a pandemic was coming. He told them they needed to get to work right away to develop an effective vaccine.

After nine days of hard work, clocking 14 hours per day, Hilleman and his colleagues found that this virus was, in fact, a new strain of the flu that could kill millions. As the Chief of Respiratory Diseases at the Walter Reed Army Research Institute, Hilleman had access to large numbers of serum obtained from people of various ages that had been collected in previous years. He could not find any evidence from available serum samples of any antibodies that would provide immunity to this new strain. However, he did find a small number of serum samples with antibodies after reaching out to other health departments. It turned out that all of the people in this small set were in their 70s and 80s, and they also were survivors of the "Russian Flu" pandemic of 1889-1890.[15]

Armed with this knowledge, Hilleman immediately issued a press release announcing that a new flu pandemic would be arriving soon from Asia. He predicted and that it would reach the U.S. by September 1957.[16] This announcement created quite an uproar in government circles, as well as in the media. There was a great deal of concern that Hilleman's statement would "create panic." However, Hilleman believed from prior experience, that some degree of urgency was a good thing when it came to preparing for pandemics. The generally lethargic government bureaucracy and elected officials needed to be woken up with a bucket of cold water thrown in their faces when an occasion like this justified it.

Hilleman's dramatic gambit paid off, and when he got the desired attention of the public and the private vaccine manufacturing companies, he got all of the assistance and cooperation that he needed. The vaccine manufacturers agreed to work with him and his government team on an emergency and expedited basis. Hilleman had concluded that the country needed 100% vaccination coverage, at least for school-age children. No detail was too small for Hilleman's attention. Since a large number of fertilized chicken eggs would be needed for vaccine production, he reminded the companies manufacturing the vaccine that they should tell the farmers not to kill their roosters at the end of the hatching season.

Making a vaccine for a new flu strain may be quite different than making a vaccine for a novel SARS-type virus. But any project of this size and urgency requires the total and immediate mobilization of all the vast resources of the federal government and private industry. It also requires the ability to cut through the red-tape and "business-as-usual" attitudes that are often prevalent in regulatory agencies. Hilleman was able to accomplish all of this brilliantly during 1957, resulting in the saving of thousands of lives through the distribution of an effective Asian Flu vaccine on schedule.

When the new flu strain hit the U.S. in September 1957, just as Hilleman had predicted, forty million doses of vaccines were prepared and ready for distribution.[17] The Asian Flu virus did succeed in killing an estimated 116,000 Americans and up to 1.1 million people worldwide.[18] Still, without the vaccine, it was estimated that upwards of one million Americans would have lost their lives. There can be no question, therefore, that the rapid development of a vaccine and other effective responses to the pandemic had an immense and positive impact. By comparison, the Spanish Flu of 1918-1919, for which there was no vaccine, killed an estimated 675,000 Americans and 50 million people worldwide.[19]

After completing his successful research to develop an Asian Flu vaccine, Hilleman left the government. He joined Merck & Co., where he developed most of the 40 experimental and licensed vaccines that are his legacy. Of the 14 vaccines routinely recommended in current vaccine schedules, he developed eight of them.[20] His vaccines include those for measles, mumps, hepatitis A, hepatitis B, chickenpox, meningitis, pneumonia, and Haemophilus influenzae bacteria.[21] He also played a role in the discovery of the cold-producing adenoviruses, the hepatitis viruses, and the potentially cancer-causing virus SV40.[22]

Hilleman's development of a mumps vaccine began in 1963 when his daughter Jeryl Lynn came down with the mumps. He took saliva samples from her and used them as the basis of a mumps vaccine. The Jeryl Lynn strain of the mumps vaccine is still used today. It is currently used in what is known as "the trivalent" (measles, mumps, and rubella) MMR vaccine that he is credited with developing. The MMR vaccine was the first-ever approved that incorporated multiple live virus strains.

Hilleman and his group also invented a vaccine for hepatitis B by treating blood serum with pepsin, urea, and formaldehyde.[23] The vaccine was licensed in 1981, but withdrawn in 1986 and replaced by a vaccine that was produced in yeast. By 2003, there were 150 countries using it, and it is still in use today. Since Hilleman developed the hepatitis B vaccine, the incidence of the disease in the U.S. in young people had decreased by 95%.

Hilleman also was one of the early vaccine pioneers to warn about the possibility that simian viruses might contaminate vaccines.[24] The best-known of these viruses was SV40, a viral contaminant of the polio vaccine, whose discovery led to the recall of Salk's vaccine in 1961 and its replacement with Albert Sabin's oral vaccine. Contamination occurred in both vaccines at very low levels. Still, because the oral vaccine was ingested rather than injected, it is primarily used in countries, such as in India and parts of Africa, where logistics make it difficult to vaccinate large numbers of people by injection.

For his heroic efforts, Hilleman was awarded the National Medal of Science in 1988 for his contribution to public health.[25] He died on April 11, 2005, in Philadelphia, where he was teaching at the University of Pennsylvania. To this day, Hilleman's work is believed to have saved more lives worldwide than any other medical scientist in the 20th Century.

Now that we are well into the 21st Century, facing new pandemics with no vaccines, no known cures, and not much testing, we are ready for the next Maurice Hilleman to step up and save the day. Time will tell.

6

THE SARS AND SWINE FLU PANDEMICS

(2003 AND 2009)

The U.S. response to the SARS pandemic of 2003 and the H1N1 Swine Flu pandemic of 2009 – like the 1957 response to the Asian flu pandemic – were textbook examples of how a deadly outbreak of a virus should be handled. Tragically, the Trump administration seems to have misplaced or ignored the preparation and response playbooks that were successfully used in all three of these prior pandemics. The failure to apply the knowledge learned during these previous pandemics is now unfolding before us with disastrous consequences.

The SARS Pandemic of 2003

SARS (severe acute respiratory syndrome), which also involved a coronavirus (SARS-CoV), was first identified in Guangdong Province in China, adjacent to Hong Kong.[1] Although it must have started sometime in 2002, the People's Republic of China belatedly notified the World Health Organization about this outbreak on February 10, 2003.[2] At the time, they reported 305 cases, including 105 healthcare workers and five deaths.[3] Later, China stated that the outbreak in Guangdong had peaked in mid-February 2003, but there were 806 subsequent reported cases and 34 deaths.[4]

By the time the pandemic was over, W.H.O. reported a total of 8,098 people from 29 different countries and territories were infected, with 774 deaths worldwide.[5] W.H.O. declared SARS to be contained on July 5, 2003; however, several SARS cases were reported until May 2004.[6]

Early in the epidemic, the Chinese government discouraged its press from reporting on SARS. They delayed reporting to W.H.O., and initially did not provide information to their Chinese citizens outside Guangdong province, where the disease is believed to have originated.[7] In fact, a W.H.O. team that traveled to Beijing was not allowed to visit Guangdong province for several weeks.⁸ China's conduct resulted in widespread international criticism. By early April 2003, the criticism seemed to have led to a change in policy when the Chinese government started becoming more transparent about the spread of the virus.

Despite the delay in the release of information from Chinese authorities, the CDC acted with commendable speed in responding to this pandemic and preventing any significant spread of the disease in the U.S. On March 14, 2003, when the outbreak of a severe form of pneumonia of unknown origin in China was still unnamed, the CDC activated its Emergency Operations Center.⁹ On March 15, the CDC issued its first health alert to the U.S. media.¹⁰ The Center hosted a media telebriefing about this atypical pneumonia now named SARS. They also issued interim guidelines for state and local health departments and a "Health Alert Notice" for travelers to the U.S. from Hong Kong and Guangdong Province (China).

On March 24, 2003, a CDC laboratory analyst reported a new coronavirus that might be the cause of SARS. Thirty-nine suspected cases were identified in the U.S. by then.¹¹ On March 27, 2003, the CDC issued interim domestic guidelines for the management of exposures to SARS for hospitals and other healthcare providers.¹² The following day, March 28, realizing that the SARS outbreak was more widespread than initially expected, the CDC began "pandemic planning."¹³ By March 29, the CDC had extended its travel advisory for SARS to include all of mainland China and elsewhere in Asia.¹⁴ The CDC quarantine staff began screening passengers from planes, cargo ships, and cruise ships coming either directly or indirectly to the U.S. from China, Singapore, or Vietnam. Health advisory alert cards were also distributed to travelers.

By April 4, 2003, the number of suspected U.S. SARS cases was 115, covering 29 states.¹⁵ On April 14, the CDC published a sequence of the virus believed to be responsible for SARS.¹⁶ The sequencing was of critical importance since the identification of the genetic sequence of a new virus was an essential first step in prevention and treatment efforts. This breakthrough came just 12 days after a team of scientists and technicians began working around the clock to grow cells taken from the throat culture of a SARS patient.¹⁷ On May 6, 2003, the CDC declared success in the war on SARS, announcing that containment had been achieved. There were no new SARS cases in the U.S. for the prior 24 hours, and there was no evidence of ongoing transmission in the U.S. for the previous 20 days.[18]

In short, the CDC and its sister federal government agencies worked efficiently and effectively with the W.H.O. and all state, city, and local health departments in the 50 states to stop SARS. They investigated all possible cases of SARS in the U.S., collected clinical specimens from every SARS patient, and conducted extensive laboratory testing to determine the cause of the disease.[19] The CDC's Emergency Operations Center was able, from the very start, to provide round-the-clock coordination, response, and deployment of a small army of medical officers, epidemiologists, and other specialists. They conducted on-site investigations around the world.

Through this proactive approach to the pandemic, including implementation of draconian "top-down" containment and quarantine measures, the U.S. was able to interrupt all human-to-human transmissions of SARS completely. The approach effectively eradicated SARS in the U.S.[20] The strict monitoring for suspected patients through "syndrome surveillance," the prompt isolation of patients and strict enforcement of quarantine of all contacts, combined with social distancing and, in some areas, community-level quarantine, stopped SARS in its tracks.[21] The number of secondary cases from infected patients was substantially reduced since infected patients were isolated within four days of the onset of symptoms.[22]

Despite the striking similarities between SARS and COVID-19, which is caused by another one of the SARS family of viruses, the U.S. utterly failed to contain the spread of COVID-19 after it was first reported.[23] By April 21, 2020, there were 802,583 reported cases in the U.S., with 44,575 deaths,[24] and by the end of August there were 5.7 million confirmed U.S. cases, and over 177,000 reported deaths.[25]

The similarities between SARS-CoV (the 2003 strain) and SARS-CoV-2 (which causes COVID-19) go way beyond just the similarities in names.[26] The whole genome of SARS-CoV-2 has a 86% similarity with SARS-CoV.[27] Both viruses share high degrees of similarity to SARS-like coronaviruses isolated in bats, suggesting that bats are the probable origin of both of these SARS viruses.[28] Live animal markets in China selling multiple species of wild and domestic animals in proximity to large densely housed populations are thought to be the most likely sources of both outbreaks.[29]

The disease transmission routes for both viruses are also similar, in that the main transmission route appears to be respiratory droplets or the touching of surfaces harboring the virus.[30] Also, the angiotensin-converting enzyme 2 (ACE2) found in the lower respiratory tract of humans has been identified as the receptor used for cell entry for both SARS-CoV and SARS-CoV-2.[31] Both SARS and the virus causing COVID-19 also have a median incubation time of about five days.[32] The risk factors for severe outcomes from both of the viruses are old age and underlying health conditions, such as heart disease, respiratory disease, and diabetes.[33] The advancement to acute respiratory distress syndrome is 8-20 days after onset of the first symptoms.[34] Lung abnormalities on chest C.T. scans show the highest severity about ten days after the initial onset of symptoms.[35]

To be sure, COVID-19 has proved to be a more formidable foe than SARS. There appears to be a delay in some people between the time of infection and the onset of fever and flu-like symptoms, which highlights the critical importance of widespread public testing. Tragically, extensive testing got off to a late start in the U.S. Testing was not available on any broad basis until well after the virus had already passed its peak in major urban areas.

In contrast, South Korea had widespread public testing available from the very start of the crisis.[36] The screening not only flattened the curve but also led to a markedly reduced per capita mortality rate as compared to the U.S.[37] Asian countries also demonstrated success with public temperature screening, both during the 2003 SARS outbreak and during the current COVID-19 crisis. The U.S. had no such widespread testing and surveillance programs in place when some of the states started to relax social distancing restrictions and to open up their economies. Having failed to follow the lessons learned in 2003 during the SARS outbreak, the U.S. faced a catastrophic crisis in 2020 that was exponentially greater than it should have been.

The 2009 H1N1 Swine Flu Pandemic

The response by the CDC and other U.S. federal government agencies to the 2009 Swine Flu pandemic was as swift and effective as it had been in response to SARS in 2003. This 2009 Swine Flu outbreak was the second H1N1 influenza virus pandemic, the first being the devastating Spanish Flu pandemic of 1918.

The Swine Flu was first noticed in Mexico in March and April 2009.[38] It appeared to be a new strain of H1N1, combining elements of bird and human flu viruses with a Eurasian pig flu virus;[39] thus the name "swine flu."[40] Some studies estimated 11 - 21 percent of the global population at the time – or around 700 million to 1.4 billion people (out of a total of 6.8 billion) – contracted the illness.[41] Swine Flu infected more people than the 1918 Spanish Flu pandemic,[42] but only resulted in about 150,000 to 575,000 fatalities.[43] A follow-up study done in September 2010 showed that the risk of serious illness resulting from the 2009 H1N1 flu was no higher than that of the yearly seasonal flu.[44] For comparison purposes, the W.H.O. estimates that 250,000 to 500,000 people die of seasonal flu annually.[45]

Unlike most strains of influenza, the Swine Flu 2009 H1N1 did not disproportionately infect adults older than 60 years. This made the Swine Flu significantly different than the prior 1918 H1N1 virus, which particularly struck both the elderly and the very young.[46] The likely explanation for this is that older people seemed to have built up enough immunity to the group of viruses that H1N1 belongs to, so they weren't severely affected by the 2009 H1N1 illness. A small percentage of those infected with the 2009 H1N1 flu virus developed pneumonia or acute respiratory distress syndrome (ARDS).[47] In November 2009, a *New England Journal of Medicine* article noted that Swine Flu patients whose chest X-rays indicated pneumonia were effectively treated with both antivirals and antibiotics.[48]

The number of 2009 H1N1 patients did not overwhelm hospitals in most urban areas where it was most prevalent. Medical facilities in the U.S. and elsewhere were generally able to handle the influx of patients. With proper treatment, the survival rate was high. Although it was feared that the Swine Flu would kill millions worldwide, this 2009-2010 pandemic "only" killed between 151,700 and 575,400 people, according to the CDC.[49]

In 2009, U.S. and state officials also urged communities, businesses, and individuals to make contingency plans for possible school closures, multiple employee absences for illness, surges of patients in hospitals, and other effects of potentially widespread outbreaks.[50] Disaster response organizations such as Direct Relief helped by providing protective items to clinical workers to help them stay healthy throughout the flu season.[51]

Of the 60.8 million cases of Swine Flu in the U.S. between April 2009 and April 2010, there were over 274,000 hospitalizations and nearly 12,500 deaths — a mortality rate of about 0.02%.[52] This relatively low mortality rate is likely because there was already some "herd immunity" in the U.S. population to seasonal flu. Those who were already immune to the seasonal flu were also immune to the 2009 H1N1 infection. Others who did not already have immunity were partially protected since their immune systems had successfully fought related diseases.

By contrast, COVID-19 is caused by a SARS-type virus, not an H1N1 flu virus, which is why the mortality rate for COVID-19 appears to be closer to 2.3%.[53] The difference may not seem like a great deal at first glance. Still, it can mean hundreds of thousands or millions of more deaths worldwide when extrapolated out. So far, COVID-19 is much more deadly for people over 60 than the 2009 H1N1 virus ever was. At the highest risk are older people with underlying health conditions like diabetes, cardiovascular disease, or respiratory disease.[54]

Those who were infected with the 2009 H1N1 virus tended to show obvious flu-like symptoms quickly. COVID-19 patients also have flu-like symptoms such as fever, dry cough, and shortness of breath.[55] The significant difference is that COVID-19-infected people may be asymptomatic. An infected person may look and feel completely "normal" for an extended period while he or she is unwittingly spreading it to others. The virus appears to have an incubation period of between four and 14 days, which means an individual could be carrying (and spreading) the virus for up to two weeks before experiencing any illness.[56]

The 2009 H1N1 flu was also less contagious than the novel coronavirus causing COVID-19. The primary reproduction number also called the "R-nought value," is the expected number of individuals who can catch the virus from a single infected person.[57] For the 2009 H1N1 virus, the mean R-nought value was 1.46, according to a review published in the *Journal BMC Infectious Diseases*.[58] For COVID-19, the R-nought value is estimated to be between 2 and 2.5 – at least for now.[59]

In addition to the greater lethality of COVID-19, the primary reason it has brought the world to its knees is that the U.S. was better prepared for a pandemic in 2009 than it is today. In both epidemics (2009 H1N1 and COVID-19), the U.S. responses got off to the same start, and then widely diverged. The genetic sequences of the virus were publicly released within a matter of days in both cases, so the U.S. and other countries could create diagnostic tests as soon as possible. On April 24, 2009, just nine days after the initial detection of H1N1, the CDC uploaded genetic sequences of the virus to a public database, and it had already begun the development of a vaccine.[60] Similarly, on January 12, 2020, five days after the novel coronavirus was isolated, Chinese scientists published the virus' genetic sequence.[61]

There were also some initial similarities between the U.S. response to the 2009 Swine Flu pandemic and the current COVID-19 pandemic. In the case of Swine Flu, the U.S. declared Swine Flu to be a public health emergency on October 24, 2009, eleven days after the first confirmed U.S. case in 2009.[62] Similarly, the U.S. Dept. of Health and Human Services (HHS) declared a COVID-19 public health emergency on January 31, 2020, which was 11 days after the first COVID-19 case was identified in the U.S. on January 20.[63]

But that is where the similarities end between the response of the U.S. government to these two pandemics. Within four weeks of detecting H1N1 in 2009, the CDC had begun releasing health supplies from the federal stockpile that could prevent and treat influenza.[64] Most states in the U.S. had labs capable of diagnosing H1N1 without verification by a CDC test.[65] There was a technological ability being developed to use thermal imaging cameras at airports, and other critical facilities to detect elevated body temperature, one of the signs of Swine Flu.[66]

By the time the 2009 H1N1 virus hit the U.S., the CDC and other federal agencies had been on high alert for the prior six years. The alert was from concerns about a resurgence of SARS and H5N1 influenza, which had first emerged in Asia in 1997. H5N1 killed about 60% of the several hundred people infected, starting in 2003.[67] Public health authorities in the U.S. and elsewhere took steps following these SARS and H5N1 outbreaks to try to prevent the spread of any of these viruses or similar viruses out of Asia.[68] When the H1N1 virus was detected in early 2003, the CDC and other U.S. government agencies[69] wisely used the 2009 summer lull to take stock of the U.S's response to the H1N1 flu. There was a significant attempt to patch any gaps in the public health safety net before the flu season started in early autumn.[70] Preparations included planning a second influenza vaccination program in addition to the one for seasonal flu, and improving coordination between federal, state, and local governments and private health providers.[71] On October 24, 2009, President Obama declared Swine Flu to be a national emergency, giving Secretary of Health and Human Services Kathleen Sebelius immediate authority to grant waivers to requesting hospitals from general federal requirements.[72]

In 2009, the Obama administration and the entire U.S. government prepared for the worst-case scenario to hit the U.S. as the 2009 H1N1 virus began to spread.[73] The HHS, the CDC, and the Department of Homeland Security (DHS) triggered a crash program to develop updated guidance, including the making of a video for employers to use as they developed plans to respond to the H1N1 outbreak.[74] The advice suggested employers consider and communicate their objectives, such as reducing transmission among staff. Efforts were also undertaken to protect people who were at increased risk of influenza-related complications.[75]

The CDC estimated in 2009 that 40% of the U.S. workforce might be unable to work at the peak of the pandemic.[76] This 40% included the need for many healthy adults to stay home and care for a family member.[77] The CDC further advised individuals to have plans in place if businesses and workplaces had to be closed down, and they would be required to work from home.[78] The CDC also recommended that persons in the workplace should stay home for seven days after getting the flu, or 24 hours after symptoms ended, whichever was longer.[79]

By late 2010, the world could breathe a collective sigh of relief, having dodged a significant public health bullet posed by the 2009 Swine Flu. But the Obama administration did not let down its guard. When the Swine Flu crisis had passed, the CDC and other federal agencies interpreted it as a warning sign that a deadlier virus would be coming. The U.S. needed to be preparing for it right away. The CDC and federal agencies had kept careful records regarding their prompt and effective response to the 2009 Swine Flu pandemic. They also had good records of the U.S. response to the 2003 SARS pandemic. The Obama administration used this detailed information to develop a comprehensive response plan. The plan would be in place so that the country would be able to respond quickly when the next pandemic struck the U.S.

Unfortunately, however, these plans – based on actual successful responses to prior pandemics – were either misplaced or ignored by the Trump administration when the COVID-19 crisis hit the country in January 2020. The federal government's belated, erratic, and often contradictory actions (and inactions) during 2020 led to an unnecessary increase in the number of coronavirus cases and deaths. If prompt federal action had been taken sooner, many of the deaths and illnesses could have been avoided.

For example, on February 5, 2020, the CDC began sending diagnostic testing kits for COVID-19 to about 100 public-health laboratories across the country.[80] Most of these kits proved to be faulty, resulting in a significant delay in widespread testing, which most experts agreed was a key element of any effective response plan. It also was decided that testing would only take place at the CDC headquarters until the agency could develop and send out replacement kits, which resulted in further delays.[81] These faulty tests meant that COVID-19 continued to spread, undetected for weeks. Meanwhile, a W.H.O. test developed in Germany was available.[82] The CDC made the fateful (and wrong) decision not to use the perfectly good and accurate W.H.O. testing kits, for reasons of professional pride or some other spurious reason. As a result, people have needlessly died – and continue to die – who could have been spared if the Trump administration had gotten its act together sooner.

FDA Commissioner Stephen Hahn then waited until February 29, 2020, before announcing the agency would allow labs across the country to begin using their tests for coronavirus without prior approval.[83] The labs were required to take essential steps to validate the tests and submitted an "emergency use authorization" (EUA) application within 15 days of the notice.[84]

By March 10, 2020, seven weeks after the first confirmed case in the U.S., the CDC finally announced that 79 state and local health labs in the U.S. could test people for COVID-19.[85] But by then, the virus was already rapidly spreading. The Federal Government had lost the critical lead time needed to get ahead of the pandemic as it raced across the United States.

* * * * *

In short, the federal government's anemic response to the COVID-19 pandemic is in sharp contrast to the proactive and vigorous responses to the 2003 SARS and 2009 Swine Flu pandemics. The reasons for these tragic developments are manifold. They include the Trump administration's dismantling of government programs that were in place to provide early warnings and emergency response plans. As a result, we are paying an extraordinarily high price for this lack of preparedness and response planning.

We will be doing so for some time to come.

7

THE RAPID U.S. RESPONSE TO THE 2014 EBOLA CRISIS

Ebola virus disease (EVD), also known as Ebola hemorrhagic fever, originated in West Africa in the area adjacent to the Ebola River (hence its name) in the Democratic Republic of the Congo.[1] Like other deadly viruses, such as SARS and the virus causing COVID-19, it was transmitted to people from wild animals (such as fruit bats, porcupines, and primates) and then spread in the human population.[2] The primary means of transmission of the Ebola virus is through direct contact with the blood, secretions, organs or other bodily fluids of infected people, or with surfaces and materials (e.g., bedding, clothing) contaminated with these fluids.[3] However, like SARS or COVID-19, it could also be spread by sneezing, coughing, or similar means.[4] Ebola is much deadlier than COVID-19 and most flu viruses, with a fatality rate of around 50%.[5]

The 2014 Ebola outbreak in West Africa was the largest and most complex Ebola outbreak, primarily hitting the West African countries of Guinea, Liberia, and Sierra Leone. On September 30, 2014, the CDC declared its first U.S. case of Ebola virus disease after Thomas Eric Duncan became infected in Liberia and traveled to Dallas, Texas on September 20, 2014.[6]

On September 26, Duncan fell ill and sought medical treatment, but was sent home with antibiotics. He returned to the hospital by ambulance on September 28. At that point, he was placed in isolation and tested for Ebola.[7] He died on October 8, 2014.[8] Two nurses who had treated Duncan tested positive for the virus on October 10 and 14, 2014. They were declared Ebola-free later in October.[9] A fourth Ebola case was identified on October 23, 2014.[10] Craig Spencer, an American physician who had returned to the U.S. after treating Ebola patients in Western Africa, tested positive for the virus.[11] Spencer recovered and was released from the hospital on November 11, 2014.[12]

One of the first decisions made by the Obama administration was to provide medical assistance to the Ebola victims in West Africa. The theory was that if the outbreak could be contained in West Africa, this would reduce the risk that infected people would travel to the U.S. In September 2014, the United States Africa Command, working through United States Army Africa, committed up to 4,000 U.S. Army troops to this aid mission, called Operation United Assistance.[13] The initial plan was to build 17 hospitals around the country of Liberia, each with a 100-bed capacity.[14] However, in late November 2014, this plan was reduced to 10 treatment centers with 50 beds each.[15] A 25-bed hospital planned for health workers staffed by U.S. Public Health Service Commissioned Corps officers was opened November 7, 2014, near the Liberian capital of Monrovia.[16]

In mid-October 2014, President Obama appointed Ron Klain as the Ebola Response Coordinator, more popularly known as the "Ebola Czar."[17] Klain reported to White House Homeland Security Adviser Lisa Monaco and National Security Advisor Susan Rice.[18] Nicole Lurie, Assistant Secretary for Preparedness and Response (ASPR), had responsibility for coordination with hospitals and the United States Public Health Service.[19] President Obama attempted to reassure the public regarding the federal government's Ebola response efforts by holding almost daily press briefings detailing the efforts that were being made. Obama even went so far as to invite nurse Nina Pham to the White House after she had been cured. Photographs of her hugging the president were widely circulated.[20]

President Obama also announced the formation of rapid response teams to travel to hospitals where there were newly diagnosed Ebola patients.[21] The second set of teams prepped hospitals in cities deemed most likely to treat Ebola cases. In announcing the formation of the teams, President Obama explained,

> We want a rapid response team, a SWAT team, essentially, from the CDC, to be on the ground as quickly as possible, hopefully within 24 hours, so that they are taking the local hospital step by step through what needs to be done.[22]

The CDC had developed two sets of teams, identified by the acronyms CERT (CDC Ebola Response Team) and FAST (Facility Assessment and

Support Teams).²³ The CERTs had 10 to 20 people each, who could be sent to any hospital with a suspected and laboratory-confirmed Ebola virus case.²⁴

Starting in October 2014, U.S. government officials also began questioning airplane passengers. These travelers were screened for fever at five U.S. airports: John F. Kennedy International Airport in New York, Newark Liberty International Airport in New Jersey, O'Hare International Airport in Illinois, Washington Dulles International Airport in Virginia, and Hartsfield–Jackson Atlanta International Airport in Georgia.²⁵ Combined, these airports received more than 94% of passengers from Guinea, Liberia, and Sierra Leone – the three countries most affected by Ebola.²⁶ On October 23, 2014, the CDC announced that all passengers from these countries would be monitored for 21-days.²⁷

In addition to the proactive and timely steps being taken by the federal government to address the Ebola crisis, several state governors took further actions. On October 7, 2014, for example, Connecticut Governor Daniel Malloy signed an order authorizing the mandatory quarantine for 21 days of anyone, even if asymptomatic, who had direct contact with Ebola patients.²⁸ Nine people were quarantined on October 22, following the Connecticut order.²⁹ At a joint news conference on October 24, 2014, New York Governor Andrew Cuomo and New Jersey Governor Chris Christie announced that they were imposing a mandatory 21-day quarantine on all air travelers returning to New York or New Jersey from West Africa who had any prior contact with Ebola patients.³⁰

Even though the Obama administration's response effort to the Ebola crisis generally received good grades from experts and the American public, it was not without its detractors. One of the most outspoken critics of the U.S. Ebola efforts was Donald J. Trump. He repeatedly publicly insisted that the U.S. had botched its response to the Ebola virus threat entirely. He felt the only positive step was a permanent change in the way that people greeted each other: there would be no more handshaking.³¹

Six years later, Trump seemed to have forgotten how he had publicly lectured President Obama and the American public on the need to take aggressive steps to reduce the possibility of dangerous viruses reaching the

U.S. He also seems to have forgotten his vocal advocacy during the Ebola crisis for the federal government's imposition and strict enforcement of quarantines and isolation measures applicable to any infected persons who made it into the U.S.

Despite his extreme statements during the course of the Ebola crisis regarding the need to avoid the shaking of hands and other rigorous public health practices to stem any possible transmission of the virus, Mr. Trump has been seen regularly shaking hands with health experts and others at his daily COVID-19 briefings. Trump announced during the crisis that he would not be wearing a face mask, even though the White House coronavirus task force was recommending this practice.[32] During a daily briefing, Trump said that it would be hard for him to envision wearing a face mask in the Oval Office. He explained: "Wearing a face mask as I greet presidents, prime ministers, dictators, kings, queens — I just don't see it."[33] Despite the improbability that any world leader would be visiting Trump amid a global pandemic, Trump's cavalier attitude served to undercut the CDC's guidance to the public.

Trump's low-key approach to the crisis also sharply contrasted with his apocalyptic warnings during the Ebola pandemic. According to Trump, the "Ebola plague" (which he described as "a plague like no other") would devastate America and its way of life. He bitterly criticized both Obama and the CDC for not recognizing that a catastrophic Ebola outbreak was about to take place throughout the U.S.[34] In fact, Trump was so enraged that a doctor who contracted Ebola was allowed to fly back to New York from West Africa that he demanded in a tweet: "Obama should apologize to the American people & resign."[35]

However, once Trump moved into the White House, he quickly pivoted from his prior role as the chief prophet of doom during the Ebola crisis to the COVID-19 pandemic's Denier-in-Chief. It was not until late March 2020, when the number of infected patients and deaths forced him to change his tune, that Trump even acknowledged the crisis was real and that it was severe. Forgotten were his claims from late January to mid-March that the coronavirus pandemic was some Democratic "hoax" or "fake news" scandal manufactured by a biased media intent on taking him down.

In short, Trump did not take the 2020 COVID-19 crisis that took place during his own administration as seriously as he took the 2014 Ebola crisis handled by the Obama White House. Nor does it appear that the Trump team kept a copy of the successful playbook used by the Obama administration to handle the Ebola crisis. If Trump had followed the detailed roadmap left for him by prior administrations as to how to handle pandemics successfully, the U.S. response to COVID-19 would have been much more forceful, organized, and effective.

Unfortunately, the Trump administration did not do so, and the country is paying the price.

8

THE TRUMP ADMINISTRATION IGNORES EARLY WARNING SIGNALS AND DISMANTLES PANDEMIC-PREPARATION PROGRAMS

By March 2020, COVID-19 was spreading like wildfire across the U.S. The virus was overwhelming health care systems in New York, New Orleans, Detroit, and other cities. Trump tried to justify the federal government's woeful lack of preparedness by arguing they could not have known of the looming crisis in advance – that it was unexpected. At his daily briefing on March 19, 2020, Trump responded to criticism of his administration for lack of preparedness by saying: "I would view it as something that just surprised the whole world."[1] Later he claimed that it was "uncharted territory," saying, "Nobody knew there would be a pandemic or epidemic of this proportion."[2] He continued, "So there's never been anything like this in history," adding, "And nobody's ever seen anything like this."[3]

However, over the past two decades, White House planning groups, federal agencies, and military intelligence warned that a deadly pandemic was *the* primary threat to the U.S. They cautioned that an effective emergency plan had to be in place *before* a major pandemic hit the U.S. and that if such a response plan was not in place, the consequences could be devastating. Indeed, the White House received specific intelligence reports in November and December 2019, warning that the growing outbreak in Wuhan would be potentially catastrophic.[4] Yet the White House failed to take any action. Here are some of the warnings received and ignored, and the agencies dismantled by the Trump administration that could have served as an "early warning system" for the coming pandemic:

The National Intelligence Council Warnings

Starting in at least 2004, the National Intelligence Council (NIC) gave the White House annual warnings as to the national security threat posed by a pandemic. In the 2004 edition of "Global Trends," the NIC reported: "Some experts believe it is only a matter of time before a new pandemic appears, such as the 1918-1919 influenza virus that killed an estimated 20 million worldwide."[5] It foresaw that a pandemic would "put a halt to global travel and trade during an extended period, prompting governments to expend enormous resources on overwhelmed health sectors."[6]

2017 Pentagon Plan Identifies a "Novel Influenza Disease" As National Threat #1

Similarly, a 2017 Pentagon plan circulated among officials in the Trump administration containing a section on "Enemy/Threat," identifying "the most likely and significant threat is a novel respiratory disease, particularly a novel influenza disease."[7] The plan referenced coronavirus on several occasions, saying that "[c]oronavirus infections [are] common around the world,"[8] and explained that a respiratory disease "will result in debilitating illness in military forces at significant enough [levels] to degrade combat readiness and effectiveness . . . ."[9] The plan concluded: "[a]n outbreak in a single community can quickly evolve into a multinational health crisis that causes millions to suffer, as well as spark major disruption to every facet of society."[10] It anticipated the scarcity of medical equipment needed to combat the effects of the disease would itself pose a global and regional threat, as countries competed for scarce medical resources. "Competition for and scarcity of resources will include … non-pharmaceutical MCM (Medical Countermeasures) [e.g., ventilators, devices, personal protective equipment such as face masks and gloves], medical equipment, and logistical support." The plan also predicted: "Even the most industrialized countries will have insufficient hospital beds, specialized equipment such as mechanical ventilators, and pharmaceuticals readily available to adequately treat their populations during [a] clinically severe pandemic."[11]

The Office of the Director of National Intelligence (DNI) Worldwide Threat Assessment – January 29, 2019

The 2019 Worldwide Threat Assessment by the Director of National Intelligence (DNI) unequivocally warned, "[t]he United States will remain vulnerable to the next flu pandemic or large-scale outbreak of a contagious disease that could lead to massive rates of death and disability, severely affect the world economy, strain international resources, and increase calls on the United States for support."[12] Not only did the Trump administration ignore this warning, but they also held up the release of the 2020 report, which largely repeated the same dire warning. The DNI was scheduled to deliver the 2020 Worldwide Threat Assessment to the House Intelligence Committee on February 12, 2020, but the hearing was inexplicably canceled.[13] The 2019 Worldwide Threat Assessment further warned:

> Although the international community has made tenuous improvements to global health security, these gains may be inadequate to address the challenge of what we anticipate will be more frequent outbreaks of infectious diseases because of rapid unplanned urbanization, prolonged humanitarian crises, human incursion into previously unsettled land, expansion of international travel and trade, and regional climate change.[14]

The National Center for Medical Intelligence (NCMI) Report – Late November 2019

In late November 2019, before the first press reports of a growing epidemic in China, analysts with the National Center for Medical Intelligence (NCMI) - part of the Defense Intelligence Agency (DIA) - warned the spreading coronavirus disease in Wuhan could become a "cataclysmic event."[15] The NCMI prepared and circulated an intelligence report documenting its concerns that the initial stages of a pandemic were already taking place.[16] The Joint Chiefs of Staff at the Pentagon, the National Security Council, and the White House were briefed on these sobering findings.[17]

Although the National Security Council may not have been formally briefed on the matter until December, the Trump administration was aware of the contents of the report as early as Thanksgiving (November 28, 2019).[18] The NCMI report had been made widely available to administration officials who had access to intelligence community alerts.[19] According to U.S. intelligence, the Chinese leadership knew the epidemic was already widespread as of late November 2019.[20] They claimed China was withholding crucial information from health department officials both within and outside of China, as well as foreign governments and China's citizens.[21]

The President's Daily Briefs (PDB) – January and February 2020

The *Washington Post* reported on April 27, 2020, that, during January and February 2020, Trump received more than a dozen warnings from U.S. intelligence agencies about the coronavirus threat.[22] These warnings were contained in classified briefings prepared for Trump and inserted in the President's Daily Brief (PDB), a sensitive report that is produced early each day. The brief is designed to call the president's attention to the most significant global developments and security threats.[23] Versions of these PDBs were also shared with Cabinet secretaries and other high-ranking U.S. officials.

These PDBs traced the spread of the virus and the Chinese government's suppression of information about the transmissibility and lethality of the disease. They also raised alarms about the prospect of dire political and economic consequences for the U.S.[24] Although it was widely known that Trump never read the PDBs, he did receive oral summaries of them two or three times per week.[25]

During the same time frame that he was receiving these dire warnings, Trump regularly downplayed the coronavirus threat, minimizing the potential impact of the pandemic on the U.S. and comparing it to the common flu.[26] Trump, for example, insisted publicly on February 26 that the number of cases "within a couple of days is going to be down to close to zero," saying the following day that "it's like a miracle, it will disappear."[27] As late as March 10, Trump was falsely reassuring the American public that "it will go away."[28] No effort was made during this time frame to mobilize a coordinated federal response or to obtain the supplies and equipment that would be necessary for an effective response to the pandemic once it reached the U.S. in full force.

On April 28th, one day after *The Washington Post* broke the story about Trump's PDBs in January and February 2020, Trump tried to defend his administration's inaction by saying that, in late February, he was being told by his top advisors that the coronavirus pandemic "is no problem."[29] "Even professionals like Anthony [Fauci] were saying this is no problem," Trump told reporters at the White House, "[t]his is late in February. This is no problem," he said. "This is going to blow over."³⁰ In response to specific questions as to whether any of the PDBs warned him of the coronavirus threat, Trump said: "I would have to check," adding that "I want to look as to the exact dates of warnings."³¹

The last most notable instance of a president ignoring a major warning contained in a PDB was August 2001, one month before 9/11, when President George W. Bush's PDB warned that al-Qaeda chief Osama bin Laden was "determined to strike in U.S."³²

Center for Strategic and International Studies Simulation – October 2019

In the fall of 2019, the Center for Strategic and International Studies in Washington, D.C. ran a pandemic simulation involving a coronavirus virtually identical to the COVID-19 virus that hit the U.S. in late 2019 or early 2020.³³ The purpose of the exercise was to advise U.S. Cabinet officials and other leaders on how to plan for a pandemic before it struck the country. This simulation predicted around a 3% mortality rate, a virus transmissible before symptoms showed, and highly contagious.³⁴ For comparison, the W.H.O. estimated that 3.4% of the reported COVID-19 cases had died.³⁵ One of the exercise's most important insights was that early and preventative actions were critical.³⁶

HHS Report on "Crimson Contagion" Influenza Pandemic Exercise

In October 2019, the HHS completed a long-awaited and much-anticipated draft report.³⁷ HHS summarized the results of a hypothetical influenza outbreak, code-named "Crimson Contagion."³⁸ The hypothetical model ran from January to August 2019.³⁹ The exercise simulated an influenza epidemic that spread to the U.S., eventually infecting 110 million Americans, leading to 7.7 million hospitalizations and 586,000 dead.⁴⁰ According to this scenario, the hypothetical outbreak of this deadly respiratory virus began in China.⁴¹ It was quickly spread around the world by air travelers, who ran high fevers. In the U.S., it was first theoretically detected in Chicago, and 47 days later, the W.H.O. declared a pandemic. By then, it was too late. Due to the delay and lack of preparation by the federal government regarding this pandemic, 110 million Americans were estimated to have become infected, leading to 7.7 million hospitalized and 586,000 dead.[42]

The 2019 HHS simulation and the draft report graphically detailed how underfunded, underprepared, and inept the federal government would be if confronted with a life-and-death struggle with a virus for which no treatment existed.[43] The lack of overall national guidance and leadership left cities and states to their own devices, causing a hodge-podge of school closings, quarantines, and stay-at-home orders, varying from city to city and state to state.[44]

Warnings From Trump's Former National Security Council Member Luciana Borio – January 2020

Trump and his senior advisors also received clear-cut warning signals about the coming pandemic from numerous highly experienced medical experts and epidemiologists outside the federal government. Luciana Borio was one of the many experts who were publicly urging the Trump White House to take immediate action to either avert an American coronavirus epidemic or to prepare and mobilize the resources to fight it effectively. Borio had worked on President Trump's National Security Council and had also been the Director of the Office of Counterterrorism and Emerging Threats to the U.S. Food and Drug Administration. She wrote an op-ed piece in The Wall Street Journal on January 28, 2020, entitled, "Act Now to Prevent an American Epidemic." The article outlined the simple steps that should be taken to ensure that the U.S. was ready for widespread testing and beefed up hospital preparedness.[45]

Dismantling of The White House's National Security Council Directorate for Global Health Security and Biodefense – May 2018

Even if the Trump White House had not ignored the general warnings of a pandemic threat, the administration's ability to respond to a pandemic would have been severely impaired. The White House had dismantled the infrastructure within the National Security Council that had the responsibility of preparing for and responding to a pandemic. Specifically, in 2018, the global health unit of the National Security Council was disbanded by Trump's then-NSA Director John Bolton.

When President Trump took office in 2017, the White House's National Security Council Directorate for Global Health Security and Biodefense survived the transition from the Obama administration.[46] It had been established in 2015 after the Ebola pandemic of 2014 to help mobilize federal resources to prepare for the next outbreak of disease and prevent it from becoming a global pandemic.[47] However, in May 2018, John Bolton took over as Trump's National Security Advisor. He reorganized the White House's National Security Council, disbanding the pandemic office. He combined its staff and functions with the directorate responsible for biosafety preparedness. As a result, when the COVID-19 crisis arrived, there was no clear White House structure in place to oversee this country's coronavirus response. The result was the squandering of several critical weeks that could have made a world of difference. What could have been a swift and effective response was instead a sluggish and ineffective one. In doing so, the Trump White House broke the cardinal rule in a public health security crisis, which is that speed is essential.[48]

The Trump Administration Also Dismantles USAID "Predict" Program – September 2019

While the Trump administration was receiving dire and urgent reports of a coming super pandemic, it was focused on shutting down the U.S. Agency for International Development's PREDICT program.[49] This program, which was strongly backed by both the administrations of George W. Bush and Barack Obama, tracked early-stage viruses and diseases all over the world. The USAID-funded project worked with teams in 31 countries, including China.[50] It was an essential piece in an emerging global network for infectious-disease surveillance.[51] It gave scientists in the U.S. a head start in understanding pathogens that could eventually reach U.S. shores. If PREDICT's field teams had been active and detected the new coronavirus early, American scientists would have begun work on tests, treatments, and cures much earlier.[52] When it was in operation, PREDICT succeeded in collecting more than 100,000 samples and found nearly 1,000 new viruses, including a new Ebola virus.[53] PREDICT also trained and supported staff in 60 foreign laboratories — including the Wuhan lab that identified SARS-CoV-2, the new coronavirus that causes COVID-19.[54]

Partners in the PREDICT program trained local teams in the West African countries of Guinea, Liberia, and Sierra Leone on biological safety. They collected tens of thousands of diagnostic samples in Guinea, Liberia, and Sierra Leone, especially from bats.[55] The program's teams in those countries also used their knowledge to teach people in local villages how to reduce the risk of animal-to-human transfers of viruses, and these teams also connected villagers with government and health care workers who could use PREDICT's training to help them stay safe.[56]

It is estimated that there are about 600,000 unknown viruses with the ability to jump from animals to people.[57] Researchers look in disease hotspots where wildlife and humans intermingle, such as forests that are razed for development or agriculture, or markets that sell bushmeat.[58] Sampling tends to focus on species with "high viral loads," such as bats, rats, and monkeys. Scientists run laboratory tests to find out if newly discovered viruses can infect human cells with "spillover" microbes.[59] Investigators also try to look at the various ecological and social factors that can bring disease-carrying wild animals and humans together.

Over its 10-year life span, from 2009 to 2019, the PREDICT program identified 1,100 different viruses, provided aid to 60 disease detection laboratories, and trained 6,200 people in 30 countries.[60] Researchers were particularly well aware that coronaviruses, one of which caused severe acute respiratory syndrome (SARS), could be a recurring threat. This pathogen (SARS-CoV) first surfaced in China in 2002 and spread to nearly 30 countries.[61] In 2007, researchers from the University of Hong Kong published a paper stating that the presence of many other SARS-like viruses in bats made this type of pathogen a "time bomb."[62] They noted that in southern China, there was a culture of eating exotic animals that could pick up such viruses from the bats, and this practice made it easier for them to make the jump to people.[63] These fears were realized in 2019 when the virus that causes COVID-19 turned out to be so similar to the 2002–2003 microbe that it was named "SARS-CoV-2."

In the case of virus and pathogen surveillance, the truism that an ounce of prevention is worth a pound of a cure aptly applies. The PREDICT program received approximately $200 million over its decade-long life span.[64] This amount, however, was a mere pittance when compared to the first installment of $2 trillion in emergency-relief spending authorized by Congress as a response to COVID-19 and signed into law on March 27, 2020.[65]

Although even the best surveillance system is not foolproof, USAID's PREDICT program quickly became severely understaffed and underfunded once Trump took office on January 20, 2017. The negative impact on the program's effectiveness was immediate. A surveillance program like this is often compared to a fishing net with some holes in it. Without sufficient funding or staffing, the holes keep getting larger, while the money to repair the holes dries up. "We've been gutting surveillance for too long," said Michael Buchmeier, a virologist and associate director of the Center for Virus Research at the University of California, Irvine, "[w]e're creating blind spots in our ability to identify and contain threats of infectious disease in the world."[66]

Thus, with too little money and human resources committed to the program, and with the effective termination of the program in September 2019, it was virtually powerless to identify any new deadly viruses, such as COVID-19. The early warning surveillance system had been effectively turned off.

Kevin Olival, a disease ecologist at the EcoHealth Alliance, a New York City-based nonprofit research group, part of the PREDICT program, confirmed that researchers at EcoHealth were working with the information they had received in late 2019 from the Wuhan Institute of Virology in China.[67] WIV had identified many SARS-related coronaviruses in bats.[68] But by then, the virus was already beginning its deadly spread in Wuhan, and would soon be galloping its way around the globe.

It is too late to now reinstate the PREDICT program for purposes of the current crisis. It is not too late, however, to get ready for the next pandemic. All of the U.S.'s programs like the PREDICT program could be strengthened to identify early on what spillover virus we will have to face next. The U.S. should also be working with other countries to eliminate the root causes of these spillover viruses. Efforts must be made to close wild animal markets, the proximity between bats and humans, and other problem areas that can be mitigated to reduce global risks. Getting a better grasp on animal-human exchanges is critical to predicting these spillovers. What is needed is more detailed knowledge of local ecology, maps of species distributions, an understanding of people's behavioral interactions with other species, and an awareness of what Kevin Olival refers to as the "cultural and economic drivers of the animal trade."[69]

These types of analysis and assessments are necessarily complex, taking a lot of scientists and facilities, as well as training and money. With inadequate resources, surveillance cannot be carried out at all of the high-risk markets where wildlife is butchered and then sold as food. Without closing down all of these markets, or having a small army of "surveillance officers" monitoring these markets, there is no practical way to ensure that the people who work in and around these markets do not come into contact with infected animals.

In a late January 2020 letter to USAID, Senators Angus King of Maine and Elizabeth Warren of Massachusetts demanded to know why PREDICT was being shut down.[70] They expressed concern that even as COVID-19 "threatens public health in the U.S. and abroad, programs like PREDICT are winding down rather than winding up."[71]

It is impossible to assess whether the PREDICT program would have identified the COVID-19 virus as a world killer before it became a pandemic. However, the prior experience the U.S. had with Avian flu, SARS, Ebola, and other outbreaks is clear. The earlier we know a potential epidemic is on its way to the U.S., the better chance we have to prepare and adequately respond.

The Trump administration thus ignored the clear-cut warning signals, and it dismantled the early-warning systems that had been working so successfully for at least the prior ten years. All Americans are now paying a huge price for this recklessness and gross incompetence.

9

WHAT IS COVID-19?

"Know Thy Enemy, Know Thyself"
Sun Tzu's Art of War

COVID-19 (SARS-CoV-2) is shorthand for "coronavirus disease, 2019." It is sometimes referred to as the "new" or "novel" coronavirus. The name "coronavirus" is derived from the Latin word corona, meaning "crown" or "wreath."[1] The name was coined by virologists June Almeida and David Tyrrell in 1967 while they were first studying human coronaviruses at St. Thomas Hospital in London.[2] When looking at these new viruses under the microscope, they noticed they "had a kind of halo surrounding them."[3] The word was first used in print in 1968 by an informal group of virologists in the journal *Nature* to designate the new family of viruses.[4] This halo or solar corona effect is created by the club-shaped protein spikes projecting from the surface of the virus.[5]

The virus is an "enveloped virus" since it is a single-stranded RNA genome wrapped in a protein shell.[6] Inside the viral envelope, there is the nucleocapsid, which is formed from multiple copies of the nucleocapsid (N) protein, which are bound to the positive-sense single-stranded RNA genome in a continuous beads-on-a-string type conformation.[7] The lipid bilayer envelope, membrane proteins, and nucleocapsid protect the virus when it is outside the host cell.[8]

Using an electron microscope, Almeida and Tyrrell were able to show that two types of the virus with the distinctive club-like spikes (B814 and 229E) were morphologically related to each other, as well as related to infectious bronchitis virus (IBV).[9] Also, in 1967, a research group at the U.S. National Institute of Health was able to isolate another member of this new group of viruses with club-like spikes, naming this virus strain "OC43."[10]

Human coronavirus 229E and human coronavirus OC43 continued to be studied in subsequent decades, with some important research papers about them being published in 2012.[11] However, there does not appear to have been any research conducted on the development of a vaccine for these strains of coronavirus, since there was not a high incidence of these viruses found in human populations. Meanwhile, the coronavirus strain B814 was somehow (and incredibly) lost, so it is not known whether any of the present known strains of coronavirus that are now causing the current pandemic are related to B814.[12] Other human coronaviruses were later identified, including SARS-CoV in 2003, HCoV NL63 in 2004, HCoV HKU1 in 2005, MERS-CoV in 2012, and the archvillain of them all: SARS-CoV-2 (COVID-19) in late 2019.[13] There has also been a large number of animal coronaviruses identified since the 1960s.[14]

Infected animal or human carriers shed coronaviruses into the environment by coughing, sneezing, or other means.[15] These viruses can be suspended in microscopic droplets in the air before they fall to a surface or are aspirated (breathed in) by another potential host.

Once the virus invades the body of the new host, the coronavirus spike protein interacts with its complementary cell receptor in the host.[16] Coronaviruses mainly target epithelial cells, which line the outer surfaces of organs and blood vessels throughout the body.[17] They are transmitted from one host to another host, depending on the coronavirus species, by either an aerosol, fomite (a surface capable of carrying infectious agents) or fecal-oral route.[18] Human coronaviruses infect the epithelial cells of the respiratory tract.[19] SARS coronavirus, for example, infects the human epithelial cells of the lungs, via an aerosol route,[20] by binding to the angiotensin-converting enzyme 2 (ACE2) receptor.[21]

There are two known strains of coronavirus, which are named "S" and "L." The S-type strain is the original, "ancestral" strain of the disease that mutated from a coronavirus transmissible between bats.[22] The S-type strain is the milder of the two strains and is less likely to cause serious illness or death.[23] The L-type strain, which is more aggressive, at least in its transmission, evolved from the S-Strain and was initially believed to be responsible for most of the COVID-19 infections.[24] The difference between the L-Strain and S-Strain involves two specific amino acids, which have been compared to changing two lines of code in a computer program.[25]

There is some evidence that the S-type strain may have made a resurgence to the point where it is the more prevalent strain in causing coronavirus infections. Even though it is less aggressive than its close cousin, the L-type strain, it may have spread more widely in the human population because people are able to tolerate it better, and it is not out to kill the host. As explained by Dr. Nicole Saphier on Fox News: "The 'L' strain tends to be the more lethal or severe strain, while the 'S' strain seems to have more mild symptoms ... So what we are seeing is ... more of the mild strain of the virus because it doesn't actually want to kill the host."[26]

COVID-2019 is an RNA virus, which means it uses ribonucleic acid to encode its genetic material instead of DNA.[27] RNA viruses, which include viruses like Ebola, influenza, rabies, and even the common cold, tend to mutate extremely frequently because their polymerase enzymes used for reproduction aren't as good at "proofreading" for errors when transcribing genetic code.[28] The constant mutations make COVID-19 and other RNA viruses more of a moving target, which makes it harder to develop an effective vaccine and may require annual updates of the vaccine to keep up with the mutations of the virus.

How Contagious is COVID-19?

The transmission rate of COVID-19 is relatively high and is higher than the rate of SARS, another coronavirus. Early research indicates that one person who can spread it, on average, to between 2 and 2.5 others.[29] One study found that the rate was higher, with one case spreading to between 4.7 and 6.6 other people.[30] By comparison, one person who has the seasonal flu will pass it to between 1.1 and 2.3 others.[31]

Scientists at the Los Alamos National Laboratory published a study on May 7, 2020, indicating the now-prevalent strain of coronavirus is a more contagious version of the pathogen first reported in Wuhan, China.[32] The study was published on BioRxiv.org, a website used by medical researchers to facilitate the speedy collaboration on studies of potential treatments of coronavirus. Scientists affiliated with the Los Alamos lab, which is run by the U.S. Department of Energy, collaborated with researchers at Duke University and the University of Sheffield in England.[33] The researchers concluded that a mutation of coronavirus that occurred sometime in early February in Europe made the pathogen more contagious, such that the mutated strain rapidly migrated to the East Coast of the U.S. and has been the dominant strain of coronavirus worldwide since March.[34] According to Bette Korber, a Los Alamos biologist, "The story is worrying, as we see a mutated form of the virus very rapidly emerging, and over the month of March becoming the dominant pandemic form," adding, "When viruses with this mutation enter a population, they rapidly begin to take over the local epidemic, thus they are more transmissible."[35]

Where Am I Most Likely to Catch It?

By now, you have heard at least a thousand times that, in order to protect yourself or those around you from a coronavirus infection, you must wash your hands regularly, wear a mask when in public, and stay at least six feet away from people when outside your home. But what you may not know is that the risks vary from place to place and that your home, public transportation, your workplace (when your state's stay-at-home orders are eased), and the grocery store all present different challenges and risks.

A mid-May blog post by Dr. Erin Bromage, an expert on infectious diseases and a professor at the University of Massachusetts Dartmouth, titled "The Risks - Know Them - Avoid Them," identified some of the highest risk areas that may not be what you would expect.[36]

According to Dr. Bromage, you are at the highest risk when you are with a lot of people in an enclosed environment with poor airflow, and when there is a lot of talking or singing going on. This often leads to a great deal of new infections. Other than nursing homes and meatpacking plants, the biggest outbreaks that have been reported can be traced to religious ceremonies, choir practice, indoor sporting events, prisons, and even birthday parties.[37] As Bromage explained in an ABC interview, "You've got a lot of people in an enclosed space with lots of huffing, puffing, or yelling, which just led to large outbreak events," he said. Prolonged contact and lots of direct talking, breathing, and yelling between individuals increase the direct exposure to viral particles, which increases the likelihood of infection.

Bromage further explained that the risk of infection increases with the amount of time that you are exposed to a virus, so that if you are passed on the sidewalk by a jogger, you may be momentarily exposed to the virus, but it is less likely that you will be infected than if you are in an enclosed space and exposed to the virus for a prolonged time period. Scientists refer to this amount of exposure to the virus that leads to infection as the "infectious dose." The highest infectious doses come from exposure to a sneezing and coughing release, which causes the highest amounts of viral material to be exposed into the air. A single sneeze, according to Bromage, has been estimated to release about 30,000 droplets that can travel up to 200 miles per hour, which means it could easily cross a room.[38] A cough releases round 3,000 droplets that can travel around 50 miles per hour. These particles may drop to the ground or could hang around in the air for a short period of time. Of course, the amount of the virus that is released when a person sneezes or coughs varies depending on the infected person's "viral load," which is the amount of the virus detected in a test sample from a patient and reflects how fast the virus is replicating.

Of particular note is that, in very high-risk situations, such as when there are multiple people in a confined space for a prolonged period of time, even the following of social distancing guidelines may not protect you from getting infected, since a low dose of the virus in the air in a poorly ventilated room can reach you from more than a six-feet distance and may be enough to infect you.

While there are risks involved with grocery shopping, if you observe all the usual safety rules such as avoiding other shoppers and not speaking to anyone directly more than necessary, there should not be any high risk of exposure as long as you limit the time period that you are in the store as much as possible. Public bathrooms are much riskier even if there are few people in the bathroom at the same time, due to the fact that there are a lot of surfaces to touch - like door handles, faucets, and countertops – where the virus may be lurking. This risk, however, is substantially mitigated by thorough hand washing and avoiding touching your face.

If social restrictions have been eased in your area, and you are planning to get together with family or friends for a social gathering, you can make it as safe as possible by meeting outside or in a well-ventilated location, and agreeing in advance to not shake hands, bring your own food, and space the chairs out at least 6 feet a part. Common sense and caution also go a long way to assessing what are acceptable risks for you and your family members, taking into account your age, health and especially whether you have any immune-compromising conditions.

How Dangerous Is This Virus?

Although the World Health Organization estimated early on in the pandemic that the death rate for COVID-19 would be 3.4%, China was reporting a lower death rate of 1.4% as of March 19, 2020.[39] Dr. Deborah Birx, a U.S. health official and member of the White House coronavirus task force, called this "unrealistically low," suggesting that China was playing fast-and-loose with its numbers.[40] In any event, it appears that the overall COVID-19 death rates will be significantly below that of the 1918 Spanish flu pandemic, but higher than that seen in the 2009 HINI flu outbreak.

COVID-19 is five to 10 times more deadly than the flu for those between the ages of 0 and 45.[41] It is 12 1/2 times more deadly than the flu for those over 85.[42] During the 2018-19 flu season, about 35 million people in the U.S. contracted the flu, and about 34,000 died, according to the CDC.[43] Flu-related deaths were thus about one out of every 1,000 people. The CDC estimates the total number of flu infections in the U.S. via its influenza-surveillance system, which gathers flu data from state and local partners and projects nationwide totals using infectious-disease models.

While about 0.1% of people who get the flu die, the coronavirus' global death rate is about 4.7%.[44] The death rate in the U.S. from coronavirus as of March 30 was 1.8%,[45] but it has been rising. The mortality rates have varied widely around the world, with Italy reporting an 11% death rate as of the end of March.[46]

However, it is highly probable that the actual number of coronavirus cases and related deaths is much greater than being reported. It is estimated by some public health experts that the actual case totals in Italy and the U.S. could be at least ten times higher than officially reported, which would also mean that the death rates are correspondingly higher.[47] "There are a lot of deaths that we probably will never know if they were coronavirus deaths or not," said Elizabeth Halloran, a biostatistician at Fred Hutchinson Cancer Research Center and University of Washington, adding, "There could be a lot more people infected than we thought."[48]

The Italian research group Instituto Cattaneo estimated that, as of April 1, the number of coronavirus deaths in Italy was almost double the total reported by the Italian Department of Civil Protection.[49] In the U.S., the reported spikes in "excess deaths" by states suggests that that the actual number of coronavirus deaths could be between 30% and 50% higher than officially reported.[50]

What Don't We Know About COVID-19?

The plain truth is that more is not known about COVID-19 than is known about it. As of now, there is no known cure, highly effective treatment or vaccine for this disease. That is why we have reverted to the medieval and partially successful "mitigation" methods of combatting the disease, such as quarantine and isolation. Despite all our modern technology and scientific achievements, we are now completely exposed to the ravages of the virus, and the best we can do is huddle in our homes, "social distance," and wear masks when we venture outside.

While the reader is encouraged to carefully read the CDC and other websites to learn more about the practical "good hygiene" measures that should be taken to reduce the spread of COVID-19, the extraordinary "take away" from a review of relevant websites is how much is not known about this virus or the diseases it causes.

- **No Vaccine.** There is no coronavirus vaccine yet, although intense research is underway to develop one or more vaccines. Vaccine testing in humans started in March 2020. More than 100 vaccine projects are in various phases of development. One vaccine candidate that's in human trials, developed in part at Oxford University, uses a version of the common cold virus that has been mixed with part of SARS-CoV-2.
- **Cure?** No, but they are working on it. Stay tuned.

- **Coronavirus Treatment.** There's no specific treatment for COVID-19. People who get a mild case can mitigate their symptoms with the same techniques you would employ in the event of the seasonal flu or bad cold, like rest, fluids, and fever control. Over-the-counter medications are often taken for a sore throat, body aches, and fever. At a hospital, people with coronavirus are typically treated with "fluids to reduce the risk of dehydration, medication to reduce a fever, [and] supplemental oxygen in more severe cases," according to Healthline.
- **Antibiotics.** Since antibiotics treat bacteria, not viruses, they are not effective against this coronavirus. However, if a person infected with COVID-19 develops a secondary infection, antibiotics are sometimes used to treat the infection.
- **Antiviral Medications and Other Possible Treatments.** The FDA issued an emergency use ruling for **hydroxychloroquine** and **chloroquine.** These medications are approved to treat malaria and autoimmune conditions like rheumatoid arthritis and lupus. Studies on their use against COVID-19 have had mixed results, but due to possible cardiac complications and lack of any clear evidence that they are effective, they are not now being recommended for the treatment of COVID-19.

    Nevertheless, President Trump surprised everyone by announcing at the White House on May 18 that he was taking hydroxychloroquine, although there was considerable skepticism as to whether this was really true. Medical experts, including those on Fox News, quickly reacted by cautioning the public that the use of this drug as a preventative measure was ill-advised and that there were risks involved in taking this drug, especially for prolonged periods.

    Several studies focused on an antiviral medication called **Remdesivir**, which was created to fight Ebola. An emergency FDA ruling lets doctors use it for people hospitalized with COVID-19 and in clinical trials. According to Katherine Seley-Radtke, a Professor at the University of Maryland, remdesivir works by "blocking the coronavirus RNA polymerase," which is one of the key enzymes it needs to replicate its genetic material and multiply in the body."[51] Clinical trials are also underway for **Tocilizumab**, another medication used to treat autoimmune conditions. The FDA is also allowing clinical trials and hospital use of **blood plasma** from people who've had COVID-19 and recovered to help others build immunity. This is often referred to as "**convalescent plasma.**"[52]

- **Antibody testing.** In answer to the simple question as to whether a test showing that there are antibodies in your blood means that you are immune from catching COVID-19 again, the answer is "Maybe." While the presence of antibodies means that you were infected and have recovered, and medical experts expect that this will confer some immunity, they simply don't know at this point and must await the results of ongoing studies. Some doctors have reported seeing the same patients twice with coronavirus infections.

COVID-19 and High Blood Pressure

Another major issue that is still up in the air is whether a person with high blood pressure and no other underlying health condition is more susceptible to contracting coronavirus and, if so, is more likely to become seriously ill from it. The CDC's current position with regard to the possible association between COVID-19 and high blood pressure is as follows:

> At this time, we do not think that people with high blood pressure and no other underlying health conditions are more likely than others to get severely ill from COVID-19. Although many people who have gotten severely ill from COVID-19 have high blood pressure, they are often older or have other medical conditions like obesity, diabetes, and serious heart conditions that place them at higher risk of severe illness from COVID-19.[53]

While the correlation of high blood pressure and increased risk of coronavirus infection is still being studied, there is no serious dispute that high blood pressure, when combined with other risk factors, results in a greater likelihood of COVID-19 infection and complications. Data from China indicates that 25% to 50% of people who came to hospitals with coronavirus had high blood pressure and other health condition like cancer, diabetes, or lung disease.[54] In Italy, 76% of people who died had high blood pressure and another underlying condition.[55]

There are two theories as to why there is a high correlation between high blood pressure and high risk of disease from coronavirus. One theory is that high blood pressure weakens the immune system, making it less able to fight off the virus. Nearly two-thirds of people over 60 have high blood pressure,[56] so age also increases the risk of a serious infection from coronavirus.

Another possibility is that the higher risk comes not from high blood pressure itself, but from certain drugs used to treat it -- ACE inhibitors and angiotensin receptor blockers (ARBs).[57] This is just a theory since there's no research yet on what impact, if any, these medications might have on COVID-19. The concept is based on the fact that ACE inhibitors and ARBs raise levels of an enzyme called ACE2 in your body, and to infect cells, the COVID-19 virus must attach itself to ACE2.

Is It Just A Respiratory Virus, Or Does It Also Attack Others Systems?

COVID-19 often attaches to the lungs and can cause serious illness or death as a result of respiratory complications such as pneumonia. However, there is a growing recognition the novel coronavirus is far more unpredictable than a simple respiratory virus. It can also strike anywhere in the body, from the brain to the toes.[58] Keeping a patient breathing is, of course, the first priority in the emergency room or ICU, and many patients have to be intubated and attached to ventilators to keep them breathing by mechanical means while they are given time to recover from a coronavirus infection.

Many patients, though, are at risk from inflammatory reactions triggered by the disease, kidney and heart ailments, and it has the capacity to cause blood clots or stroke.[59] "We don't know why there are so many disease presentations," said Angela Rasmussen, a virologist at the Center for Infection and Immunity at Columbia University's Mailman School of Public Health, "Bottom line, this is just so new that there's a lot we don't know." [60]

In addition to weakening the heart's muscles and disrupting its rhythm, it can also attack and disable the kidneys, forcing coronavirus patients onto dialysis equipment while, sometimes at the same time, the patient is unable to breathe on their own. It also impacts the nervous system, leading to an inability to taste and smell in many patients, and sometimes attacks the brain.[61] Often the most lethal effects are when it creates blood clots that can quickly lead to death, and it inflames blood vessels throughout the body.[62]

What Are the Most Serious Symptoms of COVID-19?

COVID-19 symptoms include cough, fever, shortness of breath, muscle aches, sore throat, unexplained loss of taste or smell, diarrhea, and headaches. It can cause severe illness throughout the body, most commonly to the following systems:

- **Lungs:** SARS-CoV-2 infects both the upper and lower respiratory tracts, eventually working its way deep into the lungs, clogging and filling tiny air sacs (alveoli) with cells and fluid that choke off the flow of oxygen. This can cause pulmonary embolism from breakaway blood clots and micro clots.
- **Immune system:** There is often an exaggerated, overactive response from the body's immune system, a storm of killer "cytokines" that attack the body's cells along with the virus as it seeks to defend the body from an invader.
- **Brain:** It can cause strokes from blood clots, as well as neurological issues.
- **Blood:** The virus often attacks the blood vessels, leading to a phenomenon being referred to as "sticky blood" and clots that can range from microscopic to sizable. Patients have suffered strokes and pulmonary emboli as clots break loose and travel to the brain and lungs. A study in The *Lancet*, a British medical journal, showed this may be because the virus directly targets the endothelial cells that line blood vessels.
- **Heart:** Weakens heart muscle; causes dangerous arrhythmias and heart attacks due to small clots.

- **Kidneys:** Damage to structures that filter waste from blood; patients often require dialysis.
- **Gastrointestinal system:** Vomiting and diarrhea sometimes occur.
- **Eyes:** Pinkeye.
- **Nose:** Loss of smell and taste (anosmia).
- **Skin:** "COVID toes" or fingers are purple rashes from the virus's attack on blood vessels.[63]

How Does COVID-19 Affect Children?

It was initially thought that COVID-19 generally bypassed young people to concentrate its lethal firepower on the elderly and adults with pre-existing conditions, such as high blood pressure, obesity, or asthma. This assumption had to be revised, however, when hospitals started seeing dozens of cases where children were stricken with a rare inflammatory reaction with cardiac complications.[64] On Friday, May 8, New York Gov. Andrew M. Cuomo announced 73 children had fallen severely ill in the state, and a 5-year-old boy in New York City had become the first child to die of the syndrome.[65] Two more children had succumbed to the syndrome the following day.[66] COVID-19 is the seventh coronavirus to have crossed over to human hosts, but it is far and away the most deadly virus in the coronavirus family. COVID-19 has been described as a combination of "the infectiousness of its cold-causing cousins with some of the lethality of SARS and MERS."[67]

In short, little is known about COVID-19, other than that it is fairly highly contagious and more dangerous and deadly than the seasonal flu. Conversely, much is unknown about it, and there is as yet no highly effective therapeutic medication (i.e., "cure") or vaccine for it. Diagnostic testing for coronavirus is relatively reliable, but there is still a severe shortage of widespread diagnostic testing. Antibody testing is generally available, but of the 70 or so antibody tests that are available and on the market, only twelve have been approved by the FDA as of early May.[68] However, there is a serious question as to whether the results of antibody testing are very meaningful. All you know for sure if you test positive for antibodies is that there are antibodies in your blood that were developed as a reaction to a

COVID-19 infection. It does not necessarily mean that you are immune and that you can't catch the disease again. So for now, at least, it is unlikely that any states will be issuing you an "immunity passport," certifying that you have immunity from the coronavirus just because you have been tested and found to have antibodies.

*****

Sorry to be so depressing. But on the bright side, it could be worse. Most people who catch the disease recover from it relatively unscathed. And while the infection and transmission rate may be high, it is not as deadly a killing machine as the Spanish Flu, which killed off large numbers of young adults and middle-aged people, in addition to the very young and very old. COVID-19 particularly targets for serious illness the elderly, those with underlying diseases, and especially those who are already ill in nursing homes and other long-term care facilities.

So COVID-19 is likely to be with us for quite a while. As they say in the Marine Corps, we must "improvise, adapt and overcome." We really don't have much choice. Darwinian natural selection is fully at play here. It is either COVID-19 or us, unless we can reach some sort of accommodation with it whereby we can co-exist, which is possible. Humans have been on this planet for about 6 million years, and Homo sapiens have been around for 300,000 years, so we are unlikely to be permanently felled by a mere virus, even one as ingenious as COVID-19. Let's keep looking at the sunny side of the street (from your window, of course if you are in quarantine).

So other than that, Mrs. Lincoln, how did you like the play?

10

COVID-19 BREAKS OUT IN CHINA

AND THE CHINESE GOVERNMENT COVERS IT UP

Because of the culture of secrecy and self-censorship that imbues every aspect of life under the authoritarian regime in China, the initial reaction was for the Chinese government to throw a blanket of secrecy and silence over the coronavirus crisis. As a result, the origins of the outbreak in Wuhan are still partially shrouded in mystery. Much, however, is known about the efforts of Chinese authorities to suppress information on the nature and scope of the outbreak. This web of secrecy and misinformation had significant implications on how the U.S. and the rest of the world reacted to the pandemic, and will doubtlessly impact China's relations with the U.S. and other countries for the foreseeable future.

The Mysterious Origins of COVID-19

The first known case of coronavirus arose in early December 2019 in Wuhan, China, when a man was admitted to a Wuhan hospital after a 7-day history of fever, cough, and other symptoms.[1] His wife, a 53-year-old woman who had no known history of exposure to the market, was also hospitalized with pneumonia.[2] Whether this first reported case of coronavirus can be described as "Patient Zero" is questionable. There is a high likelihood others were infected with the virus earlier and did not seek treatment. It is also reasonable to assume that other earlier cases were not correctly identified.

According to Dr. Wu Wenjuan of Wuhan's Jinyintan Hospital, one of the earliest case clusters involved four people in the same family.[3] These people included a 49-year-old Hua'nan market vendor and his father-in-law.[4] The vendor got sick on December 12, 2019, while the father-in-law, who had no exposure to the market, fell ill seven days later.[5] By January 2, 2020, there were 41 people hospitalized with this illness in Wuhan hospitals, according to an article published by the medical journal *Lancet*.[6] Of those patients, 27 of them had direct exposure to the Hua'nan seafood market, which sold live animals as well as seafood.[7] The others did not.

Although the Hua'nan market has been suspected of being "Ground Zero" for the coronavirus outbreak in Wuhan, this is not necessarily so. First of all, no bats were sold at the market, so there could not have been a direct transmission of the virus from bat to a human at the market. However, there is a good possibility the bat coronavirus may have been transmitted from bats to one of the wild animals sold at the market, and then to a human host.

U.S. intelligence agencies, among others, explored another possibility. Less than 300 yards from the seafood market is the Wuhan branch of China's CDC. Researchers from that facility and the nearby Wuhan Institute of Virology (WIV) have, for many years, posted articles about collecting and studying bat coronaviruses from around China.[8] U.S. intelligence sources are pursuing the possibility one of the samples being analyzed leaked, or hazardous waste from one of these labs was deposited in a place where it could spread.[9]

The WIV had the highest biosafety rating (Biosafety Level 4). However, the Wuhan CDC, which also studies bat coronaviruses, only had a Biosafety Level 2 rating. A level 2 facility provides only minimal protection against accidental releases.[10] There were also some stories circulating that a Wuhan CDC staffer collected bat coronaviruses with inadequate personal protective equipment and used other unsafe operational practices. Two articles described Tian Junhua, the Wuhan CDC researcher, capturing bats in a cave.[11] They claimed that the researcher "forgot to take protective measures" and that "bat urine dripped from the top of his head like raindrops."[12]

In January 2018, the U.S. Embassy in Beijing sounded the alarm about the lax safety standards at the WIV.[13] This warning came even though WIV had already received its Level 4 rating in 2015. The U.S. Embassy sent senior science diplomats to the WIV, including Jamison Fouss, the consul general in Wuhan, and Rick Switzer, the embassy's counselor on the environment, science, technology, and health.[14] These representatives tried to impress on WIV officials that the lab had safety and management weakness.[15] The U.S. delegation thought that the matter was particularly urgent since the lab was actively engaged in extensive research work on bat coronaviruses. This kind of lab work always posed a potential risk of human transmission and a new SARS-like epidemic.[16] Strangely, although the WIV issued a news release in English about one of these U.S. official visits to the lab, the statement was later deleted from its website. However, it remained archived on the internet.[17]

A cable sent on January 19, 2018 by the U.S. Embassy team in Wuhan reported: "During interactions with scientists at the WIV laboratory, they noted the new lab has a serious shortage of appropriately trained technicians and investigators needed to operate this high-containment laboratory safely."[18] The cable further advised that the U.S. representatives had met with Shi Zhengli, the head of the research project, who had been publishing studies related to bat coronaviruses for many years.[19] In November 2017, Shi Zhengli and her team published a research article showing horseshoe bats collected from a cave in Yunnan province were likely from the same bat population that spawned the SARS coronavirus outbreak in 2003.[20] This information was significant since these WIV lab researchers established that various SARS-like coronaviruses could interact with ACE2. ACE2 is the human receptor identified for SARS-coronavirus, suggesting the likelihood of additional transmissions from bats to humans.[21]

If, in fact, the coronavirus linked to the Wuhan outbreak accidentally originated from one of these two Wuhan labs, this would be truly ironic, since the primary mission of these labs was to *prevent* any future virus transfers to humans.

Support for the theory that an accidental release caused the outbreak also comes from a paper published by Botao Xiao and Lei Xiao from Guangzhou's South China University of Technology in February 2020.[22] The article appeared on an internet site, "ResearchGate." In the paper, the scientists concluded: "In addition to origins of natural recombination and intermediate host, the killer coronavirus probably originated from a laboratory in Wuhan. Safety level may need to be reinforced in high-risk biohazardous laboratories."[23] The article was later withdrawn. When asked about it by a *Wall Street Journal* reporter in February 2020, Botao Xiao stated that he had removed the paper because it "was not supported by direct proofs."[24] It was strongly suspected, however, that he had withdrawn the paper under pressure by Chinese authorities.

China Clamps Down Hard On Media Coverage of the Outbreak

Whether the coronavirus outbreak in Wuhan started at the seafood market or in one of the two government-run laboratories is unclear. But what is certain is that the virus outbreak originated in Wuhan. What we also know for sure is that, from the very start, the Chinese government placed a total lockdown on information relating to the virus origins and the extent of the outbreak. China failed to fully cooperate with U.S. investigators and those from other countries and the W.H.O. regarding the outbreak. A Shanghai laboratory published the genome of this novel coronavirus on January 11, 2020, but the lab was quickly shut down by authorities for "rectification."[25] Also, at least as of mid-April 2020, the Chinese government failed to provide U.S. experts with actual samples of the virus, which were urgently needed for further research.[26]

Reports of the outbreak of a new type of SARS virus began to appear in late December 2019. A doctor at Wuhan's Fifth Hospital, Lü Xiaohong, told the *China Youth Daily* she became alarmed when some of the medical staff at two Wuhan hospitals were quarantined after being infected with a mysterious type of viral pneumonia.[27] One week later, Dr. Ai Fen, an emergency room doctor at Wuhan Central Hospital, reported the case of another seriously ill patient who was also suffering from a virus of unknown origin.[28] Dr. Ai alerted hospital authorities and ordered the medical staff in her hospital department to wear masks.[29] That night, the hospital's disciplinary department summoned Dr. Ai and rebuked her for "spreading rumors." Although she tried to argue that the disease could be contagious, the hospital administration concluded that her action had caused "unnecessary panic" and "damaged the stability" of Wuhan.[30]

Another Wuhan doctor, Dr. Li Wenliang, quickly became a national and international celebrity after he started sharing information on the "SARS coronavirus" with his medical colleagues. On December

30, he saw a patient's report from Dr. Ai containing a reference to the newly discovered "SARS-type virus." The same day, Dr. Li wrote to a group of other doctors who participated in a private WeChat group: "7 confirmed cases of SARS were reported [to hospital] from Huanan Seafood Market."[31] He also posted the patient's examination report and C.T. scan, confirming that this was a new type of coronavirus infection that still needed to be subtyped."[32] Li asked the WeChat group members to inform their families and friends to take protective measures.

Given the electrifying nature of Li's communication, the information quickly went viral on social media platforms and elsewhere on the internet.[33] Screenshots of Li's widely-circulated WeChat messages came to the attention of the Wuhan Public Security Bureau, and Li was interrogated on January 3. The Wuhan authorities gave him a warning notice and censured him for "making false comments on the Internet."[34] He was forced to sign a "letter of admonition" promising not to do it again. He was further warned that he would be prosecuted if he continued to engage in "rumormongering."[35]

After the warning, Dr. Li returned to work in the hospital, where he contracted the virus from an infected patient on January 8. Li was admitted to the intensive care unit of Wuhan Central Hospital on January 12, where he was quarantined, treated, and tested positive for coronavirus.[36] On January 31, Li published on social media his account of his experiences at the police station, including the fact that he was forced to sign a letter of admonition. After his post went viral, he became an overnight hero for millions of ordinary Chinese citizens who were feeling angry and frustrated over the government's handling of the crisis. Many, including some within the all-powerful Chinese Communist Party, started questioning why a doctor who gave early warnings about the outbreak was being silenced.[37]

Li vowed in his internet communications that he would return to the medical front lines to fight the coronavirus as soon as possible, but it was not to be.[38] His condition became critical on February 5 and he died shortly thereafter.[39] Although the Chinese state media initially reported Li's death in social media posts on February 6, it quickly became apparent that the state media had jumped the gun and that reports of his death were premature. Official reports were revised to say that Li was still in "critical condition" and that "we are doing our best to rescue him."[40] The hospital confirmed Li's actual death the following day, on February 7, with more than 17 million people watching the drama on live stream updates.[41]

The widespread frustration among the Chinese people that the Dr. Li drama tapped into continued to smolder in Wuhan and throughout China. Government officials were being less than honest with their own people and with the foreign media, and China's massive propaganda machine quickly went into overdrive to control and manage the unfolding narrative. The truth itself was far less important than what people could be led to believe was the truth. Even after Chinese doctors and local authorities were well aware that the virus was being spread from person to person, Chinese President Xi Jinping continued to deny the virus could be spread among humans.[42] Chinese authorities also had to manage the negative press fallout from the disastrous decision to go ahead with a Chinese Lunar New Year banquet involving tens of thousands of families in Wuhan in the midst of a rapidly expanding epidemic.[43]

Much like President Trump would later try to rewrite history as to the U.S. response (or lack thereof) to the coronavirus crisis, Chinese officials spent an enormous amount of energy on the public relations or "crisis management" aspects of the outbreak. They tried to convince their people and the world press that they had acted promptly and forcefully. In a February 23 teleconference with 170,000 officials and world press, President Xi categorically rejected all criticism of China's coronavirus response.[44] He asserted the country's vigorous response had "bought time" for the rest of the world.[45]

China also tried to suppress the plain fact that President Xi was personally responsible for the decision to allow about five million people to leave Wuhan without screening before a lockdown was eventually imposed. This ill-advised decision, which accelerated the virus's spread throughout the country and the rest of the world, was made despite the detailed knowledge by President Xi and the rest of the Chinese leadership as to the extent and global dangers of the Wuhan outbreak.

President Xi also waited until January 20 to publicly admit that the virus was spreading between humans,[46] and he delayed until January 23 the decision to lock down Wuhan and three other cities. Even though it should have been ordered sooner, this near-total lockdown did succeed in finally slowing down the spread of the virus within China's borders. By then, however, the virus had already jumped to other countries. If the Chinese government had taken proactive measures at an earlier date, a strong argument could be made that the virus would have been contained within China's borders. If that had occurred, there might not have been a worldwide pandemic.

China did communicate some information directly to U.S. authorities in early January, but the information was incomplete and potentially misleading. On January 3, CDC Director Robert Redfield received a phone call from his counterpart at China's CDC, informing him only there was some sort of a respiratory illness spreading in Wuhan.[47] However, there was no disclosure that the virus was contagious and could be spread from person-to-person, or that it posed an immediate and significant danger of spreading beyond China's borders. Redfield relayed this news to HHS Secretary Alex Azar, the agency that oversees the CDC and other public health entities. Azar, in turn, notified the White House, and he instructed his chief of staff to inform the National Security Council.[48]

However, on the very same day (January 3), China was intensifying its efforts to prevent any embarrassing details regarding the outbreak from leaking out. Top health officials at China's National Health Commission and the Hubei Health Commission issued gag orders directing that Wuhan pneumonia samples be moved to testing facilities or destroyed. The massive cover-up was then broadened when the National Health Commission ordered all Chinese institutions not to publish any scientific information related to the virus or the outbreak.

Based upon the erroneous information being announced by Chinese authorities on December 31 and thereafter, the W.H.O. issued a grossly misleading and erroneous statement, as follows: "Based on the preliminary information from the Chinese investigation team, no evidence of significant human-to-human transmission and no health care worker infections have been reported."[49] The W.H.O. later regretted having so willingly and perhaps so naively accepted China's erroneous pronouncements. This also gave President Trump some basis, along with some subsequent misstatements by W.H.O. and praise for China's response efforts, as "proof" that the W.H.O. was somehow complicit in China's cover-up. He also accused W.H.O. of being "biased" in China's favor.

On January 6, the CDC offered Beijing its technical expertise to help with the virus.[50] The Chinese government ignored the offer for over a month, along with additional offers of assistance from Secretary Azar and other senior U.S. officials. Also, on January 6, the CDC sent a letter to Chinese officials seeking samples of the virus.[51] The samples were critically important to the development of diagnostic tests and a potential vaccine. However, these overtures from the U.S. were either rebuffed or went unanswered.

China's official party line regarding the country's "perfect" response to the crisis began to crack in early March 2020. Zhong Nanshan, one of China's most highly regarded epidemiology experts and leader of China's National Health Commission's task force on the epidemic, said officials had identified a coronavirus by December 31.[52] He confirmed China took too long to confirm human-to-human transmission publicly.[53] In this unusual display of candor, Dr. Nanshan admitted that if the government had taken action earlier, "the number of sick would have been greatly reduced."[54]

These concessions by a leading Chinese spokesperson, however, were not enough to stem the tidal wave of criticism of China's for its early secretiveness and total lack of candor and transparency concerning the Wuhan outbreak.

Trump Turns Up the Heat On China

As early as March 18, Trump personally ratcheted up the rhetoric against China for the devastation caused by the pandemic that had originated in Wuhan. Labeling it the "Chinese virus,"[55] Trump made clear his personal view that Beijing should have acted faster to warn the world of the pandemic.

He also refused to condemn an unnamed White House official who had privately termed it the "kung flu," which was widely condemned as racist.⁵⁶

On May 1, 2020, Australia's *Daily Telegraph* reported that a research paper compiled by the U.S. and allied intelligence services (the so-called "Five Eyes" intelligence alliance), concluded that China intentionally hid or destroyed evidence as to the severity of the coronavirus outbreak.⁵⁷ The 15-page document, which was compiled by the intelligence agencies of the U.S., Canada, the U.K., Australia, and New Zealand, suggested that China's secrecy and misrepresentations of fact may have resulted in the loss of tens of thousands of lives around the world.⁵⁸

This intelligence report included references to China's initial denial that the virus could be transmitted between humans, and that this fundamental misrepresentation was later picked up by the W.H.O. According to the intelligence report, the Chinese government's denial that the virus was not easily communicable was made "despite evidence of human-human transmission from early December."⁵⁹ The report also asserted that the W.H.O. made this misrepresentation even though it should have known better, and that at the time that "officials in Taiwan raised concerns [that human-to-human transfer was possible] as early as December 31, as did experts in Hong Kong on January 4."⁶⁰ It also called attention to the silencing or "disappearing" of doctors who tried to speak up, the destruction of evidence in Chinese laboratories, and China's refusal to provide live samples to international scientists working on a vaccine.⁶¹

The report confirmed prior reports that China began censoring news of the virus on search engines and social media beginning December 3, 2019, deleting terms such as "SARS variation," "Wuhan Seafood market," and "Wuhan Unknown Pneumonia."⁶² It also confirmed that on January 3, China's National Health Commission ordered virus samples to be moved to designated testing facilities or destroyed, and that the government issued a "no-publication order" related to the disease.⁶³ It is further noted that on January 5, Wuhan's Municipal Health Commission stopped releasing daily updates on the number of new cases and failed to resume them for 13 days. Also, on January 10, Wang Guanga, a respiratory specialist at Peking

University First Hospital who had been investigating the outbreak, was reported by the Chinese government-controlled media as saying that the outbreak was "under control" and largely a "mild condition."[64] Two days later, on January 12, a Shanghai professor's lab was closed down after it shared data on the virus's genetic sequence with the outside world.[65] On January 24, Chinese officials stopped the Wuhan Institute of Virology from sharing virus samples with a lab at the University of Texas.[66]

The intelligence report also documented China's duplicity throughout the critical month of February, during which time "Beijing [pressed] the U.S. [sic], Italy, India, Australia, Southeast Asian neighbours [sic] and others not to protect themselves via travel restrictions, even as [China] impose[d] severe restrictions at home."[67] At the same time, the report stated: "Millions of people [left] Wuhan after the outbreak and before Beijing lock[ed] down the city on January 23."[68] The report further recounted China's successful efforts to get European Union diplomats who were preparing a report on the pandemic to "strike language on [China] disinformation."[69]

Even before the release by the *Daily Telegraph* of information on China's extensive cover-up and disinformation campaign, President Trump was already pointing the finger at China for much of the U.S.'s pandemic travails. For example, on April 30, President Trump even speculated that the release of the coronavirus from China could have been intentional.[70] However, this theory was dismissed by the Office of the Director of National Intelligence (DNI), the clearinghouse for the web of U.S. spy agencies.[71] The DNI issued a statement ruling out the virus being human-made but was still investigating the precise source of the global pandemic.[72]

As an alternative theory and line of attack, Trump speculated that China could have unleashed the coronavirus on the world due to some kind of horrible "mistake." U.S. intelligence agencies did back Trump up on this possible theory, confirming they were still examining the notion that the pandemic may have resulted from an accident at a Chinese lab.

As time went on, the calls for China to be held accountable grew increasingly loud as further evidence was revealed as to China's misrepresentations and cover-up of the extent and severity of the COVID-19 outbreak. However, China's wrongdoing and gross negligence still could not completely explain away or absolve the U.S. government for its pathetically anemic response to the coronavirus pandemic, despite early warnings that it was soon to arrive.

11

THE TRUMP WHITE HOUSE DOWNPLAYS THE PANDEMIC AS IT HITS THE U.S.

"It's Completely Under Control"
- Donald J. Trump

The first English language reports of the new virus were published on December 31, 2019, when the *Associated Press* reported that the outbreak in Wuhan was being compared to the 2002-2003 SARS epidemic.[1] The CDC started an investigation on the same day, issuing an alert on January 6, 2020, warning Americans to take precautions when traveling to China; a second alert was issued on January 8.[2]

However, the threat of a global pandemic was not a priority of the Trump White House in November and December 2019, despite the multiple warning by several U.S. agencies and experts both within and outside the federal government. By January 2020, Trump was totally preoccupied with the unfolding Congressional impeachment proceedings against him. More importantly, there was no White House-based group that was solely focusing on potential pandemic threats. There also were no senior advisors in the White House with any expertise or interest in pandemics.

There was little discussion of the coronavirus issue in the White House, other than the logistical challenge of getting U.S. personnel out of China and back to the U.S. On January 18, HHS Secretary Alex Azar gave Trump, who was at Mar-a-Lago, a substantial briefing about the coronavirus threat.[3] In this phone call, Azar assured Trump that the issue was being worked on and closely monitored, which it was not. Trump largely dismissed the matter, telling Azar that he (Azar) was being an "alarmist."[4]

The White House Decides to Downplay the Crisis

The first confirmed COVID-19 case in the U.S. was on January 21, 2020, which was that of a man in Washington State who had returned from

Wuhan on January 15.⁵ The following day during a *CNBC* interview at the global economic forum in Davos, Switzerland, Trump dismissed the significance of this case. He referred to it as "one person coming in from China," and that the situation was "under control" and "it's going to be just fine."⁶

On January 22, before Trump's return to Washington, HHS Secretary Azur spoke to Robert O'Brien, Trump's National Security Adviser, and convinced O'Brien to have the National Security Council (NSC) assert control over the federal government's coronavirus response.⁷ O'Brien put his deputy, Matthew Pottinger, in charge of coordinating the still non-existent U.S. response.⁸

On January 26, there were five cases of the new virus confirmed in the U.S.⁹ All the cases involved people who had traveled to Wuhan, the epicenter of the outbreak.¹⁰ U.S. health officials started expanding the screenings of international travelers on January 28, 2020.¹¹ Still, federal officials continued to insist there was no serious health risk to Americans. For example, Azar told reporters on January 28: "At this point, Americans should not worry about their safety."¹²

Azar did instruct subordinates to establish a nationwide surveillance system to track the spread of the coronavirus. This system was a stepped-up version of what the CDC does every year to monitor new strains of the ordinary flu.¹³ But an effective national surveillance system at this point was virtually impossible since HHS and CDC lacked a diagnostic test that could accurately identify those infected with the new virus. Even if they had an effective test, the HHS and CDC did not have the capability of producing test kits on a mass scale for deployment throughout the United States.¹⁴ Meanwhile, the World Health Organization was far along in developing an effective test, but the CDC and HHS made the fateful decision not to use the W.H.O. test, but rather to rely upon a CDC test that was still under development and would prove to be defective.

On January 29, there were 195 Americans evacuated from Wuhan, who underwent three days of testing and monitoring at a California military base.¹⁵ Pottinger and Trump's acting chief-of-staff, Mick Mulvaney, started organizing a series of meetings at the White House with senior officials from HHS, the CDC and the State Department, including Azar and Dr.

Anthony Fauci. This group became the core of the White House's coronavirus task force. Still, it primarily focused on efforts to keep infected people in China from traveling to the U.S. while, at the same time, evacuating thousands of U.S. citizens. The group did not deal with the urgent issue of how the federal government was going to ensure there would be enough testing capacity for the entire country. Nor did it address the question of whether the emergency federal stockpile had enough of an inventory of personal protective equipment, respirators, ventilators, and other items to respond to significant outbreaks in the country.

HHS Secretary Azar Forms a Coronavirus Task Force (Sort of)

The day the first U.S. case of coronavirus was reported, Alex Azar appeared on *Fox News*, giving false assurances to the American people. He stressed that the U.S. government was fully prepared to respond to the coronavirus outbreak reported from China.[16] "We developed a diagnostic test at the CDC, so we can confirm if somebody has this," Azar said. "We will be spreading that diagnostic [test] around the country so that we are able to do rapid testing on site."[17] Azur falsely reassured the country that, while the coronavirus detected in Wuhan was "potentially serious," America was prepared since it "was one for which we have a playbook."[18] What Azur did not disclose was that the Trump White House did not have anything that could seriously be considered to be a "playbook." If it did have one, it was being ignored.

Unfortunately for America, Azur also was misleading the country about the availability of a viable diagnostic test at CDC. As we are now painfully aware, two of the agencies Secretary Azar oversaw at HHS - the CDC and the FDA - took an excruciatingly long 5 ½ weeks after Azar's January 21st announcement to develop a workable coronavirus test.[19] Other countries and the World Health Organization had already prepared their tests.[20]

An early indication that the Trump administration was not taking the pandemic threat very seriously was Azar's appointment of Brian Harrison to lead HHS's COVID-19 response effort.[21] Harrison had no public health experience. His principal – if not only - qualification for the job was that he was one of Azar's long-time cronies. Harrison's most significant life accomplishment before being appointed as "Coronavirus Czar" was that he was the owner and CEO of the company "Dallas Labradoodles." The company bred and sold Australian Labradoodles (a cross between a Labrador Retriever and a Poodle).[22]

Azar's appointment of Harrison to this critical position was akin to President George W. Bush's appointment of Michael "Brownie" Brown as the FEMA chief in 2003. Brown's major prior experience was as Commissioner of the International Arabian Horse Association, from which he resigned amid charges of conflicts of interest. Shortly after Hurricane Katrina struck the Gulf Coast in August 2005, President Bush gave Brown what soon became one of the most infamous endorsements in history. At a stop at the Mobile (Alabama) Regional Airport on September 2, 2005, Bush praised Brown by saying: "Brownie, you're doing a heck of a job."[23] Only a few days later, on September 9, 2005, Brown was relieved of all on-site relief duties along the Gulf Coast after the full extent of FEMA's disastrous response to the hurricane crisis started becoming more widely known.[24]

One colossal mistake that Harrison made early on had to do with the decision as to who should have a seat on the coronavirus task force. On January 29, representatives of the CDC, FDA, and National Institutes of Health were listed as members of the Task Force, including CDC Director Robert Redfield and Dr. Anthony Fauci, director of the National Institute of Allergy and Infectious Diseases.[25] For some inexplicable reason, FDA Commissioner Stephen Hahn's name was omitted. The FDA was not included in this group until Vice President Mike Pence took over the leadership of the Task Force in February 2020.[26] Without representation by the FDA on the Task Force, its ability to mobilize all of the federal government's resources was sharply limited. The FDA was such an integral part of any national testing effort that it was impossible to have a meaningful federal testing plan without FDA involvement.

On January 31, during a Coronavirus Task Force briefing, Azar continued to maintain his low-key approach to the crisis publicly. "I want to stress: The risk of infection for Americans is low," he said.[27] The next week, on February 7, in another press conference, Azar repeated the message. "The immediate risk to the American public is low at this time," he announced.[28] Again, on February 14, Azar continued to maintain that "the immediate risk" to Americans was low. Those travel restrictions had worked, "[s]o I think so far, our measures have been quite effective," he told National Public Radio (NPR).[29]

However, some federal officials still thought it was their job to alert the American people to the looming crisis. On February 25, Dr. Nancy Messonnier, director of the National Center for Immunization and Respiratory Diseases, dropped a bombshell at a press conference. She stated what was plainly evident to most public health professionals: "It's not so much of a question of if this will happen anymore," she said, "but rather more of a question of exactly when this will happen."[30]

In response to Dr. Messonnier's refreshing candor, Azar immediately went into damage control mode by appearing on *Fox News* the same day (February 25), falsely reassuring an increasingly edgy media and the public by saying: "But thanks to President Trump's historically aggressive containment efforts, we've actually contained the spread of this virus here in the United States at this point," adding, "I think part of the message to the American people is we all need to take a bit of a deep breath here . . . The government is working on this. You've got the right people on this."[31] As it turned out, the government was not seriously making any real preparations for the looming crisis. Further, it most definitely had the wrong people assigned to do it.

By the end of February, Azar and Harrison were no longer running the White House Task Force. Vice President Pence took over control, and the FDA and Hahn were now actively involved.[32] Meanwhile, acting on the principle that when you receive bad news, the first thing you do is to shoot the messenger, Dr. Nancy Messonnier's position in the federal coronavirus response effort was downgraded. She never again appeared in public as a national spokesperson. Such is the price for public honesty and transparency.

Peter Navarro Delivers Some Bad News to Trump

On January 29, Peter Navarro, Trump's trade advisor and a member of the White House coronavirus task force, issued a disturbing memo.[33] Navarro starkly warned Trump and other administration officials that the coronavirus crisis could put millions of Americans at risk of illness or death.[34] It also warned that it cost the U.S. economy trillions of dollars. Navarro noted in the memo, "The lack of immune protection or an existing cure or vaccine would leave Americans defenseless in the case of a full-blown coronavirus outbreak on U.S. soil," adding, "This lack of protection elevates the risk of the coronavirus evolving into a full-blown pandemic, imperiling the lives of millions of Americans."[35] The memo was widely circulated in the West Wing and throughout the administration.

Following receipt of Navarro's warning memo, Trump continued to minimize the dangers of COVID-19. At a speech at a Michigan manufacturing plant, Trump reassured the audience that "we have very little problem in the country," emphasizing that there were only five cases.[36] At the same time, the W.H.O. had declared a global public health emergency. In response, Trump expressed the view: "We think we have it very well under control. We have very little problem in this country at this moment — five [reported cases] — and those people are all recuperating successfully."[37]

The following day, on January 31, the Trump administration declared a public health emergency.[38] Travel restrictions for travelers from China were imposed.[39] Nonetheless, little was being done by the White House to prepare for the inevitable U.S. outbreak of the virus.

Trump later would repeatedly compliment himself by suggesting that he had boldly imposed a complete travel ban on China. For example, on Friday, April 3, Trump proclaimed during a briefing, "I cut off China very early."[40] If only this were true. By April 4, nearly 40,000 more Americans and authorized travelers had come into the U.S. from China after the imposition of the partial travel ban.[41] During this intervening two month period, 279 flights from China had arrived in the U.S.[42]

Meanwhile, the coronavirus pandemic continued its inexorable and deadly attack on an unprepared country.

12

TRUMP BLAMES CHINA, THE WORLD HEALTH ORGANIZATION, THE OBAMA ADMINISTRATION, THE GOVERNORS, ETC.

"I don't take responsibility at all"
-Donald J. Trump

In March 2020, the COVID-19 crisis was well on its way to overwhelming health care systems in New York, New Orleans, Detroit, and other cities across the country. Knowing that his administration would be blamed for its virtually non-existent early response to this crisis, Trump went into a full defensive mode, casting about for scapegoats to deflect attention from himself and others in his administration. President Harry S. Truman famously had a sign on his White House desk saying: "the buck stops here." Trump's desk was uncluttered by such aphorisms; he also took every opportunity possible to remind the press and the public that he took no responsibility for the unfolding debacle of a federal response.

Trump's first line of defense for the federal government's woeful lack of preparedness was to argue that his administration could not have known of the looming crisis in advance because it was totally unexpected. For example, at his daily briefing on March 19, Trump responded to criticism that his administration was not prepared for the crisis by saying: "I would view it as something that just surprised the whole world," adding later that it was "uncharted territory" and saying, "Nobody knew there would be a pandemic or epidemic of this proportion."[1] "So there's never been anything like this in history. There's never been," he said. "And nobody's ever seen anything like this."[2]

However, Trump's attempts to revise history cannot erase the record of the warnings given him by the NCMI and other intelligence sources, starting in November 2019, that the China virus outbreak was quickly evolving into a global pandemic that would soon be hitting the U.S. with the ferocity of a cyclone. It also ignores the January 18, 2020 detailed briefing that Trump received from HHS Secretary Azar, who particularly emphasized the threat that the coronavirus posed to the U.S., and the January 29 memo by White House Adviser Peter Navarro to Trump and senior officials at the White House, sounding the warning alarm and flashing red lights about the national disaster about to happen.

As a result of the White House's inaction, the country lost valuable weeks to properly mobilize federal resources to prepare for widespread testing and upgrading in hospital preparedness. Trump's approach to the imminent crisis was not for lack of warnings from U.S. intelligence sources and some of those in his administration. In addition to the Navarro letter of late January 2020, Trump's briefing by Secretary Azar on January 18 about the crisis severely undercut his after-the-fact argument that this stealthy virus blindsided him.

And yet, despite ample evidence that the federal government was ill-prepared for the looming pandemic challenge, Trump instead chose to treat the problem as a public relations issue that could be solved with an upbeat and optimistic message, as if wishing the virus to go away would make it so. After all, despite the dire predictions that the Asian Flu, SARS, MERS, and Ebola viruses might strike devasting blows to the U.S. population and economy, the country survived with minimal deaths and economic damage from all of these prior pandemics. The last devastating epidemic was in 1918 when we did not even have antibiotics, ventilators, and the other wonders of modern medicine at our disposal. So, more than 100 years later, in 2020, was the "worst-case scenario" actually realistic?

Trump had dodged some dangerous bullets before, including the Russia probe, the Mueller investigation, and impeachment, so why shouldn't he bet all his chips on his gut instinct that the coronavirus threat was being blown out of proportion and that this crisis would blow over like all the other ones?

The trouble, though, with betting that your luck will hold out, rather than preparing for the worst-case scenario, is that if you bet all your chips on red, and the roulette wheel stops at black, you are completely wiped out. The results will be catastrophic. And so it came to pass.

After the first death in the U.S. was reported in Washington State on February 29,[3] Governor Jay Inslee declared a state of emergency,[4] an action that was followed by Florida, California and other states.[5] Schools in the Seattle area canceled classes on March 3,[6] and by mid-March, schools across the country were closing, and most of the country's students were out of school.[7]

Even as the number of COVID-19 cases rapidly grew in the U.S, Trump continued to maintain his dismissive tone regarding the severity of the crisis. By March 5, even though the number of cases had grown by a factor of 25, he tweeted: "Only 129 cases."[8]

The following day, on March 6, even though he falsely claimed that the number of U.S. cases was "lower than just about" any other country, Mr. Trump signed the Coronavirus Preparedness and Response Supplemental Appropriations Act, which provided $8.3 billion in emergency funding for federal agencies to respond to the outbreak.[9] By March 12, when the number of cases had jumped tenfold, to over 1200, Trump continued to argue that the U.S. had "very few cases" compared to other countries.[10] He also began to misleadingly refer to the coronavirus as "no worse than the flu," spreading disinformation regarding the deadly virus on March 27, by saying: "You call it germ, you can call it a flu. You can call it a virus. You can call it many different names. I'm not sure anybody knows what it is."[11] Trump also inferred that the annual flu was more dangerous than the COVID-19 pandemic, citing the number of flu deaths in March to be "25,000 to 69,000", and saying that it was as high as "100,000" in 1990.[12] The actual number of fatalities during the 1990 flu season was 33,000, and in the past decade, the flu had killed an estimated 12,000 to 61,000 U.S. residents each flu season.[13] In actuality, though, the coronavirus is ten times more deadly than the flu, and unlike the flu, no vaccine or cure yet exists for it.

Trump has also been a font of disinformation regarding the fatality rate in prior epidemics, stating that the Ebola death rate "was virtually 100 percent," when in truth, the average fatality rate was around 50%.[14] Trump also publicly misrepresented the fatality rate during the 1918 flu pandemic, saying on Tuesday, March 24: "you had a 50/50 chance or very close of dying."[15] The actual numbers were nowhere near that.

While the federal government largely fumbled the ball in the early days of the COVID-19 crisis, the private sector and local and state governments took matters into their own hands, imposing restrictions even in the absence of federal government guidance on these critical public health issues. Corporations imposed employee travel restrictions, canceled conferences,[16] and encouraged employees to work from home.[17] Sports events and entire seasons were canceled, including the National Basketball Association (NBA) and Major League Baseball (MLB)'s spring training.[18] Starting on March 15, 2020, many businesses voluntarily closed or reduced hours throughout the U.S. to try to combat the virus.[19]

Still, these responsible steps by states, municipalities, and private corporations to protect their citizens, employees, and customers were not matched by the federal government, despite the near-universal outcry that the Trump administration step up into a leadership role.

When the Trump Administration finally did something, it was just too late. The administration seemed to be always playing catch up in an unfolding crisis where events were moving ever more swiftly. For example, the White House waited until March 13, 2020 to belatedly declare a national emergency, which finally made federal funds available to respond to the crisis.[20] However, the administration was failing miserably in ramping up testing for the virus, which was universally recognized as an essential first step in a multi-pronged response to the pandemic.

When asked about the government's slow response at a White House press conference, Trump refused to take any responsibility: "I don't take responsibility at all," Trump said, regarding the government's failure to produce enough tests; instead, he blamed existing rules set by prior administration for limiting his options: "We were given a set of circumstances, and we were given rules, regulations, and specifications from a different time," he said, attempting to cast blame onto the prior Obama administration.[21]

Trump also claimed not to know that his administration dismantled a pandemic preparedness team within the National Security Council in 2018. On March 13, Trump threw a very public temper tantrum during a press briefing at the White House, referring to a question by *PBS* reporter Yamiche Alcindor about the 2018 dismantling of the White House pandemic unit as "nasty," he said categorically, "I didn't do it."[22]

On Thursday, March 26, the U.S. gained the dubious distinction of being the nation with the largest number of reported coronavirus cases, with 81,321 Americans known to have been infected with the coronavirus, and with more than 1,000 deaths.[23] And this was only the beginning. The same day – March 26 – Trump appeared on *Fox News* and expressed doubt about reported shortages of medical supplies, boasting about the country's testing capacity despite reliable reporting to the contrary. Never missing an opportunity to bash his predecessor, he criticized Barrack Obama for his response to an earlier outbreak in the country. He claimed that the Obama Administration "acted very, very late" during the H1N1 Swine flu epidemic in 2009 and 2010.[24] In actuality, President Obama took prompt action to quarantine affected areas after the first death was reported, thus substantially stopping the spread of the virus in its tracks and minimizing its damage.

On *Fox News*, Trump also questioned the truth of New York Governor Andrew Cuomo's statements about an acute shortage of ventilators. He then reversed course the following day, claiming on Friday, March 27, that urgent steps needed to be taken for the U.S. to produce more ventilators.

In his Thursday, March 26 *Fox News* interview, Trump also spread the false rumor that because of the U.S. travel ban on China, "a lot of the [Chinese] people decided to go to Italy instead."[25] In fact, the opposite was true; Italy had issued a wide-ranging ban on travel from China even earlier that the U.S.[26]

Meanwhile, President Trump also broadcasted a confusing message to the public regarding the availability of current treatments or "cure" for COVID-19. From late February to early March, Trump repeatedly promised that a vaccine would be available "relatively soon" despite being told by public health officials and pharmaceutical executives that the process would take at least 12 to 18 months.[27] Later, he promoted unproven treatments against the virus, falsely suggesting that they had already been "approved" and available when they were not. He also promoted a website developed by a company affiliated with Google, incorrectly saying that insurers were covering the cost of treatment for COVID-19 when they had only agreed to waive co-payments for testing. Trump also prematurely declared that automakers were making ventilators "right now."[28]

In short, Mr. Trump was trying desperately to create a parallel reality where he had taken early and decisive action to combat the spread of the virus into and around the U.S.; that even though the virus was spreading here, it was not that big a deal and we shouldn't worry too much about it; that the response effort was really the responsibility of the states, with the federal government playing a backup role, and that the federal government was doing everything in its power to minimize and mitigate the impact of the epidemic in the U.S. Unfortunately for Trump, however, the American public saw a consistently different and much darker picture of the crisis being portrayed by the press. Trump's response was to call it "fake news." Who are you going to believe anyway: what I am telling you or your own lying eyes?

13

THE FAILURE TO CONDUCT ADEQUATE TESTING STALLS THE U.S. RESPONSE EFFORT

"It begins with testing. We can't defeat an enemy if we don't know where it is."
-Bill Gates

By March 6, when Mr. Trump made the blatantly false statement that testing was available to all Americans, the U.S.'s coronavirus response effort was already on the brink of collapse. Although the White House must have known about the contingency plans formulated by prior administrations in response to various public health crises, it refused to follow them. There had been virtually no discussion within the administration as to what the federal government should or could do to make a significant difference in the trajectory of the pandemic as it reached the U.S. But by far and away, the most colossal blunder was the government's failure to provide for adequate testing.

While anyone in the White House could, no doubt, get tested to determine if they were positive for the coronavirus, the reality was quite different for the rest of America. The availability of testing varied widely from state to state and city to city, but nowhere was it adequate. During the early months of the pandemic in the U.S., it was very difficult for many - if not most - Americans who suspected that they had the virus to get tested. Early every morning outside Elmhurst Hospital in Queens, New York, people would start lining up to get tested. They would stand in the line all day through the cold and the rain, hoping upon hope they would get tested. Often, they would have to come back the following morning to go through this agonizing and often hopeless ritual once again. Paramedics in New York City told reporters that many patients who died at home were never tested for the coronavirus, even if they showed telltale signs of infection.[1]

The lack of available testing was not just a New York phenomenon. It was happening all over the country. And it made no difference whether you were still living, or if you had recently died. A coroner in Indiana, for example, wanted to know if the coronavirus had killed a man in early March.[2] Still, testing was denied by the health department due to a shortage of testing equipment. In Virginia, a funeral director prepared the remains of three people after health workers cautioned her that each of them had tested positive for the coronavirus. But only one of the three had the virus noted on the death certificate.[3] Julio Ramirez, a 43-year-old salesman in San Gabriel, California, came home from a business trip suffering from a fever, cough, and body aches. By the next day, he had lost his sense of taste and smell and died shortly thereafter.[4] His wife's attempts to get him tested were unsuccessful. "I kept trying to get him tested from the beginning," she said.[5] When calls to the CDC to get a post-mortem test failed, Mr. Ramirez's widow hired a private company to conduct an autopsy. Nineteen days after his death, Ms. Ramirez received a call from the L. A. County Department of Public Health, reporting that a sample taken from her late husband's body at the funeral home had tested positive for coronavirus.[6]

The widespread lack of testing capability severely impaired the ability of medical personnel to make accurate and informed decisions regarding the treatment of patients. It also made it likely that the number of coronavirus cases and fatalities being reported each day in alarming numbers were inaccurate and on the low side. On April 14, New York City felt forced to revise its statistics by adding another 2,700 cases to its official tally of coronavirus-related deaths.[7] These cases brought the total above 10,000, including many cases who had their "cause of death" reported as "pneumonia" or "influenza," but which were more accurately related to coronavirus infections.[8] Coroners were having the same problem outside New York City, particularly in rural areas where they did not have the tests they needed to detect the disease.

With no uniform system for reporting coronavirus-related deaths in the U.S., and a continued shortage of tests, many cities, states, and counties were left to improvise as to how they counted their dead. "We definitely think there are deaths that we have not accounted for," said Jennifer Nuzzo, a senior scholar at the Johns Hopkins University Center for Health Security, which collected statistics on the coronavirus pandemic.[9]

The CDC Fails to Develop An Effective Test

Throughout the critical early stages of the crisis, the U.S. did not have a reliable diagnostic test for COVID-19. Even if there had been a reliable test available, the federal government would have still been unable, by itself, to mass-produce a sufficient number of testing kits, as well as the necessary swabs and chemical reagents. One major reason for this is that the government did not do what other countries successfully did. They did not reach out to private industry, private laboratories, and university labs for assistance. Taiwan, South Korea, Iceland, and Germany all entered into effective public-private partnerships to meet their countries' testing needs.[10] The U.S. government did not do so until it was too late. As a result, the federal government and the American public were left flying flying without any radar throughout most of the crisis. The government had no way of knowing how many Americans were infected in the hardest-hit cities and states. The reason for this was that the number of people who tested positive for coronavirus was only a fraction of those who were actually infected. In most cities, the only Americans tested were those who were taken to the hospital by ambulance or were otherwise admitted. If you did not feel well and wanted to get tested to see if you were infected with the coronavirus, the odds were that you would not be tested. This was especially true if you did not have a fever or other obvious symptoms. There were relatively few testing kits to go around, so many – if not most – hospitals were carefully rationing them for use on only the sickest of patients.

South Korea and the U.S. announced their first coronavirus cases at about the same time.[11] The similarities between the two countries' response efforts end there. South Korea immediately ramped up the production of tests, while the U.S. did not.[12] As a result, South Korea already had tested 290,000 people by March 18, while the U.S. had only conducted about 60,000 tests.[13] This disparity was particularly huge when you consider the fact that South Korea has a population of only 51 million, while the U.S., with about 330 million people, is almost 7 times larger.[14]

As early as January 27, South Korean government officials met with leading South Korean manufacturing companies and sought their assistance in developing a reliable test.[15] These South Korean companies were assured that they would have full government support for their efforts. One week after this January 27 meeting, South Korea's CDC approved one of the private company's diagnostic tests and approved another company's test kits shortly thereafter.[16] By the end of February, South Korea had drive-through screening centers and was testing thousands of people daily.[17] Within seven weeks, over 290,000 Koreans had been tested, and over 8,000 positive cases were identified.[18] By March 18, South Korea had passed its peak, and fewer cases were being reported each day.[19] Ninety-three were reported on March 18, down from a daily peak of 909 two weeks earlier.[20] Meanwhile, at that point, the outbreak in the U.S. was just warming up.

Compared to South Korea, the U.S. testing response to the crisis was virtually non-existent. With only about 60,000 tests run by March 18, federal, state, and local officials in the U.S. had no real grasp of the number of Americans who were infected.[21] As Roger Klein, a former lab medical director at the Cleveland Clinic, put it, "You cannot fight what you cannot see."[22] Without testing, you cannot see the extent of the spread of COVID-19.[23]

It had not always been that way in the U.S. During the battle against the Asian Flu in 1957, the U.S. government had enlisted the assistance of private labs and pharmaceutical companies as soon as the virus was identified. In contrast, the Trump administration delayed seeking assistance from these private sources for several critical weeks during the current crisis. The CDC did not ask the private labs and the university labs for help until the CDC-developed test was found to be flawed, and its attempts to correct these tests failed.[24] When the government finally turned to the private sector and academia for assistance, the waiver of standard protocols and regulations still proceeded slowly. The U.S. Food and Drug Administration (FDA) did not approve the use of any test other than the CDC's test until February 29, more than five weeks after discussions with outside labs had begun.[25]

Meanwhile, in the absence of enough testing kits, the CDC insisted for weeks on narrow criteria for testing. The CDC recommended testing only when a person had recently been to China or other hot spots or had contact with someone known to be infected.[26] As a result, the federal government failed to screen an untold number of Americans and missed a critical window of opportunity to contain the spread.[27] Dr. Anthony Fauci candidly admitted while testifying before a House committee on March 12 that the U.S. testing efforts had been "a failing," explaining, "The idea of anybody getting [tested] easily the way people in other countries are doing it, we're not set up for that."[28] This delay in U.S. testing undoubtedly cost lives that could have been saved if there had been testing available earlier on.

As reports of COVID-19 began to dominate the news cycle, members of the White House coronavirus task force seemed unaware that the U.S. was not ready to do mass testing.[29] The Task Force members were erroneously reassured that the CDC had developed a diagnostic model that would be rolled out quickly. But when the deadly virus began spreading like wildfire across the U.S., there was still no large-scale testing of people who might have been infected. The reasons for this colossal failure may be many, including technical flaws in the CDC's diagnostic model. However, the incompetence and lack of any sense of urgency by the federal government's elected and bureaucratic leaders on many levels appear to be the most decisive factors.

The U.S.'s abysmal failure to develop an effective testing strategy is particularly puzzling since the U.S. is (or was) generally recognized as a global leader in public health, with access to many of the world's most highly trained scientists and infectious disease specialists. Nevertheless, the U.S. leadership squandered the critical four to six-week window that it had to develop a robust and effective testing program for the spreading virus. America was left flying blind in the face of the largest catastrophe it had faced since perhaps the Civil War.

Although he acknowledged to Congress that the U.S. government's testing efforts had been a failure, Dr. Fauci admitted during a *Science Magazine* interview that he did not know why we were not able to mobilize on a broader scale.[30] Hopefully, a Congressional investigative committee or "blue ribbon" panel will someday get to the bottom of this question. A significant piece of the puzzle seems to be that the CDC had no realization of the sheer volume of testing that would be needed until it was too late. Secondly, there was a total lack of understanding that the CDC labs themselves were unable to "scale up" to the number of testing kits needed. The government simply did not understand until it was too late that the assistance of private industry and university labs was essential.

The CDC did not realize until February that there were fundamental flaws in the test that it had developed, and it took weeks to correct these flaws.[31] Federal officials acknowledged on April 18 that the CDC engaged in sloppy laboratory practices that caused test contamination, rendering the country's first coronavirus tests ineffective.[32] It was discovered that two of the three CDC laboratories in Atlanta created the coronavirus test kits in violation of their manufacturing standards.[33] The result was that this agency sent tests that did not work correctly to nearly all of the 100 state and local public health labs.[34] A spokesperson for the FDA admitted, in a classic bureaucratic understatement: "CDC did not manufacture its test consistent with its protocol."[35] Problems ranged from researchers entering and exiting the coronavirus laboratories without changing their coats and assembling test ingredients in the same room where researchers worked on positive coronavirus samples.[36] Those practices created contaminated tests that were then sent to public health labs, rendering these faulty tests unusable.[37]

The CDC compounded these errors by placing unnecessarily tight restrictions on who was eligible to be tested. The restrictions created a slow roll-out of "community-based surveillance," a standard screening practice to detect the spread of any virus.[38] If the U.S. had a robust testing program in place early on, it would have been able to track COVID-19's movements and identify hot spots requiring local quarantines. It did not have this capability, so there was never enough data to implement effective containment and quarantine procedures.

Meanwhile, the FDA dropped the ball by imposing regulations that made it more difficult for hospitals, private clinics, and companies to deploy diagnostic tests on an emergency basis. Other countries, such as South Korea and Taiwan, were testing tens of thousands of people daily. At the same time, there were fewer than 100 tests per day on average in the U.S.[39] Given the scale of the problem, the testing numbers in the U.S. were not much better than if there had been no testing at all.

The Department of Health and Human Services (HHS) compounded the problem in that HHS Secretary Azar, who chaired the coronavirus task force until Vice President Mike Pence took over in late February, passively went along with Trump's strategy of focusing on the public relations aspects of this national health crisis, instead of focusing on the substantive work needed to prepare for this unfolding natural disaster.[40]

Even by the end of February, Trump was still telling the American public that the fear of the virus was overblown and largely concocted by a biased left-wing mainstream media. Trump predicted, "It's going to disappear. One day — it's like a miracle — it will disappear."[41] By early March, when the federal government finally acknowledged the need for more extensive testing, it was too late. The horse was already out of the barn and galloping cross country at a breakneck pace. Even by late March, many Americans who were experiencing symptoms of COVID-19 were still not able to get tested. Without testing, there was simply no way for a possibly infected individual and his or her doctors to make an informed decision as to whether they should leave their families and go into isolation in order to avoid infecting others. As an official of the W.H.O. succinctly puts it: "You can't stop it," he warned, "if you can't see it."[42]

The CDC lulled itself and the rest of the country into a false sense of complacency when, by January 20, it thought it had developed a test that could be deployed to detect the country's first coronavirus cases. This was only two weeks after Chinese scientists shared the genetic sequence of the virus, and would have been a significant victory for the agency but for the fact that the tests were defective. Once the CDC realized that there were some defects in the tests, it took several critical weeks to fix them. At this time, it was not yet known that the virus could spread between asymptomatic people who showed no indications of infection. This lack of information meant that the virus was poised to spread much more quickly than expected, and could reach an exponentially larger number of Americans.

The CDC's original test was based on three small genetic sequences that matched up with portions of the virus's genome. Theoretically, the CDC test was more precise than the "two genetic sequences" test adopted by the

W.H.O. But shortly after the FDA cleared the CDC to share its test kits with state health department labs, it was discovered that the third sequence, or "probe," gave inconclusive results.[43] While the CDC explored the cause of this problem, the state labs were told to stop testing. This setback left the U.S. with only 100 tests per day by mid-February, which is when the nation needed it the most.[44] With little testing capability, the criteria for testing remained limited to only people who had recently traveled to China or had been in contact with someone who had the virus.

The CDC finally announced a plan on February 14 to perform "early warning" screening.[45] They targeted five high-risk cities: New York, Chicago, Los Angeles, San Francisco, and Seattle. However, these cities did not have the capability of doing any widespread testing since the federal government had still not provided them with the promised test kits and testing equipment, including the specialized swabs and reagents needed to conduct the tests.[46] The U.S., therefore, had no option other than to blindly wait for the virus to hit those cities with its full force.

By the end of February, cases started emerging in the Seattle area of people testing positive for the virus who had no known history of exposure to the virus through travel or other means.[47] Seattle was the same location where the U.S.'s first case had been detected more than a month earlier, on January 21. According to researchers, the virus had probably been spreading there and elsewhere for weeks. However, without any extensive testing data, all the epidemiologists could do was to give educated guesses.[48] Without a complete picture of who had been infected, public health workers could not do any "contact tracing." It was critical to find all those with whom any contagious people had interacted and then quarantine them to stop further transmission. But this was impossible without extensive testing capability.

The CDC's Director, Dr. Robert R. Redfield, offered false reassurances to Congress about the CDC's response to the testing crisis. In his response to a February 24 Congressional letter, he denied that there was any problem: "CDC's aggressive response enables us to identify potential cases early and make sure that they are properly handled."[49] For those few with any real knowledge of what the CDC was capable of doing at that point, this statement was sheer fantasy.

Days later, the CDC reversed its prior instructions to state and local labs. The CDC told state and local health department labs that the promised new tests that the CDC was supposed to be developing were not coming after all. These state and local labs were instructed to start using the CDC test kits that had been sitting on their shelves for the past several weeks as the CDC tried to correct the testing defects.[50] In other words, the CDC was giving up on its efforts to correct the tests and to provide new replacement kits. Instead, they were telling the states and cities to use the CDC "two-probe" test kits and to just forget about the problematic third probe.

Meanwhile, Dr. Nancy Messonnier of the CDC's National Center for Immunization and Respiratory Diseases warned on February 25 that, based on the spread of the virus in South Korea and Italy, "disruption to everyday life might be severe" in the U.S.[51] She made these widely reported comments while Trump was on a trip to India, which infuriated him. Upon his return, he directed HHS Secretary Azar to try to lull the country back into its initial state of near-comatose complacency about the viral tsunami about to hit the U.S.

Secretary Azar walked back Dr. Messonnier's warnings at a hastily announced news conference. He assured the public that all they needed to do was to vaguely "start thinking about, in their own lives, what that might involve."[52] These comments were about as helpful as the captain of the *H.M.S. Titanic* telling the passengers that the ship was going down, that nothing could be done, and that they should make peace with their maker. In other words, there was nothing in Azar's statement that would give the American public even the faintest of hopes that the U.S. actually had a plan to handle the unfolding crisis.

Meanwhile, the FDA was putting obstacles in the path of permitting private sector testing for COVID-19. Private testing was supposed to be the next necessary step in a national testing plan once the CDC ramped up its screening at public labs in the states throughout the country. Taiwan, South Korea, Singapore, and other countries had already successfully done this, so there was no reason to believe that the U.S. could not do it too. But the FDA decided on a more cautious – and disastrous – approach, keeping the FDA's often restrictive methods and rules in place before any testing and medical screening could be approved.[53]

In addition to rebuffing overtures by private and academic labs to do their testing, the federal government also failed to provide testing support for the nation's public health labs. These labs were looking to the FDA for help. In late February, Scott Becker, chief executive of the Association of Public Health Laboratories, wrote to FDA Commissioner Hahn, stating: "We are now many weeks into the response with still no diagnostic or surveillance test available outside of CDC for the vast majority of our member laboratories." He added, "We believe a more expeditious route is needed at this time."[54]

The FDA's so-called "emergency use authorizations" (EUAs) were intended to speed along the FDA approval process for tests and vaccines, which generally could take a year or more.[55] However, the EUAs relating to COVID-19 testing involved almost as much federal regulation and delays as the standard procedures. The FDA seemed incapable of cutting through the red tape to address the crisis. As a result, even though several prominent private and academic-based research institutions had the capability of creating COVID-19 tests, the FDA's approval process hindered them from doing so.[56]

Researchers at Stanford University, for example, had a functional test by February.[57] The tests were based on protocols published by W.H.O., which had delivered more than 250,000 of German-designed W.H.O. tests to 70 laboratories around the world.[58] Doctors and researchers at the Stanford lab wanted to make sure that the U.S. was prepared for the pandemic by testing coronavirus samples themselves and developing an effective test. However, the Stanford clinical lab was prevented from doing any of this critical test development until early March, when the FDA finally relaxed the rules.[59] By the time an effective test was developed, however, it was already too late to help out in hotspots such as New York and Seattle, where the deadly virus was hitting the hardest. As a result, these new tests sat unused at labs around the country.

Similarly, bioMérieux, the multinational diagnostic testing company, did not receive FDA emergency approval for its COVID-19 testing until

March 24.⁶⁰ If it had received approval earlier, there is a strong likelihood that bioMérieux would have been able to provide an effective testing system when it was most needed. This company had a countertop testing system for the common flu and other respiratory illness that was already being used by 1700 hospitals across the country.⁶¹ These testing platforms, which provided results within 45 minutes of testing, could have been modified fairly quickly to test for COVID-19.

The Trump administration was also painfully slow in identifying one "point person" for the coronavirus response effort. Previous presidents had moved quickly to confront major disease threats by installing a "czar" to coordinate the response efforts from within the White House. During an outbreak of the Ebola virus in 2014, for example, President Barack Obama tapped Ron Klain, his vice president's former chief of staff, to direct the response from the West Wing.⁶² As previously discussed, the Obama administration later created an office of global health security inside the National Security Council to coordinate the responses to future crises. But faced with the coronavirus, Trump chose not to have the White House lead the planning until nearly two months after the crisis began. The Obama global health office had been disbanded more than a year earlier, in 2018. And until Vice President Pence took charge, the Task Force also lacked a single White House official with the power to compel any federal action.

Not until late March did U.S. testing begin to ramp up quickly, with nearly 100 labs at hospitals and elsewhere performing them.⁶³ On Friday, March 27, the health care giant Abbott received emergency approval for a portable test that could detect the virus in five minutes.⁶⁴

Yet, despite these improvements, many hospitals and clinics across the country still denied tests to those with milder symptoms, trying to save their scarce testing supplies for the most severe cases. Also, those who were tested often had to wait a week or more for results. In tacit acknowledgment of the shortage, Trump asked South Korea's president to send as many test kits as possible, since South Korea was producing far more than required for its own needs.⁶⁵

The number of lives that could have been saved in the U.S. if adequate testing had been available sooner will probably never be known. Still, it seems clear that the federal government's delayed response to the COVID-19 crisis with adequate testing capacity was a major contributing cause of the runaway spread of the virus in New York, New Jersey, Washington, Louisiana, Michigan and elsewhere in the U.S. The harsh reality is that it took the U.S. a full three months after the disease was first disclosed in China to develop a significant testing capability to identify where the disease was located and who actually was testing positive for the virus. An effective and coordinated response to the virus simply could not take place without adequate testing capabilities. Hence, the delay in testing left a gaping hole in the national response effort to the crisis. America was left in a desperate position, trying to play "catch-up" rather than staying out in front of the pandemic.

By late April and early May, the lack of testing also became a massive impediment to the emerging plans by various states to start to reopen their schools, businesses, and economies. As Microsoft co-founder Bill Gates and other experts on the pandemic emphasized, testing was the key to both containment and response to the virus, but also to any plans to reopen. As Gates explained:

> It begins with testing. We can't defeat an enemy if we don't know where it is. To reopen the economy, we need to be testing enough people that we can quickly detect emerging hotspots and intervene early. We don't want to wait until the hospitals start to fill up, and more people die.[66]

Trump Belatedly Announces Testing "Blueprint"

After telling the states for three months that they were mainly on their own with regard to testing, Trump was finally forced by the mounting public uproar to come up with some semblance of a federal plan on testing. On Monday, April 27, he announced what the White House called a "blueprint" for increasing testing capacity.[67] However, Trump's testing "plan" still left most of the onus on the states to develop their plans and rapid-response programs. According to the document released by the White House, the federal role would be limited to "strategic direction and technical assistance," as well as the ability to "align laboratory testing supplies and capacity with existing and anticipated laboratory needs."[68] The federal government was described as the "supplier of last resort."[69]

Trump outlined the effort at an April 27 White House news conference where he was joined by executives from Abbott Laboratories, CVS, and other major retailers. They said they had ramped up the rate of testing and the production of medical supplies, and it was predicted that testing would accelerate in the coming month.[70] The Trump administration's top testing official, Adm. Brett Giroir, promised that the federal government would conduct at least 8 million tests a month by the end of May.[71] But this promise was skeptically received by many knowledgeable observers since a previous announcement of a high-profile public-private testing initiative had fizzled out with barely a trace.

Senate Minority Leader Chuck Schumer of New York blasted Trump's testing "blueprint" as "pathetic."[72] Schumer, among others, expressed frustration that Trump had not used the Defense Production Act to ramp up U.S. production of testing kits and necessary testing supplies. "There will be no way to ramp up and get the number of tests, and the auxiliary things like the swabs that we need unless the federal government takes over," said Schumer, adding, "Other countries are way ahead of us."[73] Addressing Trump directly on *MSNBC*, Schumer said, "Mr. President Trump, Donald Trump, you're hurting the recovery you want so badly, by not having the tests. The best way to recover quickly is testing, testing, testing."[74]

Trump Reveals Why He Is Ambivalent About Widespread Testing: Less Testing Means Fewer Reported Cases

While medical professionals and experts were warning that the lack of widespread testing in the U.S. was resulting in a gross underreporting of cases and COVID-related deaths, President Trump did not view this as a bad thing. In fact, he viewed it as a positive development. After all, in Trump World, if a person was not tested for coronavirus, then the person's case cannot be officially recorded as a COVID-19 case. If a person is tested, however, and tests positive for COVID-19, then it is recorded as a case, and the official record of COVID-19 cases in the U.S. ticks up one more notch. So, if testing is limited, it then logically follows that there will be fewer cases officially reported, and the numbers look "better" for the White House.

Of course, this strategy does not actually reduce the number of COVID-19 cases; it just artificially deflates the official numbers, which is a good result in the Trump playbook. If you do not widely test and have accurate numbers regarding the number of cases and the number of COVID-19 deaths, it is difficult for the epidemiologists and other experts to track the route and severity of the virus's movements throughout the country. But that apparently was of little concern to the Trump White House.

After touring the medical supply distributor Owens and Minor in Allentown, Pennsylvania, on Wednesday, May 13, Trump talked about his plans for expanding the Strategic National Stockpile and praised his administration's coronavirus response, including increased testing.[75] He noted that "America has now conducted its ten-millionth test,"[76] while failing to mention that the rate of testing based upon the size of the country's population (over 330 million) was actually much lower than that of other countries.

Trump then explained his bizarre theory that the reason why the U.S. had more reported coronavirus cases than any other country was that it had done so much testing. "And don't forget, we have more cases than anybody in the world," he said. "But why? Because we do more testing. When you test, you have a case. When you test, you find something is wrong with people. If we didn't do any testing, we would have very few cases."[77]

In other words, fewer tests meant fewer reported cases. It makes no difference that the numbers bear no real relationship to reality. In Trump World, the actual status and extent of the virus's spread in the country is of little importance. Rather, the important thing is politics and perceptions and keeping the official numbers as low as possible.

"So we have the best testing in the world," Trump added. "It could be the testing's, frankly, overrated? Maybe it is overrated. But whatever they start yelling, we want more [testing], we want more. You know, they always say we want more, we want more because they don't want to give you credit."[78]

The Window of Opportunity For Widespread Testing in the U.S. Closes Shut

By the latter part of May, the U.S. finally started showing some significant improvement in its nationwide testing figures, doubling the number of completed tests from the previous month to 300,000 tests per day.[79] But the country still needed to triple its capacity to at least 900,000 tests a day, and as many as 20 million tests had to be completed in order to get an accurate view of the outbreak, according to experts.[80] This increased testing was particularly needed in states that were lifting their stay-at-home and other restrictions during May, and the testing data was simply not available for them to properly track the consequences of easing up on these restrictions and reopening the states for business again.

In short, the Trump White House completely missed the opportunity during the critical months of February to May 2020 to do what other democratic governments had done. The U.S. utterly failed to establish a nationwide testing plan as one of its highest priorities. This failure was shocking, given the U.S.'s proud history of rising to the occasion when presented with great threats and challenges. In the last century, the U.S. government met the challenges posed by World War II, converting America's industrial capacity into the mightiest war machine the world has ever seen. At the same time, it successfully undertook the Manhattan Project to develop an atomic bomb before Germany got one. After World War II, the U.S. almost singlehandedly rebuilt Western Europe through the Marshall Plan.

So, when the U.S. was confronted with the greatest challenge yet of the 21st century - the coronavirus crisis - what prevented the U.S. from taking its traditional world leadership role? Was this the same U.S. government that was out in front of every response effort to every major crisis ever to face this country? Are we as Americans willing to accept without objection the novel theory that the federal government's only role in a major national crisis is to provide "back up" for the states? Has it really come to this? Has America sunk so low?

Time will tell, but the seismic rumblings of change can already be heard throughout the land.

14

THE ANTIBODY TEST DEBACLE

After having been inexcusably slow in authorizing the use of any non-CDC tests to detect coronavirus infections, the Food and Drug Administration (FDA) went to the other extreme when it came to antibody testing.[1] On March 16, the FDA allowed more than 120 antibody tests to flood the market without prior review, including those of dubious quality or reliability.[2] The result was a "Wild West" scramble by dozens of companies to cash in on the coronavirus crisis, some of whom had extensive experience in the development of reliable tests, and some that had no idea what they were doing, but wanted a piece of the action.

By April 1, Congress sounded the alarm after early data from researchers in California who "tested the tests" showed troublingly high rates of false results.[3] One in three antibody tests they analyzed produced false positives more than 10% of the time.[4] "No one would be happy with those results," said Dr. Alex Marson, a physician and microbiologist at the University of California, San Francisco, who was conducting the research. As he explained on *NBC News*, "If we give people a false impression, for whatever reason, that they may be in fact protected when they're not, that would be not only irresponsible, it would be dangerous to individuals."[5]

There are two different types of tests for antibodies, which are produced by the human body to fight off infections and disease and are used to identify people who were previously infected by COVID-19. The first and fastest type of antibody testing involves so-called "rapid testing," which uses a small amount of blood from a finger prick and may cost as little as $20 or less. The other type of antibody testing relies on traditional blood draws and cost considerably more. Many of the finger-prick tests are being marketed for use in doctors' offices and pharmacies, even though the government requires all unauthorized tests to be run in Clinical Laboratory Improvement Amendments (CLIA), labs that are certified to conduct high complexity testing.[6]

Antibody testing is quite different from diagnostic testing, which tells whether or not you are presently infected with the coronavirus. Diagnostic testing is, of course, most important in the early stages of a pandemic, when it is critically important to know whether a person is infected so he or she can be isolated and unable to infect other people. Diagnostic test results are also vital for doctors and medical personnel to know when they are treating a coronavirus patient so that they can take appropriate protective measures to avoid contagion and properly treat the patient.

As previously discussed, the Trump administration failed miserably to roll out any sort of national program for diagnostic testing for reasons of indifference, incompetence, and other factors. However, there was another reason for lack of diagnostic testing, and this was a political one: more diagnostic testing could only mean that additional positive coronavirus cases would be identified, and Trump wanted to keep the numbers down because it would hurt his re-election chances in November. Simply stated, if the U.S. government did not make widespread testing available, then thousands of positive cases would not be identified, and the number of reported cases would be lower. To paraphrase Joseph Stalin, "No victims, no problem!"

The unavailability of widespread testing even artificially depressed the statistics of coronavirus-related deaths, since if a patient is not tested for coronavirus, or if the person dies at home without being tested, the "cause of death" that ends up on the death certificate will usually not be recorded as "coronavirus-related," even if that is strongly suspected to be the cause.[7]

The political calculations on antibody testing are quite different. Anyone who tests positive for antibodies (assuming that the test result is not a "false positive") only means the person had coronavirus in the past and survived, usually without being hospitalized. The more "coronavirus survivors" there are, the greater likelihood they have some degree of immunity and can return to the workplace. This supports the Trump's administration's (and Trump re-election campaign's) goal of reopening the country's economy as soon as possible since he could then forcefully argue that the coronavirus crisis was behind us and that the country could move on since more people have already passed through the crucible of coronavirus infection and recovery.

However, such a superficial political analysis does not address the harsh reality that a positive antibody test only means the person has been exposed at some point to the coronavirus. It does not indicate when or to what extent.[8] It could mean that the person only had a quick exposure that triggered a mild immune system response without ever having produced any symptoms. Many such positive results are really just vague indications of at least some limited exposure, but these people could very well get sick later on with full-blown COVID-19.

On April 15, President Donald Trump misleadingly oversimplified the issue by announcing that Abbott Laboratories has developed an antibodies test that can determine whether someone has previously been infected with the coronavirus, inferring that such a positive result meant that the person had developed an immunity.[9] Trump announced the test at a coronavirus task force press briefing, saying the U.S. would provide the test for up to 20 million Americans "in a matter of weeks."[10]

On April 28, the Trump administration posted an update to its plan to reopen the U.S. economy, which called for local government to administer two antibody tests per person under some circumstances, an approach that could enhance both the positive and negative predictive values compared to a single antibody test.[11]

It also was reported on April 28 that the Trump administration was planning to launch a pilot program that would involve widespread testing of New York City residents for antibodies to the coronavirus.[12] This federal program, called "Restore America," was discussed in an internal Trump administration document produced by the Department of Homeland Security and shared with other departments within the federal government that were working on the pandemic response.[13]

However, if an antibody test is unreliable – which is the case for many of the tests being sold and used on the market – then the test results from such defective tests can be worse than having not been tested at all. If you take an antibody test and it is a "false positive," meaning that the results say that you have antibodies in your blood but you actually do not, then you may tend to act differently - and improperly - than if you never took the test and did not know whether you had caught the virus or not. Simply stated, if a test erroneously tells you that you have antibodies and you do not, then you might think it safe to visit grandma on the theory that you are most likely immune since you have antibodies and the risk of infecting grandma is significantly reduced.

Even if you have an antibody test and the test correctly shows that you do have antibodies in your blood, this does not mean that you are immune. In fact, it does not tell you anything other than you were infected by the coronavirus and developed antibodies as a result of that infection. It does not necessarily mean that you are immune. Many scientists and reputable public health organizations, including the W.H.O., say that even high-quality antibody tests lack evidence to prove someone has immunity from the coronavirus and is no longer at risk of being re-infected.[14] In fact, the W.H.O. has flatly said that there is no evidence serological (antibody) tests can show whether a person has immunity or is no longer at risk of becoming re-infected.[15] Dr. Maria Van Kerkhove, head of the W.H.O.'s emerging diseases and zoonosis unit, announced at an April 17 press conference that while there were "officials of many countries suggesting these tests would be able to capture what they think will be a measure of immunity," the W.H.O. was holding to its position that "[r]ight now, we have no evidence that the use of a serological test can show that an individual is immune or protected from re-infection."[16]

Similarly, a negative antibody test – even if correct – does *not* necessarily mean that the coronavirus has never infected you. In fact, if you receive a negative antibody test within the early incubation period, your body may have not yet had a sufficient chance to develop enough antibodies to be detected through testing, or you may have recovered from an infection and, for some reason, your body did not generate sufficient antibodies to be identified by the antibody test.[17]

One of the reasons for the uncertainty in antibody testing is that most, if not all, of the current COVID-19 antibody testing done on a large scale is designed to detect "binding antibodies" and does not measure "neutralizing antibodies."[18] A neutralizing antibody (NAb) is an antibody that defends a cell from a pathogen or infectious particle by neutralizing any effect it has biologically.[19] Neutralization renders the particle no longer infectious or pathogenic.[20] A binding antibody will bind to the pathogen, but the pathogen remains infective; the purpose can be to flag the pathogen for destruction by the immune system.[21] Since most COVID-19 antibody tests will return a positive result if they find only binding antibodies, they cannot reveal that the person being tested has generated any NAbs which would give him or her protection against re-infection.[22]

These questions as to the reliability and usefulness of antibody testing were highly relevant to the ongoing debate as to whether the economies of various states and countries should be opened up, and if so, how much. Prodded by such concerns, the FDA stepped up warnings and joined other agencies, including the National Cancer Institute, to try to determine whether the unvetted tests actually worked. On Thursday, April 19, FDA Commissioner Stephen Hahn warned that "people should be very cautious" about tests that had not undergone the rigorous process of getting emergency authorization from the FDA.[23] So why, you may ask, did the FDA permit so many antibody tests to flood the market in the first place, only later to warn the public about using "unapproved" tests?

The FDA must have been asking itself the same question since, on Monday, May 4, the FDA tightened up its rules on antibody tests after learning that some of the test manufacturers were making false claims and that the tests were giving a high percentage of inaccurate results.[24] The agency acknowledged that they had received numerous complaints from hospitals and state and local governments about some of the 160 tests that had been launched in the U.S. since the coronavirus crisis erupted and that some of the companies had engaged in deceptive and false marketing about their products.[25] Some even claimed that they could be used at home, which the FDA had not approved.[26] The former CDC director, Dr. Tom Frieden, said in an interview on April 13 that many of the coronavirus antibody tests on the market were "junk."[27] Right now, Frieden said, "there are many tests on the market and many of them – now that I can speak very freely that I'm not in the government – many of them are junk."[28]

Two high-profile examples of either fraud or just faulty testing equipment involved the purchase of large numbers of antibody tests from Chinese manufacturers by the U.K. and Indian governments, which found them to be useless since they provided inaccurate or unreliable results. The British government was particularly embarrassed by the transaction since it paid $20 million upfront for the antibody tests, even before they had undergone confirmation testing at any U.K. lab. Even more embarrassing for the FDA and other U.S. regulators was that these defective tests — manufactured by Guangzhou Wondfo Biotech, Zhuhai Livzon Diagnostics, and Hangzhou AllTest Biotech — were still available for purchase in the U.S., according to the FDA's own website.[29]

Even if these tests had worked, the usefulness of these test results would be questionable since scientists still did not know the level of antibodies needed to make someone immune from the virus, or how long protection might last.

In tightening up its regulations on May 4, the FDA said in a statement: "We, unfortunately, see unscrupulous actors marketing fraudulent test kits and using the pandemic as an opportunity to take advantage of Americans' anxiety."[30]

Numerous state and local health departments had warned consumers and doctors to avoid tests that had not yet been FDA authorized. In San Diego County, officials shut down a "pop-up" antibody testing site at a community college, citing a lack of documentation about the test.[31]

One antibody test that was marketed by ARCpoint Labs of Edina, Minnesota, and which had not been FDA approved, raised concerns, according to Scott Becker, the executive director of the Association of Public Health Laboratories.[32] The information sheet relating to this antibody test represented that the presence of specific antibodies suggested a person had "functional immunity" and could safely "discontinue social distancing."[33] However, as of early May, scientists and researchers still did not know enough about antibody testing to say definitively whether the presence of antibodies meant that a person was immune, and if so, for how long. Therefore, any definitive representations by an antibody testing company as to the significance of the test results on the question of a person's immunity would be misleading, or at the very least, premature.

The FDA belatedly revised its rules to require its authorization for the marketing and sale of any antibody tests and noted that it had granted emergency authorizations for 11 antibody tests. Companies with antibody tests on the market without FDA authorization would now be required to submit their formal applications to regulators within ten business days.[34] Companies that launched their products at a later date would have to submit applications to the FDA within ten days after validating the tests.[35]

Some experts questioned whether even reliable antibody test results would really be that helpful in the process of deciding how local, national, and world economy should be opened back up. Unless a positive antibody test was an accurate predictor of immunity, and unless it was known how long the immunity would last, just knowing that a person has been infected was of limited utility. Antibody test results will, no doubt, be a helpful research tool in determining how widely the coronavirus spread among the U.S. population, but beyond that, it is unclear what useful information an antibody test result could provide. "We're spending a lot of time and resources on something that is not really a panacea for reopening," said Kamran Kadkhoda, a lab director at the Cleveland Clinic.[36] Even FDA Commissioner Stephen Hahn had to concede the limited utility of antibody testing. He told reporters: "Whether [an antibody] test should be a "ticket for someone to go back to work as the sole item, my opinion on that would be no because there are a lot of unanswered questions."[37]

Early on in the coronavirus crisis, there had been some serious consideration to issuing "immunity passports" to critical workers who tested positive for antibodies and were, therefore, presumed to be immune from any risk of transference of the disease to others and immunity from any re-infection by the virus.[38] With "immunity passports," the theory went, America would be able to get immune workers back into the workforce more quickly. However, since the presence of antibodies in a person's blood does not necessarily translate into immunity, this approach made little sense. Only with the completion of more studies on the correlation between antibodies and immunity will this critical question be answered. Unfortunately, some early studies on this issue did not contain good news.

The hope that antibodies would provide immunity against COVID-19 was somewhat dimmed by the report in early May that a new mutant strain of the coronavirus had been identified by scientists at Los Alamos National

Laboratory in New Mexico.[39] To make matters worse, this mutant strain appeared to be more contagious than the original versions that spread in the early days of the COVID-19 pandemic.[40] This new strain appeared in February in Europe, migrated quickly to the East Coast of the U.S., and soon became the dominant strain across the world since mid-March.[41] In addition to spreading faster, this mutant strain may make people vulnerable to a second infection after a first bout with the disease, a report warned.[42]

Scientists at major organizations working on a vaccine or therapeutic drugs to treat COVID-19 cases told *The Los Angeles Times* that they were pinning their hopes on initial evidence that the virus was stable and not likely to mutate the way influenza virus does, requiring a new vaccine every year.[43] The Los Alamos report could upend that assumption and make the development of an effective vaccine or treatment drug more difficult – or impossible. For example, some of the compounds in development were supposed to latch onto the coronavirus spike or interrupt its action. If they were designed based on the original version of the spike, they might not be effective against the new coronavirus strain. Even more depressingly, if the pandemic fails to wane seasonally as the weather warms, the virus could undergo further mutations just as research organizations were preparing the first medical treatments and vaccines based on the last iteration of the virus.[44]

Perhaps the most practical use of antibody test results was that it could identify people who could then donate their blood for use as "convalescent plasma" to be used in the treatment of active coronavirus cases.[45] The theory is that the antibodies in the blood serum will help the infected person fight off the infection. The effectiveness of this treatment approach, however, is still undergoing study. For example, as of early May, the University of Virginia Health System launched a new clinical trial to test the effectiveness of convalescent plasma for patients with COVID-19.[46] The trial tested whether using plasma from patients who have recovered from the coronavirus actually worked to help treat those currently suffering from COVID-19. Patients at UVA who had tested positive for the coronavirus were being offered the opportunity to participate in the trial. According to Dr. Scott Heysell, Associate Professor of Infectious Diseases, "That type of therapy has been used with success for other coronaviruses, including MERS and SARS, and has even been used recently in the Ebola outbreak in West Africa."[47]

* * * * *

The Trump administration's belated reliance on antibody testing did little or nothing to stem the first wave of the coronavirus pandemic from washing over the U.S. Moreover, the FDA's reckless decision to let several dozen untested, unapproved and oftentimes defective tests to be marketed and sold in the U.S. at the height of the pandemic was a dangerous distraction from the lack of diagnostic testing throughout the U.S.

15

CALIFORNIA AND OTHER WEST COAST STATES TAKE THE LEAD IN THE BATTLE AGAINST COVID-19

In retrospect, it should not have been so surprising that California would take the lead in the U.S.'s response to the coronavirus crisis. Although only one of 50 states, California's status is more like that of the city-state of Venice in Italy. During the Middle Ages and early Renaissance, Venice was one of the dominant world trading powers for almost 1,000 years. California is often referred to as a "nation-state," and this is not much of an exaggeration. With nearly 40 million residents, it has a larger population than either Canada or Australia. Its population is one third larger than that of the next most populous state, Texas, and surpassed New York to become the most populous state way back in 1962.[1]

If California were a sovereign nation, it would rank as the world's fifth-largest economy, with a $3.137 trillion gross state product as of 2019.[2] California has a larger economy than that of India, which has over 1.35 billion people, and just behind Germany, which has more than twice California's population, at 83 million.[3] In addition to being an economic powerhouse, California is also at the cutting edge of – well – everything. It is often said that if you want to see the future, go to California. California's Silicon Valley, in the Santa Clara Valley just south of San Francisco, is home to some of the world's most successful technology companies, including Apple, Alphabet Inc./Google, Facebook, and Twitter. Over 10% of the Fortune 1000 companies are based in California, the most of any state.[4]

California also has the dubious distinction of having, arguably, the most natural disasters of any state, requiring it to be on a perpetual state of alert for earthquakes, wildfires, mudslides, drought, floods, and every other manner of pestilence, natural and man-made. The San Francisco fire of 1851 destroyed almost three-quarters of the city, and the 1906 earthquake destroyed 80% of the city.[5] By the time the 1918-1919 Spanish Flu epidemic ended, 45,000 San Franciscans were sickened, and 3,000 died during these two waves of the influenza pandemic, resulting in one of the highest death rates in the country.[6] Since then, wildfires and blackouts have become a way of life for some areas of the state. On the plus side, California does have an enormous and highly sophisticated emergency response structure in place at the state, county, and local levels. Its citizens and communities have historically shown a great deal of resilience in facing and overcoming emergency challenges of every conceivable nature.

California responded to the 2020 coronavirus pandemic with the same proactive and organized energy as it responded to former crises. Its response efforts were so successful that it was able to lend a helping hand to other less-fortunate cities and states around the country. Acting more like the president of an independent country than governor of a state, Governor Gavin Newsom announced the state was spending $1 billion to buy 200 million masks (both N95 protective masks and surgical masks) per month from a Chinese company, BYD North America.[7] BYD was the first company that the FDA approved for emergency delivery of respirator masks.[8] BYD had previously been best known as a significant global player in the electric vehicle and lithium battery markets and had no history of making personal protective equipment.

Gov. Newsom explained that he had made this secretive purchase "to combat a growing need for masks in California and to secure them before other states and countries sign similar deals."[9] California had only received 1 million N95 masks from the federal government, which was a minute fraction of the over 41 million N95 masks that the state had already used by early April.[10] The state saw no alternative other than to take an aggressive position on the open market to secure the protective equipment that it would need for the foreseeable future. Gov. Newsom explained why in an interview with *MSNBC*. "We've been competing against other states, against other nations, against our own federal government for PPE — coveralls, masks, shields, N95 masks — and we're not waiting around any longer."[11] He continued, "In the past 48 hours we have secured — through a consortium of nonprofits and a manufacturer here in the state of California — upwards of 200 million masks on a monthly basis that we're confident we can supply the needs of the state of California, [and] potentially the needs of other western states."[12] Governor Newsom also announced California was prepared to lend 500 state-owned ventilators to other COVID-19 hot spots in need.

However, California's relative success in dealing with the coronavirus crisis was far from an inevitable outcome, despite its long history of successfully dealing with other crises. The virus was not an earthquake, a fire, or a drought that could be dealt with by the usual array of emergency personnel. It was the first pandemic to hit California in any significant way since the 1918 Spanish Flu pandemic. Its first responders were the state and county public health officers who were tasked with monitoring the spread of the virus on the West Coast. These state and county health officials got together and formulated a plan of action that would be effective enough either to stop the virus or at least slow its pace so that it would not overwhelm the available medical resources. Fortunately for California, and the rest of the country, Dr. Sara Cody and the Santa Clara County health department were able to take a leadership role in this successful effort.

Santa Clara and the Bay Area Order the First Lockdown in the Country

On January 31, Sara Cody, Santa Clara County's Public Health Officer since 2013, received word that the first official coronavirus case was reported in her county.[13] The case was also the first coronavirus patient reported in the San Francisco Bay Area and the seventh reported in the U.S.[14] In anticipation of the pandemic, Santa Clara activated its Medical Health Joint Operations Center (MHJOC) on January 28.[15]

The second confirmed case of coronavirus in the county came 48 hours after the first. Both of them involved travel from China. However, it was almost impossible for Dr. Cody and her California public health colleagues to get any real sense of the scope of the spread of the coronavirus at this point. The process of sending swabs for testing to the CDC in Atlanta took so long they could not do any realistic modeling of the cases in the Bay Area. It was not until February 26 that Santa Clara County was finally authorized by the CDC to use its lab for testing,[16] and on February 28, the CDC confirmed a third "positive" test for coronavirus.[17]

This third case, which would be known as a "sentinel case," proved to be a turning point for their understanding of the virus' spread across the Bay Area. This third case was a woman in her 60s who, unlike the first two, had not traveled overseas to China. She also had not been in contact with anyone who had traveled from China. This was a clear-cut case of "community transmission," meaning the woman had become infected by someone else in the community.[18] This third case was confirmed by Dr. Cody at a press conference that same day, February 28.

With each confirmed coronavirus case, Dr. Cody's team went through the meticulous process of interviewing every infected person. The team traced back every place the person had been and everyone they had contact with and monitoring them in quarantine. Their goal was to stop the chain of transmission, which they have not been able to do completely, but they did at least put a dent in it. As the number of cases escalated, it became nearly impossible to keep up the contact tracing. On March 3, Dr. Cody started issuing mitigation guidelines recommending everything from telecommuting to cancellations of large gatherings.[19]

By March 9, the woman who was the sentinel case had died, and now forty-three cases had been confirmed in Santa Clara County, the highest of any county in California.[20] Santa Clara County was now officially branded as a coronavirus "hot zone." Dr. Cody announced that the local NHL professional hockey team, the San Jose Sharks, would either have to cancel their games or play to an empty arena. She also announced the shutdown of the annual Cinequest Film Festival and the closing of bars, clubs, and other establishments that attracted large groups of people. On March 13, Dr. Cody went one step further in her mitigation orders to try to restrict the spread of the virus. At a press conference, she announced the prohibition on gatherings of more than 100 people.[21]

On March 16, Dr. Cody and her public health colleagues in the Bay Area announced shelter-in-place legal orders – the first in the country – keeping nearly 7 million people in the Bay Area at home and effectively closing all schools and non-essential businesses.[22] According to Dr. Cody, she just wanted to "slow the train down," by issuing the orders, "so that when it hits the curve in the track, it will not derail."[23] Gov. Newson followed suit with a statewide stay-at-home order a few days later on March 19.[24]

After the September 11 terrorist attacks and the subsequent anthrax scare, Dr. Cody and two of her predecessors in the Santa Clara health department, Marty Fenstersheib and Karen Smith, had joined forces. Together they built Santa Clara County's model for a massive, coordinated emergency response to a bioterrorism attack or pandemic. These planned responses included social distancing, shutting schools, and – if necessary – mandating that people stay home. This was the plan that they activated on March 16 when the shelter-at-home orders were issued to try to slow the path of COVID-19.

Indeed, these extreme mitigation measures implemented by Santa Clara County and the rest of the Bay Area helped "flatten the curve." However, the rapidly developing spike in the number of coronavirus cases, hospitalizations, and deaths in Santa Clara County and the rest of the Bay Area continued to accelerate.

By March 28, the Bay Area had surpassed 1,800 cases and recorded 46 deaths.[25] But with only limited testing and other surveillance tools available, it was impossible to calculate the real numbers. Although Santa Clara was out in front of the rest of the country on implementing proactive measures, the benefits would have been even greater if they had been implemented earlier.

Dr. Cody also conducted numerous press briefings, including the dramatic March 16 announcement of the stay-at-home orders. Still, her low-key approach and calm demeanor led to a lesser degree of notoriety than, say, New York Governor Andrew Cuomo, or the often combative White House briefings of Donald Trump. None of her interviews went viral, such as those of the more dramatic San Mateo County Public Health Officer Scott Morrow. Morrow publicly criticized violators of the stay-at-home order as the equivalent of "spitting in our face" and contributing "to the death toll that will follow."[26]

By Sunday, March 15, there were 245 people across the Bay Area who tested positive, and three had died from the virus.[27] Passengers from the *Grand Princess* cruise ship showing symptoms were holed up on the third floor of the nearby San Carlos hotel and at the Asilomar conference center in Pacific Grove, California.[28] And in Gilroy, California, 66-year-old Gary

Young was on a ventilator, in quarantine at St. Louise Hospital, one of the growing number of victims. He would die the next day.[29] Dr. Cody decided that more had to be done.

Dr. Cody got on the phone with health officers Tomas Aragon from San Francisco and Dr. Scott Morrow from San Mateo County. They compared the trend lines of COVID-19 cases in the Bay Area with Italy's a week and a half earlier, just before the situation in Italy disintegrated into the horror story that made headlines around the globe. They knew they had to do something bold and dramatic to shut down the spread of the virus. Social distancing was the only real option that they had open to them. As Dr. Cody later described the decision: "We just needed to embrace the risk and do it."[30]

Dr. Cody and her colleagues were well aware that the immediate ordering of nearly 8 million Bay Area residents to stay at home was not going to stop the spread of the virus completely. But it could hopefully buy time for hospitals to keep the number of patients each day at manageable levels. In all, Dr. Cody spoke with all seven health officers from six counties and the city of Berkeley, plus the two county lawyers. They had to make sound decisions as to what businesses would be considered essential. They also had to find ways to accommodate the students from low-income families so they could continue to receive free lunches. What could they do about those critical health care workers who might have to stay home to care for their children? What would be the impact on the community of canceling graduations, funerals, and religious services?

The final legal orders that were drafted included exceptions for hospitals, grocery stores, gas stations, and other "essential businesses," to be determined on a case by case basis. The following morning, March 16, Dr. Cody and the other six Bay Area county health officers gathered in a county briefing room. Dr. Cody spoke first, explaining that, throughout the Bay Area, 273 cases had been confirmed, and the number was accelerating: "I recognize that this is unprecedented," she said. "But we must come together to do this, and we know we need a regional response… We must all do our part to slow the spread of COVID-19."[31]

California Follows the Bay Area's Lead

On March 4, Gov. Newson declared a state of emergency.[32] On March 15, he called for the closure of all bars across the state during a Sunday press conference.[33] He also said that restaurants would have to cut their seating capacity by 50% and social distance people.[34] The following day, when Bay Area counties, issued stay-at-home orders, Newsom and his public health advisors pondered whether these orders should be broadened to the entire state. Their unanimous answer was, "Yes."

On March 19, Gov. Newsom ordered California's 40 million residents to stay at home indefinitely.[35] It was the widest-ranging directive issued by any state, even though the death toll thus far from coronavirus was only 150 in the entire U.S., and 19 in California.[36] There were about 1,000 known cases in California as of the date of the state lockdown order.[37] Exceptions were made for grocery stores, pharmacies, gas stations, farmers' markets, food banks, convenience stores, takeout and delivery restaurants, banks, and laundromats. "You can still take your kids outside, practicing common sense and social distancing," Newsom said. "You can still walk your dog."[38] The directives also exempted critical infrastructures such as food and agriculture, health care, transportation, energy, and financial services.

As of the March 19 statewide shutdown, it was estimated that up to 56% of the state's residents would become infected by the virus, a figure that would equate to more than 22 million people.[39] As of April 25, the numbers were much lower than anticipated, with only 41,338 reported cases in California and only 1,654 reported deaths.[40]

These numbers were in sharp contrast to the numbers experienced by New York, with 288,045 confirmed cases in the state and 19,966 deaths.[41] However, New York had 805,350 tests completed as of April 26, while California only had 143,800 as of that date, with 14,100 pending results.[42]

By April 14, Gov. Newsom felt sufficiently optimistic that he held a press conference announcing that the state was considering the gradual lifting restrictions.[43] He did not indicate when specifically these decisions might happen, only that "when it comes to reopening, SCIENCE – not politics – must be California's guide."[44] Newsom identified six indicators that would guide California's decision-making:

- The ability to monitor and protect our communities through testing, contact tracing, isolating, and supporting those who are positive or exposed;
- The ability to prevent infection in people who are at risk for more severe COVID-19;
- The ability of the hospital and health systems to handle surges;
- The ability to develop therapeutics to meet the demand;
- The ability for businesses, schools, and child care facilities to support physical distancing; and
- The ability to determine when to reinstitute certain measures, such as the stay-at-home orders, if necessary.[45]

Even with the easing of some restrictions, Californians were still expected to continue wearing masks in public. Gov. Newsom insisted that restaurants have fewer tables and that servers wear gloves and masks. The Governor also encouraged people to prepare for the likelihood that sporting events, concerts, and festivals would not resume by summer. He also appointed an advisory council. Former Democratic presidential candidate Tom Steyer was named to head the group. He was joined by all of the state's living former governors to oversee the restarting of the economy.

Gov. Newsom continuously emphasized, however, that the reopening of the state had to be done cautiously, explaining, "There's no light switch here. It's more like a dimmer."[46] He said that any successful easing of restrictive measures would depend, to a large extent, on individual accountability and responsibility as it relates to face coverings and physical distancing.

On April 23, when California had its deadliest day until then, with 115 deaths reported within 24 hours, Newsom warned: "We are not out of the woods yet."[47] But the coronavirus crisis was clearly over its peak in California at that point, since hospitalizations were down 4.4%, and there was a 1.2% decline in intensive care patients in the state.[48]

Gov. Newsom received high marks for having implemented some innovative programs to help those Californians who were left most vulnerable and exposed by the crisis. He announced a program called "Restaurants Deliver: Home Meals for Seniors." The program provided payment to local restaurants to deliver three meals every day of the week to at-risk seniors during the coronavirus epidemic.[49] When announcing the program, Gov. Newsom said that 1.7 million of California's 5.7 million seniors lived alone.[50] This program, closely looked at by other states, was designed not only to help seniors but also to provide essential economic stimulus to local businesses and workers that were struggling to stay afloat during the crisis.

On the same day, Gov. Newsom also announced a significant expansion of coronavirus testing capability throughout California. Testing was another crucial step forward towards the eventual easing of the state's strict stay-at-home order.

Gov. Newsom's ability to keep the lines of communication open with the White House during the crisis also paid some dividends, especially concerning the critically important issue of testing supplies. Without adequate testing, California's efforts to allow people to return to work and businesses to reopen would be severely hampered.[51] On April 24, the federal government agreed to send California a supply of testing swabs, which were in short supply. The White House was able to send 100,000 swabs immediately, and 250,000 additional swabs the following week.[52] The Governor also announced that six testing sites were being opened in the state, with particular emphasis on getting "Black and brown communities" and rural communities tested.[53] Gov. Newsom announced Abbott Laboratories provided California with 1.5 million serology (antibody) tests.[54]

Washington State Also Pushes Back Hard Against COVID-19

Washington State is really where the coronavirus saga in the U.S. started. The first U.S. confirmed case announced on January 21, 2020, was a resident of Snohomish County.[55] Washington also had the unenviable distinction of being the first state to announce a death from the disease on February 29. It later announced that two more deaths on February 26 were due to COVID-19.[56] Information later came out indicating that prior undetected cases were present in the Bay Area in California. Still, there is no question that the Seattle area was in the eye of the coronavirus hurricane. Indeed, until mid-March, when New York surpassed it, Washington had the highest absolute number of confirmed cases and the highest number per capita of any state in the country. Many of the deceased were residents of a nursing home in Kirkland, an Eastside suburb of Seattle in King County.[57] At least 37 people connected to Life Care Center of Kirkland died from coronavirus-related illness, according to King County public health officials.

By April 26, this state of more than 7.5 million people had 13, 219 confirmed cases, with 738 deaths.[58] More than a third of the cases in Washington were reported in King County, which includes Seattle.[59]

Governor Jay Inslee, a former candidate for the Democratic Party's presidential nomination, got off to a rocky start with the Trump White House as to how to deal with the coronavirus crisis. Inslee was an early and outspoken critic of the Trump administration's lackluster performance on the development of testing and other issues. This criticism triggered a sharp and very public response from Trump. On March 6, during a trip to CDC headquarters in Atlanta, Mr. Trump lashed out at Gov. Inslee, who had just had a meeting with Vice President Mike Pence the day before.[60] "I told Mike not to be complimentary of that governor because that governor is a snake," Mr. Trump said. "Let me just tell you we have a lot of problems with the governor," he added. "So Mike may be happy with him, but I'm not, OK?"[61]

With little guidance or support from Washington, D.C., Gov. Inslee quickly followed the lead of California by effectively shutting down Washington state with orders closing schools and directed people to stay at home. Inslee also ordered a halt to all elective surgeries and banned all gatherings. These orders effectively closed down all businesses, except grocery stores, pharmacies, gas stations, and other essential companies.

Washington's stay-at-home and other mitigation programs quickly reduced the infection rate. According to the CDC, Washington went from the state with the highest number of cases to the 11th-highest.[62] The University of Washington's Institute for Health Metrics and Evaluation projected that the state hit its peak in coronavirus deaths around April 1, with 24 fatalities that day.[63] In contrast, New York's infection and death rates were still sharply rising at that point.

Washington's stringent social distancing measures had a dramatic effect on the number of cases and deaths that the state was experiencing. One reason for this is that Seattle and other cities and towns in Washington are less dense than cities like New York and Chicago. Also, communities in the Northwest tended to adhere to social distancing and stay-at-home orders more closely than in some other parts of the country.

Washington's relatively low numbers can be attributed in part to the fact that state and local health officials tested more extensively than elsewhere. By finding cases of coronavirus early on, and instituting quarantine and monitoring protocols for all known cases, the numbers were held down. Washington also has first-rate health care and hospital system that was able to handle the sharp initial increase in hospitalizations the state was experiencing. "Our hospitals have been preparing, building up capacity," commented Hilary Godwin, Dean of the University of Washington School of Public Health, "Once we got to the point where we had to do social distancing because the number of cases was so great, we were really well-positioned and were able to roll those things out really systematically."[64]

The hospitals in Seattle and the rest of the state were thus better prepared to handle a surge in the capacity as the coronavirus cases accelerated. Researchers found that in late February, each infected individual in the county was spreading the virus to an average of two or three other people. However, by March 18, that number had been virtually cut in half, with people on average infecting 1.4 additional people.[65] To see an actual drop in new cases, each individual with coronavirus would need to infect, on average, less than one other person. Once this "replacement" number was down below "one," Washington state planned to have the local health departments conduct contact tracing for each newly reported case.[66]

In addition to a robust contact tracing program, Washington also recognized that, to transition out of comprehensive social distancing measures, there needed to be widespread availability of testing with very rapid turnaround time. Also needed was a sufficient supply of personal protective equipment, ventilators, and other items necessary to handle any increases in hospitalizations due to the second wave of virus infections. Washington was fortunate in that, between the state's public health laboratory and the lab at the University of Washington in Seattle, there was plenty of capacity for testing. However, the initial bottleneck was that the medical workers conducting the testing did not have enough adequate personal protective equipment for obtaining samples. There were also shortages of swabs and reagents – the enzymes and chemicals needed to conduct the testing. Once these shortages were overcome by early to mid-May, Seattle and the rest of the state were ready to begin easing social restrictions and to gradually open the state up for businesses again.

Washington State officials were well aware that the easing of social constraints and restarting of the economy could lead to a "second wave" of infections. Preparing for this possibility, the state focused on the continued buildup of its capacity to conduct testing and contact tracing. The state has also worked on expanding its hospital capacity so that it will have enough "bandwidth" to cope effectively with any resurgence of the virus.

One promising breakthrough in Washington was the development of a new testing procedure whereby people could take their own samples and then turn over the swabs to health care workers at a drive-through or other health care facility. Also, Seattle-area hospitals such as Harborview Medical Center began screening all patients admitted for any reason for COVID-19.[67] Previously, only patients with symptoms or those whose medical histories were unknown were tested. The virology lab administered the tests at U.W. Medicine, the health care system affiliated with the University of Washington, which can turn around thousands of same-day tests.[68]

Thus Seattle, the first major city to become a "hot spot" for coronavirus, was poised to become one of the first major cities to responsibly ease its social restrictions with an actual plan and resources in place to handle a potential "second wave" of cases. Seattle Mayor Jenny Durkin's response efforts were designed in coordination with Los Angeles Mayor Eric Garcetti, and the two mayors further coordinated their plans to ease social distancing restrictions and open up their businesses. But they planned to do so cautiously. As Mayor Jenny Durkin puts it, "It's a marathon, not a sprint," adding in mid-April: "We're not even really halfway through, even though we've hit the peak."[69] The key elements would be the availability of adequate testing, adequate protective equipment for front-line health care workers, and sufficient capacity in hospitals and other medical facilities.

By April 21, the crisis in Washington had sufficiently stabilized so that Gov. Inslee could announce that plans were underway for the state's return to public life. Again he emphasized it would be on a gradual basis. First, the state had to sufficiently scale up its access to rapid testing and response, and enough protective supplies for health care workers as well as the public.[70] He echoed Gov. Newsom of California by cautioning, "It will look more like the turning of the dial rather than the flipping of a switch."[71] Gov. Inslee's approach included a phased-in approach for businesses and industries, the assistance to various parts of the state with infrastructure programs to assist with the economic recovery, and a variety of economic recovery assistance measures for workers and businesses. He also emphasized the importance of social supports during the reopening process, including increased capacity for behavioral and mental health services, support for people experiencing increased anxiety and stress, payments for child care costs for parents seeking employment, and the closing of six miles of residential streets to vehicle traffic in Seattle to create more space for social distancing and for pedestrians and bicyclists during the coronavirus crisis.[72]

Oregon Also Puts Together the Key Elements Needed for a Recovery

On February 28, the Oregon Health Authority reported that the first case of a suspected coronavirus carrier in the state was a resident of Washington County.[73] The same day, Governor Kate Brown created a state coronavirus response team composed of representatives of 12 state agencies. The team was "tasked with coordinating state and local-level preparations for an epidemic" of coronavirus in Oregon.[74] She later ordered the cancellation of events for 250 or more people. She issued a statewide stay-at-home order on March 23, effective immediately.[75]

Within one month, Oregon's disciplined approach to the crisis succeeded in quickly "flattening the curve" of coronavirus cases in the state. By April 26, Oregon was reporting a total of only 2,311 coronavirus cases, with 91 deaths.[76]

One of the factors that Oregon had going for it was that - like California and Washington - it had a strong science and technology industry. Oregon partnered with the state governmental agencies and universities in the state to take on the coronavirus challenge. For example, based upon a collaborative effort between private industry and the Oregon Health & Science University in Portland, the state was able to make several breakthroughs in its response efforts. One of these was the development of a new type of ventilator created with 3D printing technology.[77] Once approved by the FDA, any hospital with access to a commercial grade 3D printer would have the ability to produce a new ventilator within a matter of hours. The ventilator design does not require electricity and operates off of a standard oxygen tank. This ventilator could go a long way to eliminating the shortage of ventilators at the state, national, and international levels.

Masks for medical workers were also in desperately short supply in Oregon until mid-April when the state was finally able to obtain millions of masks. Within one week, the state was able to secure nearly 2 million surgical masks.[78] The following week it received about 4 million KN95 masks, which are similar to N95 masks and meet the same basic requirements. About 50,000 more masks from China arrived at Los Angeles International Airport and were then transported to Oregon.[79] They were a gift from the provincial government of Fujian Province, which has been Oregon's sister state since 1984. It pays to have influential friends in China in these difficult times, especially when they have 50,000 extra masks!

Oregon also received an N95 mask disinfecting machine, which uses hydrogen peroxide to disinfect up to 85,000 masks per day.[80] Battelle, the manufacturer of the decontamination system, also deployed its systems in Ohio, New York, Massachusetts, Illinois, Connecticut, and Georgia.[81]

Oregon was able to accelerate the painfully slow nationwide buildup in testing capacity, including a deal with Walgreens to open up a drive-through testing site in a Portland suburb. Oregon health officials also announced that was considering hiring up to 600 more workers to perform coronavirus contact tracing under a plan entitled "Reopening Oregon."[82] These contact trackers would help identify people exposed to known COVID-19 infections and then monitor them to make sure they get tested and followed quarantine guidelines. Oregon tried to use contact tracing to keep pace with the spread of the virus when it first hit Oregon in late February. Still, the effort quickly became overwhelmed by the sheer volume of new infections. Oregon officials hoped the additional number of contact tracers and a reduction in the level of new infections would lead to a more successful result when the state began to reopen for business. So far, Oregon's infection rate has been relatively low, with one infection for every 20 residents tested.[83]

As Gov. Kate Brown summed it up, "One step at a time, we are making progress towards the day when we can begin to reopen our communities and safely return to public life," adding, "It's very, very clear that we need a much more robust public health strategy around contact tracing, around testing and around isolating and quarantine."[84]

The West Coast States Combine Forces

On Monday, April 13, Newsom and his fellow governors, Brown of Oregon and Inslee of Washington, announced that they, like the six East Coast states, would be forming an alliance, known as the "Western States Pact," with the intention of "restarting public life and business."[85] Shortly thereafter, two more states joined this Western alliance: Colorado and Nevada.[86] The governors explained their goal:

> COVID-19 has preyed upon our interconnectedness. In the coming weeks, the West Coast will flip the script on COVID-19 – with our states acting in close coordination and collaboration to ensure the virus can never spread wildly in our communities.[87]

Just as they had taken the lead in putting into place forceful and effective mitigation measures to slow the spread of the virus, California and its two neighboring states to the north are thus continuing to take the leadership role in the reopening of the states. To do this prudently, they carefully put together the testing and contract tracing measures necessary to begin reopening their state economies without reigniting the spread of the virus. In most countries, this kind of leadership would be found only in the central government. But in America – at least in the Trump era – these weighty responsibilities have devolved in the states. Fortunately, at least the three West Coast states – along with Nevada and Colorado - appear to be up to the task.

16

COVID-19 EXPOSES THE UGLY TRUTH ABOUT NURSING HOMES AND HOW AMERICA CARES FOR ITS ELDERLY

"For the elderly, COVID-19 is almost a perfect killing machine."
-Mark Parkinson, CEO
National Center for Assisted Living

When COVID-19 first landed in the U.S., one of the early epicenters was King County in Washington State, which includes Seattle. Kings County is also where several of the state's largest nursing homes are located. One of these nursing homes, the Life Care Center of Kirkland, became an early epicenter of the coronavirus outbreak in the U.S. At least 37 people associated with this nursing home were reported to have died from COVID-19 related complications.[1]

As different epicenters of the coronavirus began appearing, at least 4,100 U.S. nursing homes were reporting coronavirus cases by mid-April 2020.[2] There also were more than 7,000 confirmed COVID-related deaths in nursing homes during this same time period.[3] As of April 29, about two weeks later, more than 55,000 nursing home residents and staff members had contracted COVID-19, and more than 11,000 had died.[4]

By May 10, the number of coronavirus-related deaths in nursing homes and other long term care facilities had skyrocketed to the point where at least 27,700 residents and workers had died, according to a *New York Times* database.[5] The virus, as of May 10, had infected more than 150,000 individuals at about 7,700 nursing homes and long term care facilities.[6] While just 11% of the country's cases have occurred in such long-term care facilities, deaths related to COVID-19 in these facilities account for more than one-third of the country's pandemic fatalities.[7] In 14 states, the number of residents and workers who have died of COVID-related illness accounts for more than one-half of all deaths from the virus.[8] In some states, the numbers are even worse: Connecticut reported that nearly

90% of its COVID-related deaths between April 22 and April 29 occurred in nursing homes.[9]

Nursing home residents are at extremely high risk of being infected by the coronavirus and dying, according to the CDC.[10] COVID-19, the disease caused by the coronavirus, is known to be particularly lethal to older adults with underlying health conditions and can spread more easily through group health care facilities such as nursing homes, where many people live in a confined environment and workers move from room to room.

In New York City alone, at least 14 nursing homes in the city and its suburbs recorded more than 25 coronavirus-related deaths by mid-April.[11] In neighboring New Jersey, officials reported that infections had broken out in 394 nursing homes and other long-term facilities, or about two-thirds of all such facilities in the state.[12] New Jersey also reported that more than 1,500 deaths from the virus were tied to nursing facilities.[13]

Gruesome stories started emerging as the full scope of the nursing home crisis unfolded. Betsy McCaughey, a former lieutenant governor of New York, bluntly described the status of many nursing homes during the crisis: "They're death pits," she said.[14] Judith Reagan, an editor and publishing executive with a 91-year old father in a nursing home, bitterly commented: "The residents and staff are being led to slaughter." [15]

On April 15, for example, there was an anonymous report of a body being stored in a shed outside New Jersey's largest nursing home, Andover Subacute and Rehabilitation II, located in the northern part of the state.[16] When the police investigated, they found 17 bodies in a makeshift morgue inside the nursing home.[17] The body in the shed had been moved inside. The nursing home staff was completely overwhelmed as the coronavirus quickly circulated among the elderly residents in the facility, and the 17 bodies that were found were just a part of a total of 70 recent deaths at this facility.[18] Of those who died, 26 people had tested positive for the virus, and of the patients still remaining at the home, 76 tested positive.[19] In addition, 41 staff members, including the administrator, were reported to be sick with COVID-19.[20]

The coronavirus has also preyed on residents of other nursing homes in New Jersey with almost equal force, claiming more than 4,850 lives as of early May.[21] Deaths at long-term care facilities accounted for one-half of the state's COVID-19 fatalities, well over the national rate.[22] As of Sunday, May 10, New Jersey nursing homes had reported 30 or more deaths each, including four with more than 50 deaths.[23]

Other horror stories kept pouring in about deaths in nursing homes from around the country. Twenty-four residents of an Indiana nursing home hit by COVID-19 had died, while a nursing home in Iowa saw 14 deaths.[24] Chicago's Cook County set up a temporary morgue that could take more than 2,000 bodies, expecting that many of them would be coming from nursing homes.[25]

While the coronavirus struck people of all ages, its impact on the elderly was disproportionate and devastating. As the virus spread, it soon became painfully clear that older people, particularly those with pre-existing medical conditions, were the ones at most risk for serious disease and death. According to an analysis released by the CDC on March 18, 80% of the U.S. deaths associated with the coronavirus were adults aged 65 and older, even though two-thirds of the Americans known to be infected were under 65.[26] This analysis appeared to be consistent with recent data released by China, which showed 80% of the deaths there were adults aged 60 and older.[27] The average age of death for the disease in Italy was 81.[28]

There are several reasons why older people are more likely to be at risk of contracting coronavirus and dying from it than younger people. One's immune system weakens with age, and older adults are more likely to have underlying health conditions that exacerbate illness. New York Governor Andrew M. Cuomo graphically explained why older adults in nursing homes were particularly vulnerable to being struck by the disease. "Coronavirus in a nursing home can be like fire through dry grass," he said.[29] Not only are the immune systems of older adults weaker, but they also have a greater likelihood of suffering from "co-mobility," meaning that they often have chronic illnesses, such as cardiac problems, respiratory issues, diabetes, and other problems.[30] "The residents are sitting ducks," exclaimed Richard Mollot, the executive director of the Long Term Care Community Coalition.[31]

Nursing home residents are particularly vulnerable to the coronavirus, since family members and friends who regularly visited elderly nursing home residents may have been infecting them without even knowing it. We now know that the virus can be carried by someone who is not showing any symptoms of the disease, so this makes it particularly difficult to detect, especially when it is an early incubation period. Mark Parkinson, chief executive of the National Center for Assisted Living (NCAL), explained that "[t]he grim reality is that for the elderly, COVID-19 is almost a perfect killing machine."[32] Parkinson explained: "In our facilities, the average age is 84, and everyone has underlying medical conditions. So when you combine those factors together, we are dealing with perhaps the greatest challenge that we ever have had."[33]

While the temporary suspension of all visitors at nursing homes throughout the country has partially reduced the risk of "friendly fire" infections from family members, this has also led to an increased sense of isolation and loneliness by nursing home residents, which itself can have severe adverse health consequences. Moreover, family members often serve as a critical support network for nursing home residents, and if those family members are prevented for legitimate public health reasons from visiting, their family members who are residents of the nursing homes are deprived of their best advocates. Richard J. Mollot, explained this paradox: "We know that, in addition to providing company, love, and a friendly face, families provide vital monitoring and often essential care," he wrote.[34]

Although the elderly are, well, getting older, the same also can be said about all of the rest of us. The mere statistical fact, however, that a person is elderly does not mean that he or she is leading a life that is worth less than that of younger people. But some countries have not acted as if this were true. The W.H.O. has strongly suspected that some countries have responded more slowly to the coronavirus threat because they deemed it to be a condition primarily lethal to old people and that older people were expendable. As explained by W.H.O. director-general, Dr. Tedros Ghebreyesus, some countries treat their elderly as "less worthy of the best efforts to contain it."[35] In other words, in the midst of the crisis, older people are far too often being written off as necessary casualties or sacrificial lambs.

Since the coronavirus pandemic has hit, there has been a sharp uptick in "ageism" jokes and memes on the internet, such as the cruel meme referring to the coronavirus as a "Boomer Remover," an update of last year's dismissive and condescending "OK, Boomer."[36]

This attitude towards the elderly, namely, that "they are on their way out anyway," is not only grossly insensitive but also inaccurate from an actuarial standpoint. Due to increases in longevity over the past several decades, the risk of death in the next year for a 70-year-old man (at least before the COVID-19 pandemic hit) was just 2%, and an 80-year-old woman has only a 4% likelihood of dying in the coming year, according to the Stanford economist John Shoven.[37] COVID-19 may, however, have dramatically changed these actuarial numbers for the elderly residents of nursing homes and other long-term facilities.

However, getting infected by the coronavirus is not necessarily a death sentence for a nursing home resident or any other elderly person. One living example of this is Sylvia Goldsholl, who turned 108 last December and survived the Spanish Flu and every other public health crisis since then.[38] She also survived COVID-19. During April, Ms. Goldsholl's relatives received the distressing news that she had contracted the coronavirus in the New Jersey nursing home where she was located and was in isolation. Her relatives expected the worst. "This is killing people in nursing homes all over New Jersey and the country," said Nancy Chazen, a niece of Ms. Goldsholl. "Quite honestly, I thought that was going to be the end — I mean, she's 108." Two weeks later, relatives received another call. "They told us, 'She's fully recovered,'" said Ms. Chazen. Mrs. Goldsholl now has the distinction of being the oldest known COVID-19 survivor in the world.

But many nursing home residents are not as fortunate as Sylvia Goldsholl. Due to weakened immunity systems, preexisting illnesses, and other factors, a coronavirus infection is just too much for many elderly patients and thus fatal.

Even for nursing home residents who do not become infected with COVID-19, the coronavirus crisis has intensified the "normal" sense of loneliness and isolation experienced by many older people living at home or in long-term facilities. While children and grandchildren may have regularly come to visit them before the crisis, they are now often completely isolated from almost any human contact. Even if they are living in a facility, group activities and group dining have either been restricted or cancelled. The only people they see are (hopefully) dressed from head to toe in personal protective equipment (PPE) and wearing face masks.

A recent report on Twitter was by a young woman in Oregon, who described being called over to a car outside at her local supermarket by a couple in their 80s.[39] The couple had been sitting in the car in the parking lot of the supermarket for a prolonged period of time, too scared to go inside for fear of becoming infected. The couple handed the young woman a $100 bill and begged her to do some shopping for them so they would not starve.

Another elderly resident in an assisted living facility in the San Francisco Bay Area movingly wrote of the almost unbearable loneliness he was experiencing in his current living situation. He described it as "like being in solitary confinement...."[40]

In addition to age-related and chronic health issues, the extraordinarily high mortality rates among nursing home patients can be traced to quality-of-care issues that were already plaguing nursing homes and similar long-term care facilities. Many of these facilities have long histories of struggling with staff shortages, even in the best of times. Prior to the pandemic's arrival in the New York-New Jersey area, the nursing home where the 17 bodies were found (Andover Subacute and Rehabilitation II) had struggled to meet minimum regulatory standards. It had recently got a one-star rating (out of a possible 5) of "much below average" from Medicare for staffing levels, inspections, and patient care.[41]

Nursing homes and extended care facilities also have always been the poor step-sisters of the health care system. Staff members are generally paid less and receive less extensive training than their counterparts in hospitals. Many nursing assistants make less than $15 an hour, and there is high staff turnover. About 700,000 certified nursing assistants (CNAs) work at nursing homes, according to the National Association of Health Care Assistants.[42] They make up the majority of care workers at nursing homes. Unlike hospitals, nursing homes are not meant to provide critical care, and registered and licensed practical nurses, who hold higher-level positions, are far outnumbered by low-skilled care workers.

These low-income nursing home employees also often have multiple jobs, and when they return home, they are often returning to disadvantaged communities where there is a greater risk of contracting the virus. So when CNAs go to work in a nursing home, often without protective equipment, they are being asked to move from room to room on a frequent basis, which optimizes the conditions for the widespread transfer of the virus.

When the coronavirus crisis hit, many health care workers at nursing homes and long-term care facilities simply stopped showing up for work. They were either themselves infected, or they feared, with good reason, they would become infected if they went to work. In California, 83 patients with the virus had to be evacuated from a nursing facility in Riverside County after only one of 13 scheduled CNAs showed up for work.[43] Sixteen employees and dozens of patients at this facility had tested positive days earlier.[44]

Canterbury Rehabilitation and Healthcare Center in Richmond, Virginia also struggled to hire and retain nursing staff. In addition to a scarcity of protective equipment, there was very little testing equipment available. Consequently, it was impossible to determine which residents and staff members were infected and which ones were still healthy.[45] By the time local public health officials were able to test everyone, after a delay of several weeks, more than 60 residents had tested positive, including some who did not show symptoms.[46] At least 46 of the facility's estimated 160 residents died from the virus, making it one of the deadliest nursing home case studies in the country.[47]

At a nursing home outside Nashville, Tennessee, nursing home workers recently reported working 12-hour shifts six days per week, caring for between 13 to 18 elderly residents per shift.[48] Nursing aides at this facility were provided with only a single cloth face mask for each shift, with no protective gowns or N95 face masks.[49] These workers lived and worked in daily fear that, with insufficient protective equipment, a single asymptomatic resident or staff member could trigger a contagion throughout the entire facility. "We are so up close to the residents, in their faces doing their care," one nursing assistant said. "They are touching us. How are we going to stop it?"[50]

The lack of masks and other protective equipment was the most cited reason why health care workers were not showing up for work at nursing homes. "We don't have what we need to stop this," said Mark Parkinson, adding, "We have got to have masks."[51]

In addition to staff shortages, nursing homes throughout the country were reporting a severe shortage of masks and protective gear. Without such protective equipment, the nursing home staff members were unable to prevent or slow the spread of the virus to the elderly patients and still-healthy staff. There was even a severe shortage of body bags since many of the victims were left to die at the nursing home rather than being transferred to hospitals. Nursing home operators often were asked by overwhelmed hospitals to keep extremely ill patients at the nursing homes. In some cases, this was due to a shortage of available hospital beds. In other cases, however, severely ill nursing home residents were not moved to hospitals since it was believed such transfers would be futile, given the fact that most elderly patients being intubated and put on respirators were dying anyway.[52] Governor Andrew Cuomo recently estimated that only 20% of coronavirus patients placed on ventilators "will ever come off." [53]

Most of the nursing homes and long-term care facilities in New York and New Jersey were soon reeling from the devastating impact on their staff and residents. At Crown Heights Center for Nursing and Rehabilitation in Brooklyn, workers said they had to convert a room into a makeshift morgue after more than 15 residents died of the coronavirus in rapid succession.[54] They said they had contacted local funeral homes, but they could not handle all the bodies.[55] At Elizabeth Nursing and Rehabilitation Center in New Jersey, 19 deaths were linked to the virus, and of the 54 residents who remained, 44 were already sick.[56] After 13 people died in an outbreak at the New Jersey Veterans Home in Paramus, Governor Phil Murphy called in 40 combat medics from the National Guard.[57]

As the virus spread, some nursing homes went into total denial, unable to cope with the growing number of seriously ill patients in their facilities. They also did not want to "alarm" residents or their families. Promises of "transparency" quickly devolved into miscommunications with patients and families, and in some cases, facility administrators just completely stopped all communications.

Even when there was some PPE available, some facilities instructed workers not to wear protective gowns or masks so as not to "unduly worry" the patients. Staff members at Alaris Health at Hamilton Park, a 260-bed home in Jersey City, said they were instructed to tell family members that even though a patient there had tested positive for COVID-19, there was no cause for alarm. "Everything is fine," the script read, according to the handout, "We are closely monitoring all residents and staff of any signs of illness…."[58] Such reckless actions led, of course, to an even more rapid spread of the contagion among the nursing homes' staff and patient populations.

Although there was a general shortage of PPE, this shortage hit nursing homes and extended care facilities particularly hard since they were at the bottom of the pecking order when it comes to the doling out of supplies to health care facilities. Whatever scarce equipment was available was routed first to hospitals and acute care facilities. But even when the supply needs of the hospitals started being met, chronic supply shortages still continued to be reported by nursing home facilities. As explained by Scott LaRue, the chief executive of ArchCare, which operates five nursing homes in New York: "The story is not about whether there's COVID-19 in the nursing homes," he said, "The story is, why aren't they being treated with the same respect and the same resources that everyone else out there is? It's ridiculous."[59]

There is overwhelming evidence that nursing home workers are being treated completely differently than their counterparts in hospitals. While hospital workers have received well-deserved recognition as the heroes that they are, nursing home workers are largely being ignored and treated as second or third-class citizens. When hospital workers get sick, they are immediately tested for coronavirus and told to stay home until they recover, whatever their illness might be. Nursing home workers, by contrast, are rarely tested, and many of them are told to report for work even if they may be ill. "Care staff are getting sick, but they can't afford to stay home," said Richard Mollot. "They take an aspirin, and they go to work."[60]

One reason nursing homes are so vulnerable is that they were not the initial focus of the federal coronavirus response, which prioritized hospitals. According to Elaine Ryan, vice president of government affairs for state advocacy at AARP, "In many ways, nursing homes were unfairly a second priority for receiving personal protective equipment," she said, "Federal and state governments did not make them a priority, and that resulted in thousands of people losing their lives."[61]

Sterling Harders, president of SEIU 775, a labor union that represents health care workers in Washington and Montana, said nursing home caregivers are using the same N95 masks for up to a week when taking care of COVID-19 patients.[62] At one facility, Harders said workers are sterilizing the masks with a disinfectant that causes rashes on their faces.[63] Prior to the outbreak, the reuse of N95 masks would have violated CDC guidelines, but those guidelines were relaxed to conserve supplies during the pandemic.

"Our society is telling these workers, who are mostly women, women of color, and immigrants, that they are essential," Harders said, "Yet we are not paying a living wage, and we are not giving them the basic supplies they need to do their work safely."[64]

Connecticut Nursing Home Deaths Skyrocket Out of Control

One of the hardest-hit states in terms of nursing home deaths was Connecticut, where nursing home deaths comprised 60% of the overall deaths reported in the state from COVID-19, and in some weeks, nursing home deaths represented 90% of the state's coronavirus-related deaths.[65] This nursing home crisis led to a behind-the-scenes struggle between Connecticut Gov. Ned Lamont and his state health commissioner over how best to solve this problem, which was plaguing other states, but not as badly as in Connecticut.[66] On May 11, Gov. Lamont fired his health commissioner, Renee Coleman-Mitchell, who had been advocating a plan that called for segregating nursing home residents with the virus in long-term care facilities that would house only those who were infected.[67] But the plan was rejected by Gov. Lamont because it was never vetted with other public health experts, including the state epidemiologist. The plan would have required transferring healthy residents out of nursing homes to make room for infected patients, which was objected to by many relatives of nursing home residents who opposed having their family members displaced.

Instead, Connecticut established so-called recovery centers to isolate nursing home residents who had the virus and had been released from the hospital, a relatively novel approach that drew praise from public health specialists.[68] This approach seemed to be a more effective one than Gov. Andrew Cuomo's initial approach, which was to require that nursing homes accept coronavirus patients after they were released from hospitals, a position which was then reversed after the plan met with fierce opposition over the danger of infected patients being admitted to nursing homes and then spreading the virus infection within those facilities.

New York and the Other States Scramble to Tighten Up Their Nursing Home Regulations

Since the start of the coronavirus crisis, a rising storm of protest by desperately concerned family members and patient advocates has led, in many instances, to a greater degree of accountability by nursing home operators as well as state regulators. In New York State, health officials scrambled to keep pace with the cascade of emergencies arising in nursing homes and extended care facilities within their jurisdiction. They adopted a number of new regulations designed to provide increased protection for elderly residents and attempted to provide enhanced oversight of these facilities. For example, new regulations barred outside visitors and suspended all group meals and activities during the crisis; every worker also had to be tested for fever or respiratory symptoms at every shift.[69] Gary Holmes, a New York State Health Department spokesman, said that the state had acted quickly and aggressively to issue guidance specifically for these facilities on testing, infection control, environmental cleaning, staffing, visitation, admission, readmission, and outreach to residents and families."

On Tuesday, May 5, New York reported more than 1,700 previously undisclosed coronavirus deaths at nursing homes and adult care facilities in the state.[70] The new figures revealed a spike in nursing home deaths that includes people believed to have died from the coronavirus before their positive diagnosis could be confirmed.[71] At least 4,813 people died from the virus in New York nursing homes and care facilities since March 1, according to a count released by the state on Monday, May 4.[72] The exact number of nursing home and care facility deaths in the state is uncertain because the released tally does not include residents who were transferred to hospitals before dying. However, these numbers did show that 22 nursing homes, primarily in New York City and Long Island, had reported 40 or more virus-related deaths.[73] One nursing home alone, Parker Jewish Institute in Queens, reported the highest number of deaths, with 71.[74]

In a Tuesday, May 5 press conference, Gov. Cuomo stated: "Nursing homes, we said from day one, are the most vulnerable place, because it's old people — senior people — who are the vulnerable people in a congregate setting."[75] Gov. Cuomo, however, said he did not know what the state could do to better protect nursing home residents going forward, adding, "It's something we're studying. We're also doing an investigation with the attorney general to look at it." [76]At about the same time, Maryland announced that it required coronavirus testing for all nursing home residents.[77]

On Sunday, May 10, Gov. Cuomo held another press briefing, announcing new rules and restrictions to protect nursing homes from the coronavirus.[78] By then, COVID-19 had killed at least 5,380 residents and workers in New York.[79] Gov. Cuomo was facing mounting public outrage as to why more was not being done to protect vulnerable nursing home residents from the coronavirus onslaught. In particular, Gov. Cuomo was criticized for making the "no-visitation" rules so restrictive that they prevented ombudsmen from visiting nursing homes. Ombudsmen are government-appointed advocates for nursing home patients.[80]

Even prior to the May 10 press conference, New York nursing homes had already been required to transfer patients to another facility if they were unable to fully care for them with appropriate staffing, PPE, and quarantine capacity.[81] On May 10, Gov. Cuomo announced that these same rules would apply for homes that were not able to care properly for patients testing positive for COVID-19. Gov. Cuomo also announced:

- Nursing home staffs must be tested for the coronavirus twice a week;
- Hospitals would no longer be permitted to discharge a patient to a nursing home unless they tested negative for the coronavirus; and
- Nursing homes that do not follow the procedures would lose their state licenses.[82]

New York regulations previously prohibited nursing homes from denying the admission of patients on the grounds that they tested positive for the coronavirus, which state Senate Republicans criticized as having been responsible for infected patients from hospitals to have "imported the virus into places that house New York's most vulnerable."[83] New York rescinded and reversed this regulation, announcing instead that the state was no longer allowing hospitals to discharge patients to nursing homes unless they tested negative for COVID-19.[84]

At his May 10 press conference, Gov. Cuomo defended the state policy of rescinding the license of any nursing home that did not follow these new regulations, underscoring his "get tough" policy regarding nursing homeowners and operators, saying:

> This virus uses nursing homes. They are ground zero. They are the vulnerable population in a vulnerable location. It's a congregation of vulnerable people . . . If a nursing home operator does not follow these procedures, they will lose their license. Well, that's harsh. No. Harsh is having a nursing home resident who doesn't get the appropriate care. That's what's harsh.[85]

New Jersey's health commissioner also claimed that the state had moved quickly to house sick people in separate hallways or wings, and to address outbreaks by enforcing strict protocols. In fact, an entire New Jersey nursing home was evacuated, and 94 of its residents were relocated to a facility about a half-hour away after dozens of its residents and staff members tested positive for the virus.[86] New Jersey officials also urged facilities to create separate sections so that there was a firewall between those who were infected and those who were not.[87]

But serious questions have been raised by families of nursing home residents and patient advocates as to whether the tightening of state regulations will really change anything amid equipment shortages and the confusion surrounding the coronavirus response. LaDawn Chapman, a CNA, lamented: "It's so many deaths," she said, adding, "We're losing people left and right."[88] Staff members said that so many workers had fallen ill, supervisors were imploring them to come to work even if they were sick. "You had it for weeks already," one supervisor complained in a text to a sick worker, suggesting that the worker come back to work regardless of whether she was still sick or not.[89]

Veterans' Homes And Their Residents Are Decimated By Coronavirus

While nursing homes throughout the U.S. were hit hard by the coronavirus, many of the nursing homes hit the hardest were the state-run veterans nursing homes.[90] By April 15, veterans homes in 16 states had reported at least one case of the virus, according to Mark Bowman, president of the National Association of State Veterans Homes.[91]

One of the hardest-hit veterans' nursing homes was the Holyoke Soldiers' Home in Massachusetts, where 70 residents were reported to have died there of the virus.[92] The state government and the U.S. Justice Department immediately launched an investigation as to whether the nursing home's administration had been negligent in its response. There were also reports of 45 positive cases of the coronavirus in two of Alabama's four veterans homes.[93]

One of the most horrendous incidents occurred at the New Jersey Veterans Home in Paramus, a state-run home for former members of the U.S. military.[94] The home was established on the idea that those who served in the military are entitled to dignified care in their twilight years. What these aging veterans got instead was one of the largest coronavirus outbreaks in the country. The virus swept through the facility, which in late March had 314 residents, infecting 60% of its patients.[95] As of May 10, there were 74 reported deaths, all linked to the virus.[96] Of the remaining 209 veterans and their spouses, 133 had either tested positive for the virus or were awaiting results.[97] About one in five staff members has contracted the virus, and one employee died.[98] "The whole place is sick now," said Mitchell Haber, whose 91-year-old father, Arnold, an Army veteran, died at the home, "What they should really do is raze it and put a park there," he said. "It's like a mass shooting."[99]

About 35 miles south of the Paramus veterans home is another state-run home for veterans in Edison, New Jersey, which had 57 coronavirus-related deaths as of May 10.[100] An official who oversaw both homes for the state's Department of Military and Veterans Affairs, Mark Piterski, resigned after announcing that he intended to run for Congress.[101] Mr. Piterski said he had struggled to maintain staffing levels at the nursing home when 100 employees a day were calling out sick.[102] He said he had asked for help repeatedly but to no avail.[103] Two congressmen and the New Jersey commander of the Veterans of Foreign Wars demanded that a federal inquiry be launched. The state's attorney general, Gurbir S. Grewal, also opened an investigation into these veterans nursing homes and other similar facilities with high fatality rates.[104]

Families of veterans who died at the Paramus home and at other similar homes for veterans questioned how things went so horribly wrong so quickly, and why they were not told earlier about the severity of the problem. "They really kind of held the truth from everyone," said Stephen Mastropietro, whose 91-year-old father, Thomas, died at the home last month after testing positive for the virus. "They said that they had a case, but in another part of the hospital," he said, "Then 20-something people died that week."[105]

Cynthia Petersen's 91-year-old father, Harold, an Army sergeant during the Korean War, was also at the Paramus home. She said she got a call recently from the nursing home that focused not on his health, but on a billing dispute over her request for documentation related to doctors' visits last year. She could not believe they were calling her about a billing issues when most of the residents' lives at the home were in peril. "You have 230 patients, most of whom are sick, and you think you have time to spend on the phone with me?" she said, "I asked them: 'How did this get so out of control?'"[106]

New Jersey did not require nursing home staff members to wear masks until March 30, and relatives said their loved ones were routinely brought to sit in common areas at the start of the outbreak.[107] According to the residents' families, little or no information about the virus was shared with them until the first wave of deaths prompted Governor Murphy to dispatch 40 Army National Guard medics to the home.[108]

Preparing Nursing Homes for the Next Crisis

As a result of the recent crisis, nursing homes have started to receive the close public and regulatory attention that they deserve, although the precipitating cause for this increased scrutiny has unfortunately been the massive death toll among nursing home residents. Hopefully, these outcries for the provision of sufficient PPE supplies to protect nursing home workers from getting infected or passing on infections to residents will carry over into the normal practices of the nursing homes, rather than just applying on an emergency basis. There have also been calls for sufficient testing kits and equipment to test all nursing home staff members and residents, but given the general lack of testing equipment, it is unlikely that this will happen until nursing home residents become the priorities for protection they so richly deserve.

In addition, the emergency regulations that have been issued by HHS's Centers for Medicare and Medicaid Services (CMS) and state health departments will be of little long-term value unless they continue to be strictly enforced on an ongoing basis. As a good first step, the Kirkland facility in the Seattle-area that had reported two dozen coronavirus deaths was assessed a fine of over $600,000.[109] It also lost its federal funding for failure to follow federal guidelines for the protection and care of its patients.[110] Among other things, Kirkland failed to have emergency physician services available 24-hours a day or have an emergency plan in place when a physician is "unavailable to assist with a high volume of residents during a crisis situation."[111]

Now that the longstanding neglect of the elderly in this country has begun to receive the national attention it deserves as a result of the coronavirus crisis, there is an opportunity that long overdue reforms may finally be instituted. Meanwhile, in the short term, thousands of more needless deaths can hopefully be prevented through the immediate supply of sufficient PPE and testing kits to all nursing homes nationwide. Only with an adequate supply of protective gear and increased testing capacity can every nursing home staff member and resident be tested on a daily or at least regular basis. Nursing homes must also be required to send daily reports to CMS and state health departments certifying that adequate PPE is being used and that the testing kits are actually being used. Nursing homes and extended care facilities should also be required to supply a daily or at least biweekly roster of all patients/residents, identifying which ones have tested positive for COVID-19.

Once the worst of the crisis is over, other critical long-term regulatory changes must also be instituted. Only then can nursing homes and long term care facilities be prepared when the next public health crisis hits. For example, PPE and testing equipment must be required to be stored and stockpiled at the facilities, or at state and local storage facilities, so that the necessary equipment is available *before* another crisis hits, not after. In addition, the long overdue issues of health care worker compensation and training must be addressed. In fact, the American Health Care Association has sounded the alarm for years about an underpaid workforce.[112] "This issue will not be fixed overnight," it said, "Once we get through this pandemic, we need Congress to support innovative programs that will help recruit, retain, and attract people to work in long term care to ensure our nation can support the needs of our residents and patients."[113]

The Service Employees International Union (SEIU), which represents more than 10,000 workers at 100 nursing homes, most of them in the Chicago area, has also highlighted the scandalous underpayment of its nursing home workers.[114] Many of the union members are paid only the required minimum wage of $13 per hour while being asked to put their lives and health at risk caring for this critically vulnerable population.[115] Shaba Andrich of the union's nursing home division said these workers are seeking at least $15 an hour and hazard pay for working during the pandemic.[116] The workers are also demanding improved staffing, better training, and more personal protective equipment. Ms. Andrich explained: "They were already struggling to take care of their families [before the current crisis hit]," adding, "We're asking nursing homes to step up and do what's right."[117]

Providing for the safety of the elderly in this public health care crisis, and preparing properly for the next one, is not only the right thing to do, but it is also vital for our future. How we treat the elderly says much about our society. Applying this standard to how we have left our nursing home residents needlessly exposed to infection and death during this crisis does not reflect well on us. And even from a purely self-interested vantage point, those of us who do not yet qualify as "senior citizens" will – with a little luck – make it there someday. It sure beats the alternative!

17

THE PERSONAL PROTECTIVE EQUIPMENT CRISIS AND DARWINIAN FEDERALISM

Why Are Those Nurses Wearing Garbage Bags?
– unidentified patient, Elmhurst Hospital, Queens, New York

In his debut appearance at the White House daily briefing on April 2, Trump's son-in-law Jared Kushner publicly accused some state governors of requesting coronavirus response supplies from the federal government without knowing what they really needed.[1] Kushner further suggested that the governors were not resourceful enough to find the necessary equipment themselves.

Other than the fact that Jared was married to Trump's daughter Ivanka,[2] Kushner had absolutely no credentials to play a leadership role in the country's coronavirus response effort. Nor did he have any qualifications to lecture the nation's governors on their ability to procure desperately needed supplies on behalf of their states. Kushner – like Trump himself – had a real estate magnate for a father, but this hardly qualified him to be a Senior Advisor to the president. Kushner's only prior experience before following Trump to the White House was as a real estate developer and failed newspaper publisher. He had no medical background or experience with supply chain logistics, and he had no experience in government before his father-in-law's election in 2016.

Soon dubbed "Secretary of Everything,"[3] Kushner was assigned, among other things, to solve the seemingly intractable Israeli-Palestinian "problem."[4] As if that was not enough, Jared was also put in charge of improving relations with Mexico, negotiations with China, overseeing government innovation, and facilitating criminal justice reform.[5] When his Mideast Peace Plan was unveiled with much fanfare, it was, not surprisingly, panned by most experts. One expert described Kushner's plan as "the Monty Python sketch of Israeli-Palestinian peace initiatives."[6] Undeterred, Kushner got on a call with Arab and Israeli reporters, insisting that his vision was "100% workable" if only the Palestinian leadership would stop being so "hysterical and stupid."[7] Not the kind of language you would expect from someone on a sensitive diplomatic mission.

After Kushner's string of insults and attacks on Palestinian leadership was widely publicized, Trump belatedly realized that this "Boy Prince of New Jersey" might not be cut out for the diplomacy business after all. Trump, therefore, decided it was time for his son-in-law to move on to solving some easier problems – such as organizing the U.S.'s coronavirus response effort. But this new project did not work out very well either.

True to form, Kushner's attack on state governors at the April 2 press briefing was about as un-diplomatic as his prior attacks on the Palestinian leadership. Kushner's opening gambit was to misrepresent the purpose of the federal government's stockpile of equipment. During the briefing, he described the federal reserve as "our stockpile," insinuating that it was the White House's property, not that of the American people.[8] "It's not supposed to be state stockpiles that they then use," Kushner insisted.[9] However, according to the U.S. Department of Health and Human Services (HHS) website, the Strategic National Stockpile "is to supplement state and local supplies during public health emergencies."[10] This definition on the website was, however, revised later in the day to conform to Kushner's novel theory that it was only supposed to be "our stockpile."[11]

Kushner also could not resist lecturing the state governors on what he perceived was their incompetence, noting that some leaders are "better managers than others."[12] "Some governors you speak to . . . they don't know what's in their state," he commented.[13]

Unaware (or undeterred) that his son-in-law's performance was triggering a storm of negative reaction, Trump doubled down on Kushner's new line of attack on Democratic "blue state" governors. Following up on Kushner's critique of the governors for having failed to prepare for the crisis properly, Trump said, "We're a backup. We're not an ordering clerk."[14]

Darwinian Federalism

Trump had previously touched on the subject of federal-state relations at a March 30 press conference. "We are letting governors do, in their states, pretty much what they want with our supervision," he told reporters in the Rose Garden.[15] "And they consult with us in all cases. Some go further than others, as you know. I could give you plenty of examples, but I am not going to do that because we never want to be controversial."[16]

Although the reviews of Kushner's performance were universally negative (except on Fox News), Trump appeared to be pleased with Kushner's defense of the indefensible. He forcefully pushed back against the barrage of criticism and negative press that Trump had been receiving. These well-founded critiques were based on the undeniable fact that the federal government was not doing enough to assist the front-line hospitals in coronavirus hot zones that were being quickly overrun with COVID-19 patients. The hospitals were quickly running out of PPE, ventilators, and other critical supplies. Indeed, there were reliable reports that New York nurses were wearing garbage bags for lack of surgical gowns.[17] Other protective equipment that had been promised by the federal government also was never received.[18]

The major takeaway from Kushner's remarks was that, overnight, the Trump White House had turned the pandemic into a reality-TV show competition. Just as the rivals in *The Apprentice* had to do battle to get Trump's approval, governors in every state were expected to compete with each other. The states also were competing with the federal government in a mad scramble to acquire medical supplies needed to test and treat coronavirus patients.[19]

This divide-and-conquer approach was undoubtedly designed to deflect attention from the federal government's pitiful response to the crisis. However, some darker and more sinister forces may have also been at work. Trump and Kushner were signaling a fundamental shift in the traditional relationship between the federal government and the states since the country's founding. This change marked a shift to a new type of federalism.

Trump's new theory of the U.S. government's relationship with the states can best be described as "Darwinian (or *Hunger Games*) federalism."[20]

This strategy calls, first, for the federal government to hold back its resources, waiting to see who were the winners and who were the losers among the states competing for scarce global supplies. The second stage would then be to dole out the federal supplies on a patronage-type basis. The only states that would get the sorely needed medical supplies would be those governors who lavished praise and gave proper thanks to President Trump for his beneficence.

Senior Trump administration aides quickly picked up Trump's Darwinian federalist theme. They argued the coronavirus response was not a test of Trump's national leadership. Instead, they argued it was a test of the leaders of the states and cities to find their way out of the crisis. Since the White House and the rest of the federal government was only there to provide "back up" to the states, it was up to the governor to determine their own state's fate on their own.[21]

Leading Democrats, of course, vocally rejected this approach. "That is a Darwinian approach to federalism; that is states' rights taken to a deadly extreme," commented Martin O'Malley, the former Maryland governor.[22] O'Malley added: "The better read of federalism is that the states and federal government work together when the U.S. is attacked, whether it is by imperial Japan or a pandemic."[23] He further noted that only the president had the power to invoke the Defense Production Act, how to allocate the federal stockpiles, and how to give FEMA reserves.

Kushner's "Shadow Task Force"

Weeks before his debut at the April 2 press conference, Kushner also had been tasked by Trump with forming a "shadow task force."[24] The group would operate separately from the official coronavirus task force headed by Vice President Pence. Kushner already had reached out to high tech companies in Silicon Valley to brainstorm about websites, apps, and other tech solutions to the coronavirus problem. Kushner's "shadow task force" was supposed to get supplies and resources to the hotspots which most urgently needed them before they hit their peaks. But this didn't happen.

The Kushner team was also supposed to help volunteer organizations around the country transport the supplies they had to where they were most needed. The most prominent of these volunteer groups was a coalition of grassroots organizations informally known as the "PPE Coalition." The alliance included colorfully named groups like "Operation We Can Sew It to Get Them PPE."[25] The organizations were linked through various websites and prepared to ship their supplies to wherever they were needed. These groups were reassured by Kushner and other members of his "shadow team" that FEMA would coordinate the shipment of their critical supplies to where they were most needed.[26] But this never happened either.

Kushner and his team just dropped the ball, leaving thousands of well-intentioned Americans and their volunteer organizations in the lurch. One of the volunteers, Jennifer Pahlka, kept trying to reassure herself and other volunteers, saying, "There's no way we should be doing this alone."[27] Pahlka, who had founded the tech group "Code for America," served as deputy chief technology officer in the Obama White House. Now helping with a coronavirus-relief group, U.S. Digital Response, Pahlka explained: "In our community, we have sweatshirts and T-shirts and stickers that said, 'No one is coming. It's up to us.'"[28] They, of course, never thought this was true and that the slogan "No one is coming" was just a slogan, and the federal cavalry would come riding in to save the day.[29] That's what General Custer may have also thought would happen at Little Big Horn.

Meanwhile, Kushner and his team were well embedded at FEMA. They were supposed to report to Navy Rear Admiral John Polowczyk, who took the lead at FEMA, overseeing the supply-chain problems.[30] These problems had significantly held up the federal government's coronavirus response efforts. However, it appears that Kushner failed to inform Polowczyk that he had recruited eight junior analysts from Insight Partners, a New York–based investment fund.[31] Kushner assigned them to work at FEMA's headquarters to help source protective gear and test kits for medical workers from vendors.[32] But when these volunteers started using their personal Gmail accounts in their communications with vendors, many vendors suspected they were being "scammed." The unprofessional emails led to a flurry of urgent phone calls to FEMA to see whether Kushner's people were authentic and had the authority to speak on behalf of FEMA.[33] In one case, FEMA advised a vendor to report the contact to the police, not realizing at the time that the email had come from one of the volunteers.[34]

The FEMA volunteer program was conceived by both Kushner and Adam Boehler, chief executive of the U.S. International Development Finance Corp.[35] Kushner and Boehler had met during a summer college program a couple of decades ago. Once the coronavirus outbreaks erupted in the U.S., they got together over a drink to come up with a solution to the crisis. The more they talked, the more they became convinced that they needed to take charge of the federal government's sputtering coronavirus response efforts. Their plan was to show America how private enterprise could provide the initiative to jump start these foundering efforts while, at the same time, identifying lucrative investment and acquisition opportunities.

What they did not plan on, however, was that the Wall Street volunteers had only agreed to work for a couple of weeks, which was hardly enough time to get anything accomplished. The Wall Street volunteers packed up and left FEMA headquarters by April 10.[36] This meant that, as pressure on FEMA intensified during April to get much-needed supplies from vendors to the states, the Kushner team was already gone.

Even while Kushner's Wall Street volunteers were still working at FEMA, their work was heavily influenced by political cronyism. In fact, they were directed to basically ignore offers of needed equipment that came from sources who lacked sufficient political connections with Kushner and the White House.[37] Instead, they were told to prioritize tips from political cronies and associates of President Trump. These priority tips were tracked on a spreadsheet called "V.I.P. Update," according to a *New York Times* investigation.[38] Among these tips from VIPs were leads from Republican members of Congress, as well as from the Trump youth activist, Charlie Kirk, and a former "Apprentice" contestant.[39] A Pennsylvania dentist once featured at a Trump rally is also reported to have dropped the president's name as he pushed the agency to procure test kits from his associates.[40] As the *Times* report concluded, Kushner's FEMA involvement was typical of Trump's style of governing, "in which personal relationships and loyalty are often prized over governmental expertise, and private interests are granted extraordinary access and deference."[41]

Trump and Kushner's penchant for mixing public and private interests created irreconcilable conflicts of interest that would have been enough to bring down almost any other federal administration in U.S. history. For example, the so-called Teapot Dome Scandal almost crippled the administration of President Warren G. Harding during the period from 1921 to 1923. Often referred to as the greatest and most sensational scandal in American history prior to Watergate,[42] this Senate investigation led by Senator Thomas J. Walsh focused on the lease of Navy petroleum reserves at Teapot Dome in Wyoming, as well as two locations in California, to private companies without competitive bidding. Secretary of the Interior Albert Bacon Fall was convicted on charges of accepting bribes from the oil companies, earning him the dubious distinction of becoming the first presidential cabinet member to go to prison.

Not only did the efforts of Kushner's shadow task force reek of conflicts of interest and "no-bid" political cronyism in the dispensation of federal contract monies, but the sole focus on following up on "VIP tips" actually impeded FEMA's otherwise legitimate response efforts. In late March, two of the Kushner volunteers passed along procurement forms submitted by Yaron Oren-Pines, a Silicon Valley engineer who said he could provide more than 1,000 ventilators. These forms were forwarded to senior officials in New York, who assumed the Kushner group at FEMA had vetted Mr. Oren-Pines, which was not the case. Oren-Pines' only qualification that had been checked was that his name appeared on the "VIP list" that the volunteers were given. New York awarded him a contract and paid him $69 million, but never received any of the desperately needed ventilators that had already been paid for.[43] This was at a time when New York started "splitting" ventilators, with two patients being forced to share the same ventilator due to the ventilator shortage.[44]

Meanwhile, legitimate tips were being ignored by FEMA and the Kushner team since the names of people and companies who were legitimate potential suppliers were not on the VIP list. For example, Dr. Jeffrey Hendricks, a South Carolina physician with longstanding manufacturing contacts in China, reached out to FEMA with an offer to help procure millions of face masks from established suppliers in China.[45] His offer was diverted to the Kushner volunteers, who never followed up.

Kushner's Wall Street volunteers at FEMA also assisted a politically-connected Pennsylvania dentist, Dr. Albert Hazzouri, who used his White House connections to repeatedly press FEMA officials to buy 100,000 test kits from a supplier in Mexico.[46] Dr. Hazzouri, a frequent visitor to the president's private Florida club at Mar-a-Lago, had been referred by Representative Brian Babin, a Texas Republican and die-hard Trump supporter.

In addition, some of Trump's associates sought special treatment from FEMA. Jeanine Pirro – a vocal Trump cheerleader and *Fox News* host – succeeded in using her Trump connections to get FEMA to divert 100,000 masks to her favorite hospital.[47]

The history of Kushner's amateurish FEMA project would be an amusing tale in more tranquil times. But in the midst of a life-and-death crisis, the consequences could be – and probably were – fatal. FEMA and the rest of the federal emergency response efforts were in shambles, even before the arrival of the volunteer Wall Street brigade. This was not an opportune time to turn major responsibilities over to private-sector volunteer reinforcements who are going to be leaving after a couple of weeks. This is especially true when the volunteers had no experience or expertise with supply-chain issues. Kushner's toxic brew of incompetence and cronyism meant that some sorely needed supplies from FEMA never made it in time to the coronavirus hot spots in New York, New Orleans, Detroit and elsewhere.

FEMA Fails to Deliver Critical Supplies In Advance of "Death Week"

By the end of March, the FEMA response effort and that of other federal agencies were being accurately described by the *Associated Press* as "a fragmented procurement system now descending into chaos."[48] Not a single shipment of medical-grade N95 masks arrived in the U.S. during March.[49] Incredibly – and unforgivably – the federal government did not even begin placing bulk orders for the urgently needed supplies until mid-March. It was not until March 21 that the first large U.S. government order was placed with one of the largest U.S. producers, 3M. This $173 million order was for N95 masks.[50] The order did not require supplies to be delivered until the end of April, far too late to help with the thousands of cases already overwhelming hospitals in New York, New Orleans, Detroit, and elsewhere.[51]

In late March and early April, when FEMA started becoming involved in the supply procurement issues, FEMA's efforts came into conflict with those of some of the states. Trump and others in his administration had told the states that they should go out and buy their PPE and other medical equipment that they needed. Now FEMA started raiding the supplies that the states were able to procure. In Massachusetts, for example, a large order by that state for personal protective equipment for their health workers was, in essence, confiscated and seized by FEMA.[52] In Kentucky, the head of a hospital system told Congress his broker canceled an order of four shipments of medical gear after FEMA commandeered the supplies.[53] Meanwhile, Gov. Jared Polis of Colorado thought his state had secured 500 ventilators before they were "swept up by FEMA."[54] In other words, it seemed as if FEMA's belated efforts were causing more harm than good.

On Monday, April 6, the Inspector General for HHS released a survey of 323 hospitals in 46 states, D.C., and Puerto Rico, finding "widespread shortages of PPE" and also other equipment, such as ventilators and masks.[55] This shortage could not have come at a worse time, since the week of April 6 was expected to be the peak "death" week in hot spots such as New York, New Jersey, Connecticut, and Michigan. Brett Giroir, HHS assistant secretary for health, predicted: "It's going to be the peak hospitalization, peak ICU week and, unfortunately, peak death week."[56]

According to the HHS Inspector General's report: "One hospital reported receiving a shipment of 2,300 N95 masks from a state strategic reserve, but the masks were not useable. The elastic bands had dry-rotted."[57] Hospitals also had severe shortages of testing supplies and extended waits for test results, which limited the hospitals' ability to monitor the health of patients and staff.[58] "Hospitals reported that they were unable to keep up with COVID-19 testing demands because they lacked testing kits, or they lacked the swabs, reagents, and other materials needed to complete the tests."[59]

In support of its conclusions, the 41-page report cited several specific examples of the federal government's lack of pandemic preparedness. One hospital reported receiving two shipments of PPE supplies that had expired a decade earlier.[60] It turned out that some of the masks were not N95 masks at all, but rather construction masks.[61] Another health system reported that it had received 1,000 masks, but that it desperately needed a much larger resupply.[62] Further, 500 of the 1,000 masks received were for children and, therefore, unusable by the health system's adult staff.[63] Another hospital administration told HHS assistant inspector general Ann Maxwell that, due to the shortages, some of the hospital staff were sent into the neighborhood to procure masks and gloves from auto part shops. They also "shopped" for supplies at home supply stores, beauty salons, and art supply stores.[64]

After the Inspector General's report was released, Trump's reflexive reaction was to attack it, tweeting that it was "Another Fake Dossier!"[65] He attacked the principal deputy Inspector General who prepared it, suggesting that she was politically biased since she had served during the Obama Administration. Trump failed to note, however, that she had also served in the Clinton and Bush administrations.[66] On Friday, May 1, Trump announced that he was firing the HHS Inspector General, Christi Grimm, and that he was nominating a loyal (and presumably more compliant) replacement.[67]

The critical shortage of PPE and other equipment was inevitable and predictable. The Trump administration had frittered away the brief window of opportunity it had to properly mobilize all necessary resources to meet the required supply needs. On February 13, the Center for Global Development (CGD), a nonpartisan Washington think tank, warned in a report about the "urgent but closing window" for the U.S. government to prepare.[68] CGD urgently recommended (a) an immediate review of the PPE supply chain; (b) the creation of a plan for the distribution of supplies and the public communication of that plan; and (c) the development of "options for addressing PPE shortfalls," which ranged from increasing manufacturing to coming up with new "parameters for reuse in crisis conditions."[69] The recommendation was made in mid-February, a full month before Trump deputized Kushner to step in, and before the first orders for PPE and equipment went out.

Jeremy Konyndyk, who co-authored the CGD report, said he did not anticipate there would be such widespread confusion.[70] Within and outside the U.S. government, no one knew who was in charge of the federal government's pandemic response. Nor did anyone foresee that Trump would hold the states solely responsible for the lack of PPE.

The Trump Team "Misplaces" the Obama Pandemic Playbook

The Trump administration's abdication of federal responsibility was inconsistent with the approach to pandemics by every previous administration, both Democratic and Republican. The pandemic playbook developed during the Obama Administration, which was titled "Playbook for Early Response to High-Consequence Emerging Infectious Disease Threats and Biological Incidents," was intended to share the lessons learned during the Ebola and Zika outbreaks.[71] This 69-page National Security Council guidebook developed in 2016 had the stated goal of assisting administration officials "in coordinating a complex U.S. Government response to a high-consequence emerging disease threat anywhere in the world." It outlined questions to ask, who should be asked to get the answers, and what critical decisions should be made.[72]

After *Politico* first unearthed a copy of the Obama playbook in March,[73] Senate Majority Leader Mitch McConnell denied that the Obama administration had ever provided the Trump administration with any such information about the threat of a possible pandemic.[74] However, when the White House press secretary was forced to concede that the Trump team did, in fact, have a copy of the playbook, the White House took the fall back position that it was not very useful. Of course, if a playbook is not used, there is no way that it can be "useful."

Information also started leaking out about similar playbooks that were developed by the Obama administration for the CDC and HSS.[75] "To say there was no playbook was ridiculous," said Nicole Lurie, who served as the assistant secretary for preparedness and response at HHS during both terms of the Obama administration.[76]

The States Try to Fill the Leadership Vacuum

With no real alternative, the states were forced to take matters into their own hands. On April 7, California Governor Gavin Newsom announced a deal to spend nearly a billion dollars to buy two hundred million medical masks a month.[77] In New York, Governor Andrew Cuomo called for states to form a new consortium under the aegis of the National Governors Association, in order to buy the supplies the federal government told them to get on their own.[78] In a pandemic, Gov. Cuomo said, there needs to be a "master strategist" and chief "purchasing entity," and that would generally be the federal government.[79] The current status quo of cities and states bidding against one another, Gov. Cuomo added, was "just madness."[80]

However, the consortiums formed between and among states in the various regions of the country would come too late for New York City, New Orleans, and for the other cities that were the first epicenters of the pandemic. However, other towns, cities, and states who were not as far down the road of the pandemic cycle could hopefully benefit from the coordinated regional efforts by the state governors. The federal response effort either was never intended by Trump to be effective, or if it was so intended, the effort was hopelessly bungled. Either way, America paid a massive price for it.

The Trump administration's "leave it to the states" approach to federalism did not make a lot of sense in the context of a pandemic response. The virus certainly had no respect for borders between states. Trump's Darwinian Federalist approach was no doubt calculated to win over states with Republican-conservative governors. They were instinctively wary of federal government intervention and had taken a "go-slow" approach to social distancing.[81] Arizona Governor Doug Ducey, for example, permitted many small businesses, such as barbershops, to stay open.[82] In most other states, barbershops were closed. Meanwhile, Ron DeSantis, the Governor of Florida, made a name for himself on conservative media outlets for carving out exemptions for churches to continue to hold large gatherings.[83]

Trump's apparent haphazard approach to crisis management also helped out one of the most important segments of his "base," namely, big business. One good example of this was the comment made during a White House press conference by Rear Admiral Polowczyk, where the Admiral said that the ventilators and other equipment the Navy was airlifting from overseas would be turned over to private companies to sell to the highest bidder.[84] Polowczyk explained: "This product that we are moving is primarily a commercial product that would enter the commercial system and be distributed through financial business transactions between hospitals and these distributors."[85] But if ever there was a good time to disrupt the "business-as-usual" approach to the supply of critical medical equipment in a crisis, this was the time to do it. In March and April 2020, when the crisis was at its peak, only the federal government had the power to cut through the usual red tape and get the supplies to where they were most needed. But the Trump team seemed to lack any real sense of urgency.

The adage that "one man's misery is another man's opportunity" seems to have been the guiding principle for many of the decisions – or non-decisions – by the Trump White House. Former Obama official Andrew Slavitt reported that one of the governors told him that "FEMA is buying all the vents in the market. We can't buy any."[86] Slavitt also noted, "One of the governors is trying to buy them at $45,000 per ventilator. The typical cost is $15,000 per ventilator . . . They are all bidding against each other. State vs. state."[87]

Clearly, there was a lot of money to be made from the coronavirus response and disaster relief effort. But a catastrophe on this scale is not a time for wartime profiteering. During the Civil War, unscrupulous war profiteers made fortunes by selling recycled wool to be used for uniforms and making cardboard shoes that were then passed off as leather. This sad chapter in American history should not have been repeated in the coronavirus crisis. Unfortunately, profits seem to have taken precedence over principle at the Trump White House.

18

A TALE OF TWO CITIES: SAN FRANCISCO QUICKLY DECLARES A STATE OF EMERGENCY WHILE NEW YORK CITY DAWDLES

> *"It was the best of times, it was the worst of times …"*
> -Charles Dickens, A Tale of Two Cities

Both New York and San Francisco pride themselves on being staunchly progressive, championing environmental protection, the Green New Deal, LGBTQ+ rights, and a host of other cutting-edge social and political issues. You would expect, then, that these two cities would respond to the COVID-19 threat in a fairly similar and serious manner. Not so. This is a cautionary tale of two very different cities, one who acted quickly to recognize the pandemic for the serious threat that it posed to the health and public safety of its residents (San Francisco), while the other (New York) dithered and dawdled as the coronavirus stealthily attacked an unprepared city, wreaking death and destruction in its path.

London Breed, the 45th mayor of San Francisco, declared a state of emergency in San Francisco on February 25, 2020, even before any coronavirus case was reported within the city limits.[1] New York Mayor Bill de Blasio's declaration did not come until March 13.[2] The Bay Area counties (a nine-county area including San Francisco and Santa Clara counties) began issuing shelter-in-place orders on March 16, and California Governor Gavin Newsom implemented a mandate for the entire State on March 19.[3] New York's orders did not come until March 20, but the message to New Yorkers was garbled since New York Governor Andrew Cuomo and Mayor de Blasio had been publicly bickering for about a week over whether to shut down the City and the State, and if so, when.[4] De Blasio had told New York City residents to prepare for a stay-at-home order, but was vague about when it might actually be issued, while Governor Cuomo saw it primarily as a turf battle between himself and de Blasio, publicly warning the Mayor that only the State could shut down the City.[5] As a result, the gravity of the crisis was lost on most New Yorkers amidst the political squabbling.

The resulting COVID-19-related numbers were staggeringly divergent. By April 30, 2020, New York City had reported 4,571 deaths, while San Francisco meanwhile had only 25.[6] During this same time frame, there were 304,400 confirmed cases in New York State, and of those, 18,321 people have died as of April 30.[7] California, by comparison, had reported only 49,840 cases, with 2,014 deaths.[8] New York had the highest number of confirmed cases of any state in the U.S., with three times as many cases as neighboring New Jersey and seven times that of neighboring Pennsylvania. Most of New York State's cases occurred in New York City or its suburbs.[9]

The Bay Area (7.76 million) has roughly the same population as New York City (8.54 million), and they are both major urban areas. So, why did the Bay Area have so many fewer deaths from the coronavirus, as compared to New York? New York City's greater density may have something to do with the gross disparity in the numbers, as well as the fact that the Big Apple receives many more visitors from abroad. But the most significant factor is the difference in leadership between the two cities.

As the *New York Post* put it bluntly on April 9, 2020, New York Mayor de Blasio was slow and indecisive, while San Francisco Mayor London Breed demonstrating the kind of proactive leadership that, no doubt, saved countless lives in her city and in the Bay Area.[10]

Mayor de Blasio Fiddles While New York Burns

New York State had its first reported coronavirus case on March 1, 2020, which was a 39-year-old woman health care worker who lived in Manhattan.[11] She had returned from Iran on February 25 and had no symptoms at the time. She went into home isolation with her husband.[12] A second case appeared in New York on March 3, when a lawyer living in New Rochelle, twenty miles north of New York City, was confirmed as being infected with the virus.[13] This lawyer, who commuted to Manhattan and had an office near Grand Central Station, had traveled to Miami in February but had not visited areas known to have a widespread transmission of the coronavirus.

Two of his four children had recently returned from Israel. After first feeling ill on February 22, he was admitted to a hospital in Westchester on February 27, diagnosed with pneumonia, and released from isolation after testing negative for the flu.[14]

Even as San Francisco and other cities began taking increasingly drastic measures to slow the outbreak, Mayor de Blasio failed to take the crisis seriously. For example, he was furious as late as March 17 that the city's libraries planned to close and threatened to cut their budget in response.[15] De Blasio also initially refused to cancel the St. Patrick's Day parade, always held on March 17, claiming that the virus required "close physical proximity" beyond the level of a parade crowd to spread.[16] The event was canceled only after Mayor de Blasio confirmed on March 11 that 53 coronavirus cases had been reported in New York City.[17] And it was also widely reported that the day before bars, gyms, and restaurants closed statewide, Mayor de Blasio took a final trip to his own gym and urged New Yorkers to go out to local restaurants for one last night on the town.[18]

On March 4, the number of cases in New York State increased to eleven as nine people linked to the lawyer tested positive, including his wife, a son, a daughter, a neighbor, and a friend and his family.[19] On March 5, Mayor de Blasio said that coronavirus fears should not keep New Yorkers off the subway, riding from Fulton Street to High Street in a public press attempt to demonstrate the subway's safety.[20] On March 6, eleven new cases were reported, bringing the state caseload to 33.[21] All the new cases were tied to the first community transmission case, the lawyer.[22] At the end of the day, an additional 11 new cases were reported by the Governor, bringing the total caseload to 44, with 8 of the new cases in Westchester County and 3 in Nassau County on Long Island.[23] Also, on March 6, an article appeared in the *New York Post* stating that while Mayor de Blasio assigned responsibility for the lack of N95 masks and other personal protective equipment to the federal government, the City never ordered the supplies until that date.[24]

On March 10, de Blasio continued to give the New York public dangerously inaccurate information about the severity of COVID-19, saying in a comment similar to that articulated by President Trump – that "[t]his disease, even if you were to get it, basically acts like a common cold or flu."[25]

Consistent with the nonchalant attitude that Mayor de Blasio was communicating to the public about the coronavirus threat, New York City Commissioner of Health, Oxiris Barbot, seriously misled New Yorkers as to the dangers posed by the coronavirus, saying at a March 2 press conference that people can't contract coronavirus through casual, short-term exposure, but instead require prolonged exposure to the infected person's secretions.[26] The following day, on March 3, she further encouraged New Yorkers to let down their guard and, in fact, to ignore the coming coronavirus pandemic by stating: "We are encouraging New Yorkers to go about their everyday lives."[27] On March 4, she added: "There's no indication that being in a car, being in the subways with someone who's potentially sick is a risk factor."[28] On March 5, she said that New Yorkers without symptoms should not have to quarantine.[29] On March 20, Barbot shockingly discouraged New Yorkers not to use masks unless they were showing symptoms, saying:

> The time to use a mask is when someone is symptomatic, when they're coughing, when they're sneezing, and it's to ensure that that individual doesn't contaminate other folks. It gives people who are asymptomatic a false sense of security that if they wear this mask, they don't have to wash their hands, they don't have to cover their mouths and their noses when they cough or they sneeze.[30]

Two NYC Councilmen – Democrat Robert Holden and Republican Eric Ulrich – were so alarmed at Barbot's reckless and unprofessional statements that they wrote to Mayor de Blasio, asking him to relieve Barbot of her position "before it's too late," saying her comments on coronavirus were disastrous.[31]

Fortunately for New York, Governor Cuomo was taking the risks posed by coronavirus more seriously than Mayor de Blasio. On March 10, Gov. Cuomo announced a containment zone in the city of New Rochelle enforced by National Guard troops.[32] On March 12, Cuomo also announced restrictions on mass gatherings, directing events with more than 500 people to be canceled or postponed and any gathering with fewer than 500 people to cut capacity by 50%.[33] In addition, only medically necessary visits would be allowed at nursing homes.[34] Also on March 12, Cuomo announced that all Broadway theaters had been ordered to shut down by 5 p.m. that day, and that public gatherings in congregate spaces with more than 500 people were prohibited beginning 5 p.m. the following day.[35]

On March 14, the first two fatalities in the State occurred: an 82-year-old woman in Brooklyn with pre-existing emphysema died in the hospital,[36] and a 65-year-old person with other significant health problems who had not previously been tested for COVID-19 died at home in Suffern, Rockland County.[37]

Mayor de Blasio also inexcusably dragged his feet with regard to the closing of the enormous New York City school system. As late as March 13, the Mayor was still refusing to close New York City schools, despite pressure from parents, the teachers union, and some city council members to do so. De Blasio cited the school meals programs and child care needs as the rationale for keeping the schools open, continuing to downplay the risk of a rapid spread of the virus among schoolchildren and their families.[38] Finally, on March 15, Governor Cuomo decided the issue by announcing that New York City schools would close the following day and gave the city 24 hours to come up with a plan for child care and meals.[39] Public schools in Westchester, Suffolk, and Nassau counties closed on March 16.[40]

Mayor de Blasio also finally (and belatedly) announced that all schools, bars, and restaurants in the city were to be closed starting 9 a.m. on March 17, except for food takeout and delivery.[41] It quickly became public knowledge that the Mayor had to be pushed, practically kicking and screaming, to make the painfully obvious decision to shut down New York City's businesses. On March 16, The *New York Times* reported that for the prior week, the Mayor's "top aides were furiously trying to change the Mayor's approach to the coronavirus outbreak. There had been arguments and shouting matches between the Mayor and some of his advisers; some top health officials had even threatened to resign if he refused to accept the need to close schools and businesses, according to several people familiar with the internal discussions."[42]

On March 17, as the number of confirmed cases rose to 814 citywide, with seven deaths, Mayor de Blasio announced that the city was considering a similar shelter-in-place order within the next 48 hours.[43] De Blasio's comments were quickly rejected by Gov. Cuomo's office, and again later by the Governor himself in an interview with CNN's Jake Tapper.[44] Melissa DeRosa, secretary to the Governor, issued a statement during the Mayor's briefing, clarifying the state government was not considering shelter-in-place orders at the time.[45] Gov. Cuomo said later that morning, "We hear 'New York City is going to quarantine itself.' That is not true. That cannot happen. It cannot happen legally. No city in the state can quarantine itself without state approval. And I have no interest whatsoever and no plan whatsoever to quarantine any city."[46] On March 18, Gov. Cuomo reaffirmed that he would not approve a "shelter-in-place" order for New York City: "That is not going to happen, shelter in place, for New York City," Cuomo said, "For any city or county to take an emergency action, the state has to approve it. And I wouldn't approve shelter in place."[47]

On March 20, Mayor de Blasio – now a true believer in the lethality of coronavirus only after seeing New Yorkers starting to die off in exponentially increased numbers – called for drastic measures to combat the coronavirus outbreak: "We have to go to a shelter-in-place model," he said, praising California's "stay at home" model.[48]

Finally, Gov. Cuomo announced a statewide stay-at-home order, also known as the "NYS on Pause Program," with a mandate that all non-essential workers work from home beginning at 8 p.m. on March 22.[49] Only businesses declared as essential by the program were allowed to remain open.

On March 24, Gov. Cuomo warned that New York hospitals and health care workers were running short of critical supplies, such as personal protective equipment and ventilators, and that the City and State were rapidly approaching a breaking point, with 25,000 cases and at least 210 deaths.[50] He also complained that the State desperately needed assistance from the federal government.

On March 26, the crisis in New York sharply accelerated to the point where Governor Cuomo felt compelled to announce that the state would, on an emergency basis, allow two patients to share one ventilator using a technique he called "splitting," where a second set of tubes would be added to the ventilator.[51] COVID-19 patients generally needed ventilators for between 11 and 21 days, while under normal circumstances, patients usually only required them for three to four days. Gov. Cuomo also said the state was considering converting anesthesia machines to use as ventilators.[52] In the 24 hour period between March 25 and March 26, there were 100 deaths statewide, with the number of hospitalized patients skyrocketing by 40 percent in New York City.[53] Meanwhile, the NYC Mayor said that the city would run out of supplies by April if the federal government did not send 3 million N95 masks, 50 million surgical masks, 15,000 ventilators, and 45 million surgical gowns, gloves, and face shields.[54] Some EMS workers expressed frustration at being asked to wear the less-effective surgical masks.[55]

By late March, the situation at Elmhurst Hospital Center in Queens, New York was described by one of the doctors there as "apocalyptic."[56] As elsewhere, family members of coronavirus patients were not allowed in the hospital, which in many cases deprived them of the opportunity to say "goodbye."[57] On March 25, several news outlets reported Elmhurst Hospital was at its "breaking point" after 13 patients died within a 24-hour period.[58] Admissions decreased during the first week of April, but doctors said that the reason was that they were sending home patients who would have been admitted if there were space for them.[59] Dr. David Reich, President of Mount Sinai Hospital, announced that the hospital was converting its lobbies into extra patient rooms to "meet the growing volume of patients" suffering from coronavirus.[60] A 68-bed COVID-19 respiratory care unit was set up in Central Park in Manhattan.[61] At the end of March, at hospitals such as Lenox Hill Hospital on the Upper East Side of Manhattan, sidewalk morgues were set up on city streets to deal with the overflow of corpses from the pandemic.[62]

On March 28, The *New York Times* reported that the City's 911 emergency response system was "overwhelmed" due to the large number of coronavirus patients needing transport to the hospital.[63] Dispatchers received more than 7,000 calls on March 26, a record since the September 11 attacks.[64] Emergency workers had to decide which cases to prioritize, and some patients were being left at home without medical care. In addition, paramedics lacked sufficient protective gear.[65]

Also on March 28, Governor Cuomo threatened Rhode Island Governor Gina Raimondo with a lawsuit over a new state quarantine policy, which would require people from New York to self-quarantine for 14 days upon arrival in Rhode Island.⁶⁶ On March 29, Raimondo repealed the order that specifically referred to New Yorkers, and broadened it to include any out-of-state traveler entering Rhode Island with intent to stay.⁶⁷

On March 30, a field hospital began operations at the Javits Convention Center on the West Side of Manhattan, and that month the U.S. Army also dispatched soldiers from the Army Corps of Engineers field hospitals in Fort Campbell, Kentucky and Fort Hood, Texas to New York City to convert the Javits Center into a 2,910-bed civilian medical hospital.⁶⁸ It was later announced that field hospitals would be set up in Central Park and at the Billie Jean King National Tennis Center in Queens.⁶⁹

On March 31, it was revealed that Governor Cuomo's brother Chris, a New York City resident and CNN journalist, had been diagnosed with COVID-19.⁷⁰ Chris Cuomo continued to appear on his regular weeknight CNN show, *Cuomo Prime Time*, even after contracting COVID-19 and quarantining in the basement of his home. During the first week or so of his illness, Chris Cuomo allowed his viewers to vicariously experience through his own illness the fever, shaking and intense pain of the disease, from which he finally fully recovered. He regularly had CNN's Dr. Sanjay Gupta on his show during the course of his illness, who clearly explained from a medical perspective what Cuomo was going through. Governor Cuomo also frequently appeared on the show, engaging in heartfelt good cheer and friendly banter with his "little brother" and "best friend." For thousands of viewers, Chris Cuomo's nightly show brought some much needed sense of humanity, drama and good humor into what was otherwise the tedious boredom and stress of life in stay-at-home lockdown.

On April 15, Gov. Cuomo signed an executive order requiring all New York State residents to wear face masks or coverings in public places.⁷¹ On April 16, Gov. Cuomo extended the state's stay-at-home order and school closures through May 15, amid signs of the rate of hospitalizations slowly declining.⁷² He warned that any change in behavior could reignite the spread of coronavirus.⁷³ Gov. Cuomo announced April 22 that the state would be starting a contact tracing program in coordination with New Jersey and Connecticut as a preliminary step to any loosening of the stay-at-home order.⁷⁴ The Johns Hopkins Bloomberg School of Public Health announced that it would develop an online curriculum that will be used to train 35,000 students in medicine and related fields at the SUNY and City University of New York schools.[75] Michael Bloomberg, former New York City mayor, contributed $10.5 million to this program.[76]

The San Francisco Experience

San Francisco's first coronavirus case appeared on March 5,[77] a few days after New York City got its first case on March 1.[78] In sharp contrast to New York's approach, however, Mayor Breed and the rest of the City's leadership took it extremely seriously. Even before any cases had been identified in San Francisco, Mayor Breed issued the February 25 state of emergency declaration, and on March 16, health officials throughout the Bay Area issued a shelter-in-place order, closing all but essential businesses.[79] The California state government had already banned large gatherings four days before that. "We were maybe a week up on New York," one UC Berkeley public-health expert told the *San Francisco Chronicle*. "That doesn't sound like much time, but in terms of the spread of this pandemic, it's enormous."[80]

In the first week of March, California and New York were still neck and neck on cases of COVID19, but by late March, New York case counts doubled every few days, and by March 25, New York State had ten times the cases California had: 25,000 to 2,500.[81] Early and very vocal efforts by San Francisco and other Bay Area officials to discourage people from gathering in crowds and then following up with shelter in place orders most likely had a dramatic impact, even if they came only a few days ahead of those in New York. Bay Area officials conveyed their concern and even alarm to the public, while New York City downplayed the crisis until it hit the City like a two-by-four.

Mayor Breed, for example, sent out a string of public tweets advising residents to prepare for "a disruption."[82] De Blasio also posted some public health warning messages, but these were far overshadowed by his other tweets urging New Yorkers to, for example, go out on the town and enjoy themselves before the lockdown went into effect.[83] In one March 2 tweet, Mayor de Blasio wrote: "Since I'm encouraging New Yorkers to go on with your lives + get out on the town despite Coronavirus."[84]

Governor Cuomo of New York Becomes "America's Governor"

As New York became the epicenter of the coronavirus epidemic in the U.S., Gov. Cuomo started holding televised daily briefings from the Javits Center on the westside of Manhattan or the Red Room at the State Capital Building in Albany, New York. These daily briefings quickly developed a huge audience and became a near-addictive source of desperately needed information for both New Yorkers and other Americans throughout the country – as well as the world. These briefings were what Americans were craving from President Trump, but which he was incapable of delivering. After all, in a time of crisis, Americans are used to seeing a calm and somber president appear on TV to clearly explain the scope of the crisis and what the country was doing to deal with it. It is supposed to be informative, but also calming and reassuring. In a public health crisis, we are used to having daily or at least weekly briefings from CDC headquarters in Atlanta, but the CDC stopped holding daily briefings just as the crisis was building to a crescendo. As the coronavirus crisis literally exploded in certain regions of the country, the CDC – until then, the best and most well-reputed public health organization in the world – went silent under pressure from the White House. And then to the country's horror, the White House briefings turned into an embarrassing circus of disinformation, prevarication, and a forum for President Trump to air his grievances against the press, the World Health Organization, Democratic governors and just about anyone else who dared question the unfolding disaster of a response effort by the federal government.

Nature abhors a vacuum, and Gov. Andrew Cuomo's daily briefings filled it. Carried live on several local and national networks, his appearances had a regular routine and flow that was in itself reassuring. Cuomo started each briefing with an update on the coronavirus numbers in New York, followed by a PowerPoint presentation of what the state government was doing to address the crisis. He then transitioned to announcing new directives to control the spread of the virus and provide medical treatment for those that were infected. Then the Governor would get personal, talking about how emotionally draining and frightening the coronavirus was, how it has affected his own family, and how he knew Americans would get through it together.[85]

For millions of Americans, as well as countless people in Europe and around the globe, Gov. Cuomo became the "must-see" center of the coronavirus information universe for about one hour every weekday. His ratings climbed even higher than Trump's daily White House briefings, which tended to be more meandering, chaotic, less (or non) informative two-hour marathons that many people had largely tuned out and turned off. England's *Sky News* reporters were regulars at Cuomo's briefings, as were French and other European reporters, many of whom stopped covering Trump's on-air briefings later each day.

Most leaders have little difficulty looking good and appearing to be reasonably competent when things are going well. The real test of a leader is when, as now, times are tough and they are in the midst of a crisis. Whether the crisis involves an actual war or a monumental public health challenge, what is required from the start is a firm, decisive and articulate leader to guide both the government and the citizenry through the troubled times to calmer waters. In order to win and sustain the confidence of the people, an effective leader must also tell the truth. In addition to executive competence, a "wartime" leader must also provide moral and spiritual leadership in a time of crisis. Facts and statistics are vitally important, but so too is the ability of a leader to empathize with the millions of people who are huddled in their homes around the TV – isolated and scared – looking for a leader who can identify with what they are going through and have the instinctive ability to strike a responsive chord with ordinary people.

Fortunately for New Yorkers and their fellow citizens, Gov. Cuomo was one of those rare leaders who were thrust into the public spotlight through circumstances beyond their control and rose to the occasion. His ability to connect both intellectually and emotionally with Americans was also enhanced by his evening appearances on his younger brother's cable news show. These moving on-air exchanges with Chris Cuomo showed that both of these brothers, like their father before them (the late Governor Mario Cuomo), had a strong sense of familial love and kindness that widely extended to their friends, neighbors and broader community.

On Tuesday, March 24, in one of his daily briefings, Gov. Cuomo reminded us that "New York is the canary in the coal mine," telling his fellow Americans elsewhere: "New York is your future."[86] Gov. Cuomo also made an impassioned plea on that day for thousands of ventilators to be sent to New York within the next 14 days to deal with an expected severe shortage given the wave of patients expected to be infected with the coronavirus.[87] Without ventilators to assist seriously ill patients to breathe, many or most of those in critical condition would die. He urged the Trump administration to use the Defense Production Act to get corporations to produce the equipment, as well as send the state the 20,000 ventilators sitting in a federal stockpile.[88]

March 24 was a particularly rough day for New York. On that single day, there were 13 fatalities at Elmhurst Hospital in Queens, and news cameras showed a multitude of sick people lined up outside the hospital, desperately trying to get admitted to the Emergency Room to be tested. Meanwhile, a refrigerated truck was parked outside to collect the dead bodies.[89] As much of America watched this disaster unfold, Gov. Cuomo's reassuring air of competence and compassion seemed like just the right tonic to ease our collective pain.

Adam Nagourney of the *New York Times*, who has been covering Gov. Cuomo for years, has referred to him as the "human bulldozer" for the zeal and tenacity with which he had tackled any major problem facing the state. One of the Governor's former advisors puts it another way: "The Governor thinks he's a hammer. So everyone looks like a nail."[90]

Progressives and Democrats across the country suddenly began wondering why Gov. Cuomo has been overlooked as a potential presidential candidate this year. After all, Bill de Blasio, New York City's Mayor, made a brief run for the Democratic presidential nomination, so why didn't the New York Governor give it a try?

The current New York governor's father, Mario Cuomo, also seemed like an obvious choice to be the Democratic Party's presidential nominee in 1988, after he made his eloquent "Tale of Two Cities" speech at the Democratic National Convention in 1984, and had an excellent reputation and record as New York's Governor. But Mario Cuomo, the New York governor from

1983 to 1994, was dubbed "Hamlet on the Hudson" for good reason since he did not have the ego or "fire in the belly" required for a politician to reach for the ultimate brass ring in American politics. So, Mario Cuomo sat out the 1988 presidential primary, which produced the disastrous candidacy of Massachusetts Governor Michael Dukakis.

In any event, Gov. Andrew Cuomo's brashness, and what many considered as a cold, calculating demeanor, morphed almost overnight into a caring and passionate advocate for ordinary New Yorkers and an overstressed health care system as the number of coronavirus patients and fatalities began to skyrocket in New York City. Comedian and political commentator Bill Maher even suggested that the Democratic Party should consider "switching out" Biden for Cuomo as their presidential candidate: "He's unlikable, which I really like."[91]

Gov. Cuomo also came to exemplify the single New Yorker having to learn to survive in relative isolation in New York. After his 2005 divorce from Kerry Kennedy and split from the Food Network chef and author Sandra Lee, Cuomo has been living alone with his dog, a Northern Inuit named Captain, in the mostly empty 40-room Victorian brick mansion on Eagle Street in Albany that is reserved for New York governors. Cuomo hit a responsive chord with all New Yorkers and other Americans who were living in isolation and quarantine during the crisis, when he admitted that he sometimes got annoyed with his dog for no good reason.

Gov. Cuomo also talked poignantly about having to warn his sisters about bringing their kids to see his 88-year old mother, Matilda, who was particularly vulnerable to the virus. He shared that his mother was a little annoyed with him when he named a social distancing guideline for the most vulnerable "Matilda's Law" in her honor. Gov. Cuomo was quick to come to his mother's defense – and all the other elderly in the country – by pushing back at the suggestion of Dan Patrick, the lieutenant governor of Texas, that older Americans might be willing to sacrifice themselves for the good of their grandchildren's economy after President Trump called for the reopening of America on Easter, April 12, 2020.[92] Gov. Cuomo declared: "My mother's not expendable."[93] He also tweeted: "You cannot put a value on human life. You do the right thing. That's what Pop taught us."[94]

In sharp contrast to Trump's self-centered view of the universe and social Darwinism, Gov. Cuomo offered a different – and, to most of us, more familiar – view of what it means to be an American, often offering quotes from his father about the government being like a family, with "mutuality, the sharing of benefits and burdens for the good of all, feeling one another's pain, sharing one another's blessings – reasonably, honestly, fairly, without respect to race or sex or geography or political affiliation."

After the agonizing 2016 presidential run by Hillary Clinton, political handicappers and oddsmakers included Andrew Cuomo's name among the top 10 likely Democrats to run against President Trump in 2020. But although he tested the waters, he decided not to make the grueling marathon run for the presidential nominee, deciding to hunker down in Albany and concentrate on the Empire State's many issues.

When Trump surprisingly told the assembled press and American people on Monday, April 13th, that he alone had the authority to reopen the American economy,[95] Governor Cuomo scornfully retorted: "We don't have a king; we have a president."[96] In a separate appearance on *MSNBC*, Gov. Cuomo warned that if Mr. Trump tried to force an economic reopening on the states, it could lead to "a constitutional crisis like you haven't seen in decades, where states tell the federal government, 'We're not going to follow your order.'"[97]

Gov. Cuomo further expressed his astonishment during an interview on *MSNBC*: "You want to say now the federal government is in charge?" He added, "Which, by the way, is a shift because the federal government didn't close down the economy. Right? They left it to the states. It was state by state, it was a whole hodgepodge, the governors had to close the economy, which was not politically easy to do, but now the federal government says it can open it? Well then, why didn't you close it if you can open it?"

Governor Ned Lamont of Connecticut joined in Gov. Cuomo's critique of Trump's suggestion that a president can preempt the powers that the U.S. has reserved to the states, stating that Trump's "verbal hand grenades" should not "distract from a lot of other good work that's going on."[98]

Trump had obviously not consulted with any legal experts before declaring his "absolute power" as president; nor could he have read the U.S.

Constitution. The Tenth Amendment to the Constitution states: "The powers not delegated to the United States by the Constitution, nor prohibited by it to the States, are reserved to the States respectively, or to the people." Since there is nothing in Article II of the Constitution giving the president the power to decide when the economies of the states are closed or reopened, it is crystal clear that these powers are reserved to the states.

Mayor de Blasio Also Starts Taking a Proactive Role, While Continuing His Ongoing Feud with Gov. Cuomo

As Mayor of America's largest and hardest-hit city, Bill de Blasio also played a prominent role in New York's response. On Tuesday, April 14, for example, Mayor de Blasio announced that New York City would start producing its own coronavirus test kits.[99] "We said if people can make them around the world — why not us," de Blasio said during a conference call with reporters.[100] De Blasio announced that the City would be producing 50,000 test kits by May "with components put together right here with companies, universities, New York City workers," he said. "It means commercial labs and academic institutions in this city working together to produce testing kits which are made up of three parts – nasal swabs, a liquid solution and tubes."[101] In addition, the Mayor announced that Carmel, Indiana agreed to donate 50,000 COVID-19 tests to New York City, and city officials there had "confirmed that they can produce them regularly for New York City."[102]

However, Mayor de Blasio and Gov. Cuomo could not restrain themselves from publicly renewing their ongoing feud as to which one of them had control over the immense New York City school system. The issue that precipitated this verbal outbreak between these two New York leaders was the issue over who had the final say as to when the school system should reopen. On Saturday, April 11, Mayor de Blasio announced that he was closing New York City schools through the summer as a way to protect educators and children.[103] The Mayor had told a select few advisers the day before that he was making the move, as well as Dr. Anthony Fauci, one of the doctors leading the White House's response to the virus.[104] However, de Blasio's team apparently neglected to touch base with Gov. Cuomo before making the announcement, which must have raised temperature levels in

Albany. The Mayor's announcement did not sit well with the Governor, who used his news conference later that day to address "the mayor's opinion" because, in the Governor's eyes, de Blasio did not have the authority to close the schools: "There has been no decision on schools," Gov. Cuomo said bluntly. "That's his opinion, but he didn't close them, and he can't open them."[105]

New York Takes the Lead in a Northeast Coalition of States

One thing that both Gov. Cuomo and Mayor de Blasio agreed on was the importance of New York's leadership position in formulating and carrying out a regional plan to carefully phase in the easing of restrictions and the reopening of the New York economy and that of its nearby sister states. In fact, on the same day that Trump was giving his "absolute power" press conference at the White House (April 13), Gov. Cuomo was on a conference call with the governors of six other northeastern states, announcing that he had reached an understanding with the governors of New Jersey, Connecticut, Rhode Island, Massachusetts, Pennsylvania, and Delaware to coordinate the "reopening" of their states on a gradual basis, once the necessary testing and health surveillance infrastructure was in place.[106]

"Everyone is very anxious to get out of the house, get back to work, get the economy moving. Everyone agrees with that," said Gov. Cuomo, who presided over the conference call from the state capitol in Albany. "What the art form is going to be here is doing that smartly, and doing that productively, and doing that in a coordinated way, doing that in coordination with the other states that are in the area and doing it as a cooperative effort where we learn from each other, and we share information."[107] Gov. Cuomo added that each State would provide a public health official, an economic development official, and the Governor's chief of staff to form the working group.

New Jersey Governor Phil Murphy added another word of caution, saying that the plan to reopen the states would take time, emphasizing that "the house is still on fire."[108] Gov. Murphy added: "We still have to put the fire out, but we do have to begin putting in the pieces of the puzzle that we know we're going to need … to make sure this doesn't reignite."[109]

Trump's juvenile response was to send out a tweet, comparing these East and West Coast working groups to the mutineers in the movie of "Mutiny on the Bounty," who justifiably took over the ship from a despotic Captain Bligh, who was cruelly and shamelessly abusing his crew.[110]

Trump, unfortunately, repeated this same pattern throughout the crisis. Responsible governors of some of the most heavily impacted states did everything within their power to contain the spread of the virus through stay-at-home orders and requirements that masks be worn in public. At the same time, they did whatever was necessary to obtain the personal protective equipment and other essential support so that the medical professionals in their states could respond to the increased number of COVID-related cases without having their hospitals overwhelmed by the crisis. Meanwhile, President Trump chose to gripe and snipe at these hardworking governors from the sidelines, and in some cases, actually obstructing their efforts to confront the crisis. Some necessary federal supplies and equipment were actually withheld from blue state governors who were unwilling to sufficiently bend the knee and grovel before Trump. Moreover, FEMA actually commandeered some desperately needed equipment that the states had purchased from overseas sources and was being shipped directly to the states.

In other words, the White House did not just fail to provide leadership to find a solution to the problem. Trump was also making himself part of the problem.

19

HOW THE FACE MASK ISSUE TURNED INTO A POLITICAL CULTURE WAR

"Wearing a Face Mask With My MAGA Hat Just Doesn't Feel Right!"
-unidentified Trump supporter
Tulsa, Oklahoma

From January through March 2020, the first three months of the coronavirus crisis in the U.S., health officials repeatedly warned Americans that they should not wear face masks to prevent the spread of the infectious illness.[1] The CDC, HHS, and the U.S. Surgeon General were in unanimous agreement that masks were unnecessary – and even counterproductive – for the general public.[2] The U.S. Surgeon General, Jerome Adams, issued a February 29 warning on twitter urging the public to "STOP BUYING MASKS!" "They are NOT effective in preventing the general public from catching #Coronavirus, but if healthcare providers can't get them to care for sick patients, it puts them and our communities at risk!"[3]

During a January 30 briefing, Dr. Nancy Messonnier, director of the National Center for Immunization and Respiratory Diseases (NCIRD), which is part of the CDC, misleadingly stated: "The virus is not spreading in the general community," adding, "We don't routinely recommend the use of face masks by the public to prevent respiratory illness. And we certainly are not recommending that at this time for this new virus."[4]

Dr. Messonnier's assertion that the coronavirus was "not spreading in the general community" was incorrect and highly misleading, especially given the fact that it was already known that the virus had been spreading widely throughout Wuhan, elsewhere in China, and several other countries. CDC also knew at that point that the virus was being spread from person-to-person in the U.S. Indeed, on the very same day that Dr. Messonnier made the statement, the CDC disclosed an Illinois case involving the transmission of the disease between a husband and wife.[5] There was, therefore, simply no basis for the assumption that the spread of the virus would be restricted to family members and was not readily transferrable in the broader general community beyond immediate families. The logical and scientific assumption that should have been made by the CDC was that if the virus could spread between family members, it was likely to spread within the general community and it was only a matter of time before it did so.

The CDC also knew that face masks were being widely used at that time in Wuhan and other hotspots in China to try and control the spread of the virus and that the general use of face masks by the pubic was already leading to positive results. It also knew that the use of face masks was precisely what had helped stop or at least slow down the spread of prior outbreaks, such as the Spanish Flu epidemic in 1918.

It was, therefore, irresponsible for the federal agencies tasked with controlling the spread of the virus in the U.S. to take the position that the use of face masks by the general public was not warranted. Indeed, if the CDC had made the recommendation in late January or early February that face masks should be used, and encouraged social distancing in public, it is highly likely that the spread of the virus could have been slowed.

At the same time that the CDC downplayed the risk of the community spread of the virus, the CDC announced in a January 30 press release that COVID-19 (2019-nCoV) "had spread between two people in the United States, representing the first instance of person-to-person spread with this new virus here."[6] The CDC explained that " this latest 2019-nCoV patient has no history of travel to Wuhan, but shared a household with the patient [in Illinois] diagnosed with a 2019-nCoV infection on January 21, 2020."[7] The CDC further confirmed that it knew even earlier that COVID-19 "could potentially spread between people," which is why it had "been working closely with state and local partners to identify close contacts" with confirmed cases.[8] The CDC further confirmed that "MERS and SARS, the other two coronaviruses that have emerged to cause serious illness in people, have been known to cause some person-to-person spread."[9] Even though the CDC knew of this person-to-person spread, CDC Director Robert R. Redfield sought to reassure the public (erroneously as it turned out) that "we still believe the immediate risk to the American public is low."[10]

There was also evidence emerging by late January that the virus was being transmitted by infected persons who were not yet exhibiting any typical signs and symptoms of the illness. Thus, Dr. Messonnier's comments to the effect that the use of face masks "for people who have not been directly exposed to the virus was not justified" made little sense since it was impossible for someone to know whether or not they had already been exposed.[11] The CDC's "guidance" on the use of a face mask was inconsistent with the real danger of asymptomatic transfers of the virus. The CDC was thus doing the public a disservice by advising people to wear a mask only if they were displaying symptoms of coronavirus or "taking care of a person with suspected 2019-nCoV infection."

Even if the virus could not be transmitted from an asymptomatic person to someone else (which is not true), it still made no sense for the CDC to advise the public to wear a mask only if they knew they were "directly exposed to the virus," since the fact that the virus can be transmitted in microscopic droplets suspended in the air makes it virtually impossible for someone to reach an informed judgment of whether or not they had been exposed to the virus. It is one thing to know you have been exposed to the virus when you are living with a spouse, partner, or family member who tests positive for the virus, but without such testing, it is little more than a deadly guessing game. So logic and common sense dictate that everyone should take the precautionary measure of wearing an ordinary cloth face mask to avoid infecting others if we ourselves are infected but do not know it yet since we are not showing symptoms and have not been tested. Conversely, if others around you are wearing face masks, they are basically protecting you and others from being infected by them. This mutual and communal wearing of face masks also strengthens the social bonds in the community, since the wearing of a mask is an outward signal that you care about the health not only of yourself, but also others in the community.

Although the CDC and other federal agencies prided themselves on making public health decisions that were "science-based" or "evidence-based," their "guidance" to the public regarding the use of face masks was based on neither fact nor science, and was just plain confusing. At the same time that the CDC was recommending against the wearing of face masks by the public, HHS Secretary Alex Azar was also cautioning the public against the wearing of masks, but focused his objections on the use by "the average American" of an "N95 mask."[12] His explanation for this was not that an N95 respirator mask is not effective in protecting the user from the inhalation of a dangerous virus, but, rather: "If it's not fitted right you're going to fumble with it," adding, "These are really more for health care providers."[13]

This recommendation against the use of N95 masks by the general public, and the suggestion that they only be reserved for use by medical professionals, was far more understandable than a blanket recommendation against the use of all face masks by the public. N95 masks are tighter-fitting than surgical masks that protect against small droplets and large particles, and since there were only 30 million N95 masks in the national stockpile as of the end of February and the beginning of March, it made sense to restrict their use only to active health care workers. Azar pointed out that "as many as 300 million masks [will be] needed in the U.S. for health care workers," so it made sense to conserve all of those more-sophisticated masks for health professionals.[14]

The public fully understood that more sophisticated N95 masks, which were in critically short supply, should only be used by doctors, nurses, and other health care professionals. What the public had difficulty understanding at the time was the official discouragement of the use of even the most rudimentary cloth face masks by the general public. Public health officials going back to at least the 1918 Spanish Flu pandemic had recommended the use of face masks by the general public, and there was a general consensus that these were helpful in preventing an infected person wearing a mask from coughing or sneezing infected droplets onto passers-by.

The federal government's position that "you don't need a mask" policy continued for more than two months after the CDC's January 30 press conference. On March 8, Dr. Anthony Fauci, the government's leading infectious disease expert, appeared on CBS's "60 Minutes", stating, "There's no reason to be walking around with a mask."[15] Dr. Fauci explained that while masks may block some droplets, they do not provide the level of protection people think they do. He also cautioned that wearing a mask may also have unintended consequences: People who wear masks tend to touch their faces more often to adjust them, which can spread germs from their hands.[16] Dr. Fauci also expressed concern that the increased demand for masks might outstrip the supply, saying, "It could lead to a shortage of masks for the people who really need it."[17]

There must have been many skeptics among the general American public regarding this "mask or no mask" issue, since as early as late February and early March, Walgreens, Duane Reade, and other pharmacies reported a sharp increase in demand for face masks across the country.[18] Several sites sold out of face masks entirely. Target also reported that its brand of face masks was completely out of stock, and Amazon, 3M, Home Depot, and CVS started running dangerously low on their supply of face masks.[19]

Finally, on April 3, after weeks of downplaying the highly contagious nature of the coronavirus and telling Americans they did not need face masks, the CDC completely reversed itself on the face mask issue. It announced that all Americans should now wear cloth face coverings and that the use of face masks should not be limited just to medical workers.[20]

On Wednesday, April 15, New York Gov. Cuomo publicly expressed his agreement with the CDC's new policy of recommending that face masks be worn in public. He even took this recommendation one step further by ordering all New Yorkers to cover their faces in public when they could not maintain proper social distancing: "You're walking down the street alone? Great! You're now at an intersection, and there are people at the intersection, and you're going to be in proximity to other people? Put the mask on!"[21]

Also, in mid-April, Mayor Bill de Blasio called for all grocery stores in New York City, the epicenter of the coronavirus pandemic in the U.S., to insist that customers wear masks while shopping. "I'm asking every store to put up a sign that you're required to wear a face covering. This is another one of the things we have to do to protect each other," he said at his daily press briefing.[22]

New Jersey Gov. Philip Murphy also signed an order making it mandatory for all people over the age of two who are in grocery stores, pharmacies or any essential businesses in that state to wear some kind of cloth mask:

"People talk about a new normal, I think that's a reality," adding that social distancing may need to continue until 2022.[23]

The takeaway from the "mask or no mask" issue is that it showed exactly how our governmental leaders and public health professionals should *not* deal with the American people. The insistence for months by the CDC, Surgeon General, and others who we have traditionally looked to for professional guidance in a public health care crisis unnecessarily tarnished their credibility. It led many to question not only their competence, but also their honesty in dealing with this important public health issue. The communicable nature of the coronavirus disease from person-to-person was known from a very early stage in the pandemic, and there was also clear evidence early on that it could easily spread in communities on a person-to-person basis. Some of the early cases that were diagnosed in Washington State were people who had never been in China and had not been in recent contact with anyone who had recently returned from China.

U.S. public health officials also had no basis to assume that the virus could only be spread by a person who was already symptomatic, and it was irresponsible for them to rely upon this erroneous assumption. If they did not know at the time whether or not the disease could be spread by an asymptomatic carrier, they should have assumed that yes, in fact, it could be carried by someone not showing symptoms of the disease, not the opposite assumption.

The application of the "precautionary principle" to public health issues is not something new and should have been applied by the CDC and the Surgeon General to the "mask or no mask" issue. It should have also been applied to other public health decisions and recommendations that the government was making about the coronavirus crisis. The "precautionary principle," as applied to public health issues, simply says that when approaching issues of potential harm when extensive scientific knowledge on the matter is lacking or inconclusive, caution should be applied when making important decisions as to the public health, and choices that are the least potentially harmful to the public if later proved to be wrong should be made, as opposed to decisions that may prove disastrous.[24]

The CDC, HHS, and other federal agencies should have candidly told the public that they did not have enough information to make an informed decision on whether or not the public should wear face masks, if that were the case. Or they could have taken a cautious approach by recommending that people wear face masks on the theory that, if the virus turned out to be extremely contagious, the face masks might have done some good. Or if the virus proved not to be terribly contagious, then no one would have been injured by the wearing of an unnecessary mask.

What the CDC did was to take the worst possible course of action, which was to recommend that the public not wear face masks when they either should have known that masks would have helped stop or slow the spread of the virus in the community or, if they did not have enough data yet on the "community spread" issue, to err on the side of caution and recommended the public use of face masks anyway.

Instead, the CDC and other federal public health officials seem to have let the scarcity of masks influence their public guidance, fearing that a run on masks by the general public would deprive health care workers of necessary protective equipment. If this were the case, then public health officials, by "shaping the message," were misleading the public about the efficacy of face masks for perhaps a noble goal, but they paid for it with a loss of public credibility. Much of the public already put zero weight on Mr. Trump's pronouncements and prognostications, with good reason, but at least we had Drs. Anthony Fauci, Deborah L. Birx, and Nancy Messonnier to rely on to tell us the truth about the virus, what was being done about it, and what we ourselves should be doing. Now the public may not be so sure. Trust is a tricky commodity. It is hard to earn and easy to lose.

If the public was told that face masks could be helpful and partially successful in limiting the spread of the coronavirus infection, but that we should forego buying them for the time being until health care and other front line workers had a sufficient supply of them, the public would have gotten the message and complied, at least to a large extent. The generosity and altruism of the American public is virtually limitless, and a likely response would have been to trigger fundraising drives for surgical and N95 masks for health care workers and first responders. In this crisis, more than ever, there was a need for transparency and honesty, not less of it.

It should also be kept in mind that some of the countries who handled their pandemic responses better than the U.S. – like Hong Kong, Taiwan, and South Korea – put in place social distancing and universal mask-wearing requirements almost immediately, resulting in their ability to bring the pandemic in those countries under control more quickly than in the U.S. In fact, Taiwan responded to the coronavirus by immediately ramping up mask production, which not only met all the local and national requirements but gave them a surplus supply that they started sharing with the U.S.[25]

Finally, the widespread or universal use of masks is an important psychosocial message to others in our community and around the country that in a crisis, it is not "business-as-usual," and that we are all acting in solidarity with our health care workers, first responders, grocery store clerks and other members of our community who are doing all they can do to fight the good fight against this powerful and persistent enemy.

The danger of public cynicism regarding the mask issue increased exponentially on April 15 when it was reported that since mid-March, during the time period when the CDC and the Surgeon General were still defending their "no mask" orders for the general public, the White House staff was scrambling to obtain enough masks and to protect themselves from the advancing pandemic.[26] On March 14, a National Security Council team within the White House made an urgent appeal to Taiwan's government for help amid growing reports that the nation's stockpile of protective gear was at risk of running dangerously low.[27] The Taiwan government responded positively, and 3,500 of the masks were earmarked for White House staff and officials.[28] The NSC was apparently not taking the CDC's public "no masks necessary" announcements seriously, and they were taking whatever steps they could to make sure that they were protected to the maximum extent possible against infection and transmission, and this meant wearing masks. As a result, the NSC staff had masks available to them a full two weeks before the CDC and the White House took a U-turn on the mask issue.

"Real Men Don't Wear Masks" (Or Do They?)

While U.S. health experts finally reached a consensus that masks should be used in public, many Americans have been reluctant to follow this directive, and many more have been outright opposed to it. One reason for this is that their president and vice president were not leading by example. In fact, the message they were sending was that, while there was nothing wrong with other people wearing a mask, they were not going to. Many of their followers quickly fell into line.

When President Trump announced on April 3 that the CDC was now recommending Americans wear cloth or fabric face masks in public to help prevent the spread of the deadly coronavirus,[29] he then completely undercut this important public health message by quickly adding that he himself would not be wearing one. He also emphasized that the CDC recommendation was completely "voluntary," insisting that you don't have to do it.[30] Trump explained his own decision not to wear a face mask despite the CDC urging it, saying he could not imagine being seen in a mask while greeting "presidents, prime ministers, dictators, kings, queens" in the Oval Office.[31]

Trump's rationale for not wearing a mask was somewhat odd since all of Trump's meetings with foreign leaders have been canceled because of the coronavirus.[32] The White House had already announced it was postponing a meeting with the king of Spain that had been scheduled for mid-March.[33] The administration also canceled the in-person G-7 meeting of the world's largest industrialized economies that had been set for June. It also seemed rather strange that none of Trump's supporting cast at the April 3 White House press conference wore any protective mask over their faces, including the medical doctors present.

Later that month, during a visit to the Mayo Clinic in Minnesota on Tuesday, April 28, Vice President Mike Pence was captured on camera without a face mask, which explicitly violated Mayo Clinic's policy that all patients and visitors wear masks during the coronavirus pandemic.[34] All members of the press pool with Pence complied with the mask rule. The Mayo Clinic confirmed that Pence was informed of the policy ahead of time, but later deleted the tweet.[35] Some of the images flashed on the news channels pictured Pence near masked staff members and a masked patient, even though he was without a mask. When Pence received some withering press criticism for not wearing a mask, he ended up apologizing – something Trump has never done. Pence's concession of wrongdoing was so atypical of the Trump Team that there were some murmurings in the White House as to whether Pence was really tough enough to be Trump's "wingman."

Republican officeholders throughout the country clearly understood the "no mask" signals from Trump and Pence meant they now had a permanent "hall pass" from any mask-wearing requirements. After all, wasn't it part of the American creed (or mythology) that we are supposed to be rugged individualists who can defy conventional wisdom (such as public health directives)? Some Republicans even reached for religious grounds for their non-compliance. For example, Republican Ohio State Representative Nino Vitale, who is a vociferous critic of Ohio Gov. Mike DeWine's stay-at-home orders during the COVID-19 pandemic, announced that he was refusing to wear a face mask to slow the spread of the disease, claiming that to do so would violate his "Judeo-Christian Principles."[36] Vitale added, "[t]his is the greatest nation on earth founded on Judeo-Christian Principles . . . [o]ne of those principles is that we are all created in the image and likeness of God. That image is seen the most by our faces. I will not wear a mask."[37] In other words, Vitale argued that since God does not wear a mask, neither would he.

Thus very quickly, the "mask or no mask" issue became more of a political weathervane than a matter of public health. Most of the American public understood and supported these public health mitigation measures, such as the wearing of masks in public, particularly in dark blue states on the East and West Coasts. A COVID-19 Impact Survey showed that about 8 in 10 Americans reported wearing a mask in response to the coronavirus pandemic, with an overwhelming 9 in 10 adults in California and New York saying they wore masks.[38]

Overwhelming public compliance with public health directives is something of an American tradition. But then again, this appears to be the first time in American history that compliance with protective measures such as the public wearing of masks had become a political rather than a public health issue. In 1918, the U.S. Surgeon General recommended that masks be worn in public by everyone, and many of the state governors and local governments legally required it.[39] Guides were even published in newspapers showing how to make a cloth mask properly. Photographs of the period show that almost everyone followed the state and local rules on mask-wearing in public.

The distancing and mask-wearing requirements set by state and local governments were generally complied with, at least on the East and West Coasts. However, an increasing number of Americans – primarily Republicans and Trump supporters – felt that the defiance of these public health laws and regulations could be characterized as a political statement to be used against mostly Democratic state governors who had ordered stay-at-home and other pandemic mitigation orders.

Trump actively encouraged protesters in at least three states to defy stay-at-home and other mitigation orders on Friday, April 17, when he sent out three tweets to protesters in Minnesota, Michigan, and Virginia, urging them to "LIBERATE" their states.[40]

With some of their most prominent leaders foregoing masks, the unwritten and often unspoken code among Trump supporters and protesters against state restrictions became: "Real men (and women) don't wear masks!"

Of course, one would expect Democrats and European liberal leaders like French Prime Minister Emmanuel Macron to comply with mask requirements during a global pandemic. But real macho men (or Neanderthals from another perspective) like Donald Trump or U.K. Prime Minister Boris Johnson would never be caught dead wearing a mask, even if it had some macho logo on it like the stars-and-bars of the Confederate flag or the skull and crossbones. Indeed, Boris Johnson had bragged that he was going to go on shaking hands with COVID-19 patients no matter what happened. And sure enough, he himself ended up in the hospital with a bad case of COVID-19, in critical condition.[41]

As Florida lifted some of its coronavirus restrictions over the first weekend in May, Floridians were invited to enjoy the newly opened parks and beaches, as long as people wore masks and kept their distance.[42] Many turned out to enjoy the sun and outdoors, but few were seen with masks. In addition, it was reported that over three days in early May, more than 7,300 people showed up at Miami Beach parks without covering their mouths and noses, according to police reports.[43] Hundreds more violated the mandated six feet of social distancing. "There is no way to effectively enforce social distancing when hundreds of individuals refuse to do so," Miami Beach City Manager Jimmy Morales told CNN.[44]

These Florida scofflaws had plenty of company around the country, as people in many states resisted guidelines that encouraged or required face masks in public spaces to prevent the spread of the coronavirus. Even though they probably drove to the protest rallies or parks with their seat belts on without giving it a second thought, some people expressed the view that the public health mandate regarding the use of face masks was an unnecessary intrusion into their personal lives, or even akin to a civil rights violation. In at least one incident, a dispute over the face mask issue has escalated completely out of hand. Police in Decatur, Illinois, for example, arrested a man who had shoved a gas station clerk who insisted he wear a mask while paying for fuel on the first day of the state's newly imposed rules that require people to cover their faces inside businesses.[45] In Michigan, the police announced they were searching for a man who had allegedly wiped his nose on a Dollar Tree employee's sleeve on Saturday, May 2.[46] Also, in Michigan, a man shot and killed a security guard at a Family Dollar store after the guard argued with a woman who refused to comply with the statewide executive order that requires people to wear masks inside shops.[47]

Faced with tremendous opposition to his statewide order requiring the wearing of masks in public, Ohio's Republican Gov. Mike DeWine had to rescind the order as businesses reopened, conceding that the measure was "a bridge too far," telling ABC News that people are "not going to accept the government telling them what to do."[48] In Stillwater, Oklahoma, city officials also had to rescind a mandatory mask order for local restaurants and businesses after employees were threatened and verbally abused by non-complying residents. Stillwater city manager Norman McNickle explained the dilemma that he and other city officials faced: "Many of those with objections cite the mistaken belief the requirement is unconstitutional, and under their theory, one cannot be forced to wear a mask," he said. "No law or court supports this view ... It is further distressing that these people, while exercising their believed rights, put others at risk."[49] Nevertheless, the city withdrew the "face mask" ordinance since a large portion of the Oklahoma citizenry were influenced by right-wing Republican and conservative political figures and commentators who were recklessly encouraging their fellow-citizens to defy public health orders that had been proven time and time again to have effectively reduced the spread of contagious viruses such as COVID-19.

Politicization of the "mask issue" intensified as protesters wearing MAGA hats and no face coverings started descending on state capitals, protesting state stay-at-home and face mask orders. On April 30, some 400 to 700 protesters descended on the Michigan Capitol building in Lansing to demonstrate against Democratic Gov. Gretchen Whitmer's stay-at-home order, which was issued in March following the declaration of a state of emergency that was set to expire at the end of the day.[50] (She later signed executive orders that put in place a new state of emergency through May 28).

Speaking with CNN's Jake Tapper, Whitmer said that the protesters, whom President Donald Trump sided with, dredged up "some of the worst racism and awful parts of our history in this country," adding, "the Confederate flags and nooses, the swastikas, the, you know, behavior that you've seen in all of the clips, is not representative of who we are in Michigan. And the fact of the matter is, I mean, we're in a global pandemic," she said, adding that "we need to listen to the expertise and our institutions of higher learning and our health system and make decisions that are going to protect the lives of everyone."[51]

Meanwhile, solidly blue state governors on the East and West Coasts continued to hold firm on the extension of enforcement of "public mask" orders, confident that the overwhelming majority of the citizens of those states would continue to comply with the order until the crisis was over. On Monday, May 4, Gov. Cuomo reminded New Yorkers that it was "disrespectful" for people to refuse to wear a mask in public. "You can literally kill someone because you did not want to wear a mask. How cruel and irresponsible would that be?"[52]

The "face mask" issue exploded into a mini-crisis at the White House on Friday, May 8, when it was learned that Vice President Pence's press secretary, Katie Miller, had tested positive for the coronavirus.[53] This news followed a report earlier in the week that one of Trump's personal valets had tested positive for COVID-19.[54] With no sense of irony, Trump apparently went ballistic when he heard about his valet's test results, chastising his staff for not having required the valet to wear a face mask when he was around Trump. Katie Miller, who is married to senior Trump advisor Stephen Miller, had been photographed on numerous occasions at White House briefings and other occasions without a face mask. The White House reporters and others that she spoke to on a frequent basis were all wearing masks.

Trump said he was "not worried" about the virus spreading in the White House.[55] Nevertheless, the White House belatedly stepped up the implementation of mitigation efforts, such as the wearing of face masks, that had already been recommended by the CDC on April 3 and universally supported by public health experts. The president and vice-president started being tested daily, as well as some staffers who closely interacted with Trump.[56]

On Monday, May 11, a memo was circulated within the White House, instructing most officials and staff there to wear masks or face coverings in the West Wing, as well as to avoid "unnecessary visits" there.[57] Trump, of course, was not expected to wear a mask in the White House, as if the force of his personality was enough to stave off infection. In a sign of the confusion and "death spiral" that had descended upon the White House's coronavirus response policy, it was reported that several senior administration officials inside the White House were still arguing that masks were unnecessary for people getting regular testing.[58] At a Rose Garden news conference that day, Trump himself was without a mask, although all of his aides wore them. However, the White House staff present at the briefing inexplicably failed to engage in any social distancing, which was one of the major mitigation strategies that the CDC and other agencies were recommending to the public. Trump tried to rationalize his "no mask for me" policy by saying: "In the case of me, I'm not close to anybody. . . . Obviously, in my case, I'm very far away from everyone."[59]

Trump further needlessly polarized the "mask issue" when he defied requests by the Ford Motor Company to comply with company regulations by wearing a mask when he toured one of their plants in Michigan on May 21.[60] Trump also ignored a written warning from the Michigan state attorney general, Dana Nessel, reminding him that it was the law in Michigan that everyone should wear a mask in such a setting: an indoor venue with many people in attendance.[61] Nevertheless, Trump, maskless, was photographed touring the plant in Ypsilanti, Michigan, which has been recast to produce ventilators and personal protective equipment. Surrounded by Ford executives who were wearing masks, Trump told reporters he had put one on earlier, out of the view of cameras: "I had one on before. I wore one in the back area, but I didn't want to give the press the pleasure of seeing it."[62] By refusing to wear a mask, he wanted to convey a sense of defiance to his followers. He knew that they would tend to emulate him by defying state and local public health directives, which was fine by him since he knew that he could get some political mileage out of it.

Michigan Attorney General Nessel responded by publicly referring to Trump as a "petulant child."[63] "The president is like a petulant child who refuses to follow the rules. This is not a joke," she told CNN, adding that Trump's behavior was "extremely disappointing" and that thousands of people in Michigan have died from coronavirus.[64] She also put Trump on notice that he was not welcome to return to the state, given the fact that he was now a scofflaw: "If he fails to wear a mask, he's going to be asked not to return to any enclosed facility inside our state."[65]

Clearly, Mr. Trump and his allies were cynically polarizing and politicizing the country's response to the coronavirus crisis, turning defiance of public health directives into a symbol of right-wing identity and honor. When Trump loyalists saw him without a mask and encouraging the lockdown protesters to "liberate" their states, science and data be damned, they naturally accepted their leader's re-characterization of this public health issue as an ideological and political issue.

But it would be wrong to view this division as a class issue. Even though many of Trump's die-hard supporters are working-class folk without a college education, they are the ones most likely to be working the highest-risk jobs as they are ordered to go back to work. And in places where coronavirus cases were still growing, and the virus was far from being under control, they were justifiably angry and terrified at being treated as the sacrificial lambs so that the elite could continue to work from the safety of their homes.

In the end, public health measures that are put in place during a public health crisis such as this one can only be effective if there is a high degree of public compliance with those directives. Compliance is driven by the degree of public and social trust that the sacrifices that are being asked of the public are for legitimate purposes of public health and safety. Do most of the citizens trust their government leaders when they tell them that they have to comply with certain public health restrictions not only for their health but the health of those around them and the entire community? And is that bond of trust between the government and its citizens impaired when senior government officials say that the public should do one thing, but refuse to do it themselves? Handwashing is an act of social trust. Covering your mouth when you cough is a matter of social trust. Maintaining a six-foot distance between yourself and others is a matter of social trust. And, yes, wearing a mask is a matter of social trust.

Only in America would a simple public health tool such as a face mask become a political football, with possibly deadly consequences. We will never know how many lives were put at risk – and how many were lost – as a result of Trump's cynical conversion of a public health care issue into a political one. But we do know that when a sitting president undercuts his own administration's public health directives for political ends, he has disgraced the office that he temporarily holds in trust for the American people.

20

CONSPIRACY THEORIES, SNAKE OIL SALESMEN AND THE HYDROXYCHLOROQUINE HYPE

"Try it, What do you have to lose?"
- Donald J. Trump

Conspiracy theories flourish in both good times and bad, but in the midst of a global crisis such as this one, they thrive even more. There are theories that the virus was man-made in a Wuhan laboratory and intentionally released, that cellular data 5G networks are spreading the virus, that it is part of a globalist government takeover, and that the crisis is being exaggerated and overblown by a liberal media and their Democratic allies in order to embarrass President Trump. None of these sensationalist theories have any reliable basis in fact, but that does not stop their widespread dissemination at a speed faster than the spread of the virus itself.

In times of crisis, conspiracies are nothing new. 9/11 was so horrific that many people believed the widely circulated theory that President George W. Bush was behind the tragedy or at least knew about it beforehand and let it happen. The mass shooting of children and teachers at Sandy Hook Elementary School in Newtown, Connecticut on December 14, 2012 also was so terrible and hard to comprehend that some people instead believed the alternate conspiracy theory promoting it did not actually happen.

Similarly, every pandemic has its own set of rumors and conspiracy theories on where it came from and who or what was responsible for it. During the AIDS epidemic of the 1980s, it was difficult for many Americans to accept the fact that the HIV virus in fact caused AIDS, or that the HIV virus was dangerous enough to cause a case of life-threatening AIDS. An otherwise reputable scientist, Peter Duesberg, at U.C., Berkeley, expressed the view at the time that HIV was a harmless virus and that it had nothing to do with AIDS.[1] Many people believed him, to their own peril.

During the H1N1 Swine Flu pandemic of 2009, conspiracy theories based on existing concerns about globalization and the pharmaceutical industry gained traction worldwide.[2] For example, some people in the U.S. believed that undocumented migrants were being used by "terrorists" to spread the virus within American borders, while some people in Mexico and Central and South America argued that American authorities were purposely spreading the virus for the benefit of pharmaceutical companies. In addition, on April 27, 2009, the Chilean newspaper *El Ciudadano* published an article on the origins of the Swine Flu that suggested a U.S. biodefense agency was working to "weaponize" avian influenza and that former U.S. Defense Secretary Donald Rumsfeld stood to benefit from the outbreak.[3] This article pointed to Rumsfeld's longstanding role with Gilead Laboratories in California, which manufactured Tamiflu, a possible treatment for highly pathogenic avian influenza (HPAI).[4]

The COVID-19 "Infodemic"

The false rumors and disinformation circulating during the coronavirus crisis reached such epidemic proportions that the World Health Organization declared that it was an "infodemic" as early as February 2020. The myths about the coronavirus included the notion that the disease could be cured by drinking methanol, which led to more than 700 deaths in Iran. In addition, the rumor that it was spread by 5G transmitters convinced arsonists in Britain to carry out more than 90 attacks on phone towers.

Republicans, Trump supporters and conservatives tended to believe in false narratives in much larger numbers than Democrats, which is not surprising since one of the basic tenants of right-wing orthodoxy in the U.S. is that you should not trust intellectuals, academics, scientists, journalists and any other fields that rely heavily on facts and rational thought processes. These professions have long been conservative targets. Rush Limbaugh, the conservative talk-show host, often speaks of the "four corners of deceit": the media, scientists, academia and the government.

The Pew Research Centre found in March that 30% of Republicans believed the virus was created intentionally, nearly twice the percentage of Democrats.[5] In May, a poll by YouGov.com found that 44% of Republicans thought Bill Gates wanted to use COVID-19 vaccines to implant microchips in people; only 19% of Democrats agreed. The false belief that the virus was being intentionally spread by China, the U.S., or both was so widely circulated that a clip of the film "Plandemic" went viral when it was uploaded on May 4, and quickly registered 8 million viewers. The film promoted the theory that a worldwide shadowy elite conspired to start the outbreak and facilitate its spread as part of its plan for world domination and trillions in profits. The star of the film, Judy Mikovits, who is also a leading "antivaxxer," i.e., an anti-vaccine advocate, has written two books - *Plague* and *Plague of Corruption* – which are on Amazon's bestseller list.[6]

During the coronavirus crisis, there has been growing support for social media platforms to take a harder line with false COVID-19 stories and content. It is generally believed that false stories and rumors are easier to identify than, for example, stories with political content. It should, therefore, be easier to censor apocryphal coronavirus stories. In March, Mark Zuckerberg said Facebook had no problem taking down "things like 'You can cure this by drinking bleach.' I mean, that's just in a different class." In America, 84% of the people surveyed said social networks should delete posts that they suspect contain inaccurate information about COVID-19.[7] Half that number said they should do so without confirming the posts are false. Tech firms thus began to add warnings to false information and signposts to reliable sources.

One major problem that has been identified is that social networks' algorithms have steered people towards polarizing content, which is more likely to provoke "engagement" and thus generate advertising revenue.[8] In 2018, an internal report at Facebook warned that users were being directed to divisive material. Facebook then developed a plan to highlight less controversial posts—a project dubbed "Eat Your Veggies"—but this plan was sidelined, partly because of concerns that the changes would affect conservative users more than others.[9] And, of course, there would be a sharp drop in advertising revenue, which may have been the real reason for dropping this public-spirited initiative.

One reason why Republicans have no real incentive to bridge the gap between conservatives and those on the more liberal side of the political spectrum is that there are political advantages to polarization. As Ezra Klein argues in his book, *Why We're Polarised*, ultra-partisanship works well for conservatives since liberals, who draw from support primarily in the cities and suburbs, have to win votes from moderates in order to prevail. Conservatives, on the other hand, can win elections by just getting out their base, who are to be found in more rural areas and states which have a disproportionate influence in the Electoral College. As politics becomes more polarized, energizing the base gets easier, and winning over moderates harder.[10]

What distinguishes COVID-19 deniers from prior conspiracy theorists is that the coronavirus-deniers – at least at the start of the crisis – included President Trump himself. It was as if President Ronald Reagan during the 1980s denied that there was actually an AIDS epidemic and that it was just a scare tactic intended to divide the American people, or that it was an epidemic that had actually been engineered in a Russian lab, weaponized, and then released on an unsuspecting American public. Sounds preposterous, doesn't it?

The COVID Denier-in Chief

Fast forward to the COVID-19 crisis, and we have a president who uses his bully pulpit in the White House to deny for weeks that the U.S. had any real coronavirus problem, that it was being overblown by media purveyors of fake news with the malevolent intent of taking him down. And then when he had to acknowledge that it was for real, he dismissed it as no more of a threat than the common cold or flu. On January 30, 2020, Trump described the handful of U.S. coronavirus cases as a "very little problem" and said those people were "recuperating successfully."[11] On February 10, 2020, Trump continued to reassure the American public: "I think the virus is going to be — it's going to be fine." On the same day at a political rally in New Hampshire attended by thousands of his supporters, Trump declared that "by April, you know, in theory, when it gets warmer, it miraculously goes away."[12] On March 24, Trump again downplayed the crisis by comparing it to the common seasonal flu, arguing that the flu leads to 36,000 deaths per year, "but we've never closed down the country for the flu."[13]

Brazil President Jair Bolsonaro took an equally blasé attitude towards the coronavirus crisis. Perhaps taking his cue from President Trump, he described the coronavirus to reporters as "a little flu," and that it was largely a media invention.[14] Not to be outdone, Mexico's President Andrés Manuel López Obrador told reporters in mid-March that he was using amulets as protection against the coronavirus; he also argued that "not allowing corruption" prevents the disease.[15]

Coronavirus Skeptics Join Forces With Climate Change Deniers and Tea Party Activists

With the current occupant of the White House acting as "Denier-in-Chief" regarding the seriousness of the crisis, it was almost inevitable that his followers would actively oppose the stay-at-home and other mitigation measures imposed by governors in most of the states. In mid-April, a few thousand demonstrators took to the streets in the state capitals of Michigan, Ohio, Minnesota, and Virginia, protesting "lockdown" and social distancing orders, saying restrictions to prevent the spread of the virus were dooming small businesses.[16] In Frankfort, Kentucky, protesters nearly drowned out Democratic Governor Andy Beshear as he held a news conference.[17] Demonstrations also took place in Raleigh, North Carolina, where at least one protester was arrested.[18]

At an "Operation Reopen" rally at the state capitol in Austin, Texas on April 18, the notorious rightwing conspiracy theorist Alex Jones was photographed shaking hands with several fellow protesters and coronavirus skeptics, ignoring warnings by public health officials regarding the importance of social distancing and avoidance of handshaking in the fight against COVID-19. Jones, who has been praised by President Trump in an appearance on his InfoWars show, has become a prominent "resister" to the lockdown and stay-at-home orders issued by numerous state governors and recommended by the White House's own coronavirus task force. Jones has also claimed that the White House gave its approval for the phony coronavirus remedies that he sells on his program, including "Superblue Silver Immune Gargle."[19] On March 12, New York Attorney General Letitia James sent a notice to Jones ordering him "to immediately cease and desist selling and marketing products as a treatment or cure for the coronavirus."[20] Undeterred, Jones continued his marketing of "The Real Red Pill," which he said contained various secret ingredients that could ward off coronavirus. Previously, he had falsely claimed that a colloidal silver toothpaste he sold "kills the whole SARS-corona family at point-blank range."[21]

Shouting through a bullhorn at the Austin Rally on Saturday, April 18, Jones called the coronavirus crisis as "a hoax" and blamed – in no particular order - the Chinese government, globalists, communists, reporters and the Deep State for damage done by pandemic, which he called "a bioweapon meant to shut down our economy."[22] Jones also compared the efforts of the state governments and health care officials to slow down the spread of the virus through social distancing other mitigation measures as a form of "Nazi-style suppression." "We don't live in fear of some made-up virus!" Jones yelled. "We know the globalists and the media are the enemy!" Following Trump's lead, other demonstrators at the Austin, Texas rally called for the firing of coronavirus task force spokesman Dr. Anthony Fauci. Trump had approvingly retweeted a call for Fauci's firing.

On April 15, an "Operation Gridlock" protest succeeded in its goal of snarling traffic on the streets of the State Capitol in Lansing, Michigan, drawing a few thousand demonstrators, many of whom chanted "Lock Her Up" slogans directed at Governor Gretchen Whitmer, who had been the focus of much of President Trump's criticism of Democratic governors.[23] In addition to the typical stay-at-home orders and business closures in place in other states, the Michigan state government also banned interstate travel, closed garden stores, and halted motor boating.[24] Michigan was one of the midwestern states that were hardest hit by the coronavirus crisis, with nearly 2400 fatalities as of mid-April, and with about 1 million workers filing for unemployment, about 24% of the workforce in that state.[7]

Some of the Michigan demonstrators were affiliated with the Tea Party and displayed the "Don't Tread on Me" logo that is the unofficial slogan of that movement.[25] Some of the Michigan protesters waved Confederate flags and prominently displayed an array of firearms.

Governor Whitmer responded forcefully to the protests by accusing Trump's Secretary of Education Betsy DeVos of having provided the dark money financing at least one of the protest groups who organized the demonstrations. The Michigan Freedom Fund, one of the sponsors of the demonstration, has long-established connections with the wealthy DeVos family.[26] Gov. Whitmer called on her fellow Michiganders to condemn the group's open violation of social distancing guidelines during the pandemic.[27] "This group is funded in large part by the DeVos family," Gov. Whitmer told reporters in a press briefing.[28] "And I think it's really inappropriate for a sitting member of the United States president's cabinet to be waging political attacks on any governor," she added. Whitmer, citing those connections, called on DeVos to disavow the group's actions and to encourage participants in future actions to "stay home and be safe."[29]

Meanwhile, in Washington, President Trump took a break on April 17th from his weighty constitutional duties to basically incite an insurrection against the Democratic governors of three of the states with strong stay-at-home orders in place that were consistent with the Trump administration's own guidelines on social distancing: "Liberate Michigan!" he tweeted. "Liberate Minnesota;" "Liberate Virginia."[30] Trump further made favorable reference to the demonstrators, who were flouting social distancing orders, by referring to the protesters as "very responsible people."[34] It was eerily reminiscent of Trump's now-infamous equivalency comments on August 12, 2017, following the Charlottesville, Virginia demonstrations by white supremacists chanting racist and anti-Semitic slogans, remarking that "you also had people that were very fine people, on both sides."[35]

White House economic advisor Stephen Moore went even further than Trump in his praise of this rebellion against reasonable public health restrictions; he compared the protesters to the civil rights activist, Rosa Parks, who sparked a nationwide effort to end racial segregation in public facilities when she refused to surrender her seat on a segregated bus in Montgomery, Alabama.

Many of the "coronavirus skeptics" seeking to downplay the dangers posed by the COVID-19 pandemic, and who supported the protest rallies at various state capitals, were also the same people who railed against climate change scientists, who have been warning for decades that climate change and global warming was an even more serious threat to human life on the planet than pandemics. The blog "DeSmog," an organization that tracks false online information about the climate crisis, identified about 70 individuals and groups who have been "climate change deniers" as being now in the forefront of the disinformation campaign regarding the seriousness of the coronavirus crisis and pushing for an end to social distancing.[36]

One of the most vocal opponents of the lockdown orders by various states was the Heartland Institute, which simultaneously questioned the dangers posed by global warming and the science surrounding the human health risks posed by COVID-19. In a podcast on March 15, Jim Lakely, Heartland's communications director, compared the virus to a bad flu season.[37] A video by The Media Research Group said: "This is exactly how they incite mass panic: through lies and deception and exploiting ignorance. It's how they convince people that we're all going to die because Trump doesn't believe in science or something."[38]

As one might expect, the fossil fuel industry and its supporters also capitalized on the pandemic to emphasize the high economic costs of trying to mitigate the impacts of climate change and any other efforts to protect the planet. Alex Epstein, the founder of the Center for Industrial Progress, a group connected with the rightwing billionaire brothers Charles and David Koch, called the current recession a "mild preview of the Green New Deal," adding, "our biggest ally in the fight against coronavirus is the fossil fuel industry."[39]

The links between climate science deniers and opponents of COVID-19 lockdown orders also extended outside the U.S. In the U.K., James Delingpole, a rightwing commentator and longstanding skeptic as to the connection between fossil fuel use and climate change, called doubters of quarantining measures "lockdown skeptics," and referred to those who support social distancing as "hysterical bedwetters."[40] In a recent podcast, he also accused the media of promoting panic in "hysterical tabloids."

Enter the Snake Oil Salesmen

In addition to attracting coronavirus doubters, climate change deniers, and a wide-ranging array of conspiracy theorists, the pandemic also attracted a rogue's gallery of hucksters, scam artists, and snake oil salesmen who come out of the woodwork in times of disaster. These opportunists saw it as a golden opportunity to cash in on the collective suffering and fears, and to fleece the public through the sale of worthless merchandise "guaranteed" to prevent or cure coronavirus infections.

The term "Snake Oil Salesman," which has come to refer to any seedy profiteer or quack trying to exploit an unsuspecting public through the sale of fake cures, originated with the sale of "snake oil" and other worthless "patent medicines" that gained popularity in the late 1800s as a cure-all for a wide variety of ailments, including chronic pain, headaches, "female complaints" and kidney disease.[16] While Alex Jones' miracle cure for coronavirus definitely qualifies as "snake oil," and was clearly 100% fraudulent, he is by no means the most famous of the coronavirus-cure hucksters. After all, Donald J. Trump, who has made a career successfully hyping himself, his brand, real estate with his name on it and a wide variety of merchandise, could not resist for very long the reflexive impulse to promote coronavirus-cure products.

"Up Like Lazarus" - The Hydroxychloroquine Hype

The most widely publicized of the drugs that the president has promoted is the anti-malarial drug hydroxychloroquine. After seeing it promoted on *Fox News* for days, Trump quickly embraced this drug as the wonder-cure for all of our coronavirus problems. At his March 19 White House briefing, Trump kicked off a month-long promotional campaign for hydroxychloroquine and its first cousin, chloroquine, with an unqualified endorsement: "It's shown very encouraging — very, very encouraging early results," Trump said.[42] "And we're going to be able to make that drug available almost immediately ... I think that's a tremendous — there's tremendous promise, based on the results and other tests ... I think it's going to be great," he added a bit later in the news briefing.[43]

Over the next month, Trump mentioned these drugs at least 44 times.[44] Trump's hype for this anti-malaria drug got more hyperbolic over time, to the point that the president was representing that, with the possible exception of the development of antibiotics, hydroxychloroquine could be "one of the biggest game-changers in the history of medicine" and should "be put in use immediately."[45] If only it were true.

On April 4, President Trump escalated his marketing blitz on behalf of hydroxychloroquine by hyping his administration's success in acquiring huge amounts of it.[46] "We have millions and millions of doses of it—29 million to be exact," he said,[47] ignoring the fact that many of the state governors across the country had not been requesting this drug, but rather, had pleaded for federal support to acquire tests, ventilators, and protective gear for health care workers. Trump's promotion of the drug ran counter to the collective opinion of the federal government's top interagency working group of clinicians and scientists, who determined on March 24, 2020 in an internal consensus statement, that chloroquine-based COVID-19 treatments be studied only in controlled, hospital-based clinical trials because their safety and efficacy was "not supported by data from reliable clinical trials or non-human primates" and carried "potential risks."[48] One of the factors that gave these government scientists pause was the fact that the drug was known to have potentially serious side effects, including heart arrhythmias.[49]

The Trump White House and its closest political allies within the federal government decided to ignore the March 24 internal consensus statement and, immediately after the April 4 press conference, White House officials pushed ahead with a massive behind-the-scenes pressure campaign on the government's top health officials to deliver huge amounts of chloroquine drugs to just about anyone who wanted them.[50] Brett Giroir, the assistant secretary for health in the Department of Health and Human Services, sent an email with the subject line "Hydroxychloroquine" to a group including FEMA administrator Pete Gaynor, HHS assistant secretary for preparedness and response Robert Kadlec, and Navy Rear Admiral John Polowczyk, who led the supply-chain task force at FEMA, stating:

W.H. call. Really want to flood Ny and N.J. with treatment courses. Hospitals have it. Sick outpatients don't. And can't get. So go through distribution channels, as we discussed. If we have 29 million, perhaps send a few million ASAP? W.H. wants follow up in AM.[51]

Vice President Pence and the rest of the Trump administration quickly fell into line behind the president's expressed wishes that this drug treatment should have the full backing of the entire U.S. government. Vice President Pence had already previously announced on March 24th that the FDA was approving the "off-label" use for the anti-malarial drug hydroxychloroquine to treat coronavirus patients. He made the comments during a *Fox News* coronavirus town hall in response to a question from media personality Dr. Mehmet Oz, who himself endorsed the drug by saying that he would take the drug if he felt sick.[17]

Not coincidentally, hydroxychloroquine was mentioned repeatedly on the *Fox* channels, day after day over several weeks.[18] On Friday, April 3, *Fox News* Host Laura Ingraham, who talked about the drug on her show virtually incessantly, brought two doctors who frequently appeared on her show to the White House to sell Trump on the medication as a cure-all for coronavirus.[19] Just two days later, Trump asserted that "a lot of people are saying" that the drug should be used to treat coronavirus patients.[20] Trump's touting of the drug was against the best advice of his leading infectious disease expert, Dr. Anthony Fauci, who had reportedly urged the president against touting the drug. Nevertheless, Trump insisted that he "feels good" about it, saying, "what do you have to lose?"[21]

At one point during a White House news conference on April 6, when a reporter asked Dr. Fauci as to what he thought about hydroxychloroquine as a treatment for coronavirus, Trump jumped in and silenced Fauci. It was clear that Trump did not want Fauci to express his standard cautionary remarks to the effect that the drug's efficacy could not be determined until the results of clinical trials were in.[22]

One of the reasons why President Trump seemed highly motivated to promote hydroxychloroquine as an accepted treatment for COVID-19 was that Trump himself has a small personal financial interest in Sanofi, the French pharmaceutical company that makes Plaquenil, the brand-name version of hydroxychloroquine.[23]

In addition to the fact that Trump appears to have had "something to gain" from the sale of the brand-name version of this anti-malaria drug, it also came to light that coronavirus patients did, in fact, have "something to lose" by taking this medication. According to genetic cardiologist Michael Ackerman of the Mayo Clinic, who treats patients predisposed to heart arrhythmias because of genetic conditions, chloroquine and hydroxychloroquine have the potentially fatal side effect of causing a type of irregular heart rhythm that may lead to cardiac arrest.[24] When hydroxychloroquine is used in combination with azithromycin, there is an increased risk of cardiac death. The small risk of cardiac death for patients on these drugs stems from a well-known side effect: a condition called Q.T. prolongation, a delayed response for the heart muscle recharge between beats.[25] On April 21, it also was reported that this anti-malarial drug promoted by President Trump had no benefit and was linked to higher rates of death for Veterans Affairs patients who were hospitalized with coronavirus.[26] The study by the Veterans Administration and academic researchers showed that the rates of death in the groups treated with the drugs were worse than those who did not receive the drugs.[27]

A study released by the medical journal *Lancet* on May 22 further confirmed that more patients treated with this anti-malaria drug for COVID-19 died than recovered.[28] This published study, which was the largest of its kind until then, came five days after Trump said that he was taking hydroxychloroquine to ward off COVID-19. The study concluded: "We were unable to confirm a benefit of hydroxychloroquine or chloroquine when used alone or with a [an antibiotic], on in-hospital outcomes for COVID-19."[29] Further, the study concluded that these drugs "were associated with decreased in-hospital survival and an increased frequency of ventricular arrhythmias when used for treatment of COVID-19."[30]

However, in early June, the *Lancet* study was back in the news when three of the authors of the study retracted their support for the study's findings, which concluded that hydroxychloroquine, taken either alone or with an antibiotic, was of no benefit to a COVID-19 patient and actually increased a patient's risk of dying.[31] The underlying data for the study had been collected by a private company called Surgisphere, whose founder, Spaan Desai, was a co-author of the study. Concerns were raised about the accuracy of the data when more than a hundred scientists and clinicians asked the *Lancet* journal to provide details about the data and called for the study to be independently validated. The problem was that when *Lancet* launched an independent review and asked Surgisphere to transfer their complete database for evaluation, the third party reviewers were unable to access all of the data. Surgisphere said that it could not release all of the data because it would violate client agreements and confidentiality requirements. This led the three authors to withdraw their support for the article's conclusions.

Aside from the efficacy of these anti-malaria drugs for the treatment of COVID-19 patients, and whether or not there were serious medical risks associated with the taking of these drugs themselves, one other potential negative effect of Trump's promotion of these drugs was that the public demand for them was causing a shortage of the drug for legitimate uses. Hydroxychloroquine had been proven to be an effective treatment for existing rheumatic and autoimmune diseases like lupus, and the run on the drug by those who wanted to use it experimentally for coronavirus depleted the supply for people who already needed the drug to survive. Trump's promotion of the drug at his March 19 news conference immediately led to a stampede of surging demand for it, and by March 23, supplies were running low at pharmacies that were already supplying existing clients who took the drug to treat other diseases.[32]

The potential problems posed by this anti-malaria drug certainly did not deter *Fox Nation* star Laura Ingraham from promoting it to her nearly four million viewers on a nightly basis. Ingraham assured her viewers that hydroxychloroquine was "a game-changer" in the fight against coronavirus.[33] She featured recovered patients on her show to describe the "miracle turnaround" they experienced once they used the drug, gushing that the amazing results were "[l]ike Lazarus, up from the grave."[34] She denigrated anyone who questioned the drug's efficacy as being "in total denial."[35] Ingraham dismissed the caution displayed by public health experts by saying that "they want a double-blind controlled study on whether the sky is blue."[36]

Another *Fox News* prime-time host, Tucker Carlson, had a guest on his show named Gregory Rigano to promote the drug. Mr. Rigano, who claimed that hydroxychloroquine was "100% effective" against coronavirus, was identified as an advisor to Stanford University School of Medicine. Stanford, however, denied knowing him.[37]

After having induced Mr. Trump to jump on the hydroxychloroquine bandwagon, *Fox News* almost completely shut down its promotional program for the drug once the Veterans Administration test results came out questioning both the efficacy and the safety of the drug.[38]

Firing the Real Scientists; Replacing Them With Charlatans

Trump, apparently feeling that Ingraham and his other friends at *Fox News* had left him in the lurch on the hydroxychloroquine issue, lashed out at a target within the federal bureaucracy that had been criticizing Trump's fixation on this drug as a cure-all. Dr. Rick Bright, the director of the Department of Health and Human Services' Biomedical Advanced Research and Development Authority (BARDA), was fired from his position in late April.[39] Dr. Bright, the official who led the federal agency involved in developing a coronavirus vaccine, had been pressing for rigorous vetting of hydroxychloroquine. He accused the Trump administration of putting "politics and cronyism ahead of science," and claimed that he had been pressured to direct money towards hydroxychloroquine, which he described as one of several "potentially dangerous drugs promoted by those with political connections."[40] In a statement, Dr. Bright stated: "I am speaking out because to combat this deadly virus, science — not politics or cronyism — has to lead the way."[41]

Don't Drink the Clorox (and no gargling with Lysol either)!

Within days after Trump was forced to draw back on his hydroxy-chloroquine hype and the firing of Dr. Bright, Trump started a new campaign, promoting the power of sunlight and ultraviolet rays, as well as disinfectant, as the new sure-fire cure-all for coronavirus.

During his daily White House marathon on April 23, Administrator William N. Bryan, the head of science at the Department of Homeland

Security, told the briefing that the agency had tested how sunlight and disinfectants — including bleach and alcohol — can kill the coronavirus on surfaces in as little as 30 seconds.[42] Trump could barely contain himself. "Supposing we hit the body with a tremendous — whether it's ultraviolet or just very powerful light," Mr. Trump mused out loud, gesturing to Mr. Bryan, "And I think you said that hasn't been checked, but we're going to test it?" He then continued, sharing with all his other brilliant idea: "And then I said, supposing you brought the light inside the body, either through the skin or some other way."[43]

Mr. Trump then turned to Dr. Deborah Birx, the White House coronavirus response coordinator, who had already turned pale with a frozen smile on her face. He asked her to confirm his theory that sunlight was an effective tool against viruses, and more specifically, the coronavirus.[44] "Not as a treatment," Dr. Birx replied. "I mean, certainly fever is a good thing when you have a fever. It helps your body respond. But not as — I have not seen heat or . . . "[45] Dr. Birx's response helplessly floated off into oblivion.

Undeterred by Dr. Birx's less than enthusiastic endorsement, Trump then pivoted to his alternative theory about the possible medical benefits of disinfectants in the fight against the virus. "And then I see the disinfectant where it knocks it out in a minute — one minute — and is there a way we can do something like that by injection inside, or almost a cleaning?" he asked. "Because you see it gets in the lungs, and it does a tremendous number on the lungs, so it would be interesting to check that."[46]

Trump's suggestion of injecting a disinfectant inside the body doubtlessly caused at least one of his medical advisory team to suffer a severe anxiety attack, and it set off alarm bells throughout the country, and indeed the world. Experts warned that ultraviolet lamps could cause skin cancer when exposed outside the body, so it is reasonable to assume that any exposure inside the body would be equally or more dangerous. Bleach and other disinfectants may kill microbes when properly used outside the body, but if swallowed or otherwise ingested, they can kill you. That is why bottles of bleach and other disinfectants carry dire warnings of ingestion dangers.

Emergency management officials in Washington State immediately responded by posting a warning on Twitter: "Please don't eat Tide pods or inject yourself with any kind of disinfectant," they wrote, before urging the public to rely only on official medical advice about COVID-19. "Just don't make a bad situation worse."[47]

The maker of the disinfectants Lysol and Dettol also issued a statement warning against the improper use of their products: "As a global leader in health and hygiene products, we must be clear that under no circumstance should our disinfectant products be administered into the human body (through injection, ingestion or any other route)," the company said.[48] The company's concerns that the public might take the president's remarks seriously were understandable, especially since an Arizona man had died on March 24 and his wife hospitalized after the couple ingested a form of chloroquine used for cleaning fish tanks.[49] They apparently were following what they thought was an endorsement of the drug by President Trump, who had described it as a possible "game-changer" in the fight against coronavirus.[50]

* * * * *

Unfortunately, the tangled web of pandemic deniers, conspiracy theorists, and snake oil salesmen led by the president himself as Huckster-in-Chief further crippled the U.S. response effort to the COVID-19 crisis. And yet the leaderless ship-of-state forged ahead through the stormy waters of the pandemic, with the governors of the states and mayors of the largest cities stepping up to meet the challenge as best they could.

21

HOW COVID-19 AND THE U.S. RESPONSE TARGETED MINORITIES

"It's awfully close to genocide by default"
- Gregg Gonsalves, Professor, Yale University

COVID-19 has often been referred to in the media as "the great equalizer,"[1] as if to suggest that it is an equal-opportunity disease putting everyone equally at risk regardless of race, ethnicity, or income. This is not true. The virus is not color blind; rather, it has been targeting people of color and Native Americans at an alarmingly disproportionate rate.

As of May 11, when the country was starting to close in on the 80,000 mark for the number of U.S. deaths from coronavirus, an analysis from the American Public Media (APM) Research Lab showed that 17,155 Black Americans were known to have died due to COVID-19.[2] These approximately 17,000 known African American deaths were out of nearly 65,000 fatalities for which race and ethnicity data were available. To put those numbers into context, although African Americans only make up 13% of the total population from which the data was derived, 25% of all COVID-19 deaths were African Americans.[3] Other studies have put this percentage of coronavirus-related minority deaths at closer to one-third. By contrast, about 62% of the population in places reporting race and ethnicity are white; however, white residents make up 49% of COVID-19 deaths, the research showed.[4]

In Georgia, African Americans make up 80% of people hospitalized for coronavirus, although they comprise only 31% of the state's population.[5] In Chicago, 72% of those who died of the disease were Black, despite making up only 30% of the city's population.[6] In Louisiana, African Americans make up 32% of the population but account for around 70% of deaths.[7] In North Carolina's Mecklenburg County – home of Charlotte, the state's largest city – Black Americans make up 32.9% of residents but accounted for

43.7% of reported coronavirus cases as of April 4.[8] In Milwaukee County, Wisconsin, Black Americans make up about 27% percent of the population but comprised almost half of all COVID-19 infections and 71% of all fatalities.[9] Next door in Michigan, state health officials report that 33% of COVID-19 cases have occurred among Blacks, ten percentage points higher than whites, and more than twice the state's percentage of Black residents.[10] Black Americans also accounted for 41% of deaths in Michigan, compared with 28% among whites.[11] The statistics in Detroit were particularly disturbing, where Black Americans make up 80% of the city's population. Detroit represented only 7% of Michigan's population, but 26% of the state's infections and 25% of its deaths.[12]

Other minority groups have also been hit disproportionately hard by the virus. In New York City, Latino Americans make up about 29% of the city's population but represent nearly 34% of the patients who had died of COVID-19.[13] And almost 28% of the city's known deaths were among Black Americans, who represent about 24% of the population.[14]

Native Americans have also been particularly hard hit by the virus. The Arizona Department of Health Services reported during April that Native Americans make up 16% of the state's COVID-19 related deaths, despite representing only 6% of the state's population.[15] In New Mexico, Native Americans make up less than 10% of the population but over one-third of coronavirus cases.[16] The Navajo Nation, which includes areas of Arizona, Utah, and New Mexico, reported 1,197 positive coronavirus cases and 44 deaths as of April 24.[17] If it were a state, it would rank third in the country for confirmed cases per 100,000 population, behind only New York and New Jersey.[18]

Many health departments did not even include Native Americans in their racial demographic data, even in areas with high numbers of Native residents. A large number of Native Americans live in urban areas, such as New York City and Los Angeles. But neither city explicitly includes Native Americans in the breakdowns of their COVID-19 data.[19]

Studies outside the U.S. also showed the same disproportionate burden that this deadly disease placed on Blacks and other minorities. In the U.K., a study released on May 7 showed that Black people in the U.K. were dying of coronavirus at a rate more than four times greater than whites and even when these numbers are discounted for age and demographic factors, Blacks would still be dying from the disease at more than twice the rate of whites.[20]

Racial and Ethnic Disparities in Access to Health Care Equals Poorer Health

There are many reasons for the health disparities along racial and ethnic lines in the U.S., starting – in the case of African Americans – with a history of slavery, racism, segregation, and discrimination. Black Americans have more serious medical issues and less access to health care. Blacks are more likely to live in more impoverished and disadvantaged communities, often downwind from polluting industrial smokestacks or toxic waste dumps. Black Americans also have had traditionally high rates of unemployment and are often the first to be laid off when there is an economic downturn, as there is now.

Racial disparities in health care were more pronounced in the South, in part because a number of governors, including former Louisiana Governor Bobby Jindal, rejected Medicaid expansion under the Affordable Care Act. It was not until Democratic Governor John Bel Edwards took office in 2016 that Medicaid was expanded in Louisiana. The 2016 expansion, which covers 10% of the people in the state, decreased annual mortality in Louisiana, cut insurance rates in half, and expanded access to care.[21] However, Louisiana was the only state in the "Deep South" to embrace the ACA.

Even before the coronavirus pandemic began, African Americans and other minorities were coming up short with regard to almost every generally accepted public health and actuarial yardstick. Life expectancy for African American men and women has always been shorter than for non-Hispanic whites,[22] which is unsurprising since the disease and death rate for chronic illnesses has typically been higher for Black Americans than for whites. According to the U.S. Department of Health and Human Services' Office of Minority Health, the disease and death rate for Black people is generally higher than that of whites for "heart disease, stroke, cancer, asthma, influenza and pneumonia, diabetes, HIV/AIDS, and homicide."[23]

Fifteen years ago, according to the CDC, Black Americans had a life expectancy at birth of 71.8 years, compared to whites, where the figure was 77.3 years.[24] Over the years, this gap narrowed, and by May 2017, Black Americans had a life expectancy of 75.6 years, only a few years less than the average life expectancy for whites at 79 years.[25] One reason for the closing of this gap was that heart disease, the leading cause of death in the U.S., was killing Black and white Americans at about the same rate. However, Black Americans aged 35 to 64 were found to be 50% more likely than whites to have high blood pressure.[26] With the onset of the coronavirus pandemic, it is suspected that the gap may begin to widen again, but any definitive conclusions will have to await a new study after the worst of the coronavirus crisis has passed.

Lack of access to adequate health care has also been a major contributor to the generally poor health experienced by many Native Americans. The CDC has also reported that Native Americans experience diabetes three times more than any other racial or ethnic group in the U.S., and have the highest rates of asthma among racial groups.[27] Before the pandemic, the federal health system serving Native Americans was already chronically underfunded, "[h]ealth disparities are nice words for systematic racism... it's the residual effects of the founding of this country," said demographer Desi Rodriguez-Lonebear (Cheyenne).[28]

Factors Leading to Poorer Outcomes For Minorities When COVID-19 Strikes

Factors such as less access to reliable health care, plus a higher incidence of serious underlying illnesses in minority and Native American communities, make minority communities much more vulnerable to the coronavirus pandemic. Minorities are more likely to have a more serious course of illness when coronavirus strikes since many people of color also have "co-morbidities" and thus are more vulnerable to the ravages of the disease. When the virus hits people with underlying health issues, there is an increased likelihood of hospitalization and even death. Certain chronic conditions prevalent in minority communities, such as renal failure, require the patient outside the home for treatments like dialysis, which makes them even more vulnerable to coronavirus since the risk of getting infected by the virus increases every time they leave their home.

Dr. Philip Levy, a professor of emergency medicine and assistant vice president at Wayne State University in Detroit, explained the close association between hypertension and poor health outcomes that Black Americans in Detroit were experiencing: "What we are seeing is that because of the way [COVID-19] attacks the body, in terms of what it does in the lungs and how it interacts with the part of the body that controls the blood system, people with hypertension are more susceptible to the illness itself."[29] Dr. Levy further pointed out that it was not just elderly Black people who are falling prey to the virus: "[t]here's a high degree of hypertension among younger individuals here, where they have elevated blood pressure on a higher basis," he said, "Young people think they are invincible, but they might have hypertension at 30 and succumb to this infection."[30]

Racial and Ethnic Stereotypes, Biases and Misconceptions In Health Care

As if COVID-19 was not enough of a challenge for minorities, some studies have concluded that white doctors have shown an unconscious bias against minority patients. These studies showed that not only were white doctors spending more time with white patients than Black or other minority patients, but the white doctors also prescribed different treatments for these differing demographics.[31] Since the start of the coronavirus crisis, this unconscious bias has continued. Initial indications are that doctors are less likely to refer African Americans for testing when they visit a clinic with symptoms of COVID-19.[32] Since the disease can progress quickly, it is reasonable to infer that a disparity in testing can lead to considerably worse outcomes. In addition, reports of a lack of early communication regarding the threat of COVID-19 in minority communities, as well as confusing messages, produced an information vacuum in some Black communities that allowed rumors to circulate, such as the false rumor that Black people were immune to the disease.[33]

African Americans were similarly stereotyped during the yellow fever epidemic in Philadelphia during the 1790s. Dr. Benjamin Rush, a respected white Philadelphia physician, and others advanced the idea that Black people were somehow biologically immune to yellow fever. According to Rush's theory, since Black people were immune, they should be relied upon to care for the sick, dig graves, and cart away and bury bodies.[34] Rush and his cohorts seem to have ignored the uncomfortable fact that 240 Black residents of Philadelphia died during the worst of the yellow fever outbreaks there.[35] Unfortunately, these kinds of racial myths in medicine remains a part of the U.S. psyche even today.

Although there are no inherent biological differences between the races when it comes to susceptibility to virus diseases, there most certainly are disparities in access to health care and living environments between predominantly minority areas of a city and the more affluent and whiter neighborhood. For example, in Chicago, even before the pandemic hit, officials had calculated that white Chicagoans had an average life expectancy of 8.8 years longer than Black Americans.[36] "These communities, structurally, they're breeding grounds for the transmission of the disease," Dr. Sharrelle Barber, an assistant research professor of epidemiology and biostatistics at Drexel University, said, "It's not biological. It's really these existing structural inequalities that are going to shape the racial inequalities in this pandemic."[37]

Arline Geronimus, a professor of public health at the University of Michigan, said that one factor that might make the coronavirus more devastating for African Americans is that they experience high levels of stress-mediated wear and tear known as "weathering."[38] Stresses like exposure to toxins, lack of sleep, and racial discrimination, Dr. Geronimus said, can cause a kind of accelerated aging. The coronavirus is most lethal in people over 65, but members of minority communities that are aging at a faster rate may have weakened immune systems and other signs of aging even before they hit 65.

But there is a fundamental lack of race-related data being collected during the coronavirus pandemic to analyze these issues properly. Some of the hardest-hit states — such as California, New Jersey, New York, and Washington — have not provided statewide information about the race of patients.[39] Senators Elizabeth Warren, Kamala Harris, and Cory Booker have demanded that the Trump administration collect race and ethnicity data on coronavirus testing and treatment.[40] And Jumaane D. Williams, the public advocate for New York City, has strongly requested that Mayor Bill de Blasio release a breakdown of cases by race.[41]

To the extent, however, that data is available, this data has confirmed the anticipated trends, which is that race is a significant factor in determining that a case of COVID-19 is much more likely to lead to a serious illness and fatality. "This current crisis lays out what we have known for a long time, which is that your ZIP code is often a determinant of your health outcome," said Dr. Mandy Cohen, secretary of the North Carolina Department of Health and Human Services.[42]

Racial Discrimination in Availability of Testing

During the coronavirus crisis, National Public Radio (NPR) conducted an investigation of the location of public testing sites in Texas during the May time-frame when Texas was re-opening.[43] Specifically, NPR wanted to determine whether testing sites were equally distributed in various diverse neighborhoods, or whether there was a bias in favor of predominantly white neighborhoods. The investigation found that in four out of six of the largest cities in Texas, testing sites were disproportionately located in whiter neighborhoods, which was troubling since Black and Latino communities were being hit much harder by the disease. Also, as a result of these disparities, there was a higher likelihood that public health professionals would miss pockets of infection and hotspots in minority communities that could evolve into new large outbreaks. "If you're casting a very small net, and you're shining a flashlight on a small portion of infections that are out there, you might think you're doing OK," said Dr. Jennifer Nuzzo, lead epidemiologist for the Johns Hopkins COVID Testing Insights Initiative. "Whereas there's this whole pool of infections that you haven't seen."

This NPR investigation highlights the larger problem that most states and cities across the country either do not track or do not report the racial breakdown of tests that are conducted, and certainly the locations where testing sites have been set up in those states and cities. Although hard data is not available, NPR tentatively concluded that the racial disparities in testing found in Texas were typical of what was happening elsewhere around the country.

Is This A Genocide By Default?

Gregg Gonsalves, a professor of epidemiology and law at Yale University, has concluded that the U.S. response to the coronavirus is "awfully close to genocide by default." "How many people will die this summer, before Election Day?" Professor Gonsalves has asked. "What proportion of the deaths will be among African Americans, Latinos, other people of color? This is getting awfully close to genocide by default. What else do you call mass death by public policy?"[44]

Although there is no evidence that the Trump administration has any carefully thought-out secret policy to kill off large portions of minority groups in this country through intentional exposure to COVID-19, Professor Gonsalves has argued that "what is happening in the U.S. is purposeful, considered negligence, omission, failure to act by our leaders."[45] In other words, it is possible – and indeed probable – that the Trump administration's inaction and failure to design and implement a vigorous coronavirus response plan may well have been the result, at least in part, on a recognition that the disproportionate brunt of the serious illnesses and deaths would fall on minority populations. And since minorities may be reliably assumed to vote Democratic, this result would not necessarily be seen as a bad thing in the eyes of some White House and Republican strategists.

Even experts who may not necessarily go so far as to accuse the Trump administration of a quasi-genocide are justifiably appalled by the federal government's disastrous response (or non-response) to the coronavirus crisis. They are also deeply troubled by the grim data showing which segments of the population are most severely impacted by the coronavirus crisis. The CDC itself has recognized that a disproportionately large percentage of the "essential workers" that risk infection every day are people of color, and that these minorities fall within the most vulnerable sectors of the population when it comes to the likelihood of a serious illness from an infection and a higher incidence of death. According to the CDC website, "The risk of infection may be greater for workers in essential industries who continue to work outside the home despite outbreaks in their communities, including some people who may need to continue working in these jobs because of their economic circumstances."[46]

Even if they are not technically "essential workers," minority peoples tend to be employed in jobs that do not permit them to stay "sheltered-in-place" and to work remotely from home. As New York Governor Andrew Cuomo has explained: "There are more public workers, Latino and African-American, who don't have a choice, frankly, but to go out there every day and drive the bus and drive the train and show up for work—and wind up subjecting themselves to, in this case, the virus, whereas many other people who had the option just absented themselves."[47]

The Trump Administration Implies That Minorities Are Responsible for Their Greater Share of COVID-19 Illnesses and Deaths

There has always been a subterranean strain of bias and thinly disguised racism among some medical professionals and public officials that suggests that certain minority cultures, particularly African American culture, does not sufficiently emphasize the importance of maintaining a healthy lifestyle and good diet, and this lack of focus on good health has inevitably resulted in poor minority health, increased hospitalizations, and shorter life spans. The Trump administration has toyed with this theory to try and explain away the high death rate from COVID-19 in the U.S., especially among Blacks and other minorities.

Alex Azar, Secretary of Health and Humans Services, actually tried to explain away some of the high coronavirus death numbers that the U.S. was experiencing by suggesting that the underlying health conditions of Americans, in particular in minority communities, contributed significantly to the death toll from the coronavirus: "Unfortunately the American population is very diverse," said Secretary Azar in a *CNN* interview with Jake Tapper, adding,"It is a population with significant unhealthy co-morbidities that do make many individuals in our...minority communities particularly at risk here because of significant underlying disease health disparities and disease co-morbidities – and that is an unfortunate legacy in our health care system that we certainly do need to address."[48]

When Tapper pushed back, asking Azar if he was implying the reason so many Americans had died from COVID-19 was because they were at fault and were "unhealthier than the rest of the world," Azar said no, that was not what he meant. However, Secretary Azar continued to emphasize that the U.S. had a "significantly disproportionate burden of co-morbidities... (including) obesity, hypertension, diabetes," adding that "these are demonstrated facts that do make us at risk for any type of disease burden."[49] Secretary Azar further described the problem by emphasizing that U.S. people generally have risker profiles.[50]

One of the Scientists Leading the Search for a Vaccine is a Young Black Woman

Although members of minority communities have had difficulties breaking into the upper ranks of scientific research, one of the government scientists leading the search for a vaccine against this disease that has been disproportionately targeting people of color is a young Black female. Kizzmekia Corbett, Ph.D., who is one of the leading viral immunologists at the National Institutes of Health in Bethesda, Maryland, briefed President Trump, Dr. Anthony S. Fauci, and other officials in early March on the progress that had been made in developing a vaccine there and in coordination with other public and private laboratories.

Dr. Corbett, who is now in her 30s, grew up surrounded by tobacco and soybean farms in rural Hurdle Mills, North Carolina. Identified by her teachers at an early age for her exceptional talent, she had the good fortune of being set on a path that ultimately led her to the National Institute of Health and her current key position in the battle against the coronavirus. When Corbett was in the 10th grade, a teacher recognized her potential and recommended her for Project SEED, a program for gifted minorities. This program, in particular, allowed her to study chemistry in labs at the University of North Carolina at Chapel Hill. Shortly thereafter, she won a full scholarship for minority students interested in studying science at the University of Maryland, where she was first introduced to NIH. Corbett and her team are now working at a furious pace in coordination with the Kaiser Permanente Washington Health Research Institute in Seattle.

In addition to being a brilliant scientist, Corbett has also made waves as an outspoken advocate for minority rights on the internet and in the media. On February 27, Corbett posted a tweet lamenting the lack of diversity on President Trump's coronavirus task force: "The task force is largely people (white men) he appointed to their positions as director of blah blah institute. They are indebted to serve him, NOT the people."[51] Also, as public health officials started reporting the data showing how the virus was disproportionately killing African Americans, Corbett vented on Twitter. "I tweet for the people who will die when doctors have to choose who gets the last ventilator and ultimately … who lives," she wrote March 29.[52] When someone responded that the virus "is a way to get rid of us," Corbett replied, "Some have gone as far to call it genocide. I plead the fifth."[53]

Corbett's outspoken comments triggered a storm of protest in the right-wing and conservative media. One commentator charged her of "appear[ing] to be an anti-white racial grievance monger who believes the coronavirus is being used to commit genocide against Black Americans…"[54] *Fox News* host Tucker Carlson read several of her tweets aloud on his show and questioned her "commitment to scientific inquiry and rational thought."[55] He further accused Corbett of "spouting lunatic conspiracy theories."[56]

Dr. Corbett has not personally responded to these attacks, but other prominent African Americans have leaped to her defense. For example, Robert Bullard, a professor of urban planning and environmental policy at Texas Southern University in Houston, has said, "What I've seen parade across that stage in the task force, other than the surgeon general, are all white people," adding, "To look and see these horrific disproportionate numbers of African Americans dying of coronavirus vindicates her tweet. She knew this virus would be like … a heat-seeking missile that would target the most vulnerable."[57]

* * * * *

The virus's disproportionate assault on people of color has left some health care professionals and academics wondering if the coronavirus pandemic will ultimately become a Black and minority pandemic.[58] Once the wealthy and whiter portions of the population feel that the virus is under control, at least with regard to their own communities, there is a serious question as to whether America still really cares that it mostly continues to ravage Black and brown communities. Will racial demographic information in testing and health be used to improve treatments for this disease among communities of color, or will it be used for more perverse and discriminatory purposes? These are urgent and open questions that must be answered at the national level.

22

TRUMP DECLARES "MISSION ACCOMPLISHED," AND THEN COVID-19 ATTACKS THE WHITE HOUSE

On May 1, 2003, President George W. Bush landed in a fighter jet on the aircraft carrier *USS Abraham Lincoln*, which was returning from the Persian Gulf following the U.S. invasion of Iraq. As President Bush got out of the fighter jet, wearing a flight suit and helmet, a massive banner with the words "Mission Accomplished" was emblazoned across the ship's superstructure for the TV cameras and all America to see.

In a brief speech given on the deck of the carrier with the ship's crew assembled behind him, Bush announced: "Major combat operations in Iraq have ended. In the battle of Iraq, the United States and our allies have prevailed."[1] To be sure, major combat operations against the Iraqi regime of Sadaam Hussein may have ceased at that point, and American troops may have seized the capital city of Bagdad, but little did President Bush or any other American know, or even suspect, at that point, was that American troops would remain in Iraq for many bloody years.

At first, White House staffers said that the "Mission Accomplished" banner was made by Navy personnel on their own, in a spontaneous outpouring of support for the president. Then the White House staff members backtracked, admitting that they made the banner, but that U.S. Navy personnel hung it. White House spokesman Scott McClellan told CNN, "We took care of the production of it. We have people to do those things. But the Navy actually put it up."[2] According to John Dickerson of *Time Magazine*, the White House later conceded that they hung the banner but still insisted it had been done at the request of the crew members. And so it goes. Presidents may come and go at the White House, but the impulse of White House senior staffers to overstage a photo op and then try to spin the story with gratuitous embellishments never changes.

For critics of the Iraq war, the photo-op became a symbol of the Bush administration's false pretenses and outright lies to the American people regarding the reasons why the country was being led into a totally unnecessary and extremely wasteful war, both in terms of human life and in treasure. The banner also came to symbolize the supreme irony of Bush giving a victory speech only a few weeks after the beginning of a war that would last seven years.

Fast forward to Wednesday, April 29. Presidential son-in-law and heir apparent to the Trump crown, Jared Kushner, appeared on camera on the administration's unofficial news outlet, *Fox News*, to declare victory over coronavirus. It was truly another Mission Accomplished moment, breathtaking in its audacity as only a bald-faced lie can be. "We're on the other side of the medical aspect of this [coronavirus crisis]," Kushner said. "We've achieved all the different milestones that are needed. The federal government rose to the challenge, and this is a great success story."[3]

Which part of the "great success story" that Kushner was referring to was unclear. Perhaps it was the part where President Trump repeated downplayed the threat that the virus, which was already working its way across China, posed to America. Or was it the utter failure of the Trump administration to organize a timely and coherent federal response to the pandemic and to assemble the massive amounts of protective gear, equipment, and testing capacity that was needed to address this looming crisis? Or was it the shameless presidential promotion of an anti-malarial drug that his own experts were telling him was ineffective and, indeed, dangerous? Or perhaps it was his refusal to set an example for the rest of the country by swallowing his pride for once and wearing a mask in public? How about the moment of "success" in late April when the U.S. hit the 1 million case milestone, with over 60,000 Americans dead from the virus? Was it the "strength" he displayed by never ever acknowledging the pain that so many families were going through as a result of a loss of a loved one to the virus?

Vice President Mike Pence confirmed to reporters on Tuesday, May 5, that the White House might look to close down the special coronavirus task force he had been leading, possibly in early June.[4] After all, since Trump and Kushner were declaring victory, it was time to fold up the tents, close down the task force and change the subject to something – anything – else. "It really is all a reflection of the tremendous progress we've made as a country," Pence said. "The president stood up the White House coronavirus task force … to marshal a national response." "And as I've said before," Pence continued, "as we continue to practice social distancing and states engage in safe and responsible reopening plans, I truly believe — and the trend lines support it — that we could be in a very different place" by late May or early June.

This would all have been wonderful if it had been true. However, an expert analysis conducted at that time suggested that the number of coronavirus-related deaths nationwide could double by August to 135,000. This turned out to be on the low side since there were over 177,000 fatalities by the end of August.

The real reason for the closing of the White House task force (which was technically continued in the face of widespread public criticism, but was effectively DOA as of early June) was that the Trump administration could now shift responsibility for the fiasco that the federal response had turned into back to the CDC, FEMA, Homeland Security, and the other agencies. Then, as anticipated, the chorus of Congressional and press finger-pointing that would inevitably follow could be redirected at the leadership of those federal agencies, not the White House itself. The state government and the governors could also take some of the blame as the full story of what happened to the U.S. in the age of coronavirus was finally told.

The Trump administration was fully gearing up for the fall re-election campaign, and the lingering consequences of the pandemic were the last thing that Trump wanted handing around his neck like a millstone, threatening to drag him underwater. So when faced with a disaster, he did what every other crafty leader throughout history has done, which is to declare victory and move on. And if the feared "second wave" of the virus struck the country in the fall, he could blame it on the states and the federal agencies, arguing that he had everything under control by early summer.

On Monday, May 11, President Trump said that the number of coronavirus cases was going down "almost everywhere," even though a White House report that had not yet been released showed infection rates spiking across the United States.⁵ "We have met the moment, and we have prevailed," Trump told reporters during a White House briefing.

The following day, however, on May 12, two of the Trump administrations senior health officials – Dr. Anthony S. Fauci and the CDC Director, Dr. Robert R. Redfield - painted a grim and entirely different picture of the situation, telling a Senate panel that the coronavirus pandemic was far from contained. These two officials further noted that the U.S. still lacked critical testing capacity and the ability to trace the contacts of those infected.⁶ "If we do not respond in an adequate way when the fall comes, given that it is without a doubt that there will be infections that will be in the community, then we run the risk of having a resurgence," said Dr. Fauci. He further elaborated: "If states reopen their economies too soon, he warned, "there is a real risk that you will trigger an outbreak that you may not be able to control," which could result not only in "some suffering and death that could be avoided, but could even set you back on the road to trying to get economic recovery."

In other words, the Trump administration and the country had not "prevailed" as Trump had said as if the mere statement of wishful thinking would make it so.

The Virus's Sneak Attack On the White House

At about the same time that Trump, Kushner, and Pence were declaring victory over the country's number one viral enemy, and as Trump was exhorting his countrymen: "We have to get our country open again," 1600 Pennsylvania Avenue itself became a target of opportunity for the virus. Three top officials leading the White House response to the pandemic quarantined themselves after two Trump administration staff members — a valet to President Trump and Katie Miller, the press secretary for Vice President Mike Pence — tested positive for the virus.

Like many other members of the White House staff, Ms. Miller did not regularly wear a mask while at work. Indeed, just hours after receiving a negative diagnosis, she was seen on television talking without a mask within a few feet of several reporters, all of whom were wearing one.

One senior White House advisor summed up the sentiments of most of those who worked there: "It is scary to go to work," Kevin Hassett, a top economic adviser to the president, said on the CBS program "Face the Nation." Rumors were quickly spreading that the administration was having trouble containing a coronavirus outbreak as the disease rapidly spread through the warren of cramped offices that make up the three floors of the West Wing.[7]

When reports that Vice President Pence was in quarantine went "viral," administration officials stated on May 11 that Pence would not alter his routine or self-quarantine. However, it was confirmed that Dr. Fauci, Dr. Redfield, and Dr. Stephen Hahn, the FDA Commissioner, would be quarantined for two weeks. As a result, they had to testify via a video link with the Senate the following day.

The Navy's top admiral, Michael M. Gilday, also had to be quarantined after coming into contact with a family member who has tested positive for the coronavirus. It was further reported that a second member of the Joint Chiefs of Staff, Gen. Joseph L. Lengyel, the chief of the National Guard Bureau, tested positive for the coronavirus, although to further confuse the picture, there were questions raised about the reliability of the testing. A further alarm was also raised when a photograph of a meeting of the Joint Chiefs with President Trump over that weekend showed that neither Trump nor the military officials seated around the table wore masks.

Of course, there was ample testing for White House employees. All employees were being tested at least weekly, officials said, and a handful of Trump's top aides who regularly interact with the president were being tested daily. Outside the White House, however, most workplaces that President Trump was asking workers to return to did not have such ready access to such testing. Most restaurants, offices and retail stores do not have the ability to regularly test all their employees and quickly track down and quarantine the contacts of anyone who got infected.

Despite Trump's aversion to the wearing of a face mask, the White House culture was transformed virtually overnight as employees there were told to either work from home or to wear masks while in the White House. Members of the Secret Service who worked at the White House also started being seen wearing masks regularly. People who entered the White House campus, which includes the Eisenhower Executive Office Building, where many White House staff members work, started to be asked by medical doctors whether they had any of a list of symptoms. And the people closest to Mr. Trump — including Kayleigh McEnany, the White House press secretary; Mark Meadows, the chief of staff; and Hope Hicks, a senior adviser — started being tested daily.

Even as it struggled with an outbreak in the White House itself, the Trump administration continued in the early part of May to hold up the release of CDC's guidance on when and how states and businesses could start opening up again. The White House, which considered the CDC draft report on reopening to be too restrictive, was reported to be hard at work watering down the CDC draft so that businesses could open up more quickly, regardless of the consequences. "The virus is in the White House, any way you look at it," said Juliette Kayyem, a former assistant secretary of homeland security under President Barack Obama. "Whether it's contained or not, we will know soon enough. But the fact that a place — secured, with access to the best means to mitigate harm — is not able to stop the virus has the potential of undermining confidence in any capacity to defeat it."[8]

* * * * *

As the virus breached the secure perimeter of the White House, people around the country properly started asking themselves the obvious question: If it is so hard to maintain a healthy environment at 1600 Pennsylvania Avenue, with all of its unlimited resources, then how can businesses across the country that lacked the White House's resources effectively establish a safe space for their workers?[9] Nevertheless, President Trump and his administration officials continued to vigorously urge the states and businesses around the country to open up as soon as possible, without any clear guidance from the CDC as to how they could implement the conditions necessary to protect their employees, and in most cases, without the essential testing capabilities to monitor their employees' health.

23

COVID-19 AND THE ENVIRONMENT

*"Look, the sky is really blue!
Why can't it be that way all the time?"*
-unidentified child in Central Park, New York City

Nature and the environment strongly rebounded while coronavirus had driven at least 1 billion people indoors. Air pollution was down about 50% in New York and in every other U.S. city.[1] Photographic images of some of the pollution capitals of the world – such as New Delhi, Mexico City and Los Angeles – showed crystal clear blue skies free of their usual yellow-brown hue of soot and smog. Pictures of the San Zulian canal in Venice showed crystal clear waters with the seabed visible below.

As people stayed off the streets and sheltered in place, the world's wildlife grew increasingly bolder. Photographs of the downtown areas of major cities around the globe showed an almost post-apocalyptic vision of empty streets and roaming packs of wild animals. Coyotes were sighted wandering the streets of San Francisco and Chicago; mountain lions strolled in San Mateo with not a person in sight; Great Orme Kashmiri goats were seen foraging in the seemingly deserted seaside town in Wales; groundhogs munched on leftover pizza on Philadelphia streets; wild boars roamed downtown Barcelona and Haifa; red foxes sauntered through Nashville and made their home under the boardwalk in Toronto; and sea turtles nested on semi-deserted Florida beaches.

When you mess with Mother Nature, she has a way of eventually getting even. It was payback time for humanity. And, yes, payback's a bitch!

Throughout history, mankind has generally viewed wildlife and most of nature as its natural enemy, something to be conquered and subdued. We have largely succeeded in that endeavor, but at great cost to the natural components – especially the fresh water and clean air – that make this such a unique planet and hospitable place to live. In return, we have not been very good stewards of the environment with which we have been so blessed. Mankind has plundered the natural environment as if its resources were limitless and were put there solely for our own pleasure and consumption. We have destroyed much of the primordial rainforests and woodlands, and shamelessly polluted the air and the water resources of the planet. And finally, we have tampered with the earth's thermostat so much that it is rapidly rising towards a level where life as we know it will no longer be possible on much of the planet.

Of course, there were some environmental laws enacted along the way, and every Earth Day (until Earth Day 2020) speeches and demonstrations around the globe warned of the danger we humans have on the irreversible climate change, and that strong, concerted and immediate action must be taken on a global scale. This made most people feel good about themselves, but after everyone went home, most government leaders turned their attention to what they perceived as more important issues, such as re-election and profiting from their public position before leaving office.

The Obama Administration Makes Progress on Climate Change

And then America elected a president who rolled back hard-won environmental regulations, and announced that he was withdrawing the U.S. from the Paris Climate Accords, an effort by 195 countries to save the planet by reducing greenhouse gases that were a primary cause of the rapid warming trend over the past several decades.

The historic Paris Climate Accords were agreed to by the Obama administration on December 2015, and these Accords became part of a larger package of international environmental law under the United Nations Framework Convention on Climate Change (UNFCCC).[2] Due to the status of the U.S. and China as the greatest emitters of carbon dioxide, President Obama's support and his cooperation with China on climate change issues were one of the major factors leading to the convention's early success.[3] The primary objective of the Accords was to hold the increase in the global average temperature to well below 2 °C above "pre-industrial levels." This could only be done by all of the countries who were parties to the Accords to agree to substantially reduce greenhouse gas emissions, such as coal fired power plants and other heavily polluting industries. The emission-reduction targets for each nation were separately negotiated and were supposed to be voluntarily enforced, leading U.S. officials to regard the Paris Accords more like an executive agreement rather than a legally binding treaty. This removed the requirement for ratification of the agreement by the U.S. Congress.[4]

In addition to committing the U.S. to make significant reductions in greenhouse gas emissions, the Obama administration also committed the U.S. to contributing $3 billion to the Green Climate Fund, which had a goal of raising $100 billion a year by 2020.[5] The world seemed well on its way to finally taking some serious action to slow the pace of Climate Change and to keep its temperature ranges within habitable limits. This all sounds reasonable, doesn't it? And then a not-so-funny thing happened.

Trump Pulls the U.S. Out of the Paris Accords and Dismantles Obama's Environmental Regulations

On November 8, 2016, four days after the Paris Accords entered into force in the U.S., Donald Trump lost the popular vote by several million ballots but was elected anyway as President by an anachronistic Electoral College. To put it mildly, this was not a good development for the causes of pandemic prevention or for Climate Change mitigation. Despite the fact that 99.99% of the world's scientists believed that industrial activity and other man-made activities were a major contributor to Climate Change, Trump and a few conservative Republicans were among the dwindling ranks of climate change skeptics.[6] In 2012, Trump tweeted that he believed the concept of global warming was created by China in order to impair American competitiveness.[7] Since many of the swing states in the 2016 presidential campaign were also coal producing states, Trump used this skepticism to his political advantage. He promised to reinvigorate the coal industry, which was providing much of the CO_2 and other gases that were direct contributors to climate change.

In order to support the coal industry and other heavily polluting industries, Trump vowed to dismantle all those annoying Obama environmental regulations that stood in the way of industry's goal of emitting as many tons of pollutants into the atmosphere and American waterways as possible. The razor-thin margins that put Trump over the top in the November 2016 election were his victories in several swing states that either had large coal industries or relied heavily on power plants that burned coal. Trump showed his gratitude to these industries during the first few months of his presidency by issuing executive orders reversing President Obama's Clean Power Plan and other environmental regulations.[8]

The Interconnectivity Between Pandemics and the Environment

While the recent industrial slowdowns and reduced pollution during the coronavirus crisis are at least temporary good news for the environment, it is likely to only be a momentary respite, and the planet will continue to warm unless drastic measures are taken.

Not only is the existential threat of climate change not going away anytime soon, but it is more closely linked to the coronavirus crisis than we might realize. The global climate changes that we are already experiencing at an accelerating rate are, in fact, the same forces that have unleashed the coronavirus killer virus, as well as the next ones that will be coming.

There are some very real connections between COVID-19 and climate change, but not as the coronavirus protesters and climate change deniers would have us believe.[9] Neither one of them is "a hoax;" they are both very real and interrelated. There is already strong evidence emerging that air pollution is increasing the odds that people will die from COVID-19. A one microgram per meter-cubed increase in particulate matter (particles in the air) raises the chances of death from COVID-19 by 15%.[10] In other words, a very small change in air quality leads to a substantial increase in risk of people dying.

An analysis by the Medical Research Council Toxicology Unit at Cambridge University compared regional data on total COVID-19 cases and deaths against levels of three major air pollutants.[11] The study used data from seven regions in England, where a minimum of 2,000 infections and 200 deaths were reported from February to April 8, 2020; a comparison was made between COVID-19-related illnesses and deaths to air pollution records from more than 120 sites in 2018 and 2019.[12] The study concluded that fatalities from coronavirus infections were greater in London and other parts of the U.K. where the levels of pollutants (primarily nitrogen dioxide and nitrogen oxide) were the highest, primarily from traffic fumes.[13]

Research conducted by the Harvard T.H. Chan School of Public Health also showed that air pollution was associated with higher COVID-19 death rates. This study looked at 3,000 U.S. counties and compared COVID-19 deaths and levels of fine particulate matter in the air.[14] They found that even small increases in long-term exposure to the pollutants led to significantly higher mortality, which makes sense since this disease primarily attacks the lungs.[15]

This correlation between healthier environments and reduced COVID-related illness and death was encouraging news for New York City and other cities that have been hardest hit by the coronavirus crisis. In March, for instance, researchers at Columbia University calculated that carbon monoxide emissions in New York City, mostly coming from vehicles, fell by 50%.[16] Therefore, a dramatic improvement in public health could be anticipated, including the ability of infected New Yorkers and other Americans to resist COVID-19 and other infectious diseases that will inevitably come in the future.

Since environmental pollution is a contributing cause to COVID-19 deaths, and pollution is also a contributor to global warming and climate change, the global battle against the coronavirus and the global campaign to prevent climate change have a common enemy: carbon emissions, nitrogen oxide, nitrogen dioxide and other pollutants. In other words, climate solutions are pandemic solutions.

In addition to pollution, another direct connection between the coronavirus crisis and climate change is the massive deforestation of the planet. It is estimated that about 20% of carbon emissions relate in some way to deforestation, and deforestation is strongly suspected to have a correlation to an increase in infectious disease pandemics, such as COVID-19.[17]

Since the current working assumption is that most coronavirus outbreaks among humans originate from bats, COVID-19 origins are, most likely, similar to that of the Ebola virus. The Ebola virus originated from bats who were driven into closer proximity to human settlements in West Africa by the destruction of forests in the region. This deforestation is likely to have resulted in increased incidents of animal-human encounters, leading to the crossover of the Ebola virus (and probably many other viruses) directly from bats to humans, or from bats to animals to humans. Similarly, it is reasonably believed that the destruction of the Amazon rainforest in South America had much to do with malaria outbreaks.

What seems to be missing, therefore, in the current search for a "cure" for COVID-19 is the recognition of the environmental factors that have contributed to the increased outbreak and "cross-over" of viruses to humans. The prevention of any further net deforestation on the planet, and even programs to expand forested areas, is likely to reap benefits both for our immediate human health – through the prevention or at least delay in the arrival of the next pandemic – and for the longer-term health consequences of climate change.

Some of the public "social distancing" measures that have been instituted by many cities in both the U.S. and Europe may also have a profound positive effect on human health. Bike and pedestrian lanes and road closures have been sprouting up in Seattle, San Francisco, New York and other cities, with the ostensible goal of permitting people who are outdoors to be able to maintain at least six feet of distance from the next bike rider or pedestrian. However, these innovations also have the incidental desirous effect of reducing car and truck traffic in downtown areas and thus reducing pollution levels, which we now know is a contributing cause to both increased coronavirus vulnerability as well as climate change.

There are additional health benefits from these "public" social distancing measures, such as bike and pedestrian lanes and road closures. We know that "co-morbidities" such as obesity, diabetes and other indicia of poor health increase the likelihood of a "poor outcome" (i.e., longer illness or death) to a coronavirus infection. While coronavirus may be the latest epidemic to hit the U.S., the longstanding epidemics of obesity and diabetes have exacerbated and accelerated the coronavirus crisis. So to the extent that towns and cities can persuade citizens to get out of their cars or leave them where they were throughout most of the crisis (in the garage), and to walk or bike to work or the store, then the general health of the populace will be improved, and there will be reduced levels of obesity, diabetes and other chronic ailments that severely degrade the health of a huge number of Americans. Many European countries, such as Holland, have successfully encouraged the use of bicycles rather than cars, and the resulting health benefits have been significant.[18] There is no reason why the U.S. cannot replicate this model as well, leading to improved health as well as taking a bite out of the coronavirus crisis and climate change at the same time. If we are smart about it (a big "if"), we would be much better served if we do not return to the old "normal" as the coronavirus crisis abates. With changes in our lifestyles – more walking, more biking and less driving and less flying – we will be healthier and generating less pollution. In other words, we can both "flatten the curve" on the coronavirus pandemic and the next one to come, as well as "flattening the curve" on air pollution and climate change.

Global Benefits From Reduced Air Pollution in China

It is possible that the improved air pollution in China that was the direct result of the coronavirus lockdown of its major cities will ultimately result in the saving of as many lives as were lost to coronavirus. In February 2020, as the country ground to a halt, industrial emissions fell by 25% in China, according to an analysis by the climate group Carbon Brief.[19] When Carbon Brief did a follow-up analysis in early April, it found that China's 2020 emissions could fall by 5.5% from its 2019 levels.[20] If the same is true of the U.S. and Europe, as an unintended consequence of the mitigation restrictions imposed during the coronavirus crisis, then these countries may actually meet the goals agreed to for the reduction of their emissions as part of the Paris Accords. In other words, the pandemic may have the unintended positive consequence of bringing the world closer to its ultimate goal of keeping global warming below 2 degrees Celsius above pre-industrial global temperatures.

The 5.5% in reduced emissions from China tops the 3% reduction in emissions that followed the 2008 financial crash, when economies also slowed, and people traveled less. The same can be true for the U.S., if only the country collectively resolved to keep the carbon emissions at a lower level than before the crisis, for the sake of our health and the health of the planet. During the past three years, with the loosening of environmental regulations by the Trump administration, air pollution has actually gotten worse in the U.S. As the coronavirus crisis eases, there is no reason why the country has to go back to its prior polluting ways through excessive reliance on fossil fuels.

As we can all plainly see, Americans are driving their cars less due to the stay-at-home orders in their state, the voluntary impulse to keep as much "social distance" between themselves and others, unemployment, or just general reduced economic activity. This anecdotal evidence has been confirmed by Northern Arizona University climate scientist Kevin Gurney, who found that the amount of gasoline supplied in the U.S. – a close measurement of direct consumption – fell by 50% over the two-week period ending April 3.[21] Interestingly, the amount of diesel supplied has remained fairly stable, which is probably due to it being more of a commercial fuel, used for the semi-trailer trucks that are still making deliveries while the rest of us keep our cars in the garage.

* * * * *

Both the Climate Change and the coronavirus crises are clear warning signs. Mother Nature is not to be trifled with. The natural world – through various climate change mechanisms and the evolution of various microscopic yet highly infectious micro-organisms – has put us on notice that it stands ready to reclaim the planet that we have hopelessly trashed if we do not mend our ways. We are way beyond the point where vague feel-good promises made once a year on Earth Day will be enough to make up for our failures as the chosen "stewards" of the planet. Hopefully, we have heard the wake-up call and are prepared to take the necessary action. The day of reckoning is truly upon us.

24

HOW COVID-19 AND LAX HEALTH SAFETY STANDARDS ARE DEVASTATING WORKERS AT U.S. MEAT AND FOOD PROCESSING PLANTS

"They treat you like you're nothing, like you're an animal."
-meat processing worker, Greeley, Iowa

By mid-April, just as New York, New Jersey, Detroit, and other East Coast hot spots were reaching their peaks, the states that had primarily dodged the crisis up to that point were hit hard by the virus. Many of the new COVID-19 hotspots developed near towns and cities in states where large meat processing plants were located. The spread of the coronavirus also reached workers in processed food facilities, which make frozen dinners, baked goods, and dairy products. And finally, the outbreaks arrived at the farms and ranches where the poultry, pigs, and cattle originated. The spread of the disease throughout these meat and food processing plants reached epidemic proportions, engulfing both the workers in the plants as well as the residents in nearby communities where the workers lived.

Before the arrival of the coronavirus, these meat and food processing facilities were already some of the most dangerous workplaces in the country. The coronavirus pandemic made them even deadlier. By mid-May, almost half the current COVID-19 hotspots in the U.S. were linked to meat processing plants where the nation's poultry, pigs, and cattle are slaughtered and packaged for consumption.[1] As of May 15, at least 12 of the 25 hotspots identified in the U.S. – that is, counties with the highest infection rates – originated in meat factories where employees work side by side in cramped conditions.[2] In Nebraska, five counties had outbreaks linked to meat plants including Dakota County where about one out of every 14 residents tested positive, which was the second-highest per capita infection rate in the U.S.[3] Five Nebraska counties with meat processing plants accounted for almost half the state's 9,075 positive cases, according to data tracking by The *New York Times*.[4]

As of mid-May, the 11th highest rate of infection in the U.S. was in Dodge City, located in Ford County in the neighboring state of Kansas. In Ford County, one out of 28 residents were infected with COVID-19, likely linked to the meat processing plants there.[5] Indeed, all four of the hardest-hit Kansas counties have meat processing plants with infected employees that were driving the infection and death rates in these counties.

In North Texas, at least 220 workers at the Tyson Foods plant in Sherman tested positive for COVID-19 as of May 27, with some of those infected living in surrounding communities throughout Dallas-Fort Worth.[6] Some employees at the plant had already tested positive for the virus when, just two weeks earlier, Texas state officials conducted a large round of tests on more than 1,600 workers over a two-day period.

In Minnesota, another state home to numerous meat and food processing plants, was also hit by coronavirus outbreaks. In Nobles County, almost 500 workers at a large Brazilian-owned JBS pork plant tested positive.[7] The outbreak rapidly spread through the county, with 1,291 confirmed cases as of mid-May compared with just a handful in mid-April.[8] About one in 17 people in the county were testing positive.[9]

COVID-19 outbreaks were also reported at meat and food processing facilities in 15 other states, according to the CDC, including a beef plant in Colorado, a pork plant in Iowa, and a hamburger plant in Pennsylvania.[10]

Based on data collected by the Food and Environment Reporting Network, as of May 28, at least 237 meatpacking and food processing plants had confirmed cases of COVID-19, and at least one meatpacking plant and four food processing plants had closed.[11] In total, at least 20,649 workers in the food processing and meatpacking industries (18,437 meatpacking workers, 1,240 food processing workers, and 972 farmworkers) tested positive for COVID-19, and at least 73 workers (67 meatpacking workers and six food processing workers) died.[12]

In addition, nearly 300 USDA inspectors, whose jobs were to visit and inspect the 6,500 meat and food processing plants, were sickened by the virus, or under self-quarantine due to exposure.[13] At least four of these inspectors died.[14]

A Brief History of Slaughterhouses

The struggle for good hygiene in slaughterhouses and meat processing plants goes back to the 19th Century. In England, slaughterhouses were carefully regulated by law to ensure that good standards of hygiene were observed, that the spread of disease was minimized, and that needless animal cruelty was avoided. Slaughterhouses were equipped with specialized water supply systems to clean the operating areas effectively. Veterinary scientists, such as George Fleming and John Gamgee, campaigned for more stringent levels of inspection to prevent outbreaks of epizootics, such as rinderpest.[15] A devastating outbreak of rinderpest in 1865 interrupted England's meat supply for a period of many months. The Public Health Act of 1875 required local authorities in England to monitor slaughterhouses, and they were finally given powers to close unsanitary slaughterhouses in 1890.[16]

In the U.S., the Humane Slaughter Act of 1958 required that all swine, sheep, cattle, and horses be stunned unconscious with the application of a stunning device by a trained person before being hoisted up on the line.[17] However, unsanitary conditions in U.S. slaughterhouses continued for at least several more decades, particularly in the Chicago area. Upton Sinclair's novel *The Jungle* gave a fictionalized but accurate account of the unsanitary conditions in slaughterhouses and the meatpacking industry during the 1800s. This led to an investigation commissioned by President Theodore Roosevelt, and to the passage of the Meat Inspection Act and the Pure Food and Drug Act of 1906. This 1906 Act established the Food and Drug Administration (FDA).[18]

Worker Safety Pre-COVID-19

American meat processing workers are three times more likely to suffer serious injury than the average American worker.[19] National Public Radio (NPR) reported in 2016 that pig and cattle slaughterhouse workers are nearly seven times more likely to suffer repetitive strain injuries than the average U.S. worker.[20] In July 2018, The *Guardian* reported that, on average, there are two amputations a week involving U.S. slaughterhouse workers.[21] At Tyson Foods – the largest meat producer in America – it is estimated that one employee's finger or limb is amputated each month.[22] According to the Occupational Safety and Health Administration (OSHA), the meat and food processing industry were riddled with "serious safety and health hazards ... including dangerous equipment, musculoskeletal disorders, and hazardous chemicals."[23]

The worker safety statistics in the U.K. have been equally abysmal. The Bureau of Investigative Journalism reported that over a period of six years, 78 slaughter workers in the U.K. lost fingers, parts of fingers or limbs, more than 800 workers had serious injuries, and at least 4,500 had to take more than three days off due to accidents.[24]

Even if a meat processing worker survived with all of his or her limbs and digits intact, the worker would still be in serious danger of suffering major psychological trauma.[25] Some slaughterhouse workers are instructed to wear ear protectors to protect them from hearing the constant screams of animals being killed.[26] A 2016 study in *Organization* suggested that slaughterhouse workers consistently experience lower physical and psychological well-being along with increased incidences of negative coping behavior.[27] In particular, slaughterhouse workers are "at risk of Perpetration-Inducted Traumatic Stress, which is a form of post traumatic stress disorder and results from situations where the concerning subject suffering from PTSD was a causal participant in creating the traumatic situation."[28]

There is also a close correlation between slaughterhouse work and criminal or antisocial behavior. A 2009 study by criminologist Amy Fitzgerald indicated, "slaughterhouse employment increases total arrest rates, arrests for violent crimes, arrests for rape, and arrests for other sex offenses in comparison with other industries."[29] As the *PTSD Journal* explained, "These employees are hired to kill animals, such as pigs and cows that are largely gentle creatures. Carrying out this action requires workers to disconnect from what they are doing and from the creature standing before them. This emotional dissonance can lead to consequences such as domestic violence, social withdrawal, anxiety, drug and alcohol abuse, and PTSD."[30]

At Least 50% of Meat Processing Workers Are Immigrants

Given the extremely stressful and dangerous nature of the work, it is unsurprising that most native-born Americans avoid working in meat processing facilities if there are other options open to them. Consequently, slaughterhouses in the U.S. commonly employ immigrants, many of them illegal.[31] In 2010, Human Rights Watch described slaughterhouse line work in the U.S. as a human rights crime.[32] As reported in an Oxfam America study, slaughterhouse workers were not allowed breaks, which forced some employees to wear diapers; many of the workers were also paid below minimum wage.[33]

A recent investigation by *USA Today* disclosed that many meat processing workers were "victims of trauma and dislocation, and they hail from some of the most troubled places in the world."[34] Some of them are "diversity visa lottery winners," including many of those that work at the Columbus Junction Tyson Foods hog processing plant, where, as early as April 24, more than 180 of the 1,400 workers had tested positive for the virus.[35] Many of these foreign-born meat and food processing workers, who generally live from paycheck to paycheck, come from conflict areas such as the Democratic Republic of Congo, Somalia, Myanmar, Guatemala, El Salvador or elsewhere in Central or South America. In total, immigrants comprise about one-half of the workforce at all of America's meat and food processing plants.[36] Roughly half of those immigrants are undocumented, and many have limited English skills.[37] At some plants, there are up to 30 languages spoken at any one time.

While many of the immigrant workers are fearful and resentful at being forced to work without proper protective equipment, they are also afraid of being labeled "troublemakers" and getting fired.[38] One worker confided to a *Mother Jones* reporter that her father, who had worked at the JBS meat processing plant in Greeley, Iowa, and then died of COVID-19, had told them before he died: "They treat you like you're nothing, like you're an animal."[39] But still, the workers generally did not feel that there was much they could do, especially since the new U.S. guidelines on conditions in meat and food processing plants are voluntary, rather than mandatory.

When given a choice as to whether to comply with a "suggested" regulation or not, the owners of the plants generally opt-out, since the modification of the plants to improve the safety of the workers costs money.

The mean annual salary for meatpackers in the U.S. is about $29,600.[40] On average, line workers start at $13/hour, and, if they remain on the job for six months, they qualify for health insurance.[41] However, the high turnover rates at a typical plant mean that approximately a quarter of meat and food processing workers have no health insurance. They are part of what can accurately be described as a highly vulnerable working underclass of America. And in the midst of the coronavirus, they are largely being treated as expendable "essential workers."

Despite some improvements in safety measures over the past few years, meat and food processors almost invariably carry the scars on their bodies from slipped blades and knives, and they almost all have the gnarled knuckles and swollen ankles that are byproducts of the repetitive motions of assembly-line labor. The processing lines are primarily designed for speed and efficiency, not worker safety. Workers are required to stun (kill), bleed out, de-hide, de-hair, gut, and split the carcasses of upwards of 5,000 cattle carcasses per day. The hanging halves are chilled and aged, before a line of workers, standing along a snaking conveyor system, butchers each into individual cuts for packaging.[42] Visitors and tourists are generally not encouraged to view this process, since merely watching this brutal process has been known to cause PTSD and drive people into swearing off the consumption of red meat – at least for a while.

Failure to Supply Workers With Protective Equipment

During the course of the 2020 coronavirus crisis, many meat processing and food companies failed to provide their workers with masks and other protective gear, leaving the virus to spread quickly through the ranks of both the managers and the line workers at these plants. Although unions and some public officials called for the companies to provide adequate protective equipment for their employees and sanitary work conditions to reduce the spread of the virus among workers, these urgent cries often fell on deaf ears.

The physical requirements for the work inside many of the plants, when added to the noise levels, make it difficult for many workers to wear masks while, at the same time, effectively communicating with one another and with their supervisors. Thoroughly disinfecting the plant and equipment every day is also a near-impossible undertaking since the plants often operate up to 24 hours per day, and the company owners and managers are very much aware that the company's profits drop each time a line is stopped.[43]

The companies that own and operate the plants have been slow to change their management practices during the pandemic, which often continue to provide bonuses and other incentives to workers who continue to work even while they are still sick. In an interview with CNBC, president Marc Perrone of the United Food and Commercial Workers International Union (UFCW), representing 1.3 million workers in the U.S. and Canada, said that meat processing workers not only need high-quality protective gear such as N95 respirator masks during the current coronavirus pandemic, but that plants must also be reconfigured to allow 6 feet of social distance in addition to any plexiglass barriers.[44] Perrone also said workers must have expanded access to both diagnostic and antibody testing. However, these demands by workers and their union representatives have met with significant resistance from company owners and management, especially since the federal government has refused to make any of these sensible health safety measures mandatory.

By early May, almost all of the country's meat processing facilities were reporting coronavirus cases, with Iowa reporting the highest percentage of workers who tested positive.[45] Upwards of 18.2% of the employees in two of the meat processing plants in Iowa were testing positive for COVID-19.[46] South Dakota also reported that 17.3% of the workers at two of the state's plants tested positive.[47]

In some cases, where dangerous working conditions persisted, the workers walked off the job. In central Minnesota, for example, some workers at the Pilgrim's Pride poultry plant in Cold Springs walked out in late April to protest the company's abysmal record on worker safety.[48] Mohamed Goni, an organizer with Greater Minnesota Worker Center, said the company was not sharing information about the condition of sick fellow workers, and had not implemented social distancing on the line.

In addition, workers at the plant who were out sick were forced to return to work after only just two or three days, even though they had not recovered from the coronavirus disease. Some workers who developed symptoms – even very severe symptoms – were not allowed to leave to go home. County public health officials confirmed that employees at both Pilgrim's Pride in Cold Spring and the Jennie-O turkey processing plant in Melrose, Minnesota, were still actively working at the plants despite having tested positive for COVID-19.[49] The federal government offered some non-binding "guidance" to the companies owning these plants but declined to issue regulations that actually required these plants to take the necessary safety measures. As a result, little or nothing was done to reduce the spread of the virus among the workers.

Meanwhile, as cases started being filed in federal courts by workers seeking injunctions requiring the plants to take prudent safety measures, processing plants around the country started closing down for fear that they would be hit with massive damages lawsuits if they stayed open and continued to require their employees to work under dangerous conditions.[50]

Interruption of the Meat Supply Chain

By early May, Wendy's was out of fresh hamburger at some locations.[51] Costco and Kroger (which includes Ralphs, Food 4 Less, Fred Meyer, and many more retail outlets) started limiting the amount of pork and beef customers could buy. Meat processors – including Smithfield, Hormel, and Tyson – were forced to at least temporarily shut down plants amid virus outbreaks. About 20 to 30% less meat was being processed than it was a year earlier, before the start of the 2020 coronavirus crisis.[52]

More than 20 meatpacking plants, including two of the nation's largest, closed temporarily under pressure from local authorities and their own workers because of the virus.[53] Tyson suspended operations at its pork plant in Waterloo, Iowa, after a slew of infections.[54] Prior to closing, the Waterloo plant had already slowed production because many of its 2,800 workers had been calling in sick.[55] The Black Hawk County health department, which includes Waterloo, linked the Tyson plant to 182 of the county's 379 COVID-19 cases.[56] Due to coronavirus outbreaks among workers at other plants, Tyson also closed another pork processing plant in Columbus Junction, Iowa, and further announced that it would be closing another pork plant in Logansport, Indiana.[57]

In addition, Smithfield Foods, a wholly-owned subsidiary of WH Group of China, halted production at its meatpacking plant in Sioux Falls, South Dakota, after an outbreak infected 853 workers there.[58] This huge Smithfield plant, which was linked to nearly 1,000 COVID-19 cases, had the unenviable distinction of being the nation's largest single-source coronavirus hot spot, with 44% of South Dakota coronavirus cases directly linked to that plant.[59] There were also coronavirus outbreaks among the workers at the JBS pork plant in Worthington, Minnesota, a Hormel food processing facility in Rochelle, Illinois, and a ConAgra food processing plant in Marshall, Missouri.[60] Union leaders complained that the plant owners waited too long to introduce safety measures and, instead, had encouraged employees to continue to meet the surging demand for their products during the pandemic.[61]

The United Food and Commercial Workers International Union, which represents 1.3 million food and retail workers, announced on April 28 that 20 food-processing and meatpacking union workers in the U.S. had already died of the virus and that an estimated 6,500 were sick or had been exposed while working near someone who tested positive. The 15 largest pork-packing plants account for 60% of all pork processed in the U.S., and the country has already seen a 25% reduction in pork slaughter capacity, according to UFCW.

The White House to the Rescue (of the Meat Processing Companies)

Although it was the workers in the meat processing facilities that desperately needed protection from the spread of the disease within the plants, it was the corporate owners of those plants who got Washington's attention. Seeing that the corporate owners of these plants needed protection from the complaints and lawsuits that they were starting to get hit with, the Trump White House immediately stepped in to provide these corporate owners with protection from legal liability.

The Trump White House seized on this cascade of plant closings to bail out the struggling meat processing industry without imposing any additional safety requirements on the companies. On April 28, Trump issued an executive order stating: "Such closures threaten the continued functioning of the national meat and poultry supply chain, undermining critical infrastructure during the national emergency."[62]

Even though the White House had declined to use the full powers of the Defense Production Act to secure desperately needed personal protective equipment for health care workers on the front lines of the coronavirus crisis, Mr. Trump did not hesitate on April 28 to cite this authority under the Defense Production Act to issue an executive order mandating that food supply chain workers return to work in unsafe and dangerous plants: "It is important that processors of beef, pork, and poultry ('meat and poultry') in the food supply chain continue operating and fulfilling orders to ensure a continued protein supply for Americans."[63] Many of these meat processing plants had already closed because so many employees had already contracted the coronavirus, and thousands of other workers remained vulnerable to infection.[64]

This action by the White House followed the publication of a full-page ad by the Chairman of Tyson Foods on Sunday, April 26 in The *New York Times*, The *Washington Post* and other major newspapers around the country warning that as more meat plants were being forced to close amid the coronavirus crisis, "millions of pounds of meat will disappear from the supply chain" and that America's food chain was in danger of breaking.[65]

Trump's order did nothing to increase the protection or safety of workers in food plants from the ravages of coronavirus being spread among the workers. But since the executive order was signed under the authority of the Defense Production Act, mandating that the plants continue to function, one of the goals of the executive order was to give companies such as Tyson Foods Inc and other meat processing companies more liability protection in case employees caught the virus as a result of having to go to work. Trump made it clear to reporters in the Oval Office on Tuesday, April 28: "We're working with Tyson . . . we're going to sign an executive order today, I believe, and that will solve any liability problems where they had certain liability problems."[66]

Senate Democratic Leader Chuck Schumer, speaking to reporters on a teleconference the same day, commented on the push by Senate Republicans for business liability protections as the meat processing companies moved to reopen their operations. "Is he [Senator Mitch McConnell] saying if an owner tells a worker he needs to work next to a sick person without a mask [the owner] wouldn't be liable? That makes no sense," Schumer said.[67]

Even after the issuance of the Executive Order requiring that the plants be reopened, and the workers return to work, the CDC and the Occupational Safety and Health Administration (OSHA) continued to steadfastly maintain the position that any "guidance" or suggestions that they had as to workplace safety requirements were not being issued on a mandatory basis. In essence, the federal government was saying that if the companies wanted to provide their employees with protective equipment or to provide testing, that would be nice, but it was not required.

The unions representing the plant workers expressed their deep frustration over this laissez-faire approach by the federal agencies. "We only wish that this administration cared as much about the lives of working people as it does about meat, pork, and poultry products," one union official bitterly commented.[68] Kim Cordova, president of UFCW Local 7, which represents 3,000 workers at the JBS meat processing plant in Greeley, Colorado, added that Trump's executive order "will only ensure that more workers get sick, jeopardizing lives, family's income, communities, and of course, the country's food supply chain."[69]

The Resurgence of Plant-Based Meat Companies

If there was any silver lining in the coronavirus assault on large, traditional meat processing plants throughout the U.S., it was that it gave at least a temporary shot in the arm to the plant-based meat companies. These companies are offering plant-based sources of protein as an alternative to animal protein from traditional meat products. Plant-based meat alternatives are claimed to be better for your health, since they are much lower in saturated and total fat, lower in calories, higher in protein and fiber, and lower in cholesterol.

As of the start of the coronavirus crisis, plant-based meats made up only about 1% of the overall meat market and 2% of retail sales for packaged meat in the U.S.[70] However, with all the COVID-19 problems faced by traditional meat companies and their plants throughout the U.S., and the growing scarcity of "real meat" in the supply chain, the plant-based meat industry may have received an unexpected boost. One major advantage this industry may have is that their processing plants were generally designed in a way that made it much easier for workers and managers to exercise good hygiene practices during the crisis, with minimal dislocation or slowdowns in production. According to a recent Nielsen report, demand for these "meatless" products has increased 278% since the prior year.[71]

By early May, two plant-based meat companies saw an increase in sales as meat processing plants were hit with coronavirus outbreaks.[72] "Beyond Meat" reported its first-quarter revenue increased 141% from the prior year (2019). Its net income in the first quarter of 2020 was $97.1 million compared with $40.2 million during the same time period in 2019.[73] Meanwhile, "Impossible Foods" reported that it was rolling out its plant-based products at an additional 777 grocery stores in California, Nevada, and the Chicago area as demand surged.[74] Many of their orders came from Americans who were eating at home under "shelter-in-place" orders. The surge in sales was also due to the fact that traditional meat processing plants in more than a dozen states had shut down, at least temporarily, due to the coronavirus outbreaks throughout the mostly rural midwestern, Great Plains and other "middle American" towns and cities where these meat processing plants were located.

Since plant-based meat companies are generally safer and provide better wages and benefits for their workers and their products may be healthier for you, the expansion of this sector of the protein market may yield one of the more positive outcomes of the food supply chain issues during the coronavirus crisis.

25

SACRIFICING HEALTH CARE AND OTHER ESSENTIAL WORKERS

"If you're not in a casket, you better show up for work."
-unidentified hospital supervisor

In any natural or man-made disaster, it is the emergency and essential personnel - those frontline workers who must continue working during a disaster - who inevitably end up joining the list of casualties. The most recent pandemic was no exception to this general rule. Essential workers in the health care and food supply services have been required, at considerable personal risk, to continue doing their jobs without being provided with proper protective or safety equipment.

Of the 2,977 victims killed in the terrorist attacks on Sept. 11, 2001, 412 were emergency workers in New York City who responded to the World Trade Center. This included 343 firefighters (including a chaplain and two paramedics) of the New York City Fire Department (FDNY);[1] 37 police officers of the Port Authority of New York and New Jersey Police Department (PAPD);[2] 23 police officers of the New York City Police Department (NYPD);[3] 8 emergency medical technicians and paramedics from private emergency medical services;[4] and one patrolman from the New York Fire Patrol.[5]

On Sept. 11, immediately after American Airlines Flight 11 crashed into the North Tower of the World Trade Center, NYPD and PAPD officers were ordered into the twin towers to assist with stairwell evacuations, while others helped with evacuations in the plaza and subway station. Then, United Airlines Flight 175 hit the south tower. Many of these officers died when the two towers collapsed.

However, the deaths of police, fire and emergency workers on 9/11 itself was only the beginning of an unfolding tragedy. From the moment the towers collapsed, a toxic cloud filled with asbestos particles, shards of fiberglass and other toxins shrouded ground zero. Consequently, as many as 40,000 first responders and volunteers who spent days and even months at the World Trade Center site – most of whom had no protective respiratory equipment - reported a slew of irreversible and chronic illnesses ranging from upper and lower respiratory ailments to gastro-esophageal reflux disease, sarcoidosis, a disease that scars lung tissue, post-traumatic stress disorder and cancer.[6] Respirators were scarce commodities in the early days of the cleanup, and the EPA erroneously assured 9/11 responders and the rest of New York the air around the disaster site was safe to breathe.[7]

Just as there was a serious shortage of personal protective equipment (PPE) for emergency and medical personnel during the recent coronavirus pandemic, there was a serious lack of full-faced air-purifying respirators available for the 9/11 responders during the critical first few weeks after the attack.[8] Even when such PPE was available, many of the emergency workers at Ground Zero did not wear respirators since there was a culture of "toughness" and casualness among the workers that led many of them to avoid wearing necessary protective equipment. In addition, the design of the respirators themselves was an impediment, making them uncomfortable to wear, especially since they were fit-tested, and the design itself did not allow responders to communicate with one another.

In contrast to the informality and lack of proper respiratory equipment at the World Trade Center, the Pentagon site management following the 9/11 terrorist attack there was tightly controlled, requiring workers to follow rigid HAZMAT rules. Many fewer first responders there experienced the respiratory and other ailments that plagued the first responders at Ground Zero for many years.

As a study conducted by the New York City Fire Department and Montefiore Medical Center later revealed, hundreds of emergency medical workers who came to the aid of victims of the terrorist attack themselves became victims, suffering from chronic health conditions for years thereafter. This study, which was published on April 15, 2015 in *Occupational & Environmental Medicine*,[9] involved more than 2,000 emergency medical service (EMS) workers from the fire department from September 11, 2001 through December 2013. These injuries included Rhinosinusitis (RS), which is an inflammation of the nasal passages and sinuses, Gastroesophageal reflux disease (GERD), Low serum IgA and airway injury, cancer and mental health issues, including depression, and Post Traumatic Stress Disease (PTSD).[10] The EMS workers who arrived earliest to the scene were 7 times as likely to have suffered from mental health issues, including PTSD, and nearly 4 times as likely to have acid reflux and rhinosinusitis.[11]

The lessons learned and "takeaway" from the 9/11 emergency response efforts was that the country and every major American city needed an emergency stockpile of respiratory and other PPE so that such equipment would be immediately available in the event of another local or national emergency.

As with the 9/11 disaster, in the current crisis America is relying on its frontline health care and other essential service personnel to combat this viral scourge. However, the lessons learned in the aftermath of 9/11 did not, for some reason, result in the stockpiling of adequate PPE and other emergency equipment needed by emergency and frontline workers to perform their essential services safely.

As a result, by the end of April, thousands of health care workers nationwide had become infected because of a lack of protective equipment, and many of them died. The CDC estimated that, as of April 28, about 9,300 health care workers had already been infected with the coronavirus.[12] This meant that between 10-20% of all U.S. coronavirus cases were health care workers. By May 26, the CDC was reporting that more than 62,000 doctors, nurses, and other health care providers on the front lines of the U.S.'s COVID-19 crisis had become infected, and at least 291 have died.[13]

On April 21, registered nurses protested in front of the White House, trying to draw attention to their predicament and the dangers that they faced on a daily basis due to a lack of protective equipment. One week later, on April 28, one of the unions representing thousands of nurses and other health care workers – The American Federation of Teachers – called on the federal government to investigate their complaints against hospitals and other health care providers for failing to protect their workers during the coronavirus crisis properly.[14]

The AFT union filed 40 complaints with the Occupational Safety and Health Administration (OSHA), alleging that hospitals were forcing them to work with defective equipment and to ration masks and gowns. The union's president, Randi Weingarten, said it is "immoral" that OSHA was "refusing to issue and enforce guidelines" to protect health care workers and their patients.[15] The 40 complaints, which covered 20,000 workers from 40 different union locals, claimed that the hospitals where they worked were "placing workers at grave risk of infection and death from the coronavirus."[16] The union locals are located in 10 states: Alaska, Connecticut, Maryland, Montana, New Jersey, New York, Ohio, Oregon, West Virginia, and Wisconsin.

In New York, where health care workers were particularly hard hit, another nurses union filed multiple lawsuits accusing the state and two hospitals of "grossly inadequate and negligent protections." Also, in April, HCA Healthcare nurses in Kentucky, Texas, Florida, and a handful of other states protested the company's "lack of preparedness" and shortages of personal protective equipment.[17] Their union claimed that workers had been given defective equipment and were forced to ration masks and gowns. In addition, the hospital staffs were sometimes not told when a room had a patient with COVID-19 in it, and some nurses contracted the disease while working in units that were meant for non-COVID patients. In another case, hospital management refused to allow employees to wear protective masks. When one nurse tested positive for the disease, she was told by the hospital's human resources department to file for unemployment insurance.

Dr. Iahn Gonsenhauser, chief quality and patient safety officer at the Ohio State University Wexner Medical Center in Columbus, said he felt "great sadness and loss" upon learning that so many colleagues had been affected by COVID-19.[18]

Nursing home workers in Chicago also claimed they had been fired for demanding PPE.[19] Greg Kelley, president of SEIU Healthcare Illinois, said that the suspension of two nursing home workers in the Chicago area for raising safety issues was just an example of the firing and disciplining of many health care workers whose concerns were disregarded by nursing home owners. The workers were employed at Bridgeview Health Care Center and Walden Lakeland. Tanika Somerville, a Certified Nursing Assistant at Bridgeview Health Care Center, said she feared bringing the virus home to her eight kids because she was not provided with adequate protective equipment. She said that the facility never told her that one of the residents she was caring for had died of COVID-19, and was never given the opportunity to be tested for the virus. Ms. Somerville only heard about the deaths at the nursing home through social media. When she and a group of other employees went to the nursing home's administrator to ask for help in getting the PPE, she was fired.[20]

One of the primary reasons why hospitals and other health care employers were not properly protecting health care professionals and other workers was that OSHA had never developed any adequate or enforceable rules and regulations to protect workers from infectious diseases in their workplaces. Although the CDC had issued "guidance" to protect health care workers, the guidance was not binding on hospitals and other health care providers, leaving health care workers unprotected, since OSHA had no enforceable standard to protect workers from airborne infectious diseases. This was fundamentally unfair, especially since the nation's frontline health care workers were at an elevated risk of exposure to the coronavirus at a time when the country and sick patients needed them the most.

On Mar. 10, 2020, Representative Bobby Scott of Virginia, the Chairman of the House Committee on Education & Labor, along with Representative Donna Shalala of Florida and 19 other House Democrats, introduced legislation to protect the safety of health care workers who were caring for patients suffering from COVID-19. The *COVID-19 Worker Protection Act of 2020* (H.R. 6139) would require OSHA, which is part of the U.S. Labor Department, to issue an Emergency Temporary Standard to ensure health care facilities implement comprehensive infectious disease exposure control plans to keep frontline health care workers safe during the COVID-19 pandemic, the most significant infectious disease crisis that this country has faced in over a century.[21]

The *Occupational Safety and Health Act* gives the Department of Labor the authority to issue an Emergency Temporary Standard if employees are exposed to grave danger from new hazards. Before introducing H.R. 6139, House Democrats called on OSHA to issue an Emergency Temporary Standard, but the Labor Department indicated it had no plans to implement any mandatory rules and regulations. The bill would also require the government to track and investigate coronavirus infections and ban retaliation against health care workers who report infection control problems.

Other Essential Workers Were Also Denied Protective Equipment

Governor Andrew Cuomo issued frequent reminders at his pressconferences that "we are all in this together." He referred to the coronavirus crisis as "The Great Equalizer." While this is a catchy phrase, it is, of course, not entirely true. Equality has always been an elusive ideal in this country since its founding, and the crisis has only increased the yawning gap of inequality in the country. Many of us are permitted to stay home, seamlessly working on our computers and phones, while other more essential and generally underpaid workers are out there delivering packages, processing food, keeping our telecommunication services going, collecting garbage and keeping our streets clean, working check-out counters at grocery stores, and doing other essential tasks so the rest of us can shelter-in-place.

While the economy is working very well for the wealthy and the massive corporations, it has been stagnating for those further down the economic ladder. From 1980 to 2014, wages for the bottom half of income earners grew by one percent, while wages for the top one percent of earners grew by 205 percent.[22] This inequality, stagnation, and instability for so many is not a long-term health sign for a well-functioning economy or a truly democratic political system. Nor is it the inevitable or "natural" result of an evolving economy. Instead, it is the direct result of pro-corporate and anti-worker policy choices over decades that have stripped workers of the power to stand together and bargain for fairer wages, benefits, and working conditions.

Unions have been critical throughout the modern history of our country in the successful effort of working men and women to win decent wages and, in particular, to participate meaningfully in the post-World War II economic expansion. Unions have also played a critical role in every effort to address income inequality based on gender and race. However, the pendulum has swung back over the past few decades in favor of big business, as special interest-funded attacks have eviscerated important parts of the labor laws and eroded union membership. Today, union members earn over 13% more than those with similar education, occupation, and experience in a non-union workplace.[23] However, anemic labor laws have been exploited by unscrupulous employers, which has successfully reduced union membership from 33% in 1956 to just 10% in 2018.[24]

Once the global pandemic hit the U.S., the country was graphically reminded of the profound disconnect between the value that essential workers produce and what they get in return. This is especially true when they are being asked to put themselves at risk during a public health crisis. These workers were mostly invisible before, in no small part because a disproportionate percentage of them were women, immigrants, Blacks, and Latinos. Not only have they been chronically underpaid, but even more outrageous has been the fact that many essential workers have been fired for raising legitimate health and safety concerns about the spread of coronavirus in their workplaces.

Low-wage essential workers were more likely to face dangerous working conditions than high-wage workers, even before the COVID-19 pandemic. Now, with the added risk of contracting coronavirus, the dangers to essential workers have only increased. In a study involving 1,600 essential workers released in early June, Jasmine Kerrissey, an Assistant Professor at the University of Massachusetts Amherst, and Clare Hammonds, a Professor at the same university, found that across income levels, roughly two-thirds of essential workers – including grocery clerks, home health aides, and delivery workers – were unable to practice social distancing.[25] Low-wage essential workers include grocery clerks, home health aides, and delivery drivers, while high-wage workers include nurses, doctors, and managers. Although they do crucial jobs, many essential workers are low wage, earning under $20 an hour.

However, low-wage workers were two to three times more likely than high-wage workers – workers earning over $40/hour – to lack other forms of protection, including access to masks, hand sanitizer, training on how to prevent COVID-19 transmission or regular hand-washing opportunities.[26] Not surprisingly, low-wage workers reported feeling less safe at work than high-wage workers. While 44% of high-wage workers reported not feeling safe, this percentage increased by 10 points to 54% for low wage workers.[27]

Even though these essential workers were working under increasingly risky conditions, a large percentage of those surveyed in mid-April reported that they were not making enough money to make ends meet, such as paying the rent while continuing to buy enough food to feed themselves and their families. One of the essential workers surveyed wrote, "We are risking infecting our family by working, and they don't give us anything extra in our paychecks to be able to buy more food. What we earn is for paying rent, electricity, insurance, and the rest is barely enough to buy food."[28]

Workers who have raised their voices in protest over safety issues have been disciplined and fired, with little or no consequences to the employers for engaging in such blatant retaliation. In late March, for example, Amazon fired Chris Smalls, a worker at its Staten Island, New York warehouse who had organized a walkout at one of its warehouse facilities.[29] Smalls and other workers were demanding greater protections from the company amid the coronavirus outbreak.[30] "They pretty much retaliated against me for speaking out," said Smalls, "I don't know how they sleep at night."[31] He and dozens of other employees at the warehouse walked off the job to demand that Amazon temporarily close and clean the facility after a worker tested positive for COVID-19 there. There were 5,000 workers at this one warehouse facility, and the workers reasonably requested that Amazon pay them for their time off when they became ill from the coronavirus or needed to otherwise self-quarantine.

Calling the firing "disgraceful," New York Attorney General Letitia James said her office was considering all legal options and called on the National Labor Relations Board to investigate the incident. "In New York, the right to organize is codified into law, and any retaliatory action by management related thereto is strictly prohibited," James said in a statement, adding, "At a time when so many New Yorkers are struggling and are deeply concerned about their safety, this action was also immoral and inhumane."[32]

On May 1, workers at retail and delivery companies throughout the country, including workers at Amazon, Walmart, Target, and delivery apps such as Instacart, walked off the job for the day to demand better pay and treatment.[33] Organized under the hashtag #essentialworkersday, the protests were timed for May Day or International Workers' Day – a date typically marked around the world by labor marches. Kerri Blair, a mother of five in Akron, Ohio, who usually picked up extra income delivering orders for Shipt, joined the walkout, saying, "People who work at Whole Foods, at Target, at Walmart. . . there's no way to get around not being around people. That is your job. . . We're out there in the public. . . doing things for other people."[34]

To keep up the surging volume of online orders during the lockdowns in cities and states across the country, Amazon, Instacart, Shipt, and other online shopping and delivery services have gone on hiring sprees to handle new orders. Some of the companies offered increased pay, at least on a temporary basis, and some instituted health and safety measures, such as regularly providing workers with masks, and thoroughly cleaning all stores and warehouses. However, many other companies have maintained the status quo, requiring their workers to do their jobs at the same fairly low salary levels without factoring in the increased health risks they were asking their employees to endure.

Target was one of the companies to give their employees a temporary pay increase. "In recognition of the significant contributions of our front-line team members amid the coronavirus, we've invested more than $300 million, including $2 an hour higher hourly wages, which we've extended until May 30," Target said in a statement.[35] Target also said that it had established "dozens of new measures" aimed to keep both workers and shoppers safe during the pandemic. However, after May 30, while the company was still in the midst of a pandemic, Target workers were being required to assume the additional health risk of traveling and showing up at work each day, but were no longer receiving the $2 hourly bonus.

At about the same time, Amazon announced it would spend its entire operating profit in the second quarter — an estimated $4 billion — dealing with the coronavirus. That included providing protective equipment to workers, paying them more, cleaning warehouses, and testing employees for COVID-19. An Amazon spokesman said: "Health and safety is our top priority, and we expect to spend more than $800 million in the first half of the year on COVID-19 safety measures."[36] However, some workers said they were still having trouble getting the protective gear they had been promised, and that this and other large retailers were not being fully transparent about how many employees had fallen ill or died from COVID-19.

Whole Foods, which is owned by Amazon, also seemed to be on the right track during the crisis by temporarily paying their workers an additional $2 an hour for "hazard pay" during the crisis.[37] Whole Foods employees at most stores also got their temperature checked before each shift and were required to wear face masks while at work. They also received text alerts when colleagues get sick with the coronavirus. Whole Foods also tried to boost morale by giving employees T-shirts that said: "Hero" on the front and "Hard Core" on the back. But the extra money they had been receiving during the pandemic disappeared by the beginning of June. This decision to end so-called hazard pay upset most of the workers, who were still at risk of contracting the coronavirus, which by that time had infected at least 1.8 million Americans and killed at least 107,000. "The hazard — the thing we're getting paid extra for — is still around. Coronavirus has no cure," said an employee who feared losing his job by speaking out, "If we need to wear a mask, it's because there's a hazard. That's not part of our standard job operation."[38]

Delivery personnel is another category of essential workers who were being asked to put themselves in harm's way without proper protective equipment. For example, delivery drivers working for Cort Furniture Rental were ordered to make deliveries in the coronavirus "containment zone" in New Rochelle, New York, even though they did not have face masks or other protective equipment.[39] The area was being patrolled at the time by National Guard troops who were enforcing a quarantine in the area. This was apparently standard operating procedure for workers employed by this and other companies owned by Warren Buffet, the third richest American, with a fortune of at least $75 billion. Buffett's Berkshire-Hathaway conglomerate employs more than 370,000 people, few of whom are represented by unions who could negotiate for safety conditions as well as pay and benefits.[40]

Like Walmart and Amazon, the Warren Buffet non-union companies do not have to worry about engaging in heavy-handed union-busting tactics since there is no functioning National Labor Relations Board (NLRB) to handle complaints. This also means that whistle-blowers and other workers who are subject to retaliation for raising questions about their health and safety during the coronavirus crisis have little or no legal recourse. Throughout the Trump presidency, the NLRB could not act on a complaint because it lacked a quorum. That was because Trump had failed to appoint replacements for those who left the board, just as he had done with some other federal boards and commissions.

From giant companies such as Amazon to mid-size and smaller companies such as Cort Furniture Rental, numerous other companies have been accused of terminating workers who spoke out against unsafe working conditions and a lack of proper protective equipment during the pandemic. "It's very difficult to stand six feet away from somebody when delivering to their home," said Anthony Salcedo, a Cort delivery man, "The majority of our pickups and deliveries come from [New York City]—the epicenter [of the COVID-19 pandemic in our country]. I have a family—my biggest fear was coming into contact with someone with coronavirus and passing it onto my wife and kids."[41] Nevertheless, the company refused to provide protective masks and gloves. The workers were told they had the option of taking a leave of absence, using their vacation days if they felt unsafe or just staying home without pay. One Cort manager is quoted as telling workers, "Unless you plan on living the rest of your life in a bubble—keep on working."[42] After many weeks, when the company finally did provide gloves, most of them were so small that they simply tore when they tried to put them on.

In the midst of the coronavirus crisis, some of the workers at Cort filed a petition seeking a March 10 vote on unionizing the company.[43] When management got wind of the petition, however, they began bringing in subcontracted drivers to do their work. The Cort employees saw this as a blatant attempt at intimidation and union-busting. The company also required its drivers to use a new app while on duty. With it, drivers had to report all stops on their route to their manager– even bathroom breaks.[44]

Essential Workers Protection and Compensation Act

While a comprehensive plan for dealing with this or any future pandemic requires adequate testing capability, sufficient health care equipment and supplies, and enough hospital beds and other capacities, it also requires a plan for maintaining essential services without exploiting the workers providing such vital services. They must be adequately compensated and given benefits, and they also must be provided with a safe working environment, which means that they must have adequate protective equipment.

While there have been bills introduced in Congress with titles such as the "Essential Workers Protection Act,"[45] they have been primarily designed to enhance the coordination between the U.S. Department of Labor and other federal agencies that may have some jurisdiction over worker safety. For example, on April 29, Representatives Haley Stevens and Chris Pappas introduced the *Essential Worker Protection Act* (HR 6631), a bill to create an interagency task force focused on worker protection as millions of essential workers continue to perform their duties despite the risk of exposure to COVID-19.[46] While increased coordination between and among the federal agencies is, of course, a laudable goal, it only skims across the surface of the fundamental safety, fair compensation, and other pressing issues facing America's essential workers.

The *COVID-19 Health Care Worker Protection Act of 2020* (HR 6139), another bill introduced in the House, calls for an important first substantive step to be taken by the U.S. Department of Labor, which would be the promulgation of emergency and then permanent occupational safety and health standards to protect essential employees from occupational exposure to COVID-19.[47] These standards would apply to health care sector employees and other employees identified as having an elevated risk for exposure. However, this and other similar legislation will be of no assistance to essential workers unless passed by both the House and Senate and signed into law by the president.

The Center for American Progress and other progressive-leaning "think tanks" have outlined various requirements that should be guaranteed to essential workers through state and federal laws and regulations, so they can continue doing their jobs with the dignity and safety they richly deserve.[48] These core reforms that are urgently needed for essential workers include the following:[49]

Safety Standards

Under the Obama administration, OSHA was working to develop an infectious disease workplace standard that would have prepared workers for a pandemic such as the one we are presently experiencing. However, the Trump administration halted this work. As a result, OSHA has mainly been "AWOL" in the current crisis and has done little or nothing to address safety issues as it relates to protective equipment needed by workers who may be exposed to airborne infectious diseases such as COVID-19. OSHA already has regulations pertaining to bloodborne pathogens, such as HIV and Hepatitis-B, but does not have similar regulations relating to the airborne pathogens in the workplace. Congressional action to pass the *COVID-19 Health Care Worker Protection Act of 2020* (HR 6139) or even more comprehensive legislation would address this glaring omission in OSHA's regulatory scheme. Guidelines and training for how essential workers can minimize the risks of infecting their families is another element that should be addressed by federal and state regulations.

Adequate Compensation

Even when essential workers are provided with safety protections, they are still taking an increased risk, for which they should be adequately rewarded. Essential workers should be paid at least the prevailing wage rate that government contractors must pay, or $15 per hour, whichever is higher. If the worker is categorized as an independent contractor rather than an employee, they should be paid a premium rate for the additional costs they must bear. Finally, on top of these minimums, essential workers should also receive a hazard pay supplement. Pay for essential workers should be higher than the level of the emergency unemployment benefits they receive if they have been temporarily laid off. Workers should have a financial incentive to return to work, rather than continuing to receive unemployment benefits.

This can be accomplished by raising pay for essential workers, not by cutting unemployment benefits.

Paid Family and Medical Leave

As many as 96 million workers were left out of the emergency paid leave provisions included in the *Families First Coronavirus Response Act (FFCRA)* and the *Coronavirus Aid, Relief, and Economic Security (CARES) Act*.[50] In fact, many essential workers are explicitly exempted from coverage. Through the FFCRA, qualifying workers became eligible for up to two weeks of short-term paid leave if they were sick, self-quarantining, or caring for a family member. They were also eligible to receive an additional ten weeks of paid childcare leave to care for a child whose school or place of care was closed. This amount of leave, however, was insufficient for many workers who become ill or need to care for a family member diagnosed with COVID-19. In addition, this law provides that any paid leave used for caregiving, short or longer-term, would only be paid at two-thirds of the worker's regular wages, capped at $200 per day. This unfairly devalued caregiving and had a disproportionately negative impact on the economic security of women, who are more likely to be the caregivers in their families.

Also, many essential workers did not even qualify for these protections, based on loopholes and exemptions that were added during the negotiations process. Employers could deny paid leave to otherwise-qualifying health care providers and emergency responders, including "any individual who is capable of providing health care services necessary to combat the COVID-19 public health emergency." Incredibly, this meant that essential frontline workers in the health care field were cut out of the legal protections and benefits being provided to other categories of essential service workers. In addition, employers with more than 500 employees, a category that includes almost all major grocery stores and pharmacy chains, were exempted from providing any guaranteed paid leave to their workforces.

In short, the very people who are necessary to ensure the public health of their communities were explicitly singled out to be denied the right to paid leave if they themselves fell ill or needed to care for their loved ones. These gaping holes in the paid leave safety net should be repaired as soon as possible if we are to have anything approaching justice for our essential workers.

Access to Affordable Health Care

Essential workers fall within the ranks of the millions of Americans who do not have access to affordable health care, especially in states that opted not to participate in expanded Medicaid programs and other programs that could have been available under The Affordable Care Act. Congress has generally provided for access to no-cost testing, but the cost of treatment for COVID-19 can still fall on Americans, including essential workers, who can least afford it. Ultimately, America will be forced to reckon with the inescapable truth that all Americans, including essential workers, need and deserve guaranteed universal health coverage. But as the first step in this crisis, Congress must ensure that essential workers have access to no-cost treatment for COVID-19.

Quality Child Care

For frontline health care workers and millions of other essential workers, the ability to work is dependent on access to childcare. Schools and childcare centers across the country closed in compliance with state orders and social distancing guidelines. This created an urgent need for emergency childcare to serve children of essential workers who did not have the luxury of staying at home. However, now that childcare workers and early childhood educators are recognized as essential workers, steps must be taken to ensure that they are adequately compensated for their essential services. These workers now make, on average, less than $12 per hour, which means that they are severely underpaid for their services and often do not receive any benefits.

Private Right of Enforcement of Workplace Standards

Just as federal and state anti-discrimination and civil rights statutes give individuals a private right of action to enforce those laws and seek damages for violations in state and federal courts, the statutes and regulations settling forth workplace standards for essential workers should contain provisions that permit essential workers the right to bring private actions on their own against companies that violate their rights. Government enforcement of these provisions should also be vigorous, but all too often, the limited resources that are made available for government enforcement are inadequate to enforce these laws and regulations. Statutory private rights of action are needed, which should include provisions that allow workers to receive back pay, damages, attorneys' fees, and injunctive relief.

Access to Unions

Essential workers, whether they are categorized as employees or independent contractors, should have their rights to unionize and collectively bargain protected by the enactment of the Protecting the Right to Organize Act of 2019 (H.R. 2474), which already passed the House in early February but languished in the Republican-controlled Senate.

The *Protecting the Right to Organize Act* ("PRO") is the most significant and progressive piece of legislation in the past 80 years designed to strengthen workers' ability to organize. It would amend the county's outdated labor laws to potentially grant hundreds of thousands of workers collective bargaining rights that they do not currently have. Studies have estimated that hundreds of thousands to millions of workers are misclassified as contractors when they should be employees, an issue that has become the subject of intense debate in progressive states such as California.[51]

The Act would also add penalties for companies that violate labor law and would also weaken "right-to-work" laws in 27 states that allow employees to forgo participating in and paying dues to unions.[52] Incredibly, no penalties now exist in the labor laws to punish companies who violate them, which means that companies that are subject to union organizing efforts have no disincentives to breaking the law. According to federal data obtained by the Economic Policy Institute, about 40% of the companies where workers have voted to unionize have violated federal laws during union campaigns, but without any penalties being imposed.[53] This Act would give the NLRB the power to enforce these federal labor laws, with the right to impose penalties of up to $50,000 per violation. It would also award workers compensation for the damages they experience when they are retaliated against, not just back pay, to which workers are currently entitled.

This would mean that employers could not force workers to attend anti-union meetings or sign arbitration agreements that prevented their right to organize. This would also mean that essential workers would have the ability to communicate with each other about collective issues. With greater access to union membership and collective bargaining, essential workers would be in a better position to negotiate with their employers regarding wages, benefits, and working conditions. While legislated standards are critical to setting a floor for working conditions and compensation for essential employees, collective bargaining would help them enhance those minimum requirements so that they can securely join America's embattled middle class.

* * * * *

Of course, these seven core reforms included in the Essential Workers Protection Act should apply to all employees, but you have to start somewhere. So, let's start with essential employees now that there is some public attention being paid to them for a change. Later on, once the crisis has abated, the country needs to fix the more fundamental structural problems of the American economy, which leaves lower-level salaried employees largely failing to participate in the growth of the economy. Permanent reforms that protect worker rights and increase worker participation in the economic benefits of an expanding economy will provide benefits not only for these salaried workers and independent contractor "gig" employees, but will also lead to a country that is more resilient to the inevitable future challenges that we will face in a post-COVID world.

26

THE FAILED LEADERSHIP OF BORIS JOHNSON OF THE U.K., DONALD TRUMP OF THE U.S., AND JAIR BOLSONARO OF BRAZIL

"Send in the clowns…Don't bother, they're here."
- From *A Little Night Music* by Stephen Sondheim

Let's play a little guessing game.

The leader of this country sports long, blondish hair and has a boisterous, even buffoonish personality. He comes from a privileged background, but claims that he really represents "the working man." A showman to his core, he rose to prominence by appearing on a popular T.V. show, has a well-deserved reputation as a philanderer who engaged in serial extra-marital affairs. He spouts lies and half-truths on a constant basis, and never apologizes even when caught in a red-faced lie. He makes profoundly offensive and derogatory statements about racial, ethnic, and religious minorities, and rose to political prominence by appealing to the fear, prejudices and baser instincts of his fellow white citizens.

No, we are not talking about Donald J. Trump. We are talking about Prime Minister Boris Johnson of the United Kingdom. Just as Trump rose to prominence with The Apprentice, Johnson's early claims to fame were on the British quiz show "Have I Got News for You." Like Trump, who breezily refers to "shithole" countries in Africa, a large part of Johnson's popularity with his white, working-class "base" has been his offensive comments about minority groups, gay men, Muslim women, and Africans.

At the start of the coronavirus crisis, both Trump and Johnson sent confusing and contradictory signals to the citizens of their respective countries about the dangers posed by the pandemic during the critical months of January through mid-March, and their governments' responses to the crisis were, to put it charitably, disorganized and mostly ineffective. As a result, both the U.K. and the U.S. experienced more coronavirus cases and COVID-19 related deaths than other similarly situated countries that had more serious and effective leadership, such as the U.K.'s next-door neighbor, Ireland, or the U.S.'s neighbor, Canada.

The U.K. and Boris Johnson

As the virus spread to Europe in mid-February, an alert European leader would have taken immediate charge of the response preparations, aware that a possible pandemic posed a grave danger to their country. Instead, Prime Minister Boris Johnson vanished from public view for 12 days, most of it spent on a private holiday with his pregnant fiancée at a stately country house. It was not until the end of February, with 80,000 known coronavirus cases worldwide and the World Health Organization on the edge of declaring a pandemic, that Johnson began mobilizing his government to respond to the crisis. But by that time, there were already 20 confirmed cases and one death in Britain, and this was just the beginning.

On February 28, Johnson finally announced that the virus was the U.K.'s top priority, and then insisted on acting to the contrary by taking off for a long weekend. The following week, he – like President Trump in the U.S. – continued to send out confusing signals to his fellow countrymen and women by reassuring them that "we should all basically just go about our normal daily lives" so long as they washed their hands for 20 seconds, several times a day.[1] Much like Trump reveled in his refusal to wear a face mask even when his own administration was recommending that everyone do so, Johnson similarly undercut his government's advice about not shaking hands and limiting physical contact with others. He boasted that he was still shaking hands, as he had very publicly done at a hospital with several virus patients. This air of reckless bravado was an important – and almost fatal – part of his persona, as it was for Trump.[2]

Despite the rapid spread of the virus from late February through the entire month of March, the U.K. government waited until March 20 to shut down all schools,[3] restaurants, pubs, and other indoor entertainment venues.[4] On March 23, the government imposed a lockdown on the entire population, banning all "non-essential" travel and contact with people outside one's home, and shutting almost all businesses, venues, facilities, and places of worship. People were told to practice social distancing when in public, and the police were given the power to enforce the lockdown under the Coronavirus Act of 2020,[5] the most stringent use of emergency powers since the Second World War.[6]

By mid-April, the U.K. National Health Service announced that it could now cope with all new cases showing up in the emergency rooms,[7] and it was reported that social distancing had "flattened the curve" of the epidemic.[8] In late April, it was announced that the U.K. had passed the peak of its outbreak,[9] and as of May 3, the U.K. had 186,599 confirmed cases and 28,446 deaths overall, a rate of about 418 dead per million population. More than 90% of those in the U.K. who died had underlying illnesses[10] or were over 60 years old.[11] London had the highest number of cases and the highest rate of infections.[12] Of the regions that comprise the United Kingdom, England and Wales had the highest recorded death rate per capita, while Northern Ireland had the lowest recorded death rate.[13]

Since the U.K. got off to a slow start in its response to the crisis under Johnson's leadership, the number of cases and coronavirus deaths in the U.K. was strikingly higher than in Ireland, its neighboring country, even accounting for the disparity in their population levels. The U.K. had 28,446 deaths as of May 3, while Ireland had 1,303 up to that date.[14] Adjusting for population, this means that there have been about 7.4 deaths in Ireland for every 100,000 people, while in the U.K., there have been 17 deaths per 100,000.[15] In other words, people were dying of coronavirus in the U.K. at more than twice the rate they were dying in Ireland.[16] The actual disparity between the two countries was probably even more significant since the U.K. was only reporting hospital deaths. Ireland, however, was reporting deaths not only in hospitals, but also in nursing homes and at home.

The primary reason for this disparity in outcomes from the pandemic was the fact that both the Irish and the English peoples took their cues from their political leaders, and the leaders of these countries were sending very different messages. While the Irish Taoiseach (Prime Minister) was regularly communicating to the Irish public the seriousness of the coronavirus threat and took early actions to close down Irish schools and universities, the U.K. prime minister, Boris Johnson, took a more lackadaisical approach to the crisis, telling people to wash their hands, and not much more.[17] Unsurprisingly, Johnson himself contracted a severe case of COVID-19, which landed him in the ICU unit of a London hospital. Johnson fortunately recovered, but the absence of cohesive and coherent leadership during the most serious weeks of the crisis left many with the impression that the U.K. was acting much like a rudderless ship foundering in a storm.

Irish citizens knew that the virus threat was very serious when the government canceled St. Patrick's Day celebrations. In contrast, the government in the U.K. permitted various major events and festivals to go ahead as planned, with tens and hundreds of thousands of people being thrust together in cramped spaces, which they should have known was an ideal super-spreader environment for the virus. A huge concert took place in Cardiff, Wales featuring the Welsh group "Stereophonics" over the weekend of March 14-15, as well as another huge March 13 concert the previous day in Manchester, England. These and other concerts that were permitted to proceed may have been decisive factors in turbocharging the spread of the virus throughout the U.K., leading to the exponential growth of the pandemic there.

In contrast, while the Irish models forecasted 3,000 new coronavirus cases a day by the end of March, the daily increase proved to be only about 300 cases per day, one-tenth of what was predicted.[18] In short, the Irish government's serious and proactive approach to the pandemic reaped tremendous rewards and likely saved countless lives.

Ireland also eclipsed the U.K. in the amount of testing that it conducted. While the U.K. faced enormous delays in testing, Ireland's testing rate was about twice that in the U.K. This lack of testing in the U.K. also significantly depressed the reported number of coronavirus cases and related death there. As of May 3, official U.K. figures showed the number of daily tests conducted fell to 76,496, just days after the government touted its ability to do more than 100,000 tests per day.[19] The U.K. testing rate actually fell to around 20,000 tests per day.[20]

The U.K.'s lack of testing quickly went from tragic to farcical when, facing a global scramble for materials, British officials paid $20 million for two million unproven antibody testing kits from China in a gamble that exploded in the government's face.²¹ British officials took the deal, paid the $20 million upfront, and then confidently promised tests would be available at pharmacies in as little as two weeks. "As simple as a pregnancy test," boasted Prime Minister Johnson, "It has the potential to be a total game-changer."²² There was one problem, however: the tests did not work.

Ireland also had another advantage over the U.K., which is that it enlisted the support of one of Ireland's most famous groups, U2, to lend a helping hand in obtaining urgently needed medical supplies to fight the coronavirus.²³ Bono, the U2 frontman, reached out to South Korean president, Moon Jae-in, and Apple's co-founder Tim Cook, in the hope that they could assist him in finding personal protective equipment (PPE) and other supplies for Ireland's health service. The band donated the equivalent of $10.9 million to aid the search for and purchase the personal protective equipment that Ireland needed.²⁴ These supplies were obtained and flown into Dublin Airport by an Irish aircraft leasing company. The third flight arrived in Dublin from Shenzhen, China on Sunday, May 3, carrying two million face masks and 32,000 surgical gowns for Irish healthcare workers.²⁵ In addition to the financial contribution made by U2, an Irish businessman from Cork, Ireland, Liam Casey of PCH International, arranged for the transaction with the Chinese and flew back from China on one of the flights carrying the medical supplies.²⁶ This third air cargo shipment contained 2.1 million "Type IIR" surgical face masks and surgical gowns, which were priority items requested by the Irish government.

Jair Bolsonaro of Brazil

Since the beginning of the pandemic, Brazilian President Jair Bolsonaro, like Donald Trump, showed disdain for any fact-based news or scientific recommendation that was not to his political liking. Like Trump, he dismissed COVID-19 by describing it as a "measly cold," as if demeaning the virus would embarrass it and make it go away. Also, like Trump's attack on the liberal media for spreading "fake news" about the virus, Bolsonaro said that the people would soon see that they'd been "tricked" by the governors and the media when it came to the outbreak. On April 12, when more than a thousand Brazilians had already died, he proclaimed that "the matter of the virus" was "starting to go away."[27] Trump made a similar prediction that the virus would "disappear" with the coming of spring and warmer weather. When Bolsonaro's prediction proved to be wrong, he spent his days fighting against state and municipal shutdowns, arguing that they were economically disastrous for the country.

Bolsonaro also fired Brazil's health minister, Luiz Henrique Mandetta, for supporting the isolation measures while resisting Bolsonaro's attempts to promote chloroquine and hydroxychloroquine as miracle treatments for COVID-19.[28] He also continued to attend pro-government street rallies, shaking the hands of his supporters and drawing large crowds that became super-spreader events for the disease.

On April 23, when Brazil registered more than 3,300 deaths in one day, President Bolsonaro was asked about the rising toll. His response was classic: "I'm not a gravedigger," he replied. Five days later, as the death toll continued to rise rapidly, he said: "So what? I'm sorry. What do you want me to do?"[29] On the day Brazil reached 11,653 deaths, with no peak yet in sight, Mr. Bolsonaro issued an executive order classifying gyms, barbershops and beauty salons as essential businesses that could reopen.[30] A few days later, the new health minister, Nelson Teich, resigned from his post after less than a month on the job.[31] The interim minister was an active-duty army general who had no experience in public health and immediately appointed nine other fellow army officers with even less public health experience to the ministry.

Although the W.H.O. had strongly recommended a nationwide lockdown in Brazil to stem the frightening increase in coronavirus-related cases and deaths, President Bolsonaro resisted such comprehensive lockdown measures, following President Trump's lead by threatening to pull Brazil out of the body, accusing it of being a "partisan political organization."[32]

By late May, Brazil was rapidly overtaking the U.S. as the country with the highest daily rates of coronavirus-related cases and deaths.[33] The actual numbers were probably much higher than Brazil's reported numbers since there was minimal testing. While the growth curve of cases was flattening out in most of the rest of the world, it was actually spiking in Brazil in late

May and early June. Hospitals were on the brink of overflowing. In the Amazonian city of Manaus, deaths soared to the point where the main cemetery was burying five coffins at a time in shared graves. Even in the midst of this crisis, many Brazilians did not follow social distancing measures, since they were taking their contemptuous cue from their president.

By June 6, as Brazil was registering 1,000 coronavirus-related deaths for four straight days and the criticism of Bolsonaro's bungling of the crisis was reaching a deafening crescendo, Brazil took the unprecedented step of removing months of data on COVID-19 from a government website.[34] It also inexplicably stopped reporting coronavirus-related cases and deaths on a cumulative basis. Bolsonaro's explanation was that the cumulative data did not reflect "the current picture." At this point in early June, Brazil had more than 640,000 confirmed cases and more than 35,000 coronavirus-related deaths, the third-highest national toll, but the number was believed to be much higher because of insufficient testing.[35] Even more ominously, Brazil's rates were spiking with no clear indication when they would peak.

On Tuesday, July 7, after months of downplaying the severity of the pandemic, President Bolsonaro joined Boris Johnson as yet another leader of a major country who had tested positive for coronavirus.[36] By this time, Brazil's caseload had exponentially exploded to more than 1.5 million reported cases and 65,000 deaths, a two-fold increase in just one month.

* * * * *

All three of these major countries that were hard hit by the coronavirus crisis – the U.S., the U.K., and Brazil – experienced far higher numbers of cases and deaths than they otherwise could have had if they had been led by leaders who took the pandemic seriously and moved quickly to contain and mitigate the disease's spread. In each one of these countries, the leadership was slow to acknowledge the true scope of the viral threat, and once the reality of the pandemic's spread throughout their countries could no longer be avoided or denied, they failed to promptly implement response plans containing all of the universally recognized component elements, including quarantine, lockdown, social distancing, mask-wearing, testing, and contact tracing. The citizens of all three countries suffered unnecessarily from this lack of leadership during a time of crisis. They paid an especially high price for the contempt shown by all three leaders for fact-based scientific and expert advice that, if implemented early and aggressively, would have resulted in more favorable outcomes for their countries and their countries' citizens.

27

TAIWAN, ICELAND, GERMANY, SOUTH KOREA, IRELAND, AND NEW ZEALAND RISE TO THE CHALLENGE

SO, HOW WERE SO MANY OTHER COUNTRIES ABLE TO GET IT RIGHT?

As the states and federal government review the hard lessons learned to date and are working their way through the crisis towards a (hopefully cautious) reopening, it is instructive to see how some other countries have approached the coronavirus crisis in their respective countries and to see if some lessons can be learned from them now, as well as for future planning purposes.

As we are now painfully aware, there is much more to solving this complex puzzle than just "flattening the curve" and then hoping for the best once the worst of the storm passes. Any reopening has to be done slowly and intelligently, and it obviously needs to be done in the context of widespread testing to determine not only who is currently testing positive for the virus, but who has had it in the past and now have antibodies and possibly some degree of immunity.[1]

Taiwan

Taiwan's response to the COVID-19 pandemic established a gold standard for pandemic responses and provides a model that should be integrated into the response plans for the U.S. and other countries to any future public health crisis on this scale.

Sitting directly off the coast of mainland China, this island nation of 24 million people was registering the second-highest number of cases in the world (after China) by late January 2020.[2] It appeared to be on a collision course with a major disaster. However, by June 5, Taiwan only had 443 cases, and seven deaths reported.[3] Amazingly, these results were accomplished without any severe mitigation restrictions, such as lockdowns or school closures. By comparison, during this same time period, there were 1,917,101 coronavirus cases reported in the U.S., with 109,979 deaths.[4] Based on the Taiwan model and accounting for the difference in the size of the populations of both countries, the number of U.S. deaths by early June would have been around 83.[5]

One reason for Taiwan's successful response efforts is that it was (unlike the U.S.) prepared. In 2003, there were a total of 183 people who died on this island from the Severe Acute Respiratory Syndrome (SARS) outbreak that year.[6] In response, the Taiwan government established a Central Epidemic Command Center (CECC), which stood ready to be activated in the event of another serious outbreak. When the first case was identified in Taiwan, the CECC was activated on January 20, 2020, and was able to implement stringent containment and response measures immediately. Since a plan had already been carefully laid out in advance, it was activated without the delay that bogged down the U.S. response.

Taiwanese officials immediately imposed travel restrictions on anyone coming from the Wuhan area of China and began boarding and inspecting passengers for fever and pneumonia symptoms on flights from Wuhan. Officials also started updating the public in daily briefings.

Within a three week period, the CECC also was able to put 120 action items into place.[7] In addition to the air travel restrictions, it proactively tested anyone who got off cruise ships and even retested people previously diagnosed with influenza or pneumonia to make sure they had not been misdiagnosed and were infected with the coronavirus. Taiwan officials also cross-checked national health insurance data with customs and immigration databases to create real-time alerts for the already sick, the elderly, and other vulnerable sectors of the populations. Taiwan already had an excellent health data system in place, which played an essential role in the monitoring of the spread of the disease and early detection of those infected. Everyone who saw a physician for respiratory symptoms triggered a record in the national health insurance database and, if warranted, would be followed up on immediately.

Taiwan authorities also quickly implemented a plan to quarantine all infected individuals, trace their recent contacts, and to monitor quarantined individuals electronically via government-issued cell phones. It used "digital fencing" for close to 55,000 people in home quarantine, where alarms would sound if a quarantined person wandered too far from home.[8] While the aggressive use of these technical surveillance methods by the Taiwan government may raise serious privacy concerns if left in place after the emergency is over, there is no question that these technological aids have been a highly effective part of Taiwan's comprehensive approach to the crisis.

Although Taiwan did not impose strict social distancing measures until April 1, 2020, the quarantine, testing, and tracking mechanisms that had already been implemented proved to be highly effective in combatting the spread of the virus.

Taiwan's innovative approach to its successful coronavirus response included humor as a tool in fighting the pandemic. Speaking at the TED conference, Taiwan's digital minister Audrey Tang explained how a tactic called "humor over rumor" had effectively quashed misinformation about COVID-19.[9] Every time a hoax surfaced on social media, Tang and her band of civic hackers unleash a joke containing the facts of the matter within two hours of spotting the post. This approach was based on the idea that since people like to share funny memes on social media, the government was able to take control of the narrative by acting proactively on the internet. Tang also said that government agencies had employed professional comedians as "engagement officers" to help in the cause. Tang's team also located some of the perpetrators and recruited them as allies in Taiwan's coronavirus effort.

In short, there was a robust and coordinated response by the Taiwan government with the full support of Taiwan citizens, who were receiving clear-cut information and instructions each day as to what they should do or not do in response to their national emergency. The U.S. would be well advised to borrow a page or two from the Taiwan playbook.

Indeed, Taiwan's successful response to the coronavirus threat reaped benefits far beyond just the public health and safety of its own citizens. It also helped enhance Taiwan's reputation and prestige in the world community, as it mass-produced millions of face masks emblazoned with the words "Made in Taiwan," which it shipped to countries hit hard by the crisis. Although Beijing has been trying for decades to isolate Taiwan from the rest of the world and has never acknowledged its independent political and diplomatic existence, the positive public relations boost that Taiwan has received from its model pandemic response efforts and donations of protective equipment to other countries has reinvigorated the country's efforts to promote itself as a model of self-rule and democracy.[10] "We can see that this is a good opportunity for us to let people know that Taiwan is a good global citizen," commented Taiwan's Vice President Chen Chien-Jen.[11]

Iceland

The fundamental difference between Iceland's response to the coronavirus crisis and that of the U.S. is that, in the U.S., we have a federal government that promised there would be testing available for everyone, while in Iceland, the government actually accomplished universal screening. Widespread testing has been crucial to Iceland's low number of infections and deaths, with only around 1,700 people having been infected in Iceland, and eight deaths.[12]

Like Taiwan, Iceland quickly responded to the crisis through the quarantine of all infected persons and contact tracing, combined with close monitoring. After six cases were confirmed on March 3, 2020, Iceland immediately issued quarantine measures for all travelers returning from Italy and increased travel restrictions. A national emergency was declared on March 6.[13]

Iceland's rapid response has meant that it has been able to stay on top of the outbreak without being unduly restrictive. Groups of up to 20 could still meet, as long as they stayed 2 meters (about 6.5 feet) apart from each other.[14] Universities were closed, but schools and nurseries were still open, allowing at least one parents to continue working.

One key to Iceland's success was that it effectively used its police force to assist public health personnel with contact tracing to identify every person who has been in contact with every diagnosed coronavirus case.

Iceland also implemented a highly effective testing program through a public-private partnership between the National University Hospital of Iceland and the biotech company deCODE Genetics. Iceland was able to test 10% of its population by the second half of April 2020, and quickly expanded the program thereafter.[15] Among other things, this testing found 528 mutations of the coronavirus, which could provide an important key to decoding the virus and developing an effective vaccine.

Icelandic officials also made an app available for people to download, to help chart the spread of the virus and log where the user had been.[16] Users did not have to share their data with authorities, but many of them did so voluntarily to help the authorities with contact tracking.

By mid-May, Iceland had not only flattened the curve of coronavirus cases but it had virtually eliminated it. There were reports of only two new coronavirus cases each week by May in the entire country, and contract tracers and the police were able to monitor and deal with each new case quickly. Amazingly, Iceland achieved this result without ever imposing a lockdown, and only a few types of businesses – such as night clubs and hair salons – were temporarily closed down.[17] Hardly anyone in the capital city of Reykjavík needed to wear a mask by early June, which was when Iceland started heavily promoting its tourism industry again, seeking to attract people from North America and Europe who were tired of the lockdown doldrums and wanted to get away to a vacation spot that did not require any quarantine period.

South Korea

South Korea, like Taiwan, had absorbed the lessons learned from past virus outbreaks and had a plan in place to respond to the next microbial threat quickly. Although it was mostly unaffected by the SARS outbreak in 2003, only reporting three cases and no deaths at all, it had the unfortunate distinction of becoming the worst-impacted country outside the Middle East when the 2015 MERS outbreak occurred.

During the first few months of the COVID-19 crisis, fewer than one in every 100,000 people in South Korea's population died from the virus, compared to approximately eight in every 100,000 in the U.S.[18] The four keys to South Korea's success appear to have been as follows: early testing, early diagnosis, early quarantine, and early treatment.

As early as January 3, 2020, South Korea was quick to implement quarantine and screening measures for people arriving from Wuhan, more than two weeks before South Korea's first infection was even confirmed.[19] Authorities quickly rolled out a series of travel restrictions soon thereafter. South Korea also started rigorous contact tracing, and when it traced one case to a religious group in the city of Daegu, it was able to quarantine the entire area and conduct intensive testing within the quarantine area.[20] These prompt actions prevented the further spread of the virus from this hot spot.

Drive-through testing also quickly found widespread use in South Korea, and these highly accessible tests were largely free, quick, and done by well-trained staff who worked from a safe distance. The U.S. tried the same "drive through testing" model in some states, but it did not become nearly as universally available here as it was in South Korea.

Since South Korea is one of the most technologically advanced and innovative countries in the world, it was also able to win widespread acceptance and use of an app to monitor people in quarantine and to track potential coronavirus cases.[21]

South Korea's success with its testing program was exemplified by its agreement on April 20 with Republican Governor Larry Hogan of Maryland and his Korean-speaking wife Yumi to supply 500,000 testing kits to Maryland to ease Maryland's shortage of testing equipment.[22] "The [number] one problem facing us is lack of testing," said Governor Hogan, who was among the many critics of the Trump administration's repeated claims that states had adequate testing equipment. He added, "We can't open up our states without ramping up testing."[23]

By early June, South Korea was still experiencing a small but steady stream of new coronavirus cases, most of which were related to nightclubs and other crowded spaces, but the government was generally able to deal with these hot spots though quick investigations, contact tracing and individual quarantines.[24] As summer got underway, South Korea was able to open up some of its famous water parks, such as one called "Caribbean

Bay" in Yongin, southeast of Seoul, but it had strict social distancing rules in place for people both in the pools as well as locker rooms and other facilities. Visitors were required to first fill out an online form to list any potential symptoms, and then have their temperatures checked before being allowed in. Officials also required that the water park operator conduct disinfection operations every hour. Everyone was also required to wear protective face masks when not in the water, and the park provided plastic bags to keep masks dry when not in use.

Ireland

The pandemic hit the Republic of Ireland at about the same time as it arrived in the U.K, its closest neighbor across the Irish Sea. The results, however, were markedly different, with the U.K. experiencing almost twice the death rate as Ireland. The first coronavirus cases were reported in Ireland on February 29, 2020,[25] and within three weeks the virus spread to all of Ireland's counties.[26] On March 12, when Acting Irish Taoiseach (Prime Minister) Leo Varadkar was still in Washington, D.C. for some pre-St. Patrick's Day festivities,[27] he announced the virtual shutdown of Ireland with the closing of all schools, colleges, childcare facilities, and cultural institutions.[28] As part of his televised address on Irish TV, Varadkar spoke with the authority of the medical doctor that he was, explaining to his Irish audience why the extensive mitigation measures were necessary, and further appealing to the traditional Irish respect for their elders:

> We know that older people and those with chronic diseases are at real risk. We have a duty as a society to protect ourselves and, above all, to protect others – our parents and grandparents, our family and friends, co-workers, and neighbors. We have not witnessed a pandemic of this nature in living memory. This is unchartered territory. We said we would take the right actions at the right time. We have to move now to have the greatest impact.[29]

Ireland then canceled the annual St. Patrick's Day festivities in Dublin – which were expected to attract about 2 million people on March 17. The last time that these St. Patty's Day events had been canceled in Dublin was in 2001 when there was a hoof-and-mouth infectious disease scare.[30] On March 24, all remaining "non-essential" businesses were shut.[31] The Garda Siochana (National Police) was given the power to enforce the restrictions, which were extended through May 18 at the earliest.[32] In addition to the severe economic impact on Ireland caused by these shutdowns, the Irish were temporarily deprived of their cherished sporting events, which were an integral part of Irish culture. These sporting events that were canceled included football (soccer), Gaelic football, and hurling (an outdoor team game of ancient Gaelic Irish origin). The Dublin Horse Show was also canceled for the first time since 1940.

By mid-April, the Irish National Public Health Emergency Team reported that the growth rate of the pandemic had been driven "as low as it needs to be,"[33] that the curve had flattened and that there was no peak coming.[34] As of May 3, the Irish Department of Health had confirmed 21,506 cases and 1,303 deaths.[35] More than 90% of those deaths were over 65,[36] and most also had underlying illnesses or live in care homes.[37]

For purposes of comparison, people were dying of coronavirus in the neighboring U.K. at more than twice the rate they were dying in Ireland.[38] The likely reason for this disparity in outcomes from the pandemic was the fact that both the Irish and the English peoples took their cues from their political leaders, and the leadership of these countries was sending very different messages. While the Irish Taoiseach was regularly communicating to the Irish public the seriousness of the coronavirus threat and took early actions to close down Irish schools and universities, the U.K. Prime Minister, Boris Johnson, like President Trump in the U.S., was constantly sending mixed messages as to whether or not the pandemic should really be taken seriously.[39]

In a show of solidarity between the Irish people and Native Americans, donors in Ireland sent money to certain Native American tribes badly hit by the coronavirus in recognition of the debt that Ireland owned these tribes since the time of the Great Famine in Ireland in the 1840s.[40] Navajo and Hopi communities in North America set up a GoFundMe campaign to raise money for food, water, essential supplies, and personal protective equipment. By early May, they had raised more than $1.6 million, with some of the donations coming from Ireland, inspired by the help provided to Ireland by the Choctaw Nation tribe during the Great Famine. This native American tribe had donated $170 — the equivalent of $5,000 today — to help the Irish people in 1847.[41] This donation was particularly significant since the Choctaw had themselves experienced great suffering and loss, with around 60,000 Native Americans, including the Choctaw, being forcibly relocated from their ancestral homelands through what became known as the Trail of Tears. During this forced relocation, thousands died from starvation, disease, and exposure. A message from one Irish donor, Pat Hayes, said: "From Ireland, 170 years later, the favour is returned! "To our native American brothers and sisters in your moment of hardship."[42]

Germany

The coronavirus crisis hit Germany with force, with more than 100,000 laboratory-confirmed infections as early April, more than any other country except the United States, Italy, and Spain.[43] Although Germany's coronavirus infection rate was high, it was able to keep its death rate down to about four people for every 100,000, which was about one-half the U.S. rate (eight for every 100,000), and well below that of Italy (35 per 100,000) and the U.K. (18 out of 100,000).[44] Germany's well-resourced universal health system had such a large capacity that its hospitals started treating people for coronavirus from Italy, Spain, and France. With a superb health care system, German authorities were able to treat people with even moderate symptoms in hospitals well before their condition dangerously deteriorated, and there was evidence that this early treatment improved the chances for survival for many patients.

Germany's success was also primarily based upon its ability to make mass testing available. Like Taiwan, South Korea, and Iceland, Germany devised an effective diagnostic test for coronavirus, which it rolled out with a large number of testing kits early on, even before the country reported its first death. The German government also had a good working relationship with the private sector, including private labs, which ensured that the ambitious mass testing program was actually carried out.

Germany's successful campaign against COVID-19 can be measured by its relatively small number of cases and fatalities, as compared to the U.S. and its European neighbors, taking into account the relative size of various countries' populations. As of April 20, 2020, Germany had

147,065 confirmed cases of coronavirus, according to data compiled by Johns Hopkins University (JHU), and had registered 4,862 deaths.[45] In stark comparison, as of that date, Spain recorded 20,852 deaths (and over 200,000 cases of the virus), Italy had seen over 24,000 deaths, France over 20,000 deaths, and the U.K.'s death toll had risen to 16,550.[46] In addition, as of Friday, April 17, Germany's announced that the reproduction or transmission rate (the number of people that each infected person goes on to infect) had dropped below one for the first time.[47] This closely-watched measure led Germany Health Minister Jens Spahn to declare: "as things stand today, the outbreak is again controllable."[48]

By mid-April, German Chancellor Angela Merkel felt confident enough to announce that the country would begin scaling back its lockdown, while continuing with its intensive testing program, including antibody testing, to monitor whether the increased social contact between people would lead to a second wave of infections. Germany also planned to rely upon an excellent contact tracing program in place throughout the country, so that any additional cases that were identified could have all their recent contacts traced, tested, and isolated if necessary.

Due in no small measure to these robust nationwide testing and contact tracing programs it already had in place, on Monday, April 20, Germany started tentatively reopening its economy, with smaller retailers of under 800 square meters being allowed to reopen, as long as social distancing and good hygiene measures could be maintained.[49] Larger car dealerships, bike shops, and book shops were also allowed to open. The country's vital car industry had lobbied hard for lockdown measures to be eased, resulting in the opening of one of the Volkswagen manufacturing plants in Germany, in the city of Zwickau, with more plants to following shortly thereafter.[50]

Germany also announced that schools would reopen on May 4, with priority given to students taking exams. Large mass gatherings, however, remained banned until August 31, 2020, and bars and restaurants, movie theaters, and large retail stores remained closed. As it had previously done in past crises, Germany developed a clear plan as to how to reopen its economy, and carefully monitored each step of the reopening process very closely.

By May 6, Germany's new infection numbers had fallen to the point where Chancellor Angela Merkel announced that the country was in a position to reopen most aspects of its economy and society that had not already begun to reopen.[51] "We can afford a little audacity," Ms. Merkel said.[52] Germany's relatively quick recovery was due, in large measure, to the kind of cautious, science-led political leadership and widespread testing that sharply distinguished it from the U.S.'s generally haphazard response, which was more in the nature of "let's reopen whether we are really ready to do so or not." Germany shut down early and then systematically tested its way back to some semblance of normality. Face masks and social distancing quickly became the new normal throughout Germany, which allowed for the reopening of hotels, restaurants, and bars under strict restrictions to prevent the spread of the virus.

There were also indications that Germany's recovery might even get a boost from the fact that it seems to be in the lead – or at least in the lead pack – of the countries that are racing to develop an effective COVID-19 vaccine. The German biotechnology company BioNTech announced that it had developed a vaccine candidate in collaboration with the American pharmaceutical company Pfizer, and that it had been approved for clinical testing in Germany.[53] According to Ugur Sahin, an immunologist and co-founder of BioNTech, "We are pleased to have completed preclinical studies in Germany and will soon initiate this first-in-human trial ahead of our expectations."[54]

With new case rates dropping in all parts of the country by early June, and widespread testing capability in place, Germany was well on its way to an orderly reopening of its commercial and social life. "We can say today that the first phase of the pandemic is behind us," Ms. Merkel announced with confidence.[55] In stark contrast, the infection rates were continuing to rise in some U.S. states by early June, and the country still did not have the extensive testing capabilities available in many key cities and states.

New Zealand

On Monday, June 8, New Zealand celebrated the complete eradication of coronavirus, as the last known patient in the country had recovered.[56]

There had been no new coronavirus infections in New Zealand for the past 17 days. The country had seen only around 1,500 total cases out of a population of about 5 million, with 20 reported deaths.[57] Prime Minister Jacinda Ardern, who had placed the country on strict lockdown at the end of March, announced at a press conference: "We can hold public events without limitations. Private events such as weddings, functions, and funerals without limitations," she said, "Retail is back without limitations. Hospitality is back without limitations. Public transport and travel across the country is fully opened."[58]

New Zealand's success was primarily based on its "go hard, go early" lockdown strategy, which was supplemented by vigorous testing and contact tracking program. Its successful response efforts were also due in part to strong border control measures, with the country banning entry of all non-residents, and requiring returning citizens to be tested upon arrival and quarantined for two weeks.

New Zealand entered a level 3 lockdown on March 23, which meant that non-essential businesses were closed, discretionary domestic air travel was banned, and all events and gatherings had to be canceled. It then entered into a level 4 lockdown 48 hours later, which required all citizens and residents to maintain contact only with those with whom they lived.[59] Even earlier, on March 19, New Zealand closed its borders, banning all inbound travel to the country with the exception of returning New Zealanders and some essential health workers.[60] On April 27, New Zealand lifted some of its lockdown measures, moving back into the level 3 stage and allowing people to expand their social "bubbles" to reconnect with close family outside of their households.[61] Some schools and businesses were also allowed to resume.

In addition to putting lockdown measures in place quickly, New Zealand also ramped up testing to the point where it had the capacity to process up to 8,000 tests per day, meaning New Zealand had one of the highest testing rates per capita in the world. Without any mitigation measures, COVID-19's R0 rating would be around 2.5, while under lockdown, the R0 of the virus had dropped to 0.4, meaning each infected person would only transmit the virus to less than half a person.[62]

The New Zealand government also clearly communicated with its citizens. Prior to the lockdown being implemented, for example, emergency text messages were sent to residents with a concise explanation of what the level 4 lockdown would entail. The emergency message read: "This message is for all of New Zealand. We are depending on you ... Where you stay tonight is where you must stay from now on ... it is likely level 4 measures will stay in place for a number of weeks."[63]

By completely eradicating the disease and reopening with reliable precautions in place by early June, New Zealand reaped the rewards of its nimble and proactive response efforts, and could look forward to having its economy rebound sooner than that of many other countries still in lockdown or, like the U.S., still experiencing COVID-19 outbreaks and increases in cases throughout the country.

28

DID SWEDEN AND THE OTHER SCANDINAVIAN COUNTRIES TAKE THE RIGHT APPROACH?

The Scandinavian (Nordic) countries – Sweden, Norway, Finland, and Denmark – share a similar cultural, geographical, and sociological attribute. However, Sweden took a much more relaxed and "hands-off" approach to the coronavirus crisis than its three other Scandinavian neighbors, who took a more aggressive approach.[1]

Denmark announced widespread closures on March 11 and was among the first in Europe to close borders, shops, schools and restaurants, and to ban large gatherings.[2] Norway began introducing travel restrictions in mid-March and closed schools and daycare centers, prohibited the use of vacation properties, canceled events and closed businesses such as hair and beauty salons.[3] Finland declared a state of emergency on March 16, ordering the closure of schools and banned gatherings of more than ten people, and followed up by closing restaurants, cafes, and bars on April 1.[4]

Sweden only closed down its high schools and colleges while keeping its preschools, grade schools, pubs, restaurants, and borders open. It even kept its world-famous ski slopes open.[5] It would be inaccurate, however, to conclude from Sweden's more relaxed approach to the crisis that it was not taking the pandemic seriously or that the country was not serious about the health and safety of its people. The country's leader and health officials stressed the importance of handwashing, social distancing, and protecting people over the age of 70 by limiting contact with them. The country's leading epidemiologist, Anders Tegnell, forcefully asserted in an interview that Sweden's strategy, which was based on science, saying, "We are trying to slow the spread enough so that we can deal with the patients coming in."[6] In other words, Sweden's most important goal was not to let its hospital and health care system be overwhelmed with a large influx of cases all at once. As long as the country had the hospital and equipment capacity to handle the increased caseload, Sweden's leadership felt that the country was fully capable of riding out the pandemic storm.

Sweden's approach was consistent with the country's tradition of the public's self-restraint and sense of responsibility, Mr. Tegnell explained: "That's the way we work in Sweden. Our whole system for communicable disease control is based on voluntary action. The immunization system is completely voluntary, and there is 98 percent coverage."[7] Sweden's system of government is also relatively unique when it comes to public health issues since there are restrictions placed on the ability of elected officials to countermand the views of the public health professionals.

Although it is still too early to project what the long-term impact of the pandemic will be on Sweden and its closest neighbors, there is no escaping the fact that the death rate in Sweden was significantly higher than many other countries in Europe by the end of April. Sweden's death rate reached as high as 22 per 100,000 people, according to figures from Johns Hopkins University.[8] As of April 28, Sweden had registered 18,926 coronavirus cases and 2,274 deaths among its population of 10.3 million people.[9] By contrast, Denmark recorded just over 7 deaths per 100,000 people, and both Norway and Finland less than 4 deaths.[10] To put it in perspective, by the end of April, Denmark had 9,049 cases and 427 deaths in a population of 5.8 million; Norway had 7,599 cases and 206 deaths among its 5.4 million people; and Finland had 4,695 cases and 193 deaths in its population of 5.5 million.[11]

Based on their ability to "flatten the curve" and that they were well past their peaks of hospitalizations and coronavirus-related deaths during April, these three countries - Denmark, Norway, and Finland - started in late April to ease their lockdowns, with children returning to school, using smaller class sizes and floor markers to help keep children and faculty six feet apart. Beauty salons and other businesses with one-to-one contact also started reopening in Norway in late April, while Finland extended its restrictions until May 13.[12]

Although Sweden had more deaths on a per 100,000 population basis than its Scandinavian neighbors, it had far fewer deaths than did Italy or Spain, which recorded around 45 and 51 deaths per 100,000 people, respectively.[13] It also had far fewer deaths than the U.K., where there were about 32 deaths per 100,000 of the population.[14] But there are various complex differences between Sweden and these other European countries that make direct comparisons more difficult. Italy, for example, has an older population, more smokers, and a more significant number of multigenerational households, where infections can travel more freely.

Although Sweden's approach led to more cases and deaths than its Nordic neighbors, at least in the short term, the question as to whether the coronavirus pandemic could actually be stopped prior to the development of an effective vaccine, or if the world population can reach "herd immunity," remains unanswered. This concept can best be described as the point at which the virus stops spreading in the population at a rapid rate because a sufficient percentage of the population is already immunized since they have recovered from the virus infection and have sufficient antigens in their blood system to ward off future infections.

Mitigation measures such as "shelter-in-place" orders and the closure of businesses and schools unquestionably "flatten the curve" in the infection rate so that health care systems are not overwhelmed within a short period of time by unacceptably high numbers of cases. But mitigation measures hold no guarantee that, over time, the virus will not infect 60-70% or more of the population. At some point, the virus cannot find enough new uninfected hosts to keep the pandemic going. The only other possible scenarios, in the long run, is for a therapeutic "wonder drug" cure for COVID-19 to be discovered, or that there is an effective vaccine developed.

The argument in favor of Sweden's looser approach to the coronavirus crisis is that is has been able to work, more or less, because it has an excellent healthcare system that has reasonably been able to cope with the increase of coronavirus cases requiring hospitalizations. Peter Lindgren, managing director at the Swedish Institute for Health Economics, told *CNN* that the number of people treated in intensive care units was stable, "[s]o, in that aspect, it has to be successful."[15]

The Swedish Public Health Agency forecast that COVID-19 would have infected almost a third of people in Stockholm County (later revised down to 26%) by May 1.[16] Mr. Tegnell said that Sweden would likely be in a better place to withstand a second wave of coronavirus because so many people in the country had already been exposed to the virus.[17] Indeed, it can reasonably be assumed that Sweden – like the U.S. and the rest of the world – may have to undergo multiple waves of the virus until herd immunity is attained, or that a vaccine or highly-effective therapeutic drug is discovered or developed. Simply stated, the theory is that as the percentage levels of antigen-driven immunity increase in the population, the reproduction infection rates will fall, and the pandemic will stall. Of course, whether antigens in your blood give you some degree of immunity or not, is still an open question.

Sweden's approach to the crisis diverged from not only that of its Scandinavian neighbors but also most other nations. India, for example, imposed a virtual lockdown of 1.3 billion people. Germany banned gatherings of two or more people, except for families. French citizens were required to fill out a form stating the purpose of each errand that they run when they leave their homes.

However, Sweden's approach to the crisis has been followed by The Netherlands. On March 16, Dutch Prime Minister Mark Rutte said that his country of 17.1 million was opting for "controlled spread" of the virus among Dutch groups that were least likely to get seriously ill and argued that it was too late to shut down the country completely.[18] As of April 25, Holland was reporting more than 9,700 cases of the virus and 639 deaths.[19]

Many American health care experts followed the developments in Scandinavia very closely since the outcomes there were likely to be important for a long-term understanding of the coronavirus crisis and how different populations responded to the pandemic. In America's health care debates that were ongoing long before the outbreak of the current coronavirus crisis, the region often looked to as a model was Scandinavia.[20] When *US News & World Report* ranked best health care systems in the world earlier in 2020, Denmark, Sweden, and Norway were rated in the top four. The United States came in 15th.[21] It makes sense that since Scandinavia is a traditional world leader in both health care and in social responsibility, the policies and outcomes of those policies by these countries will be highly relevant to our planning for any future pandemic or health care crisis.

One reason for the relatively high infection rates in Scandinavia is that the increased availability of testing in those countries accounts for those higher – and more accurate – numbers. South Korea, another country with a high per capita number of recorded cases, also tested extensively, which may be giving the rest of the world the wrong message that countries who do the right thing and have extensive testing platforms available may be "punished" with higher infection and death rates. Johan von Schreeb, a professor of global disaster medicine at Sweden's Karolinska Institute, has suggested that the coronavirus-related data in the U.S. is artificially depressed since the U.S. has not done nearly the same degree of extensive testing as have Sweden and South Korea.[22]

In fact, tests conducted on 200 blood donors by Sweden's Karolinska Institute, together with Karolinska University Hospital, showed that at least 11 out of 100 of the participants had antibodies to COVID-19.[23] This means that more than one in 10 people in Sweden may have been infected with the coronavirus since the outbreak began, based on these preliminary results of this new COVID-19 antibody study. If these results are truly indicative of the viral spread in society, they suggest that Sweden, which has roughly a population of 10 million, has more than a million people who may have been infected. In a population of around 330 million, like the U.S., this infection and potential immunity rate would translate to 33 million Americans, assuming that the 10% infection rate is roughly the same from country to country. However, as of April 28, the U.S. official tally for reported coronavirus cases hovered only around 1 million (981,246 cases), with over 50,000 deaths (55,258), and by June 9, those numbers had doubled to 2,008,728 cases and 113,099 deaths.[24]

An indication that all of the Scandinavian countries may have been on the right track is that their health care systems have done an excellent job of handling the increased influx of coronavirus patients as indicated by the relatively low number of COVID-19 reported deaths. A large percentage of the fatalities in three of those countries – 206 in Norway, 427 in Denmark, and 2,274 in Sweden – came from nursing home residents, and each one of these countries has taken emergency measures to reduce the unacceptable and excessively high number of fatalities being traced to nursing homes.[25]

Since the Scandinavian countries all seemed to have passed their peaks by mid-April 2020, the countries that had shut down the hardest – Norway, Denmark, and Finland – eased up on restrictions as early as late April and May. Because the number of coronavirus cases and patients on ventilators had been trending downwards, Norway's Minister of Health and Care announced that the outbreak in that country was "under control" and that restrictions would be gradually lifted.[26] The Norwegian Prime Minister Erna Solberg also encouraged all Norwegians to download a new app designed to track the spread of the virus. This "Smittestopp" app has also been used to alert users when they are close to someone infected with the coronavirus.[27] Similarly, the spread of coronavirus infections had slowed sharply in Finland to the point where health officials in that country started considering easing restrictions as early as April 27.[28]

One of the long-term factors that were being closely watched in Scandinavia as well as in other countries was the general health of each country's people and their susceptibility to serious illness or death from a coronavirus infection. The better the general health of those being infected, the more likely their immune systems would have the ability to fight off a serious virus infection and to develop sufficient antigens to possibly qualify as immunity.

The Scandinavian diet, unlike the diet of most Americans, has reduced starchy carbohydrates and usually includes healthy servings of local sources of protein, such as cold-water fish, and organic vegetables.[29] Cooking is a significant part of the Scandinavian culture, and something children are generally taught to do from an early age. "Combined with almost-universal access to fresh produce and fish, Scandinavians generally eat healthier than most Americans," according to Christel Oerum, diabetes advocate originally from Denmark, who is now living in Los Angeles.[30]

Scandinavians also generally believe that junk food is, well, junk. Out of all the countries, the U.S. and U.K. take the top spots for consuming the most junk food, including pizza and deep-fried foods. Swedes consume the least. Scandinavians are also generally obsessed with saunas, with Finland alone having over 2.2 million saunas. A study conducted by scientists at the University of Eastern Finland found that a 30-minute sauna reduced blood pressure and increased heart rates to levels comparable with moderate exercise.[31] Saunas also help sweat out toxins and alleviate stress.

Although it is difficult to generalize about Americans, since they cover such a wide diversity of communities and cultures, Scandinavian people are more homogeneous and generally take a more moderate approach to all things in life, including work, leisure time and meals. This way of living is called *lagom*, or "just the right amount," is key to Nordic philosophy, which does not place any arbitrary restrictions on any activities but requires that whatever you do, you should not do it in excess.

Almost all Scandinavian cities also are designed for easy biking and walking. In Copenhagen, 50% of the locals commute to work by bike daily, and another 25% walk or use a combination of public transportation and walking. And it does not matter what the weather is like. Even in the snow, sleet, or freezing cold, you will see more people biking to their destinations than you will see taking public transportation.

Scandinavian countries also put a high priority on family and maternity leave, mandating up to 16 months of paid family leave after a baby's birth or adoption. The state-run health system also has a strong emphasis on preventative health and a "wellness" to health. Although there is a stereotype of Scandinavians as heavy drinkers, studies have shown that Norwegians, for example, drink far less than people in many other countries, including the U.S. and the U.K. Scandinavians also forge strong social relationships through exercise classes and sports clubs. One in three people in Denmark belongs to a private sports club, such as a soccer or tennis club, making them a large part of social life in all of Scandinavia.[32] Americans, by contrast, either tend not to exercise regularly, leading to obesity and diabetes, or if they do go to gyms or health clubs, they usually are found exercising individually, rather than in groups.

* * * * *

Although Sweden took a slightly different path than its neighboring counties in its response to the coronavirus crisis, all of the Scandinavian countries ended up doing reasonably well, thanks in no small measure to their sophisticated and well-equipped national health systems, all of which included adequate testing and contact tracking capabilities.

29

COVID-19, RELIGIOUS FREEDOM AND THE STATES' RIGHTS TO RESTRICT RELIGIOUS SERVICES

"If beer is 'essential,' so is Easter."
-U.S. District Court Judge, Justin Walker

As of mid-May, approximately 1,300 state and federal lawsuits had been filed against states, challenging state restrictions imposed since the start of the COVID-19 pandemic.[1] Many of these lawsuits related specifically to state restrictions on places of worship. These legal challenges were generally based on the claim that such restrictions violated the right to freedom of religion as protected by the First Amendment of the U.S. Constitution.

State restrictions on religious services - all of which were imposed in an effort to stem the transmission of coronavirus infections - ranged from complete bans on religious services to restrictions on the number of people who could attend church services at any one time. Most states (approximately 22) permitted religious gatherings to take place if the gathering was limited to 10 people or less, a third of the states (about 15) did not limit size, and only ten states had prohibitions of religious gatherings altogether.[2]

By mid-May, the states where houses of worship were already allowed to open in some form included Alabama, Florida, Indiana, Kentucky, Louisiana, Maryland, and Virginia. Places of worship in Colorado were technically able to open since stay-at-home orders were lifted, but many congregations are still limiting services and gathering virtually. The states where houses of worship were never required to close included Pennsylvania, although Governor Tom Wolf advised religious leaders not to hold in-person services.[3]

While various churches throughout the country opposed such restrictions, it should be noted that most churches and faith groups willingly complied with public health restrictions on their services in states throughout the country. Most Roman Catholic, Episcopal, and other churches suspended in-person religious services while stay-at-home state orders were in effect. Instead, these churches streamed their religious services online for their congregants and all others who wished to view these services on their home computers. Muslim groups also generally agreed to celebrate Ramadan at home rather than in mosques.[4]

The Right of the States To Impose Public Health Quarantine Restrictions Versus Freedom of Religion

The right to Freedom of Religion is enshrined as the first enumerated right in the First Amendment of the U.S. Constitution. The First Amendment reads: "Congress shall make no law respecting an establishment of religion, or prohibiting the free exercise thereof; or abridging the freedom of speech, or the press; or the right of the people peaceably to assemble, and to petition the Government for a redress of grievances."

As strange as it may seem to us three centuries later, the early American colonies were not particularly tolerant of forms of worship that deviated from that of the prevailing religious orthodoxy. For example, the colony of Rhode Island was founded after Roger Smith fled the Massachusetts Bay Colony to escape religious persecution by the dominating Puritans there. In 1660, the religious persecution of the Quakers in New England led to the public hanging of English Quaker Mary Dyer in Boston, Massachusetts. After three other Quakers were executed in Boston, King Charles II issued an edict in 1661 explicitly forbidding Massachusetts from executing any more Quakers.[5] The Pilgrim and Puritan settlers were also virulently anti-Catholic.[6] In 1647, Massachusetts passed a law prohibiting any Jesuit Roman Catholic priests from entering territory under Puritan jurisdiction.[7] The penalty for a first offense was banishment from the colony; a second offense carried the death penalty.[8]

The major exception to religious intolerance in the American colonies was in Maryland, founded by the Catholic Lord Baltimore in 1634, which was the first colony to adopt the concept of religious freedom as a principle of government.[9] In 1649, the Maryland Toleration Act was enacted by the colonial assembly, allowing freedom of worship for all Christians in Maryland who believed in the Holy Trinity, but sentenced to death anyone who denied the divinity of Jesus.[10]

The Religious Freedom Restoration Act (RFRA) was enacted by Congress in 1993 to prevent other federal laws from substantially burdening the free exercise of religion.[11] RFRA explicitly states that the "Government shall not substantially burden a person's exercise of religion even if the burden results from a rule of general applicability." However, even with the passage of the RFRA, religious groups and their exercise of religion are still subject to laws where these laws have a "compelling state interest" and in which states used the "least restrictive means."

The states have jurisdiction over police powers regarding matters of public health and safety under the Tenth Amendment to the U.S. Constitution, which is part of the Bill of Rights. The Tenth Amendment states: "The powers not delegated to the United States by the Constitution, nor prohibited by it to the States, are reserved to the States respectively, or to the people." In other words, the 10th Amendment makes it clear that the states hold all of the powers under our federalist system of government, except for those specifically delegated to the federal government under the Constitution.

There has never been a nationwide quarantine in the history of the U.S., even during the 1918 Spanish Flu pandemic that killed an estimated 675,000 Americans.[12] Although, in theory, the Public Health Service Act of 1944 or the Commerce Clause could arguably give the federal government the right to impose a nationwide quarantine, such a draconian step has never been seriously considered. Therefore, to the extent that U.S. courts have reviewed the legality and scope of quarantines, these have been quarantines imposed by states, municipalities, or other local governmental entities.

In 1902, the Supreme Court first reviewed a state's power to quarantine a large geographical area around New Orleans in its decision in *Compagnie Francaise &c. v. Board of Health*.[13] In that case, the Supreme court upheld a Louisiana statute that permitted the state to isolate or restrict healthy persons from entering an area where there were contagious persons infected with an illness, and which restricted infected persons from entering any area where healthy people were located.[14]

Similarly, in 1905, in the case of *Jacobson v. Commonwealth of Massachusetts*,[15] Justice John Marshall Harlan upheld a compulsory state vaccination law for smallpox as a legitimate exercise of state police powers against charges that it unduly interfered with personal liberties.

Over a century later, these two Supreme Court cases remain good law and have been cited in support of quarantines as recently as the Ebola outbreak.[16]

However, a state's power to issue quarantine orders or to take other steps to protect its citizen's public health and safety is not limitless. Courts had sometimes struck down quarantine orders when they were found to be arbitrary and unreasonable in relation to their goal of protecting public health. In one 1900 case, for example,[17] a California federal court found that sealing off an entire section of San Francisco to prevent the spread of the bubonic plague was "unreasonable, unjust, and oppressive."[18] Such an overbroad order, the Court declared, was "not in harmony with the declared purpose" of preventing the spread of the disease.[19] In an 1889 decision, the New York Court of Appeals also rejected as overbroad a blanket quarantine of individuals who refused vaccination, where there was no reason to believe they had been infected or even exposed to the disease.[20]

Thus, although the states clearly have the authority to impose quarantines and other reasonable public health restrictions on an emergency basis, the Supreme Court and other federal courts have never completely determined constitutional limits on the state's authority to do so.[21] This is because the Supreme Court has rarely, if ever, reviewed cases regarding the legality of quarantine. Perhaps this is because involuntary quarantining has not been common since World War II.[22] The only clear guidance the Supreme Court has provided was in the 1905 decision in *Jacobson*, where the Court explained that each state and community has the duty and "right to protect itself against an epidemic of disease which threatens the safety of its members."[23]

With the onset of the coronavirus crisis, the issues of quarantines rose to the legal forefront when states and cities started issuing orders to individuals who tested positive for COVID-19 but refused to self-isolate themselves. For example, when a 53-year-old Kentucky man who tested positive refused to self-isolate, state officials there obtained a court order to force him to isolate himself.[24] They also posted a law enforcement officer outside the man's home.

Attorney General Barr Warns the States About Restrictions on Individual Rights

Since the Trump administration was pushing the governors to reopen their states for business as soon as possible, Attorney General William P. Barr directed all 93 U.S. attorneys on Monday, April 27, to "be on the lookout for state and local directives" that curtail individual rights in the name of containing the novel coronavirus.[25] In a two-page memo, Barr warned: "Many policies that would be unthinkable in regular times have become commonplace in recent weeks," adding that, "we do not want to unduly interfere with the important efforts of state and local officials to protect the public. But the Constitution is not suspended in times of crisis."[26]

During an interview with conservative radio host Hugh Hewitt, Barr further elaborated on the Justice Department's strategy, which was first to try to intimidate governors into backing away from policies the Trump administration opposed, and then if that did not work, to use the judicial system to achieve the administration's goals: "If we think one [restriction] goes too far, we initially try to jawbone the governors into rolling them back or adjusting them," he said. "And if they're not and people bring lawsuits, we file statements of interest and side with the plaintiffs."[27]

Barr was obviously correct that, even in the midst of a public health crisis, state policies cannot violate the Constitution. However, it has long been settled U.S. law that restrictions on the operation of businesses, including houses of worship, are constitutional as long as they are reasonable and non-discriminatory. In other words, public health restrictions ordered by the state and municipal governments are lawful as long as they do not unduly single out churches and other religious institutions. Such restrictions can only run afoul of the First Amendment right to freedom of religion if these restrictions are more onerous than restrictions placed on comparable businesses, such as movie theaters, concert halls, and sports arenas, where large numbers of people are allowed to congregate for prolonged time periods.

The Mississippi Church Cases

The first case that the U.S. Justice Department intervened in was a case brought by the Temple Baptist Church in Greenville, Mississippi, which sued over the city's efforts to shut down drive-in religious services.[28] In its legal statement of interest filed in support of Temple Baptist Church, the Justice Department took the position that the city ordinance suggested that the city singled out churches for disparate treatment, which, if true, would be unconstitutional.[29] The Department of Justice's statement of interest noted that "individual rights secured by the Constitution do not disappear during a public health crisis," citing to the Fifth Circuit Court of Appeals decision, *In re Abbott*, which was decided on April 7.[30] The Fifth Circuit, in that case, emphasized that individual rights, including the protections in the Bill of Rights made applicable to the states through the Fourteenth Amendment, are always in force and restrain government action.[31]

The Temple Baptist Church case was particularly compelling since the church was holding the religious services in its parking lot. Worshippers stayed in their cars while the church broadcasted its service over a low-power FM station. The church did not have a website, and most of its members do not have social media or the ability to participate in Zoom calls or to watch services online.[32] For the congregants, the only opportunity that they had to participate in services was from the parking lot.

These "parking lot" services also seemed to be in full compliance with CDC and state public health guidelines requiring social distancing. Nevertheless, the city of Greenville dispatched eight uniformed police officers to ticket the church member, issuing $500 tickets to people merely sitting in their cars with their windows rolled up.[33] The DOJ argued in its statement of interest that, even though the city ordinance listed church services as "essential," it treated the church more strictly than it did other essential businesses.[34] The city also permitted drive-in restaurants to operate freely, with the restaurant customers sitting in their cars with their windows rolled down, but penalized churchgoers who similarly sat in their vehicles during religious services with their windows rolled up. The Justice Department's intervention in the Greenville case achieved its desired goal since the city ultimately backed down and lifted the restriction on the drive-in religious services.

The First Pentecostal Church of Holly Springs, Mississippi, was not so fortunate. On Easter Sunday, April 12, the church service was interrupted when police served a "cease and desist" order on the pastor for violating stay-at-home state orders and directed that the religious service be terminated. After having unsuccessfully challenged these restrictions in Court,[35] the church burned down during the early morning hours of May 20, apparently as a result of arson. A spray-painted message read: "I Bet you stay home now you hypokrits [sic]."[36]

Churches in Kansas Also Challenge State Restrictions

The Alliance Defending Freedom, a conservative Christian advocacy organization, filed suit in Federal Court on Thursday, April 16, challenging statewide shelter-in-place directives ordered by Kansas Governor Laura Kelly that placed a limit on "gatherings of more than ten congregants or parishioners in the same building or confined or enclosed space." The Kansas Supreme Court had previously upheld the Governor's executive order. [37]

The two Baptist church pastors in Kansas who were the are plaintiffs in the lawsuit - First Baptist Church of Dodge City and Calvary Baptist Church of Junction City - argued that the Governor's order discriminated against churches since it exempted 26 types of secular activities from this gathering ban, including bars, restaurants, libraries, shopping malls, retail establishments, and office spaces.[38] The churches claimed they were unfairly targeted for restrictions, since restaurants and bars were exempted as long as they maintain six feet between tables and bar stools, and in some cases, state or local authorities had held that establishments serving food provide an "essential" service.

The Kansas lawsuit also argued that Governor Kelly's executive order singled out "churches and other religious services or activities" and did not take into account whether social distancing, hygiene, "and other efforts to slow the spread of COVID-19 were practiced." The complaint asserted the fundamental religious liberty principle that religious gatherings cannot be treated worse under the law than similar gatherings. While many Kansas churches had moved services online, the pastors and churches that brought the federal court action against Governor Kelly said they believed that God required them to engage in "corporate" prayer.

On Saturday, April 18, U.S. District Judge John Broomes, sitting in federal Court in Witchita, issued a decision that effectively blocked Kansas from limiting attendance at in-person religious worship services or activities to 10 people or fewer.[39] In his ruling, Judge Broomes wrote: "Churches and religious activities appear to have been singled out among essential functions for stricter treatment." Broomes noted the Governor's order recognized some exceptions for "essential" businesses and called the disparate treatment of churches "arbitrary."

Judge Broomes' order, however, did not let the churches have services without any restrictions. Instead, he ordered them to abide by recommendations for social distancing that people stay 6 feet apart and to continue following other practices the churches said they had imposed, such as not using collection plates. Governor Kelly's order had limited in-person religious services or activities to 10 congregation members but did not limit the number of pastors, choir members, and others who could put on the service, so long as they practiced social distancing.

Following the decision, Governor Kelly responded in a statement: "This is not about religion. This is about a public health crisis." Kelly's office said the six deaths and 80 cases were tied to religious gatherings. Broomes' action was welcomed by the Republican-controlled Kansas Legislature, which had been strongly advocating that the Governor's stay-at-home order be lifted. Republican legislators had moved in the Kansas state courts to challenge Kelly's order on church gatherings. However, the Kansas Supreme Court let the Governor's order stand on technical grounds, without deciding whether it violated freedoms guaranteed by the U.S. or Kansas constitutions.[40]

Following Judge Broomes' grant of a temporary restraining order to the two churches, temporarily exempting them from the state restrictions, Governor Kelly and attorneys for the two churches reached what they described as a "temporary truce," whereby both sides filed a motion in Federal Court on April 25 promising that a new executive order would be issued, allowing church services and other large gatherings as long as people stayed 6 feet apart from each other and followed other protocols to check the spread of the coronavirus.[41] This compromise was designed to prevent the spread of the infection at church services and other gatherings while gradually opening up commerce in the state.

The "First Legacy" Church Case in New Mexico

In a New Mexico case, the First Legacy Church sought a restraining order in Federal Court in Albuquerque, seeking to prevent enforcement of a state order issued by Governor Michelle Lujan Grisham, who added churches to the state's list of nonessential services the day before Easter.[42] The state ordinance restricted church services to no more than five people. The church argued that it needed at least 30 people to put on the service that would be live-streamed to church members. The church pastor also argued that his building was large enough so that even the 30 members could socially distance within it. The state, however, took the position that the physical presence of 30 people in the church was an unjustifiable risk to public health: "[S]uch large public gatherings, even at just one church, have significant potential to lead to an outbreak of COVID-19 affecting thousands of people, causing more deaths."[43]

In denying the church's request for a temporary restraining order against enforcement of the Governor's executive order, the Court concluded that "[t]he public's interest in limiting the COVID-19 outbreak in the state, a compelling interest, outweighs the right to gather."[44] The Court thus found that the state order limiting gatherings to five persons was not discriminatory to churches. "Religious activity's relatively late recategorization stemmed not from hostility toward religion, but rather solicitousness towards religion," the judge said, adding the New Mexico state government "sought to preserve religious organizations' leeway to conduct services as long as possible until COVID-19 became too severe to continue affording such latitude."

The "On Fire Christian Church" Case in Kentucky

In a Kentucky case, On Fire Christian Church sued Louisville Mayor Greg Fischer for prohibiting drive-in church services on Easter.[45] Worshippers arrived in and stayed in their cars, did not roll their windows down, and otherwise followed CDC social distancing guidelines. On Fire's lawyer argued that, to prohibit the drive-in services despite these precautions, "unlawfully target[ed] houses of worship."[46] The church argued that these restrictions against "parking lot" church services were particularly draconian since the ordinance permitted liquor stores to stay open, labeling them as "essential businesses."[47]

The U.S. District Court judge, Justin Walker, ruled in favor of the church, reasoning that "if beer is 'essential,' so is Easter."[48] The Court further wrote in its decision that the mayor's decision to prohibit such religious services was "beyond all reason" and "unconstitutional."[49]

Wisconsin Supreme Court Invalidates All State Restrictions

On May 14, the Wisconsin Supreme Court voted 4-3 in favor of overturning Wisconsin Governor Tony Evers' coronavirus stay-at-home order on the grounds that he had not sought legislative approval for an extension of the lockdown ban.[50]

Evers' stay-at-home order had gone into effect in March, affecting schools and nonessential businesses. It was set to end on April 24, but Health and Human Services Secretary Andrea Palm, who was appointed by the Governor, extended it to May 26, launching a legal battle with the state legislature, which wanted to reopen the state.[51]

One of the dissenting judges on the Wisconsin Supreme Court, Justice Rebecca Dallet, wrote that the decision would "undoubtedly go down as one of the most blatant examples of judicial activism in this Court's history.

And it will be Wisconsinites who pay the price."[52] As Wisconsinites turned out in droves in bars and restaurants across the state, Democratic Governor Tony Evers accused the high Court and Republican-controlled legislature of causing "chaos." Governor Evers told *MSNBC*'s Ali Velshi: "We're the Wild West," reacting to scenes depicted on news channels of celebration in various Wisconsin bars, "There are no restrictions at all across the state of Wisconsin ... So, at this point in time ... there is nothing that's compelling people to do anything other than having chaos here."[53]

The Oregon Supreme Court Declines to Lift the State Restrictions Requiring Social Distancing During Religious Services

On May 18, four days after the Wisconsin Supreme Court issued its bombshell decision invalidating all state stay-at-home and social distancing restriction, an Oregon county judge declared Oregon Governor Kate Brown's coronavirus social distancing restrictions on religious services "null and void" because the legislature did not approve the emergency orders after the initial 28-day period.[54] The 10 Oregon churches that brought the lawsuit argued that the emergency powers of the Governor only extended for one month and that the permission of the state legislature was required for the executive order to be extended.[55] Baker County Circuit Judge Matthew Shirtcliff agreed with the church plaintiffs, holding that the Governor's social-distancing directives were unconstitutional. "The governor's orders are not required for public safety when plaintiffs can continue to utilize social distancing and safety protocols at larger gatherings involving spiritual worship," he wrote.[56]

Governor Brown immediately appealed the ruling to the state Supreme Court to try to keep the emergency orders in effect, which affected all businesses in the state, not just churches. Governor Brown said that an injunction against the enforcement of the county judge's decision was necessary to "ensure we can continue to safeguard the health of all Oregonians — including frontline health care workers, those living in nursing homes, workers in agriculture and food processing plants, and Oregonians with underlying health conditions — while the legal process moves forward."[57]

Later the same day, May 18, the Oregon Supreme Court stayed the county circuit judge's order invalidating the extension of the Governor's stay-at-home order without legislative approval.⁵⁸ The Supreme Court's ruling stayed Judge Shirtcliff's decision pending review by all the Supreme Court justices.

Governor Brown praised the Supreme Court action, stating: "There are no shortcuts for us to return to life as it was before this pandemic. Moving too quickly could return Oregon to the early days of this crisis when we braced ourselves for hospitals to be overfilled."⁵⁹

The U.S. Federal District Court in Virginia Upholds the State Prohibition Against Large Gatherings

The pastor of the Lighthouse Fellowship Church in Accomack County, Virginia, was charged with violating Virginia Governor Ralph Northam's prohibition on large gatherings after holding a Palm Sunday service on April 5.⁶⁰ The church argued in its lawsuit that it had maintained social distancing on Palm Sunday and only had 16 worshipers, in a space with a capacity of 225 people. It was further noted in the lawsuit that businesses were allowed to have more than ten people if proper precautions were taken.⁶¹

On May 4, the Justice Department filed a "statement of interest" supporting the church, arguing that Virginia "has offered no good reason for refusing to trust congregants who promise to use care in worship the same way it trusts accountants, lawyers and other workers to do the same."⁶²

Despite its support from the Department of Justice, the church lost its First Amendment-based challenge in Federal Court on Thursday, May 21, when the federal judge refused to enjoin the enforcement of the Governor's order stopping the religious services there.⁶³ "Although the existence of a pandemic might be considered extraordinary," U.S. District Judge Arenda L. Wright Allen, sitting in Norfolk, Virginia Allen, wrote in her opinion, "it does not call for federal intervention in state proceedings. If anything, the once-in-a-century nature of a pandemic strengthens the important state interests that counsel against federal intervention."⁶⁴

This was the second rejection of the suit filed by the Lighthouse Fellowship Church. Judge Wright previously denied the emergency request for a temporary restraining order against Governor Northam on May 5, and on May 21, she also rejected a request for an injunction pending appeal of her ruling.[65] Judge Wright further noted that the Governor was immune from such a suit unless he was involved in enforcing such orders.[66] She further found that no injunction of the enforcement of the ordinance was warranted since federal courts should generally refrain from interfering with pending state proceedings and that in this case, there was a criminal case against Pastor Wilson still pending.[67]

After the suit was filed and the Justice Department's statement was written, Governor Northam issued new orders on May 8 that allowed religious gatherings up to 50% of capacity with proper social distancing and cleaning.[68]

Trump Declares That Churches Provide "Essential Services"

Trump and his White House advisors saw the restrictions being placed on religious services as a much-needed opening for him to reinvigorate the support of white evangelicals, which was one of the critical elements of his political "base" that he needed to carry overwhelmingly if he had any shot at all of being reelected in November 2020. The president's strength with these religious supporters had slipped somewhat. Among white evangelical Protestants who favor Republicans, 77% said Mr. Trump was doing a good job dealing with the pandemic, down from 83% who thought so in March, according to a Pew Research Center poll.[69] Catholic voters who previously approved of his virus response were rating it negatively by May. Trump could not risk further slippage with the country's religious right, so he leaped into the middle of the controversy with a White House briefing on the subject.

On May 22, the day following the Virginia federal court decision in the *Lighthouse Fellowship Church* case, President Trump announced that all houses of worship would be considered "essential services" and urged governors to "do the right thing" and reopen them immediately—adding that he would "override" them if they didn't.[70] "Today, I am identifying houses of worship, churches, synagogues, and mosques, as essential places that provide essential services," Trump declared in a White House briefing.[71]

At the time that he made this statement, Trump must have known that he did not have any constitutional or other legal authority to "override" decisions by the states' governors on these issues, but this did not matter to him. The important thing was that it seemed to play well with his religious support base of Christian evangelicals, 80% of whom had voted for him in the 2016 presidential election.[72] "Religious conservatives are the most solid core of Trump's voter base, and he needs an especially strong turnout from that community in what appears to be an uphill run for re-election," said Mark J. Rozell, the dean of the Schar School of Policy and Government at George Mason University and a longtime scholar on religion and politics, adding, "These are Trump's voters, and he needs them to turn out big this year."[73]

As anticipated, Trump's announcement drew praise from evangelical supporters. "We feel vindicated in the fact that this is what we have said all along, that churches are essential to our communities," said Jim Franklin of Cornerstone Church in Fresno, California, one of the 1,200 California pastors who had vowed to resume services on May 31 even if limits have not been lifted. "We feel very secure in our position in opening the churches."[74] Mark Rienzi, the president of Becket, a religious liberty law firm representing several Minnesota churches, also praised the president's statement: "We hope that local officials across the country will heed the president's words and respect houses of worship, including our clients," he said, "Religion is an essential service for the well-being of society that cannot be subordinated to the economic interests of the states."[75]

Other religious leaders, however, took a more cautious approach. Bishop Kenneth H. Carter, the head of the Florida Conference of the United Methodist Church, said its 700 churches would look at reopening sometime after June 15. "God will reassemble us when we know it is safe. This requires our trust, assurance, maturity, civility," he said, "Our purpose is to love God and our neighbor. Our purpose is to do no harm, to do all the good we can."[76]

Trump's demand that churches be reopened appeared aimed at Democratic governors of states with whom he had been having political skirmishes, including Governor Gavin Newsom of California, Governor J.B. Pritzker of Illinois and Governor Gretchen Whitmer of Michigan. Governor Whitmer banned large gatherings but also said houses of worship would not be subject to penalties, leaving the final decision on whether to impose social restrictions in the hands of religious leaders.[77]

California Governor Newsom responded to Trump's comments by saying that he had been consulting with faith leaders and was drafting guidelines. "We look forward to churches reopening in a safe and responsible manner," he said.[78] The California guidelines distinguished between megachurches and smaller venues, deal with the configuration of pews and "sanitation protocols," the Governor said, "We deeply respect and admire the faith and devotion and the cause that unites millions and millions of Californians, people of faith."[79]

Illinois Governor Pritzker said he would "continue to operate based on science and data" when deciding when it was safe to reopen.[80] "I'm as anxious as anybody to make sure that our churches, our mosques, our synagogues open back to where they were before COVID-19 came along," he said, "We're gradually moving in that direction. But there's no doubt the most important thing is, we do not want parishioners to get ill because their faith leaders bring them together."[81]

David Postman, the chief of staff to Washington Governor Jay Inslee, said the state was working with an interfaith group to develop guidelines. "We don't believe the president has the ability to dictate what states can and cannot open," Mr. Postman said.[82]

Trump's threat to "override the governors" if they did not immediately lift the restrictions on religious services had no legal or constitutional basis, but those impediments never stopped him before, and he was not about to let them stop him now. "He could make a statement, and even call it an 'order,' but there is no legal compulsion for the state governors to comply," said Harold Hongju Koh, a Yale Law School professor and former Obama administration official.[83]

J. Michael Luttig, a former Republican administration official and circuit appeals court judge, agreed: "The president does not have the unilateral authority to override a governor's decision temporarily to prohibit the assembly of church congregants because of COVID-19," he said.[84]

The Supreme Court Steps in To Uphold California's Restrictions on Religious Services

On Friday, May 29, the Supreme Court decided for the first time the balance that should be struck between state restrictions during the current public health crisis and the U.S. Constitution's protection of religious freedom. In a 5 to 4 vote, with Chief Justice John C. Roberts, Jr. casting the decisive vote along with the Court's four liberal justices, the Court, in *South Bay United Pentecostal Church v. Newsom*, denied a California church's request to issue an injunction blocking enforcement of state restrictions on its religious services that were designed to reduce the spread of the coronavirus.[85]

In so ruling, the Supreme Court affirmed the decision handed down the day before by a divided three-judge panel of the United States Court of Appeals for the Ninth Circuit, sitting in San Francisco, which found that the shutdown orders did not single out houses of worship for unfavorable treatment.[86] The Ninth Circuit majority found that California state officials had struck an appropriate balance,[87] writing: "We're dealing here with a highly contagious and often fatal disease for which there presently is no known cure," the majority wrote. In so holding, the Ninth Circuit majority went on to quote a famous dissent from a 1947 Supreme Court decision,[88] stating: "In the words of Justice Robert Jackson, if a 'court does not temper its doctrinaire logic with a little practical wisdom, it will convert the constitutional Bill of Rights into a suicide pact.'"[89]

In his dissent in the Ninth Circuit decision in *Newsom*, Judge Daniel P. Collins wrote that California had failed "to honor its constitutional duty to accommodate a critical element of the free exercise of religion — public worship. I do not doubt the importance of the public health objectives that the state puts forth," Judge Collins wrote, "but the state can accomplish those objectives without resorting to its current inflexible and overbroad ban on religious services."[90]

The primary thrust of the church's argument in both the Ninth Circuit Court of Appeals and the Supreme Court in the *Newsom* case was that the state-imposed limits on how many people can attend their services violated constitutional guarantees of religious freedom. The church said it regularly had 200 to 300 people attend its services, and that the 100-person limit was unduly restrictive. Another church submitted a brief in the Supreme Court supporting an injunction against the state restrictions against houses of worship, noting: "A review of California's sector-specific guidelines shows that the only two industries with percentage caps are retail and houses of worship," the brief said, "and retail is set at a 50 percent cap. Offices, manufacturing, food packaging, museums, and every other sector has no percentage cap."[91]

In his concurring opinion in *Newsom*, Justice Roberts rejected these arguments, noting that similar or more severe limits applied to concerts, movies, and sporting events "where large groups of people gather in close proximity for extended periods of time."[92] He further noted that "the [California] order exempts or treats more leniently only dissimilar activities, such as operating grocery stores, banks, and laundromats, in which people neither congregate in large groups nor remain in close proximity for extended periods."[93]

The dissenting judges – Clarence Thomas, Samuel A. Alito Jr., Neil M. Gorsuch, and Brett M. Kavanaugh – disagreed with the majority's conclusion that the church and its congregants were being treated equally to comparable secular businesses. Justice Kavanaugh wrote in dissent that the restriction "discriminates against places of worship and in favor of comparable secular businesses. Such discrimination violates the First Amendment."[94] Kavanaugh pointed to supermarkets, restaurants, hair salons, cannabis dispensaries, and other businesses that were not subject to the same restrictions. In the dissent, Justice Kavanaugh further noted: "California already trusts its residents and any number of businesses to adhere to proper social distancing and hygiene practices," suggesting that churches should be trusted to act in a similarly responsible manner.[95] Justice Kavanaugh also quoted from an appeals court decision in another case, writing that a state cannot "'assume the worst when people go to worship but assume the best when people go to work or go about the rest of their daily lives in permitted social settings.'"⁹⁶

On the same day that the Supreme Court decided the *Newsom* case, the Court decided another case where a church was challenging an Illinois state regulation restricting its right to hold religious services.⁹⁷ This second case was brought by two Chicago-area churches, Elim Romanian Pentecostal Church and Logos Baptist Ministries. They challenged an order by Illinois Governor Pritzker, claiming that his ordinance restricting church services to ten people discriminated against houses of worship. These Chicago churches argued that "a unique 10-person limit on religious worship services [was discriminatory] since it was not imposed on customers or employees of 'big box' retail stores, liquor stores, restaurants, office buildings, warehouses, factories or other businesses and activities which, like worship services, have been deemed 'essential'" by the Governor.⁹⁸

The United States District Court for the Northern District of Illinois, located in Chicago, had refused to block the order restricting religious services to 10 congregants, deciding that the regulation was rational and sensible. "Gatherings at places of worship pose higher risks of infection than gatherings at businesses," wrote Judge Robert W. Gettleman of the U.S. District Court in Chicago, in *Elim Romanian Pentecostal Church v. Pritzker*.⁹⁹ "The congregants do not just stop by Elim Church. They assemble to sing, pray, and worship together. That takes more time than shopping for liquor or groceries."¹⁰⁰

A unanimous three-judge panel of the United States Court of Appeals for the Seventh Circuit, in Chicago, refused to stay Judge Gettleman's ruling while the churches pursued an appeal. In a preliminary decision of the case, the Seventh Circuit panel wrote that "the executive order does not discriminate against religious activities, nor does it show hostility toward religion."¹⁰¹ The panel further wrote: "It appears instead to impose neutral and generally applicable rules," adding, "The executive order's temporary numerical restrictions on public gatherings apply not only to worship services but also to the most comparable types of secular gatherings, such as concerts, lectures, theatrical performances or choir practices, in which groups of people gather together for extended periods, especially where speech and singing feature prominently and raise risks of transmitting the COVID-19 virus."¹⁰² "Worship services," the panel further wrote, "do not seem comparable to secular activities permitted under the executive order, such as shopping, in which people do not congregate or remain for extended periods."¹⁰³

The Supreme Court Narrowly Supports Nevada's Restrictions on Religious Services

On July 24, 2020, the Supreme Court, in a narrow 5-4 decision, denied an application for injunctive relief filed by the Calvary Chapel Dayton Valley against Steve Sisolak, the Governor of Nevada.¹⁰⁴ Chief Justice John Thomas once again refused to join with his four conservative colleagues on the Court - Justices Samuel Alito, Brett Kavanaugh, Neil Gorsuch and Clarence Thomas – in their quest to turn a public health issue into another religious crusade. The church in this rural area of Nevada went to the Supreme Court, claiming that their right to the free exercise of religion was being infringed by Nevada regulations that prevented it from having 90 people at one worship service instead of the permitted 50. The church never fully explained why they could not hold another church service the same day with another 40 or 50 attendees, or why they could not hold an outdoor church service under a tent with the desired 90 people. The state order had raised to 50 (from the original 10) the number of people who can gather indoors at most places, including movie theaters, lecture spaces, museums, trade schools and churches. Churches were also given the option to hold their services outdoors, with no limit on the number of people who can gather outside, as long as they observed proper social distancing. Restaurants and theme parks in Nevada were capped at 50 percent of capacity, as were the state's casinos.

Like many other cases around the country that were challenging COVID-19 related regulations restricting the size of religious and all other public gatherings, Calvary Chapel was represented by the Alliance Defending Freedom, which in the pre-covid era had focused primarily on representing people seeking a religious exemption from having to do business with couples in same-sex marriages.

Calvary Chapel had been holding its services online, but its application to the Court claimed that it could not continue to do so because of its belief that the Bible requires in-person worship. "If a body of believers fails to hold in-person gatherings, Calvary Chapel views it as ceasing to be a church in the biblical sense," according to the emergency appeal filed on its behalf by the Alliance Defending Freedom.

Despite the fact that the federal courts have generally acknowledged that they are ill-equipped to strike the delicate balance between public health requirements and religious freedoms, and that there is a well-documented correlation between religious services and the spread of the virus, the Calvary Chapel application was denied by only a razor-thin 5-4 majority.

The main dissenting opinion, written by Justice Alito and joined by Justices Thomas and Kavanaugh, portrayed the Nevada regulations as a frontal attack on religious freedoms. This 11-page blistering dissent attacked the regulations as an infringement on the Free Exercise clause because casinos were allowed to have more than 50 people congregate inside the casino as long as the number did not exceed 50 percent of capacity: "The Constitution guarantees the free exercise of religion," intoned Justice Alito. "It says nothing about the freedom to play craps or blackjack, to feed tokens into a slot machine, or to engage in any other game of chance." He added, "But the governor of Nevada apparently has different priorities." The state, he said, "blatantly discriminates against houses of worship."[105]

* * * * *

Thus, court decisions dealing with First Amendment's Freedom of Religion clause in the context of the COVID-19 public health crisis have made it clear that the states have the authority and the responsibility to regulate matters of public health and safety under the 10th Amendment to the U.S. Constitution, and state and municipal stay-at-home orders and other restrictions reasonably designed to prevent or reduce the spread of infection during a public health crisis apply equally to houses of worship as they do other businesses. However, the developing case law also makes it clear that such restrictions must be non-discriminatory and apply equally to other similarly situated enterprises, such as theaters and stadiums, where large groups of people may be expected to congregate in restricted spaces for prolonged time periods.

It is vitally important to note, however, that the Supreme Court's only decisions so far on the subject of the interplay between the First Amendment's religious freedom clause and the states' right to regulate public health and safety during a pandemic were made on a razor-thin 5-4 split between the nine Supreme Court justices. The outcome would have been entirely different if Chief Justice John Roberts, who was appointed by Republican President George W. Bush, had not taken the bold step of joining the four liberal justices of the Court to uphold the California and Illinois executive orders restricting in-person religious services in those two states as reasonable emergency public health measures during a pandemic.

So, the coronavirus crisis triggered a series of significant legal and constitutional disputes, starting with First Amendment issues relating to freedom of religion and freedom of assembly arising from stay-at-home orders and restrictions on public gatherings. However, as time went on, and especially following the brutal police killing of George Floyd in Minneapolis, a tidal wave of other constitutional and legal issues arose, including the rights of citizens to peacefully assemble and petition for redress of injustices without getting teargassed and beaten in the process, and issues of police brutality, racial targeting, and systemic racism.

It soon became clear that the post COVID-19 world would never be the same again. Fundamental and longstanding flaws in the American system had been even more clearly exposed during the public health and economic crisis. Some major changes need to take place before we could ever honestly refer to it again as a true democracy that guarantees, as engraved on the Supreme Court building, "Equal Justice Under Law."

30

THE BACKLASH AGAINST CHINA AND THE WORLD HEALTH ORGANIZATION LEADS TO A NEW COLD WAR

For weeks during March and early April, President Trump faced relentless criticism for having overseen a slow and ineffective response to the coronavirus pandemic, failing to quickly implement public health measures that could have prevented the disease from spreading.[1] Polls began to appear showing that more Americans disapproved of Mr. Trump's handling of the virus crisis than approved of it. Trump and his senior advisors in the White House, anxiously fretting over the barrage of negative press reports, desperately searched for some way to change the "narrative."

"Whenever things are going bad, and you are in trouble, blame someone else." That was the invisible sign posted on Trump's desk in the Oval Office, just as Harry S. Truman had famously placed a sign there saying, "The buck stops here." In sharp contrast to the Truman approach to the presidency, which was to accept ultimate responsibility for actions taken by his administration, Trump consistently tried to duck responsibility for those acting under his command. When asked directly in mid-March whether he would accept blame for the lack of testing capacity in the country, Trump responded, "I don't take responsibility at all."[2]

It was not surprising, therefore, that on Tuesday, April 14, Trump shifted the entire blame for the chaos that had engulfed the U.S. response effort onto China and the World Health Organization.[3] Trump announced that he was ordering his administration to halt funding for the W.H.O., claiming the organization had made a series of devastating mistakes as it sought to battle the virus, and should be therefore punished for it. He said his administration would conduct a review into whether the W.H.O. was responsible for "severely mismanaging and covering up" the spread of the virus. "So much death has been caused by their mistakes," the president told reporters during a White House briefing.[4]

In effect, Trump was accusing the world's leading health organization of making all of the same mistakes that he had made since the virus first emerged in China. The attack on the W.H.O., which was founded after World War II as part of the United Nations "to promote and protect the health of all peoples," was the latest example of the president's attempt to shift the blame throughout the crisis. Previously, Mr. Trump has accused the news media, governors, Democratic members of Congress, and even former President Barack Obama of being responsible for the pandemic reaching the U.S. But these accusations were so preposterous that even the Trump faithful were having trouble accepting them uncritically.

Trump's attack on the W.H.O. for having been duped by China in the early days of the pandemic at least had a thin veneer of truth to it. The core of Trump's claim against the W.H.O. was that the organization had been too quick to believe information about the virus coming from the Chinese government at a time when it should have been more critical. "Had the W.H.O. done its job to get medical experts into China to assess the situation on the ground objectively and to call out China's lack of transparency, the outbreak could have been contained at its source with very little death," Trump said.[5] He added that the W.H.O. "willingly took China's assurances at face value" and "pushed China's misinformation."[6]

But if the W.H.O. was guilty of being too gullible when it came to China, then Trump was doubly to blame for the same naivety, since he himself had gone out of his way to publicly and repeatedly praise the Chinese government for its handling of the virus at the beginning of the year when his administration was negotiating a trade deal with China. Even if the W.H.O. could have more swiftly sounded the alarm that a global pandemic was developing, this fact would not have exculpated Trump's inaction even after the W.H.O. started issuing statements and taking actions to stop the spread of the virus. Thousands of Americans would be alive today if President Trump spent more time listening to the W.H.O., instead of trying to destroy it.[7]

On January 24, for example, Trump issued a statement on Twitter, praising China's efforts to combat COVID-19: "China has been working very hard to contain the Coronavirus. The United States greatly appreciates their efforts and transparency. It will all work out well. In particular, on behalf of the American People, I want to thank President Xi!"[8] Again, on January 30, in a *Fox News* interview, Trump complimented China for "working very hard" on its coronavirus containment efforts, adding, "We'll see what happens. But we're working very closely with China and other countries."[9]

Trump's effusive praise for China continued throughout February. On February 7, for example, Trump announced on Twitter, "Just had a long and very good conversation by phone with President Xi of China. He is strong, sharp, and powerfully focused on leading the counterattack on the Coronavirus. He feels they are doing very well, even building hospitals in a matter of only days . . . Great discipline is taking place in China, as President Xi strongly leads what will be a very successful operation. We are working closely with China to help!"[10]

On the same day (February 7), Trump further noted that the CDC and the W.H.O. were working in close coordination with China on a coronavirus response, adding that China was "doing a very good job."[11] Three days later, on February 10, in a *Fox Business* interview, Trump again predicted that China was "going to have it under control fairly soon," and that there was little to worry about since the coronavirus "dies with the hotter weather."[12] For the remainder of the month, Trump basically reiterated the same theme, showering China and President Xi with compliments on their coronavirus response efforts every chance he got. On February 26, during a trip to New Delhi, India, he underscored the point that China was "getting it under control more and more." On February 27, at a Coronavirus Task Force press conference, Trump reassured the American public that "the spread has gone down quite a bit" and had "actually gotten smaller."

Two days later, on February 29, at another Coronavirus Task Force press conference, Trump characterized China's relationship with the U.S. over the coronavirus pandemic as highly cooperative. "They've been talking to our people, we've been talking to their people, having to do with the virus," he said.[13]

For decades, China had been trying to buy its way into world respectability and world-class power status. Until the coronavirus hit the country like a bombshell in or around December 2019, China was mainly succeeding in that objective. With the onset of the pandemic, China's "transparency" and truthfulness as to what it knew about the virus and when it knew it started being called into question. This is why Trump's complimentary statements about China were so welcomed by the Chinese leadership.

With Trump's backing, the Chinese government's propaganda machine was able to fend off criticism of Beijing's handling of the coronavirus outbreak for months.[14] The U.S.'s benevolent view of China was joined by a host of other voices, including the W.H.O., the Serbian government, and the rapper Cardi B, who praised China for being responsive to the crisis.

But as word of China's cover-up of its intentional dissemination of misinformation started to leak out, countries and leaders around the globe began to reconsider their early praise for China. It soon became clear China deliberately failed to inform the world as to the real existential dangers posed by the coronavirus outbreak in Wuhan. This lulled the world into a false sense of complacency and security for the critical months of January, February and March 2020.

Even previously friendly foreign leaders and governments, such as Iran, began to question whether China had lied about its number of reported coronavirus cases and deaths. A top European diplomat warned that China's aid to the continent was a mask for its geopolitical ambitions, while a Brazilian official suggested the pandemic was part of China's plan to "dominate the world."[15]

China's critics, including the Trump administration, blamed the Communist Party's authoritarian leadership for exacerbating the outbreak by initially trying to conceal it. But China fought back with its increasingly sophisticated global propaganda machine, casting itself as the munificent, responsible leader that triumphed where others had stumbled. The stakes were high as to which narrative would prevail. In addition to the importance of who won the "blame game," the implications were significant for the ongoing struggle for global leadership, which is still in considerable flux.

As the U.S. pulls back from its international commitments and traditional global leadership role, China is more than willing to fill the void. Whether it can do so depends, in significant part, on how its reputation emerges from the current coronavirus crisis. If its reputation is ultimately tarnished and the world's verdict is that it had primary responsibility for the severity and duration of the pandemic, then China's global ambitions will suffer a setback. However, if China is able to take control of the narrative, or if it is the first country to come up with a vaccine, then it will be able to exercise significant leverage over which countries get priority status in the distribution of the vaccine, and the current criticism of China is likely to dissipate quickly.

Even if the W.H.O. Was Too Cozy with China, U.S. "Defunding" of it was Reckless and Irresponsible

Trump's announcement that he would halt American funding for the W.H.O. just as the world was facing a raging pandemic was a dangerous attempt to find a scapegoat for his own failings. It was like taking away a fire department's trucks in the middle of a blaze and then blaming them for not putting out the fire.

The U.S. preparedness plan, which had been passed on by the Obama administration to the Trump team (and then filed away and ignored), emphasized the critically important role that the W.H.O. played in organizing and coordinating a global response to a pandemic. With an annual worldwide budget that was less than that of some American hospital centers, the W.H.O. had generally done an admirable job in fighting Ebola, Polio and a host of other diseases and has been credited with saving countless children's lives and keeping the world safe from pandemics. It has promoted safe childbirth, and thanks to the efforts led by the W.H.O., the number of women dying in childbirth has been cut almost in half over the last 25 years.[16]

The W.H.O. may bear some responsibility for the fact that the coronavirus pandemic was not nipped in the bud like previous threats, but given the abysmal record of the Trump administration, the W.H.O. was only one of several parties, including China and the U.S. itself, who must take ultimate responsibility for this worldwide crisis.

A close look at the chronology indicates that the W.H.O. actually gave the U.S., Europe, and the rest of the West enough advance notice of the coming pandemic to implement precautionary measures. The W.H.O.

tweeted its first warning about the coronavirus as early as January 4 and then rang alarm bells, culminating at the end of that month when it declared a "public health emergency of international concern."[17] It then quickly developed an effective diagnostic test for the coronavirus that is used in dozens of countries worldwide, while the CDC and the rest of the U.S. government totally fumbled the ball by failing to develop a reliable test and to implement a robust testing plan.

If Trump had not played jingoistic politics and had adopted the W.H.O. test when it was offered, thousands of American lives would have been saved. Instead, the Trump administration made the grievously arrogant decision to reject the W.H.O. test for use in the U.S. while the CDC was simultaneously working to develop its own test. This decision would have taken the extreme pressure off the CDC to develop a test, knowing that there were already people dying in New York and other epicenters for lack of a reliable test. Instead, the CDC made some critical unforced errors in the development of its own test, which probably would not have been made if it had not felt that it was under pressure to shortcut normal protocols and rush the development process.

In view of the fact that the Trump administration made zero effort to provide global leadership against the coronavirus pandemic, Trump's efforts to crush the one organization that tried – albeit imperfectly – to fill that critical leadership role was reckless and irresponsible. Pressed on why he was taking steps to defund the W.H.O. in the middle of the global fight against this pandemic, Trump's only response was to insist that the W.H.O. was very "China-centric." Even if it were true that W.H.O. had a bias in favor of China, it was unclear as to what the W.H.O. could have done differently to slow the spread of the virus.

The W.H.O. Responds to Trump's Attacks

The W.H.O. responded to Trump's attacks as best it could, using the language of diplomacy rather than of confrontation. In a statement issued on the evening of April 14, António Guterres, the secretary-general of the United Nations, defended the W.H.O., saying it "must be supported, as it is absolutely critical to the world's efforts to win the war against COVID-19."[18]

Guterres said that "it is possible that the same facts have had different readings by different entities," but insisted that the middle of a pandemic was not the time to resolve those differences. "It is also not the time to reduce the resources for the operations of the World Health Organization or any other humanitarian organization in the fight against the virus," he said.[19]

Trump Announces That the U.S. Is "Terminating" Its Relationship with the W.H.O.

The U.S. followed up its April 14 "defunding" of the W.H.O. with further steps signaling the U.S.'s further withdrawal from international or multi-national cooperation in the battle against the coronavirus pandemic and the economic devastation it was causing. On Friday, May 29, Trump announced that the U.S. was "terminating" its relationship with the W.H.O. for its failure to enact reforms in the face of concerns over its handling of the coronavirus pandemic and its pro-China bias.[20] "Because they have failed to make the requested and greatly needed reforms, we will be today terminating our relationship with the World Health Organization and redirecting those funds to other worldwide and deserving urgent global public health needs," Trump said at a Rose Garden event.[21]

Although Trump's remarks were directed at the W.H.O., this international organization was being increasingly viewed by senior Trump administration officials as a proxy for China, which was assuming an increasingly greater role in the financing and administration of W.H.O. China's greatest fear was that world opinion would coalesce against it and that it would once again become increasingly isolated. "I think that the Chinese remain very fearful about what will happen when we finally all get on top of this virus, and there is going to be an investigation of how it started," said Bonnie Glaser, the director of the China Power Project at the Center for Strategic and International Studies in Washington, "They're just trying to repair the damage that was done very early on to China's reputation."[22]

Evidence Emerges that China Misled the W.H.O., the U.S. and the Rest of the World Community As to the Extent of the Outbreak There

In addition to its delay in reporting the start of the coronavirus outbreak in Wuhan, China consistently understated the number of cases and deaths in that country. Starting in late March, China consistently reported zero or single-digit new local infections, and on Wednesday, April 8, it lifted its lockdown in Wuhan, where the outbreak began. As of that date, China reported only 84,000 cases and about 3,300 deaths, which was a suspiciously low number considering that is where the pandemic started. It was also suspiciously low, considering that the U.S., Spain, and Italy were reporting larger numbers by then, with the U.S. reporting 399,000 cases, and Spain and Italy each with more than 135,000 cases.[23]

If true, China's reported numbers would support its argument that its response was quick and responsible, and that its tactics should have been the model for the rest of the world. In contrast, Chinese officials have, with a good factual basis, compared China's own response with that of the U.S., which was late in coming, confused, and marred by shortages of testing kits and ventilators. While China argued that it set an example and bought precious time for the world, Hua Chunying, a spokeswoman for China's foreign ministry criticized the U.S. for not using this valuable time "to enhance preparedness."[24]

While the more likely outcome of any post-crisis investigation will be to confirm China's critique of U.S. preparedness, it is also probable that is will confirm the almost universal skepticism of experts and U.S. officials of the accuracy of China's data regarding its case numbers and deaths. For example, *Caixin*, a respected Chinese newsmagazine, reported that a truck driver brought thousands of urns to just one funeral home in Wuhan, though it was unclear if the urns were only being used for coronavirus victims.[25] China also refused for weeks to follow W.H.O. guidance, which recommended that countries include asymptomatic patients in their official counts. China only started doing so on April 1, after considerable public outcry.

The U.S. Knew That China Was Under-Reporting the Numbers

The C.I.A. was well aware that China was under-reporting its numbers since at least early February. In addition, a four-page Department of Homeland Security report dated May 1, which was obtained by the *Associated Press*, concluded that Chinese leaders "intentionally concealed the severity" of the pandemic from the world in early January.[26] The analysis further found that one reason why China had downplayed the outbreak in Wuhan and elsewhere was that China was increasing its imports of medical supplies while, at the same time, decreasing its exports of those critical supplies.[27] China then strategically attempted to cover up their stockpiles of medical supplies without alerting the international community;[28] it "denied there were export restrictions and obfuscating and delaying the provision of its trade data," according to this Homeland Security analysis.[29]

These revelations came as the Trump administration intensified its criticism of China, with Secretary of State Mike Pompeo accusing China of being responsible for the spread of disease and demanding that it had to be held accountable. Appearing on ABC's *This Week*, Pompeo said he had no reason to believe that the virus was spread deliberately by China, but added, "Remember, China has a history of infecting the world, and they have a history of running substandard laboratories."[30]

Other countries quickly adopted the newly critical U.S. point of view regarding China's role for causing the pandemic and failing to respond to it early enough. Of course, these countries well knew that the U.S. rising rhetoric against China coincided with mathematic precision to the mounting criticism of the Trump administration's response to the looming crisis. But still, they found some valid factual basis to criticize China. Even Iran's health ministry finally joined the chorus, calling China's reported numbers "a bitter joke."[31] Chinese officials quickly shot back, calling the accusations "immoral slanders." They suggested that the U.S. was casting doubt on China to distract from the fact that American officials had ignored early warnings from experts. "We sympathize with Americans, as they are facing a severe situation, and I can imagine why some in the United States are trying so hard to shift the blame," Ms. Hua said.[32]

While China's propaganda must be discounted, it cannot be completely dismissed, since it has a large kernel of truth in it. As explained by Yanzhong Huang, who leads the global health center at Seton Hall University in New Jersey, "The complacency, the lack of action, the efforts to downplay the serious of the problem by our own governments ... actually help China to make a strong case that they are not the cause of the problem," he said.[33]

It also must be conceded that the Chinese government's strict, top-down response helped stop the outbreak more successfully than in many other countries. Public health experts in other countries initially criticized China's draconian Wuhan lockdown when it was first imposed as doomed to fail. But such measures – while harsh – proved to be effective, especially in view of the fact that other means, such as widespread testing, a cure, or a vaccine, were unavailable. Stay-at-home orders, lockdowns, and quarantines have universally proven to be the best stopgap measures while the world waits for an effective treatment and a vaccine.

Ultimately, China's characterization of its reporting as to the nature and extent of the outbreak does not bear close scrutiny, at least for the early days and weeks of the reported outbreak in Wuhan. In January, Chinese government spokespersons were still comparing the outbreak to the flu and accusing the U.S. of "fear-mongering" when it began evacuating citizens from Wuhan. When Italy suspended flights to and from China, a senior Chinese official summoned the Italian ambassador to criticize the "overreaction." In early February, China prematurely declared that it had "effectively contained the cross-border spread" of the virus.[34]

In late March, China did make a belated effort to seal its own borders, barring practically all foreigners and stranding many Chinese citizens overseas, with no other means to return home. China also embarked on an ambitious public relations campaign to win over the hearts and minds of world public opinion. China announced that it had supplied medical equipment to 120 countries, but officials in Italy and other countries noted that many of these so-called gifts were actually exports.[35] Some countries also complained that many of the test kits and masks that they received from China were defective. The European Union's top diplomat, Josep

Borrell, warned in a blog post that China was seeking to use the "politics of generosity" to undermine European solidarity.[36]

China invested millions, if not billions, of dollars in building up its global propaganda machine in an attempt to blunt the growing criticism. When Cardi B praised China's containment measures, she cited a documentary about the lockdown in Wuhan which had been produced by the state-run China Global Television Network, with English narration and subtitles.[37] This propaganda campaign was also filled with reminders that China was the world's largest manufacturer of desperately needed medical gear, and few countries wanted to directly bite the hand that was gifting or selling them this equipment for fear that China could cut off the spigot.

Some of the early critics even had to walk back their criticism. For example, after the Chinese ambassador to Iran objected to Iranian criticism, the Iranian official who called China's numbers "a joke" tweeted that China's support of Iran would "never be forgotten."[38] Similarly, the Brazilian official who accused China of maneuvering for "world domination" later deleted his Twitter post after a similar backlash. The fact that China is the biggest trading partner for both Iran and Brazil undoubtedly played a role in these reversals.

31

THE RACE FOR A VACCINE AND A CURE

Vaccines already developed to combat various diseases have saved millions of lives. The CDC estimates that vaccinations prevented more than 20 million hospitalizations and 732,000 deaths among children over the past two decades.[1]

Right now, the world record holder for the quickest development and delivery of a vaccine from "scratch," i.e., from the research laboratory to the clinic, is Dr. Maurice Hilleman. His development of the Avian Flu vaccine in less than one year in 1957 (discussed in Chapter 5) is the stuff of legend. He also holds the record for the second-fastest vaccine ever developed, which was the mumps vaccine.

The development of the mumps vaccine started at around 1 a.m. on March 21, 1963, when Dr. Hilleman's 5-year-old girl, Jeryl Lynn Hilleman, woke up her father. She had come down with the mumps, and her swollen jaw was making her feel miserable. Fortunately, her father just happened to be the pre-eminent vaccine developer in the U.S. So, he told Jeryl Lynn to go back to bed, drove to his lab at Merck to pick up some equipment, and returned to swab her throat. Dr. Hilleman refrigerated her sample back at his lab and soon got to work weakening her virus samples until they could serve as a mumps vaccine. In 1967, it was approved by the F.D.A.

Vaccines typically take ten to fifteen years of research and testing. And only six percent of the vaccine projects that scientists start end up with a safe and effective vaccine. So, Dr. Hillman's development of a mumps vaccine in a few years was considered to be extraordinary.

For a world in the grips of COVID-19, the story of Dr. Hillman's record-breaking development of vaccines is not particularly reassuring. The U.S. and the rest of the world do not want to consider the possibility that the development of a vaccine for COVID-19 may take years, or, even more horrifying, may never be developed. Even a four-year wait for a vaccine, while millions die and economies remain crippled, is not an acceptable option or potential reality that anyone wants to talk about.

Some of the leading contenders for a coronavirus vaccine are now promising to have the first batches ready in record time, by the end of 2020 or the start of the following year. They have accelerated their schedules by collapsing the standard vaccine timeline. They are combining trials that used to be carried out in sequential order. They are pushing their formulations into production, despite the risk that the trials will fail, leaving them with millions of useless doses.

Some experts want to speed up the vaccine development process even further by using techniques that push the envelope of ethical science to its limits, and perhaps beyond. In March 2020, the inventor of the current rubella vaccine and a leader on the vaccine field, Stanley A. Plotkin, proposed that a carefully designed "human challenge" trial could offer clear proof of a vaccine's worth at blinding speed.[2] "We're talking 2, 3 months," says Plotkin, adding, "People who are faced with a terrifying problem like this one will opt for measures that are unusual. And we have to constantly rethink our biases."[3]

Another team of researchers published an article in March in The *Journal of Infectious Diseases*, stating, "Such an approach is not without risks, but every week that vaccine rollout is delayed will be accompanied by many thousands of deaths globally."[4]

Challenge trials were used in the early days of vaccine research, but now are carried out only under the strictest of conditions and only for illnesses, like flu and malaria, that have already established treatments. Since COVID-19 is new, the use of challenge trials would be outside established norms. In Congress, Representative Bill Foster, Democrat of Illinois and a physicist, and Representative Donna E. Shalala, Democrat of Florida and the former secretary of the Department of Health and Human Services, organized a bipartisan group of 35 lawmakers to sign a letter asking regulators to approve such trials.[5] The organizers of a website set up to promote the idea, *www.1daysooner.org*, say they have signed up more than 9,100 potential volunteers from 52 countries.[6]

Even without challenge trials, accelerated testing may run the risk of missing potential side effects. A vaccine for Dengue Fever, and one for SARS that never reached the market, were abandoned after they made some people more susceptible to severe forms of the diseases, not less.

"It will be extremely important to determine that does not happen," said Michel De Wilde, a former senior vice president of research and development at Sanofi Pasteur, the French vaccine maker.[7]

While there was no vaccine available that could be used effectively to combat COVID-19 as of June 2020, there were more than 130 teams of researchers around the world working at breakneck speed on vaccine candidates, with 22 of the vaccines already having reached various stages of human trials.[8] There were several radically different approaches being taken, so it is unlikely that any potential stone would be left unturned in the search for a vaccine.[9]

In some cases, researchers started from scratch, while in other cases, past research on SARS and MERS vaccines has identified potential approaches. COVID-19 is in the SARS family of viruses, so some of the prior research appears to be promising in the efforts to try to jump-start the development process.[10] Under most aggressive but realistic scenarios, it appeared that the earliest date for a vaccine to be developed would be sometime in the spring of 2021. However, as discussed below, one crash program funded by the U.S. government was hoping to get a vaccine out as early as October 2020.[11]

The Traditional Vaccine Approach

Most vaccines in use today incorporate an inactivated or weakened form of a virus that is not able to cause disease. Simply stated, these traditional vaccines expose the body to a virus or other pathogen in order to allow the body to build up immunity in a controlled way. In theory, the body's immune system reaction stops this foreign virus or microbe in its tracks at the site of injection. The key to vaccine success is that, after inoculation with the vaccine, the immune system starts to create fast-response antigens that will circulate throughout the body and be able to recognize and fend off the same pathogen in the future.[12] These antigens themselves may be grown in a lab setting, isolated, mixed with preservatives or stabilizers, and then used to trigger the immune system.

Current conventional vaccines include those for influenza, chickenpox, measles, mumps, and rubella. However, in order to make these vaccines, viruses must first be grown in large quantities. They are typically grown in chicken eggs, and other vaccines are developed in tanks full of floating cells. These procedures can take months to produce a batch of new vaccines. Sinovac and other companies, for example, are working on developing a conventional kind of COVID-19 vaccine.[13]

Genetically Engineered Vaccines

Genetically engineered vaccines do not deliver the virus or other pathogen itself into the host cells. Instead, they deliver some or all of the genetic code of the virus. This type of vaccine uses genetically engineered RNA or DNA that has instructions for making copies of the coronavirus's S protein.[14] As previously discussed,[15] coronaviruses have a spike-like structure on their surface called an S protein. The spikes create the corona-like or crown-like structure, an appearance that gives the viruses their name. The S protein attaches to the surface of human cells. A vaccine that targets this protein would prevent it from binding to human cells and stop the virus from reproducing.[16] These genetically engineered vaccines prompt an immune response to the virus without actually infecting the host person. No genetically engineered vaccines have been fully developed or licensed yet for any human use, including to combat COVID-19, although several are in the works. These genetically engineered vaccines generally fall into two categories: DNA Vaccines and RNA Vaccines.

DNA Vaccines

These genetic vaccines deliver a circle of engineered DNA into cells. The cells read the viral gene, make a copy in a molecule called messenger RNA, and then use the mRNA to assemble viral proteins. The immune system detects the proteins and mounts defenses. Prototype DNA vaccines target the so-called spike proteins that cover the virus and help it invade human cells.[17] The immune system can develop antibodies that latch onto spike proteins and stop the virus. A successful DNA genetic vaccine for the COVID-19 would teach people's immune systems to make antibodies against the virus without actually causing the disease. The protein can then stimulate the immune system to produce antibodies and help mount other defenses against the coronavirus.

DNA vaccines have been approved for veterinary cases such as canine melanoma and the West Nile virus in horses. There are no approved DNA vaccines for use in humans, but researchers are running trials to see if they might be effective for diseases such as Zika and the flu. Now they are also researching the use of DNA vaccines for COVID-19. Companies researching the use of DNA vaccines include Inovio.[18]

RNA Vaccines

Some genetic vaccine researchers are trying to skip the DNA stage and instead deliver messenger RNA directly into cells. The cells read the mRNA and make spike proteins that trigger an immune response. The biotech company Moderna has already completed a small safety trial with eight volunteers that showed promising early results against the coronavirus.[19]

There are no approved RNA vaccines, but they are in clinical trials for MERS and other diseases. Companies such as Moderna, Pfizer, BioNTech, and CureVac are working on RNA vaccines.[20]

Viral Vector Vaccines

In the 1990s, researchers began working on vaccines that enlisted human cells to help train the immune system to make antibodies. The foundation of these vaccines was typically a virus called an adenovirus. The adenovirus can infect a person's cells but is altered so that it does not cause any illness. Scientists can add a gene to the adenovirus from the virus they want to fight, creating what's known as a viral vector. Several virus vector vaccines are used to vaccinate animals against rabies and distemper. Johnson & Johnson has developed HIV and Ebola vaccines using an adenovirus.[21] Both have proven safe in humans and were in efficacy trials by June of 2020.

Researchers at the University of Oxford and the Chinese company CanSino Biologics created a viral vector vaccine for COVID-19, and by

June of 2020, they had started safety trials on volunteers.[22] Others, including Johnson & Johnson, were also planning to launch trials of their own. Researchers at Johnson & Johnson were trying to make a five-dose vial to save the precious glass, which might work if a smaller dose is enough for vaccination.

Protein-Based and Virus-Like Particle Vaccines

Protein-based vaccines would use a coronavirus protein or a protein fragment. Similarly, virus-like particle vaccines use particles that contain pieces of viral proteins. They cannot cause disease themselves because they are not actual viruses, but they can still show the immune system what coronavirus proteins look like. The vaccine for Human Papillomavirus infection (HPV) falls into this category. Companies such as Medicago and Doherty Institute have been working on this type of vaccine for coronavirus.[23]

Recombinant Vaccines

Yeast or other cells can be engineered to carry a virus's gene and spew out viral proteins, which are then harvested and put into a vaccine. This category includes some vaccines for shingles and hepatitis B. A coronavirus vaccine of this design would contain whole spike proteins or small pieces of the protein. Novavax is one of the companies working on this type of vaccine for the coronavirus.[24]

Problems That Must Be Overcome to Develop a Vaccine

Past research on vaccines for coronaviruses identified some significant problems (or "challenges" as researchers prefer to call them) in developing a COVID-19 vaccine based on prior research on SARS and MERS. There has not yet been developed a proven treatment or vaccine against SARS, MERS, or any of the SARS or coronavirus families of viruses. Infectious disease experts warn that many vaccine candidates take years to perfect. In addition to the time factor, some vaccine candidates fail despite the effort to develop them, or cause such severe side effects that human trials are halted.

China's history with the development of vaccines is a cautionary tale regarding the dangers of trying to shortcut the established steps for developing a safe and effective vaccine. The Wuhan Institute of Biological Products was involved in a 2018 scandal in which ineffective vaccines for diphtheria, tetanus, whooping cough, and other illnesses were injected into hundreds of thousands of babies.[25] The Chinese government confiscated the Wuhan Institute's "illegal income," fined the company, and punished nine executives. However, the company was allowed to continue to operate, and it is now running a coronavirus vaccine project along with two other Chinese groups that have been allowed to combine their safety and efficacy trials. Several Chinese scientists questioned the decision, arguing that the vaccine should be shown to be safe before testing how well it works.

In China, there are now a total of nine Chinese COVID-19 vaccines in development, involving 1,000 scientists and the Chinese military.[26] China's CDC predicted that one of the vaccines could be in "emergency use" by September 2020, meaning that in the midst of the presidential election in the U.S., Trump might see television footage of Chinese citizens lining up for injections. "It's a scenario we have thought about," one member of Trump's coronavirus task force was quoted as saying, "No one wants to be around that day."[27]

In addition to safety factors, the lack of effectiveness of the vaccine can be a significant obstacle to a vaccine development project. Of the vaccines for SARS that have been tested on animals, several of them have improved the animals' survival but did not prevent the virus infection itself. Thus, some of the experimental vaccines did not provide immunity or only offered limited immunity. After infection with coronaviruses, re-infection with the same virus — though usually mild and only happening in a fraction of people — is possible after a period of months or years. An effective COVID-19 vaccine will need to provide people with long-term infection protection.[28]

When a person encounters a pathogen, such as the novel coronavirus, there is no way to predict whether it will induce a mild or severe form of disease or how the body will react.[29] Traditional vaccines are selected to contain either a weakened (active) or dead (inactive) form of the disease-causing germ that can spark an immune response. Live vaccines that use a weakened (also referred to as "attenuated") form of the virus or other pathogen that causes a disease prompt an immune response without themselves causing the disease. Live vaccines are now being used to protect against measles, mumps, rubella, smallpox, and chickenpox. As a result, the scientific and manufacturing infrastructure is already in place to develop these kinds of vaccines.

However, live virus vaccines generally require extensive efficacy (effectiveness) and safety testing. Since there is always a slight chance that live viruses are inadvertently transmitted to a person who is not immunized, unintentionally causing disease, this is always a concern, especially for people who already have compromised or weakened immune systems.

Inactivated vaccines use a dead (inactive) version of the pathogen (e.g., the coronavirus) that causes a disease. This kind of vaccine induces an immune response but not an infection. Inactivated vaccines are now being used to prevent the flu, hepatitis A and rabies. However, inactivated vaccines may not provide protection that is as strong as that produced by live vaccines. In addition, this type of vaccine often requires multiple doses, followed by booster doses, to provide long-term immunity. Producing these types of vaccines might require the handling of large amounts of the infectious virus.

Vaccines may also affect people differently, depending on their age. People over age 50 are at higher risk of having a more severe case of COVID-19. Older people usually do not respond to vaccines as well as younger people, since a person's immune system generally weakens over time.[30] An ideal COVID-19 vaccine would work well for every age group, but particularly this age group and people of all ages who are already immune-compromised.

Logistical Delays

Logistical and delay issues are a significant problem for most vaccine development programs. Once a vaccine is approved, it will take time to manufacture, produce, distribute, and administer to the global population. The problem is that each vaccine type has its own manufacturing process, to very exacting standards, so companies are reluctant to invest millions of dollars before they know whether there will be a return on their investment. One way to "fast track" this manufacturing process, which has been championed by philanthropist Bill Gates, would be to select several promising vaccine candidates in the development pipeline and construct factories in advance.[31] That could be costly because some will not be needed, but the advantage is that a factory would be ready sooner for a successful vaccine candidate. The "waste" of money on building factories that would never be used would be worth it, given the enormity of the dire emergency that this country and the rest of the world is facing.

Another "fast track" approach proposed by Gavi, the global vaccine alliance, would be to have governments provide an "advanced market commitment," in which the governments promised in advance to buy large quantities of vaccine.[32] This would give an incentive to pharmaceutical companies to invest in the needed equipment. Gavi has proposed an initial $2 billion pledge to purchase enough vaccine to protect 20 million healthcare workers.[33]

Another obstacle to a comprehensive vaccine program for the entire U.S. and world community is that, because the human species has no prior history of immunity to the COVID-19 virus or any other SARS-type virus, it is likely that each person would require two vaccinations, three to four weeks apart. People would likely start to achieve immunity to the COVID-19 virus one to two weeks after the second vaccination. Given the fact that there are about 7.5 billion people on the planet, the logistical hurdles obviously will be formidable. Who gets the vaccine first? Should all of the people in the country that first develops the vaccine be declared the "winners" and get the first shot at vaccination before people in other countries? Or should there be some international agreement whereby, for example, the health care workers and other essential workers around the globe get immunized first? What if a large percentage of the population proves to be "anti-vaxxers" and refuse to be vaccinated? These are just some of the issues that must be addressed well before the development of a safe and effective vaccine.

What are the Steps in the Development of a Vaccine?

Once a vaccine candidate is developed in the lab, it is first tested in animals to see if it works and is safe. This testing must follow strict lab guidelines and generally takes three to six months. The manufacturing of vaccines also must follow quality and safety practices.

Next comes testing in humans. A small phase I clinical trial evaluates the safety of the vaccine in humans. During phase II, the formulation and doses of the vaccine are established to prove the vaccine's effectiveness. Finally, during phase III, the safety and efficacy of a vaccine need to be demonstrated in a larger group of people.

Because of the seriousness of the COVID-19 pandemic, some of these normal steps are being fast-tracked, hopefully without compromising safety. But even at "warp speed," as the Trump administration refers to the development of a vaccine, it is unlikely that a COVID-19 vaccine will become available sooner than six months after clinical trials start. The average time for the development and testing through human clinical trials is 12 to 18 months. This all assumes that an effective vaccine for this virus is, in fact, possible.

The U.S. Vaccine Effort Makes Progress

Some of the early research and development of a vaccine for the novel coronavirus (COVID-19) showed promising results in animal and human trials during the spring of 2020. By early June, three separate coronavirus vaccine Phase 3 trials were scheduled to be run in the U.S. during the summer of 2020, under government supervision.[34] The potential vaccines all needed to clear the final stages of clinical trials and prove they could prevent COVID-19 infections before being approved for general use.

Dr. Anthony Fauci confirmed that, as of June 2020, three of these would be used in extensive Phase 3 trials funded by the U.S. government.[35] "The coronavirus vaccine effort is progressing very well, and we expect more than one candidate vaccine to be in advanced clinical testing by early summer," Fauci told CNN. "This is good news for the overall coronavirus vaccine effort," he said.[36]

Oxford University and AstraZeneca Jump Out to An Early Lead

In mid-March, as the pandemic was just reaching its full force in Europe and North America, a lab at Oxford University had already developed what was undoubtedly the most precious drops of liquid on the planet. Carefully packed in dry ice, several tiny vials filled with a few drops of "seed stock" were sent to Advent, a lab just south of Rome in Italy.[37] This "seed stock" was a starter kit of sorts for the production of a potential vaccine for COVID-19. This was the West's best, and perhaps only, chance to develop and produce a viable vaccine by the end of the year. The Italian government provided Advent with all the assistance and resources it could marshal. Italy's health minister, Roberto Speranza, said in an interview, "This is the vaccine our scientists think will arrive before the others. In this moment, there is no other company saying we could have the vaccine by the end of the year."[38]

Advent's mission was to turn these few droplets into an amount large enough to conduct large-scale trials involving 13,000 people on several continents.[39] The hopes and prayers of millions, if not billions, of people around the world depended on what Advent did within the next month or two. "We could really feel the pressure," said Francesco Calvaruso, the production manager of Advent, which needed the next two months to grow, filter, and purify a trial vaccine known as "AZD1222."[40]

Oxford had already manufactured its own vaccine for use in the earliest small trial, known as Phase 1. But for the far larger ongoing trials, which had to involve tens of thousands of people, it needed the expertise of Advent, a division of a larger group known as IRBM, which had been focusing on experimental vaccines using adenoviruses for more than a decade.[41] The notion of having a vaccine so quickly — when the process of experimentation and approval typically takes a decade — seemed a near impossibility at the beginning of the outbreak. But the Oxford University project had done the near-impossible and was now poised to complete the development process.

The large-scale Phase 3 trials were scheduled to take place in the U.K. Ironically, however, one of the obstacles that the Oxford scientist ran into was the steep decline in the rate of new infections in the U.K., which made it more difficult to prove the effectiveness of their vaccine candidate. Ethics rules generally prevent researchers from deliberately infecting test participants. This meant that unless enough test participants who were given a placebo become infected with the virus in the community, the researchers could not prove that the potential vaccine does its job. Oxford solved this problem by partnering with the huge Anglo-Swiss company AstraZeneca, which was able to get the approval to conduct a trial in Brazil, as part of its effort to seek volunteers in parts of the world where the pandemic was still raging.[42] Advent also started producing a batch of doses to be used in trials in several African countries.[43]

On May 21, 2020, the U.S. Department of Health and Human Services (HHS) announced it would provide "up to $1.2 billion" to AstraZeneca to develop a potential coronavirus vaccine based upon the samples developed at Oxford University.[44] HHS would make the funding through the Biomedical Advanced Research and Development Authority (BARDA), which was in the process of distributing billions of dollars to AstraZeneca and other companies to develop a coronavirus vaccine.[45]

The deal with AstraZeneca was the fourth and by far the most substantial vaccine research agreement disclosed by HHS. The money would pay for a Phase 3 clinical trial of a potential vaccine in the U.S. during the summer of 2020 involving about 30,000 volunteers.[46] The HHS statement said the agency and AstraZeneca "are collaborating to make available at least 300 million doses," and projected that the first doses could be available as early as October 2020.[47]

AstraZeneca succeeded in entering into a licensing agreement with perhaps the most promising research and development effort by Oxford University, and then quickly moved the project into the kind of large-scale testing necessary to prove safety and effectiveness. Building on efforts to develop a vaccine against a similar disease, the Middle East Respiratory Syndrome (MERS), the Oxford scientists in the U.K. began a Phase I trial in April 2020 of their potential vaccine against COVID-19, involving 1,100 participants.[48] A combined Phase II and Phase III trial involving 5,000 participants began in Britain at the end of May.

AstraZeneca's accelerated timetable was viewed with skepticism by most public health experts and scientists, who continued to caution that a viable, mass-produced vaccine would probably not be available until sometime next year, at the earliest. AstraZeneca, however, defended its schedule and confirmed that it had reached agreements with several governments and other organizations to produce at least 400 million doses, and had "secured manufacturing capacity for one billion doses."[49] AstraZeneca also said it was discussing deals for simultaneous production by other companies, including the giant Serum Institute of India, a major supplier of vaccines to the developing world.

Moderna, Johnson & Johnson and Sanofi Are Also in the Running

In addition to its substantial financial commitment to AstraZeneca, HHS, through BARDA, also agreed to provide up to $483 million to the biotech company Moderna Therapeutics, and $500 million to Johnson & Johnson, for their separate vaccine efforts.[50] Another $30 million was also allocated to a coronavirus vaccine effort by the French company Sanofi, building on a larger contract announced in December 2019 for making flu inoculations. However, when Sanofi suggested in May that the U.S. – which had helped fund the research – might be given early access to any COVID-19 vaccine that it developed, the French government said that it would not permit this French drug giant to let the U.S. be first in line to receive the vaccine.[51] "For us, it would be unacceptable if another country had privileged access under a financial pretext," Agnès Pannier-Runacher, the junior economy minister, told Sud Radio.[52]

The controversy started when Paul Hudson, Sanofi's chief executive, told *Bloomberg News* that "the U.S. government has the right to the largest pre-order because it's invested in taking the risk."[53] Sanofi later said in a statement that it was "committed in these unprecedented circumstances to make our vaccine accessible to everyone," and noted that it has manufacturing plants around the world.[54] The issue was a delicate one for President Emmanuel Macron of France, who repeatedly took the position that

Europe needed to develop its "economic sovereignty" to depend less on the U.S. and China for strategic technological and medical goods.[55]

Dozens of current and former world leaders signed an open letter in May urging that any coronavirus vaccine not be patented and be shared among all nations. However, the Trump administration remained non-committal on the issue, and after months of mutual vilification between the U.S. and China over the origins of the virus poisoned the well of potential cooperation between these two superpowers, any international hopes for multi-national collaboration on the development of a vaccine that included the U.S. seemed remote.

By early May, the U.S. government was already warning that American innovations and technologies, including any vaccine developed by the U.S., had to be protected from theft by China or other hostile foreign power.[56] "Biomedical research has long been a focus of theft, especially by the Chinese government, and vaccines and treatments for the coronavirus are today's holy grail," warned John C. Demers, the U.S. assistant attorney general for national security, "Putting aside the commercial value, there would be great geopolitical significance to being the first to develop a treatment or vaccine. We will use all the tools we have to safeguard American research."[57]

Indeed, the intensity of the global research efforts and competition to produce a vaccine as early as possible was leading governments and companies to building production lines before they had anything to produce. "We are going to start ramping up production with the companies involved," Dr. Anthony S. Fauci said on NBC, adding, "You don't wait until you get an answer before you start manufacturing."[58]

Moderna Announces in May That It Has Reached An Important Milestone

On Monday, May 18, Moderna Therapeutics announced some of the results of its first-phase trial, saying that its vaccine candidate had proven safe and that it had provoked an immune response in 8 of 45 people.[59] Moderna noted that the first coronavirus vaccine to be tested in people appears to be safe and able to stimulate an immune response against the virus. The findings were based on results from the first eight people who each received two doses of the vaccine, starting in March.[60] Those people, healthy volunteers, made antibodies that were then tested in human cells in the lab and were able to stop the virus from replicating — the critical requirement for an effective vaccine. The levels of those so-called neutralizing antibodies matched the levels found in patients who had recovered after contracting the virus in the community.

Moderna further said that it is proceeding on an accelerated timetable, with the next phase involving 600 people. It said it was working on this accelerated timetable with partners at the U.S. National Institute of Allergy and Infectious Diseases (NIAID) and the Swiss company Lonza. Moderna had already received approval to move to a second phase involving 600 people and said it would also begin a third stage in July with thousands of healthy people.

According to Dr. Tal Zaks, Moderna's chief medical officer, a vaccine could become available for widespread use by the end of this year or early 2021, if the trials went well. Although Moderna was somewhat vague as to the number of vaccine doses it planned to have ready by then, Dr. Zaks said, "We're doing our best to make it as many millions as possible."[61]

Moderna was using a genetically engineered RNA technology in the development of the vaccine, which involved a segment of genetic material from the virus called messenger RNA, or mRNA. Moderna said that additional tests in mice that were vaccinated and then infected found that the vaccine could prevent the virus from replicating in their lungs and that the animals had levels of neutralizing antibodies comparable to those in the people who had received the vaccine.

Three doses of the vaccine were tested: low, medium, and high. These initial results were based on tests of the small and medium doses. The only adverse effect at those doses was redness and soreness in one patient's arm where the shot was given. But at the highest dose, three patients had fever, muscles, and headaches, Dr. Zaks said, adding that the symptoms went away after a day.

Trump Fires the Head of BARDA

The efforts by BARDA to partner with these private companies to develop a vaccine ran into trouble when President Trump dismissed Rick Bright, the head of BARDA.[62] Bright had filed a highly publicized whistle-blower complaint contending he had been pressured to seek approval for specific treatments for COVID-19 favored by Trump.

In mid-May, Trump named Moncef Slaoui as Bright's replacement to lead the BARDA and HHS effort to develop a vaccine referred to by the Trump administration as "Operation Warp Speed." Slaoui was a venture capitalist and longtime vaccine executive at GlaxoSmithKline; he was also a board member of Moderna. As a lead scientist for this federal effort, Dr. Slaoui's financial ties to multiple drug companies came under close scrutiny. However, since he was working for the federal effort as a contract employee, he was exempt from conflict-of-interest and disclosure rules that applied to most executive and federal employees. Dr. Slaoui responded to these concerns by saying that he had sold his stock in Moderna and donated some of his capital gains from the stock sale to cancer research.

Moderna was the first company to kick off Phase 3 trials in July, followed by AstraZeneca's Oxford candidate a month later. The third vaccine project being backed by the U.S. government was that of Johnson & Johnson, the huge pharmaceutical company, although J&J had not announced any vaccine results as of June 2020 and had not yet started Phase 1 trials. According to The *Wall Street Journal*, J&J planned to start the first human trials in the second half of July and would move to Phase 3, pending the outcome of the first stage and subsequent regulatory approval.

Pfizer and BioNTech Were Still in the Running, But Not With U.S. Financing

Surprisingly, Pfizer, Inc. and BioNTech SE, a German company, were not included in the NIAID program as it was announced in June 2020. The two companies partnered on Phase 1 trials in Germany and the U.S. a few weeks previous to that, with the BioNTech vaccine being a genetic drug similar to Moderna's concept. Pfizer was also scheduled to begin its Phase 3 trial in July. On May 5, The *Wall Street Journal* had reported that researchers have begun giving healthy volunteers in the U.S. an experimental coronavirus vaccine developed by Pfizer.[63] Researchers at the New York University Grossman School of Medicine in Manhattan and the University of Maryland School of Medicine in Baltimore confirmed they had begun injecting people with the first of four vaccine candidates from Pfizer and BioNTech. The testing of the vaccine candidates in Germany already had started.

It was expected that these clinical trials would help the researchers evaluate whether their vaccine candidates were safe, which produced the strongest immune response, and what the dose should be.

Novavax Promised $1.6 Billion From U.S. To Develop A Vaccine

On July 7, Novavax, a Maryland-based company that had never brought a product to market before, announced that it had been awarded $1.6 billion by the U.S. – the biggest deal to date – to expedite the development of 100 million doses of a coronavirus vaccine by the beginning of 2021.[64] The deal was the largest that the Trump administration had made up to that date with a company as part of the federal government's multiagency effort known as "Operation Warp Speed." In so doing, the Trump administration was placing a massive bet on a company with a non-existent track record in actually producing a product that reached the market.

In an interview on Sunday, July 5, Novavax's president and chief executive, Stanley C. Erck, initially said he was not sure where in the government the $1.6 billion was coming from. The company later said the money was coming from a "collaboration" between the Health and Human Services Department and the Defense Department. Mr. Erck acknowledged that the U.S. government was taking a significant risk. "The risk they're taking is that a company like ours — which doesn't have a pipeline of already commercialized products — can we get to the big leagues and scale-up?" he said. "And I think they're placing the bet that we can."

Novavax had previously been awarded $388 million in May by an international group known as the Coalition for Epidemic Preparedness Innovations, upon the company's commitment to making the vaccine available globally.[65]

The U.S. Refuses to Commit to a Multi-National Effort

On Thursday, June 18, the Trump administration's nominee to lead its coronavirus vaccine initiative – General Gustave F. Perna – refused during his Senate confirmation hearing to commit to the U.S. working with any nation that could further the U.S.'s efforts to develop a COVID-19 vaccine by early next year.[66] In questioning by members of the Senate Armed Services Committee, General Perna, who had been nominated by President Trump to become a chief operating officer of "Operation Warp Speed," declined to clarify the degree to which the U.S. would participate in international scientific collaboration in the government's plan to provide 300 million vaccine doses by January.

During his confirmation hearing, Perna, who also served as head of U.S. Army Materiel Command, was asked by Senator Richard Blumenthal (D-Conn.) whether he would commit to working with "any nation that offers cooperation or information relevant to developing vaccines or a therapeutic."[67] Perna responded that he would commit "to working with all nations that we deem are friendly to our national security" and would apply his "best military advice" to the question of international cooperation. Blumenthal, who noted that the U.S. engages in trade or treaties with nations that are rivals or competitors, called Perna's answer "insufficient." Senator Mazie Hirono (D-Hawaii) later asked Perna whether the list of countries the U.S. would collaborate with on a vaccine included China. "Right now, for me, it does not," Perna replied. "But as I said, it would be my best military advice."[68] Hirono responded, "It could very well be, General, that China might be the one that actually develops an effective vaccine, and then where does that put us?"[69]

The Multi-National Vaccine Effort (Without the U.S.)

While the U.S. was working alone in partnership with a few companies to develop a vaccine and pouring billions of dollars into its own research efforts, most other major countries were collaborating with each other in an extraordinary multi-national effort. During a three-hour fund-raising conference on Monday, May 18 organized by the European Union and conducted over video link, representatives from around the world — from

Japan to Canada, Australia to Norway — took turns announcing their countries' contributions to fund laboratories that had promising leads in developing and producing a vaccine. The European Commission, the executive branch of the European Union that spearheaded the initiative, said that the goal was to raise $8 billion that would be spent over the next two years.[70] For example, Romania contributed $200,000, and Canada donated $850 million for the cause.[71] Prime ministers, a king, a prince, and even Madonna all chipped into the $8 billion pot to fund a coronavirus vaccine.[72] Their goal was to deliver universal and affordable access to a vaccine and medications to fight COVID-19. Senior Trump administration officials did not explain why the U.S. did not attend the European-organized conference, but they did confirm that the U.S. had already spent $2.6 billion on research and development for a vaccine.[73]

Will There Really Be a "Winner" in the Race for a Vaccine?

The U.S. was not the only country that decided to move ahead with the development of its own vaccine on a national basis. China also financed some of the clinical trials relating to the development of a vaccine. And in India, the chief executive of the Serum Institute of India — the world's largest producer of vaccine doses — said that most of its vaccines "would have to go to our countrymen before it goes abroad."[74]

George Q. Daley, the Dean of Harvard Medical School, warned that this kind of "America first," or "China or India first" approach made little practical sense since it "would involve squandering the early doses of vaccine on a large number of individuals at low risk [in one country], rather than covering as many high-risk individuals globally" — health care workers and older adults — "to stop the spread" around the world.[75]

According to some experts, and given the proliferation of vaccine projects, the best outcome would be for no company or country to emerge as a clear winner. "Let's say we get one vaccine quickly, but we can only get two million doses of it at the end of next year," said Anita Zaidi, who directs the Bill and Melinda Gates Foundation's vaccine development program,

"And another vaccine, just as effective, comes three months later but we can make a billion doses. Who won that race?"[76]

Who Gets the Vaccine First in the U.S.?

As early as April, when the development of a vaccine was still in its early stages, the CDC and an advisory committee of outside health experts began working on a ranking system on who would get the first doses of a vaccine. Even if an effective vaccine were to be available for public use by the winter of 2020-2021, there would be a several month gap between the time that the first vials of the vaccine started being shipped from the manufacturing plants and when tens of millions of doses would be generally available to the public.[77]

The CDC's advisory committee – which was tasked with making life-and-death recommendations affecting every American – included 15 voting members selected by the secretary of HHS who come from the fields of immunology, infectious disease, and other medical specialties, 30 nonvoting representatives from across the health field, and eight federal officials focused on vaccines.[78] The group generally conducts its work in secrecy, given the critical importance and delicacy. "It's a back-room kind of thing," said Dr. Nancy Bennett, a health professor at the University of Rochester who led the advisory committee from 2015 to 2018.[79]

According to a preliminary plan, the first approved vaccines would be offered to vital medical and national security officials first, and then to other essential workers and those considered at high risk, such as the elderly and people with underlying conditions. Children and the relatively healthy would be forced to wait. Many thorny questions remained unresolved for months, however, such as how to define "essential workers" and whether pregnant women and teachers should be given priority.

By far the hottest topic for debate was the proposal under consideration as to whether Black and Latino people should be given priority, in view of the fact that COVID-19 had disproportionately impacted them. Statistics were showing that Black and Latino people had become infected with the virus at three times the rate of whites, and were dying at nearly twice the rate.[80] The increasingly heated debate within the CDC and its advisory board involved the question of whether racial justice was a proper scientific and ethical factor to be considered in developing a vaccine distribution policy. This issue was particularly sensitive since the U.S. has a history of racism in the experimentation of cures for infectious diseases. In the infamous Tuskegee syphilis study, for example, the federal government deliberately let hundreds of Black men go untreated even when there was a known cure for the disease.[81]

Since Black and Latino people have a disproportionately high incidence of underlying diseases, such as diabetes and high blood pressure, an argument could be made that prioritizing Americans with underlying conditions would automatically enhance the position of these minority groups. Dr. Sharon Frey, a professor of infectious diseases at St. Louis University, has pointed to health disparities among Black and Latino people, suggesting that perhaps priority for a vaccine need not be given to entire minority groups, but only to those people who are living in urban areas with inadequate housing, crowded conditions and less access to health care.[82] Dayna Bowen Matthew, Dean of the George Washington University Law School, agreed with the view that some recognition must be given to racial and ethnic disparities in formulating a vaccine distribution plan: "It's racial inequality — inequality in housing, inequality in employment, inequality in access to health care — that produced the underlying diseases."[83]

Harald Schmidt, an assistant professor of medical ethics and health policy at the University of Pennsylvania, has predicted that courts would strike down any guidelines explicitly based on race and ethnicity, but would be receptive to an index approach that took into account education, income, employment, and housing quality to rank neighborhoods by socioeconomic disadvantage. "Because of Tuskegee and structural racism within the health care system, you have to make a case much more strongly to the African American population," Dr. Schmidt said.[84]

In addition, the White House and Trump administration political appointees focused on the political consequences of these critical public health decisions, as they were doing with the decision to open up schools and reopen the economies of the states. At the public advisory committee hearing, held in mid-June, a Defense Department representative said the operation would address the distribution plans in the coming weeks. It was clear, however, that in order to speed distribution, the vaccines that were furthest along in the approval process would start being produced even before they cleared the final stages of clinical trials and approved for public use by the F.D.A.

"Desperation Science" Confuses the Search for a Cure

While the effort to develop a vaccine was ongoing, doctors and scientists were also in a desperate rush to find an effective therapeutic drug to treat COVID-19. The danger of rushing this search, however, was that doctors, government agencies, and drug companies were placed under tremendous pressure to use shortcuts that compromised established rules and procedures for scientific research. These scientific research procedures and protocols were not designed for speed; instead, they were designed for accuracy and fact-based results. As a result, this corner-cutting actually slowed down, in many cases, the ability to gain a true understanding of the disease and delayed the ability to determine which drugs were actually effective in combatting and treating it. "People had an epidemic in front of them and were not prepared to wait," said Dr. Derek Angus, critical care chief at the University of Pittsburgh Medical Center, adding, "We made traditional clinical research look so slow and cumbersome."[85]

The use of drugs on patients before they have been thoroughly tested has sometimes led to tragic results in the past. For example, lidocaine was routinely used for decades to prevent heart rhythm problems in people suspected of having heart attacks. However, a study in the mid-1980s showed the drug actually caused the problem it was meant to prevent.[86] During the 1990s, there was a major effort to get insurers to cover bone marrow transplants for breast cancer until a study showed that these transplants actually made patients sicker without improving their chances of survival. During the Ebola outbreak in 2014, the use of an antibody combo called ZMapp was promoted without any hard evidence that it actually worked, and later studies showed that it was not effective. During the 2009-2010 Swine Flu outbreak, the experimental drug Peramivir was widely used without a formal review. Later test results showed that Peramivir was only effective for less severe cases of flu and not for severely ill hospitalized patients.[87]

With the onset of the coronavirus crisis, many doctors treating COVID-19 patients frantically scrambled to find a cure by using a "hit-and-miss" method, which involved experimentation on their patients with medicines for stroke, heartburn, blood clots, gout, depression, inflammation, AIDS, hepatitis, cancer, arthritis, and even stem cells and radiation. Dr. Steven Nissen, a Cleveland Clinic researcher, commented: "Everyone has been kind of grasping for anything that might work. And that's not how you develop sound medical practice … Desperation is not a strategy. Good clinical trials represent a solid strategy."[88]

In addition to desperation, the search for an effective treatment was also hampered by politics, especially when President Trump began relentlessly promoting hydroxychloroquine, saying, "What have you got to lose?"[89] Meanwhile, the country's top infectious disease expert, Dr. Anthony Fauci, warned, "I like to prove things first." For three months, weak studies emerged that gave conflicting views regarding the efficacy of hydroxychloroquine until several more reliable ones found it ineffective. The Trump administration's hype and controversy over this anti-malaria drug reflected the prevailing Republican view that was highly suspicious of science and fact-based research, relying more on hunches and wishful thinking to drive policymaking. The obvious problem with this gunslinger approach was that it distracted from any real rigorous analysis of scientific data relating to the vast array of potential cures.

Even well-respected researchers started taking shortcuts and bending the rules in a rush to find a "wonder drug" to cure the disease, and scientific journals began rushing to publish the results of incomplete studies. More than 2,000 studies were conducted regarding COVID-19 treatments, using hundreds of potential therapeutic elements and drugs, from azithromycin to zinc.

Trump compounded the dangers of a lack of scientific rigor in these tests and studies by publicly promoting the taking of a drug cocktail of hydroxychloroquine with azithromycin, an antibiotic that, like hydroxychloroquine, can cause heart rhythm problems. After criticism, "Doctor" Trump modified his prescription by saying, "You should add zinc now … I want to throw that out there."[90] In May, he said he was taking the drugs himself to prevent infection after an aide tested positive. Given his record for truth-telling, few believed him.

It was not until later that a U.K. study found hydroxychloroquine to be ineffective for treatment, as did other studies by the U.S. National Institutes of Health and the World Health Organization. All of a sudden, all but a few doctors stopped promoting the drug, and even *Fox News* backed off the strong endorsement of its use.

Remdesivir was another experimental medicine administered through an IV that showed promise against other coronaviruses, in that it tended to curb the ability of coronaviruses to copy their genetic material. Doctors in China began studies of Remdesivir in the care of severely and moderately ill hospitalized patients. The drug's maker, Gilead Sciences, also started its own studies, and the NIH launched the most rigorous test, comparing Remdesivir to placebo IV treatments.[91] While these studies were underway, Gilead also gave away the drug on a case-by-case basis to thousands of patients.

In late April, Dr. Fauci revealed preliminary results from the NIH trial showing Remdesivir shortened patients' recovery time by 31%, 11 days on average versus 15 days for those just given usual care.[92] This data, however, was inconclusive since the studies could not be continued due to ethical concerns about continuing to provide the placebo for the control group of patients when the benefit of Remdesivir started becoming apparent.

* * * * *

The race for a vaccine and a cure for COVID-19 thus proceeded with breakneck speed but was seriously impaired by a lack of scientific rigor and overuse of "shortcuts." These efforts were also complicated by a toxic mix of politics, hucksterism, and wishful thinking by President Trump and others who took his lead. Science gave way to highly politicized viewpoints, with Trump supporters taking their leader's "pro-hydroxychloroquine" point of view, while the rest of the world (including Dr. Fauci) persisted in their faith in science and the scientific method.

THE COVID-19 CRISIS HIGHLIGHTS THE NEED FOR AN OVERHAUL IN THE U.S. HEALTH CARE SYSTEM

As the coronavirus pandemic continued its rampage across the U.S., medical professionals and experts acknowledged that the additional strain on the U.S. health care system exposed significant flaws that must be remedied if the country is to successfully face its next public health crisis.[1]

America's generally lackluster response to the crisis was due, in large measure, to the fact that its balkanized and disjointed health care system was less prepared for a pandemic than countries with more fully integrated and comprehensive health systems.[2] According to Cynthia Cox, director of the Peterson-Kaiser Health System Tracker, "The U.S. performs worse than average among similarly large and wealthy countries across nearly all measures of preparedness for a pandemic."[3] The data supporting this indictment of the U.S. health care system is formidable. Even though health care costs in the U.S. are the highest in the world, Americans die at much higher rates from preventable causes.[4] In addition, a bigger share of the U.S. population lacks health insurance than in any other developed country. In fact, Americans carry much more medical debt as compared to citizens of other countries, which causes Americans to delay seeking medical help until it is often too late.

The root causes of America's deeply flawed health care system are simple to identify. Long before the coronavirus crisis hit this country, the U.S. had fewer doctors and fewer hospital beds per capita than most other developed countries. The U.S. has 2.6 doctors per 1,000 people, well below the average for comparable developed countries of 3.5 per 1,000 people.[5] Experts point to the extremely high cost of medical schooling in the U.S. for this lack of doctors.

America's relatively few hospital beds create a potential shortage during a pandemic under even the best of circumstances. The U.S.'s number of hospital beds is about the same as that of Canada or the U.K., which have far fewer people. This chronic shortage of hospital capacity is compounded by the fact that the U.S. has higher rates of hospitalizations for chronic conditions that, with proper management, should not require hospitalization. Those chronic conditions that could usually be treated on an outpatient basis include congestive heart failure, diabetes, and asthma. However, Americans with these conditions often end up in the hospital more frequently than in other countries, due to lack of access to primary care and the high costs of such routine primary care even when it is available.[6]

As a result, when the COVID-19 crisis hit, emergency rooms and ICU beds filled up quickly to overflowing capacity even before many cities and states reached their peaks. It took only two or three weeks for the New York City health care system to start buckling under the strain of the public health crisis that descended on it virtually overnight. There was little reserve capacity of supplies, equipment, and ICU beds to meet the overwhelming demand.

As we all are now painfully aware, the U.S. was also totally unprepared to conduct the level of testing needed in the current pandemic. However, this should not have come as a big surprise since the U.S. healthcare system is mostly a for-profit system, and having large stockpiles of testing equipment sitting around in a warehouse waiting for the next pandemic is not a profitable investment. U.S. drug and pharmaceutical research companies are primarily in the business of making profits for their shareholders, not creating therapeutic drugs and vaccines for an illness that does not yet exist or has not yet reached the U.S. There is simply not enough of a profit incentive for private companies to spend millions or even billions of dollars on the development of diagnostic tests and vaccines for the virus which may or may not come. If a particular virus does not result in a pandemic, all of the investment will have been for "nothing." "Emergency preparedness" are just not words in the vocabulary of the U.S. health care system when it comes to tests and vaccines for diseases that have not yet arrived.

Countries with universal health care, by contrast, invest far more in public health research and testing, which is why those countries – such as the Scandinavian countries, Germany, South Korea and Taiwan – were able to test far more people per capita than the U.S. Not surprisingly, these same countries with universal health care systems generally had lower COVID-19 death rates than the U.S. Any universal health care system requires centralized planning, which is always an asset in times of crisis.

Taiwan, for example, saw a remarkably low level of coronavirus cases despite its proximity to and high traffic with mainland China. As of May 1, Taiwan had just 429 coronavirus cases, and only six deaths, out of a population of nearly 24 million.[7] It also had a very aggressive testing program, which meant that it was unlikely that it was overlooking many unreported cases. In Taiwan, with its single-payer health program, every citizen has their digital medical records loaded into the same system, and during the coronavirus outbreak, the country added travel records to these online medical files. As a result, every doctor in the country could easily check whether their patients visited any areas affected by the outbreak. Taiwan also got off to a quick start in its response to the crisis, which was able to markedly lower the number of cases and prevent the number of cases from overrunning the health care capacity.

Since many Americans are uninsured or have high out-of-pocket costs, they have had a longstanding tendency to delay seeking care for many of the underlying health conditions that made them more susceptible to more serious or fatal outcomes to COVID-19 infections.[8] The higher the cost barriers to medical care, the more likely that people will delay or forgo care they need, including for serious conditions. A 2019 study found that one-third of Americans told researchers that cost-related barriers delayed their decision to get medical care, and 25% said they even postponed care for a severe condition. Moreover, Americans are far more likely to neglect paying medical bills and avoid making follow up visits to the doctor when their insurance plan refuses to cover some or part of their medical claims. This compares to only 7% of patients in Germany, who reported that they delayed medical care due to costs.[9]

When the pandemic hit, many Americans were already programmed to worry about the medical costs involved with COVID-19 and thus delayed seeking treatment once they became infected with the coronavirus. During the start of the pandemic, they tended to be wary about going to the doctor at all because they could not afford the check-up or testing fees. If someone were to get a positive COVID-19 diagnosis and require hospitalization, they would have to face hospital and doctors' bills, as well as costs involved in any follow-up treatment. This reluctance to seek medical treatment for a fever or other symptoms associated with COVID-19 led many sick Americans to delay seeking treatment until their condition deteriorated to the point where a 911 call for assistance was unavoidable. This, in turn, led to unnecessarily extended hospital stays, more acute illnesses, and, in many cases, death.

In addition, the rabbit warren patchwork of public and private medical labs made it difficult, if not impossible, for the U.S. to scale up to the level of testing needed to maintain the tens of thousands or millions of daily tests that experts were saying was required for effective monitoring of the disease. This testing capacity was especially needed as lockdown and social distancing restrictions were eased, but was generally just not available to most Americans who needed testing the most.[10]

To be sure, the existence of a country's universal health care was not in itself enough to spare countries such as Italy from the devastating impact of the pandemic. Parts of northern Italy were ravaged with a massive volume of cases and deaths, especially among the elderly. Some Italian towns reported a "hollowing out" of an entire generation in their 70s, 80s and older. Nevertheless, it is generally agreed that the situation in Italy would have been far worse if it did not have a first-rate universal health care system to ride out the crisis. Italy has far more hospital beds and doctors per capita than the U.S., and a much smaller population. As a result, even though the Italian health care system was severely stressed during the worst part of the outbreak in that country, its health system still had the capacity to handle the massive surge in patients that it experienced.

The Existing Financial Structures of the Privately-Owned U.S. Hospital Systems Left Them Wide Open to A Financial Crisis In the Midst of the Pandemic

Even the most prestigious and well-managed U.S. hospital systems quickly ran into financial trouble when the coronavirus crisis hit this country. For example, the Mayo Clinic in Minnesota lost millions of dollars a day when it suspended all non-emergency medical care in late March to deal with coronavirus cases.[11] Previously, in 2019, this hospital network produced $11.6 billion in annual patient revenue and $1 billion in net operating revenue. Of that revenue, 60% came from privately insured patients, and only 3% from Medicaid.[12] Most of the rest of the revenue came from Medicare.

However, during the height of the 2020 coronavirus pandemic, the Mayo Clinic projected an annual loss of $900 million for 2020, even after furloughing workers, cutting doctors' pay, and halting new construction projects.[13] About 30,000 staff employees were either furloughed or had their hours reduced, which represented almost half its workforce, as the Mayo Clinic tried to stem the financial hemorrhaging it was experiencing.[14] Similarly, Johns Hopkins, another elite hospital system based in Baltimore, estimated a loss of nearly $300 million going into 2021, forcing it also to make significant cost reductions.[15]

In the past, the Mayo Clinic, Johns Hopkins, and other premier hospital chains showed consistent financial strength, benefitting from their worldwide reputations. They attracted wealthy patients and clients from across the country and around the globe who either paid premium rates for the elective surgeries and other medical services they received or their private health insurance policies paid their bills for them. These high-end hospital systems promoted their services to well-off patients, delivering quality health care alongside luxury amenities such as hotel-like suites with fluffy bathrobes, private dining rooms, and access to gourmet meals.[16]

In a typical year, more than a million patients traveled to the Mayo Clinic's 21 hospitals from all 50 states and 140 countries.[17] Many were seen at its 2,000-bed Rochester, Minnesota campus. The Mayo Clinic had aggressively expanded its services abroad, opening a facility in London in the fall of 2019, and was building a 741-bed for-profit facility in Abu Dhabi, in the United Arab Emirates.[18]

However, suddenly with the onset of the coronavirus crisis, elective surgeries were either canceled or postponed so that these hospitals could help meet the growing demands of COVID-19 patients in their areas. In addition, many of these traditional well-to-do clients became hesitant to rely on air travel and airport connections to meet their medical needs, opting instead to use hospitals closer to home. As a result, these hospital systems were forced to rely more heavily on local and regional residents, especially those low-income patients enrolled in the Medicaid program.

Almost overnight, the U.S. privately owned hospitals and health care systems saw a dramatic drop in their income and profit projections, since their patient base of wealthy and privately insured patients who paid premium rates for elective surgeries dried up. In addition to the suspension of elective surgeries during the crisis, millions of Americans who were suddenly unemployed lost their private insurance coverage, since these health insurance policies were tied to their jobs.

At the same time, privately-owned for-profit and ostensibly "not-for-profit" hospitals and health care systems were squeezed from the other end, since public programs like Medicare and Medicaid negotiated lower rates for medical services, thus reducing profit margins for the hospitals. For example, Minnesota's private insurers pay the Mayo Clinic $566 for each obstetric ultrasound, approximately five times the Medicaid price.[19] For an echocardiogram, the difference is tenfold. As a result, the previously lucrative health care model that had worked so well for decades has been turned on its head. "Health care has always been viewed as recession-proof, but it's not pandemic-proof," said Dr. David Blumenthal, president of the Commonwealth Fund, a health research organization, adding, "The level of economic impact, plus the fear of coronavirus, will have a more dramatic impact than any event we've seen in the health care system in my lifetime."[20]

By the middle of May, U.S. hospitals were losing an estimated $50 billion a month, according to the American Hospital Association.[21] Based on the Bureau of Labor Statistics data, 134,000 hospital employees were among the estimated 1.4 million health care workers who lost their jobs in April.[22] Across the country, hospitals reported seeing between 40-70% fewer patients from late March through early May, many of them scheduled for valuable services like orthopedic surgery and radiological scans.[23] This decline affected both large and elite hospital systems as well as suburban hospitals and small rural facilities that were already financially stressed. Hospitals that treated high numbers of coronavirus patients reported having been hit especially hard, as they had to spend heavily on protective equipment and increased staffing just as their most profitable services were halted. These patients often had long stays in intensive care units, requiring expensive equipment like ventilators. "We began ordering everything at a feverish pace," said Kenneth Raske, president of the Greater New York Hospital Association. "The costs were sometimes 10 or 20 times normal. We were scrounging all over the world for supplies."[24] His organization estimated that, across New York City, large academic medical centers lost between $350 million and $450 million each last month.[25]

Urban Institute, a nonprofit organization, projected between eight and fifteen million new Medicaid enrollments among those losing the private insurance they had through employers.[26] An additional five to ten million Americans who lose such plans are expected to become uninsured, and four to eight million will transition to the Affordable Care Act's individual market plans or other sources of private insurance.[27]

The Trump administration has earmarked $12 billion in relief funds for hospitals that treated 100 or more coronavirus cases, meant to offset the high costs of caring for patients whose hospital stays could last weeks.[28]

The States Take An Important First Step to Reduce the Costs of Testing and Treatment for COVID-19

In the U.S., several governors and state legislatures made proposals and issued executive orders that would eliminate or reduce the cost of medical and hospital treatments for COVID-19. New York Governor Andrew Cuomo announced that New York would require insurers and the state Medicaid program to cover treatment and testing for free while the state's emergency declaration was effective.[29] States also had some discretion as to the coverage of their Medicaid programs, and several states, including

California and New York, opted for Medicaid coverage of COVID-19 medical treatments and testing. However, as is the case with a computer virus, a temporary patch for the treatment of a real virus such as this one will only work – well, temporarily – and a more permanent fix must follow.

States are limited, however, in what they can do to make medical and hospital services more financially accessible during a public health crisis, since federal law, through the Employee Retirement Income Security Act (ERISA), regulates the large employer health insurance plans that cover about 100 million Americans. This presents a major barrier to what state officials can do by themselves to relieve the burden on ordinary citizens for coronavirus-related health care costs. Given the decentralized nature of most of the health care system, a major overhaul at the federal level would be necessary if the U.S. really wanted to transform what we now have into a first-class health care system. Congress must, therefore, take up this critical task so the country will be prepared to respond to any more waves of the coronavirus or any future health care crisis.

There are already some signs that the U.S. is starting to address some of the major flaws in the country's health care system. Representative Tony Cardenas of California, for example, introduced HR 6616 in Congress on April 24, which would amend the Social Security Act to allow states to provide coverage under the Medicaid program for vaccines and treatment for COVID-19 for uninsured individuals without the imposition of cost-sharing requirements. This would be an essential first step that could improve the U.S. health care system and move it closer to the universal health care coverage systems that have become the norm in other developed countries.

Even the Trump administration, which has not demonstrated any progressive leanings when it comes to the funding of health care costs, agreed that the federal government should take primary responsibility for the costs associated with COVID-19 treatment and testing. Vice President Mike Pence announced COVID-19 testing and treatment would be treated as an "essential health benefit," a standard established by the Affordable Care Act to permit coverage under the ACA. However, this coverage would still not apply to the self-funded ERISA plans or Medicare.

Private Equity Firms Ruin the Health Care Industry and then Cash In On the Federal Emergency Aid Programs

Private equity firms have been significant contributors to the sorry state of the U.S. health care system. In the decade preceding the coronavirus crisis, private equity funds acquired hundreds of healthcare companies, primarily targeting large hospitals, dermatology clinics, and dental practices. In the past five years alone, private equity firms have invested more than $10 billion in medical practices, with a special focus on dermatology, which has been a "growth industry" because of the aging population.[30] In addition to buying up medical practices in the U.S., private equity firms like Blackstone, Apollo Global Management, The Carlyle Group, KKR & Co. and Warburg Pincus have spent more than $340 billion to buy healthcare-related operations around the world.[31]

Cerberus Capital Management, a $42 billion investment firm run by Steve Feinberg, owns Steward Health Care, which runs 35 hospitals and a multitude of urgent care facilities in 11 states.

Warburg Pincus, headed up by former Treasury Secretary Timothy Geithner, owns Modernizing Medicine, an information technology company that helps health care providers ramp up profits through medical billing and, to a lesser degree, debt collections.

The Carlyle Group owns MedRisk, a leading provider of physical therapy cost-containment systems for U.S. workers' compensation payers, such as insurers and large employers.

KKR & Co., Inc., a global investment firm based in New York, with annual revenues of $1.79 billion, paid $9.9 billion in 2018 for EmCare, which provides healthcare services such as ambulatory surgery and anesthesiology. EmCare is part of Nashville, Tennessee-based Envision Healthcare Corp.

Apollo Global Management, a $330 billion investment firm overseen by Leon Black, owns RCCH Healthcare Partners, an operator of 88 rural hospital campuses in West Virginia, Tennessee, Kentucky, and 26 other states.

The encroachment of private equity financing into the health care field has been a relatively recent phenomenon since for-profit investors have long been prevented by standards set by the American Medical Association (AMA) from buying doctor's offices and medical facilities. Direct corporate ownership is also prohibited by law in many states, including Texas and New Jersey. For most of the past 100 years, if you wanted to make money on a medical practice, you needed to have a medical license. During most of the 20th Century, hospitals were generally owned by nonprofit entities with religious affiliations or by states and cities with ties to medical schools. For-profit hospitals existed, but it was not until recently they came to dominate the health care field.

And then some bright and crafty lawyers devised an ingenious structure that allowed investors to buy medical practices without technically owning it. The MSO (or management service organization) was thus born. The way it works is that when an investment firm buys a doctor's office, it is technically only buying the office's "nonclinical" assets. In theory, physicians control all medical decisions and agree to pay a management fee to a newly created company, which handles administrative tasks such as billing and marketing. In reality, though, investors exercise substantial influence over medical decision-making, since all decisions in a medical practice have an impact on what is the only thing of importance to investors, which is profits. "When we partner with you, it's a marriage," said Matt Jameson, a managing director at BlueMountain Capital, a $17 billion firm that's backed medical groups in fields such as gastroenterology.[32]

The rapidly rising rate of such acquisitions (or "marriages" as some equity funds prefer to call it) has transformed the health care industry, but not for the better. To be sure, it has created an immense concentration of wealth in the major private equity firms that own and trade health care systems for fun and profit like it was a game of Monopoly. It has propelled equity fund managers into the upper ranks of America's plutocrats. Most of those who head major private equity firms are reported to be billionaires, like the two men who head Blackstone: Stephen Schwarzman, a close adviser to President Donald Trump, and Hamilton "Tony" James, a major donor to Democrats.

Private equity acquisitions in the health care field follow a standard "playbook," which is designed for one purpose and one purpose only: to cut costs and maximize profits, regardless of the negative fallout and damage that is done in the process. The first step involves the acquisition of the health care company or medical practice, where individual doctors generally receive $2 million to $7 million each, with 30% to 40% of that paid in equity in the group.[33] After the acquisition, doctors usually get lower salaries and are asked to help recruit other doctors to sell their practices or to join as employees.

The acquisition phase is followed by the drastic cutting of costs, often involving major cuts in preventative health medicine and other crucial but low-profit health care areas. In order to cut salary overhead, these for-profit companies make liberal use of so-called "physician extenders," like nurse practitioners, to see patients instead of actual doctors. Because such "extenders" require less training than doctors, their salaries are correspondingly lower. Generally speaking, a health care company can hire three nurse practitioners for the cost of one doctor.[34] Private equity-owned firms also use doctors with less experience or training to save money.

In the nursing home field, the negative impact of cost-cutting maneuvers by private equity firms has been perhaps the most dramatic. A recent in-depth study of private equity-owned nursing homes concluded that these private equity profiteers were basically ruining the nursing home field, which had more than its share of challenges before the private equity firms targeted them. "In the nursing home setting," the study concluded, "it appears that high-powered profit-maximizing incentives can lead firms to renege on implicit contracts to provide high-quality care, creating value for the firms at the expense of patients."[35]

The final stage of the private equity playbook in the health care field is to sell off the company for a profit, with an average expected annualized return of 20% to 30% within a three to five-year time frame.[36] "I know private equity does this in other industries, but in medicine, you're dealing with people's health and their lives," says Michael Rains, a doctor who worked at U.S. Dermatology Partners, a prominent private equity-backed chain, "You can't serve two masters. You can't serve patients and investors."[37]

When the coronavirus crisis struck, hospitals owned by private equity funds were some of the first to experience a shortage of personal protective equipment, ventilators, and other necessary equipment needed to treat COVID-19 patients. This is because these hospitals were already staggering financially with excessive debt taken on at the time of purchase by the private equity firms. Then when these companies slashed hospital costs, the first budget items to be eliminated were "excess" capacity of beds, protective gear, and equipment that were unlikely to be needed in normal times, but would be critical during a pandemic.

In the business of health care, as opposed to the practice of medicine, the drive for profits often runs counter to the goal of helping patients and protecting workers. The excess debt of these hospitals also gives them little or no financial cushion to weather an economic storm like the one that hit them as a result of the coronavirus crisis, depriving of their major income streams such as elective surgeries.

When the coronavirus pandemic severely damaged the finances of many hospitals and other health care providers, Congress stepped in with a huge bailout program, including interest-free loans, administered by the U.S. Department of Health and Human Services (HHS). Some of the first health care providers to benefit from this program were those that were owned by cash-rich private equity firms such as KKR. For example, EmCare IAH Emergency Physicians, a Houston staffing company owned by private equity firm KKR, applied for a $317,379 interest-free loan.[38] Almost 300 entities affiliated with KKR-owned Envision also received HHS loans, according to an analysis by *Bloomberg*.[39] The loans included $1,963,697 for the River Drive Surgery Center in Elmwood Park, New Jersey; $1,049,804 to the Bend Surgery Center in Oregon; and $610,850 to the Surgery Center of Allentown in Pennsylvania. These loans were made through two existing HHS programs administered by the Centers for Medicare & Medicaid Services — the Advance Payments Program and the Accelerated Payments Program — that were expanded under the CARES Act to help healthcare companies cope with the pandemic.

HHS distributed $100 billion through the programs, starting in late March.[40] The loans, which were structured as advances on future payments the companies expected to receive from the government, were interest-free for the first seven months to a year. The loans to companies owned by private equity firms came in addition to hundreds of millions of dollars in COVID-19 relief grants that HHS automatically sent to health facilities when it disbursed funds to providers that have treated Medicare patients during the past two years. That money, which was allocated according to billings, did not have to be repaid.

More than $60 million of the HHS loans went to 300 subsidiaries of KKR-owned companies.[41] The fact that the ultimate beneficial owners of many of these companies were well-financed and profitable hedge funds and investment firms such as KKR – who were generally sitting on cash hoards of millions if not billions of dollars – was not a factor considered by HHS in doling out these interest-free loans, as long as the applicants of record were registered Medicare-enrolled providers.

The HHS loans were made to KKR-owned companies even though KKR was at the center of a 2019 congressional investigation of the shady billing practice known as "surprise billing," where the KKR-owned companies such as EmCare staffed in-network emergency rooms and surgical centers with out-of-network doctors. The patients, who were unaware that the ER doctors who were treating them were "out of network" physicians, were then sent large bills and subject to aggressive collection practices. EmCare's profit margins heavily depended on its ability to collect on those expensive and often inflated claims, and it financed a robust lobbying effort in Congress to block attempts to ban the practice.

The private equity firms that benefited the most from the HHS loan programs were the ones who least needed the cash. KKR, for example, had more than $58 billion of cash to invest. Similarly, another private equity firm owning a slew of health care facilities, Apollo Global Management, started the year with about $46 billion cash in hand. Nevertheless, Apollo received at least $500 million in HHS loans. Subsidiaries of Apollo-owned LifePoint Health Inc. received more than 90 loans, ranging from $439 for a small hospital in Paris, Kentucky, to $39.7 million for a bigger one in Marquette, Michigan.[42]

Cerberus Capital Management, another large private equity firm, which threatened to close a hard-hit Pennsylvania hospital, received at least $400 million in HHS loans. Even as it was applying for these interest-free government loans, Cerberus was hard at work, quadrupling the size of one of its investment funds to $750 million. Even though it was awash in cash,

Cerberus and its subsidiary, Steward Health Care System L.L.C., which operates 37 community hospitals and has 42,000 employees, issued an ultimatum to Pennsylvania Governor Tom Wolf, threatening to close its hospital in Easton, Pennsylvania if the state did not comply with its demand that it cover all operating costs and liabilities for the hospital. Since it was in the middle of the coronavirus crisis, the state had no alternative other than to cave in to Cerberus's extortionate demand.

On April 2, Cerberus Capital and Steward Health Care created another firestorm when it suspended intensive care unit admissions at Nashoba Valley Medical Center, a hospital in rural northeastern Massachusetts, and redeployed equipment and staff elsewhere to meet COVID-19 demand. Hospitals are not supposed to close such units without first notifying state authorities and holding community hearings, but Cerberus apparently answers to a higher authority: its investors.

As for KKR-owned Envision, which also received HHS loans, it saw its credit rating downgraded even deeper into "junk bond" territory in April by Moody's Investors Service, which said the company had deployed an "aggressive financial strategy characterized by high financial leverage, shareholder-friendly policies and the pursuit of acquisitive growth. This is largely due to its private equity ownership by KKR since its leveraged buyout in 2018."[43] Soon afterward, Envision said that it was considering bankruptcy as it sought to restructure its existing debt.

KKR and Envision appear to be following the tried-and-true strategy successfully employed by hedge fund and private equity firms on numerous occasions, which is to load up companies with debt, siphon off the cash, and then leave the creditors and debt-holders holding the bag. In other words, "Heads I Win, Tails You Lose." The biggest losers of this game are the patients who are forced to accept watered-down medical care, something that no one would accept when buying whiskey, but which the country seems to have docilely accepted in life-and-death health care matters. Another set of likely losers will be U.S. taxpayers, who are funding the multi-billion dollar corporate bailouts disguised as coronavirus crisis relief funds.

Private Equity Owned Health Care Companies Lay Off Emergency Room Medical Professionals To Cut Costs During the Pandemic

As the coronavirus crisis was unfolding in the U.S., Emergency Room doctors, nurses, and other medical staff were on the front lines of the epic battle against COVID-19. ERs and ICU units were filled to overflowing, the medical staff was working long shifts or even 24/7 as necessary to try to stem the tide of illness and death that they faced every minute of every waking hour. They were often the only ones who were there to try and comfort those who would otherwise die alone, and in many cases, it was the medical professionals who were themselves dying for lack of proper protective gear. Yes, these were the true heroes of the crisis, and, no doubt, statues will be erected and parades gave in their honor when this is all over.

For private equity firms that owned the staffing companies and hospitals where these ER and ICU medical professionals worked, this was the least profitable part of the business. It is well known in health care investment circles that the real action and the money is in dermatology and expensive elective surgeries, with ER and ICU staffing considered only as a "loss leader" or low-profit margin venture. Since elective surgeries were being suspended and delayed as a result of the crisis, private equity firms started cutting other costs to try to keep a strong "bottom line" for their companies, notwithstanding the fact that they were in the middle of an unprecedented health care crisis. So, they started laying off ER doctors to the extent they could, and when they could not reduce the ER staff any further, they cut their pay.

Companies controlled by private equity firms also discharged doctors and other medical staff members who complained about hospital safety, lack of equipment, or other critical health care matters during the crisis. Dr. Ming Lin, a veteran ER doctor at PeaceHealth St. Joseph Medical Center in Bellingham, Washington, brought his concerns about the facilities' preparedness for the pandemic to the attention of the hospital administration.[44] Frustrated by what he considered to be their inadequate response, Lin took to social media, criticizing the hospital's operations in a series of posts. Several days later, the hospital removed Lin from the rotation in the emergency department.

Although Dr. Lin wanted to protest his removal, he could not complain to PeaceHealth, since the hospital was not his employer. Instead, his employer was TeamHealth, a physician practice and staffing company that provided the hospital with emergency room services. TeamHealth is owned by Blackstone Group, one of the largest equity finance companies, which bought it for $6.1 billion in 2016.[45] Dr. Lin's due process rights as an employee turned out to be non-existent. He never got a hearing. "One of the objectives is to point out any deficiencies in the system that may harm the patient," Dr. Lin told *NBC* News, "Because private equity has taken over health care, it has made that difficult."[46]

Mark Reiter, a program director of emergency medicine for the University of Tennessee and past president of American Academy of Emergency Medicine, has been blunter in his critique: "Private equity-backed health care has been a disaster for patients and for doctors," he told *NBC* News, adding, "Many decisions are made for what is going to maximize profits for the private equity company, rather than what is best for the patient, what is best for the community."[47]

Eileen Appelbaum, co-director of the Center for Economic and Policy Research in Washington, D.C., agrees that private equity firms have no legitimate role to play in the health care field. "We should not be running our health care system as a profit-making operation on steroids," she said, adding, "Health care is not so much anymore about taking care of patients. It's way more about making money."[48]

The COVID-19 Crisis Highlights the Urgent Need for a National Health Care System

As the coronavirus epidemic was exploding in New York, Governor Andrew Cuomo had the misfortune of experiencing "up close and personal" the consequences of the inefficiencies, conflicts of interest, balkanization, and confusion of the health care system as it scrambled to deal with the COVID-19 epidemic. As he said in mid-April, "No one hospital has the resources to handle this. There has to be a totally different operating paradigm where all those different hospitals operate as one system."⁴⁹ This "different operating paradigm" should be a national health care system.

The health care system in the U.S. has mostly failed to efficiently and effectively address this health care crisis since it is primarily designed to provide maximum short-term profits for private equity firms and other entrepreneurs, not to serve the general public and the greater good by making sure that it is prepared for this as well as the next health care crisis. In a crisis, there must be a coherent plan in place and someone clearly in charge of executing that plan. This can only be done through a national system. There must also be a national inventory stockpile of necessary equipment and health care supplies. Billionaire-owned private equity firms promote "just-in-time inventory management" that is good for profit margins but leaves these hospital systems vulnerable to shortages during a crisis.

* * * * *

If the U.S. learns anything of long-term significance from the coronavirus crisis, it is that the problems with our fragmented health care system are not just limited to the number of beds in our hospitals or the supply of personal protective equipment and ventilators. It is that we need a national health care system that is designed to meet the needs of the 21st Century, not the last one, and that is designed to provide the maximum health care coverage for all Americans at the lowest possible cost, not one designed to maximize the profits of private equity fund investors. The cost-cutting efficiencies and "just-in-time" model of health care systems designed to maximize profits for shareholders have proven to be disastrous when the health care system is confronted with a massive crisis such as that posed by COVID-19.

One of the reasons that New York City's medical care system rapidly approached a state of paralysis after only two or three weeks of the crisis had nothing to do with the inadequate emergency room and ICU capacity, or a lack of PPE and other vital equipment. Instead, it had to do with the fact that there was an almost total suspension of all normal health care activities that are the usual lifeblood and major revenue streams that hospitals depend on, including scheduled outpatient visits, procedures, and operations, as well as chemotherapy treatments.

Even though primary care is the most important sector of a health care system in terms of preventive medicine and treatment, primary care is a low-margin to negative-margin business for hospitals. Fancier elective operations and cancer therapy and things of that nature have much higher profit margins, which are then used by health care systems to remain profitable or at least break even, since they offset the losses from primary care.

If the Treasury Department and other federal agencies continue on their present course of action, which is to repeatedly commit billions of dollars for bailouts of the largely-broken health care systems, then the public and American taxpayers are entitled to a serious discussion in Congress about the re-organization of the health care system into something approaching a coherent national health care system. For far too long, our fractured health care system has been responsive to the business plans of private equity investors, not public policy.

While we are entering into a similar debate on systemic racism and policing in America, we urgently need to have a serious discussion as to what kind of health care system we want for our country. How can we make it more responsive to the genuine health needs of our communities and universally available to all Americans through existing payment mechanisms, such as Medicare, Medicaid, and the ACA? Or do we need some new comprehensive system of health insurance coverage?

Whatever the changes, they should involve a complete overhaul of the financial incentives for existing hospital systems. If they need to be bailed out with federal funds in times of crisis, we need to rethink both the short-term and long-term future of the health care system. In the short term, the most obvious solutions are to require hospitals to increase their excess capacity and stockpile more equipment so that elective surgeries and other medical treatments do not have to be completely suspended due to lack of capacity when the next health care crisis hits.

A greater emphasis on primary care, including "wellness" and preventative medicine, must be required either by regulatory reform or financial incentives, or both, if we are actually going to move forward to a truly effective health care system that is focused on the health and welfare of all Americans, not profits for the mega-rich.

33

ANXIETY, STRESS AND PSYCHOLOGICAL TRAUMA IN THE AGE OF COVID

"It felt like there was an anvil sitting on my chest."
-COVID-19 survivor describing panic attack

By mid- June 2020, more than two million people in the U.S. had been sickened by the coronavirus,[1] and there had been over 7.5 million cases worldwide.[2] By mid-July, over 135,000 had already died from the disease in the U.S. by then, with the number still rising at the rate of over 1,000 deaths per day. By mid-August, there were over 5 million cases and death toll was approaching 177,00 cases in the U.S. related to COVID-19.

But these are just dry statistics. They do not give the rest of us who had not yet caught the virus a sense of how frightening and traumatic the illness can really be. To be sure, some of us saw Chris Cuomo shaking with fever and chills on CNN as he broadcast his weekday evening show from his basement during his quarantine and recovery period. Knowing that he had a reputation of being a very physically fit and otherwise healthy person, seeing him on TV in such an obviously debilitated and weakened state gave us some sense of how severe this disease could be and how much more powerful and damaging it could be when compared to the seasonal flu.

The New York Times conducted extensive interviews with COVID-19 survivors, giving us some firsthand accounts of what it felt like to get slammed with the disease:[3]

- "I woke up with a headache... like someone inside my head was trying to push my eyes out... I put some onions in the Instant Pot to sauté. I put my face in the pot, but I couldn't smell the onions. My partner had a cough and shortness of breath. I would just start sobbing...We got nasal swabs together, and it felt like they took a piece of our brain."

    Aaron M. Kinchen, 39, Jersey City, New Jersey

- "Everything hurt. Nothing in my body felt like it was working. I felt so beat up like I had been in a boxing ring with Mike Tyson. I had a fever and chills — one minute, my teeth are chattering, and the next minute I am sweating like I am in a sauna. And the heavy, hoarse cough, my God. The cough rattled through my whole body."

    LaToya Henry, 43, Lathrup Village, Michigan

- "I felt like there was an anvil sitting on my chest...I've never really had a panic attack before, but I'd never felt anything like this ... What I was experiencing was not extreme difficulty breathing — it was panic about whether I had extreme difficulty breathing."

    David Hammer, 45, New Orleans, Louisiana

- "It's not like a common cold, where you feel a sore throat and sniffles. It just goes straight into your lungs, and you feel other symptoms coming from it. My stomach pain was so bad, it felt like I had appendicitis. I also had a bad cough, shortness of breath, and a heavy feeling in my lungs. I slept 19 hours a day, and it still didn't feel like enough... When it was over, I woke up feeling like a weight let go of me. It feels like I got a get-out-of-jail-free card now that I can move around outside a little more freely."

    - Thoka Maer, 35, New York, New York

- "Walking made me lose my breath. I was just gasping. It felt like drowning."

    Clement Chow, 38, Salt Lake City, Utah

- "It was just a loss of all energy and drive. There was no horizontal surface in my house that I didn't want to just lay down on all day long... I didn't want to do anything. And my brain wasn't working very well. I was calling it "the corona fog.""

   Mark Backlund, 73, *Anacortes, Washington*

- "It was chills on a level that I've never experienced. Intense shivering. It was very hard to move. I had really intense body aches. It felt like I was in a U.F.C. match and beaten up."

   Jared Miller, 27, *Brooklyn, New York*

- "My chest was tight, I was feverish... I lost seven pounds... They put me in an isolation room, took my vitals, swabs, and did a chest X-ray. It came back showing multifocal pneumonia. An E.R. doc said to me: "You can still breathe on your own. You're better off going home. If something changes, let me know, but we are about to run out of equipment in six days.""

   Lauren Taylor, 71, *New York, New York*

- "Attached to the ventilator, I slept for the next six days or so...When I woke up, I felt like Rip Van Winkle. It was as if those six days never happened. In my first conversation with my husband after extubation, I returned to the exact same topic we had been discussing right before I was intubated."

   David Lat, 44, *New York, New York*

- "I've never felt so bizarre. My body felt like it was not my own. I had crazy back pain. Sometimes I felt like I couldn't move my shoulders. I had a raw, dry cough, and the fevers spiked in the night. I have a C-section scar from 10 years ago that hurt again because I was coughing so much."

   Kadambari Wade, 44, *Chadler, Arizona*

The Long-Term Emotional and Psychological Impacts of COVID-19

While those who survived the infection were obviously far better off than those who did not, their status as "survivors" did not automatically mean they had fully recovered and were back to the same level of generally good health as they were experiencing before their bout with the virus. And many of the survivors continued to suffer from long-term physical effects from the disease. For example, impaired lung function from the coronavirus infection often affected other organs like the heart, kidneys, and brain, with significant health impacts that could last well after the patient had substantially "recovered" from the infection's initial onslaught. Many surviving patients who had COVID-19 developed acute respiratory distress syndrome (ARDS), which placed them at higher risk of long-term health issues.[4] Others who had lost their sense of taste and smell never fully recovered these two senses.[5]

But in addition to these physical symptoms and risks that COVID-19 patients faced, there were also risks of psychological trauma and what is generally known as "hospital delirium."[6] One coronavirus survivor, Kim Victory, reported feeling like she was paralyzed on a bed and burned alive.[7] According to Ms. Victory, someone rescued her just in time, but suddenly, she was turned into an ice sculpture on a fancy cruise ship buffet. Next, she believed that she was a subject of an experiment in a lab in Japan and that she pleaded with the Japanese scientists to release her, telling them, "I am an American, and I have a right to eat a cheeseburger and drink Coca-Cola," she recalled. Ms. Victory also imagined that cats were attacking her.

These nightmarish visions seemed so real and terrifying that while still in the hospital on a ventilator for severe respiratory failure caused by the coronavirus, she became so agitated that she pulled out her breathing tubes. "It was so real, and I was so scared," said Ms. Victory, who lives in Franklin, Tennessee.[8]

Reports from hospitals and researchers suggest that about two-thirds to three-quarters of coronavirus patients in ICU's have experienced hospital delirium in one form or another. Some have "hyperactive delirium," or paranoid hallucinations and agitation, while others have "hypoactive delirium," which is internalized visions and confusion that cause patients to become withdrawn and incommunicative. Some have both.

Some recover reasonably quickly, while others have lingering long-term effects. "There's increased risk for temporary or even permanent cognitive deficits," said Dr. Lawrence Kaplan, director of consultation-liaison psychiatry at the University of California, San Francisco Medical Center, "It is actually more devastating than people realize."[9]

The incidence of hospital delirium among coronavirus cases is particularly acute since ICU patients have long stints on ventilators and are usually heavily sedated and sleep deprived. Patients on ventilators are forced to be immobile for long periods of time and are often restrained to keep them from accidentally disconnecting tubes. Patients have been cut off from social interactions with family members, and the only people they see are medical providers who wear face-obscuring protective gear.

The oxygen depletion and inflammation that many seriously ill coronavirus patients experience can affect the brain and other organs besides the lungs. Kidney or liver failure can lead to a buildup of delirium-promoting medications in the blood. Some patients develop small blood clots that do not cause strokes but can trigger subtle circulation disruption that may lead to cognitive problems and delirium.[10]

The Looming Health Care Crisis

However, no matter how hard we try to manage the increased stress and anxiety of this pandemic on our own, there are tens and indeed hundreds of thousands of us who either suffered from severe anxiety, depression or other mental illnesses before this crisis ever hit, and are now at an even higher risk than before of having our health care issues entirely overwhelm us. The daily barrage of negative news that we feel forced to follow in excruciating detail is extremely difficult, if not impossible, for all but the healthiest and most resilient of us to handle without professional help. In addition, the isolation and both reasonable and unreasonable waves of fear that people are experiencing are, according to many experts, generating widespread psychological trauma.[11]

Federal agencies and experts warn that a historic wave of mental-health problems is fast approaching, including depression, substance abuse, post-traumatic stress disorder, and suicide.[12]

Just as the initial COVID-19 outbreak caught hospitals unprepared, the U.S. mental health system may be even less prepared to handle the coming surge of serious mental health cases that are being precipitated by the pandemic. "That's what is keeping me up at night," said Susan Borja, who leads the traumatic stress research program at the National Institute of Mental Health, "I worry about the people the system just won't absorb or won't reach. I worry about the suffering that's going to go untreated on such a large scale."[13]

The suicides of two New York health-care workers highlighted these increased risks. Lorna Breen, a New York emergency room doctor, committed suicide after having spent weeks contending with coronavirus patients flooding her hospital.[14] She had no history of mental illness but was reported to have had increased difficulties coping with the emotional weight of handling a massive volume of coronavirus cases and death every day. In addition, there were reports that a Bronx emergency medical technician, John Mondello, had killed himself after less than three months on the job.[15] Mr. Mondello expressed his reservations about his new position to a fellow EMT colleague, mentioning his dislike for the job due in part to the constant exposure to death.[16] He had no previously reported mental health diagnosis.[17]

It is not unusual for the rates of suicides, overdose deaths, and substance abuse disorders to go up after a natural disaster, and the current pandemic certainly qualifies as a natural disaster of global proportions. Meanwhile, therapists and community behavioral health centers have had severe difficulties in maintaining their practices online and in connecting with vulnerable people. There are both licensing restrictions imposed by states for them to maintain online practices, and insurance companies and the government often make it difficult to obtain payment or reimbursement for their services.

"If we don't do something about it now, people are going to be suffering from these mental-health impacts for years to come," said Paul Gionfriddo, president of the advocacy group Mental Health America.[18] Gionfriddo also mentioned that as individuals flood emergency rooms with panic attacks, overdoses, and depression-related symptoms, the economy could be harmed due to the constant stress and anxiety put on workers in the medical field.[19]

In order to deal with the surge in mental and behavioral health needs, the country's capacity to provide mental health screenings is as important as the availability of diagnostic testing for coronavirus. There also needs to be better access to counseling and therapeutic service through online telehealth and additional funding for mental health programs at federal, state, and local levels.

Coronavirus Depression and Opioid Overdoses

Drug overdoses have sharply accelerated since the pandemic began.[20] This alarming increase in drug overdoses quickly developed into a hidden epidemic within the pandemic. The continued isolation, economic devastation, and disruptions to the drug trade since the start of the crisis contributed to this surge in drug overdoses. Suspected overdoses nationally jumped 18% in March compared with the prior year (2019), 29% in April, and 42% in May, according to the Overdose Detection Mapping Application Program.[21] In some jurisdictions, such as Milwaukee County, dispatch calls for overdoses have increased by over 50%.[22]

When the pandemic hit, some authorities hoped it would lead to a decrease in overdoses by disrupting drug traffic as borders closed and cities shut down. The opposite seems to be happening. As traditional supply lines were disrupted, people who use drugs appear to have sought out new suppliers and substances they are less familiar with, increasing the risk of overdose and death. Synthetic drugs and less common substances started increasingly showing up in autopsies and toxicology reports.

Social distancing has also sequestered people, leaving them to take drugs alone and making it less likely that someone else will be there to call 911 or to administer the life-saving overdose antidote naloxone, also known as Narcan.

In addition, many treatment centers, drug courts, and recovery programs have been forced to close or significantly scale back during shutdowns. With plunging revenue for services and little financial relief from the government, many had to close their doors as they faced financial collapse.

Even before the pandemic, the nation's infrastructure for helping people with substance use disorders was underfunded and inadequate. Without substantial government intervention, it is a virtual certainty that overdoses and deaths will continue to climb during the pandemic, and the existing system will be swamped. Emergency funding is desperately needed to keep these treatment programs, recovery centers, and needle-exchange programs afloat. Medical associations have also urged federal officials to relax restrictive barriers to opioid treatments such as buprenorphine, and called for broader distribution of naloxone.

The Trump administration repeatedly cited the possible rise of overdoses and suicides as a reason why the states and businesses needed to reopen quickly. Yet, of the nearly $2.5 trillion approved for emergency relief, Congress and the Trump administration have designated only $425 million — barely more than a hundredth of 1% — for mental health and substance use treatment.[23]

The Close Correlation Between Economic Upheaval and Mental Health

Mental-health experts are especially worried about the ongoing economic devastation. Research has established a strong link between economic upheaval, suicide and substance use. A study of the Great Recession that began in late 2007 found that for every percentage point increase in the unemployment rate, there was about a 1.6% increase in the suicide rate.[24] Using such estimates, a Texas nonprofit — Meadows Mental Health Policy Institute — created models suggesting that if unemployment amid the coronavirus pandemic ends up rising 5% points to a level similar to the Great Recession, an additional 4,000 people could die of suicide and an additional 4,800 from drug overdoses.[25] But if unemployment rises by 20% points — to levels recorded during the 1930s Great Depression — suicides could increase by 18,000 and overdose deaths by more than 22,000.[26]

So, just as the federal government should have implemented a more robust early warning system to alert Americans to the spread of the pandemic to the U.S., the country also needed to engage in immediate health system planning for the inevitable increases in suicides and overdoses. The problem is that the reporting of an increase in suicides can itself cause a contagion of additional suicides. "Could the numbers go up? Yes, but it isn't inevitable. We know suicide is preventable," said Christine Moutier, chief medical officer for the American Foundation for Suicide Prevention.[27]

There is a wide range of prevention and treatment options when faced with a mental health crisis. The ready access of people at risk to rapid screening for suicidal thoughts, and the treatment of underlying psychological conditions to ensure access to therapy and crisis hotlines is essential. More than 250 mental health groups, including the National Institute for Mental Health, announced that they were coordinating a national response to the problem of pandemic suicide.[28] Their first priority was to provide mental health support to front line workers, such as health care providers, grocery store workers, delivery people, and others who were especially vulnerable during the ongoing crisis.

"It Chips Away at Your Soul"

The medical staffs of hospital ERs and ICUs were particularly hard hit by the fallout from the daily stress and anxiety they had to try to deal with. A study of 1,257 doctors and nurses in Wuhan and other areas of China during that country's coronavirus crisis in late 2019 and early 2020 found that 50% of the medical staff reported depression, 45% said they experienced anxiety, and 34% reported insomnia.[29] It is estimated that the incidence of mental distress was about the same in New York City and other U.S. epicenters of the outbreak in this country, and anecdotal stories from doctors and nurses in New York actively supported this assumption.

Day after day, ER and ICU medical personnel had to watch the same heart-wrenching scenes of families pleading and crying in hospital ambulance bays, not being able to enter the hospital with their loved ones and knowing they may never see them again. Inside the hospitals, there were the beeping sounds of crashing patients and respiratory arrests every few minutes. Other patients were being sent home because they were not quite sick enough, knowing they would probably be coming right back the next day. Or never at all. The survival rate for patients intubated and put on ventilators was so abysmal that sometimes only 10% of those patients survived.[30] The recent introduction of the use of Decadron (dexamethasone) on intubated patients has improved survival rate on ventilators by 30%, but this still means that most of the patients put on ventilators do not survive.

"It chips away at your soul," said Dr. Flavia Nobay, who had come all the way from Rochester, New York to volunteer as an ER in Queens. "You have to hold on to the positive and how you're helping in the ways you can. That hope is like medicine. It's as important and tangible as Tylenol."[31]

Even before the coronavirus crisis erupted, doctors and nurses were psychologically burning out due to the pressures of long hours, workloads, and the general chaos and disorganization of an increasingly dysfunctional health care system. "We're now hitting a period of uncertainty where a lot of people are asking themselves how long they can keep it up," said Liselotte Dyrbye, a Mayo Clinic doctor and a leading researcher on burnout, "The teapot can only boil for so long."[32]

While some of these problems may be transitory, such as increased stress and insomnia, more severe issues such as post-traumatic stress disorder and severe depression require treatment by a mental health professional. "To control the virus, it's all about testing, testing, testing. And for the mental health problems ahead, it's going to be all about screening, screening, screening," said Paul Gionfriddo, CEO of Mental Health America.[33] These screening questionnaires, which are readily available on most websites of mental health organizations, are the first important step in the evaluation process for mental health problems. Since the pandemic began, those daily screenings have increased by 60 to 70%.[34]

The Mental Health Crisis Is Only Getting Worse

In the U.S., research shows that one in five adults suffers from some form of mental illness each year.[35] And that was before the coronavirus crisis hit. Yet less than half of those who experience some form of mental illness receive any treatment, according to federal statistics.[36] As suicide rates have fallen around the world, the rate in the U.S. has risen every year since 1999, increasing 33% in the past two decades.[37] Although no clear statistics are available in the age of COVID, all indications point to a further spike in the suicide rate during the coronavirus crisis.

A significant part of the problem is the markedly different way the U.S. treats mental illness compared with physical illness. If you have a heart attack, you will probably be seen almost immediately by a cardiologist in the ER of your local hospital, and if necessary the EMTs who take you to the hospital by ambulance have the equipment and training to maximize your chances of survival. But if you are having a mental health crisis, the chances of you quickly seeing a psychiatrist or other mental health professional in the ER or elsewhere are much smaller. You may not even get admitted to the hospital if your insurance coverage does not cover it. Especially during a pandemic, the likelihood of getting any attention for your mental health issues is slim to none unless you do something dramatic, like try to commit suicide or engage in some bizarre behavior; however, that will often land you in jail rather than a hospital psych ward. Hoarding all of the toilet paper from the local grocery store will probably not be enough to get you arrested, but it will probably not take much more than that to draw the attention of your local law enforcement.

As the mental health crisis worsened, the American Psychological Association, the American Psychiatric Association, the National Alliance on Mental Illness, and 12 other organizations asked federal officials to save community mental health centers facing financial collapse.[38] In a letter to Congress in early April, these mental health organizations estimated that $38.5 billion was needed to save treatment providers and centers and that $10 billion more was needed to respond to the coronavirus pandemic.[39] The federal Substance Abuse and Mental Health Agency (SAMHA) said it had awarded $375 million to states and local organizations and allocated another $425 million in emergency funding to deal with this mental health epidemic, but this was only a small fraction of the amount that these mental health groups said was needed.[40]

These mental health organizations also asked the federal government to lift reimbursement restrictions that have prevented therapists from using "telehealth" phone calls to treat patients.[41] Without receiving insurance reimbursements for therapy sessions with patients by phone, Skype, Zoom, or other electronic means, these health and drug addiction centers were facing financial collapse, which would obviously prevent them from providing any additional mental health services just when it was needed the most. More than 60% said they were running out of funding and had already closed some programs.[42]

While Congress recently authorized $100 billion in emergency funds for hospitals and medical providers, very little was earmarked for mental health and addiction service providers because they mainly receive funding through Medicaid. And most of the emergency provider money is being distributed through Medicare. "We are facing the loss of mental health centers and programs at a time when we are going to need them more than ever," said Chuck Ingoglia, president of the National Council for Behavioral Health, which represents 3,326 treatment organizations.[43]

* * * * *

As the U.S. is haltingly and inconsistently dealing with the physical symptoms caused by COVID-19 infections and illnesses, it must also deal with what will inevitably be the equally dangerous but less noticed "second wave" of the coronavirus crisis: the heightened mental health epidemic that has engulfed our nation. Without a vigorous response to this mental health crisis, the number of "collateral damage" victims of the pandemic will be far greater than the mere COVID-19 case statistics indicate.

34

"LIVE AND LET DIE": SOME STATES RECKLESSLY TRY TO REOPEN WITHOUT MEETING FEDERAL GUIDELINES, WITH DISASTROUS RESULTS

"People will die. People do die."[1]
– Quote from a Wall Street Investment Banker

On Wednesday, July 29, the U.S. passed the grim milestone of 150,000 reported coronavirus-related deaths, a number higher than in any other country and nearly a quarter of the world's total.[2] Of the 20 countries with the biggest outbreaks, the United States ranked sixth in deaths per capita, at 4.5 fatalities per 10,000 people. Only the U.K., Spain, Italy, Peru, and Chile had higher per capita rates, with U.S. deaths making up nearly 23% of the global total of 660,997.[3]

All 50 states had started easing coronavirus-related restrictions by late June, but some states that did so without meeting the federal guidelines for reopening were forced to reimpose some restrictions when the number of cases and deaths sharply rose.[4] "You have 50 different governors doing 50 different things," said Andrew Noymer, an associate professor of public health at the University of California, Irvine, "There will be states that open too soon or states that are too conservative. It is hard to thread the needle."[5]

Experts warned that the number of cases and COVID-related deaths would increase in states that eased restrictions without adhering to the federal guidelines, including the requirement that there be a downward trajectory for at least 14 days in the number of cases before a state should start reopening.[6] Ashish Jha, director of the Harvard Global Health Institute, emphasized that "the first part of the criteria is sustained decline. And we don't see that."[7]

In addition to the "14-day decline" criteria for a state to reopen, "Phase One" of the federal guidelines also required that states meet a benchmark regarding the number of daily tests conducted in each state, with the minimum number of tests varying depending on the state's population.[8] The minimum recommended number of coronavirus tests performed by these states was 152 tests per 100,000 people daily.[9]

Harvard's Global Health Institute proposed that, overall, the U.S. should be doing more than 900,000 tests per day as a country if it safely wanted to start reopening its economy.[10] This research team at Harvard published a simulation projecting the amount of testing needed in each state by May 15, finding that 41 states fell short of that benchmark.[11] Only nine states were near or had already surpassed the testing minimums projected by Harvard: Alaska, Hawaii, Montana, North Dakota, Oregon, Tennessee, Utah, West Virginia, and Wyoming.

Dr. Anthony S. Fauci took the opportunity during an interview on NBC's "Today Show" to emphasize: "The guidelines are very, very explicit, and very clear. There's a lot of leeway because we allow the governors to be flexible, but you have to have the core principles of the guidelines. You can't just leap over things and get into a situation where you're really tempting a rebound."[12] Deborah Birx, the White House coronavirus task force coordinator, also called on the states to follow the guidelines, saying, "We've made it clear what the gating criteria is."[13]

Many of the States Play A Deadly Game of "Russian Roulette" By Reopening Too Soon

By early May, numerous states – such as Georgia, Texas, Indiana, Colorado, North Dakota, and Florida – had relaxed social distancing guidelines even as the number of people testing positive in their states was continuing to increase, and testing in those states was lagging behind.[14] President Trump himself strongly supported the push by these states to reopen, notwithstanding the lack of compliance with the federal guidelines. Trump downplayed his administration's own guidelines in favor of a broad economic reopening that many experts said was courting disaster in terms of the danger of fanning the flames of the coronavirus brushfires still burning throughout the country. Trump even went so far as to criticize some Democratic governors for not easing up on their state restrictions. Trump singled out Virginia Governor Ralph Northam, a pediatric neurologist by profession, for his reluctance to quickly ease social distancing measures, telling Fox News that it was one of the states that "aren't going fast enough."[15] Trump also expressed support for protesters in two other states – Michigan and Wisconsin – tweeting about the need to "LIBERATE"[16] those states from the restrictions imposed by their Democratic governors, even though the federal guidelines indicated that those states should remain in lockdown.

Trump did momentarily break character when he criticized Georgia Governor Brian Kemp, a fellow Republican, for starting to open up his state in defiance of the federal guidelines. On April 23, Trump said that he was "not happy" with Governor Kemp's decision to open up tattoo parlors, nail salons, and barbershops, that cannot be operated without violating social distancing rules.[17] Two weeks later, however, Trump was fully back in character, denying that he had criticized the Georgia Governor: "I didn't say that," Trump flatly said when his quote about Governor Kemp was read back to him.

Unsurprisingly, the states that jumped the gun and started reopening without meeting these federal guidelines saw their cases numbers and deaths sharply increase. The data during the month of May showed that the number of new coronavirus cases was increasing in about one-third of the states; that most of the states were still hovering around the same levels; and that a few of the states – such as New York, New Jersey, and Connecticut – had case numbers that were declining, although still substantial.[18] The downward trajectory of cases in the tri-state area did not necessarily indicate that these three states had contained the outbreak. Cases in New York, for example, were still averaging more than 3,000 new cases daily during May,[19] which meant that it was still too early to open up New York City and the surrounding downstate New York area where most of the cases were occurring.

In contrast to the states that kept most of the social distancing restriction in place and continued to show a downward trajectory in their case and death numbers as of mid-May, new coronavirus cases were notably rising in Texas, Alabama and North Dakota, three of the states that have begun to lift shutdown measures.[20]

In Texas, for example, new cases were down in mid-April but began to rise in early May. Nevertheless, Texas Governor Greg Abbott, a Republican, went ahead with a plan to reopen the state's stores, restaurants, movie theaters, and malls provided that they operated at less than 25% of capacity.[21] Almost like clockwork, on May 16, Texas reported its single-day high in new cases as well as deaths, which was about 14 days after the beginning of the state's phased reopening.[22]

Tennessee Governor Bill Lee, also a Republican, let the state's stay-at-home order expire in late April despite the increase in reported cases and replaced it with a far less restrictive set of rules that allowed restaurants, shops, and fitness centers to reopen in nearly all of the state.[23] Hair and nail salons were permitted to open about one week later.[24]

Expert Studies Warned of a Rebound In Case Numbers and Deaths In Up to 24 States

Experts warned of a rebound in coronavirus outbreaks and hot spots. "We don't have the testing. We don't have the contract tracing. We can't detect a rebound," said Jeffrey Shaman, an epidemiologist at Columbia University, "It's a really problematic place to be. This is not where we want to be."[25]

An analysis of cellphone data in late May ominously showed that people were moving around much more than before, and that it was probable the coronavirus was already starting to spread rapidly in 24 states, particularly in the South and Midwest, which had reopened too quickly or without sufficient precautions.[26] Researchers at Imperial College London found that an examination of cellphone data showed that people sharply reduced their movements after stay-at-home orders were broadly imposed in March, but that when these restrictions were eased, and mobility increased approaching Memorial Day weekend, the unofficial start of summer, there was a dramatic increase in people's movement.[27]

The Imperial College researchers estimated the virus's reproduction number, known as "R_0," or "R naught."[28] This is the average number of infections generated by each infected person in a vulnerable population.

The researchers found the reproduction number had dropped below 1 in the District of Columbia and 26 states, and that in those places, as of May 17, the epidemic was waning.²⁹ If the R0 number dropped below 1, it meant that the virus had hit a lot of dead ends and could not continue to multiply its infection rate because the people already infected have been isolated or were practicing social distancing to the point where they could not infect others.³⁰

However, in the other 24 states, the model showed a reproduction number over 1, which meant that the virus could still rapidly spread through the population. Texas topped the list of these "high at-risk" states, followed by Arizona, Illinois, Colorado, Ohio, Minnesota, Indiana, Iowa, Alabama, Wisconsin, Mississippi, Tennessee, Florida, Virginia, New Mexico, Missouri, Delaware, South Carolina, Massachusetts, North Carolina, California, Pennsylvania, Louisiana, and Maryland.³¹

In some of the states that were still experiencing some of the highest infection rates, the governors were among the most aggressive in discarding all restrictions and opening up their states to the maximum extent possible. For example, in Mississippi, where the Imperial College model predicted a rapid rise in infections, Republican Governor Tate Reeves said he was ready to reopen the last few businesses that remain closed in the state, including racetracks and water parks: "We will be out of the business of closing down anybody, I hope," Governor Reeves said.³² Similarly, on Thursday, May 21, Alabama Republican Governor Kay Ivey staunchly defended her decision to reopen concert venues, movie theaters, and other businesses despite rising case numbers: "We cannot sustain a delayed way of life as we search for a vaccine," she said, "Having a life means having a livelihood, too."³³

Although many of these governors said that they would clamp the lid back down if the number of cases started to spike upwards, this would be virtually impossible to do once the genie was out of the bottle. After all, there was generally a two to three week lag between an outbreak in virus infections and when hospitals started reporting their ERs and ICU units were being flooded with new COVID-19 cases, so the re-deployment of stay-at-home orders and other restrictions would only come, if at all, several weeks after the epidemic had taken off again. As David Aronoff, director of the Vanderbilt University Infectious Disease Division, put it, "If a surge happens, the tricky part will be putting the toothpaste back in the tube" by shutting down again.[34]

Some Federal and State Officials Start Manipulating the Data For Political Purposes

Not all of the chaos relating to testing was inadvertent. Some of it was intentionally distorted for political purposes. Federal and state officials across the country deliberately altered or hid public health data crucial to tracking the coronavirus' spread, hindering the ability to detect a surge of infections as President Donald Trump pushed the nation to reopen rapidly.[35]

According to an investigation by *Politico*, at least a dozen state health departments inflated testing numbers or deflated death tallies by changing criteria for who counts as a coronavirus victim and what counts as a coronavirus test.[36] Some states even shifted the metrics for a "safe" reopening. For example, Arizona sought to clamp down on bad news at one point by simply closing down its pandemic modeling. In addition, about a third of the states stopped reporting hospital admission data, which was a bright red flag suggesting a resurgence of the virus in those states.[37] Perhaps the most shocking example of data manipulation was by a federal agency, when the previously well-reputed CDC blended diagnostic and antibody tests, artificially boosting the nation's overall testing numbers and giving President Trump a meaningless "talking point" during his marathon White House daily briefings.[38]

This inconsistent and spotty data flow was extremely troublesome, especially for public health officials who were trying to help Americans decide how and when to venture out and start going about their lives again safely. The lack of accurate and consistent COVID-19 data, coupled with the fact that the White House no longer was holding regular briefings where officials could reinforce the need for ongoing social distancing, made it increasingly difficult for state officials to convince citizens that it was still crucial for them to comply with mitigation measures.[39]

New examples of states improperly manipulating data emerged on an almost daily basis. For instance, in late May, the District of Columbia used a "community spread" metric — excluding nursing homes, correctional facilities, and others from official statistics— as a justification for reopening.[40] Similarly, Iowa Governor Kim Reynolds told reporters that the state would only share information about outbreaks at meatpacking plants upon request.[41] Moreover, Georgia failed for weeks to differentiate between diagnostic and antibody testing, the two types of coronavirus tests that were being conducted. It instead just merged them into a lump sum for testing totals that were being publicly released, rendering the results misleading or, at the very least, relatively meaningless.[42]

Irwin Redlener, a public health expert at Columbia University, said, "All these stories about undercounts, overcounts, miscounts, are undermining our ability to deal with the pandemic."[43] The country, he said, was confronting an "unheard-of level of chaos in the data, the protocols, the information."[44]

Meanwhile, some officials within the Trump administration started using inaccurate scientific evidence and models to bolster their arguments favoring a quick reopening. HHS Secretary Alex Azar, for example, warned that if the country does not get back to normalcy soon, the U.S. could see an additional 65,000 "deaths of despair" from increased suicides and drug overdoses.[45] However, an ethics center at Harvard quickly rebuked the White House for misleadingly citing numbers from one of its studies to buttress the administration's "reopen America" campaign.[46] "Some might use this report to argue that this is why our economy needs to open up fast. But that's NOT what we are saying," wrote the authors of the report, which was published by the American Academy of Family Physicians and Well Being Trust.[47] "Even as of today parts of the country are opening, data suggest that this is premature due to a lack of consistent testing, which allows public health authorities to trace, treat and isolate to prevent further spread."[48]

The White House Drags Its Feet In Issuing Expanded CDC's "Reopening" Guidelines

While states started reopening in breach of the existing federal guidelines, the CDC had still not issued a more expansive set of guidelines that had been promised to give the states additional guidance on how they could reopen safely. On Tuesday, May 12, during a Senate hearing, CDC Director Redfield said that an expansive set of CDC guidelines for states to open would be released "soon," but did not specify precisely when "soon" would be.[49] "Soon isn't terribly helpful," Senator Chris Murphy, Democrat of Connecticut, replied in a heated exchange about whether his state, which has a stay-at-home order expiring in the next few days, would know how to reopen correctly.[50] Mr. Murphy said the existing guidelines released by the White House in April were inadequate. A draft CDC report, which was leaked to The *Washington Post* in early May, predicted a sharp increase in both cases and deaths beginning May 14, with the surge reaching about 200,000 cases per day by June 1, with more than 3,000 deaths each day.[51]

On Thursday, May 7, the *Associated Press* reported that the White House shelved a report from the CDC detailing how local governments and businesses can begin reopening during the pandemic.[52] The report, entitled "Guidance for Implementing the Opening Up America Again Framework," was supposed to be released the following day, but CDC scientists were told it "would never see the light of day," according to an anonymous CDC official.[53] The guidance from the CDC was intended to help guide religious leaders, business owners, educators, and state and local officials as they begin to reopen amid an increase in business closures and unemployment claims.[54] However, according to internal government emails obtained by the *Associated Press*, the guidance had been approved by CDC Director Redfield, who had sent the documents up the chain to top officials. However, political appointees reportedly decided the shelve the guidance.[55]

On May 14, the CDC released a dumbed-down version of the guidance relating to reopening, which consisted of six one-page guides called "decision tools" to be used by workplaces, restaurants and bars, schools, childcare centers and mass transit systems that were reconsidering opening during the pandemic.[56] This was a heavily edited version of a draft report written at least one month previously that had been shelved by Trump administration officials. Senator Charles Schumer of New York objected vociferously to the shelving of the CDC's entire report, stating: "America needs and must have the candid guidance of our best scientists unfiltered, unedited, uncensored by President Trump or his political minions. The CDC report on reopening the country is an important piece of that guidance."[57]

To try and fill this vacuum created by the decision of the White House to hold up the issuance of any sensible protocols to guide the states in their reopening process, more than 20 experts banded together to formulate some clear guidelines, published under the hashtag "#OpenSafely." This group was led by former Centers for Medicare and Medicaid Services (CMS) acting administrator Andy Slavitt, former FDA commissioner and CMS administrator Mark McClellan, and about 20 other experts. These unofficial guidelines set forth the conditions that needed to be in place before the states could safely reopen, including a 14-day consistent reduction in the number of new coronavirus cases and a yardstick for measuring whether there was enough testing capacity in each state that was reopening.[58]

Public Pressure Forces the CDC to Release the Edited "Guidance" Document

On May 20, the CDC quietly posted a 60-page document on its website without a formal announcement setting forth guidance for reopening schools, mass transit, and nonessential businesses. This new release, entitled "Opening Up America Again"[59] - which was vaguely dated "May 2020" without specifying any particular day - came after numerous states had already lifted their stay-at-home orders and begun the reopening process. The CDC did not hold a briefing form the public and the press to announce this highly important document, just as the CDC had not held any other briefing on the pandemic for the past two months.

The CDC's May 2020 document was extremely dense, complex, and difficult to follow, almost as if it was intended to create more confusion than clarity. Experts who read it commented that it was unlike any other CDC document previously issued. This often-contradictory document outlined a "three-phased approach" for reducing social distancing and proposed the use of six "gating" indicators to assess when to move through another phase. The "gating" indicators included decreases in newly reported COVID-19 cases and emergency room visits as well as a "robust" testing program.⁶⁰ However, it failed to define what the criteria was for a finding that a state's testing program was sufficiently "robust."

Oddly, this "Opening Up America Again" document was released by the White House, rather than the CDC, which highlighted the extent to which the Trump administration had sidelined this premier health agency during the coronavirus crisis. In addition, the release of this watered-down "guidance" after most of the states were already beginning to reopen for business came far too late to have any real impact on the decisions being made by state officials.

The Reopening of the States Becomes a Political Football, Rather Than a Public Health Decision

In some political swing states, such as Wisconsin, Michigan, and Pennsylvania, the reopening issue became a political football, especially where Democratic governors and Republican-controlled legislatures were taking contrary positions.⁶¹ In Wisconsin, the Republican-controlled Legislature filed a lawsuit in state court challenging the statewide stay-at-home order issued by Democratic Governor Tony Evers.⁶² And on May 13, the Wisconsin Supreme Court sided with the state legislature, completely overturning the state's lockdown orders and, overnight, allowing the bars, restaurants, and other businesses to reopen immediately.

In Michigan, the stay-at-home and other mitigation orders issued by Democratic Governor Gretchen Whitmer also precipitated political protests, as hundreds of protesters, many of them armed, turned out at the State Capitol in a drenching rainstorm. The confrontation became so intense and supercharged that the state capitol was temporarily closed, and the legislative session was canceled after death threats were directed toward Governor Whitmer.⁶³

In Pennsylvania, some county lawmakers defied the Democratic governor's orders to keep nonessential businesses closed. This protest movement won the support of President Trump, who then flew to Allentown, Pennsylvania, to tour a medical supply facility (not wearing a mask, of course).⁶⁴ Democratic Governor Thomas Wolf forcefully responded to the Republican legislators who were defying the stay-at-home directives: "To those politicians who decide to cave in to this coronavirus," he said, "they need to understand the consequences of their cowardly act."[65]

Trump Makes It Clear That the Reopening of the Economy Was A Higher Priority Than Public Health

On May 5, during a tour of a Honeywell factory in Arizona that had switched from manufactured aerospace equipment to producing respirator masks, Trump again refused to wear a face mask, despite signs near the factory floor announcing safety guidelines that included the admonition, "Please wear your mask at all times." He delivered blatantly partisan political remarks after touring the plant, but it was the strange soundtrack that played in the background that attracted the most press attention. As Trump made his usual political pitch about how great the federal response was to the coronavirus crisis, the soundtrack of "Live and Let Die" by the classic hard rock band Guns N' Roses blared over loudspeakers. Late-night talk show host Jimmy Kimmel commented on the moment: "I can think of no better metaphor for this presidency than Donald Trump not wearing a face mask to a face mask factory while the song 'Live and Let Die' blares in the background," he wrote on Twitter.[66]

During his Honeywell plant tour in Arizona, Trump also made it clear that additional American lives had to be sacrificed to revive the economy quickly, and that his administration's efforts to short-circuit the reopening process had to be made at the expense of good public health protocols: "Will some people be affected? Yes," he said. "Will some people be affected badly? Yes. But we have to get our country open, and we have to get it open soon," Trump said, directly acknowledging there will be a real, negative human cost in prioritizing an economic revival over a more cautious approach in favor of public health. But even as the president advocated for a quick return to business as usual, Trump and his administration were being frustrated by the fact that the nation's governors remain in control of decision-making for their respective states.[67]

Trump Continues to Press States to Reopen Even Though the White House Was Privately Receiving "Doomsday" Projections About a Huge Second Wave

As President Trump pressed the states to reopen their economies, his administration was privately projecting a steady rise in the number of coronavirus cases and deaths over the next several weeks. It was estimated that the daily death toll would reach about 3,000 on June 1, according to an internal document compiled by F.E.M.A., which would represent a 70% increase from the early May numbers of about 1,750 per day.[68] These government forecasts also estimated that there would be about 200,000 new cases daily by the end of May, up from about 25,000 cases a day earlier in that month. The Institute for Health Metrics and Evaluation at the University of Washington also increased its estimates in early May to nearly 135,000 deaths in the U.S. relating to COVID-19 through the beginning of August, more than double what it was forecasting on April 17, when it estimated 60,308 deaths by August 4.[69] The Institute said that the revisions reflected "rising mobility in most U.S. states as well as the easing of social distancing measures expected in 31 states by May 11, indicating that growing contacts among people will promote transmission of the coronavirus."[70] As it turned out, the actual results were far worse than even these dire predictions, as the number of COVID-related deaths in the U.S. topped 150,000 by the end of July.

Throughout May, Trump continued to try to build a groundswell of support across the country for a reopening of the states, no matter what. When asked if he thought the number of deaths would rise as a result of reopening, Trump said, "Hopefully that won't be the case," but added, "It could very well be the case ... But we have to get our country open again ... People want to go back, and you're going to have a problem if you don't do it."[71]

On the theory that if you shut your eyes real tight and hold your breath, bad things may sometimes go away, Trump also made an aborted attempt to shut down his coronavirus task force. But when he received a chorus of opposition telling him that it was too soon for that, he reversed himself and vowed to keep the task force going "indefinitely." He also promised that by-then familiar experts like Dr. Anthony Fauci and Dr. Deborah L. Birx would remain on the task force. However, Trump signaled that the goal of the task force on a going-forward basis would be to figure out how to open up the country safely, rather than combatting the disease itself. "I thought we could wind it down sooner," Mr. Trump told reporters as he hosted a group of nurses in the Oval Office, "But I had no idea how popular the task force is until actually yesterday. When I started talking about winding it down, I got calls from very respected people saying, 'I think it would be better to keep it going.'"[72]

Trump's concentration on the issue of reopening rather than on the spread of the disease across the country and its deadly consequences seemed to reflect a growing fatalism and pessimism in the White House about its ability ever to get any real control of the situation. "I think he has given up on the hard stuff and as a consequence is writing off people's lives," said Andy Slavitt, the acting administrator of the Centers for Medicare and Medicaid Services under President Barack Obama.[73] Jacob S. Hacker, the director of the Institution for Social and Policy Studies at Yale University, described the probable consequences of opening up prematurely even more bluntly: "Doing so will result in many, many more deaths, with those deaths, of course, concentrated among less affluent Americans," he said, "And not just more deaths, but also a rationale for denying additional unemployment benefits and other vital assistance to those on the lower rungs of the economic ladder."[74]

In New York, the primary epicenter of the outbreak until mid-May, Governor Andrew Cuomo acknowledged the difficulty of making life-and-death choices between risking an increase in the number of deaths versus keeping businesses and state economies from revving up again. "The fundamental question which we're not articulating is how much is a human life worth?" he asked rhetorically at a briefing, "There's a cost of staying closed, no doubt — economic cost, personal cost. There's also a cost of reopening quickly. Either option has a cost."[75] On balance, however, Cuomo explained that both our collective sense of humanity as well as prudence dictated that he and other governors move slowly to reopen, since the process of reopening prematurely, closing back down and the reopening again later would be doubly harmful, both in terms of lives lost as well as the economic damage inflicted.

Trump, meanwhile, continued to argue that keeping the country's economy closed was not an option. "We can't have our whole country out. We can't do it. The country won't take it. It won't stand it. It's not sustainable."[76]

During unguarded moments of candor, some of the Red State governors who were defying the federal guidelines and opening up their states anyway privately admitted that their decision to allow some businesses to reopen would lead to an increased number of infections in their states. For example, in a leaked audio recording, Governor Greg Abbott of Texas acknowledged:

> Listen, the fact of the matter is, pretty much every scientific and medical report shows that whenever you have a reopening, whether you want to call it a reopening of business or just a reopening of society in the aftermath of something like this, it actually will lead to an increase in spread. It's almost ipso facto.[77]

On Saturday, May 16, as Governor Abbott coldly predicted, Texas reported the most new coronavirus cases in a single day with 1,801 new diagnoses (the previous single-day high was 1,450 just three days earlier).[78] The *Texas Tribune* reported that the rise was mainly due to an outbreak of over 700 new cases in the Texas panhandle, home to many Latinos who work in area meat-processing factories that have been COVID-19 hotbeds.[79]

Similarly, coronavirus cases more than doubled in Alabama's Montgomery County since May 1, as the governor continued to ease restrictions, allowing many businesses, including bars and taverns, to reopen with some social distancing.[80] This increase may have been partially due to increased testing capacity, but it is also likely that the easing of restrictions was a factor in this jump in the numbers.

So, by mid-May, the trends were fairly easy to discern. States that jumped the gun and eased restrictions without having the decreasing case numbers and available testing called for in the guidelines started to experience a burst of new cases. Those states that followed the guidelines continued to have either flat or decreasing case numbers and deaths. But for President Trump, it was not about the math. It was not about how best to save lives. It was about getting the economy humming again at all costs, including the needless loss of additional lives, since he knew that come election day on November 3, 2020, he did not have a snowball's chance in hell of getting re-elected if the economy was still in a tailspin.

The U.S. Pandemic Drags into the Summer of 2020

By mid-June, the pandemic was far from over in the U.S. The northeastern states that had been hardest hit early on in the crisis – New York, New Jersey, Connecticut, and Massachusetts – were well over their peaks, trending downward or "flatlined" at relatively low levels, but 24 states – especially in the South and in the West – were still trending dangerously upwards, with spikes in new cases, hospitalizations, and deaths.[81]

Overall, the U.S. was still registering over 1,000 COVID-related deaths per day or about 42 deaths per hour.[82] This meant that the number of lives being lost every three days was equivalent to the lives lost in the September 11 terrorist attacks.[83] Without any meaningful national leadership, and a complete abdication of responsibility by the Trump administration, the country was subject to a highly divergent patchwork of state and local responses, with some states doing well and flattening the curve, while others were opening up despite disturbing evidence that they were nowhere near their peaks.

As of mid-June, 24 states were "trending poorly" in meeting the "14-day decline" criteria for the reduction of cases. Only 21 states and the District of Columbia were "making progress" in meeting these criteria, just five states were "trending better." Some areas of the country were particularly hard-hit within one month of reopening around Memorial Day (May 25), including Arizona, which lifted its stay-at-home order on May 15. In Phoenix, it was reported that people flooded into restaurants and bars, ignoring social distancing guidelines. Arizona also imposed no requirements to wear face masks, and it had not increased its capability to contact trace or control the number of increased cases breaking out in nursing homes. By June 12, the number of cases in Arizona had risen by 98% over two weeks.[84] Texas also experienced a resurgence in cases after opening too rapidly without meeting the guidelines, with its number of hospitalizations increasing by 54% over a 14-day period, to 2,100 hospitalizations per day for the first time during the pandemic.[85]

Other states with similar negative experiences after reopening included North Carolina, South Carolina, Florida, and Georgia. Some states tried to explain away their increased number of reported cases by saying that this was due to increased testing, but the data relating to increased numbers of hospitalizations could not be explained away.

Pence Declares Victory While U.S. Cases Start to Rise Again

By the end of June, it was clear that the virus had outwitted and defeated the Trump administration and the governors of several Red States in the South and West. June 27 marked a new milestone in the viruses' comeback, with the U.S. reaching its third consecutive day with a record number of newly reported coronavirus infections.[86]

The U.S. again gained the dubious distinction of becoming the world's leader in total confirmed cases and deaths, reporting more than 45,000 new infections on Friday, June 26.[87] The country's previous peak in daily case numbers had been 36,738 on April 24. Globally, there were nearly 10 million cases, and a record was set when the number of newly reported cases exceeded 191,000 in a single day.[88] India's caseload alone surged past 500,000 on June 27.[89]

At least six U.S. states — Florida, Idaho, Kansas, Oregon, South Carolina, and Utah — reported their highest one-day case totals, and Dr. Anthony S. Fauci, the country's top infectious diseases expert, warned that outbreaks in the South and West could engulf the country. Dr. Fauci said in a brief interview that officials were having "intense discussions" about a possible shift to "pool testing," in which samples from many people are tested at once in an effort to find and isolate those who are infected quickly.[90]

By late June and early July, Texas and Florida began to experience the full brunt of their governors' reckless decision to reopen their states' economies in May and June even though the number of coronavirus cases and related deaths were still rising. Partially closing their states back down was proving to be harder than the first time, with many Texas and Florida residents just ignoring pleas to wear face masks and practice social distancing.

Both states abruptly set new restrictions on bars, reversing prior orders that had opened them up.

As the July 4th weekend approached, the beaches in both Florida and Texas became increasingly filled with mask-less sunbathers interacting with one another in close proximity. Enjoying the good weather, beachgoers generally ignored the belated appeals of state and local officials to help slow down the spread of the virus. Local and state officials wildly vacillated over the issue of whether to shut down beaches and other public places. Mayor Carlos Giménez of Miami-Dade County in Florida signed an emergency order closing beaches from July 3 to July 7, citing a surge in new cases and fears about mass gatherings during the July 4th holiday weekend.

On Saturday, July 11, Disney World in Orlando, Florida, went ahead with its planned reopening of its Magic Kingdom and the Animal Kingdom, despite continuing concerns by health experts urging people to avoid gathering in groups.[91] However, relatively few visitors showed up, and those that did venture forth to the near-empty parks complied with directions to wear masks and observe social distancing.

The following day, on Sunday, July 12, Florida set a grim milestone, shattering the national record for the largest single-day increase in positive coronavirus cases in any state since the beginning of the pandemic, adding more than 15,000 daily cases. Florida's death toll also continued to also rise with an average of 73 deaths per day, more than doubling in only three weeks.[92]

By comparison, Italy – which was devastated by the pandemic early on – was only averaging 200 new cases per day in early to mid-July, with Florida's daily caseload running 25 times greater and Texas not far behind with 9,000 new cases per day.[93] Meanwhile, Germany, with a population four times that of Florida, had fewer than 400 new cases a day.[94]

Undaunted and unrepentant for having badly miscalculated and mismanaged his state's reopening, Florida Governor Ron DeSantis said that even with the rising rates, he still wanted the schools to reopen as scheduled in late August, incorrectly stating that children had not been proven to be vectors for the disease in states and other countries where schools had reopened or had remained open. In actuality, children were found to be able to harbor large quantities of the virus in their nasal passages without necessarily showing symptoms of the disease, which made them excellent transmitters of the disease to unsuspecting adults as well as other children.[95]

Governor DeSantis further said that while each county would have to come up with their own procedures, depending on their local infection rate, not opening the schools would exacerbate the achievement gap between high and low-performing students. Misstating the known risk of children catching and transmitting the disease, DeSantis continued: "We know there are huge, huge costs for not providing the availability of in-person schooling," he said, "The risk of corona, fortunately, for students is incredibly low."[96]

Even in California, which had beaten back the virus by imposing one of the earliest stay-at-home orders in the U.S. and was already in the process of reopening, Governor Gavin Newsom was forced to announce new restrictions on Imperial County, which had the state's highest rate of infection. "This disease does not take a summer vacation," he said.[97]

At first, puzzled by the U.S.'s chaotic and ineffective response to the pandemic, the rest of the world started drawing back in increasing horror. The U.S.'s reputation had become so tarnished that European Union officials said the bloc was getting ready to bar most travelers from the U.S. and other countries considered too risky because they have not controlled the outbreaks. And for the first time, some U.S. governors were backtracking on reopening their states, issuing new restrictions on some elements of public life.

Meanwhile, the White House and administration seemed to be withdrawing into a deep state of denial as to the viruses' rebound in Texas, Florida, California, and other key states. Vice President Mike Pence held the first public briefing that the now moribund White House coronavirus task force in almost two months, claiming a victory for the Trump administration's pandemic response. "We slowed the spread, we flattened the curve, we saved lives," Mr. Pence said, making a claim that may have been partially true in earlier months but was now completely outdated and false, given the rising number of new cases in recent weeks.[98] As yet another sign that the Trump administration had given up on trying to stop the virus, Pence did not wear a mask.

35

AMERICA EXPLODES AS THE FEAR AND ANGER OF THE COVID-19 CRISIS IS FURTHER FUELED BY RACIST ACTS AND POLICE VIOLENCE

"When the looting starts, the shooting starts."
-Donald J. Trump

By late May, there were growing signs that fear, anger, frustration, boredom, unemployment, hopelessness, and depression were combining to form a toxic and combustible brew. First, the virus descended on Black, brown, poor white, inner-city, rural and Native American communities like a heat-seeking missile, targeting the most vulnerable in our society who had already been beaten down by grinding poverty, chronic illness, diabetes, high blood pressure, opioid abuse, lack of educational and job opportunities, and hopelessness. For many, any continued references to America as "the land of opportunity" seemed like some cruel joke. A huge underclass in the country had been growing for decades, barely getting by week after week and month after month, living from payday to payday until the paydays ran out and unemployment hit them like a sledgehammer right between the eyes.

As of May 28, 2020, more than 40 million people in the U.S. – one in four American workers – had filed for unemployment benefits since the coronavirus pandemic forced the U.S. economy to shut down in March.[1] First-time unemployment claims were in the millions for ten straight weeks, rising to 40.7 million unemployed and bringing the official unemployment rate to 14.7%, but the real unemployment rate was around twice that, especially if you include unemployed Americans who had been chronically underemployed or unemployed and others who had just given up and dropped out of the job market.[2] Experts predicted that the unemployment rate would rise to at least 32% before leveling off,[3] a level of near-total economic devastation that the country had not experienced since the Great

Depression. America had never recorded a single week of 1 million jobless claims prior to the coronavirus crisis.

Even as states started to come out of the coronavirus deep-freeze, this did not necessarily mean that things would get better for most Americans. In fact, for many, it just made it worse. They were still unemployed, but the landlords of the country were starting to ask them for rent again as the moratoriums on evictions were lifted in state after state and many people had no source of income to pay for their current monthly rent, let alone the back rent they owed for March, April, and May. Those who were fortunate enough to qualify for unemployment benefits faced the prospect of these payments running out as early as July or August.

The fact that there were many other millions of your fellow Americans unemployed during this crisis was not of much comfort to you if you were one of those who was unemployed. If you got an unemployment check, you were supposedly one of the "lucky" ones. There were long delays for weeks in even getting through to the unemployment office, and half the time your employer was already out of business and not providing any proof of your continued employment. Or you had been paid in cash off the books, and there was no record that you had actually been employed. When the food ran out, you drove to the line for the food bank, where you often had to wait for hours to get a box of rations that would only last you a few days, but it was better than nothing. But sometimes your car ran out of gas waiting in line, and the cars behind you just drove around you, leaving you and your family totally stranded. When grandma and grandpa were dying in the nursing home from COVID-19, you couldn't see them to say goodbye, and you didn't have any money to pay for a proper burial, so G-d knows what the county did with their bodies.

On top of everything else, you have to wear a mask in public, which you are willing to do, but you see a lot of other people walking around without masks and not social distancing, so you start feeling kind of foolish. You see that heavily armed lockdown protesters are openly breaking the stay-at-home orders in their states and demonstrating with Confederate flags and other racist symbols and signs, without the police lifting a finger to stop them. They even were able to shut down the Michigan state legislature in

Lansing, and get their photographs taken standing around beauty salons and tattoo parlors "protecting them" from any police who might dare to try to enforce the law by closing down those businesses.

Meanwhile, amidst this rising sense of frustration, there were strong indications that the stay-at-home and social distancing laws were being unequally enforced in minority communities. A block party in a Black neighborhood in DeLand, Florida, which was an annual memorial service for a Black man murdered in 2008, drew a collection of primarily white deputies and police officers from the Volusia County Sheriff's Office on May 18th.[4] Several arrests followed amid allegations that the crackdown by the police was racially motivated and racially discriminatory, given the fact that groups of white men throughout Florida and in other states standing around without masks and with prominently displayed firearms went unchallenged by the police.

The Killing of Ahmaud Arbery in Georgia

Black joggers wearing masks have also had a rough time of it during the coronavirus lockdown period. The most notorious case was that of Ahmaud Arbery, a young Black man in Georgia who went out for a jog during the day on February 23 and was shot and killed by two white men - a father and son.[5] Even though there was a videotape of the incident, the local prosecutor initially declined to charge Arbery's killers on the grounds that their actions were rooted in Georgia's "stand your ground" law. The father-son duo had pursued Arbery in a car before confronting and killing him at an intersection. They alleged that Mr. Arbery matched the description of a man suspected in several break-ins.[6] The only similarity was that Mr. Arbery and the alleged "mystery burglar" were both young Black men.

It was not until weeks later when the case received national media attention that the Georgia Bureau of Investigation (GBI) finally got involved in the investigation, and within 36 hours, the GBI announced the arrest of both of the McMichaels on murder and aggravated assault charges.[7] In addition, William "Roddie" Bryan, who filmed the cellphone video that captured the encounter leaving Arbery dead, was charged with felony murder and criminal attempt to commit false imprisonment.[8]

The Police Killing of George Floyd

The simmering rage in Black communities around the country finally erupted into demonstrations and protests after George Floyd, a Black man, died while in police custody in Minneapolis on May 25.[9] A video of the incident, which quickly went viral, showed Floyd handcuffed on the ground with a white police officer, with his hands nonchalantly in his pockets, kneeling on his neck for eight minutes and 46 seconds. Floyd could be heard pleading, "I can't breathe." These were the same words used by Eric Garner just before he too died on July 17, 2014 in the New York City borough of Staten Island after Daniel Pantaleo, a New York City Police Department officer, put him in a chokehold after arresting him.[10]

Just as the Eric Garner killing helped catalyze the Black Lives Matter movement, the George Floyd murder sparked demonstrations not only in Minneapolis, where the police precinct was burned, but also around the country. In comparison to the gun-toting, white, anti-lockdown demonstrators in numerous cities across the U.S., the unarmed BLM protestors were treated much more harshly by the police. They were subjected to barrages of tear-gas, rubber bullets, and other sorts of riot-weaponry that can cause serious injury or even death. The demonstrations in Minneapolis were fairly peaceful until a full four days after Floyd's murder when former police officer Derek Chauvin – who had been fired along with three fellow officers immediately after the incident – still was not in police custody and still not charged with a crime. After a night of violent protests, fires, and looting throughout Minneapolis and neighboring St. Paul on May 28, Chauvin was finally taken into custody on Friday, May 29, and charged with third-degree murder and second-degree manslaughter.[11]

Demonstrations took place in almost every major city throughout the U.S., with some of them violent, including a riot in Detroit that left one man dead after a vehicle was fired upon during a demonstration. In Oakland, a federal officer was shot dead in what was described as an act of domestic terrorism. Someone fired a gun near a crowd of demonstrators in Denver, and several dozen people were arrested in New York City, where about two dozen police vehicles were torched. Seven people were shot at a protest in

Louisville, Kentucky, where crowds had turned out not only to protest the police killing of George Floyd but also to demand justice for the death of Breonna Taylor, an unarmed Black woman who was shot by police while she was asleep in her own apartment in March. After a person was fatally shot in downtown Indianapolis, police were warning residents that the city was unsafe.

In other demonstrations around the country, police cars were set aflame, freeways were blocked, windows were shattered, and authorities deployed pepper spray, tear gas, and even rubber bullets. Multiple governors activated the National Guard, and curfews were enacted in several major cities, including Atlanta, Chicago, Louisville, Denver, Miami, and Milwaukee. After New York experienced increasingly escalating violence on Saturday night, May 30 – including a demonstration where Mayor Bill de Blasio's own daughter was arrested – New York Governor Andrew Cuomo and Mayor de Blasio imposed a curfew on Sunday night.[12]

California Governor Gavin Newsom declared a state of emergency and deployed the National Guard to help enforce a citywide curfew as violent demonstrations continued on the streets of Los Angeles. Mayor Eric Garcetti initially resisted using troops because he did not want to evoke memories of the 1992 Rodney King riots. However, as violence escalated in Los Angeles and businesses were being looted, the National Guard was called in to try to tamp down the violence.[13]

Minnesota Governor Tim Walz "fully" mobilized the National Guard in the Twin Cities, and the National Guard was also activated in Georgia, Kentucky, Wisconsin, Colorado, Ohio, Tennessee and Utah.[14] Seattle called in 200 National Guard members, all of whom were unarmed.

Every other U.S. president in history would have called on American citizens for a peace and calm to such a violent and seemingly unjust episode. But Trump was not like any other president. Instead of trying to defuse the justifiable anger and outrage, and to promise that a thorough federal investigation would be conducted, he decided to pour further gasoline on the fire by threatening that demonstrators would be shot. On Twitter, Trump wrote: "When the looting starts, the shooting starts."[15] This phrase, which had not been heard by most Americans for quite a while, harkened back to racist statements by Alabama segregationist Governor George Wallace, who did everything in his power to obstruct civil rights protests and marches during the 1960s. This phrase was actually coined in 1967, when the police chief of Miami threatened police violence against peaceful civil rights demonstrators.

Trump's use of this racially charged and incendiary phrase was not inadvertent. It was almost as if he wanted to incite a civil war, justifying perhaps the imposition of martial law and, of course, the postponement of the November elections until such indefinite future date when the forces of law and order were back in full control.

Trump kept up his drumbeat of provocative tweets and public remarks, threatening protesters across the street from the White House in historic Lafayette Square with "vicious dogs" and "ominous weapons." He suggested that looters in Minneapolis should be shot and referred to protesters as "thugs."[16] He also let it be known that he was prepared to order the Pentagon to use military force against American citizens. Even though live news footage of the demonstrations showed that none of the protesters ever scaled the high fence around the White House or entered the White House grounds, Trump briefly retreated on Friday night, May 29, to the subterranean bunker which had last been used by Vice President Dick Cheney after the September 11th attacks.[17]

On Monday, June 1, after a week of protests in cities across the country, Trump held a phone call with several governors in which he ranted that they were being "weak" with protesters in their states and that they needed to "dominate" riots and make more arrests. According to an audio recording of the phone call that Trump placed from the basement White House Situation Room, Trump excoriated the governors, ordering them to respond to the protests more forcefully: "You have to dominate or you'll look like a bunch of jerks, you have to arrest and try people."[18]

In other words, Trump was basically calling on the governor to answer the protests against police violence with more police violence. After the call, several of the governors pushed back at Trump's suggestion that they were not handling the protests with an appropriate degree of force. Democratic Michigan Governor Gretchen Whitmer, a frequent target of Trump, called the phone call "deeply disturbing," adding that instead of offering support or leadership in trying to cool off the rising temperature of the protests, Trump told the governors to "put it down" or be "overridden."[19] Similarly, Massachusetts Republican Governor Charlie Baker, who was also on the phone call with Trump, described the president's tone and message as one of "bitterness, combativeness and self-interest."[20] Trump had threatened to call in the military if the state governors did not "handle" the rioting and the looting that had accompanied some of the largely peaceful protests. Baker further told reporters: "I heard what the President said today about dominating and fighting. I know I should be surprised when I hear incendiary words like this from him, but I'm not," adding, "At so many times during these past several weeks when the country needed compassion and leadership the most, it was simply nowhere to be found."[21]

Earlier in the day, Governor Baker had released a statement setting the kind of measured and conciliatory tone that Americans had come to expect from their elected representatives in tumultuous times, and which they were definitely not hearing from their current president. Baker acknowledged that the peaceful protesters in Boston had made "a powerful statement," adding:

> The murder of George Floyd at the hands of police was a horrible tragedy -- one of countless tragedies to befall people of color across the United States. The vast majority of protesters today did so peacefully, toward a common goal of promoting justice and equality.
>
> I am deeply thankful for their voices and their positive, forceful message. I also want to express my gratitude to all the police officers and other first responders working to protect the people of Boston from the individuals whose violent actions, looting and property destruction was criminal and cowardly -- and distracted from the powerful statement made today by thousands of Massachusetts residents.[22]

By June 1, when Trump vented his rage at the governors trying to deal responsibly with the protests engulfing their largest cities, the nationwide protests had become more than just a reaction to the brutal and senseless killing of George Floyd in Minneapolis, as shocking as that incident was. Protesters were raising a host of other issues involving institutional racism not only in the disproportionate use of violence against young Black men by law enforcement, but also in the wide disparities in sentences handed out to Black Americans as compared to their white fellow citizens.

In addition, the legal principle of qualified immunity for law enforcement officers came under closer scrutiny in the public discussion of systemic racism. In the 1967 case of *Pierson v. Ray*, the Supreme Court first articulated the concept of "qualified immunity" in a case involving police violence against a group of civil rights demonstrators in Mississippi.[23] The Court decided that police officers should not face legal liability for enforcing the law "in good faith and with probable cause." However, by 1982, the Supreme Court shifted the doctrine of qualified immunity into a legal defense mechanism in the case *Harlow v. Fitzgerald*.[24] Since this case, a public official may use qualified immunity as a defense unless the conduct/circumstances being questioned has been found to have not constituted "good faith" established by prior case law, thus stripping the police officer of immunity. That is a very high standard to meet, and it makes these civil rights cases nearly impossible for plaintiffs to win unless there is a prior case already on the books with an identical fact pattern, holding that the officer in question was not immune.

Supreme Court Justice Sonia Sotomayor has expressed serious concerns about the judicial drift towards an increased presumption of qualified immunity for police officers. In *Mullenix v. Luna*, she wrote in her dissent: "By sanctioning a 'shoot first, think later' approach to policing, the Court renders the protections of the Fourth Amendment hollow."[25]

Hopefully the strong judicial bias in favor of law enforcement officers in excessive force and other civil rights cases can be eliminated – or at least ratcheted back – in the coming months. The Supreme Court has considered almost one dozen cases that could give plaintiffs more of a fighting chance to prevail, at least in the most egregious cases. One case – *Corbitt v. Vickers*, involves a police officer in Georgia who, while pursuing a suspect, held a group of young children at gunpoint, fired two bullets at the family dog, missed and hit a 10-year-old boy in the arm.[26] Another case, *West v. City of Caldwell*, involves officers who used tear gas grenades to enter a home when they had been given a key to the front door.[27] The Supreme Court refused to hear both of these cases, but hopefully it will agree to hear another case that will allow it to revisit the qualified immunity issue.

The summer protests across America also triggered a lively public discussion on the militarization of police departments, who were now equipped with tanks and other military equipment just waiting to be used against the American people. It has often been said that when you have a hammer, everything starts looking like a nail. The same holds true for police officers with military-grade equipment. When you are holding a brand-new grenade launcher that needs "field testing," a large crowd of demonstrators can easily be viewed as enemy combatants justifying the use of lethal force. There were also extensive discussions around the country regarding the concept of "de-funding" police departments, so that armed police officers would not necessarily be the first responders to domestic dispute calls. In Camden, New Jersey, where the police had recently adopted some innovative reforms, including an emphasis on a "community policing" approach, officers marched alongside peaceful protesters.

In addition to law enforcement issues, the protests – which could more accurately be described as a nationwide tsunami, given its size and strength – also shined a spotlight on the racism deeply embedded in the housing, employment and education sectors of society. Not much had changed since the 1960s, when President Lyndon Johnson's Kerner Commission concluded, after studying the inequalities at the root of the 1960s riots: "White institutions created it, white institutions maintain it and white society condones it."[28]

Across the U.S., there were more than 4,700 Black Lives Matter and related demonstrations, or an average of 140 per day. These started with the Minneapolis demonstrations on May 26 and continued until at least mid-July.[29] The size of these demonstrations ranged from dozens to tens of thousands in about 2,500 small towns and large cities. More than 1,360 counties in the U.S. had protests, which represents 40% of counties in the country.[30] An extraordinary 95% of counties that have held protests since May 26 were majority white counties, and nearly three-quarters of the counties were more than 75% white – a characteristic unlike any other past BLM protest.[31]

The BLM uprising peaked on June 6, when half a million people turned out in nearly 550 places across the U.S.[32] That was a single day in weeks of protests. Four polls, including one released in mid-July by Civis Analytics, strongly suggested that about 15 to 26 million people in the U.S. had participated in BLM and related demonstrations. These figures would make the recent protests the largest movement in the country's history.[33]

Even if only half of those surveyed had actually participated in BLM demonstrations, this would mean that the seven million people who took to the streets in protest dwarfed all prior social movements in this country. The Women's March of 2017 had a turnout of about three to five million people on a single day, and this was a highly organized event. Even more amazingly, there was no central organizing committee or long-term planning for the BLM protests, which were largely spontaneous, organic outpourings of grief, anger and angst by millions of Americans of every race, color and creed. The Civil Rights Movement of the 60s triggered many marches, including the iconic March on Washington where Dr. King gave his "I Have a Dream" speech. However, when added together, these demonstrations collectively involved only a few hundred thousand people. "Really, it's hard to overstate the scale of this movement," said Deva Woodly, an associate professor of politics at the New School.[34]

After weeks of sustained levels of protests – which the country had not seen since the assassination of Dr. Martin Luther King Jr. in 1968 – many experts and commentators started expressing the guarded opinion that these protests, when coupled with the economic and psychological pressures of the COVID-19 crisis, might finally be the catalyst for some fundamental reforms that had been talked about for decades but rarely acted upon.

The polling as of June 2020 was encouraging. Sixty percent of Americans, including a majority of white people, said in a *CBS News* poll that they supported ideas promoted by the BLM movement. Almost as large a majority expressed support for a national health care plan. An astonishing 89 percent also favored higher taxes on the rich to reduce poverty in America.[35]

Darnell Hunt, Dean of Social Sciences at U.C.L.A., told a *New York Times* columnist Michelle Goldberg: "Sociologists have studied collective behavior, urban unrest for decades, and I think it's safe to say that the consensus view is that it's never just about a precipitating incident that resulted in the unrest."36 Hunt added, "It's always a collection of factors that make the situation ripe for collective behavior, unrest and mobilization."37 Keith Ellison, Minnesota's attorney general, further commented: "Many people have been cooped up for two months, and so now they're in a different space and a different place. They're restless. Some of them have been unemployed, some of them don't have rent money, and they're angry, they're frustrated."38

While the ongoing protests in at least 75 U.S. cities raised the risk of a spread of coronavirus cases among the protesters, most of them wore masks and the protests were outdoors, which tended to mitigate the risks of the protests turning into virus "super-spreader" events. Many experts also expressed the view that, on balance, the protests were morally and ethically appropriate under the circumstances since public protest against the systematic violation of civil and human rights is one of the few ways that the public can let its voice be heard.

Alexandra Phelan, a professor of global-health law at Georgetown University, drew a distinction under international law between the protests against police brutality and other fundamental injustices, and the protests earlier in the spring, which opposed state orders on requiring social distancing and the wearing of masks in public. "These protests are currently the primary channel to seek accountability for the governance systems that have led to extrajudicial killings and police violence," Phelan said, adding that the protests were also directed at "the disproportionate death from COVID-19 experienced by Black and brown Americans."39

Former President Barrack Obama also weighed in to support the thousands of peaceful protesters that had turned out to bear witness that Black Lives Matter and that immediate reforms had to take place. The "bottom line," he wrote, is that "if we want to bring about real change, then the choice isn't between protest and politics. We have to do both. We have to mobilize to raise awareness, and we have to organize and cast our ballots to make sure that we elect candidates who will act on reform."40

Obama concluded his open letter by recognizing that the pandemic had helped set the stage for a national justice movement that was gaining daily momentum: "I recognize that these past few months have been hard and dispiriting -- that the fear, sorrow, uncertainty, and hardship of a pandemic have been compounded by tragic reminders that prejudice and inequality still shape so much of American life," he wrote. "But watching the heightened activism of young people in recent weeks, of every race and every station, makes me hopeful."[41]

It is likely that Dr. King himself would have agreed that the protests and demonstrations were justifiable. In 1967, he observed that "riots are socially destructive and self-defeating," but quickly added: "It is as necessary for me to be as vigorous in condemning the conditions which cause persons to feel that they must engage in riotous activities as it is for me to condemn riots."[42]

"In the final analysis, a riot is the language of the unheard," Dr. King said. "As long as America postpones justice, we stand in the position of having these recurrences of violence and riots over and over again."[43]

In only a few short weeks, the BLM protests were producing some significant results. In Minneapolis, the City Council pledged to dismantle its police department, which would open the door to a complete rethinking of the role of law enforcement in that city. In New York, lawmakers repealed a law that kept police disciplinary records secret. Cities and states across the country passed new laws banning chokeholds, and in Mississippi, lawmakers voted to retire their state flag, which prominently featured the Confederate battle flag. Statues of Confederate generals were taken down in Richmond and other cities. Perhaps even more amazingly, NASCAR racing banned the display of Confederate flags, and the Dixie Chicks dropped the "Dixie" from their name.

At long last, it seemed that the country was coming to serious terms with its racist roots. Douglas McAdam, an emeritus professor at Stanford University, commented: "It looks, for all the world, like these protests are achieving what very few do: setting in motion a period of significant, sustained, and widespread social, political change," he said. "We appear to be experiencing a social change tipping point — that is as rare in society as it is potentially consequential."[44]

36

COVIDFEST 2020

What would happen if Trump threw one of his monster "Make America Great Again" (MAGA) rallies in a deep Red State, more than 100,000 supporters promised to show up, and then the outdoor portion of the rally had to be canceled due to poor attendance? This embarrassment and humiliation for the Trump Campaign would have been unthinkable only a few short months ago. But the world seems to have wobbled slightly on its axis, and now everything had changed, utterly changed. A terrible beauty was in the process of being born.

The murder of George Floyd in Minneapolis and the ensuing protests around the country touched a raw nerve like nothing this country has seen in recent history. Meanwhile, the virus was making its silent yet inexorable way across the South and the West, wreaking havoc on the poorly laid plans of Republican governors to reopen their states while ignoring the most basic of public health guidelines. Governors of states such as Florida and Texas, where the trajectory of coronavirus cases and fatalities was still rising, decided to play Russian roulette with their citizens' lives by recklessly reopening.

Soon, faint rumblings started to be heard in Republican circles and even among his most loyal circle of conservative commentators and Trump enablers. They began to realize to their horror that Trump was headed for political disaster on November 3 and that there was a danger that he could bring down the rest of the Republican Party with him. There was even talk that a Blue Wave might engulf the country in November, sweeping the Republican majority out of the Senate while taking the White House. Could it be possible, many Trump localists began to wonder, that perhaps their Emperor was mortal after all and that all his posturing and bluster had blinded them to the fact that he had no clothes? Trump's polling numbers were sinking, and his jokes about Joe Biden wearing a mask and "hiding" in his basement were falling flat as the virus increased its vise-like grip on the country.

By May 2020, Trump was feeling increasingly anxious and trapped in the White House, pacing around the Oval Office, muttering to himself and snapping at his aides every five minutes. He had not been permitted to leave the White House for several months now, trapped like a caged animal only because the "optics" would look bad if he snuck away to play his usual rounds of golf or visited Mar-A-Largo.

Without the regular adrenaline and ego boost of his MAGA rallies and the thousands of adoring acolytes surrounding him, he had fallen into an irritable funk that his closest advisors feared would degenerate into full-blown depression and perhaps even early dementia. His falling poll numbers were not helping any, causing Trump to erupt in rage when *CNN* had him trailing Joe Biden, the Democratic candidate, by more than ten points.[1] Trump's bonehead response was to threaten to sue *CNN* if it did not retract the poll. *CNN* naturally refused,[2] calling Trump's bluff, and Trump folded like a cheap lounge chair on the deck of the Titanic. This was a self-destructive pattern that repeated itself with other news outlets and critics with increasing frequency.

His former national security advisor, John Bolton, came out with a book trashing Trump, saying that he had begged Xi Jinping, the President of China, to help him with his re-election campaign. According to Bolton, Trump had tried to ingratiate himself with the Chinese leader by complimenting him on China's campaign of mass arbitrary detention, torture, and genocidal abuse of millions of Muslim Uyghurs and ethnic Kazakhs in China's northwestern Xinjiang region.[3] Trump must have been envious. If only he could do the same, by rounding up thousands of "leftist agitators" and sending them to remote "re-education centers." Something to think about anyway, even though it may have to be put on hold until a second term.

Obviously, the only real solution to Trump's funk would be to get back on the campaign trail. In Trumplandia, the answer to most problems was, "Let's hold a rally!" And this is precisely what they did. For reasons that remain obscure, Team Trump decided to hold his comeback "Opening America Back-Up" rally in Tulsa, Oklahoma, in an indoor arena that could hold 19,000 or 20,000 tightly packed together fans. Health experts and scientists, of course, warned that this would become a "super spreader" event for coronavirus, especially since Oklahoma, as a bright Red State with a Republican governor, was opening back up its economy even as the number of cases and deaths from coronavirus continued to rise in the state, and particularly in Tulsa.

Trump and his advisors must have known of the risks of holding a large indoor rally while the pandemic was still spiking in Oklahoma, but decided it was either worth the risk of infecting his supporters, or they saw it as a positive political statement of a leader who was still questioning the severity or scope of the disease. There was never any serious consideration given to the health of his followers, who by this time were taking their Leader's cue and thinking that the whole coronavirus scare was a Left-wing hoax to prevent the Trump Faithful from exercising both their First and Second Amendment rights simultaneously (that is when white people with MAGA hats and firearms assemble together to honor the Great Orange One).

Whether Trump or his advisers knew it at the time or not is subject to debate, but the day he chose for the rally was June 19, which is a Black holiday known as "Juneteenth" (also known as Emancipation Day), which commemorates the anniversary of General Order No. 3 in 1865, when Union Major-General Gordon Granger read General Order No. 3 to the people of Galveston, Texas, thus freeing the last remaining slaves in the U.S.[4]

June 19 was also the 99th anniversary of the notorious 1921 Tulsa Race Massacre, where hundreds of armed white vigilantes, backed by Tulsa police officers and National Guardsmen, rampaged through the Black Greenwood section of North Tulsa known as "Black Wall Street," killing more than 300 Black residents, burning down dozens of square blocks and destroying about 1,200 residences and businesses.[5] It was at the time (and remains today) the most heinous race riot and systematic public lynching and murder of African-American citizens in U.S. history. That Trump had chosen both the date and the location of this mass slaughter of Blacks by white Tulsans stunned most objective observers and commentators, as if Trump was intentionally taking a stick and poking it into the hornet's nest to provoke a violent response and thus embolden his supporters to respond in kind.

Following the murder of George Floyd in Minneapolis by police officers, the marches and protest rallies in Tulsa had been generally peaceful. However, on May 31, several people were injured when a truck drove through a crowd of protesters marching on a highway to mark the 99th anniversary of the Greenwood massacre.[6] After decades of being ignored or even suppressed, the massacre is now part of the state's school curriculum — and was a pivotal plot element in the HBO series "Watchmen."

When Trump's choice of Juneteenth as his rally day set off a storm of protest, Trump apparently asked a Black Secret Service agent what the fuss was all about. When advised that holding one of his traditionally racist-tinged rallies on one of the most sacred of days in the African American calendar, Trump surprisingly moved the gathering by one day to June 20.

Trump's "super spreader" event could better be described as "Covidfest 2020" for the near certainty that this indoor event would spread viral infections, with 19,000 screaming fans, most of whom were sure to avoid wearing masks.[7] Eric Feigl-Ding, an epidemiologist at Harvard University's Chan School of Public Health, noted that Oklahoma had the second-fastest-growing per capita rate of new coronavirus infections in the country, based on a seven-day average.[8] On the Thursday before the scheduled rally, infections were up 140% in the state, according to estimates by the Federation of American Scientists.[9]

In order to protect itself from legal liability, the Trump campaign had all attendees sign waivers promising that they would not sue the Trump Campaign if they or their family members contracted coronavirus as a result of their attendance at the Tulsa rally. The campaign said that masks would be available to people if they wanted to use them, but few did so since the "no-mask" look was becoming synonymous with the implicit declaration that "I am a Trump supporter and I am asserting my civil liberty right to infect as many of my fellow Americans as possible by attending a Trump rally without a mask." Conversely, the wearing of a face mask meant, in Trump World, that you were probably a liberal Democratic and Joe Biden supporter, or worse.

One Trump supporter, David Riniker, said that he had no fears about attending the indoor Tulsa rally, despite the fact that he had been diagnosed with cancer and Oklahoma was experiencing a surge in coronavirus cases.[10] "I don't fear anything. If today is the day I die, today is the day I die," said Riniker, who drove to Tulsa from his home in Arkansas to attend what he said was his first political rally since Ronald Reagan was running for office, "I'm not paranoid, I'm not afraid."[11]

Other Trump supporters waiting to attend the rally also said that they were not worried about contracting the illness and had no plans to follow any of the recommended precautions, such as mask-wearing and social distancing. Many Trump supporters also cast doubt on the severity or even the reality of the outbreak, saying that they had a constitutional right to refuse to comply with recommended public health precautions. "I think [the coronavirus] has been hyped up more than it is. There's flu, there's cancer, there's COVID-19," said Mary Legan of Claremore, Oklahoma.[12] Tom Todd, a retired welder, couched his decision not to wear a mask in terms of patriotism: "As far as I know, I'm still an American," adding, "This is a free country, and I can do what I want. If I want to wear a mask, I wear a mask. If I don't, I don't. If I get sick, I get sick. That's my choice."[13]

Another Trump devotee expressed a longing to return to the America of yesteryear (or even last year): "I'm not going to live my life in fear. I want to get back to the normal — not a 'new normal,' but the old normal," said Jill, who lives in Orange County, California.[14] Terri Whisenhunt was more vehement in her response to the health concerns that were being raised. "I'm not going to let those people run me off," she vowed, "And COVID-19 is not going to keep me locked in my house. I think it's all a bunch of B.S."[15] Mike Alcorn, who works in maintenance and lives in Wichita, Kansas, emphatically agreed: "It's all fake," he said, adding, "They're just making the numbers up. I haven't seen anybody die, not from coronavirus. I don't even know anybody who's got it."[16]

Some local Tulsa residents and business owners tried to get a commitment from the Trump Campaign and the arena manager that the attendees at the rally would be required to comply with the CDC recommendations for social distancing and mask-wearing, but on the day before the rally, the Oklahoma Supreme Court rejected an appeal of the lawsuit.[17] Tulsa's top health official, Bruce Dart, also appealed to the Trump Campaign to postpone the event until after Oklahoma's spike in COVID-19 cases abated and it was reasonably safe, but his pleas fell on deaf ears.

Meanwhile, Oklahoma's Republican Governor Kevin Stitt welcomed the president and the rally with open arms. "My question back to all the folks that say you shouldn't have a rally, when is the right time?" he said on *Fox News*, "Do we really think that in July or August or in November coronavirus is not going to be here? We've got to learn to deal with this. We've got to learn to be safe, take precautions, but we've got to learn to also live our lives."[18]

Trump's White House press secretary, Kayleigh McEnany, echoed Governor Stitt's fatalistic attitude, saying that she would be at the rally but would not be wearing a mask, adding that she believed the question of whether to wear a mask or not was a matter of personal choice, not a public health necessity.[19]

The day of the rally got off to an inauspicious start when community leaders in the historic Black district of Greenwood in Tulsa received word that Vice President Pence would be touring the area. Hours before Pence's scheduled visit, these community leaders rushed to cover up the Black Wall Street memorials, which honored the victims of the 1921 Tulsa Race Massacre, thus depriving Pence of the political backdrop being planned for him. "I just think his visit is an opportunity for a photo op," said community activist and educator Kristi Williams, "We say, 'Don't come for a photo op when you have not come to sit down and talk with Black leaders in the community.' We are beyond symbolism."[20]

When President Trump spoke in the Tulsa arena on Saturday night, June 20, many seats were unfilled and large sections of the arena thinly populated. There was no massive overflow audience to greet Trump, as had been planned. The area outside the stadium was mostly empty by early evening, so plans for Trump to address the audience outside were quickly scrapped. The campaign had the outdoor stage dismantled even before Trump's arrival.[21]

The sparse attendance at the highly hyped rally was a significant embarrassment to the Trump Campaign, which had promised an overflowing arena and boasted that about one million supporters had expressed a desire to attend. Most of his supporters in the 19,000-seat BOK Center were not wearing masks, only hours after the Trump Campaign had announced that six members of the advance team staffing the event had tested positive for the virus.

Trump's rambling two hours speech was, as usual, filled with so many manufactured grievances, outright falsehoods, and misleading claims that the fact-checkers were working overtime to keep track of the number of falsehoods. One major theme of Trump's speech was that Confederate flags and statues were an essential part of the country's "heritage," and that protesters and political leaders who were pursuing the removal of Confederate statues across the South were perpetrating a "desecration." He said, "The unhinged left-wing mob is trying to vandalize our history, desecrating our monuments, our beautiful monuments."[22]

During the rally, Trump also downplayed the severity of the virus, fixating on the number of names that had been used to describe it and settling on his personal favorite: "Kung Flu," a blatantly offensive racist term.

Perhaps most notably, Trump disclosed that because more testing means higher numbers of known coronavirus cases, he had directed that testing be curtailed. "So, I said to my people, 'Slow the testing down,'" he said.[23] A White House official later said the president was "obviously kidding" when he made his "slow down the testing" remarks, but when Trump was asked about it after the rally, he confirmed that he was deadly serious.

What Trump did not say in his rambling remarks at the Tulsa rally was as significant as what he did say. He did not refer to the Tulsa massacre of 1921 or the killing of George Floyd. The death at the hands of a white police officer in Minneapolis of the latter had spurred global demands for racial justice. He also did not mention Juneteenth, even though this milestone marking the end of slavery in the United States fell just a day before his rally and was acknowledged by him as the reason why the rally date had been moved by one day.

Outside the arena, there were some protesters, but most of Tulsa's community that took to the streets gathered in the historically Black Greenwood neighborhood, where people danced and mingled in an atmosphere more block party than a protest. The Black Lives Matter slogan and clenched, raised fist logo were projected onto the side of the Vernon AME Church. One local resident commented: "This is Juneteenth ... we'd be out here anyway," he said, "They're scared to come over here. I know that. They know better. We ain't playin.'"[24] Another community resident was more defiant: "Why the hell that Orange Man decided to come out here after we're celebrated Juneteenth, I will never know."[25]

Most of the Trump supporters at the Tulsa rally took the cue from their leader by couching their refusal to wear masks and to practice social distancing in terms of liberty and personal freedom. It was almost as if the Republican Party (which by now could be more aptly named the "Trump Party") had reformulated Patrick Henry's famous declaration to say: "Give me liberty *and* give me death!"[26]

At least one notable Republican at the rally, who tragically, got his death wish was Herman Cain, the President and CEO of Godfather's Pizza and former Republican presidential candidate in 2012. Cain was one of the most outspoken opponents of the wearing of face masks and any public health restrictions relating to COVID-19. Cain proudly tweeted a picture from the Trump Tulsa rally, surrounded by a large group of his smiling mask-less friends. "Having a fantastic time," he wrote.[27] Nine days later, he tested positive for the virus. On June 30, the day he was hospitalized, he praised South Dakota Governor Kristi Noem for not requiring masks at an upcoming Trump campaign event, tweeting "Masks will not be mandatory for the event, which will be attended by President Trump. PEOPLE ARE FED UP!"[28] Cain died four weeks later on July 30. White House officials immediately began warning reporters that they should not "politicize" Cain's death.

The political fall-out from the Tulsa rally debacle continued to rage long after Trump had returned to Washington. The poor showing was particularly painful since Trump had bragged about having received one million RSVP's to his "return to the campaign trail" event, tweeting that "Almost One Million people requested tickets for the Saturday Night Rally in Tulsa, Oklahoma!"

While waning interest in MAGA-style rallies by Trump followers may have played some role in the poor turnout, many, if not most, of the ticket requests were the result of a coordinated trolling campaign organized mainly through TikTok, the social media platform catering primarily to a teenage audience and for its promotion of "K-Pop" (Korean Pop Music). The plan was a simple one: encourage people to register online for the free event and then not show up.[29]

Trump campaign chairman Brad Parscale had the opportunity to lay off some of the blame on TikTok for the poor showing by the Trump faithful at the rally but was apparently too embarrassed to admit that a bunch of teenage trolls had bested him and the entire 2020 Trump campaign organization. Shortly after the rally, Parscale told CNN Sunday, "Leftists and online trolls doing a victory lap, thinking they somehow impacted rally attendance, don't know what they're talking about or how our rallies work."[30]

Despite Parscale's denials, the general consensus was that TikTok's previously non-political teenage army of video viewers had struck a significant body blow to the Trump campaign. Steve Schmidt, a Republican strategist who managed John McCain's 2008 presidential campaign, tweeted, "The teens of America have struck a savage blow against @realDonaldTrump. All across America, teens ordered tickets to this event. The fools on the campaign bragged about a million tickets. lol."

Although Trump himself never disclosed whether he held TikTok responsible for the embarrassment he suffered as a result of the Tulsa rally, on Friday, July 31, Trump announced that he planned to ban TikTok and its Beijing-based parent company, ByteDance, from the U.S. market.[31] Trump's announcement came shortly after reports emerged that Microsoft was in talks to acquire TikTok's video-sharing U.S. operations. TikTok had been accused of being a data-gathering arm of the Chinese Communist Party (CCP), and both Australia and U.K. were considering a similar ban. Of course, the potential security risks posed by TikTok and its Chinese government affiliates were all well-known to U.S. intelligence sources and the White House long before the Tulsa rally. And yet Trump characteristically waited until TikToc emerged as a social media platform hostile to his re-election campaign before taking executive action against it. The potential national security threat it posed was clearly a matter of secondary concern to the Trump White House.

THE WHITE HOUSE RAISES THE WHITE FLAG OF SURRENDER

During most of the COVID-19 crisis, the Trump administration bet heavily on a public relations strategy of wishful thinking, giving the American public optimistic and totally unrealistic predictions that never came to fruition. At first, in January and early February, the White House's initial message was that the virus wasn't a threat at all. Asked if he was worried about a pandemic, Trump said at the time, "It's one person coming in from China, and we have it under control. It's going to be just fine."[1]

When it was clear that the virus was indeed a threat that could not be wholly ignored, the White House recalibrated its message, with Trump promising that "the problem goes away in April" and predicting "packed churches all over our country" on Easter Sunday. Vice President Mike Pence chimed in, claiming that "by Memorial Day weekend, we will have this coronavirus epidemic behind us." Jared Kushner predicted the country would be "really rocking again" by July because Americans were "on the other side of the medical aspect of this."[2]

But reports that the crisis "was over" were premature. The virus never got the memo from the White House, ordering it to vacate the country by Easter or any other arbitrary deadline. It continued to act in a coldly apolitical and utterly ruthless manner. It made no difference whether its targets were in Red States or Blue States, and it did not care about the political affiliations of its victims. Unlike the Trump administration, it strictly followed the science with mathematical precision. If given the opportunity - such as at a Trump rally- where the wearing of a face mask and social distancing was considered unpatriotic, so much the better.

As Trump's arbitrary deadlines for the crisis to end came and went, and with the virus spreading even more rapidly across the country, the Trump administration finally realized that its "denial" strategy was not working. The rapidly growing crisis now posed an existential threat to his presidency. The Democratic presidential contenders were seizing on the pandemic and the administration's lackluster response to it as a key campaign issue. It began to look as if the Trump administration's legacy and Trump's reelection prospects might rise or fall on this issue.

At the same time, as of mid-March, there was a dramatic escalation of precautions within the White House that attracted a great deal of press attention. Everyone entering the building were now being screened after it was learned that Trump unknowingly interacted with at least three people who have since tested positive for the virus. Both his press secretary, Stephanie Grisham, and his outgoing acting chief of staff, Mick Mulvaney, were now isolating themselves at home after coming into direct or indirect contact with those who had COVID-19.

It soon became apparent that Trump could not continue with his Pollyanna views of where the crisis was headed. So his senior advisors persuaded him to abruptly change his message. Instead of downplaying and denying that there was a serious problem, the White House did a complete about-face. It now acknowledged that the crisis was, indeed, serious, and that Trump, as Commander-in-Chief, would save the country by swiftly crushing the evil virus in an all-out war against it.

On Monday, March 16, Trump dramatically announced at a White House press briefing that the crisis was a serious one. He delivered a somber message to all Americans that the country was now faced with a new reality that would dramatically change their lives for months to come.[3] Comparing the current crisis to World War II, Trump called upon his fellow citizens to now do the same in the battle against this "invisible enemy." Trump told reporters, "Every generation of Americans has been called to make shared sacrifices for the good of the nation," adding, "Now it's our time," he said. "We must sacrifice together, because we are all in this together, and we will come through together." Uncharacteristically, Trump even went so far as to make a direct appeal to his fellow citizens to do their part to halt the pandemic's spread. He outlined the government's newest recommendations, including urging all older Americans and those with chronic health conditions to stay home and advising everyone to avoid gatherings of more than ten people.

Similarly, on Wednesday, March 18, at a White House press conference, Trump described himself as a "wartime president" in the struggle against the virus.⁴ He invoked the Defense Production Act, which allowed the federal government to direct the private sector to ramp-up manufacturing and distribution of emergency medical supplies and equipment. When specifically asked if he saw the nation as being on a wartime footing, he said he did, describing himself again as "in a sense a wartime president."

While this "wartime" narrative was a refreshing change of tone and provided some colorful rhetoric, it was doomed from the start. The Trump administration never had any serious intention – or was simply incapable - of implementing any forceful and organized national response to the crisis. Within days, Trump quickly pivoted back into more familiar territory, aligning the White House once again with the "pandemic denial" movement of right-wing and Tea Party activists. These demonstrators were showing up at their state capitols armed to the teeth and protesting stay-at-home and social distancing orders as infringements on their "freedoms." Trump signaled his support for these protesters, who were demanding that various Democratic governors open up their states, even as the number of coronavirus cases in those states was still rising. "LIBERATE MICHIGAN!" and "LIBERATE MINNESOTA!" and "LIBERATE VIRGINIA," Trump wrote on Twitter.⁵ Shirking federal responsibility once again, Trump shifted responsibility (and blame) for the pandemic to the state governors, saying, "The federal government will be watching them very closely …."⁶

Trump was gambling once again on the possibility that if his administration shifted responsibility to the states and did basically nothing, while at the same time urging the states to open back up their economies as quickly as possible, then he would look like a genius if the virus suddenly "just faded away." He would have hit the political jackpot and sailed smoothly to reelection in November. And if the virus did not magically disappear, then he calculated that he could still duck responsibility by blaming the states for inadequately responding to the crisis. But this gamble did not work out for him. The virus did not go away, and the press and American public squarely placed much of the blame for the failed response effort for the crisis where it properly belonged: at the doorstep of the White House.

Trump was now being tagged with the worst adjective in his arsenal of insults: a "loser." The appropriate thing to do would be to apologize to the

American people for his mishandling of the crisis and ask for forgiveness from the families of those who had needlessly died preventable deaths. Then he could resign with whatever remaining dignity he could muster while accepting a pardon from the newly sworn-in President Pence. This is what happened in August 1974 when Vice President Gerald Ford had taken over from a similarly disgraced President Richard Nixon. But we all knew that this was not Trump's style.

With Independence Day 2020 rapidly approaching, the U.S. reported more than 55,000 new cases of coronavirus in one day, as of Thursday, July 2.[7] Newly reported cases of the virus were rising in all but a handful of states. Many large cities, including Houston, Dallas, Jacksonville, and Los Angeles, were seeing alarming growth. Some cities and states were reversing their openings, with bars and restaurants that were reopening being ordered to shut down again.

By July 4, 130,000 deaths had been reported linked to the virus. New cases reported in the U.S. had increased by 90% in the two weeks after Independence Day, and at least five states — Alabama, Alaska, Kansas, North Carolina, and South Carolina — reported their highest single day of cases yet.[8]

Dr. Anthony Fauci was continuing to issue dire warnings on the future of the pandemic. He testified on Capitol Hill that if current trends continued, Americans could see as many as 100,000 new cases daily.[9] In an interview with *BBC Radio* on Thursday, July 2, Fauci said: "What we've seen over the last several days is a spike in cases that are well beyond the worse spikes that we've seen. That is not good news, we've got to get that under control, or we risk an even greater outbreak in the United States."[10]

Trump's new message to America on Independence Day was one of fatalistic surrender: "It is not going away anytime soon. Learn to live with it."[11] The White House decided to emphasize the relatively low risk most Americas had of dying from the virus. At the same time, it tacitly acknowledged that the virus would continue to spread unchecked throughout America until an effective vaccine was developed. This message was premised on the completely bogus theory that the country was coming back economically, that face coverings and social distancing were optional, and that the surging number of coronavirus cases across the country was no big worry. Trump was asking Americans to basically "soldier" on through this crisis, accepting more and more casualties as inevitable.

According to the new Trump doctrine, America would just have to bite the bullet and accept the loss and the pain. A century before, in 1918, President Woodrow Wilson similarly ignored the devastation of the influenza pandemic that was wreaking havoc across the country. Also, in 1932, Herbert Hoover tried unsuccessfully to convince the American people that the Great Depression was not as bad as people were saying. He was resoundingly voted out of office because the country correctly concluded that he did not understand the extent of the national trauma and suffering.

Trump's new message was reminiscent of the "learn to love the bomb" campaign during the Cold War, where there was a prevailing school of thought in successive U.S. administrations that "mutually assured destruction" (MAD) was the best policy since both the U.S. and Russia had enough nuclear-tipped missiles pointed at each other to blow each other to smithereens several times over, so we just had to accept the fact that every day could be our last.

"We have to get back to business. We have to get back to living our lives. Can't do this any longer," Trump said in an interview with *Axios* before his campaign rally in Tulsa, where almost no one socially distanced and few wore masks. "And I do believe it's safe. I do believe it's very safe," he added.[12] A number of Trump's own campaign staffers and Secret Service agents contracted COVID-19 in Tulsa, and Donald Trump Jr.'s girlfriend (a Trump campaign staffer) tested positive for the virus just before the subsequent July 3 Trump extravaganza in an amphitheater filled with largely unmasked and tightly packed Trump supporters at Mount Rushmore.[13]

On Thursday, July 2, Trump claimed that when Pence held a recent call with governors and asked the state executives what they might need, none of them requested federal assistance. "Not one governor needed anything. They don't need anything. They have all the medical equipment they can have. Thank you, U.S. government," Trump said.[14] However, Trump either was not communicating with Pence or, more likely, was just making it up as he went along. When Pence visited places with major virus outbreaks such as Dallas, Phoenix, and Tampa, he noted that several of the governors had requested federal assistance on several levels. For example, Texas Governor Greg Abbott expressed a desire to continue federal funding for testing sites in his state that was set to expire at the end of June.[15] Similarly, Arizona Governor Doug Ducey requested additional medical personnel during his meeting with Pence.[16]

Not all of those who traveled to Mt. Rushmore on July 3 were there to greet the president. Native Americans and other protesters blocked a road leading to the monument. They were protesting not only President Trump and his policies, but also the fact that South Dakota's Black Hills were taken from the Lakota people against treaty agreements. "The president is putting our tribal members at risk to stage a photo op at one of our most sacred sites," said Harold Frazier, chairman of the Cheyenne River Sioux Tribe.[17] More than 100 protesters, many Lakota, lined the road leading from Keystone, South Dakota to the monument holding signs and playing Lakota music in 95-degree heat. Some clenched their fists in the air, while others held signs that read "Protect SoDak's First People," "You Are On Stolen Land" and "Dismantle White Supremacy." "The president needs to open his eyes. We're people, too, and it was our land first," said Hehakaho Waste, a spiritual elder with the Oglala Sioux tribe.[18]

Trump had railed against other protesters in Washington, D.C. and other cities who had tried to topple Confederate monuments and statues honoring those who have benefited from slavery. It was expected that at Mt. Rushmore, Trump would continue his attack on what he was now describing as a "left-wing mob" and proponents of "cancel culture."

In his July 3 speech in the packed amphitheater at Mount Rushmore, Trump barely mentioned the pandemic still raging across America with 53,000 new cases mounting day after day. Nor did he offer any condolences or words of support for the families of the victims who had been swept away in the relentless path of the virus. Absent were any traditional July 4 words of encouragement to those who wanted to bridge the wide chasm that was now separating the country into two Americas.

Instead, Trump turned the Mount Rushmore event into a campaign rally glorifying himself, not the great country that was celebrating its

Independence Day. He insisted on an extravagant firework display in the pine forest around Rushmore in the middle of the fire season. There was no required social distancing for the crowd. And Trump could barely disguise his egotistical dream to have his face carved next to those of George Washington, Thomas Jefferson, Abraham Lincoln, and Theodore Roosevelt. The extent of Trump's delusional thinking as to his proper place in presidential history was breathtaking. There is no equivalent of Mt. Rushmore for America's worst presidents, which is where Trump has already earned a well-deserved spot.

At Mt. Rushmore, President Trump delivered a dark and divisive speech. He railed against a "new far-left fascism" seeking to wipe out the nation's values and history.[19] Trump had first burst onto the presidential campaign scene with foreboding tales of hordes of Hispanic males pouring across the country's unprotected southern border to rape, murder and pillage their way across America's heartland. Trump now set up a new straw-man version of the bogeyman by fabricating a shadowy leftist horde inciting mayhem, pulling down monuments, and taking over the country by upending its democratic and cultural institutions.

"Our nation is witnessing a merciless campaign to wipe out our history, defame our heroes, erase our values and indoctrinate our children," Trump said ominously, "Angry mobs are trying to tear down statues of our founders, deface our most sacred memorials and unleash a wave of violent crime in our cities."[20] In the face of such a threat, only Trump, of course, could save us.

As presidential historian Michael Beschloss remarked, "Most presidents in history have understood that when they appear at a national monument, it's usually a moment to act as a unifying chief of state, not a partisan divider," he continued, "I don't think it will work, because what he is trying to do is pretend that the situation is better than it is."[21]

After flying back to Washington on Air Force One, Trump ratcheted up the rhetoric to an even higher level of hysteria the following day, July 4. He compared his new battle against an imaginary leftist conspiracy to the U.S.'s struggle against Nazi fascism. "We are now in the process of defeating the radical left, the Marxists, the anarchists, the agitators, the looters, and people who, in many instances, have absolutely no clue what they are doing," Trump declared in his July 4 speech from the South Lawn of the White House.[22] The Trump faithful that gathered on the South Lawn to hear Trump speak seemed to make a point of avoiding social distancing and the wearing of face masks. It was almost as if the Trump Team was intentionally seeking to sabotage the administration's own public health experts. Trump did make a passing reference to the coronavirus pandemic, repeating his bizarre claim that the reason that the number of reported cases was rising in the U.S. was that there was more testing being done. For obvious reasons, Trump ignored the inconvenient truth that the number of actual hospitalizations was rising sharply in some areas of the country. For example, hospitals in at least two Texas counties were reporting that they were at full capacity at the start of the holiday weekend. Arizona, Florida, and California were also reporting increasing hospitalizations.

Trump also came up with the novel theory that 99% of the cases "were totally harmless." This claim was totally at odds with data from the John Hopkins University, which estimated that there was a 4.6% fatality rate for at least 2.8 million coronavirus cases in the U.S. up to that time.[23]

On July 4, Trump also stepped up his verbal attacks on China as the party responsible for the coronavirus pandemic: "China's secrecy, deceptions, and cover-up allowed it to spread all over the world, 189 countries. And China must be held fully accountable," Trump said.[24]

Notwithstanding Trump's attempts to minimize the impact of the crisis and to shift blame for the U.S. fiasco to others, there was no hiding the fact that that the Trump administration finally threw in the towel and was conceding defeat to the wily and resourceful virus that was now occupying much of the country and refusing to leave.

38

EDUCATION IN THE AGE OF COVID

While many students were able to overcome the limitations of distance learning and made reasonable academic progress despite the fact that they were being forced to stay at home, the disrupted academic year resulted in massive learning losses for countless other children throughout America.[1] In addition to deciding whether to re-open or not in the fall, or whether to continue with a part-time or full-time "distance learning" approach, school districts across the country also had to figure out how to deal with the widening educational gaps. Do you "fail" students who refused or were unable to comply with the distance learning requirements during the lockdown, or do you move them into the next grade and try to provide additional supports in the hope that students who went A.W.O.L. from March through June were somehow able to catch up?

The data and analysis of student performance during the lockdown period in the spring of 2020 were not encouraging. Preliminary studies indicated that, by September, most students had fallen behind where they would have been if they had stayed in schools with in-person classroom instruction, with many losing the equivalent of a full school years' worth of academic gains. Racial and socioeconomic achievement gaps continued to widen, which was unsurprising given the disparities in access to computers, home internet connections, and direct instruction from teachers. According to an analysis by McKinsey & Company, the average student could be expected to fall seven months behind academically. In contrast, Black and Hispanic students could experience even more significant learning losses, equivalent to ten months for Black children and nine months for Latinos.[2] This harm to students was expected to grow as most schools continued to teach fully or partially on-line in the fall.

The reasons for low academic performance by low-income Black and Hispanic students were readily apparent. Students in poor and rural school districts were much less likely to have access to computers and the broadband to use them. The principal of one high school in Phoenix found three students huddled under a blanket outside the building on a rainy day, using the school's wireless network to complete their required schoolwork because they could not log in from their homes.[3]

Even for disadvantaged, minority, and rural students who had access to computers and access to the internet, the on-line support that they received from their schools and teachers was far less. An analysis of 477 school districts by the Center on Reinventing Public Education found that only a fifth of these school districts required live teaching over video, and that wealthy school districts were twice as likely to provide such teaching as low-income districts.[4] Rural students were especially cut off from their teachers, with only 27% of their districts requiring any direct instruction from teachers while schools were closed.[5]

The disappointing results from distance learning over a period of several months came even though most parents committed significant amounts of time assisting their children with their education. According to a Census Bureau survey in May, parents averaged about 13 hours per week helping their children with schoolwork. Lower-income parents spent about the same amount of time helping their children as wealthier parents.[6]

The assessment of most teachers who were involved with the "distance learning" efforts by their schools was consistent with these studies. They were generally finding that the stay-at-home school programs that were implemented for several months, starting in March, were less than optimal. Most teachers were well aware that the absence of face-to-face instruction would be harmful to many, if not most, students. Still, many were equally worried about endangering the health of students and themselves if they returned to the classroom in the fall. "Teachers agree that remote instruction isn't optimal," said Randi Weingarten, president of the American Federation of Teachers. "The real debate, she said, is around how to return to school safely – and the need for money to do it right."[7] She added, "Either you have to be a moron about not understanding how government or schools work, or you have to be really callous and craven that you'd wait till the end, till it's almost too late."[8]

Lily Eskelsen Garcia, president of the National Education Association, said schools needed a massive allocation of federal stimulus funds to purchase protective equipment and hire cleaners. However, even as of late July, the prospect of significant additional funding to help states and school districts cover the massive costs of re-opening in a reasonably safe matter was still very much uncertain. Senate Majority Leader Mitch McConnell said that he expected Congress to pass one final rescue package, but did not commit to including assistance to states and school districts in that package.[9]

One thing for sure is that all school districts across the nation have a lot of "catching up" to do in the 2020-2021 academic year. Different school districts handled this problem in different ways. Some emphasized the reviewing of skills and content from the last school year before moving on to the curriculum typically covered in the 2020-2021 school year. But with many districts, such as Los Angeles and San Diego, not re-opening at all, and with many other school districts trying out partial re-openings and staggered in-school scheduling, the risk that many students would continue to fall further behind was high.[10]

Whichever path they took, the hurdles and competing priorities faced by school districts were formidable, and even those who are making a herculean effort to provide an excellent academic setting while meeting new state and federal health guidelines realized that they were likely to fall short of their optimal goals. The standard in-school educational programs had to be conducted with smaller class sizes, temperature checks and increased access to sinks, soap, personal protective equipment, and disinfectants. And even then, some students who were being told to return to school would not be doing so, with many parents simply choosing not to send their children back into classrooms before a vaccine was available. Also, in the event of another virus outbreak in schools, this could lead to unanticipated school closures and further interruptions in the school year.

Further complicating the fall semester was the fact that, after months of social isolation, many students would need a significantly increased level of social and emotional support from counselors and therapists. The parents of many school-age children had lost their jobs and were still struggling to make ends meet, which inevitably led in many cases to a higher susceptibility to illness and mental health issues.

So, where was the money supposed to come from to pay for these massive added expenses faced by school districts? The finances of many states were already in a virtual freefall with added health care expenses to fight the COVID-19 pandemic and falling tax revenues. Many school districts faced significant budget cuts and were not financially prepared to cover even their usual expenses, to say nothing of the additional expected costs of safely re-opening. New York City, the nation's largest school district, announced that it would slow down the expansion of its universal pre-K program to 3-year-olds.[11] Meanwhile, California's urban schools warned that budget cuts proposed by Governor Gavin Newsom could make it impossible for them to re-open safely while simultaneously helping students catch up academically.[12]

Trump Calls for the Re-opening of Schools, No Matter What

On Tuesday, July 7, Trump hosted a gathering of health and education leaders for an event billed as a "National Dialogue on Safely Re-opening America's Schools." In a day-long series of conference calls and public events at the White House, Trump Education Secretary Betsy DeVos and other senior officials opened a concerted campaign to cajole governors, mayors, and others into resuming in-person classes in the fall.[13]

Trump and others in his administration argued that since the nation's schoolchildren had been basically out of school since the coronavirus crisis heated up in March 2020, the social, psychological, and educational costs of keeping children at home would be worse than the virus itself. Dr. Deborah Birx, the coordinator of the White House's coronavirus task force, took the position that while it was important to keep students, teachers, and administrators safe, as well as families that include older people, the best interests of the students had to be given the highest priority. "I think if we put the child at the center and say, what is best for the American child? What experiences do they need? And when we come to the conclusion that they need to be in school, then we need to really figure out how to make that a safe environment," Birx said, "We have to bring in testing into the schools."[14]

Although Trump and his team emphasized the importance of in-school education for the benefit of the children, the underlying message had more to do with economics than education. Simply stated, if the schools remained closed and America's children stayed home in the fall, that meant that millions of parents could not return to the workplace since they would still be on childcare duty for their stay-at-home children. "It's not surprising," said Douglas Harris, chair of the Department of Economics at Tulane University in New Orleans and a public-education expert, "The economy can't really open back up again until kids go back to school."[15]

However, what was not being discussed at the White House was whether the federal government would be offering any new financial assistance to states and localities struggling with the problem of restructuring their academic settings, staff, and programs. None of America's schools had been built to keep children six feet apart or cope with the requirements of preventing the spread of a virus that, as of yet, had no effective vaccine or even cure. To maintain social distancing, many schools planning to try to re-open were being forced by necessity to use lunchrooms, gyms, libraries, and trailers as classrooms. Even those school districts that were planning to re-open were planning to do so with a mix of in-person and remote education that would fall short of a traditional school re-opening. Some school districts considered rotating classes in the mornings and afternoons or three days a week. Others planned to keep older pupils online while using high-school classrooms for younger children who do not learn well via Zoom.

Further complicating the planning of school administrators for the fall semester was the fact that the coronavirus case numbers and trends kept shifting in many areas of the country, making it difficult for school districts to formulate one clear-cut plan for the fall. Instead, most districts were being forced to map out several scenarios for the fall without knowing which one would be implemented on the first day of school. In Seattle, for example, officials planned for a hybrid re-opening. Parents were asked to fill out a questionnaire with their preferences, so the district could have their input in formulating a plan. "We're focusing on making that as equitable and safe as possible," said Julie Popper, spokeswoman for the Seattle Educational Association.[16] Before opening, the Seattle school system aimed to have enough funds to spend on staff and protective equipment to meet state health and safety rules, as well as to have enough custodial workers to disinfect. They were also planning to have nurses and mental health professionals in every school.

On Thursday, July 9, the CDC announced that it would not revise its guidelines for re-opening schools despite calls from the White House to do so.[17] Trump had criticized the CDC's existing guidelines as "very tough and expensive," suggesting that some of the instructions were unnecessary to the re-opening of the nation's schools.[18] CDC Director Robert Redfield pushed back: "Our guidelines are our guidelines, but we are going to provide additional reference documents to basically aid communities in trying to open K-through-12s," he said, "It's not a revision of the guidelines; it's just to provide additional information to help schools be able to use the guidance we put forward."[19]

The CDC guidelines for schools to re-open contained elaborate steps designed to keep children safe. They called for desks to be placed six feet apart when feasible and for children to face in the same direction on one side of tables and the use of cloth face coverings. The CDC also recommended the closing of communal areas like dining rooms and playgrounds and the installation of physical barriers like sneeze guards where necessary. It also proposed that staff who are at high risk of suffering COVID-19 complications because of health conditions could telework or be assigned other duties while children with medical conditions could learn online. Conversely, the CDC guidelines warned that there would be a high risk of COVID-19 transmission if there were full-size classes, a lack of social distancing, and with children allowed to mix between lessons.

After initially holding its ground for about two weeks on the school re-opening issue, on Thursday, July 24, the CDC caved in to relentless pressure from the White House to have the agency "order" school districts around the country to re-open in the fall, no matter what.[20] Trump and his advisors viewed the re-opening of schools as the key to reinvigorating the economy and reversing Trump's alarming polling numbers. Unless some dramatic action was taken to turn things around, the odds of his winning the election and serving a second term were looking increasingly slim.

The CDC disguised this dramatic reversal on the school re-opening issue on its website as a package of new "resources and tools." However, the CDC's new posting was prefaced with a blatantly political statement, listing the numerous purported benefits for children of being in school, while downplaying the potential health risks. "Re-opening schools creates opportunity to invest in the education, well-being, and future of one of America's greatest assets — our children — while taking every precaution to protect students, teachers, staff and all their families," the CDC said.[21]

Throwing caution to the wind, and abandoning its prior position that any re-opening plan had to be based on scientific evidence, this package of materials from the CDC began with a section titled, "The Importance of Reopening America's Schools This Fall."[22] It also repeatedly described children as being at low risk of being infected by or transmitting the virus, even though these issues were still very much open and unresolved within the scientific community. While it is true that children infected by the virus are at low risk of becoming severely ill or dying, the question of how easily or how often they become infected is still not definitively known, and the question of how efficiently children can transmit the virus to others is also unknown. Indeed, recent studies indicated that children in middle and high schools could be at a much higher risk of becoming infected and transmitting the disease than those under ten years of age.[23]

Aside from the undisguised political nature of its opening statement, the CDC's July 24 release included some helpful technical guidance and checklists that had been contained in its prior versions. These included recommendations on wearing face coverings, mitigation measures for schools to take, such as keeping desks six feet apart and keeping smaller-than-usual groups of children in one classroom all day instead of allowing them to move around.[24] It also suggested planning for how to handle someone in a school testing positive, including developing plans for contact tracing.

The Open-Air Classroom Approach

One major critique of the CDC guidelines is that it did not recommend one of the most successful schooling innovations utilized in prior pandemics: the open-air classroom. There is strong evidence that the risk of the transmission of the coronavirus is substantially reduced when people are outdoors. Only one case in China involved a fresh-air transmission.[25] A 2018 study of emotional, cognitive, and behavioral challenges facing fifth graders found that those participating in an outdoor science class showed increased attention over those in a control group who continued to learn conventionally.[26] At John M. Patterson elementary school in Philadelphia, student suspensions decreased from 50 to zero in one year after a playground was built in which students maintained a rain-garden and took gym and some science classes.[27]

So why would we want to restrict the use of school playgrounds, where children would be much safer than indoors, as long as they are monitored so that they keep some "social distancing." Similarly, the idea of surrounding each child with plexiglass "sneeze guards" reduces the airflow indoors and would only add to the sense of social and psychological isolation, which runs counter to one of the chief objectives of the in-school experience.

Prior generations of Americans may not have been smarter than we are today, but in many respects, they were far more creative, especially when it came in response to a pandemic. In the early years of the 20th century, when tuberculosis ravaged American cities, innovative doctors and educators developed the idea of open-air schoolrooms to mitigate the transmission of the disease among children. In 1907, two Rhode Island doctors, Mary Packard and Ellen Stone, proposed this concept, which was already being implemented in Germany.[28] An empty brick building in Providence was converted into an open space with ceiling-height windows on every side, kept open to the maximum possible extent. During the winter, children stayed warm in wearable blankets known as "Eskimo sitting bags" and with heated soapstones placed at their feet. The experiment was a huge success. None of the children got sick. Within two years, there were 65 open-air schools around the country either set up along the lines of the

Providence model or simply held outside.[29] In New York, some schools conducted classes on the school roofs, or out in public parks in large open tents, in an abandoned ferry and other open spaces.

This kind of ingenuity is sorely lacking in the CDC's and Trump administration's insistence that all schools fully re-open this fall, which is not going to happen. As of mid-July, Betsy DeVos had no answer to the obvious question as to how schools could fully re-open safely. In New York, the nation's largest school system, the decision had already been made to only partially re-open the schools, with plans for students to attend live classes only a few days a week.[30]

The open-air alternative, if appropriately implemented, could eliminate the binary choice that most school districts have made, between having their students come to school or to stay home and try to learn remotely. However, with the greater use of accessible outdoor space, students could be rotated inside and outside the school during the school day, thus reducing the number of students in a building at any given time. This would both promote the learning process while providing for proper social distancing.

New York City is particularly well-positioned to integrate outdoor learning into its school programs. Between 2007 and 2013, the City – with the assistance of the Trust for Public Land – converted more than 250 schoolyards to green space for student and community use.[31] The New York City Housing Authority has 1,000 playgrounds that could be used for outdoor educational purposes, and the Parks Department has 35 recreation centers, all of which were equipped with gyms and bathrooms that could accommodate a few thousand children.[32] However, instead of seriously exploring this open-air learning concept, the de Blasio administration in New York City concentrated its efforts on trying to figure out what to do with the tens of thousands of students who would not be attending classes on certain school days, but could not stay home since their parents were working or otherwise unavailable. On Thursday, July 16, Mayor de Blasio announced that the City was working on a plan to provide child care to 100,000 students in libraries, community centers, and other locations on the days they are learning remotely, something that would seem less necessary if more attention were paid to the outdoors learning option.[33]

The AAP Partially Reverses Itself on the School Reopening Issue

In June, the American Academy of Pediatricians (AAP) weighed in on the issue of the school re-opening issue by strongly advocating that "all policy considerations for the coming school year should start with a goal of having students physically present in school," the group said in an update to its guidance for school re-entry.[34] The AAP asserted that "the importance of in-person learning is well-documented," and that evidence already has emerged of "negative impacts" on children due to school closures in the spring.[35] One research paper estimated that, of the 55 million U.S. children who were out of school due to the pandemic, they lost roughly a third of their progress in reading and half of their progress in math.[36]

The AAP expressed particular concern that being away from school for an extended period of time could lead to social isolation. Prolonged closures could make it difficult for schools to identify students who were struggling academically, or who were dealing with domestic abuse, substance abuse, and serious mental health concerns like depression and suicidal thoughts. School closures also had a direct negative impact on children's nutrition and their physical activity levels.

The AAP guidance came as COVID-19 cases were surging in many states, leading the AAP to call for school policies to be "flexible" and "nimble" in responding to new information on the pandemic as it arose, and saying education officials should adopt policies that could be quickly revised if case counts in a given school or community spiked.

However, the AAP pointed to data suggesting that COVID-19 had not been as serious in children and that they may be less likely to spread the virus to each other. "Although many questions remain, the preponderance of evidence indicates that children and adolescents are less likely to be symptomatic and less likely to have severe disease resulting from SARS-CoV-2 infection," the guidance said, "In addition, children may be less likely to become infected and to spread infection."[37] One of the more severe health problems linked to COVID-19, pediatric multisystem inflammatory syndrome can be life-threatening to children, but so far, such cases in the U.S. have been rare.

The AAP guidance offered ways schools could balance the desire to resume in-person learning with the need to keep students and staff safe. The plan said school districts should do what they could to promote social distancing, while acknowledging the practical challenges that presents, particularly in over-crowded schools already strapped for space. The AAP pointed to some evidence that 3-feet of space between students may be effective in combatting viral spread, particularly if coupled with mask-wearing. The AAP guidance also said that while universal masking is "ideal," it is not always realistic, particularly among younger children.[38] While noting that some people have medical exceptions, the group said that school staff and older students — those in middle or high school — generally could wear cloth masks "safely and consistently," and should be encouraged to.

On Friday, July 10, however, the AAP did a partial about-face in its position on re-opening schools in the fall, distancing itself from the Trump administration's categorical calls for the re-opening of the nation's schools, no matter what.[39] The White House had cited the AAP's initial stance in order to bolster its push to re-open all K-12 brick and mortar schools.

The AAP felt it necessary to issue a new statement urging extreme caution. "Returning to school is important for the healthy development and well-being of children, but we must pursue re-opening in a way that is safe for all students, teachers, and staff," the AAP said in a statement. "Science should drive decision-making on safely re-opening schools."[40]

In a swipe at the Trump administration's politicization of virtually every aspect of the pandemic response, including the re-opening of schools in the fall, the AAP added that public health agencies "must make recommendations based on evidence, not politics" and said, "schools in areas with high levels of COVID-19 community spread should not be compelled to re-open against the judgment of local experts."[40] In an implied rebuke of the Trump administration, the AAP further warned: "We should leave it to health experts to tell us when the time is best to open up school buildings and listen to educators and administrators to shape how we do it."[41]

Never missing an opportunity to spin a new conspiracy theory, the Trump White House pushed back against the AAP's partial reversal of its position on the school re-opening issue, spreading the baseless story that the Democrats and their allies within the medical community wanted to keep schools closed until the November election in order to hurt his re-election chances. Trump also threatened to cut off federal funding to schools that did not re-open, even though he did not have the power to withhold such financing.[42]

School Districts Start Rolling Out Their Plans for the Fall

In June, around the time that the CDC and the AAP were updating their guidance for the re-opening of schools, several states began to roll out their plans for the upcoming academic year. Some school districts and states, such as New Jersey and Connecticut, included the re-opening of in-person classrooms as part of their plans for the fall.[43] But others, like New York City — once the epicenter of the pandemic in the U.S. — had not yet firmed up their plans, although New York City hinted at the strong likelihood of a hybrid model combining some remote learning and some in-person classes.

In addition to safely controlling the risks of spreading the virus in schools that were planning to re-open for in-person learning, school districts and states around the country had to deal with the issue of how they were going to pay for the increased costs of re-opening. A report from the Council of Chief State School Officers estimated that public K-12 schools across the country would need as much as $245 billion in additional funding to open in compliance with the recommended protocols from the CDC.[44] And yet, as the summer season moved closer to fall, almost no one had any clear idea where the money would be coming from to foot the bill. Local and state budgets were stretched to the breaking point, with increased expenses and lack of income driving their budgets deeply into the red. The only realistic answer was a considerable federal bailout, but neither the Trump administration nor Congress seemed to understand the urgency of the issue enough to take action.[45] Although the CARES Act authorized the U.S. Department of Education to provide $13.5 billion in funding for K-12 schools, this was a mere drop in the bucket compared to the $245 billion that was needed.

Betsy DeVos was showing such open hostility to the nation's public-school systems throughout the pandemic period that many suspected she was using the crisis to undermine the public school systems and to strengthen the private and religious schools that she had long favored. She not only was pressuring public schools to re-open and threatening to cut off federal funds for those that refused, but she also suggested that those federal funds could be diverted to families to help pay for private or religious education.[46] Also, the U.S. Department of Education started allocating "micro-grants" to families that wanted to home-school their children in the fall.

All of these actions served to destabilize further a national public-school system that was already in crisis since the pandemic forced them to close their doors in March. Since private schools are, generally speaking, better funded than public schools, it was the private schools that were better prepared financially to implement the costly modifications necessary for them to re-open safely. So by threatening to take punitive actions against public schools that could not or would not re-open in the fall, DeVos and her Education Department were driving wealthier families to take their children out of public schools, and either place them in private schools or to home-school them with the help of private tutors. The fact that this would markedly increase the already significant inequality in education in this country was of little concern to DeVos and her department. Families with limited resources and less flexible work schedules would be forced to send their children back to less-than-safe public schools, since they could not pursue the private school or private tutor alternative.

Colleges Plan For A Partial On-Campus Experience

Colleges faced many of the same challenges as high schools and secondary schools. Some colleges did not expect to open at all in the fall for on-campus courses, while many others took a hybrid approach, planning to have some students reside on campus while directing that others stay away and study remotely. Since part of the attraction for many students is the "college experience" of living away from home as part of the transition to full adulthood, colleges generally wanted to bring as many students on campus as possible without jeopardizing the health and safety of the student and faculty bodies.

Many college administrators were worried that they would not be able to provide the same level of educational excellence under restricted circumstances but felt that they had no choice but to strike an unsatisfactory compromise between educational goals and safety. "This pandemic is among the worst crises ever to hit Princeton, or college education more broadly," Christopher L. Eisgruber, president of Princeton, said in his re-opening announcement, "Princeton's preferred model of education emphasizes in-person engagement, but in-person engagement is what spreads this terrible virus."[47] Princeton said that it planned for most undergraduates to be on campus only half the year, with freshmen and juniors in the fall, and sophomores and seniors in the spring. Harvard took a slightly different approach, with its incoming freshman to be on campus in the fall, and its seniors on campus in the spring. All other students would have to stay off-campus and take their classes remotely. Stanford planned for only freshmen and sophomores to be on campus when classes started in the fall, while juniors and seniors would study remotely from home.

Cornell University was allowing all its students back to campus, with a mixture of in-person and on-line instruction being planned. Cornell said it based its decision on an analysis that found that conducting a semester entirely on a remote basis could result in far more students becoming infected — up to 10 times as many — compared with re-opening the campus. Cornell students that returned to campus or lived in off-campus housing were subjected to enforced virus testing requirements and restrictions on their behavior, which could not be done if students remained at home and studied from a remote location.

Even those students who were allowed by colleges to live in dorms on campus were generally required to view most, if not all, of their courses remotely from their dorm rooms. Students were being told they would have to eat takeout meals from the dining halls in their rooms, and some schools even required that the students make a reservation to eat.

The social scene on college campuses would be noticeably subdued, even for the colleges with well-deserved reputations as "party schools." There would be nothing even remotely resembling a scene from *Animal House*, since parties were banned and everyone would be frequently tested for the coronavirus.[48] Many universities were requiring behavioral contracts in which students agreed to wear face masks in public, to be tested regularly for the coronavirus, and to limit travel and socializing. If they broke the rules, they could be disciplined or expelled.

Most colleges and universities did not plan to offer any tuition discounts due to the limitations and restrictions that were being imposed. One exception was Princeton, which provided a tuition discount on the fall semester to those students learning remotely of 10 percent less — $48,501 for the coming year, instead of $53,890.[49] It was unclear, however, how students receiving financial aid — who account for more than 60 percent of undergraduates — would be affected.

Many colleges suspended their usual grading policies during the 2020 spring term, substituting a pass/fail system instead. Many of them, however, said they were planning to restore normal grading policies for the fall semester.

* * * * *

Primary and secondary education programs, as well as colleges and universities, struggled with the often conflicting goals of providing a sound education and learning experience for students while ensuring a high level of safety during the coronavirus crisis. While different approaches were being planned for the fall 2020 school semester, one thing was certain: that local school districts and states did not themselves have the financial capacity to successfully fund these programs, especially in light of the increased costs that were being incurred to meet the COVID-related public health requirements. Massive federal support was clearly required, and yet Congress and the Trump administration dithered and dawdled through the summer, risking the future of our country's greatest resource: our children.

39

CORONAVIRUS AND THE COURTS

The coronavirus outbreak put extraordinary stress on our nation's local, state and federal judicial systems. The onset of COVID-19 forced lengthy delays in both civil and criminal proceedings, raising legitimate concerns about the rights of defendants.[1] Once bustling courthouses were now virtually empty, with only a few judges and clerks pemitted in most courts. All court personnel and lawyers were required to wear face masks, with hearings being primarily conducted by video.

The coronavirus pandemic forced historic changes in some 230-year-old traditions at the Supreme Court of the United States, with the first-ever telephonic version of oral arguments taking place there on Monday, May 4, 2020.[2] These proceedings were also unique in that they were available online so that members of the public and the press could view them in real-time. Instead of the usual "free-for-all" type questioning, Chief Justice Roberts conducted the telephonic oral arguments in a more regimented manner, starting with questions posed to the lawyers for both sides by the most senior member (himself) of the court, and concluding with the newest, Justice Brett Kavanaugh.[3] Aside from a few technological glitches, the oral arguments went smoothly, and even prompted a usually-quiet Justice Clarence Thomas to participate in questioning for the first time since last March.[4] Justice Ginsburg's resilience was demonstrated by her willingness and ability to participate in the telephonic oral arguments from a Baltimore hospital, where she was still recovering from a gallbladder condition.[5]

Since a majority of the Supreme Court justices were over the age of 65 and deemed to be at high risk if they contracted COVID-19, it remained unknown whether the justices would physically return to the Court for the new judicial term beginning in October, or continue with the on-line format.

During the Supreme Court's virtual hearing of oral arguments on May 12, the Court heard a highly controversial separation of powers case involving the issue of whether Congress, as well as state and local prosecutors, had the right to subpoena and review President Trump's tax returns and other financial information. During more than three hours of oral arguments, members of the Court and the participating attorneys debated whether the executive powers of the presidency protected Trump from supplying information on his business affairs to Congress and prosecutors.[6]

Several justices were skeptical of Trump's argument that he was immune from criminal investigation while in office. However, they were correspondingly receptive to the Trump lawyers' argument that the House committees had overstepped in demanding information that was too unrelated to their legislative responsibilities.[7]

On Thursday, July 9, the last day of its term, the Supreme Court issued a pair of historic rulings, ultimately rejecting President Trump's claim of absolute immunity under the law.[8] In *Trump v. Mazars USA, LLP*,[9] the Court was dealing with a White House challenge to a congressional subpoena, while the *Trump v. Vance* case[10] dealt with a challenge to a grand jury subpoena issued by the New York County District Attorney, seeking Trump's tax information and other financial documents.

In a decisive 7 to 2 vote, Chief Justice John Roberts, who wrote the Court's two decisions, declared, "[i]n our system, the public has a right to every man's evidence," and "since the founding of the Republic, every man has included the President of the United States."[11] Roberts was joined in the two cases by the Court's four liberals, plus the two justices appointed by President Trump – Neil Gorsuch and Brett Kavanaugh.

Although the subpoenas in both the Congressional and New York County grand jury cases were for similar records, the victory in the New York grand jury case was a clean win for Cyrus Vance, the New York County district attorney. It gave a grand jury convened by him broad access to a wide range of documents that had been subpoenaed from Trump's accountants and from banks that have loaned the Trump business empire billions of dollars. Following the decision, District Attorney Vance issued a statement calling it "a tremendous victory for our nation's system of justice and its founding principle that no one—not even the president—is above the law."[12]

The Supreme Court, however, allowed the *Vance* case to be sent back to the U.S. District Court in Manhattan for any additional challenges Trump would seek to make.[13] In an amended civil complaint filed in that federal court, the president's lawyers challenged the legality of the subpoena and dubbed District Attorney Vance's investigation "harassment."[14]

In contrast to the decision on the New York case, when the Court sent the congressional subpoena case back to the lower courts, it called for far more detailed legal findings. It appeared to question, to some degree, the breadth of congressional authority. That all but guaranteed that the president's financial information would not become public before the November election.

These two July 9 cases were the most significant Supreme Court decisions on presidential immunity since 1974, when the Court ruled that President Richard Nixon had to hand over tape recordings relevant to the Watergate criminal investigation to a federal grand jury.[15] Similarly, in 1997, the Court ruled that President Bill Clinton was not immune from a civil sexual harassment lawsuit even though he was the sitting president.[16] The Court said at the time that requiring Clinton to give a sworn deposition would not be unduly burdensome, and his false statements at the deposition ultimately lead to Clinton's impeachment, but not his removal from office.[17] Both the Nixon and Clinton decisions were unanimous.

In the July 9 congressional subpoena case involving Trump, the Court's opinion was a cautious one, saying that "a balanced approach is necessary" to weigh the competing interests of Congress and the executive branch.[18] Roberts went out of his way to note that the congressional subpoena case was unprecedented. "From Washington until now, we have never considered a dispute over a congressional subpoena for the Presidents records," wrote Roberts in the majority opinion, "The dispute therefore represents a significant departure from historical practice."[19] While the Chief Justice affirmed that "When Congress seeks information for 'intelligent legislative action,' it unquestionably remains 'the duty of all citizens to cooperate,'" he said when Congress subpoenas the president, that implicates "special concerns regarding the separation of powers," which the lower courts did not take into adequate account.[20]

On Monday, August 3, the Manhattan District Attorney's office suggested in a court filing that it has been investigating President Trump and his company for possible bank and insurance fraud, a significantly broader inquiry than the prosecutors had acknowledged in the past, when it was believed that the Manhattan DA's investigation had been limited to illegal hush-money payments to porn star Stormy Daniels and Playboy model Karen McDougal.[21] Prosecutors cited newspaper investigations that concluded the president may have illegally inflated his net worth and the value of his properties to lenders and insurers, as well as an article on the congressional testimony of his former lawyer and fixer, Michael D. Cohen, who told lawmakers last year that the president had committed insurance fraud.[22] This Manhattan DA's investigation was of particular concern to the Trump team since the claim of presidential immunity would not shield him from criminal prosecution on state charges.

In both the federal and state courts, one of the major issues that had to be addressed during the coronavirus crisis was how to comply with the Sixth Amendment rights of every criminal defendant to a speedy trial. In addition to guaranteeing the right to an attorney, the Sixth Amendment to the U.S. Constitution guarantees a criminal defendant the right to a speedy trial by an "impartial jury."[23] This means that a criminal defendant must be brought to trial for his or her alleged crimes within a reasonably short time after arrest, and that before being convicted of most crimes, the defendant has a constitutional right to be tried by a jury, which must find the defendant guilty "beyond a reasonable doubt." The Sixth Amendment of the U.S. Constitution applies to the states through the Due Process Clause of the Fourteenth Amendment.[24]

In New York City, the backlog of pending cases in the City's criminal courts had risen by nearly a third between February and June.[25] Hundreds of jury trials in the City were put on hold indefinitely, since it was generally agreed that a jury trial by Zoom or videoconference would not be feasible and would be fundamentally unfair to the defendants. While there had been around 570 criminal trials in the New York State courts in the spring of 2019,[26] and there were as many as 15 jury trials going on each day in Manhattan Criminal Court alone, all trials statewide in New York were postponed in mid-March 2020 until further notice. To make the move legal, Governor Andrew M. Cuomo suspended the state's speedy trial laws.[27] However, as the crisis and the restrictions on jury trials dragged on for month after month, it was expected that at some point the courts would have to start ruling on the issue of whether incarcerated defendants were being denied their right to a speedy trial and that their continued detention in jails amounted to *de facto* convictions without trial.

In June, the state courts New York and some other states took the first small steps toward physically reopening, by having judges return to their chambers.[28] Criminal arraignments, pleas and evidentiary hearings were held, but almost all of them were being held by video. However, due to the shift to virtual video proceedings, those arrested were no longer physically permitted inside a courtroom to hear the charges against them in an arraignment. Instead, they generally sat in windowless booths in courthouse cells, looking into a camera and speaking into a microphone on the wall. They also had to communicate with their attorneys this way, which no one thought was ideal, but it was considered necessary given the highly contagious nature of the disease, especially in cramped and crowded jails and prison setting.

The number of criminal prosecutions also took a sharp drop in most cities and municipalities throughout the country, as state and municipalities tried to reduce the jail and prison populations for fear of turning them into coronavirus hotspots.

The national public health crisis tested the technical capacity and ingenuity of the courts to their limits, but most courts were able to maintain a minimum semblance of normalcy by mastering the art of the video conference for both emergency hearings as well as the daily run-of-the-mill arraignments, court conferences and other proceedings.

And then just when the judicial system thought it had got things under control, the killing of George Floyd and ensuing demonstrations around the country flooded the courts with hundreds, if not thousands, of arrests. Prosecutors' offices, which had worked for weeks with skeleton staffs, were forced to spring back to full capacity, with large numbers of arraignments of arrested demonstrators held in New York City and elsewhere by video. It was, as one New York City judge described it, "a crisis within a crisis."[29]

While jury trials are generally considered to be at the heart of the Anglo-American common law system of justice, only about 5% of criminal cases ever get that far, since most cases end with a guilty plea and reduced sentence that usually take into account the fact that the defendant has "accepted responsibility" by entering a guilty plea.[30] For those cases that could not be resolved through a plea agreement with the prosecutor's office, and had to go to trial, this presented an enormous challenge to the state court systems, especially for the accused defendants who had been arrested and either were denied bail or could not post the bail amount that had been set by the court.

During the summer of 2020, New York State and many other states did not have a specific time frame in mind for renewing in-person trials or grand jury proceedings. "I can't tell you we have a precise plan," said Judge Lawrence Marks, New York State's chief administrative judge, "It will be one of the last phases."[31] The reason for this uncertainty was that, by their very nature, jury trials require people to hear evidence in close quarters, and jurors are required to deliberate together, often for extended time periods, in relatively small and cramped jury rooms. "The whole idea of '12 Angry Men' screaming at each other over a telephone, over a Zoom network, would be ridiculous," said one defense lawyer, Joel Cohen.[32]

The federal courts were generally way ahead of the state courts in preparing for the inevitability that in-court trial proceedings would have held again, and that the backlog of criminal and civil cases could not be postponed indefinitely. In Federal District Court in Manhattan, architects and carpenters were busy redesigning courtrooms to maximize the safety of judges, juries, defendants, lawyers and witnesses, all of which were required for jury trials. Jury boxes were built with additional space between the jurors, and plexiglass dividers were inserted to keep jurors safer. Shields were being put in front of witness stands and at lecterns where lawyers would argue.

The question as to whether everyone in the courtrooms should be wearing masks at all times, however, raised some thorny legal issues. "You can't put a mask on the witnesses in a criminal trial because the defendant has the right to see them," said Chief Judge Colleen McMahon of the United

States District Court for the Southern District of New York, adding, "Jury trials are way, way down the road."[33]

Oregon state courts had already succeeded in reinstating in-person jury trials during the summer of 2020, but the issue of who must wear masks and when they should be worn proved to be a significant challenge.[34] During jury selection, lawyers who regularly relied on facial expressions of potential jurors in evaluating whether they are biased against one side or the other complained that they could not do so if the prospective jurors were wearing face masks. Similarly, defendants and their lawyers raised legitimate objections to witnesses being permitted to wear face masks while testifying, claiming that it denied the defendants their constitutional right to confront witnesses testifying against them. Most of the Oregon state courts accommodated these concerns raised by defendants and their counsel, requiring potential jurors to take off their masks when they were being specifically asked questions and giving their responses, and prosecution witnesses were required to remove their masks while they were actually testifying in court.

One reason why Oregon's courts resumed holding jury trials reasonably quickly was that the state had a rigid statutory deadline for trials of 180 days after the arrest, which applies only to defendants in custody. "Most of the affected defendants were in jail only because they could not afford to post bail," said Carl Macpherson, director of the Metropolitan Public Defender, the state's largest public defense agency.[35]

In another Oregon trial during the coronavirus crisis, the defendant opted to wear a mask in court, which one of the jurors later commented made him look a little like the infamous villain Hannibal Lecter. "I would have liked to have seen his whole face," he said. "If nothing else, out of curiosity."

Oregon, however, was an exception during the summer of 2020. Most state and federal courts were putting off jury trials indefinitely, a decision that that increasingly raised constitutional concerns about possible speedy trial violations among legal experts and some judges. For example, Senior Judge Jed S. Rakoff, who also sits in the same Manhattan federal court as Chief Judge McMahon, wrote in the *New York Review of Books* that if the danger of asking jurors to hear and determine civil and criminal cases persisted for a prolonged time period, "it is not easy to see how the constitutional right to a jury trial will be genuinely met."[36]

In addition to the concerns about delays in jury trials, the use of video conferencing for arraignments, preliminary hearings and other criminal proceedings also raised serious questions as to whether a defendant's rights to confront witnesses and to be provided with the effective assistance of counsel were being compromised. Before the pandemic, lawyers generally did most of the talking in court for their clients standing next to them and told to stay mute unless specifically asked a question by the judge that could not be answered by his or her attorney. With video hearings, however, defendants are no longer in the same room as their lawyers, which can lead to some strange and unforeseen results. For example, on May 8, a man arrested in the Bronx on an assault charge became upset when a judge, sitting at home, set his bail at $5,000. Moments after being led away, the defendant ran back into the booth, incriminating himself by blurting out details of the assault.[37] A court official eventually asked him to step outside, and then muted his audio feed. But the potential damage to the defendant's case had already been done.

Another man asked a judge in Brooklyn federal court during a telephone hearing if he could have special protection because he was cooperating with the government against his fellow gang members. His lawyer hurriedly asked the judge to seal the transcript.[38]

Another potential danger for the defense of criminal cases is that a defendant and his or her lawyer are generally able to assess a witness's body language and to quietly confer about the case. With video conferences and hearings, and with defendants and their lawyers in separate rooms, this is no longer possible. When the judge, the prosecutor and the defense lawyer are all on a Skype conference link, it is generally impossible for the defense lawyer to speak to the defendant in a confidential manner. Private Skype conference rooms are possible, but they are not foolproof, and mistakes and miscommunications often happen.

One of the biggest headaches for state courts has been the inability to convene grand juries, which given their size — they are usually composed of

16 to 23 people — have been unable to gather safely. In theory, grand juries are supposed to act as a check on overzealous prosecutors, but in practice their primary value has been to assist state and federal prosecutors conduct long-term and complex investigations. Without them, the justice system would be severely hampered in both the short and long term.

In New York, anyone arrested on a felony charge generally must be freed if a grand jury fails to indict within six days. Governor Cuomo suspended that deadline, which left about 400 people in custody.[39] However, by mid-June, the number of defendants held pending grand jury action in New York dropped to 87.[40]

Unable to convene grand juries, the city's five district attorneys turned instead to the lesser-used alternative of preliminary hearings, which had not been conducted in New York in decades. At the hearings, judges hear witnesses, consider evidence and decide if prosecutors' charges are warranted. Like everything else these days, these hearings are being held by video.

The two federal courts in New York City, one located in Manhattan and the other in downtown Brooklyn, were more successful than their state counterparts in getting grand juries up and running. Federal grand juries started operating again in June in satellite courthouses in White Plains, located in Westchester County north of New York City, and in Central Islip on Long Island. In both courts, regular audio and video hearings have been held, with dial-in numbers for the public clearly posted on electronic dockets.

Even as the federal courts began gearing up for trial, the problem of screening and selecting large numbers of prospective jurors proved to be a daunting task. In one high-profile capital case scheduled for trial, an Uzbek man was accused of making a 2017 terrorist attack that killed eight people on a Manhattan bike path.[41] More than 1,000 prospective jurors filled out jury-selection questionnaires, but these potential jurors were later dismissed when U.S. Judge Vernon S. Broderick postponed the trial indefinitely because of the pandemic. The entire jury selection process will have to be redone at some future date.

Another looming question in jury selection was whether a defendant could actually get a fair trial if the jury pool contained fewer members of the community from groups that were hit hardest by COVID-19, like older residents, African-Americans and Latinos, who were more reluctant to show up. Another question was whether a jury trial could genuinely be considered to be "public" if the public was being told to stay at home and limit their forays out into the world to a minimum. These and other constitutional and practical questions remained to be answered as the coronavirus crisis wore on.

40

A TALE OF TWO COUNTRIES:

THE RICH GET EVEN RICHER AND THE POOR (YOU GUESSED IT) EVEN POORER

On March 26, the U.S. Labor Department reported that a record 3.28 million Americans filed for unemployment benefits the previous week as the coronavirus pandemic shut down much of the country.[1] Initial claims of unemployment were totaling 282,000 per week.[2] "This marks the highest level of seasonally adjusted initial claims since 1967," the Labor Department said.[3] And this was just the tip of the iceberg. The Labor Department said 20.5 million people lost their jobs in April, and by May 21, a staggering total of 38.6 million unemployment claims had been filed within the nine weeks since the crisis first started to rock the U.S. economy.[4]

Congress' response was to quickly enact an unprecedented $2.2 trillion relief act in an attempt to forestall a total economic collapse. On Friday, March 27, President Trump signed the Coronavirus Aid, Relief, and Economic Security (CARES) Act into law.[5] One of the key provisions was that most Americans would receive a one-time direct deposition of up to $1,200, and married couples would receive $2,400.[6] In addition, $250 billion was provided for supplemental unemployment payments of an additional $600 per week for four months, on top of what state programs paid. This program also applied to the self-employed, independent contractors, and gig economy workers. Also, $350 billion was allocated for small business relief, with companies with 500 or fewer employees that maintained their payroll during coronavirus could receive up to 8 weeks of cash-flow assistance. If employers maintained payroll, the portion of the loans used for covering payroll costs, interest on mortgage obligations, rent, and utilities would be forgiven. Large corporations received the most significant piece of the pie, with $500 billion being allotted to the Treasury Department to provide loans, loan guarantees, and other investments. Airlines were allocated $50 billion (of the $500 billion) for passenger air carriers and $8 billion for cargo air carriers. Over $140 billion was also appropriated to support the U.S. health care system, of which $100 billion was being injected directly into hospitals. All testing and potential vaccines for COVID-19 would be covered at no cost to patients.

The receipt of $1,200 "stimulus" checks by 140 million U.S. households was a welcome and much-needed infusion of cash into the economy. Also, the $250 billion allocated for the unemployment insurance programs provided unemployed workers with a temporary source of income to pay for food and other necessities during the crisis. However, other parts of the CARES program – particularly the $500 billion giveaway program to big business – were extremely questionable. In many ways, the CARES program appeared to be a repeat of the 2008 corporate bailout of some major corporations and financial institutions at the start of what is now referred to as the "Great Recession."

The biggest "losers" in the CARES Act were state, local and tribal governments, which would receive only $150 billion, with $30 billion to be set aside for states and educational institutions, $45 billion for disaster relief, and $25 billion for transit programs. This was only a drop in the budget compared to what the states and local governments needed, as they were hemorrhaging money due to the increased expenses of their coronavirus relief efforts, and their tax revenues had almost completely dried up due to the economic freeze. In order to get the legislation passed as quickly as possible, the Democratic leadership in the House and Senate gave up their attempt to get the states the amount of funding that they really needed to continue operating. They decided to "future" the issue and hopefully address the overwhelming needs of the states and local governments through separate legislation.

The 2008 Corporate Bailouts

The financial crisis of 2007–08 was considered by many economists to have been the most serious economic crisis since the Great Depression of the 1930s, at least until the financial crisis of 2020 hit the country. This crisis began in 2007 after governmental deregulation led to the widespread abuse of questionable financial instruments, some of which were known as "derivatives," which were freely traded as speculative investments by hedge fund traders. This led to a financial crisis precipitated by the sharp decline in the subprime mortgage market and the virtual collapse of the real estate market in the U.S. The cascading impact on the financial markets developed into an international banking crisis following the collapse of Lehman Brothers, one of the major investment banks. The insurance giant AIG also teetered on the brink of collapse, but a decision by the U.S. government that AIG was "too big to fail" led to a massive bailout by the government.[7]

The Emergency Economic Stabilization Act of 2008, more aptly referred to as the "bank bailout of 2008," was proposed by Treasury Secretary Henry Paulson, passed by Congress, and signed into law by President George W. Bush on October 3, 2008.[8] This relief act created the $700 billion "Troubled Asset Relief Program" to purchase "toxic" assets from banks. The funds for the purchase of distressed assets were mostly redirected to inject capital into banks and other financial institutions, while the Treasury continued to examine the usefulness of targeted asset purchases.

After the 2008 financial crisis, there was a lot of criticism of Congress for bailing out the very banks and financial institutions that had caused the problem in the first place.[9] After all, if these institutions were forced to declare bankruptcy and to reorganize under Chapter 11 of the U.S. Bankruptcy Code, the stockholding investors and most of the lenders would have to share some or all of the losses. If this does not happen, the argument goes, then Wall Street, big banks and big business can't really lose. It's a "heads I win, tails you lose" mentality, with big business and the big banks immunized from catastrophic losses through a "too big to fail" philosophy.

The 2020 Corperate Bailout Program

Twelve years later, the 2020 coronavirus pandemic similarly morphed into another global economic meltdown. Once again, corporate lobbyists descended on Washington, their collective hats in hand looking for another massive bailout, whether they really needed it or not. After all, what is the point of a financial crisis if you can't tap into the U.S. Treasury for a few hundred billion dollars? If the government is giving money away, corporate executives view themselves as having a fiduciary obligation to their shareholders and their corporate boards to get the maximum amount of money that they can, since every other major corporation will be doing the same.

Corporate America and their allies in the White House and Congress pointed out that there was no "moral hazard" in bailing out big business this time around via the CARES Act, as there was in 2008, since the coronavirus crisis was not a self-inflicted wound by the large corporations and financial institutions. They argued that it was more like an "act of God" or a natural disaster. But this was only half true. In 2008, the government bailed out these distressed large and interconnected financial institutions because of the havoc such failures would have wreaked on the financial system. Anticipating this government bailout, some creditors loaned these firms too much money on overly favorable terms, counting on the assumption that the government would bail them out if disaster struck and there was a complete financial meltdown. These creditors gambled and won since they were correct in their analysis that the U.S. government would, indeed, quickly conclude in 2008 that these firms were "too big to fail" and that a bailout was necessary.

The origins of the 2020 financial crisis were not really as different from the sources of the 2008 crisis as one might think. There were, in fact, similar dynamics at work. In recent years, large companies took on a tremendous amount of debt. Recent financial stability reports from the Federal Reserve, the Financial Stability Oversight Council, and the Office of Financial Research revealed record-breaking levels of nonfinancial corporate debt as a potential source of systemic risk.[10] Several factors contributed to this excessive debt, but by far, the most significant factor was the low-interest rates in the U.S. and even lower rates abroad. With money so "cheap," America's corporations could not resist piling on additional debt. So, when the coronavirus pandemic struck, many corporations were over-leveraged and had insufficient cash reserves and staying power to weather the financial storm. By bailing them out, the U.S. Treasury and Federal Reserve were rewarding them for their individual and collective lack of resilience.

In addition, there were no incentives built into the CARES bailout programs to alter these dynamics and to punish corporations that engaged in questionable corporate practices, such as excessive borrowing. When the economy eventually rebounds, as it no doubt will do so over time, the large corporations – without any disincentives to do so - will again start using their profits to reward their investors and increase their already stratospheric corporate officer salaries and bonuses. They may even continue to buy back large chunks of their stock, which the airlines and other companies were aggressively doing before this crisis erupted. Then, if another pandemic or other crisis hits, they will just stop paying on the debts and, with good reason, anticipate yet another bailout. This cyclical corporate bailout strategy is, therefore, nothing more than a thinly disguised form of corporate socialism: "Heads they win, tails you (the public) lose."

Banks and institutional creditors were also among the primary beneficiaries of the CARES corporate bailout program, since much of the bailout money going to large and small companies would then be paid over to the tune of millions and billions of dollars to the companies' creditors, namely, the banks and institutional lenders from whom they had over-borrowed the money prior to the crisis. Thus by "saving" the companies, it was really the banks and other creditors who were being bailed out, risk-free. The same was true in 2008 when the bailout of AIG was as much about bailing out investment bankers like Goldman Sachs and AIG's other creditors as it was about "saving" AIG. The dirty little secret about corporate bailouts is that it is all about protecting creditors, and the CARES bailout was no exception.

The CARES Act created a Congressional Oversight Commission, designed to oversee how that $500 billion funds known as the "Exchange Stabilization Fund" was being used. However, as of Monday, May 18, this commission still did not have a chair.[11] That person was supposed to be appointed jointly by House Speaker Nancy Pelosi and Senate Majority Leader Mitch McConnell, but like with most things, they could not agree on any one person to head it up.

Nevertheless, the Commission's four members appointed individually by congressional leaders issued its first report on May 18.[12] It mostly contained questions about how the Treasury fund was going to function. The report described the lending facilities the Treasury Department had created to operate through the Federal Reserve, noting that only one of them had received any funding.[13] The program that was already funded was "The Secondary Market Corporate Credit Facility," which was supposed to purchase corporate debt. It received $37.5 billion, but the oversight commission had no idea as to how much, if any, of that fund had actually been given to corporations and the specifics about these loans. In addition, although the $500 billion Treasury fund also set aside $46 billion to make loans and loan guarantees, mainly to the airline industry, none of that money had been disbursed as of late May.[14]

The Congressional Oversight Commission's inability to get any details as to the disposition of the $500 billion corporate bailout fund seemed to confirm the worst fears about the lack of public accountability and broad discretion that the Treasury Secretary Mnuchin had in using $500 billion in taxpayer money as he saw fit. Congressional Democrats, including Senator Elizabeth Warren, who headed a similar oversight commission after the 2008 financial crisis bailout, criticized the money as a "slush fund" for corporations.[15] The language drafted by Senate Republicans that found its way into the CARES Act allowed the Treasury Secretary to withhold for up to six months the names of the companies that received federal money and how much they got.

Senator Warren, who had made corporate accountability a big part of her unsuccessful White House campaign, was particularly incensed by the lack of transparency in the $500 billion corporate bailout program. "We're not here to create a slush fund for Donald Trump and his family, or a slush fund for the Treasury Department to be able to hand out to their friends," she said, adding, "We're here to help workers, we're here to help hospitals. And right now, what the Republicans proposed does neither of those."[16] Other Senate Democrats chimed in. "We're gonna give $500 billion in basically a slush fund to help industries controlled by Mnuchin with very little transparency? Is that what we ought to be doing?" rhetorically asked Senator Mazie Hirono of Hawaii.[17]

Tax Windfalls for the Super-Rich Are Buried in the CARES Act

While unemployed workers and small businesses were receiving relatively small slices of $2 trillion in the CARES aid package, the wealthy and well-connected joined with big corporate America in receiving windfall tax breaks in the amount of $174 billion.[18] Some of these tax breaks actually undid the limitations that had been built into the $1.5 trillion tax cut package enacted in 2017. These tax breaks had little or nothing to do with assisting businesses or individuals who were being harmed by the coronavirus. One provision even increased the amount of deductions companies were permitted to take on the interest they pay on large quantities of debt. Only companies with at least $25 million in annual receipts could qualify for that break.

Another hidden tax break in the CARES Act permitted people to deduct even more of their businesses' losses from any winnings they reaped in the stock market, sharply reducing what they owed in capital gains taxes. Only households earning at least $500,000 a year — the top 1% of American taxpayers — were eligible. And yet another provision in the CARES rescue package allowed companies to deduct losses in one year against profits that they earned years earlier.

In other words, congressional Republicans and President Trump decided to bury numerous tax breaks for the wealthy in a $2 trillion act that was specifically designed for financial victims of the coronavirus-triggered financial crisis, not as another relief act for the wealthy. Many of the tax benefits in the stimulus package were just a way of "shoveling money to rich people," said Victor Fleischer, a tax law professor at the University of California, Irvine.[19] "Under the cover of the pandemic, they are undoing the perfectly sensible limitations" that moderated the size of the 2017 tax cuts, said H. David Rosenbloom, the head of the international tax program at New York University's law school, "[a]nd taking into account the giveaways in that act, it's a joke."[20]

One provision in the rescue package provided a tax break benefitting only companies with more than $25 million in gross receipts. AutoNation, a Fortune 500 company, received $77 million in small business funds, although it returned the sum after The *Washington Post* reported on it.[21] For-profit colleges with questionable records of exploiting students through excessive student loans quickly raked in $1.1 billion.

A third tax break for large corporations and the wealthy – worth more than $13 billion over a decade – temporarily loosened 2017 restrictions on how much interest big companies could deduct on their tax returns.[22] Private equity firms, which rely on borrowed money to generate significant profits, had been urging the Treasury Department to write favorable rules governing the restrictions on how much interest on their debt companies can deduct from taxes. They finally got their wishes answered under the guise of pandemic relief.

Senator Sheldon Whitehouse of Rhode Island and Representative Lloyd Doggett of Texas, both Democrats, asked the Trump administration for all communications explaining how this particularly egregious tax break provision found its way into the 880-page CARES bill. [23]

Not to be left out of this massive raid on the U.S. Treasury, oil and gas companies that had been struggling for years with low crude oil prices were given hundreds of millions of dollars in tax refunds under a provision of the $2.2 trillion stimulus package passed by Congress in March.[24]

The COVID-19 Billionaires' Club

As tragic as the coronavirus crisis was for most Americans, it proved to be a bonanza for America's billionaire class. In the two months since March 18, roughly the start of the economic crisis, America's billionaires saw their wealth collectively grow by a whopping 15%.[25] And another 16 Americans graduated into the billionaire class during that time period. Much of this increased wealth for the wealthy came from the government bailout programs that were designed to ease the financial pain of the unemployed and other real victims of the crisis. A Brookings Institution study found that young children in one in six American households were not getting enough to eat amidst the worst economic crisis since the Great Depression, while the Trump administration was trying to cut back on the food stamp program.[26] Similarly, a Kaiser Family Foundation study found that because of layoffs, 27 million Americans as of May 2 were at risk of losing employer-sponsored health insurance.[27] And yet the Trump administration, with the complicity of both houses of Congress, passed a CARES Act that resulted in a massive windfall for the super-rich.

Who says that America is no longer the land of opportunity? As long as you already had hundreds of millions or billions on your balance sheet, the pandemic offered virtually unlimited possibilities. *CNBC's* Jim Cramer best summed it up when he commented that the coronavirus pandemic produced "one of the greatest wealth transfers in history."[28]

The stock market, which is usually a good barometer of how well the wealthy are doing in this country, generally reacted favorably throughout the early months of the pandemic. The stock market's resilience during the pandemic highlighted the widening gulf between the two Americas: those who were wealthy and well-to-do, and those who filled the ranks of the 17 million unemployed Americans who had suffered job losses, foreclosures, bankruptcies, and psychological trauma during the coronavirus lockdown period. Between January and mid-June, Amazon's stock price rose from about $1,850 to about $2,600, and the S.&P. 500 — comprising large corporate stocks dominated by technology companies — had recovered most of its recently lost value.[29] Most highly paid professionals and managers were also able to keep their jobs, and for many of them, their jobs actually got easier as they were required to work from home and permitted to maintain flexible schedules.

In other words, the coronavirus outbreak was impacting Americans in radically different ways, depending on the socioeconomic status of the individual and the size of the company. To the extent there was some economic recovery while the pandemic was still ongoing, it was a big corporation and rich man's recovery. Large businesses were given the security of long-term assistance, mainly through the actions of the Federal Reserve and its promise to buy corporate bonds (including junk bonds), to provide "liquidity backstops." The Federal Reserve was now the corporate bond buyer of last resort, lending out billions of dollars against virtually any questionable collateral that companies could put up. Collectively, these actions provided extraordinary long-term assistance to major corporations and wealthy individuals who controlled them. There can be little doubt that these benefits for big business will give them a competitive advantage and even greater economic leverage than before the crisis, unless there is some drastic restructuring of the federal bailout and stimulus program to eliminate the substantial bias in favor of big companies and the wealthy.

By contrast, the portions of the CARES Act and other federal relief bills provided only short-term and stop-gap relief for small businesses and individual workers. The $1,200 stimulus checks were, of course, welcomed by the millions of Americans who received them. However, since the majority of Americans who received these one-time checks – those at the lower end of the socioeconomic scale – were given no assurances that they would ever see another such check and could not make any short or long-term plans that relied on any future payments. Similarly, the Paycheck Protection Program – designed to lend money to employers to keep workers on payroll – was initially meant to protect small business payrolls for just eight weeks, from March until June, when the pandemic crisis was expected to be over.[30] Since then, the program was changed repeatedly, and even though it was extended for a longer-term, its criteria for loan forgiveness became increasingly complex. This made it difficult – if not impossible – for small businesses with limited resources to engage in any meaningful long-term planning. As a result, tens of thousands of small businesses and individual proprietorships, which comprise much of the backbone of the American economy, just gave up and shuttered their doors, many for good.

The HEROES Act of 2020: When $2.2 Trillion Is Not Enough

Realizing that the $2.2 trillion CARES Act was not enough to stop the economic bleeding in the country, and certainly not enough to jump-start the economy again, on May 15, House Democrats passed H.R. 6800, a $3 trillion stimulus package known as the Health and Economic Recovery Omnibus Emergency Solutions (HEROES) Act.[31] The Act replicated certain provisions of the CARES Act, including the enormously popular $1,200 direct payment to American workers and their family members, up to a maximum of $6,000 per family, and an extension of unemployment benefits, which were due to expire on July 31.³² If allowed to expire – which is exactly what happened - millions of out-of-work Americans would lose the additional $600 a week in unemployment benefits that served as a critical lifeline to many of them, making the difference between the ability to weather the coronavirus pandemic and total financial disaster. The HEROES Act also provided for the suspension of student loan debt, and it set aside $175 billion for rent and mortgage subsidies, as well as $200 billion for hazard pay for essential workers.³³

In addition, the House relief package included more than $800 billion to state and local governments with severe budget crunches caused by the coronavirus crisis. This was a major Democratic priority that did not make it into the previous CARES Act or other rescue bills, and it continued to face stiff opposition from Republicans, who characterized it as a bailout for bloated blue-state governments.

However, Senate Republicans rejected the legislation even before they saw it, reflexively describing it as a liberal wish list that would go nowhere in the Republican-led Senate. Since the new Democratic bill was assembled by House Speaker Nancy Pelosi and other House Democrats without input from Republicans or the Trump administration, it was correctly perceived as an expression of House Democrats' priorities that they hoped would resonate with the public, rather than as a compromise bill they hoped would be acceptable to the Republican-led Senate. As a result, the bill landed in limbo from mid-May – when it was passed by the House – until the last week in July when the White House and Republican Senate leader Mitch McConnell finally realized that they could no longer just ignore the looming economic disaster for tens of millions of Americans. The $600 weekly federal unemployment checks that were keeping many American families afloat were scheduled to stop being issued at the end of July if no action was taken to provide continuing relief. But as the deadline got closer and closer, the willingness of both sides to strike a compromise seemed to evaporate.

On Wednesday, July 29, Mark Meadows, the White House chief of staff, told reporters after a full day of talks with Speaker Nancy Pelosi and other top Democrats that "we're nowhere close to a deal."³⁴ This appeared to be a signal that Republicans were willing to let this $600 enhanced unemployment insurance benefits expire, since and Democrats were not willing to bite at the Senate Republican proposal to scale back the unemployment supplement to $200 per week. Trump sealed the fate of any compromise proposal, saying that "we're so far apart, we don't care."[35] He even went so far as to undercut the Republican narrow legislative package being proposed, dismissing it as "semi-irrelevant."

The confusion in Republican ranks and the President Trump's decision to personally disengage himself from the negotiations, preferring to snipe at virtually all of the participants from the sidelines, was frustrating to both Republicans and Democrats alike. Senator Chuck Schumer, the Democratic minority leader in the Senate, summed up the general consensus by saying, "We're trying to get them to come to a coherent position. We don't even know what their position is . . . You can't negotiate against a ghost."

By Thursday, July 30, the $600 per week federal unemployment insurance supplemental payment program was set to expire, as well as the federal government's moratorium on evictions and some programs providing aid to small businesses. Still, Capitol Hill negotiators seemed unable or unwilling to break the gridlock. On the same day, the other bad news shoe dropped, when it was officially announced that the American economy had shrunk at an annualized rate of 32.9% in the second quarter of 2020, virtually all of it attributable to the coronavirus pandemic.[36] Unemployment also continued at a rate that exceeded even the depths of the Great Depression, with a loss of more than 10 million jobs since the pre-pandemic employment figures in February. And if the federal unemployment insurance supplemental payments were allowed to lapse, the economic forecast would get even bleaker. Evercore ISI, a financial research firm, estimated that failing to resume the federal unemployment payments would cause a drop in consumer spending large enough to eliminate about 1.7 million jobs, roughly equivalent to the magnitude of job losses during the recessions of the early 1990s and the early 2000s.[37]

Perhaps most distressing was the stark reality that the country had not reaped the public health benefits experienced by other countries that had put their economies into a deep freeze. While Spain, France and other

European and some Asian countries that had gone into lockdown mode were experiencing virtually no new coronavirus cases and were gradually opening their economies back up, the U.S. had plateaued at the rate of around 1,000 new cases per day, with the trend going in the wrong direction in Mississippi and several other states.

Realizing that they were in danger of paying a heavy political price in November if they left for their summer recess without striking a deal, the Republicans proposed a one-week extension of the $600 payments or a longer extension at $200 per week. But the Democratic leadership promptly rejected this stop-gap measure, holding firm on the broader package of relief aid outlined in the HEROES Act passed two months earlier by the House. Among the parties suffering the most from the financial woes of the prolonged pandemic were state and local governments, whose tax revenues had been reduced to a trickle, and school districts in urgent need of federal financial assistance to continue operations either on an in-school or virtual basis.

It wasn't as if the Senate Majority Leader Mitch McConnell and the other 52 Senate Republicans didn't see this political crisis coming. Since the CARES Act was passed in March, all parties knew that some key provisions of the Act would be expiring at the end of July, and others at the end of August. And yet they did nothing until these critical relief provisions were about to expire, other than to throw together a woefully inadequate $1 trillion proposal that deliberately ignored vital provisions of the $3 trillion HEROES Act passed by the House, including substantial relief for state and local governments, as well as school districts. The proposal half-heartedly put forward by McConnell included billions of dollars for new F-35 jet fighters and other military spending that had been diverted to build a border wall. However, the Republican plan allocated not even a penny in aid for state and local governments.

McConnell and other Republicans continued to refer to the House's proposed state and local government assistance as "Blue State bailouts," ignoring the fact that as the pandemic progressed across the country, there were many Red and Purple states that were also in desperate need of financial assistance. In any event, many Senate Republicans were expressing displeasure with even the McConnell $1 trillion aid package, so even if the Senate Democrats had agreed to it, it was unclear that there would be enough Republican votes to pass it. "There's no consensus on anything," said McConnell's deputy, Senator John Cornyn of Texas.[38] Senator Josh Hawley, Republican of Missouri, was blunter in expressing his frustration, calling the McConnell proposal "a mess."[39] Republican Senator Ben Sasse of Nebraska added, "I can't figure out what this [Republican-sponsored] bill's about."[40] Even Trump seemed intent on declaring the GOP plan DOA, describing it as "sort of semi-irrelevant."[41]

The White House also started to show signs of panic, with President Trump letting it be known that he would sign anything that was put on his desk, signaling that he did not really care about the details, only the political fall-out if nothing was done. Finally, on Saturday, August 8, as negotiations on a new pandemic relief package appeared to be collapsing, President Trump signed four executive orders seeking to prolong a federal moratorium on evictions, add flexibility to student loan payments and renew at least some of the additional unemployment insurance supplement for unemployed workers.[42] It was unclear, however, as to what power, if any, Trump had to order such payments to be made without Congressional approval. These orders were sure to face legal challenges in the courts before they could be implemented. The U.S. Constitution explicitly gives Congress the power of the purse. Any changes regarding taxes or spending are supposed to come from Congress, not the Executive Branch. Trump and his advisors gave no hint at how they proposed to either wrest control of federal spending from Congress, or to execute some sort of constitutional end run.

On the same day as Trump's Saturday August 8th press conference, the White House authorized the taking of about $50 billion from the FEMA disaster relief fund to pay for unemployment benefits, but that money would only cover about five weeks of payments. Then the White House probably would again have to ask Congress for money. In other words, Trump's unilateral actions, even if carried out, would provide only limited relief. Clearly, it was all about the atmospherics and political optics as far as the White House was concerned. The substance was completely secondary.

Trump's executive order approach to the economic crisis facing millions of ordinary Americans also ignored the fact that it would take several weeks or even months to set up the machinery to get the $400 per week into the hands of the people needing it. The $600 per week payments under the CARES Act were paid directly by the federal government as a supplemental payment to the state unemployment insurance payments that were being received by those out of work. However, under Trump's new executive order proposal, 25% (or $100) of each $400 payment would have to come from the states to trigger the federal "kick-in" of $300.[43] However, most states (especially Blue States like New York and California) were almost flat broke due to lack of revenues, meaning that there was a good chance that many states would be unlikely to be unable to come up with their 25% share under the Trump proposal. The unemployment benefits trust funds of several states had already been drained, and 10 states already had borrowed nearly $20 billion from the Treasury Department to cover their share of unemployment insurance payments, which typically last 26 weeks.[44]

Even those states who could cover 25% of the payments would be required to set up a whole new internal bureaucratic structure to integrate the state unemployment insurance programs with the federal one, something that could realistically take months to complete.

But these details were of no importance to Trump or his White House advisors, since the only important factor to them was the perception that Trump was taking a bold action in the face of growing political and economic chaos. The fact that no money would reach the hands of the Americans who most needed it in the short-term, or perhaps ever, was of little consequence.

To many observers, Trump's choice of venue for his press conference about the country's economic crisis and its impact on the less fortunate was odd, or completely tone deaf. With millions of unemployed Americans facing evictions and total financial disaster, Trump failed to see the irony of his choice of venue for his Saturday news conference as his private golf club in New Jersey, a pillar of wealthy privilege if ever there was one. Nor were the political optics helped by the fact that Trump chose to surround himself with several dozen obviously well-heeled club guests, who dutifully laughed at his jokes at the expenses of the Democratic leadership in Congress. If Trump's intention was to give the impression that he was the champion of the "little guy" and those that were suffering the most during the economic crisis, his golf club press conference conveyed the exact opposite.

Amidst the mounting political chaos in Washington, and with Trump hunkered down in his opulent golf club, one thing was becoming painfully clear: The infusion of trillions of dollars in federal aid since March was little more than the proverbial drop in the bucket, with an increasing number of Americans struggling – and in many cases failing – to ride out the storm.

41

AMERICA'S UNLUCKIEST GENERATION: THE DOWNWARD MOBILITY OF MILLENNIALS

Part of the American dream is based on the premise that each generation of Americans is better off than the last one. All that is required of you is to work hard and the will to succeed. Even if you don't make a fortune, you will at least be able to live more comfortably than in your parents' generation, with a high degree of economic security and peace of mind. This is part of the American mythology that has largely proven to be true throughout the country's history. That is, until fairly recently.

The American dream was a reality for the millions of Americans who enjoyed the benefits of the country's sustained economic expansion following World War II. Baby Boomers born at the end of that War or shortly thereafter generally enjoyed incomes and lifestyles that exceeded those of their parents and elders, who had been members of the Greatest Generation. America stood astride the world economic and political order like a colossus, and the American people generally benefitted from the privileged position that the U.S. enjoyed. African Americans lagged behind their white counterparts during these decades of almost uninterrupted economic expansion due to systemic racism in education, employment, and housing, but still generally did better than their parents had done.[1]

But beginning in the 1970s, the economic ladder gradually became harder to climb, and fewer Americans were able to surpass their parents in terms of economic well-being. Especially for those Millennials, who were born in the 1980s and started turning 30 in 2010, only half earned more than their parents at the same age, according to research by a team of economists led by Raj Chetty, a Harvard professor. In other words, the American dream had largely faded by 2010, and by 2020, during a pandemic and significant economic depression, the American dream became, for many, nothing more than a distant memory. Mere survival was becoming a challenge in a precarious Darwinian world with fewer jobs and opportunities available than at any time since the 1930s and the days of the Dust Bowl.

Millennials born in the 1980s missed out on the post-World War II economic boom that lifted the Boomers to prosperity. While the economy grew during their childhoods, the gains were distributed much less evenly, as the federal government backed away from policies aimed at minimizing inequality. The winners won bigger, but more people were left behind. In 2001, the year that the youngest Millennials turned 21, the stock market collapsed, and the economy fell into recession following the September 11 Terrorist Attacks. Then just as the economy started rolling again and Millennials were clawing their way back into the job market, the Great Recession of 2008 struck, further eroded the job market. A 2019 working paper by a Census Bureau economist calculated that while millennial employment recovered from the Great Recession within a decade, millennial earnings never did.[2] On average, Millennials lost about 13 percent of their earnings between 2005 and 2017.

A major reason for the downward trajectory of earnings for Millennials was that many of them had to settle for worse jobs early in their careers, which made it even harder to find a decent paying job later on. In addition, at the same time, large companies and other major employers were flexing their economic muscles in the labor markets to depress and stagnate the wages of younger workers, who often had fewer alternative options.[3] As explained by Ana Kent, a policy analyst at the Federal Reserve Bank of St. Louis, "If people enter the labor force during a recession, and they get into lower-paying jobs, that carries forward for much of their lifelong working careers." She added: "That's going to have impacts on not only their income but their wealth and also their ability to save for a down payment and their ability to meet other lifetime goals."[4]

As Millennials started approaching their 40s, life was looking rather bleak for all but the most fortunate of them. A decade of sluggish growth has ended in an economic collapse already more severe than the last. They had more debt, less predictable employment, and less reliable access to health care. The chance that they could out-earn their parents became increasingly slim. For many, if not most, it felt as if America had not kept its promises, and even the normal life cycle of growing up, getting a good education, marrying, having children, buying a house, etc. was no longer a possibility. Many were reluctant to commit to a partner and take the big step into marriage; many others got married or had a live-in partner, but could not commit to having children since they feared that the uncertainties of life would prevent them from even providing their kids the basic benefits that they themselves took for granted when they were growing up.

Even before the pandemic hit, Millennials had extreme financial vulnerability, even those who were better educated with college and post-graduate degrees. Others, particularly those who were Black, Hispanic, or women, or who have less than a bachelor's degree, were even more financially vulnerable than their age peers. Overall, Federal Reserve data showed that about 12 percent of all workers, including Millennials, could not cover a $400 emergency expense, even with the help of family or credit cards. The 12 percent number applied to non-Hispanic white Millennials, but the figure jumped to 32 percent for non-Hispanic Black Millennials, 20 percent for Hispanic millennials, and 17 percent for millennial women. For all Millennials with less than a bachelor's degree, the inability to be able to scrape together $400 for emergency expenses was an astonishing 25 percent.[5]

Thus, after having their lives and careers scarred by multiple recessions and economic downturns, Millennials were then slammed by the coronavirus pandemic, which secured for them the unenviable title of being the unluckiest generation in modern American history. After accounting for the present crisis, statistics showed that the average Millennial had experienced slower economic growth since entering the workforce than any other generation in U.S. history.[6]

The pandemic losses were particularly acute on the jobs front. A few brutal months of the coronavirus lockdown and a deep economic freeze set the labor market back to the year 2000. In April, the economy bottomed out with about as many jobs as in November of 1999. Things improved in May, but the improvement just meant that the country was back to December 2000 levels of employment. For Millennials who came of age then, it was as if all the plodding expansions and job recoveries of the past couple of decades evaporated in a matter of weeks. Just as Millennials were entering their prime working years, between their mid-20s for the youngest and nearing 40 for the oldest, employment dropped by 16 percent in March and April of 2020.[7] This was a more significant drop than that suffered by either Gen X (12 percent) or by Boomers (13 percent). The younger generation, known as Zoomers or "Gen Z," suffered even more, with one-third of their jobs evaporating in two months. However, since they were only just beginning to enter the workforce, it can be assumed that they would be able to bounce back faster when the economy recovered.

The *New York Times* took a survey of 40-somethings, and the responses tended to confirm that they felt like America had dealt them a bad hand of cards in the game of life. One higher education administrator from Wisconsin said, "Every time I've gotten a little bit of momentum, everything just grinds to a halt."[8] Another wrote: "My financial situation is vastly worse than that of my parents, who were 40 when I was born. They always owned houses and had new cars, never worried about seeing a doctor, benefited from solid pensions, and preached that college was the secret to their success. There were opportunities for them that they were able to take advantage of. There was a ladder. I'm not sure that ladder exists anymore."[9]

Another Millennial lamented that he had "graduated into a recession" and was totally unable to make his student loan payments.[10] Student loans were frequently described as "a black cloud over your head." One responder shared, "we're talking about two generations of student loans compounded for a college degree that everyone agrees my son needs to succeed in life."[11]

Many of the comments were about the inability to get a job that corresponded even remotely to their educational degrees or training. For example, one person wrote: "I ended up working in a call center for the next seven or eight years. I could not get a job that had anything to do with my degree at all."[12] Others bitterly recalled that at least two recessions had victimized them: "This is the second big recession for us. It's not like I can just pull out money from my 401(k). I emptied my 401(k) to pay for what I needed during the last recession," adding, "Every time I've gotten a little bit of momentum, everything just grinds to a halt."[13]

One pharmacist commented: "I'm a pharmacist like my dad. I ended up taking over his store, which he started a few months before I was born... The life I envisioned having when I decided to follow in my father's footsteps has not materialized. My worries about job security, and if the store will be able to stay open in the future, are constant stressors. It's nothing like when my dad started. George W. Bush and the Medicare Part D program really changed things. Now insurance companies are just squeezing you so hard. The big guys obviously write all the rules, so it's just constantly a challenge."[14]

The lack of adequate health care coverage and the financial infeasibility of home or even car ownership was a frequent refrain among the responders. One explained: "I don't have health insurance. I've been opting out of my company's coverage because it costs so much. Our wages have not gone up that much, and I'm single. It's really hard to afford a place just on my own, and there's no way I could afford the upkeep of owning a home."[15]

Even when their parents did not have particularly well-paying jobs, they still felt like they were again falling behind their parents in the great cycle of life. One wrote: "My parents, a mechanic and a waitress in rural Alabama, were able to purchase a home and land and save money for the future... I live week to week and rent."[16] Another wrote: "I am an administrator, which you think would be a decent living. You should be able to afford a car payment and a house payment. I mean, that's what my parents could have done. It was more affordable; their fair wages went further. But that is not something that's a reality for me."[17]

There was also an almost universal desire for fundamental changes that would make America a better place to live, and that it could be the country that once again lived up to its promise. One wrote: "I really, really hope that this pandemic changes things in our country and stresses the need for health care for all and more equality in general."[18]

"I am the portrait of downward mobility...With my master's, I became an adjunct professor and barista, receiving Medicaid, and SNAP benefits. Now I am in a Ph.D. program, deferring loan payments, and watching yet another job market shrink before my eyes."[19]

The U.S. Is Lagging Far Behind in Socioeconomic Mobility

The U.S. is clearly no longer the land of opportunity that it once was. Several extensive studies of mobility in developed countries in recent years have found the U.S. among the least mobile.[20] One study found that of nine developed countries, the U.S. and the U.K. had the lowest intergenerational vertical social mobility.[21] The four countries with the highest social mobility were Denmark, Norway, Finland, and Canada, where only 20% of a person's socioeconomic status depended on having a high-income parent.[22] Nobel Prize-winning economist Joseph Stiglitz contends that "Scandinavian countries changed their education systems, social policies, and legal frameworks to create societies where there is a higher degree of mobility. That made their countries more into the land of opportunity that America once was."[23]

One major factor explaining the relatively low level of social mobility in the U.S. is that children in affluent families have access to better schools, the key to higher educational and economic success.[24] Educated workers now have a decided advantage in terms of higher-paying jobs and professions, which was not always the case. While once "working class" jobs commanded high salaries due to the strength of the labor unions and an expanding manufacturing base, unionization has dwindled except for the public sector.[25] Meanwhile, high levels of immigration of unskilled laborers also have depressed wages at the lower rungs of the socioeconomic spectrum.

The more affluent are also generally healthier, while the less affluent and the poor are more prone to chronic health problems, like obesity, diabetes, and asthma, which can sharply limit education and employment opportunities, resulting in decreased mobility.[26]

The conventional view, as expressed in a July 2012 report by the Pew Charitable Foundation, entitled "Pursuing the American Dream: Economic Mobility Across Generations,"[27] was that a four-year college degree promoted mobility upward for those at or near the bottom, and prevented downward movement for those in the middle and at the top of the socioeconomic ladder. Having a four-year college degree was found to give someone born into the bottom 20% of the economic spectrum a three times better chance of climbing into the top tiers as an adult.[28]

Similarly, a 2009 survey of young adults[29] who worked full-time found the median income of those without a high school diploma ($21,000) was below the poverty level for a family of four ($22,050),[30] and less than half of what whose with a bachelor's degree earned ($45,000)[31].

On the downside, even before the coronavirus crisis struck in early 2020, many young adults and economic researchers were beginning to have serious doubts that a college education was as good an investment as it had been in the past, and whether it was such an automatic ticket to upward economic and social mobility in this country. In recent years, about 40% of college graduates were underemployed, meaning that they took jobs that were typically filled by those with a high school diploma or even less education.[32] Thus, college increasingly became a high-risk investment, especially considering that student loans totaling about $1.5 trillion have continued to plague at least one million college graduates. This often-crushing debt will follow these graduates most of their adult lives, regardless of whether they land high paying jobs or any job at all.

During the coronavirus crisis, the payments on some of this student debt were suspended. But without a forgiveness program enacted by Congress, these loan obligations will continue to be a millstone around the necks of Millennials, continuing to destroy their credit-ratings and lives. Without this student-debt relief and other mortgage-assistance, housing and jobs programs to give Millennials and even younger Americans a fighting chance at achieving the American dream, we may well be facing the prospect of multiple "unluckiest generations."

* * * * *

The economic devastation caused by the coronavirus crisis to countless Americans has only served to accelerate and highlight a trend that has been increasingly apparent for at least the past decade: the American dream is substantially dead for many Americans and on life-support for most of the rest of us. There is something fundamentally wrong with the American economic system that no longer provides less affluent and disadvantaged

Americans with a realistic chance for upward mobility, and even those of us who come from the middle and upper rungs of the socioeconomic ladder are in serious jeopardy of taking a severe fall or seeing our children working harder but living less comfortably than we ever had to.

America has faced these challenges before and overcome them, but it wasn't easy. In the Great Depression, which started with the Wall Street Crash in the fall of 1929 and continued throughout the 1930s, it was only the massive spending and public works programs of FDR's New Deal that saved the country from a total economic collapse. These New Deal programs included the creation of millions of unskilled jobs through the Federal Emergency Relief Administration (FERA), which was replaced by the Works Progress Administration (WPA) in 1935. These programs provided not only cash and much-needed relief for the American people, but it also left a legacy of improvements to our national park system and other public spaces that we still enjoy today.

The coronavirus pandemic and the ensuing economic meltdown also have reminded us that the federal government has a critical role to play in times of national crisis. It is the only entity that can provide the kind of massive cash infusions and programs necessary to stop the bleeding and provide the fiscal stimulus to jump-start a recovery. As with the New Deal of the 1930s and the Great Society and "War on Poverty" programs of the 1960s under President Lyndon B. Johnson, it is time for Congress and the entire federal administration to take bold and decisive action. We must not only address the short-term economic problems the country is facing but also to enact and implement a New-New Deal that can restore, at least in part, the American dream and reduce the widening inequalities in our economic, social and political systems.

In the past few decades, America has abandoned even the pretense of fighting a War on Poverty. Instead, it is now conducting a war on the poor and the non-wealthy, cutting back on food stamp and housing programs, as well as other vital elements of the country's relatively sparse safety-net while a public health and economic crisis is raging throughout the land. If nothing else, the callousness and cruelty of trying to crush a large segment of the American population at a time when they are most vulnerable and when they are dying at high rates is decidedly un-American. For all its faults, America has always had a big heart, and its sense of generosity and fairness has almost always outweighed the opposite human impulses of narrow self-interest and hard-heartedness.

In the end, the struggle for justice and equal opportunity is not so much a question of economics. It is about the soul of America, which has sustained our country's democracy for generations and without which it cannot survive.

42

THE NEW NEW DEAL

Not that many months ago (it now seems like years), Senator Bernie Sanders of Vermont, an avowed "Democratic socialist," won the New Hampshire primary for the Democratic presidential nomination on February 11, 2020, running on a platform of "Health Care for All" and other progressive proposals.[1] Senator Elizabeth Warren of Massachusetts was still in the Democratic presidential sweepstakes after months of campaigning on a "big ideas" platform calling for "big structural change." Andrew "It's the Math" Yang also had won an enthusiastic national following, particularly among younger voters. Yang was advocating a Universal Basic Income (UBI), which he called the "Freedom Dividend." It would give all Americans a guaranteed payment of $1,000 per month -- $12,000 per year – with no questions asked. But all of these candidates lost.

The eventual Democratic presidential nominee, former Vice President Joe Biden, appeared to be in deep political trouble after an embarrassing showing in the New Hampshire primary. He had difficulty winning substantial support from the progressive and left side of the Democratic political spectrum. He eventually won the nomination after a coalition of loyal Black voters in the South Carolina primary and middle-of-the-road Democrats throughout the country, including party leaders, handed him the nomination. This was just as the country was hit with the full brunt of the coronavirus pandemic.

At the time, Sanders, Warren, Yang, and other candidates who put forward clearly progressive agendas were considered to be too "radical" for the middle-of-the-road Democrats who controlled the party apparatus and levers of power. "Uncle Joe" Biden, on the other hand, presented a more comfortable, traditional Democratic choice, promising a "return to normalcy," which generally meant the traditional incremental Democratic approach to the fundamental systemic problems facing the country. Even the Affordable Care Act, which delivered on its promise of bringing affordable health care to millions of Americans who were without it, was consistent with this incremental approach. The Obama Administration and most Democratic leaders backed off the more controversial, but ultimately necessary, concept of Universal Health Care for all Americans as a matter of right.

So, during the 2020 Democratic presidential primary, the Party ultimately chose a candidate who would not scare off moderates and swing voters, who tend to get nervous around talk of "Democratic socialism," "big ideas," and "fundamental changes." Such talk, Democratic party leaders calculated, would leave them open to an attack by Trump and the Republicans as the party of "Big Government" and "Big Brother." The Republican Party could then distinguish itself as the party of "Small Government," allowing the invisible hand of the market and America's entrepreneurial spirit to propel the country to continued robust economic growth. In the end, therefore, the Democratic Party rejected the candidates with clear-cut progressive agendas in favor of the fuzzier, more nostalgic candidate.

Ironically, in August 2020, as the country entered its sixth month of the largest full-scale pandemic in 100 years, the concerns by Democratic Party leaders only a few months earlier that the American electorate might not be ready for a big, bold, progressive agenda seemed like a quaint concern of a bygone era. The pandemic was like getting woken up out of a deep sleep with an electric shock from a taser gun. As the full impact of the crisis engulfed the country, one thing became eminently clear to all sentient Americans, which was the necessity of an enormous federal response and economic involvement for at least the short-term and possibly into the indefinite future. This was no longer an issue of serious debate. Big Government is precisely what is needed in a time of war or when a calamity - such as a significant pandemic – strikes. Joe Biden's early pandemic "feel good" campaign theme failed to fully acknowledge that the current public health and economic crisis was painfully exposing some of the most profound fissures in our society that had been ignored for far too long. The ambitious progressive programs that seemed far too risky and implausible only a few short months ago were now being moved into the Democratic Party platform and the "First 100 Days" plan for a Biden administration.

The fundamental changes that Andrew Yang talked about in a futuristic sense earlier in the year were now a stark reality. He had predicted that within a four-year span, 30% of stores and malls would close because of Amazon.[2] Within four weeks into the lockdown period, virtually 100% of America's stores had closed, and while many of them would reopen after the initial lockdown periods in their respective states ended, it was expected that at least 30 to 40% would not. Thousands of stores and restaurants had already closed for good by August, and with their demise and the jobs that came with them, businesses would not be coming back. Also, as Yang and others predicted, thousands of warehouse and supermarket jobs would be lost to automation, further strengthening the argument for the passage of a UBI for all Americans.

Once a subject that no leading Democrat would dare to endorse, House Speaker Nancy Pelosi recently said a guaranteed minimum income was "perhaps" worthy of attention.[3] Even Pope Francis publicly came out in support of UBI. In a publicly released letter, Pope Francis wrote, "This may be the time to consider a universal basic wage" to "acknowledge and dignify the noble, essential tasks" and to "achieve the ideal ... of no worker without rights."[4] He recognized that, for many workers, the COVID-19 pandemic lockdowns were making it difficult, if not impossible, for workers to make a living and make ends meet. "The ills that afflict everyone hit you twice as hard," Pope Francis said.[5] He also acknowledged that the concept of labor was changing and that the era of the traditional employee was being transformed, as many people were now "working on your own or in the grassroots economy, you have no steady income to get you through this hard time ... and the lockdowns are becoming unbearable."[6]

Many had begun to feel that anything might be possible now in the COVID-19 Era and that we may well be entering a transformational moment in history. "I do think there's an FDR moment," said Senator Edward Markey, Democrat of Massachusetts and co-author, along with Representative Alexandria Ocasio-Cortez of New York, of the Green New Deal resolution. "Like 1933 — which would be 2021 — we can see that it is now time to discuss universal childcare, universal sick leave, and a guaranteed income for everyone in our society," added Markey.[7]

The Green New Deal itself moved from the left-of-center and progressive wing of the Democratic Party into a core element of the Party's agenda, calling for a huge new public works program to build environmentally sustainable infrastructure. With mass unemployment resulting from the pandemic shutdowns, the Green New Deal seemed increasingly attractive as both an economic and jobs shot-in-the-arm that the country needs as well as a long-overdue comprehensive national environmental agenda. Democratic nominee Biden's environmental proposals called for a trillion-dollar infrastructure program focused on the creation of "green jobs." "In lots of ways I do think we're closer to a Green New Deal than we were before because the necessity of one has become more apparent," said Rhiana Gunn-Wright, Director of Climate Policy at the Roosevelt Institute and one of the thinkers who first conceptualized the Green New Deal.[8] Andrew Yang was particularly bullish about the prospects of some sweeping changes if the Democrats took control of both the White House and Congress. "We are going to be faced with a national rebuilding project at a scale that has never existed in our lifetimes," said Yang.

As the coronavirus crisis deepened and attempts by some states to reopen faltered, the public support for New Deal-type "big" programs increased, with the polling firm Data for Progress showing that support for a Green New Deal has risen from 48 to 59% from May 2019 to the spring of 2020.[9] Backing for "Medicare for all" went from 47% in November 2019 to 53% in March 2020, when coronavirus layoffs were just starting.[10]

Millions of Americans across the country were facing extraordinary hardships that made this crisis unlike any other in their lifetimes, with the economic crisis being compounded by a health insurance crisis. People who had their health insurance tied to their jobs were not only losing their jobs but the ability to pay for their medical bills through health insurance. Almost overnight, the resistance to "Medicare for All" concepts evaporated, at least among those who once said they cherished their private health insurance and did not want to lose it, and now had lost it along with their jobs. The concept of a large safety net for all Americans, long derided as "socialism," started becoming increasingly attractive to countless families who were being buffeted by the winds of the coronavirus crisis.

People's state of mind also began to drastically alter as they considered what jobs and people in American society should be looked up to, and even idolized. After the September 11 attacks, American culture elevated soldiers, firefighters, and police officers to heroic status. There was little opposition to the militarization of police departments as America embarked on a campaign of endless war in the Middle East. With the pandemic, however, national priorities rapidly changed, and our celebrated heroes were now "essential workers," such as doctors and nurses, but also grocery store clerks, bus drivers, meatpackers, and mail carriers. Whether we remember their sacrifice when the crisis abates remains to be seen. America tends to have a short memory. Even September 11 emergency workers had to struggle to get the health care funding that they needed.

Senator Elizabeth Warren and Representative Ro Khanna of California proposed legislation that, if enacted, would assure essential workers that they would not be forgotten. Called the "Essential Workers Bill of Rights," it incorporated many longtime progressive labor priorities, including the right to free, adequate personal protective equipment, hazard pay, universal paid, sick leave, and paid family leave. It also contained provisions protecting the rights to organize unions and a crackdown on employers that misclassified full-time employees as independent contractors, and protections for union organizing.[11]

Unions saw their coronavirus activism on behalf of worker safety and benefits as the beginning of a new era for the labor movement, and rightfully so. The same happened during the Great Depression, which started with a huge disparity in power between capital and labor and ended up with a more equitable division of profits, with workers getting at least a fighting chance through their unions to obtain higher wages and benefits when the corporations they were working for were doing well.

During the depths of the Great Depression, America once before recognized the need for some fundamental transformative changes in order to ensure the survival of our democratic system of government and way of life. "Liberty," Roosevelt said at the Democratic Party's convention in 1936, "requires opportunity to make a living — a living decent according to the standard of the time, a living which gives man not only enough to live by, but something to live for."[12] His administration, working with Congress, ensured that workers had the legal right to bargain collectively, placed restrictions on banking and financial practices, and created Social Security.

The 2020 pandemic, like the 1929 stock market crash, came at a time when economic power had been concentrated in the hands of a few. While most Americans survived week-to-week without any meaningful degree of financial security or opportunity for advancement, a relatively small group of individuals and families – the New American Oligarchs – held a hugely disproportionate percentage of the nation's wealth. Over the past decade, the wealth of the top 1% of households has surpassed the combined wealth of the bottom 80%.[13]

America, the wealthiest nation on earth, is a very comfortable place to live in – as long as you are wealthy. For the less affluent and the poor, however, life is precariously lived on the edge, with little prospect of betterment. It is estimated that about 11 million American families can barely afford an apartment, spending more than half of their incomes on rent, leaving them little left over for food, clothing, and health care.[14] And they are the "lucky" ones since they at least have a roof over their heads. On any given night, half a million Americans are homeless, and their numbers are growing.

The stark reality is that when state and local officials issued stay-at-home orders during the crisis, hundreds of thousands of Americans did not have homes to shelter in place. As in the days of the Great Depression, many of our fellow Americans are forced to sleep in public spaces. Although the City of Las Vegas was lax in its enforcement of face mask ordinances and requirements of social distancing, its implementation of these ordinances against its poorer residents was much stricter. Painted rectangles were neatly placed on designated asphalt parking lots to remind homeless residents to sleep six feet apart.[15] Just as the French writer Anatole France ironically reminded us "the law, in its majestic equality, forbids the rich as well as the poor to sleep under bridges," current law enforcement practices, in all their majestic inequality, now require both the rich and the poor who make a habit of sleeping in parking lots to practice proper social distancing.

The inequalities of wealth in this country correspond to inequalities of health. A middle-aged American in the top fifth of the income distribution in the U.S. can expect to live about 13 years longer than a person of the same age in the bottom fifth — an advantage that has more than doubled since 1980.[16] Obesity and diabetes are largely diseases of the poor, and the opioid epidemic and drug overdoses also fall disproportionately on the poor, which is not surprising, since drug abuse is, to a large extent, a "disease of despair" springing from the absence of opportunity.

These patterns of poor health suffered by the poor and less affluent means they are twice as likely to die from COVID-19.[17] In addition to generally poorer health, those at the bottom of the income spectrum are more likely to have either lost their jobs or are still holding positions that put them at higher risk of contracting the disease than the more well-heeled white-collar workers who work from the safety of their homes. Every day, they risk death just to obtain the basic necessities of life and to survive until the next payday.

These gross disparities in wealth and health correspond to the distribution of political power, which also has trended in an increasingly unequal direction. Over the last few decades, politicians and policymakers have been able to largely ignore those on the lower rungs of the socioeconomic ladder because they lack the vast amounts of money needed to drive the political engines financed by the wealthy donor class. The non-wealthy also are divided by "wedge" social issues that Trump used so effectively in the 2016 election to keep many struggling white Americans from voting in a manner consistent with their true economic self-interest and the nation's collective interests. By the end of the 2016 presidential campaign, the expenditure of billions of dollars on a nonsensical wall on our southern border somehow became more important to many voters in swing states than the expenditure of billions of dollars to rebuild the country's infrastructure.

The concept that personal liberty is only meaningful if citizens have at least some degree of stability and economic security is not a new one. As FDR told the nation in 1944, "We have come to a clear realization of the fact that true individual freedom cannot exist without economic security and independence."[18] As we now know, the country is as far away as it was in 1944 to achieving the goal of economic security for all Americans, and the truth is that the country has not really tried to do so since the Great Society programs of the 1960s had some limited success in reducing poverty and expanding economic opportunities for the country's non-wealthy citizens. Since then, the country seems to have resigned itself to the fact that we are sharply divided economically and socially into two Americas: one for the wealthy and privileged, and the other for the rest of us. Millions of our fellow citizens are trapped in poverty from one generation to the next, and many of the rest of us who are fortunate to have good health and a job are still living from paycheck to paycheck with no economic security or "rainy day fund" to fall back on when an emergency strikes.

These two Americas are divided not only based on wealth but also physically, as both urban and suburban neighborhoods in the country tend to be economically and racially segregated. Even after mortgage "redlining" was declared illegal, single-family zoning laws and mortgage requirements by banks continued to exclude low-income families, particularly minorities, from more affluent neighborhoods. And, of course, better neighborhoods have better schools, since school funding is based mainly on property taxes. So higher property valuations lead to higher taxes in "good" neighborhoods, which translates into higher school budgets to provide a better education and more support services for the children of the well-to-do in the higher end neighborhoods. It is a cyclical process where wealth begets better education and a healthier living environment for the next generation. In contrast, poverty in poorer neighborhoods – with poorly funded schools in an often unhealthy environment with more inferior air quality and higher incidence of asthma and other respiratory diseases – leads to poverty and less economic opportunity for the next generation.

There are many ways that this cycle could have been broken (or at least bent) so that children born into poverty could have access to the same good educational opportunities as that of wealthier neighborhoods. However, these opportunities were missed. In a 1973 decision in *San Antonio Independent School District v. Rodriguez*,[19] the Supreme Court approved the practice that allowed differences in school funding based on differences in local property values, rejecting the argument that this was a violation of the Fourteenth Amendment's equal protection clause. The effect was to substitute economic segregation for explicitly racial segregation. State legislatures or Congress could have, through legislation, provided for greater equality in the funding of schools, regardless of whether they were in wealthy or poor neighborhoods, through federal appropriations not tied to property taxes. But they did not.

As the economy shifted from manufacturing to services, the federal government has also, over time, assisted in the evisceration of the labor movement. The right of workers to organize and join unions have been diminished with Congress and state legislatures siding with corporations that successfully resisted the unionization of new jobs. Corporations, not coincidentally, were the largest contributors to political campaigns and had the highest-paid, high-powered lobbyists. As a result, the economic balance of power between corporations and labor shifted sharply in favor of corporations and management, resulting in the purchasing power of the federal minimum wage falling since 1968. Companies were not even required by Congress to provide employees with such basic benefits as paid family leave, and they were able to avoid taxes by labeling workers "independent contractors" instead of employees. Meanwhile, executive pay skyrocketed, and shareholders enjoyed a booming stock market as workers kept falling behind.

Unlike virtually every other developed country, the U.S. has also never even seriously considered guaranteeing its citizens affordable housing and reliable access to health care. Although the Affordable Care Act was a good start toward the goal of universal health care for all Americans as a fundamental right, most of the debate since its passage against formidable opposition had been over whether or not it should be dismantled. In addition, the cost of a college education in the U.S. is the highest in the world, and it also lags behind many other countries in infrastructure investment, education, and basic scientific research.

Now that any serious reservations as to whether the federal government must take a proactive role in rebuilding the economy have been largely swept aside, the current crisis presents the country with an opportunity to makes some long-overdue and fundamental reforms. The $2.2 trillion CARES Act missed a golden opportunity to start this process. While costly, it was little more than a stopgap measure; trillions more will likely have to be invested by the federal government just to stop the economic hemorrhaging and get the economy moving again. But even these massive expenditures will do little to provide Americans with what they most need and deserve, which is long-term economic security and equality of opportunity.

In this moment of crisis, there is still an opportunity to make some of the fundamental changes that all Americans know in their hearts are long overdue but have heretofore lacked the political will to do it. In 2008, as the stock market was in freefall and key industries, such as the automotive industry, were teetering over the abyss, the federal government squandered such an opportunity by spending billions of dollars to bail out companies that were "too big to fail." The government should have, at the same time, made a relatively small investment towards greater equality and opportunity for those who had been part of the permanent underclass for far too long. When we look back on the coronavirus crisis and its aftermath, we will either be shaking our heads and decrying the fact that another such opportunity was squandered, or we will be able to proudly say that amidst this crucible of pain and suffering, a New New Deal was forged.

The purpose of the federal government, Lincoln wrote to Congress on July 4, 1861, was "to elevate the condition of men, to lift artificial burdens from all shoulders, and to give everyone an unfettered start and a fair chance in the race of life."[20] Now is the time to give Americans a fair chance in the race of life. We must not lose this opportunity to do so as we have in the past. This investment in America and America's future will reap benefits in the long run far beyond the billion-dollar corporate bailouts now being handed out by the U.S. Treasury Department.

We will be a stronger, more just, and freer society if we do so.

43

LIFESTYLE CHANGES IN THE AGE OF COVID

"SWEATPANTS FOREVER!"[1]

The social distancing and stay-at-home lifestyle changes that accompanied the pandemic accelerated the trend towards informality in clothing and virtually every other aspect of American life for the past several decades. For anyone who watched the TV series *Madmen*, or found themselves hooked on the classic films of Hollywood's golden era, especially those staring the ever debonair Cary Grant, there was a time not so long ago when men wore suits and ties to the office, and women wore dresses. Hard to believe, but some of us Boomers even experienced this quaint phenomenon during our own lifetimes.

Then civility and decorum rapidly went downhill in the 1990s, as the dot.com and high-tech revolution led to trend-setting Silicon Valley start-ups dropping the suit and tie look as if it were radioactive, opting for more casual styles. The term "suits" became a pejorative term for those who clung to the old ways.

As Silicon Valley goes, so does the rest of the country. Soon the arbiters of office wear invented the "casual Friday" concept, where office workers opted to forego the traditional suit and tie on Friday, forcing countless men across the country to actually give some thought to what they would wear to the office on Fridays. From Monday through Thursday, you could just reflexively throw on a suit while you were still half-asleep and rushing to get to the office. But now on Friday, you had to make difficult decisions, such as whether you had slacks that matched the sports jacket you grabbed from the closet.

One of the last remaining bastions of sartorial probity was in the judicial system. Although American lawyers who go to court are not required (thankfully) to wear wigs like our barrister counterparts in the United Kingdom, we *are* required to show up in court with coat and tie (in the case of male lawyers) and appropriate business attire for women. The coronavirus crisis and the transition to a virtual court proceeding have changed all of this, virtually overnight.

Temporarily freed from the dress requirements that applied to in-court proceedings, some lawyers went overboard in their zeal to embrace the new informality of virtual court appearances. In Broward County, Florida, one judge complained that a male lawyer appeared shirtless in a video court conference, and one female attorney appeared still in bed, still under the covers.[2] Such liberties taken by lawyers led inevitably to a crackdown, with the Broward County judge issuing a new "dress code" order that lawyers appearing for court conferences had actually to get out of bed and put on a shirt or other piece of clothing before appearing on Zoom.[3] "It is remarkable how many ATTORNEYS appear inappropriately on camera," the judge wrote in a letter posted on the Weston Bar Association website, "We've seen many lawyers in casual shirts and blouses, with no concern for ill-grooming, in bedrooms with the master bed in the background, etc."[4]

Such draconian bans on in-bed video conferencing and other restrictions were soon required by most other courts throughout the country. However, some enterprising lawyers started wearing shirts only covering those portions of their upper bodies that could be seen by their computer cameras, while continuing to wear sweatpants or even boxer shorts that did not show up on video.

The fashion industry, which had been teetering on the brink of disaster for more than a decade, took a complete nosedive as the coronavirus crisis struck. Some of the giants of the industry filed for bankruptcy within a few short months, including J. Crew, Neiman Marcus, Brooks Brothers, and J.C. Penney. Gap Inc., the largest specialty store in the U.S., announced that it couldn't pay the rent on its 2,785 North American stores and sued its landlord, which then triggered a countersuit by Simon Property Group LP, alleging that Gap was using the pandemic as a pretext to avoid more than $107 million in lease payments.[5] By July, the legendary Diane von Furstenberg announced she would lay off 300 employees and close 18 of her 19 stores.[6] Countless smaller retail apparel companies and suppliers followed suit.

One of the few companies that bucked the trend and actually thrived during the coronavirus pandemic was Entireworld Enterprises LLC, based in Los Angeles, which specializes in sweatsuits. Scott Sternberg, the founder and CEO of Entireworld, had been saying for years that the entire fashion and clothing industry was a giant bubble that was bound to burst. He also had his finger on the pulse of the high degree of stress and uncertainty posed by the coronavirus crisis and its impact on virtually everyone's way of life. On March 15, Sternberg blasted out an email to his company 30,000 subscribers; he wrote: "Am I sick already? Can I leave my house? What do I tell my employees? Will my mom be OK on her flight home today? Can Zod [Sternberg's dog] get coronavirus? Did I buy enough T.P.? How long will this last? Who's in charge? What's next?"[7]

Inspired by a French children's film, Entireworld's sweatsuits come in a variety of bright colors and, in Sternberg's vision, "sort of make you look like a cross between a Teletubbie, Ben Stiller in 'The Royal Tenenbaums,' and a J.C. Penney ad from 1979."[8] On a good day before the virus struck, the brand sold 46 sweatsuits. During the pandemic lockdown, it was selling more than 1,000 daily. By the end of March, the brand's sales were up 662% over the March 2019 sales.[9]

Sternberg had correctly foreseen that the luxury market would collapse and that a company selling sweatpants for $95 would thrive. The failure of Neiman Marcus was not a surprise to him at all, he said, "Because you could see the writing on the wall."[10] Although clothing sales fell 79% in the U.S. in April – the most significant drop on record – sweatpants purchases were up 80%.[11]

The coronavirus crisis of 2020 was the second major shockwave for the global fashion industry, which includes designers, the fashion media such as Vogue and WWD (Women's Wear Daily), and retail stores that sell the clothes. Before late September 2008, Fashion Week, held in New York twice a year, was where all those entities comprising the international fashion industry met and decided what people would be wearing in the coming months. The reason spring collections were shown in the fall (and vice versa) was so they can be ordered, reviewed, and produced in time for the actual season. As with most other things in business and in life, this system, which allowed for an orderly process of planning for the future, was upended by the internet. Once consumers could view collections online, they didn't want to wait for six months to buy them; they wanted them instantly! So everything began to accelerate, and stores demanded delivery of new merchandise on an almost constant basis. This was good for business for at least a while, as buyers were buying more goods at a faster rate, designers were designing faster, and consumers were buying more.

In the fall of 2008, the international fashion industry reached its zenith, with New York Fashion Week in September drawing an estimated 232,000 attendees and generated $466 million in visitor spending.[12] Three days after it ended in September, the economy collapsed. The luxury market dried up overnight. Stores panicked and marked everything down early, trying to generate enough revenue to stay in business, and they continued with virtually permanent markdowns every year. Almost no consumer was paying retail price, with everything that was sold being sold "on sale." So detrimental was the cycle of overproduction and discounting that in 2018, Burberry, the British label, revealed that it had literally been burning $37 million worth of merchandise per year to maintain "brand value."[13]

Like other companies that have been able to survive or even thrive during the pandemic, Entireworld's sweatsuits are sold directly online at a reasonable cost and are the clothing equivalent of "comfort food" in a time when everyone needs comfort and a better way to deal with the daily stress of the crisis. The sweatsuit is made of fabric that Sternberg developed from scratch, and is described as the "sartorial version of a hug."[14] It is wide and roomy, and will not serve as a reminder to people of the extra pounds that they have put on during lockdown. It is forgiving. Entireworld's slogan is, "The stuff you live in."

If only the rest of our lives were as comfortable.

44

LOVE IN THE TIME OF COVID

As if the job losses and economic crisis was not enough of a blow to young adults, their social lives have gotten even more difficult and complicated than before. Everyone who is either qualified or not to weigh in on the subject of dating and relationships during the coronavirus crisis has done so in recent months, including advice from some unexpected sources.[1] Mayor Bill de Blasio of New York has discouraged kissing, since it is a sure-fire way of spreading the virus, and health officials across the country never cease to remind us, "You are your safest sex partner." Even Dr. Anthony Fauci has even offered advice for those who want to date during the pandemic, suggesting that those looking for love or companionship "put a mask on and, you know, chat a bit." It is almost as if we have returned to a Victorian age, where the mere glimpse of a lady's ankle was enough to make a young man's heart skip a beat.

The New York City Department of Health released a document called "Safer Sex and COVID-19," laying out the ground rules for relationships during the crisis. "You are your safest sex partner," the health department said. "The next safest partner is someone you live with," it continued. The city government urged people to "limit close contact — including sex — with anyone outside your household," while also suggesting ways to limit mouth-to-mouth proximity, such as by wearing a mask. "Maybe it's your thing, maybe it's not, but during COVID-19, wearing a face-covering that covers your nose and mouth is a good way to add a layer of protection during sex," the health department suggested.

Despite this chaste advice and the health risks involved in real-life interpersonal relationships, people are still dating. Virtual dating has boomed, perhaps because it is much safer than the old-fashion way, at least from a public health perspective. Messaging on Hinge surged 30 percent, and since March, the number of OkCupid users who have been on a video date has quadrupled.

Research from Indiana University's Kinsey Institute suggests that while everyone generally is lonelier now, single people are the loneliest. The psychotherapist Esther Perel has described the crisis is a "relationship accelerator." Unhappy marriages move more quickly to divorce. Young people rush to move in together after only a few dates. And many single people realize that they do not want to die alone.[2]

In addition to the study by the Kinsey Institute,[3] another group of psychologists began a study in March 2020 to determine the psychological effects of a decrease in face-to-face communication with their "Love in the Time of COVID" project.[4] The name of the project was borrowed from the classic novel *Love in the Time of Cholera* by Gabriel García Márquez. According to one of the researchers, Richard Slatcher, Professor of Psychology at the University of Georgia, it was readily apparent that the COVID-19 outbreak was profoundly affecting social relationships, and that changes in social relationships were having a dramatic impact on people's well-being and health. The study was designed to gain an understanding of whether people were feeling more or less connected to others, how couples were feeling about working from home together, and what were the effects of living alone.[5] "This study is really about relationships: how the pandemic is influencing how connected people feel to others," Slatcher said. "Many people will feel very isolated, both physically and psychologically, but others may actually feel more connected to their households, neighbors, and/or social networks."[6]

The COVID-19 psychological survey was translated into eight languages and, by the end of April, more than 1,000 responses had been collected. Survey respondents then received follow-up questions every two weeks so the researchers could compare their reactions as the pandemic continues. Giulia Zoppolat, a Ph.D. student at Vrije Universiteit in Amsterdam, and a researcher on the "Love in the Time of COVID" project, explained: "The way people are connecting during this time is incredibly moving—and not despite the pandemic, but because of it." He added, "We are inherently social beings, and this deep drive for connection becomes beautifully and painfully apparent in times like these."[7] The research has already helped psychologists and social scientists understand which types of people are the most psychologically vulnerable to the pandemic's effects. They have identified predictors of who will struggle the most with isolation.[8]

As valuable a social asset as online dating has become, the question of how an online relationship can lead to a traditional in-person contact is a tricky one. Since the species has not sufficiently evolved to the point where most of us no longer feel that personal intimacy is a necessary component of a fulfilling relationship, some physical contact between a couple is required. Of course, if you adhere to the de Blasio and Fauci dating scenarios, this critical step in a relationship should only come after one or two dates where the couple practices social distancing and mask-wearing.

To be sure, mask-wearing and kissing are somewhat incompatible, so personal interactions must be handled carefully. Pheromones (chemical triggers that increase sexual desire) are transmitted in the air and are very important to how people are attracted to one another. Since kissing is a very close and concentrated activity, it involves an intense exchange of pheromones. Masks, by limiting the droplets emitted, also limit the pheromones every person emits. So the bottom line is that it is really necessary (yet risky) to take off the masks to engage in traditional kissing rituals. On the plus side, masks limit bad breath, so hopefully, no big surprises are awaiting you in that department when the masks come off!

On the third date or so, research suggests that the only way that a couple can determine whether they have the right chemistry or not is to make some physical contact. Kissing is a short-term phrase for what is referred to among researchers as a "mate assessment device."[9] This kind of intimacy between partners occurs in over 90 percent of human cultures, and it is unlikely that it will become merely a quaint, obsolete practice, such as the kissing of a lady's hand upon the first introduction (the lady's hand being preferably covered with a white glove, of course).

The subject of kissing during the dating and courtship process has become a hot topic among social science researchers in recent years. For example, over 1,000 college students were tested and asked to complete questionnaires measuring kissing preferences, attitudes, styles, and behaviors.[10] Results showed that females place more importance on kissing as a mate assessment device, and as a means of initiating, maintaining, and monitoring the current status of their relationship with a long-term partner. The males surveyed seemed to confirm the male stereotype, using kissing as a means to increase the likelihood of having sex. Remarkably, over 60 percent of people reported losing interest in the other someone after kissing for the first time. Imagine the agony of spending months virtually dating someone through a pandemic, finding them witty and charming, only to discover that there is zero chemistry.[11] But such is the age in which we live.

The paradox faced by singles seeking a mate in the age of COVID is a formidable one. While kissing is the most effective way to gauge chemistry, it is also the most efficient way to contract the coronavirus. The more that an online prospect pushes for an IRL (In Real Life) date, the more you have to worry about whether it is safe to meet up with him or her. It has been suggested that dating apps will start filtering for coronavirus vigilance, which at the moment seems more relevant than other variables, such as height, good-looks, religion, or party affiliation. After all, an in-person meeting where the masks come off and there is a first kiss is a big step nowadays. All of a sudden, if you want to play it safe, you suddenly are in a monogamous relationship, at least for the required 14-day incubation and quarantine period. While the issue of safe sex may have been on the pre-COVID agenda with a potential mate, the required "talk" with a prospective partner must now revolve around their coronavirus status. Have they been tested, and do they test positive for any antibodies? What is their quarantine history (have they been living alone or with someone else), and social distancing practices?[12] An actual agreement or contract may be necessary, obligating you and the other someone to date exclusively for at least the near future, entering into a mutual "support bubble."

Not very romantic, but perhaps necessary. And here I thought that dating was complicated back in the '60s and '70s!

45

THE POST-COVID NEW WORLD ORDER

THIS IS THE NAIL IN THE COFFIN OF GLOBALIZATION

The COVID-19 pandemic has been a substantial shock to the postwar world order, established by the United States and its allies at the end of World War II.[1] In July 1945, at the close of World War II, the leaders of the U.S., Great Britain, and the Soviet Union gathered at a Prussian royal palace in Potsdam outside the German capital of Berlin to hammer out the new global order.[2] The Soviet Union under Josef Stalin had emerged from the war as a superpower, while American President Harry Truman emphatically demonstrated U.S. technological and military superiority, while he was still at the conference, by ordering the dropping of atomic bombs on Hiroshima and Nagasaki. No one ever accused Truman after that of not knowing how to make a point.

At the Potsdam conference, lines were drawn for the ideological struggle between the Communist system of government as represented by the Soviet Union, and the liberal democratic and capitalist system, as represented by the U.S. and Great Britain. Despite these fundamental differences, and despite the fact that a Cold War was brewing that would continue for the next 44 years, Truman, Stalin and Churchill succeeded in laying the foundation for global prosperity and relative peace (or at least the avoidance of nuclear annihilation) until today, 75 years later.

The institutions forming the backbone of this rules-based post-World War II world order include the United Nations (UN), the International Monetary Fund (IMF) and World Bank, the World Trade Organization (WTO), the North Atlantic Treaty Organization (NATO), the G-20, the World Health Organization, and an array of other treaties and agreements.

One of the reasons for the extraordinary success of the post-World War II world order was that the U.S. did not make the same mistakes that it had made in the post-World War I era. America had entered World War I ostensibly to "make the world safe for democracy," in the words of President Woodrow Wilson in February 1917. Wilson was seeking to justify the U.S. declaration of war on Germany, who he accused of threatening Western European democracies, such as France and England. The war, which was often referred to by Allied leaders as "the war to end all wars," was one of the deadliest conflicts in history. Starting in 1914 and lasting until November 11, 1918, there were an estimated 9 million combatant deaths and 13 million civilian deaths as a direct result of the war. In addition, the related 1918 influenza pandemic caused another 17–100 million deaths worldwide.

At the close of the war, Wilson and other Western European leaders advocated the establishment of the League of Nations, the first worldwide intergovernmental organization whose principal mission was to maintain world peace. It was founded on January 10, 1920, following the Paris Peace Conference that officially ended World War I. In 1919, President Wilson won the Nobel Peace Prize for his role as the leading architect of the League. As stated in the League's Covenant, the organization's primary goals were to prevent wars through collective security and disarmament, and the settling international disputes through negotiation and arbitration. Through this and related treaties, the League also set standards for labor working conditions, the just treatment of native inhabitants, human and drug trafficking, the arms trade, global health, and other issues.

Despite its auspicious beginnings, the League failed to succeed in its core mission to prevent further wars, in large part because America turned its back on the world, with a wave of isolationist and anti-immigration sentiment in the U.S. preventing the country from joining the League. Instead of making the world safe for democracy, the post-World War I era ended up leading to the rise of fascism and communism in Europe.

Whether the U.S. – in the post-COVID-19 era – will follow the isolationist path of the post-World War I period, which led to the rise of authoritarianism and another world war, or the global leadership and engagement model of the post-World War II period, still remains to be seen. Based on the policies of the Trump administration to date, it appears that Trump, if elected to a second term, will lead the country further down the path of isolationism and xenophobia. These have been his signature policies since he first announced his intentions to build a wall on the southern border to keep undesirable illegal immigrants from entering and wreaking havoc throughout the country.

In addition to his "America First" and anti-immigration policies, Trump also has undermined the NATO alliance, much to the delight of Putin and the rest of the Russian elite in the Kremlin. He has even picked a gratuitous fight with Prime Minister Trudeau of Canada, one of our staunchest allies.

U.S. and China relations have been on a downward trajectory since the pandemic hit, with a Cold War of both words and actions beginning to settle in. A continued downturn in the U.S. and other Western economies could lead to further protectionist policies and a full-blown trade war with China. International bodies such as the W.H.O., designed to safeguard public health, have been further weakened by the U.S. withdrawal of support. Other nations also have turned inward and closed their borders, often accompanied by a decided drift towards hyper-nationalism and authoritarianism in countries such as Hungary and Poland.

However, the U.S.'s drift towards authoritarianism and isolation is not inevitable, and can probably be reversed if Trump is voted out of office on November 3, 2020, and a Democratic regime is installed in the White House, and possibly also in the Senate. This course reversal will not be easy and will require a sustained effort to win back the confidence of both the American people and of our allies, who have been so sorely abused over the past three and one-half years. Sustaining and revitalizing the rules-based order that has guaranteed freedom, prosperity, and peace for decades requires a decisive global and U.S.-led response to the pandemic.

Even under the most optimistic scenario, the new world order that will emerge post-COVID-19 will be different than the one that has existed for the prior 75 years. First of all, the U.S. must accept the fact that the era of U.S. hegemony is over, and that, instead, the world is shifting to a new multi-polar order with the U.S., China, and the European Union at its core. The U.S. will remain a world power for the foreseeable future, but it will no longer be able to impose its will on the rest of the world unilaterally.

The emergence of China as one of the pre-eminent world powers has changed the basic international calculus for the foreseeable future and will have to be dealt with in one of two ways. Either the emerging Cold War between the U.S. and China will continue to escalate in a no-holds-barred power struggle, with potentially dangerous if not catastrophic consequences, or the U.S. and China will find a way to accommodate one another, to the extent that they will be able to jointly keep the peace and cooperate on important multilateral and global issues, such as Climate Change.

"A lot of structural problems in the international order are becoming much more glaringly apparent," said Rory Medcalf, head of the National Security College at the Australian National University. With the failure of leadership by the U.S. and China's mishandling of the COVID-19 crisis, Medcalf observed that "it does add up to a kind of perfect storm," adding, "The big test is really whether we can get through let's say the next six to 18 months without these crises coming to a head."[3]

For Medcalf, whose book *Indo-Pacific Empire* deals with the strategic rivalry in the region, the defining issue now is not just how the U.S. responds to the challenge of China's rise, but whether "middle players" including India, Australia, Japan, and Europe are prepared to work with the U.S. and, if it is willing, China, to defend the international order.

The spectacular rise of China over the past two decades and the relative decline of the U.S. – a trend that has been accelerated by the COVID-19 crisis – has brought us to this historical crossroad. The next U.S. administration in 2021 will be forced to face some unavoidable realities. China is in the process of surpassing the U.S. economically, with 35% of world growth from 2017 to 2019 coming from China, only 18% from the U.S., 9% from India, and 8% from Europe.[4] By 2050, the top five largest global economies are most likely to be China, India, the U.S., Brazil, and Indonesia.

China also is leading the largest urbanization and infrastructure development scheme on the planet. China's "One Belt One Road" initiative, established in 2013 under the leadership of Chinese President Xi Jinping, has been an ambitious and largely successful program that has invested over $900 billion in the building of new roads, communication systems, and building projects in over 65 countries, spanning the continents of Asia, Africa, and Europe. Financed by Chinese state banks and a new Chinese-backed Asian Infrastructure Investment Bank, this initiative is in the process of literally rewiring global trade from a core base in China throughout Asia, the Middle East, Africa, and Europe.

China has also become a global green powerhouse, and it has taken a leadership role on climate change reduction since signing the 2015 Paris climate agreement. By 2025, most new cars in China will be fully electric vehicles, and it has aggressively cut back on coal usage. Already, over 60% of high-speed rail in the world is in China, with ten times more high-speed rail than in Japan, its closest competitor in this sector. China also recently committed to achieving blue skies in all of its major cities, and Beijing's air is already 30% cleaner.[5]

China is also setting the global pace on a digital economy, including cashless payments. In major cities, up to 90% of all commercial and retail transactions in convenience stores and cafes are occurring through platforms such as Alipay and WeChat. E-commerce delivery in large Chinese cities through Alibaba, which has had sales of $25 billion in just one day, is currently the fastest in the world.[6] In short, the world economic and geopolitical map is being redrawn, whether the U.S. likes it or not. The sooner this country faces that reality, the better positioned it will be to protect key U.S. interests.

Ideally, the multi-polar new world order will promote healthy economic competition between the national superpowers, now including China, while at the same time mutually supporting the array of world organizations and international mechanisms, such as the UN, the WTO, World Bank and W.H.O., that have been pillars of relative stability for the past decades, and can continue to provide a rules-based global system. In addition, the G-20, regional organizations, and non-state actors such as Urban 20, an organization encouraging collaboration between and among the world's largest cities, can provide further support for a fair and stable international framework.

However, it is unclear at this point as to how the U.S. (assuming it is willing come January 2021) and other national players will be able to jump-start the process of de-escalating international tensions and creating a cooperative framework for the new world order. The Group of Seven (G-7) has been sidelined mainly due to the Trump Administration's continuing insistence that Russia be invited back into this group, despite its unapologetic invasion of and annexation of Crimea, its continued efforts to destabilize Ukraine, and other aggressive actions in violation of international law. A planned summit in September between the European Union's leaders and China President Xi was postponed indefinitely, and the proposed November G-20 meeting in Saudi Arabia remains uncertain. The UN is dysfunctional, with Russia and China both able to veto any effective action on Syria and a host of other issues.

The only really good news for the U.S. is that China has mishandled the COVID-19 crisis almost as badly as the U.S., so that the two countries are, more or less, in the same position internationally as they were before the crisis. After an initial outpouring of good-will towards China when the crisis initially erupted in Wuhan, with the U.S. and other countries sending medical supplies and offering additional assistance, China's initial lack of candor regarding the scope of the outbreak led to deep-seated resentment in the U.S., the European Union, Australia, and other countries. They shared the feeling that they would have been better prepared to deal with the crisis if they had received earlier warnings from China. Australia was particularly vocal in its questioning of China regarding the origins of the virus, and Canada is in a dispute with China over the detention by Canada of Huawei Technologies Co. executive Meng Wanzhou.

Meanwhile, India is in the middle of a border dispute with China, and Japan and the E.U. have moved aggressively to decouple their pharmaceutical and other supply chains from Chinese sources. Germany and Australia have also moved to enforce laws protecting those countries from predatory investments by China. In addition, China's crackdown on Hong Kong has created severe strains with a number of countries. U.K. Prime Minister Boris Johnson's government has offered to fast-track British citizenship to 3 million Hong Kong residents, and it has threatened to exclude Huawei from its 5G networks. Tensions were also escalating regarding China's disputed claims to the South China Sea, and the U.S. signaled through naval maneuvers there that it was prepared to come to the defense of Taiwan if it were attacked.

The End of Globalization

As country after country adopted COVID-19 emergency measures to decouple their supply chains for critical PPE, equipment, and pharmaceutical ingredients from China, the already-present pressures on governments to slow down or reverse economic globalization became further intensified. Carmen Reinhart, the chief economist at the World Bank, has declared categorically that the pandemic is "the nail in the coffin of globalization."[7] As Reinhart explained, "Not since the 1930s have advanced and emerging economies experienced the combination of a breakdown in global trade, depressed global commodity prices, and a synchronous economic downturn."[8]

Reinhart, who took a leave of absence from the Harvard Kennedy School to work for the World Bank, has also expressed the view that the enormity of the economic crisis requires a "whatever-it-takes" approach. This is not a time to worry about incurring more debt, according to Reinhart. The lockdown and social distancing policies that are the only real weapon that we have now to stop or at least slow the spread of the virus has come at tremendous economic cost. She strongly recommended that there was really no choice but to mount "large-scale, outside-the-box fiscal and monetary policies."[9] Until there is a vaccine or an effective cure for COVID-19, said Reinhart, the U.S. and the global economy must be on a wartime footing, adding, "you worry about winning the war and then you worry how you're going to pay down the debt."[10] The financial crisis will undoubtedly continue until the health crisis is solved.

Globalization has been under stress since the 2007-08 global financial crisis, but the trend towards countries seeking self-sufficiency in their critical supply chains, rather than being dependent on foreign imports, has accelerated during the pandemic. Prior to the 2007-08 financial crisis, the volume of global trade was growing about 6% a year. In the decade after the global financial crisis, growth became less than half of that, about 2.5%. Much of the global contraction in trade after 2008 and 2009 was due to the fact that European countries, such as Spain, Ireland, Greece, and Portugal, had been running big, current-account deficits, which they were financing by borrowing freely from the rest of the world. When the global financial crisis hit, the credit of these countries dried up, and they were no longer able to keep increasing their debt. The had to borrow from the I.M.F. (International Monetary Fund) to cope with the crisis, but there were onerous restrictions placed on such borrowing that further drove these economies into further recession.

The global financial crisis was then followed by Brexit and a U.S.-China trade war during the Trump administration, with a resurgence of protectionist trade policies, particularly in medical supplies, pharmaceuticals, and food supplies. The global supply chains that the U.S. and Europe had relied upon for decades began showing that they were much more fragile than had previously been thought. Trump's "America First" policy further accelerated an inward-oriented and nationalistic strategy in the U.S. The pandemic also exposed the U.S.'s dependence on China and other foreign sources for critical PPE, ventilators and other supplies needed to respond to the coronavirus crisis.

To try to stop the economic bleeding from the 2020 financial crisis triggered by the pandemic, many countries, including the European Union, are taking a regional rather than a global approach to the financial bailout efforts. The E.U. is creating its own E.U.-wide bailout fund, and other countries, including the U.S., are focusing solely on their own national financial issues. Proposals that would assist the world's poorest countries in coping with the crisis, such as a temporary debt standstill, have not gained much traction, and many countries who are burdened with international debt may likely have to default on these loans in the absence of some international assistance or restructuring. Of the G-20 countries, China is by far the largest world creditor, with more outstanding debt owned it by other countries than the remaining 19 members of G-20 combined.

The May 2020 annual meeting of the World Health Assembly, which is the general assembly of the W.H.O., demonstrated just how far America's reputation had been diminished in the eyes of the world.[11] At this meeting, China was represented by Chinese President Xi Jinping, and virtually every other country, with the notable exception of the U.S., was represented by a sufficiently high-level official, consistent with the gravity of the world crisis that was being discussed. President Xi assured the Assembly that

China had adequately addressed the crisis and that it had helped the rest of the world, particularly Africa, in dealing with its effects. France's Emmanuel Macron and Germany's Angela Merkel also gave strong messages of support for global cooperation in fighting the virus through the W.H.O. With the E.U.'s leadership, the Assembly then reached a global consensus around a resolution calling for a comprehensive review into the handling of the coronavirus pandemic, which China diplomatically accepted.

The U.S. was mostly irrelevant to this entire delicate diplomatic process. Although the U.S. eventually weighed in through a short speech by Health and Human Services Secretary Alex Azar, he did little more than parrot the bellicose accusations and threats about China emanating from the White House. Even as he spoke, the Trump administration had already launched a verbal attack on China and the W.H.O., accusing them of collusion, and the White House had previously announced that the U.S. would be leaving the W.H.O. Trump was also taking some swipes directly at the E.U., telling a gathering of state governors: "Europe has been treating us very badly. European Union. It was really formed so they could treat us badly."[12]

In short, the E.U. has already resigned itself to the fact that the U.S. is no longer able or willing to provide the kind of international leadership that the world has come to expect, particularly since the fall of the Berlin Wall and the collapse of the Soviet Union in 1989 and shortly thereafter. Trust is a precious but fragile commodity. It is difficult to build up and easy to lose. It requires moral leadership that the U.S. currently sorely lacks. The U.S.'s total silence in the face of Russia's naked aggression in Ukraine, gratuitous criticism of the NATO alliance, and its repudiation of the Paris Climate Accords are just a few examples of how the U.S. has squandered its moral leadership, and how it can be regained if the U.S. reverses course. The U.S. can still rebuild that level of trust it once had, at least with its traditional allies, but it is difficult to imagine how this can be achieved other than in a post-Trumpian America.

46

THE AWAKENING OF FAITH IN A TIME OF PANDEMIC

"And there will be great earthquakes, and famines in many lands, and epidemics, and terrifying things happening in the heavens."
The Gospel According to Luke 21:11

Christians like to think of themselves as the Easter people. This is the day that we commemorate the resurrection of Jesus from the dead, described in the New Testament as having occurred on the third day after his burial following his crucifixion by the Romans in 30 A.D. On Easter Sunday, April 12, 2020, millions of Christians celebrated this joyous holy day while sequestered in their homes and apartments around the globe. Fortunately, they were able to celebrate with one another via television, Skype, Zoom, Facebook, and other media platforms.

But is attending religious services and following religious traditions really the same without physically being there? And if you are Jewish, how do you celebrate the deliverance of the Jewish people from bondage when Passover Seders must take place on Zoom? Can Muslim families celebrate Ramadan if they cannot visit local mosques for Tarawih prayers or gather with loved ones to break the fast? The answer, for now, is that we all try our best and do what we can. It is not quite the same as actually being with other family members and your faith community, but it is better than the alternative.

In thousands of empty churches around the globe, people in their homes were able to access their Easter services on their computers and other electronic devices. Millions of people watched and listened as Pope Francis presided over a service in a nearly-empty Casa Santa Marta at the Vatican, repeating the traditional Easter proclamation: "Christ, my hope, is risen!"[1] He called his Easter message, "a different contagion," one that is transmitted "from heart to heart."[2] He said: "This Good News is like a new flame that springs up "in the night of a world already faced with epochal challenges, and now oppressed by a pandemic severely testing our whole human family."³ Christ's resurrection, he explained, is not a "magic formula that makes problems vanish," he continued, "it is the victory of love over the root of evil." This victory "does not 'by-pass' suffering and death, but passes through them, opening a path in the abyss, transforming evil into good," he added.

The Pope offered comfort and hope to those afflicted and affected by the coronavirus, describing this as "an Easter of solitude, lived amid the sorrow and hardship that the pandemic is causing, from physical suffering to economic difficulties." He also expressed his gratitude and affection to doctors and nurses and "to all who work diligently to guarantee the essential services necessary for civil society." He encouraged political leaders "to work actively for the common good," providing the means "to enable everyone to lead a dignified life and, when circumstances allow, to assist them in resuming their normal daily activities."⁴

Modern-Day Martyrs in the Age of Coronavirus

So, while the times we live in are genuinely terrifying, the Christian Easter message that hope can conquer fear is especially timely. It has been a source of strength and solace for untold generations of mankind in times of war, persecution, plagues, and pestilence. In the Judeo-Christian tradition, the Scriptures are filled with references and appeals to the faithful to not be afraid in troubling times but, rather, to have hope. The Book of Isaiah (41:10) teaches: "So do not fear, for I am with you; do not be dismayed, for I am your God. I will strengthen you and help you; I will uphold you with my righteous right hand." The Book of Genesis (15:1) and St. Luke's Gospel (1:30) reassures us: *"Do not be afraid."* Such faith helps us endure the hardship and pain which are inextricable parts of human existence and that we are eventually bound for everlasting life in a far better place.

Martyrs of Charity

As with prior pandemics, the coronavirus crisis has helped millions of people of faith throughout the world to endure the intensified sense of pain, suffering, isolation, hardship, and loss that we are collectively experiencing, and it has also led many of us to reflect on our faith and our relationship with God and with each other. Faith has also helped thousands of health care professionals and other front lines "essential" workers risk their lives day after day so the rest of us can shelter-in-place and do our own small part to slow down the spread of this deadly virus. The sacrifice for others by people of faith perhaps comes more easily to those who were raised as Christians or in another faith-based environment where a sense of charity and self-sacrifice is baked into our beings from an early age.

It was not surprising to people of faith to hear the story of the Italian priest, Don Giuseppe Berardelli, who put another's life before his own. He chose to give up his ventilator to save the life of a younger person. Father Berardelli, had served for 47 years as the Archpriest of Casnigo in the Diocese of Bergamo in Northern Italy, one of the areas hardest hit by the coronavirus pandemic. He had suffered from respiratory problems for some time, so even before the virus hit the area, his parish community had taken up a collection and bought him a ventilator to aid his breathing if his condition worsened. Once the pandemic hit the area, he insisted that the equipment be used to save others. [5]

The mayor of the town described him as "a great person ... he was always cheerful and full of enthusiasm, he gave peace and joy to our communities," adding, "He was a priest who listened to everyone, he knew how to listen, whoever turned to him knew that he could count on his help."[6] James Martin, an American priest and editor-at-large for *America* magazine, a Jesuit review of faith and culture, cited a Bible verse, John 15:13, which says, "Greater love has no one than this: to lay down one's life for one's friends."

There is no doubt that Father Berardelli's sacrifice has been repeated by hundreds, if not thousands, of other people around the world who have their faith to guide them and help others to overcome the natural trepidation we all share.[7] As with prior pandemics, the age of coronavirus also has led millions of people of faith throughout the world to reflect on their relationship with God and with each other.

Christian Churches in the South Split Over What It Means To Be Christian

The combination of the coronavirus crisis and the Trump administration's polarizing policies has exposed the deep divisions in many Christian churches in the South, particularly Baptist churches.

In early 2017, shortly after President Trump had been sworn in, Chris Thomas, a young pastor of the First Baptist Church of Williams in Alabama, gave a sermon filled with quotations from the Bible that, on its surface, should not have been considered controversial. The First Baptist Church was considered to be a relatively liberal church with a predominantly white congregation in Alabama that was fairly close to one of the Jacksonville State University's campuses, so it attracted a number of active and retired faculty members from the university. The pastor built his sermon around the Beatitudes, eight blessings for the needy Jesus is said to have given to his followers on a hillside in Galilee.[8]

"Blessed are those who mourn, for they will be comforted," went one. "Blessed are the meek, for they will inherit the earth," went another.

However, President Trump had just announced his travel ban on Syrian refugees, many of which were being sponsored by U.S. churches upon their expected admission to the U.S. as refugees. The issue had already polarized many Christian churches, particularly those in the Red States in the South, Midwest, and the West. Without mentioning the Syrian refugees, Pastor Thomas added a verse of his own: "Blessed are those who seek refuge and have the door shut on their face."[9]

Pastor Thomas' remarks triggered a backlash by some of the church members, which led to the exodus of many members of the church congregation and the eventual departure of Pastor Thomas, just as churches started reopening in Alabama. As Pastor Thomas later recalled the reaction of some of his congregants to his sermon, "They more-or-less said, 'Those are nice, but we don't have to live by them,'" Mr. Thomas recalls church members saying about the verses, which are central to Christian scripture. "It was like: 'You're criticizing our president. You're clearly doing this.' From thereon, my words were being measured."[10]

After the sermon on the refugees, churchgoers began to monitor Thomas' posts on Facebook, reporting back to each other when something the pastor "liked" was seen by them as too liberal.[11] When a group of church missionaries returned from a humanitarian trip to the Mexican border, they got a cold welcome from those who said they supported Trump's border wall plans. One family proposed a "watchdog" group to ensure new members weren't gay.[12]

Then in 2018, a small group of churchgoers led a secret attempt to oust Thomas to clear the way for a more conservative preacher. "There's no doubt the country is more polarized, and the church started to reflect it," said Bobby Burns, a former member of the church's finance committee. "The walls of this church just weren't thick enough to protect us from the world."[13]

Pastor Thomas' views on racial equality and racial justice were also out of step with the beliefs of many of the church's members. On a hot summer day, Thomas was in his office when several Black children were playing basketball outside. One of them came to ask to use the drinking fountain in the church, and Mr. Thomas pointed the child toward the door where the water was. However, when a congregant, who was white, saw the Black child approaching, he pulled the door shut to not to allow the boy inside.[14]

Even before the age of Trump and the onset of the coronavirus crisis, the issue of what it meant to be a Christian and a Southern Baptist was sharply debated. Since the 1960s, the issue of civil rights and desegregation deeply divided the South. Dr. Martin Luther King Jr. called for the integration of the Southern Baptist Churches, and his 1964 essay on the subject, "11 a.m. Sunday Is Our Most Segregated Hour," is still considered to be a classic scripture-based view that the Gospels and racial equality are not only compatible, but required.[15] The Southern Baptist Convention, the body that acted as a kind of mother church for the region's congregations, had undergone an upheaval known as the "fundamentalist takeover."[16] A group of conservative pastors who believed the church had become too liberal began a purge, banishing pastors and church leaders who dared to suggest, even elliptically, that anti-gay and racist rhetoric was not compatible with the message of the Gospels.

In 1991, a small but vocal group of moderates split from the group and named themselves the Cooperative Baptist Fellowship.[17] They pushed for more liberal theology, and even advocated to allow women to serve as pastors. Churches across the South were soon forced to pick a side.

The polarization of Christian churches is not confined to the Baptists. Episcopal and Methodist churches have experienced the same divisions, with one major part of the Episcopal Church going so far as to elect Gene Robinson, a New Hampshire clergyman, as the first openly gay bishop of the Episcopal Church. The issue of immigration, including how to treat "Dreamers," the undocumented children of illegal immigrants who have spent most of their lives in the U.S. but do not have any legal status, divide many of the mainstream denominations.

Even the reading of scriptural passages about walls – references that can be found throughout Scriptures – was viewed by many Southern Christians through a political lens. For example, biblical references to the Battle of Jericho, where Joshua brings down the city's walls with trumpets, became viewed with suspicion.[18] Was the text intended to be a subtle critique of Mr. Trump's obsession with building a wall between Mexico and the U.S., at the cost of several billion dollars?

So, then, is the Christian message of the Gospels compatible with racism and prejudices based on race, ethnicity, or national origin? The answer, of course, is no. Even a cursory reading of the Bible will leave the reader with the clear and unambiguous impression that Jesus extended his hand of love and hope to all persons, no matter their race, background, social status, or health status (remember how he ministered to the lepers?). He also included women within his inner ranks of followers, and both his mother, Mary, and his close associate (there has been much debate whether they were actual "partners" or not), Mary Magdalene. To reject or ignore these core teachings of Christ is possible, and you may still call yourself a "Christian," but then you have carved out a different type of religion from the Gospels themselves, and you have turned your so-called "Christian" faith into one that is inconsistent with the Gospels but is consistent with the social, cultural and political world in which you feel more comfortable.

What Would Jesus Do?

What, then, is the appropriate Christian response to the two converging crises that America is facing: a public health crisis that has exposed the deep divisions along racial, financial and economic lines, and the equally explosive racial justice crisis arising from the murder of George Floyd and other Black Americans at the hands of the police and white vigilantes?

Of course, acts of compassion, love, and charity to all those in our community is essential. However, the teachings of Jesus go far beyond the "love thy neighbor" and "turn the other cheek." Those teachings also require Christians to address the systemic inequalities and injustices in our society. When a global natural disaster such as this one rips the thin veneer of "normalcy" off the lid of society, the longstanding inequalities and injustices in society are more evident than ever before. This, then, is a call to action for Christians, requiring us to answer the simple question: "What Would Jesus Do?" (WWJD). What would he do if he were still here walking among us and witnessed the soul-crushing inequities in our society and our inability to work in harmony with our natural surroundings without fundamentally altering the balance of nature on the planet?

The answer to that question may be found in the beautiful stain-glass window in St. John's Episcopal Church in Stamford, Connecticut, that simply yet eloquently states: "Make No Peace With Oppression." It is a reminder that Jesus himself reacted with righteous indignation and bold action when confronted with injustice. He was the one who threw the moneychangers out of the temple where they were turning a sacred place into a marketplace, elevating commerce and materialism over faith and religion. He spent his short lifetime among the poor and the powerless, eating with them, talking with them, suffering with them, healing them, and eventually dying for them.

The answer to most WWJD questions is usually straightforward, although the solutions often less so. The disproportionate burden of the pandemic has fallen on the poor, the powerless, and the disenfranchised. The rates of sickness and death from the virus have fallen disproportionately hard on people of color and Native Americans. We know that they are more vulnerable and exposed to COVID-19 due to their lack of access to adequate health care, poor and environmentally degraded living conditions, lack of educational and job opportunities, and host of other reasons. We also know that people of color, who are by and large grossly underpaid for their services, comprise a disproportionate percentage of the lower-paid ranks of our front-line health care workers, nursing home assistants and assisted living aides, grocery clerks, delivery personnel and meatpacking workers who are risking their lives each day in hazardous jobs so that those who are more fortunate can work from the safety of our homes. So, what will we be doing from this day forward to build a more just and equitable society for all Americans, and strengthen our democratic institutions in the process? Finally, confronting systemic racism in our institutions and a New New Deal would be a good start.

So, What Is Life Really All About, Anyway?

For many of us who have been temporarily released from daily commuting to work and the humdrum of an office job, spending time at home with our families and with ourselves has given us some time to think about the broader issues of life – and death. Why are we here, and where are we going? What have we done with our lives so far, and what is the best way to make the most of the rest of it? Why have we have so badly injured the planet to the point where it takes another Great Depression to slow down the pollution of the earth and the rate of global warming that may make the planet uninhabitable?

We can't go to sporting events or the theater, school, or work. So, try as we might to fill up our days with the mundane daily thoughts and actions that used to occupy our time completely, we inevitably come face to face with larger existential questions that demand our attention. And maybe we even find some answers.

And then, one day, you realize that you really do want to leave the world a better place than you found it, that you do believe in the ideals of truth, justice, and equality, and that you have not been doing nearly enough to make a difference in the fight to make those ideals a reality. You realize that you have to work even harder than before with kindred spirits. You have to refuse to make peace with oppression until it lifts its foot from the neck of all oppressed people, and some sense of justice and equality is finally achieved in your lifetime. "If not now, when?"

You must demand an answer to this age-old question. For justice, opportunity, and equality to truly become realities, it requires a change in people's hearts as well as in their heads. It requires a change in the laws and government regulations, but more fundamentally, it requires a shift in the way that people deal with each other. We don't have to always agree with one another, but we do at least have to recognize that every other living person deserves to be treated with respect and dignity. Not to be too apocalyptic, if not now, we may never again have a chance to bring our failed and faltering species back into harmony with the planet and its environment we have so sorely abused, or back from the brink of the toxic society that we have contaminated with 401 years of racism and systemic inequality. If not now, when?

Can we afford to look back on this time of pandemic and realize that it was not just a random plague, but that it was a final warning bell that we failed to heed? It is not just a matter of doing the right thing; it is now a matter of survival. COVID-19 is the wake-up call. The murders of George Floyd, Breonna Taylor, and Ahmaud Arbery were also fire alarms that blasted across the country and around the world. They triggered the explosion of universal protests by thousands of people of all races, colors, and creeds, proclaiming that "We have had enough." The day of reckoning is truly upon us in times such as these, and we ignore the signs at our peril.

The New Great Awakening

Organized religion experienced a revival in the American colonies during the 1720s through the 1740s. This was a time when plague and disease continued to haunt the Colonies, and people, realizing the limits of secular rationalism and pursuit of wealth and material goods, longed for some broader meaning to all the suffering and travail that they were going through on a cyclical basis. This religious revival became known as "The Great Awakening" brought increased passion and energy to religion, as Christian preachers traveled from town to town, promoting a renewed enthusiasm for religious worship as an essential element of American culture.

Except for the great New England preacher, Jonathan Edwards, perhaps the most significant boost to the Great Awakening came from George Whitefield, a minister from England, who toured the colonies up and down the Atlantic coast, preaching his message. In one year, Whitefield covered 5,000 miles of America and preached more than 350 times. He had a charismatic, theatrical and expressive style, often trembling as he shouted his message to people who gathered by the thousands to hear him preach. His success reenergized a once-waning Christian faith in America and helped ignite a growing nationalism in the colonies that contributed to the American independence movement and the revolution of 1776.

In these tumultuous times, there are signs that a New Great Awakening is taking place, as people begin to question whether the crony capitalism and permanent economic plutocracy that it has created is a fair, equitable, and effective foundation for a healthy and robust democracy.

On Easter Sunday, Dr. Anthony Fauci, appearing on *CNN*'s State of the Union with host Jake Tapper, said that faith was important in helping some people through the "historic ordeal" that the U.S. was facing.[19] Fauci, who is Catholic and Jesuit educated, commented: "People with a strong foundation in faith, I think it's very, very important when you go through serious, really terrible ordeals that the country is going through, I think faith helps people through this."[20] Fauci said his father was "a man of deep, deep faith" and explained that his religion helped him through many difficult times. Dr. Fauci also expressed the view that faith was an essential vehicle for people to handle stress, and that faith during the pandemic "will take an important role."

People of Faith Join Hands with the Black Lives Matter Protesters

Since Christianity is rooted, at its core, in social justice ideals, the solidarity of Christians and other people of faith with the Black Lives Matter protests following the police killing of George Floyd in Minneapolis was a no-brainer. After all, Jesus opposed violence, the taking of life, discrimination, and economic inequality. Christian leaders and leaders of other faiths took their places among the ranks of the thousands of protesters who marched on the streets of every major city, as well as in smaller cities and town, all over America, declaring that enough is enough, that we are all children of God, and that the senseless lynching police violence against the Black community in America must stop, immediately.

The close affiliation of Christian leaders goes back, at least in my lifetime, to the Civil Rights and Anti-war movements of the 1960s and early 1970s, when Dr. Martin Luther King, Jr., himself a widely recognized leader of the Calvary Baptist Church, Dr. Ralph Abernathy and other Christian leaders in the Black community played a leadership role in the civil rights movement and also, later, the anti-war movement. Catholic Jesuit priests such as the Berrigan brothers, as well as Yale Chaplain William Sloane Coffin, also played key leadership roles in the anti-war movement starting in the late 1960s. Protesters specifically opposed U.S. escalation of the Vietnam War, which was sacrificing thousands of young American lives for nothing more than to prop up one corrupt regime after another in South Vietnam.

Jonathan Myrick Daniels was an Episcopal seminarian and civil rights activist until August 20, 1965 when he was murdered in Haynesville, Alabama, by a shotgun-wielding special county deputy, Tom Coleman. Daniels made the ultimate sacrifice for a fellow human being by shielding the 17-year-old Black civil rights activist, Ruby Sales, who was the intended victim of Coleman's racist rage. They were both working in the civil rights movement in Lowndes County, trying to integrate public places and register Black voters after the passage of the Voting Rights Act that summer. In 1991, Daniels was designated as a martyr in the Episcopal church and was recognized annually in its liturgical calendar. [21]

The triple murder of civil rights workers James Chaney, Andrew Goodman, and Michael "Micky" Schwerner in Neshoba County, Mississippi in June 1964 shocked the entire country. It also left an indelible mark on me and many of my neighbors in the small suburban New York town of Pelham, where Micky Schwerner had recently graduated from Pelham Memorial High School. Although Schwerner was older than me, we graduated from the same high school. I remembered him from the various civil rights marches and demonstrations that I attended with my parents and brothers in New York City around that time period in 1964, which was generally referred to as "Freedom Summer."

Schwerner and the two other murdered civil rights workers were associated with the Council of Federated Organizations (COFO) and its member organization, the Congress of Racial Equality (CORE). They had been working with the Freedom Summer campaign by attempting to register African-Americans in Mississippi to vote. This registration effort was a part of a concerted effort to challenge the discriminatory "Jim Crow" laws in the South, which had succeeded for over 70 years, since the 1890s, to disenfranchise potential Black voters with "poll taxes" and other hurdles that barred many, mostly poor Black people from participating in elections. The Civil Rights Law of 1964 – which was not passed by Congress until after the murders of the three civil rights workers – was designed to bar such practices, but the entrenched white ruling classes of most counties in the South still tried their best to use force and intimidation to bar Black residents from registering to vote and exercising their franchise rights.

These three civil rights workers, whose ordeal was later widely publicized in the 1988 movie "Mississippi Burning," had traveled from Meridian to the community of Longdale to talk with congregation members at a Black church that had been burned. The trio was thereafter arrested following a traffic stop outside Philadelphia, Mississippi, escorted to the local jail, and held for several hours. Later, as the three of them left town in their car, they were followed by law enforcement and Klu Klux Klan members. Before leaving Neshoba County, their vehicle was pulled over, and all three were abducted, driven to another location, and shot at close range. The three men's bodies were then moved to an earthen dam where they were buried. Since the bodies were not initially found, the disappearance of the three men was first investigated as a missing person case. Their burnt-out car was found near a swamp three days after their disappearance, but a cursory search of the area did not turn up any bodies.

An extensive search of the area was then conducted by the F.B.I., along with local and state authorities, and four hundred U.S. Navy sailors. However, the three men's bodies were only discovered two months later, thanks to an anonymous tip. It eventually was found that members of the local K.K.K., the Neshoba County Sheriff's Office, and the Philadelphia Police Department were involved in the murders.

In 1967, after the state government refused to prosecute, the U.S. Department of Justice charged eighteen individuals with civil rights violations. Seven were convicted and received relatively minor sentences for their actions. The ensuing outrage over the murders and the relatively light sentences handed out to the perpetrators gave a new shot of adrenaline to the civil rights movement and their allies in Congress, who then gained passage of the Civil Rights Act of 1964.

During this time period, thousands of young people were becoming socially conscious of not only civil rights issues but the economic, housing, and other issues that affected disadvantaged Americans across all racial and ethnic lines. At the same time that the civil rights movement was getting a full head of steam, the escalating war in Vietnam triggered a formidable anti-war movement that also shook the country to its core.

On March 31, 1968, largely due to the growing number of Americans turning out for anti-war protests in Washington and in cities around the country, President Lyndon Johnson unexpectedly announced that he would not be seeking re-election in November 1968. "There is a division in the American house now," said Johnson, saying that he could not both lead the country in a time of war and internal strife and run for re-election at the same time.

As formidable were the civil rights and anti-war demonstrations of the 1960s, they were eclipsed by the massive nationwide turnout for the Black Lives Matter protests of May and June 2020. Religious leaders throughout the country joined in solidarity with the BLM marchers, issuing statements of support. For example, on May 30, Reverend Michael Curry, the Presiding Bishop of the Episcopal Church in the U.S., a familiar figure to Americans as one of the primary celebrants of the Royal Wedding between Prince Harry and Meghan Markel, released a special message that was widely circulated in the media and online. The statement is included here since it is, in the view of this author, a masterpiece effectively summarizing why Christians were turning out in the thousands to give public witness to the protests of 2020:

> "Our long-term commitment to racial justice and reconciliation is embedded in our identity as baptized followers of Jesus. We will still be doing it when the news cameras are long gone.
>
> In the midst of COVID-19 and the pressure cooker of a society in turmoil, a Minnesota man named George Floyd was brutally killed. His basic human dignity was stripped by someone charged to protect our common humanity.
>
> Perhaps the deeper pain is the fact that this was not an isolated incident. It happened to Breonna Taylor on March 13 in Kentucky. It happened to Ahmaud Arbery on February 23 in Georgia. Racial terror in this form occurred when I was a teenager growing up Black in Buffalo, New York. It extends back to the lynching of Emmett Till in 1955 and well before that. It's not just our present or our history. It is part of the fabric of American life.
>
> But we need not be paralyzed by our past or our present. We are not slaves to fate but people of faith. Our long-term commitment to racial justice and reconciliation is embedded in our identity as baptized followers of Jesus. We will still be doing it when the news cameras are long gone.
>
> That work of racial reconciliation and justice – what we know as Becoming Beloved Community – is happening across our Episcopal Church. It is happening in Minnesota and in the Dioceses of Kentucky, Georgia and Atlanta, across America and around the world. That mission matters now more than ever, and it is work that belongs to all of us.
>
> It must go on when racist violence and police brutality are no longer front-page news. It must go on when the work is not fashionable, and the way seems hard, and we feel utterly alone. It is the difficult labor of picking up the cross of Jesus like Simon of Cyrene, and carrying it until no one – no matter their color, no matter their class, no matter their caste – until no child of God is degraded and disrespected by anybody. That is God's dream, this is our work, and we shall not cease until God's dream is realized.
>
> Is this hopelessly naïve? No, the vision of God's dream is no idealistic utopia. It is our only real hope. And, St. Paul says, "hope does not disappoint us, because God's love has been poured into our hearts by the Holy Spirit" (Romans 5:5). Real love is the dogged commitment to live my life in the most unselfish, even sacrificial ways; to love God, love my neighbor, love the earth and truly love myself. Perhaps most difficult in times like this, it is even love for my enemy. That is why we cannot condone violence. Violence against any person – conducted by some police officers or by some protesters – is violence against a child

> of God created in God's image. No, as followers of Christ, we do not condone violence.
>
> Neither do we condone our nation's collective, complicit silence in the face of injustice and violent death. The anger of so many on our streets is born out of the accumulated frustration that so few seem to care when another Black, brown or native life is snuffed out.
>
> Love, as Jesus teaches, is action like this as well as attitude. It seeks the good, the well-being, and the welfare of others as well as one's self. That way of real love is the only way there is."[22]

Not only did mainstream Christian churches weigh in on the side of Black Lives Matter, but perhaps even more significantly, evangelicals. Some evangelicals who had been assumed to be squarely within President Trump's "base" of die-hard supporters, spoke up in opposition to the brutal police killings of George Floyd, Breonna Taylor, and Ahmaud Arbery. When Senator Mitt Romney of Utah, a Mormon and former Republican presidential candidate, marched in front of the White House past Lafayette Square in solidarity with the BLM protesters, it was reported that he was marching with "evangelicals," which must have sent a collective shiver up the spines of Trump and his senior campaign advisors. [23]

Part of Trump's photo-op stunt on June 1 was to have Lafayette Square cleared with pepper spray and tear gas by the Secret Service and other federal law enforcement personnel so that he could take his now-infamous "victory walk" to St. John's Episcopal Church. In front of this historic church, Trump held up an upside-down bible, an inadvertent sign of distress as much as if an upside-down American flag had been raised by him that fateful afternoon.

* * * * *

The coronavirus crisis and the abhorrent murders of George Floyd and several other Black men and women during this public health crisis tore off the scabs covering the systemic racism and economic injustice that has festered for decades. Just as the terrible murders of the three civil rights workers helped enact the Civil Rights Act of 1964, the rash of gruesome murders of George Floyd and others around the country brought the Black Lives Matter movement to a whole new level. The BLM movement now has wide support not only in the Black community, but also among all people of goodwill.

There is growing recognition that there are two Americas and that the gulf between them is turning into a chasm. There is also a division within the Christian community as to what it means to be Christian. Some "Christians In Name Only" (CINOs) will either continue to remain silent or will actively join the forces of repression and regression led by Trump and his cohorts. However, many other followers of Christ feel strongly that the struggle for full social, racial, and economic justice in this country is a moral imperative dictated by the Gospels. They will follow the example of the true Christian in the parable of the Good Samaritan, who helped a broken man in need who lay on the side of the road. The religious leaders who passed without lending a helping hand were indifferent to his fate. Only the Samaritan, who himself was a member of a group considered as an outcast, saw the wounded stranger and took action to help another human being in need. He provided medical care and housing, and he made provision for this stranger's well-being. He helped heal a fellow child of God.

This path was also the one that Jesus took. He ate dinner with the poor, the outcasts, and the forgotten. He listened to them. He befriended them. He defended them. He healed them. He encouraged them. He loved them. He spoke out against the hypocrisy, the smug apathy, the inequality, and the systemic injustice that infected every stratum of society and every institution in it. He comforted the afflicted and afflicted the comfortable. He was persecuted for calling attention to the victims of injustice. He was arrested, crucified, and ultimately died for daring to promulgate his fundamentally radical and transformative message.

So, what would Jesus do if he were amongst us now (and most probably is)? The answer is simple if you just read the Scriptures and then follow your heart and your head. And that is what thousands of Christians are doing, just as they did in the 1960s as part of the Civil Rights movement. In fact, some of us are the same people, only older. As a sign held by an elderly marcher read at a recent rally in Washington, "I'm still marching for the same s**t that I marched for in the 60s."

And we shall not stop marching, speaking out, and doing whatever else is necessary for justice to be finally achieved.

EPILOGUE

THE STRUGGLE FOR THE SOUL OF AMERICA

On Thursday, July 29, 2020, as I was in the process of finalizing this book, The *New York Times* published a posthumous essay by John Lewis, the civil rights icon and conscience of the House of Representative and of the country. Perhaps more than any other contemporary American, Lewis had experienced in his lifetime both the depths of bigotry, discrimination and hatred that have been an indelible part of our country's psyche, as well as its spirit of generosity and longing for justice that propelled its leadership of the Free World and beacon of freedom and democracy for generations. He and others were beaten and bloodied for exercising their constitutional and civil rights while crossing the bridge in Selma, Alabama, but he also lived to see the passage of the Voting Rights Act and the election of the first African-American President that brought our imperfect democracy a few steps closer to justice and equality.

While many of us have been driven to the brink of despair as our country seems to have lost its way and slid from its position of moral leadership in the world community, Lewis kept his irrepressible sense of optimism to the end. He left us with words of encouragement, reminding us that the ideals of democracy and equality that bind this country together are greater than the partisan political differences that are pulling us apart.

In his final essay, Lewis tells us that the day before he entered the hospital for the final time, he visited Black Lives Matter Plaza near Lafayette Park and the White House, reflecting on the powerful protest movements and demonstrations that were moving America closer to justice, just as the civil rights movement had done decades earlier:

> While my time here has now come to an end, I want you to know that in the last days and hours of my life you inspired me. You filled me with hope about the next chapter of the great American story when you used your power to make a difference in our society. Millions of people motivated simply by human compassion laid down the burdens

of division. Around the country and the world you set aside race, class, age, language and nationality to demand respect for human dignity.

America is surely at one of those crossroads of history, and there is no turning back.

Either we work together to build a more just and perfect union, or we can continue to drift into a semi-autocratic and oligarchical state where the rule of law and democratic institutions can no longer provide any check or balance to an all-powerful and arbitrary executive. "Democracy is not a state," Lewis wrote. "It is an act, and each generation must do its part to help build what we called the Beloved Community, a nation and world society at peace with itself."

While it is true that our democratic institutions – particularly our Congress and our electoral system – are not working properly, and political gridlock has griped the country, the failure lies not so much in our institutions, but deep within ourselves. This is what Lewis understood and was trying to convey to us in his final words. Democracy is as much about a state of mind as it is about institutions. As the American philosopher and psychologist John Dewey explained in his 1888 essay, "The Ethics of Democracy," democracy is "a form of moral and spiritual association" that recognizes the "infinite and universal possibility" within each person and seeks to foster its expression, not for "mere self-assertion" and personal gain, but for an understanding that in order to preserve our liberties and freedoms, we must also assume individual and collective responsibility to ensure that the ethical ideals of justice and equality extend to all.

In the end, democracy must be that moral and ethical imperative that springs from the very soul of every American. For its survival, it requires each and every generation to respond forcefully whenever our democracy is imperiled, as it is today.

On July 30,[1] shortly before Lewis's funeral in Atlanta, President Trump remined us yet again of the clear and present danger that he poses to our democracy. As part of his ongoing campaign to delegitimize the upcoming elections, Trump denounced mail-in voting and again raised the idea of pushing the election back to some unspecified future date. "With Universal Mail-In Voting (not Absentee Voting, which is good), 2020 will be the most

INACCURATE & FRAUDULENT Election in history," he wrote on Twitter. "It will be a great embarrassment to the USA. Delay the Election until people can properly, securely and safely vote???"

The pandemic, which has been accompanied by a seismic economic upheaval and demonstrations demanding much-needed change across America, is one of those moments in history where great challenges also present great opportunities for positive change. In past generations, the Civil War, the Great Depression and World War II presented such engines of change. While the Civil War temporarily tore the country in two, it also provided President Lincoln and Congress the impetus to build a transcontinental railroad that tied a great country together from sea to shining sea. The Great Depression led to a vast restructuring of government and the economy, with the New Deal taking substantial steps to reduce economic equalities and provide a safety net so that Americans would no longer be starving in abject poverty. World War II led to the building of the American industrial colossus that provided economic growth and prosperity for decades.

But each of these transformative moments in American history were only possible with massive government intervention, financial spending and political leadership from Washington, and if the pandemic crisis is to lead to any similar positive results, a New New Deal, a Green New Deal or other ambitious program will require leadership and financing starting at the federal level. Even the housing and mortgage crisis of 2007, followed by the Great Recession of 2008, required a massive federal financial investment in order to stave off a complete economic collapse. It also let to the transformative election of a Democratic Congress and President Barrack Obama in November 2008, leading to a landmark and long overdue extension of health insurance to millions of Americans.

Similarly, the pandemic has changed America, and is continuing to change the country and the world, just as wars and economic depressions have done before. It is the definitive and transformative event of our generation, far more than even 9/11 or the Great Recession of 2008. As traumatized as the nation was by September 11th, people flocked back to air travel shortly thereafter, and most people working in lower Manhattan went back to work in skyscrapers and large office buildings. Similarly, the 2008 financial crisis temporarily shook the nation's confidence in Wall Street, but it did not stop investors from returning to the stock market, setting off an unprecedented rise in stock prices, albeit largely benefitting the already affluent.

The pandemic has been - and will continue to be – a much more profound and transformative event. It will continue to change not only our country's economy, but also our way of life and our politics. Some of these changes will be for the better, and many no doubt for the worse, but whether we like them or not, they are likely to be here to stay.

As Warren Buffet likes to say: "It's only when the tide goes out that you learn who's been swimming naked."[2] During the deep freeze that enveloped the country and the gradual thaw that followed as the state and national economies tried to reopen, financially weak companies or those with flawed business models evaporated, or came back in sharply reduced forms. Thousands of stores and companies that were financially vulnerable before the pandemic have disappeared or can expected to be gone in the near future. Entire industries – such as cruise ships, theme parks and movie theaters – have quickly become mere shadows of their former selves. Products and services that are "essential" have tended to survive, while non-essential air travel and other expendable products and services were sharply reduced.

Without Sears and the big box stores which closed down or went bankrupt, most of the 1,100 or so malls around the country either closed or were forced to re-invent themselves. Malls that were expected to survive could no longer count on the large retail sales stores to cover their overhead costs. Instead, they were trying to hang on until either a vaccine or an effective cure for the virus allowed them to attract customers back to mall-based restaurants, specialty shops, bowling and other sports concepts, and even "urgent care" and other medical care providers.

One of the major economic sectors that was already struggling before the pandemic hit was the newspaper industry, with local newspapers disappearing at an accelerated rate, as Google, Facebook, and Instagram cut into their advertising revenues, and print copies - the kind that left ink on your hands - give way to online subscriptions. Between 2008 and 2019,

American newspapers had already eliminated about half of all newsroom jobs, and the pandemic accelerated this trend.[3] In addition to the jobs and economic losses suffered by the newspaper industry, the negative impact on the affected communities was incalculable since local newspapers were the primary news source for millions of Americans on local politics, local businesses, and every other aspect of local community life.

Clearly, some of the pandemic's biggest winners are America's largest companies, including Amazon, Target, and Walmart, as the move to online shopping accelerated during the pandemic. Tech companies such as Apple, Microsoft, Facebook, Twitter, Google, and Zoom also flourished. As Satya Nadella, Microsoft's chief executive explained it after only two months into the pandemic lockdown period in the spring of 2020: "We've seen two years' worth of digital transformation in two months." Working from home creates its own efficiencies, with less time spent on traffic-clogged roads, and higher flexibility in work schedules. Mark Zandi, the chief economist at Moody's Analytics, noticed that the 200 economists around the world who reported to him became more efficient, with almost no in-person meetings, translating into far fewer plane trips and virtually no lost travel time. Zoom, Facetime, Google Meet, and other online meeting platforms still permitted employees to share screens and work on databases at the same time. "We've gotten used to it very quickly and like it," Mr. Zandi said. "I just don't see us going back."

Most other white-collar, professional consulting and tech-based businesses experienced similar positive results, with the days of the white-collar "road warriors" always on the move by plane or car a thing of the past. "Maybe we've discovered that we don't need to travel as much as we did before," said Cecilia Rouse, the dean of Princeton's School of Public and International Affairs. American Airlines and Delta Air Lines began offering buyouts to employees, and Airbus cut thousands of jobs, clear signs that the companies expect airline travel to be depressed for years.

The world of education also underwent a sea change with "distance learning," leaving many students to either drop off the educational radar screen or to fall far behind where they would have been in a traditional school setting. There was a consensus that at least some degree of "hands-on" education had to be restored. Still, the question of how to do so safely and who would pay for it remained largely unanswered as the fall semester rapidly approached. Meanwhile, colleges that were already feeling the pinch of falling enrollment were becoming even more financially stressed, and many would likely be closing in the coming years.

The biggest unknown as this book goes to the printer in late summer 2020 is what impact the pandemic and ensuing economic crisis will have on the political future of the country. The struggle for the soul and the future of America will continue to intensify as we get closer to election day in November when the American people will be faced with the most crucial decision of their lifetimes. Donald J. Trump will likely lose the popular vote, as he did in November 2016, but the critical question is whether he will lose the election in the all-important Electoral College, where he eked out a narrow victory the first time around. Absent a landslide victory by the Democratic candidate Joe Biden, it is likely that Trump will claim that the Democrats "stole" the election with phony mail-in ballots and other forms of election fraud.

However, if the Democrats win a majority of the Senate and thereby take control of the White House as well as both chambers of Congress, the country will be poised for one of those transformative moments equivalent to the landslide election of Franklin D. Roosevelt and Democratic majorities in Congress in 1932, or the election of Lyndon B. Johnson as President in 1964, who, with Democratic majorities in Congress in 1964, led to the enactment of the Civil Rights Bill of 1964, the Voting Rights Act of 1965, Medicare, Medicaid, Jobs Corps, and many social programs of the Great Society.

If the American people (or more accurately the Electoral College or the Supreme Court a la *Bush v. Gore* in 2000) gives Trump a second term, not much will change since it is likely that the Democrats will still control the House of Representatives and little, if any, significant legislation, such as more tax cuts for the rich, will be passed. Instead, Big Business will get even bigger. Economic power will continue to consolidate, with mega-companies that control huge sectors of the economy having the financial clout to gobble up or drive smaller competitors out of business. The federal government and the country will continue its inexorable drift to autocracy, and the already wide gap between the rich and the poor, the haves and the have-nots, will continue to grow. In short, America's torch of liberty and equality will be further dimmed, if not extinguished. "My basic fear," said Heather Boushey, a leading progressive economist, "is that it leads to a rule by the oligarchs." This is what has happened in Russia and other Eastern European countries, and America is already trending in that direction.

Although Joe Biden may not be perceived as a transformative president like Barack Obama, neither was then Vice President Lyndon B. Johnson when he took over in November 1963 after the assassination of the more charismatic young President he succeeded, John F. Kennedy. And yet it was Johnson who, in 1964, engineered the most extensive array of progressive legislation since the New Deal of the 1930s. Similarly, if the Democrats win both the White House and a majority in the Senate, where they would most certainly relegate the Senate filibuster to the dustbin of history, this country would have the opportunity to significantly reduce structural and economic inequality through higher taxes on the superrich, greater scrutiny of mega-companies through reinvigorated enforcement of the antitrust laws, new efforts to reduce racial injustice and more investments and programs for the middle class and poor, including health care, education and paid leave. Significant action could also be taken to aggressively address climate change, which has the genuine potential of causing even more global misery than the coronavirus.

The kind of transformative change can happen quickly, as it did for the New Deal and Great Society programs. All it requires is the will to do it and a resurgence of the basically good instincts of the American soul.

To paraphrase the late great John Lewis, it is now our turn to let freedom ring.

August 15, 2020   Kenneth Foard McCallion

IN MEMORIAM

GEORGE PERRY FLOYD JR.

(OCTOBER 14, 1973 – MAY 25, 2020)

Haven't you heard?
America Is the Land of Freedom
It is the Land of Justice and Equality
All you need is to dream the dream
And the will to make it so
The sky's the limit
This is just the beginning
Nothing can stop us now
The opportunities are endless
Or that is the way it is supposed to be.

Get a good education they say
Don't worry about those student loans
The jobs will be there, don't worry
Haven't you heard?
There are laws against job discrimination
There are laws against housing discrimination
Everyone has the same chance at success
No matter whether you are rich or poor
Or that is the way it is supposed to be.

After all, this is America, the land of opportunity
A rising tide lifts all ships
The stock market will rebound, it always does
You don't own stocks, you say? No matter
Every generation of Americans does better than the last
Or that is the way it is supposed to be.

Remember we are all brothers and sister in the eyes of God
Nor matter what our race, color or creed
Remember there are no blue states, or red states
No white America, no Black America
Just the United States of America
Or was that just another dream?
Is it time to wake up now?

And then the deadly virus struck
And we all stayed home
Except for those of us who couldn't
Knowing that we were all in this together
And that we are all equal, aren't we?
Well maybe some of us were more equal than others
But isn't that the way it has always been?

And then Big George ventured forth
He had lost his job and caught the virus
Or did the virus catch him?

There was no cure, no vaccine for this virus
But that is not the virus that killed him
It was the other virus
the one that has been with us since the beginning
The deadly curse of racism
That choked out the life in him for 8 minutes 46 seconds
With the police officer's knee on his neck, hands in his pocket, staring at the camera
A hint of a cruel smile on his face as
George cried, "I can't breathe,"
pleading for his life
As bystanders pleaded with the officer to stop,
To get his knee off George's neck,
that he was killing him
The ambulance finally came, but it was George's hearse.

And then something magical happened
America rose up
It would not stay silent
Black America, White America, Asian America
We were not going to take it any more
George Floyd's life mattered
Black Lives Matter.
All lives matter
Enough is Enough.

George Floyd changed the world
And that is the way it is supposed to be.

-Kenneth Foard McCallion

ENDNOTES

TIMELINE

1. Abutaleb, Yasmeen, et al. "The U.S. Was Beset by Denial and Dysfunction as the Coronavirus Raged." *The Washington Post*, WP Company, 4 April 2020, www.washingtonpost.com/national-security/2020/04/04/coronavirus-government-dysfunction/?arc404=true.
2. Sharkey, Patrick. "The US Has a Collective Action Problem That's Larger than the Coronavirus Crisis." *Vox*, Vox, 10 Apr. 2020, www.vox.com/2020/4/10/21216216/coronavirus-social-distancing-texas-unacast-climate-change.
3. Keith, Tamara, and Malaka Gharib. "A Timeline Of Coronavirus Comments From President Trump And WHO." *NPR*, NPR, 15 April 2020, www.npr.org/sections/goatsandsoda/2020/04/15/835011346/a-timeline-of-coronavirus-comments-from-president-trump-and-who.
4. Bernstein, Leandra. "Government Report Anticipates 18-Month Pandemic, 'Significant Shortages'." *WJLA*, WJLA, 19 March 2020, wjla.com/news/nation-world/government-report-anticipates-18-month-pandemic-significant-shortages.
5. Ibid
6. Miller, Greg, and Shane Harris. "U.S. Intelligence Reports from January and February Warned about a Likely Pandemic." *The Washington Post*, WP Company, 22 March 2020, www.washingtonpost.com/national-security/us-intelligence-reports-from-january-and-february-warned-about-a-likely-pandemic/2020/03/20/299d8cda-6ad5-11ea-b5f1-a5a804158597_story.html.
7. "Trump Attacks W.H.O. and Ousts Watchdog for Pandemic Fund." *The New York Times*, The New York Times, 7 April 2020, www.nytimes.com/2020/04/07/world/coronavirus-updates-news-live.html.
8. Kaplan, Sheila. "C.D.C. Labs Were Contaminated, Delaying Coronavirus Testing, Officials Say." *The New York Times*, The New York Times, 18 April 2020, www.nytimes.com/2020/04/18/health/cdc-coronavirus-lab-contamination-testing.html

INTRODUCTION

1. Lipton, Eric, David E. Sanger, and Maggie Haberman. "He Could Have Seen What Was Coming: Behind Trump's Failure on the Virus." *The New York Times*. The New York Times, 11 Apr. 2020. www.nytimes.com/2020/04/11/us/politics/coronavirus-trump-response.html?ac-tion=click.
2. Abutaleb, Yasmeen, et al. "The U.S. Was Beset by Denial and Dysfunction as the Coronavirus Raged." *The Washington Post*, WP Company, 4 Apr. 2020, www.washingtonpost.com/national-security/2020/04/04/coronavirus-government-dysfunction/?arc404=true.
3. Sharkey, Patrick. "The US Has a Collective Action Problem That's Larger than the Coronavirus Crisis." *Vox*, Vox, 10 Apr. 2020, www.vox.com/2020/4/10/21216216/coronavirus-social-distancing-texas-unacast-climate-change.
4. Lipton, Eric, et al. "He Could Have Seen What Was Coming: Behind Trump's Failure on the Virus." The New York Times, The New York Times, 11 Apr. 2020, www.nytimes.com/2020/04/11/us/politics/coronavirus-trump-response.html?ac-tion=click.

5   Bernstein, Leandra. "Government Report Anticipates 18-Month Pandemic, 'Significant Shortages'." *KOMO*, KOMO, 19 Mar. 2020, komonews.com/news/nation-world/government-report-anticipates-18-month-pandemic-significant-shortages.

6   Ibid.

7   Armus, Teo. "Social Distancing a Week Earlier Could Have Saved 36,000 American Lives, Study Says." *The Washington Post*, WP Company, 21 May 2020, www.washingtonpost.com/nation/2020/05/21/columbia-study-coronavirus-deaths/.

8   O'Toole, Fintan. "Fintan O'Toole: Donald Trump Has Destroyed the Country He Promised to Make Great Again." *The Irish Times*, 25 Apr. 2020, www.irishtimes.com/opinion/fintan-o-toole-donald-trump-has-destroyed-the-country-he-promised-to-make-great-again-1.4235928?mode=sample.

CHAPTER 1

1   Voytko, Lisette. Updated: Trump Says China Should Have Given 'Earlier Notice' about Coronavirus, Disease 'Snuck up On Us'. 18 Mar. 2020, www.forbes.com/sites/lisettevoytko/2020/03/18/trump-china-should-have-given-earlier-notice-about-coronavirus-disease-snuck-up-on-us/./

2   Blake, Aaron. Analysis | Trump Keeps Saying 'Nobody' Could Have Foreseen Coronavirus. We Keep Finding out about New Warning Signs. 19 Mar. 2020, www.washingtonpost.com/politics/2020/03/19/trump-keeps-saying-nobody-could-have-foreseen-coronavirus-we-keep-finding-out-about-new-warning-signs/

3   Ibid.

4   As of April 8, 2020 100,376 deaths were recorded worldwide, with 17,991 of those deaths in the U.S.

5   "The News Hub."AFP.com, 17 Nov. 2016, www.afp.com/en/news/15/one-third-humanity-under-virus-lockdown-doc-1q57be4..

6   The pharmaceutical giant, Johnson & Johnson, which won a $1billion contract with the U.S. government to develop a vaccine, announced on April 14, 2020 that it was aiming to produce 600 million to 900 million doses of its potential coronavirus vaccine by April 2021, if human trials set to begin in September go as planned. J&J also committed more than $1 billion of investment in partnership with the federal Biomedical Advanced Research and Development Authority, which is part of the Department of Health and Human Services, to co-fund vaccine research. See Lovelace, Jr., Berkeley."J&J can produce up to 900 million coronavirus vaccine doses by April 2021 if trials go well." CNBC, 14, Apr. 2020, https://www.cnbc.com/2020/04/14/jj-can-produce-up-to-900-million-coronavirus-vaccine-doses-by-april-2021-if-trials-go-well.html.

7   Treverton, Gregory F., and Molly Jahn. "COVID-19: We Had the Warning but We Lacked the Leadership." TheHill, The Hill, 11 Apr. 2020, thehill.com/opinion/white-house/490404-covid-19-we-had-the-warning-but-we-lacked-the-leadership.

8   Klippenstein, Ken. Exclusive: The Military Knew Years Ago That a Coronavirus Was Coming. 7 Apr. 2020, www.thenation.com/article/politics/covid-military-shortage-pandemic/..

9   Coleman, Justine.US Intelligence Warned in November That Coronavirus Spreading in China Could Be 'Cataclysmic Event': Report. 8 Apr. 2020, thehill.com/policy/national-security/intelligence/491712-us-intelligence-warned-in-november-that-virus-spreading.

10   Ibid.

11   Rogers, Katie. "Trump Now Claims He Always Knew the Coronavirus Would Be a Pandemic." The New York Times, The New York Times, 17 Mar. 2020, www.nytimes.com/2020/03/17/us/politics/trump-coronavirus.html.

12 Brown, David. "Lessons to Be Learned from 1957 Pandemic." The Seattle Times, The Seattle Times Company, 26 Aug. 2009, www.seattletimes.com/seattle-news/health/lessons-to-be-learned-from-1957-pandemic/.

13 Ortega, Bob, et al. How the Government Delayed Coronavirus Testing. 10 Apr. 2020, www.cnn.com/2020/04/09/politics/coronavirus-testing-cdc-fda-red-tape-invs/index.html.

14 Alvarez, Priscilla, and Katelyn Polantz. US to Receive 750,000 Coronavirus Tests from South Korea. 13 Apr. 2020, www.cnn.com/2020/04/13/politics/south-korea-coronavirus-tests/index.html. l

15 "New York Governor Cuomo Coronavirus News Conference." C-SPAN.org, 9 Apr. 2020, www.c-span.org/video/?471087-1%2Fyork-governor-cuomo-coronavirus-news-conference.

16 Kilgannon, Corey. As Morgues Fill, N.Y.C. to Bury Some Virus Victims in Potter's Field. 10 Apr. 2020, https://www.nytimes.com/2020/04/10/nyregion/coronavirus-deaths-hart-island-burial.html

17 Rutenberg, Jim, et al. Why Republicans Are so Afraid of Vote-by-Mail. 8 Apr. 2020, www.nytimes.com/2020/04/08/us/politics/republicans-vote-by-mail.html.

18 Ibid.

19 Ibid.

20 Mozur, Paul, et al. "In Coronavirus Fight, China Gives Citizens a Color Code, With Red Flags." The New York Times, The New York Times, 2 Mar. 2020, www.nytimes.com/2020/03/01/business/china-coronavirus-surveillance.html.

CHAPTER 2

1 Jarus, Owen. *20 Of the Worst Epidemics and Pandemics in History*. 20 Mar. 2020, www.livescience.com/worst-epidemics-and-pandemics-in-history.html.

2 Ibid.

3 Saraceni, Jessica E. *Prehistoric Mass Grave Excavated in China*. 31 July 2015, www.archaeology.org/news/3530-150731-china-prehistoric-mass-grave.

4 Smith, Christine A. *Plague in the Ancient World*, people.loyno.edu/~history/journal/1996-7/Smith.html.

5 Thucydides. *The History of the Peloponnesian War*, II (52). Translated by Richard Crawley, London Dent, 1914.

6 "The History of the Ancient World: from the Earliest Accounts to the Fall of Rome." *The History of the Ancient World: from the Earliest Accounts to the Fall of Rome*, by S. Wise. Bauer, Norton, 2007,   p. 328.

7 Thucydides. *The History of the Peloponnesian War* (2.34.1-6).

8 Ibid.

9 Thucydides, (2.36.4).

10 Thucydides, (2.43.1).

11 Thucydides, II (65).

12 Thucydides, II (48).

13 Ibid.

14 Ibid.

15 Thucydides, II (54 and 47).

16 Thucydides, II (49).

17   Ibid.
18   Thucydides, II (51).
19   Thucydides, II (53). Thucydides believed the plague contributed to the defeat of Athens, because the willingness of the people to endure suffering for the public good was destroyed by the disease.
20   Thucydides, II (54). The Athenian plague was directly contagious, probably by means of airborne droplet infection. It spread to other cities when infected individuals either traveled or fled to the new areas.
21   Ibid.
22   Thucydides, II (52 and 53).
23   Thucydides, II (52).
24   Thucydides, II (54).
25   The Editors of Encyclopaedia Britannica. "On the Nature of Things."*Encyclopædia Britannica*, Encyclopædia Britannica, Inc., 2 Feb. 2018, www.britannica.com/topic/On-the-Nature-of-Things-by-Lucretius.
26   Furuse, Yuki, et al. "Origin of Measles Virus: Divergence FROM Rinderpest Virus between the 11th and 12th Centuries." *Virology Journal*, vol. 7, no. 1, 2010, pp. 52–55., doi:10.1186/1743-422x-7-52.
27   Cassius Dio Cocceianus, Herbert Baldwin Foster, and Earnest Cary. *Dio's Roman History*. Cambridge, Mass.: Harvard University Press, 19141927.
28   Murphy, Verity. *Health | Past Pandemics That Ravaged Europe*. 7 Nov. 2005, news.bbc.co.uk/2/hi/health/4381924.stm.
29   Smith, Christine A. *Plague in the Ancient World: A Study from Thucydides to Justinian*. 1996, people.loyno.edu/~history/journal/1996-7/Smith.html.
30   "The Struggle over the Euphrates Frontier."*The Pre-Islamic Middle East*, by Martin Sicker, Praeger, Westport,, CT, 2000, p. 169.
31   "Ammianus Marcellinus and the Representation of Historical Reality." *Ammianus Marcellinus and the Representation of Historical Reality*, by Timothy David. Barnes, vol. 56, Cornell Univ. Press, 1998..
32   Niebuhr, Barthold Georg, and Connop Thirlwall. *The History of Rome*. Translated by Julius Charles Hare, Lea & Blanchard, 1844.
33   Ibid.
34   Marcus Aurelius. *Meditations*, Dover Thrift ed., Dover Publications, 1997.
35   Kohn, George C. *Encyclopedia of Plague and Pestilence: from Ancient Times to the Present*. Facts On File, 2008.
36   Pruitt, Sarah. "Microbe Behind Black Death Also Caused Devastating Plague 800 Years Earlier." *History.com*, A&E Television Networks, 31 Aug. 2016, www.history.com/news/microbe-behind-black-death-also-caused-devastating-plague-800-years-earlier.
37   Roos, Dave. "Social Distancing and Quarantine Were Used in Medieval Times to Fight the Black Death." *History.com*, A&E Television Networks, 25 Mar. 2020, www.history.com/news/quarantine-black-death-medieval.
38   Ibid.
39   Ibid.
40   Little, Becky. "When London Faced a Pandemic-And a Devastating Fire." *History.com*, A&E Television Networks, 25 Mar. 2020, www.history.com/news/plague-pandemic-great-fire.

41 Ibid.
42 Brockell, Gillian. *During a Pandemic, Isaac Newton Had to Work from Home, Too. He Used the Time Wisely.* 12 Mar. 2020, www.washingtonpost.com/history/2020/03/12/during-pandemic-isaac-newton-had-work-home-too-he-used-time-wisely/.
43 Ibid.
44 Ibid.
45 Jarus, Owen. *20 Of the Worst Epidemics and Pandemics in History.* 20 Mar. 2020, www.livescience.com/worst-epidemics-and-pandemics-in-history.html..
46 "History of Smallpox." *CDC*, n.d., https://www.cdc.gov/smallpox/history/history.html. Accessed 11 May 2020.
47 ""Guns Germs & Steel: Variables. Smallpox." *PBS*, Public Broadcasting Service, www.pbs.org/gunsgermssteel/variables/smallpox.html..
48 "Smallpox and the Conquest of Mexico." *Past Medical History*, 20 Apr. 2018, www.pastmedicalhistory.co.uk/smallpox-and-the-conquest-of-mexico/.
49 "Guns Germs & Steel: Variables. Smallpox." *PBS*, Public Broadcasting Service, www.pbs.org/gunsgermssteel/variables/smallpox.html.
50 Blair, Eric, et al. "The Fight Over Inoculation During the 1721 Boston Smallpox Epidemic." *Science in the News*, 30 Oct. 2018, sitn.hms.harvard.edu/flash/special-edition-on-infectious-disease/2014/the-fight-over-inoculation-during-the-1721-boston-smallpox-epidemic/
51 "History of Smallpox." *CDC*, n.d., https://www.cdc.gov/smallpox/history/history.html. Accessed 11 May 2020.
52 Ibid.
53 Ibid.
54 Kaiser, Jocelyn, et al. *Six Vials of Smallpox Discovered in U.S. LAB.* 10 Dec. 2017, www.sciencemag.org/news/2014/07/six-vials-smallpox-discovered-us-lab.
55 Ibid.

CHAPTER 3

1 Blake, John B. *Public Health in the Town of Boston, 1630-1822.* Harvard University Press, 1959.
2 Viets, Henry R. "Some Features of the History of Medicine in Massachusetts during the Colonial Period (1620-1770)." *Isis*, vol. 23, no. 2, 1935, pp. 389–405. JSTOR, www.jstor.org/stable/224952. Accessed 14 May 2020.
3 Ibid.
4 Becker, Ann M. *Smallpox in Washington's Army: Strategic Implications of the Disease during the American Revolutionary War.* 31 Mar. 2004, muse.jhu.edu/article/54292.
5 "American Disasters 201 Calamities That Shook the Nation." *American Disasters 201 Calamities That Shook the Nation*, by Campbell Ballard, Checkmark Books, 2008, pp. 21–22.
6 Winslow, Ola E. *A Destroying Angel: The Conquest of Smallpox in Colonial Boston.* Institute of Technology for the Citizen, 1974.
7 Becker, Ann M. *Smallpox in Washington's Army: Strategic Implications of the Disease during the American Revolutionary War.* 31 Mar. 2004, muse.jhu.edu/article/54292.

8   Tindol, Robert. "Getting the Pox off All Their Houses: Cotton Mather and the Rhetoric of Puritan Science." *Early American Literature*, The University of North Carolina Press, 4 Mar. 2011, muse.jhu.edu/article/421114.

9   Burton, John D. "'The Awful Judgements of God upon the Land': Smallpox in Colonial Cambridge, Massachusetts." *The New England Quarterly*, vol. 74, no. 3, 2001, pp. 495–506.

10 "Becoming Malaria-Free by 2020." *World Health Organization*, www.who.int/news-room/feature-stories/detail/becoming-malaria-free-by-2020.18 June 2019

11 Wood, Bradford J. "'A Constant Attendance on God's Alter': Death, Disease, and the Anglican Church in Colonial South Carolina, 1706-1750."*The South Carolina Historical Magazine*, vol. 100, no. 3, 1999, pp. 204–220.

12 Kupperman, K O. "Fear of Hot Climates in the Anglo-American Colonial Experience." *The William and Mary Quarterly*, U.S. National Library of Medicine, 1984, www.ncbi.nlm.nih.gov/pubmed/11636275.

13 Ernest Carrol Faust. "History of Human Parasitic Infections." *Public Health Reports* (1896-1970), vol. 70, no. 10, 1955, pp. 958–965

14 Merrens, H. Roy, and George D. Terry. "Dying in Paradise: Malaria, Mortality, and the Perceptual Environment in Colonial South Carolina." *The Journal of Southern History*, vol. 50, no. 4, 1984, pp. 533–550

15 Blake, John B. *Public Health in the Town of Boston, 1630-1822.* Harvard University Press, 1959.

16 Shryock, Richard H. "Eighteenth Century Medicine in America." *Proceedings of the American Antiquarian Society*, vol. 59, no. 2, 1949, pp. 275-292.

17 Ibid.

18 Ibid.

19 "CDC–Malaria–About Malaria." *Centers for Disease Control and Prevention*, Centers for Disease Control and Prevention, 12 Mar. 2020, www.cdc.gov/malaria/about/index.html.

20 "World Malaria Report 2017–World." *ReliefWeb*, reliefweb.int/report/world/world-malaria-report-2017.

21 "Becoming Malaria-Free by 2020." *World Health Organization*, World Health Organization, www.who.int/news-room/feature-stories/detail/becoming-malaria-free-by-2020.

22 "Algeria and Argentina Certified Malaria-Free by WHO." *World Health Organization*, World Health Organization, www.who.int/news-room/detail/22-05-2019-algeria-and-argentina-certified-malaria-free-by-who.

23 Gallagher, James. "Malaria 'Completely Stopped' by Microbe." *BBC News*, BBC, 4 May 2020, www.bbc.com/news/health-52530828

24 Ibid.

25 O'Neill, Scott. "How a Tiny Bacterium Called Wolbachia Could Defeat Dengue." *ScientificAmerican.com*, Scientific American, 1 June 2015, www.scientificamerican.com/article/how-a-tiny-bacterium-called-wolbachia-could-defeat-dengue/.

26 Harrisberg, Kim. "Pregnancy, Malaria and Coronavirus a 'Perfect Storm' for Preventable Deaths." *Reuters*, Thomson Reuters, 24 Apr. 2020, www.reuters.com/article/us-health-coronavirus-women-trfn-idUSKCN226335.

27 Ibid.

28 Ibid.

29 "Typhoid Fever." *Infection Landscapes*, www.infectionlandscapes.org/2011/11/typhoid-fever.html#!.

30 Jones, Gordon W. "The First Epidemic in English America." *The Virginia Magazine of History and Biography*, vol. 71, no. 1, 1963, pp. 3-10. JSTOR, www.jstor.org/stable/4246912.

31 Ibid.

32 Benenson, Abram S. *Immunization and Military Medicine.* 1 Jan. 1984, academic.oup.com/cid/article/6/1/1/399439.

33 Ibid.

34 Bauer, J.R. "Yellow Fever." *Public Health Reports* (1896-1970), vol. 55, no. 9, Mar. 1940, pp. 362-71.

35 Ibid.

36 Ibid.

37 Viets, Henry R. "Some Features of the History of Medicine in Massachusetts during the Colonial Period (1620-1770)." *Isis*, vol. 23, no. 2, 1935, pp. 389-405. JSTOR, www.jstor.org/stable/224952.

38 Ibid.

39 Bauer, J.R. "Yellow Fever." *Public Health Reports* (1896-1970), vol. 55, no. 9, Mar. 1940, pp. 362-71.

40 "*Yellow Fever Attacks Philadelphia, 1793*, eyewitnesstohistory.com/yellowfever.htm.

41 Frierson, J. G. "The Yellow Fever Vaccine: A History." *The Yale Journal of Biology and Medicine*, vol. 83, no.2, 2010, pp. 77-85.

42 "Cholera." *Doctors Without Borders–USA*, www.doctorswithoutborders.org/what-we-do/medical-issues/cholera.

43 Sacwk, D. A. et al. "Cholera". *The Lancet*, vol. 363, no. 9404, Jan. 2004, pp. 223-33. doi:10.1016/S0140-6736(03)15328-7.

44 Kelley, L. Cholera". *The Lancet*, vol. 363, no. 9404, Jan. 2004, Cholera". *The Lancet*, vol. 363, no. 9404, Jan. 2004, Cholera". *The Lancet*, vol. 363, no. 9404, Jan. 2004,. Palgrave Macmillan, 2003, p.131.

45 Hosking, G.H. *Russia and the Russians: A History.* Harvard University Press, 2001. p. 9.

46 "Pandemics that Changed History." *History*, 1 Apr. 2020, https://www.history.com/topics/middle-ages/pandemics-timeline.

47 Pyle, G.F. "The Diffusion of Cholera in the United States in the Nineteenth Century". *Geographical Analysis*, vol.1, no.1, 1969, pp. 59-75. doi:10.1111/j.1538-4632.1969.tb00605.x.

48 Byrne J.P. *Encyclopedia of Pestilence, Pandemics, and Plagues: A–M.* Greenwood Press, 2008, p. 99.

49 Lacey, S.W. "Cholera: Calamitous Past, Ominous Future." *Clinical Infectious Diseases*, vol. 20, no. 5, May 1995, pp. 1409-1419. doi:10.1093/clinids/20.5.1409.

50 "Introduction." *Naval History and Heritage Command*, 9 Mar. 2015, https://www.history.navy.mil/research/library/online-reading-room/title-list-alphabetically/d/diary-of-michael-shiner/introduction.html.

51 Sharp, J.G. "Cholera at Gosport Navy Yard 1832." *US Gen. Web Archives*, 8 Mar. 2019, http://www.usgwarchives.net/va/portsmouth/shipyard/nnysharp5.html.

52 "Cholera." N.d., *WHO*, https://www.who.int/health-topics/cholera#tab=tab_1. Aceessed 13 May 2020.

53 "Cholera vaccines: WHO position paper". *Weekly Epidemiological Record*, vol. 85, no. 13, 2010, pp. 117-128. https://www.who.int/wer/2010/wer8513.pdf.

54 Sack, D. A. et al. "Cholera". *The Lancet*, vol. 363, no. 9404, Jan. 2004, pp. 223-33. doi:10.1016/S0140-6736(03)15328-7.

55 Bruwer, J. "The horrors of Yemen's spiralling cholera crisis". *BBC News*, 25 June 2017, https://www.bbc.com/news/world-middle-east-40369804.

56 "Cholera Situation in Somalia." *WHO*, May 2017, https://applications.emro.who.int/docs/EMRO-Pub_2017_EN_19873.pdf?ua=1.

57 "Chlorea." *History*, 24 Mar. 2020, https://www.history.com/topics/inventions/history-of-cholera.

58 Singh, Neil. "Cholera and Coronavirus: Why We Must Not Repeat the Same Mistakes." *The Guardian*, Guardian News and Media, 1 May 2020, www.theguardian.com/society/2020/may/01/cholera-and-coronavirus-why-we-must-not-repeat-the-same-mistakes. see also Ali, Mohammad et al. "Updated Global Burden of Cholera in Endemic Countries." *PLoS neglected tropical diseases* vol. 9, no. 6, 4 Jun. 2015. doi:10.1371/journal.pntd.0003832.

59 Ibid.

60 Daugherty, Greg. "The Russian Flu of 1889: The Deadly Pandemic Few Americans Took Seriously." *History.com*, A&E Television Networks, 23 Mar. 2020, www.history.com/news/1889-russian-flu-pandemic-in-america.

61 Ibid.

62 Ibid.

63 Ibid.

64 Ibid.

65 Janssen, Volker. "When Polio Triggered Fear and Panic Among Parents in the 1950s." *History.com*, A&E Television Networks, 27 Mar. 2020, www.history.com/news/polio-fear-post-wwii-era.

66 Ibid.

CHAPTER 4

1 "Pandemic Influenza: an Evolving Challenge." *World Health Organization*, World Health Organization, 25 July 2018, www.who.int/influenza/pandemic-influenza-an-evolving-challenge/en//; *see also* "Influenza Pandemic of 1918-19." *Encyclopaedia Britannica*, 20 Mar. 2020, https://www.britannica.com/event/influenza-pandemic-of-1918-1919; Chodosh, Sara. "What the 1918 Flu Pandemic Can Teach Us about COVID-19, in Four Charts." *Popular Science*, Popular Science, 18 Mar. 2020, www.popsci.com/story/health/coronavirus-1918-flu-pandemic/.

2 Ibid.

3 "Ten things you need to know about pandemic influenza." *Weekly Epidemiological Record,* vol. 80, no. 49–50, Dec. 2005, pp. 428–431. https://apps.who.int/iris/bitstream/handle/10665/232955/WER8049_50_428-431.PDF.

4 "1918 Pandemic (H1N1 Virus)." *Centers for Disease Control and Prevention*, Centers for Disease Control and Prevention, 20 Mar. 2019, www.cdc.gov/flu/pandemic-resources/1918-pandemic-h1n1.html.

5 ACPinternists. "Analysis of Spanish Flu Cases in 1918-1920 Suggests Transfusions Might Help in Bird Flu Pandemic." *EurekAlert!*, 29 Aug. 2006, www.eurekalert.org/pub_releases/2006-08/acop-aos082806.php.

6 Barry, John. (2004). The site of origin of the 1918 influenza pandemic and its public health implications. Journal of translational medicine. 2. 3. 10.1186/1479-5876-2-3.

7 Klein, Christopher. "Why October 1918 Was America's Deadliest Month Ever." *History.com*, A&E Television Networks, 5 Oct. 2018, www.history.com/news/spanish-flu-deaths-october-1918.

8 Taubenberger, Jeffery & Morens, David. (2006). 1918 Influenza: the Mother of All Pandemics. Emerging Infectious Diseases. 12. 15-22. 10.3201/eid1209.050979.

9   Zhang, Jun-Ming, and Jianxiong An. "Cytokines, inflammation, and pain." *International anesthesiology clinics* vol. 45,2 (2007): 27-37. doi:10.1097/AIA.0b013e318034194e.

10 Liu, Qiang et al. "The cytokine storm of severe influenza and development of immunomodulatory therapy." *Cellular & molecular immunology* vol. 13,1 (2016): 3-10. doi:10.1038/cmi.2015.74

11 Bakalar, Nicholas. "In 1918 Pandemic, Another Possible Killer: Aspirin." *The New York Times*, The New York Times, 12 Oct. 2009, www.nytimes.com/2009/10/13/health/13aspirin.html.

12 Terry, Mark. "Compare: 1918 Spanish Influenza Pandemic Versus COVID-19." *BioSpace*, BioSpace, 2 Apr. 2020, www.biospace.com/article/compare-1918-spanish-influenza-pandemic-versus-covid-19/.

13 Ibid.

14 Martini, M et al. "The Spanish Influenza Pandemic: a lesson from history 100 years after 1918." *Journal of preventive medicine and hygiene* vol. 60,1 E64-E67. 29 Mar. 2019, doi:10.15167/2421-4248/jpmh2019.60.1.1205

15 Aimone, Francesco. "The 1918 Influenza Epidemic in New York City: a Review of the Public Health Response." *Public Health Reports (Washington, D.C.: 1974)*, Association of Schools of Public Health, Apr. 2010, www.ncbi.nlm.nih.gov/pmc/articles/PMC2862336/.

16 Ibid.

17 Ibid.

18 Ibid.

19 Ibid.

20 Ibid.

21 Ibid.

22 Ibid.

23 Strochlic, Nina, and Riley D. Champine. "How Some Cities 'Flattened the Curve' during the 1918 Flu Pandemic." *How They Flattened the Curve during the 1918 Spanish Flu*, 7 Apr. 2020, www.nationalgeographic.com/history/2020/03/how-cities-flattened-curve-1918-spanish-flu-pandemic-coronavirus/.

24 Ibid.

25 Ibid.

26 Ibid.

27 Ibid.

28 Ibid.

29 "Rapid Response Was Crucial to Containing the 1918 Flu Pandemic." *National Institutes of Health*, U.S. Department of Health and Human Services, 28 Sept. 2015, www.nih.gov/news-events/news-releases/rapid-response-was-crucial-containing-1918-flu-pandemic..

30 Ibid.

31 *Ibid.*

CHAPTER 5

1   Little, Becky. *How the 1957 Flu Pandemic Was Stopped Early in Its Path*. 18 Mar. 2020, www.history.com/news/1957-flu-pandemic-vaccine-hilleman.

2   Ibid.

3   Jackson, Claire. "History Lessons: the Asian Flu Pandemic." *British Journal of General Practice*, vol. 59, no. 565, 2009, pp. 622–623., doi:10.3399/bjgp09x453882.

4   Little, Becky. *How the 1957 Flu Pandemic Was Stopped Early in Its Path*. 18 Mar. 2020, www.history.com/news/1957-flu-pandemic-vaccine-hilleman.

5   Ibid.

6   Newman, Laura. "Maurice Hilleman." *BMJ : British Medical Journal* vol. 330,7498 (2005): 1028.

7   Ibid.

8   Ibid.

9   Ibid.

10   Ibid.

11   Tulchinsky, T. H.. "Maurice Hilleman: Creator of Vaccines That Changed the World." *Case Studies in Public Health*, 2018, pp. 443–470. doi:10.1016/B978-0-12-804571-8.00003-2. Tulchinsky, Theodore H. "Maurice Hilleman: Creator of Vaccines That Changed the World." *Case Studies in Public Health*, 2018, pp. 443–470., doi:10.1016/b978-0-12-804571-8.00003-2.

12   Little, Becky. *How the 1957 Flu Pandemic Was Stopped Early in Its Path*. 18 Mar. 2020, www.history.com/news/1957-flu-pandemic-vaccine-hilleman.

13   Ibid.

14   Ibid.

15   Ibid.

16   Ibid.

17   Ibid.

18   "1957-1958 Pandemic (H2N2 Virus)." *Centers for Disease Control and Prevention*, Centers for Disease Control and Prevention, 2 Jan. 2019, www.cdc.gov/flu/pandemic-resources/1957-1958-pandemic.html.

19   "1918 Pandemic (H1N1 Virus)." *Centers for Disease Control and Prevention*, Centers for Disease Control and Prevention, 20 Mar. 2019, www.cdc.gov/flu/pandemic-resources/1918-pandemic-h1n1.html.

20   "Viruses And Man: a History of Interactions."*Viruses And Man: a History of Interactions*, by Milton W. Taylor, Springer International PU, 2016, p. 367.

21   Offit, P. A. *Vaccinated: One Man's Quest to Defeat the World's Deadliest Diseases*. Smithsonian Books, 2008.

22   Racaniello, V. "Poliovirus Vaccine, SV40, and Human Cancer." *Virology Blog,* 13 Apr. 2010, https://www.virology.ws/2010/04/13/poliovirus-vaccine-sv40-and-human-cancer/.

23   Offit, Paul A. *Vaccinated: One Man's Quest to Defeat the World's Deadliest Diseases*. Smithsonian Books, 2008.

24   Bookchin, Debbie, and Jim Schumacher. *The Virus and the Vaccine: the True Story of a Cancer-Causing Monkey Virus, Contaminated Polio Vaccine, and the Millions of Americans Exposed*. St. Martin's Press, 2004. pp. 94-98.

25   "Dr. Maurice Hilleman: 'The Father of Modern Vaccines'."*Merck.com*, www.merck.com/about/featured-stories/doctor-maurice-hilleman-father-of-modern-vaccines.html.

CHAPTER 6

1   "SARS (Severe Acute Respiratory Syndrome)." *World Health Organization*, World Health Organization, 26 Apr. 2012, www.who.int/ith/diseases/sars/en/.

2   "Update 95–SARS: Chronology of a Serial Killer." *World Health Organization*, World Health Organization, 24 July 2015, www.who.int/csr/don/2003_07_04/en/.

3   "Severe Acute Respiratory Syndrome (SARS) Multi-Country Outbreak–Update 6." *World Health Organization*, World Health Organization, 24 July 2015, www.who.int/csr/don/2003_03_21/en/.
4   Ibid
5   Pasley, James. *How SARS Terrified the World in 2003, Infecting More than 8,000 People and KILLING 774*. 20 Feb. 2020, https://www.businessinsider.com/deadly-sars-virus-history-2003-in-photos-2020-2
6   *China's Latest SARS Outbreak Has Been Contained, but BIOSAFETY Concerns Remain – Update 7*. 24 July 2015, www.who.int/csr/don/2004_05_18a/en/..
7   Rosenthal, Elisabeth, and L. K. Altman. *China Raises Tally of Cases and Deaths in Mystery Illness*. 27 Mar. 2003, www.nytimes.com/2003/03/27/world/china-raises-tally-of-cases-and-deaths-in-mystery-illness.html.
8   Ibid.
9   "CDC SARS Response Timeline." *Centers for Disease Control and Prevention*, Centers for Disease Control and Prevention, 26 Apr. 2013, www.cdc.gov/about/history/sars/timeline.htm.
10 Ibid.
11 Rosenthal, Elisabeth, and L K Altman. *China Raises Tally of Cases and Deaths in Mystery Illness*. 27 Mar. 2003, www.nytimes.com/2003/03/27/world/china-raises-tally-of-cases-and-deaths-in-mystery-illness.html.
12 "CDC SARS Response Timeline." *Centers for Disease Control and Prevention*, Centers for Disease Control and Prevention, 26 Apr. 2013, www.cdc.gov/about/history/sars/timeline.htm..
13 Ibid.
14 Ibid.
15 Ibid.
16 Ibid.
17 Ibid.
18 Ibid.
19 *Sars*. 6 Dec. 2017, www.cdc.gov/sars/about/fs-sars.html.
20 Wilder-Smith, Annelies, et al. "Can We Contain the COVID-19 Outbreak with the Same Measures As For Sars?" *The Lancet Infectious Diseases*, 2020, doi:10.1016/s1473-3099(20)30129-8."
21 Ibid.
22 Ibid.
23 Ibid.
24 "Coronavirus Disease 2019 (COVID-19)." *Centers for Disease Control and Prevention*, Centers for Disease Control and Prevention, www.cdc.gov/coronavirus/2019-ncov/index.html.
25 Ibid.
26 Wilder-Smith, Annelies, et al. "Can We Contain the COVID-19 Outbreak with the Same Measures As For Sars?" *The Lancet Infectious Diseases*, 2020, doi:10.1016/s1473-3099(20)30129-8."
27 Ibid.
28 Ibid.
29 Ibid.
30 Ibid.
31 Ibid.
32 Ibid.

33 Ibid.

34 Ibid.

35 Ibid.

36 Yoon, Dasl, and Timothy W. Martin. "How South Korea Put Into Place the World's Most Aggressive Coronavirus Test Program." *The Wall Street Journal*, Dow Jones & Company, 16 Mar. 2020, www.wsj.com/articles/how-south-korea-put-into-place-the-worlds-most-aggressive-coronavirus-testing-11584377217.

37 Ibid.

38 *Outbreak of swine-origin influenza A (H1N1) Virus Infection —- Mexico, March—April 2009*. www.cdc.gov/mmwr/preview/mmwrhtml/mm5817a5.htm.

39 Trifonov, Vladimir, et al. "Geographic Dependence, Surveillance, and Origins of the 2009 Influenza A (H1N1) Virus." *New England Journal of Medicine*, vol. 361, no. 2, 2009, pp. 115–119., doi:10.1056/nejmp0904572.

40 Hellerman, Caleb. "Swine Flu 'Not Stoppable,' World Health Organization Says." *CNN*, Cable News Network, 2009, www.cnn.com/2009/HEALTH/06/11/swine.flu.who/index.html.

41 Roos, Robert. *Study Puts Global 2009 H1N1 Infection Rate at 11% to 21%*. 8 Aug. 2011, www.cidrap.umn.edu/news-perspective/2011/08/study-puts-global-2009-h1n1-infection-rate-11-21.

42 Ibid.

43 *First Global Estimates of 2009 H1N1 Pandemic Mortality Released By Cdc-Led Collaboration*. 25 June 2012, www.cdc.gov/flu/spotlights/pandemic-global-estimates.htm.

44 DeNoon, Daniel J. *H1N1 Swine Flu No Worse than Seasonal Flu*. 7 Sept. 2010, www.webmd.com/cold-and-flu/news/20100907/h1n1-swine-flu-no-worse-than-seasonal-flu.

45 Roos, Robert. *CDC Estimate of Global H1N1 Pandemic Deaths: 284,000*. 27 June 2012, www.cidrap.umn.edu/news-perspective/2012/06/cdc-estimate-global-h1n1-pandemic-deaths-284000.

46 Hayden, Frederick G, et al. "Clinical Aspects of Pandemic 2009 Influenza A (H1N1) Virus Infection: NEJM." *New England Journal of Medicine*, 27 May 2010, www.nejm.org/doi/full/10.1056/NEJMra1000449.

47 *Clinical Features of Severe Cases of Pandemic Influenza*. 21 June 2015, www.who.int/csr/disease/swineflu/notes/h1n1_clinical_features_20091016/en/.

48 Jain, Seema, et al. *Hospitalized Patients with 2009 H1N1 Influenza in the United States, April–June 2009: Nejm*. 12 Nov. 2009, www.nejm.org/doi/full/10.1056/NEJMoa0906695.

49 Hickok, Kimberly. *How Does the COVID-19 Pandemic Compare to the Last Pandemic?* 18 Mar. 2020, www.livescience.com/covid-19-pandemic-vs-swine-flu.html.

50 McKay, Betsy. *New Push in H1N1 Flu Fight Set for Start of School*. 19 July 2009, www.wsj.com/articles/SB124787226825260533.

51 Hutain, Jenny. *478 Community Clinics in 49 States Receiving Needed H1N1 Protective Supplies*. 26 July 2018, www.directrelief.org/2009/11/478-community-clinics-49-states-receiving-needed-h1n1-protective-supplies/

52 Hickok, Kimberly. *How Does the COVID-19 Pandemic Compare to the Last Pandemic?* 18 Mar. 2020, www.livescience.com/covid-19-pandemic-vs-swine-flu.html.

53 "COVIID-19 Is More Contageious Than Its Coronavirus Brethren, But It's Not As Fatal On A Case-By-Case Basis." *KHN*, 19 Feb. 2020, https://khn.org/morning-breakout/covid-19-is-more-contagious-than-its-coronavirus-brethren-but-its-not-as-fatal-on-a-case-by-case-basis/.

54 "People Who Are at Higher Risk for Severe Illness." *Centers for Disease Control and Prevention*, Centers for Disease Control and Prevention, 15 Apr. 2020, www.cdc.gov/coronavirus/2019-ncov/need-extra-precautions/people-at-higher-risk.html.

55 *Centers for Disease Control and Prevention*, Centers for Disease Control and Prevention, www.cdc.gov/coronavirus/2019-ncov/about/symptoms.html.

56 Ibid.

57 Hickok, Kimberly. *How Does the COVID-19 Pandemic Compare to the Last Pandemic?* 18 Mar. 2020, www.livescience.com/covid-19-pandemic-vs-swine-flu.html.

58 Ibid.

59 Ibid.

60 Ibid.

61 "COVID-19 Situation Reports." *World Health Organization*, World Health Organization, www.who.int/emergencies/diseases/novel-coronavirus-2019/situation-reports/.

62 Ibid.; Shear, Michael D., and Rob Stein. *Obama Declares H1N1 National EMERGENCY, Easing Rules for Hospitals*. 25 Oct. 2009, www.washingtonpost.com/wp-dyn/content/article/2009/10/24/AR2009102401061.html.

63 Ibid.

64 "The 2009 H1N1 Pandemic: Summary Highlights, April 2009-April 2010." *Centers for Disease Control and Prevention*, Centers for Disease Control and Prevention, www.cdc.gov/h1n1flu/cdcresponse.htm.

65 Ibid.

66 Nguyen, An V, et al. "Comparison of 3 Infrared Thermal Detection Systems and Self-Report for Mass Fever Screening." *Emerging Infectious Diseases*, Centers for Disease Control and Prevention, Nov. 2010, www.ncbi.nlm.nih.gov/pmc/articles/PMC3294528/.

67 Hines, Lora. "*Health Officials Evaluate Response to Swine Flu*". 2 June 2009, www.upmc-biosecurity.org/website/about_us/pressroom/in_the_news_2009.html..

68 Ibid.

69 Stein, Rob. "*Preparing for Swine Flu's Return*". 29 Oct. 7AD, www.citizenstrade.org/ctc/wp-content/uploads/2011/05/PreparingforSwineFlu.pdf.

70 Steenhuysen, Julie. *As Swine Flu Wanes, U.S. Preparing for Second Wave*. 4 June 2009, www.reuters.com/article/idUSN04230085.

71 Stein, Rob. "*Preparing for Swine Flu's Return*". 29 Oct. 7AD, www.citizenstrade.org/ctc/wp-content/uploads/2011/05/PreparingforSwineFlu.pdf..

72 Shear, Michael D., and Rob Stein. *Obama Declares H1N1 National EMERGENCY, Easing Rules for Hospitals*. 25 Oct. 2009, www.washingtonpost.com/wp-dyn/content/article/2009/10/24/AR2009102401061.html.

73 "Pandemic Influenza." *HHS.gov*, US Department of Health and Human Services, 13 July 2016, www.hhs.gov/about/agencies/oga/global-health-security/pandemic-influenza/index.html..

74 Ibid.

75 Inslee, Jay. *PolitiFact–President Obama Declared H1N1 a Public Health Emergency before Anyone in the United States Died*. 4 Mar. 2020, www.politifact.com/factchecks/2020/mar/04/facebook-posts/president-obama-declared-h1n1-public-health-emerge/..

76 "Community Mitigation GuIbidelines to Prevent Pandemic Influenza – United States, 2017." *CDC*, 21 Apr. 2017, https://www.cdc.gov/mmwr/volumes/66/rr/rr6601a1.htm.

77. Master, OEC Web. "CDC Press Briefing Transcripts November 12, 2009". www.cdc.gov
78. Steenhuysen, Julie. *Swine Flu Has Killed 10,000 Americans since April*. 10 Dec. 2009, www.reuters.com/article/us-flu-usa-idUSTRE5AO3Z420091210.
79. 2009 H1N1 Pandemic (H1N1pdm09 virus). (2019, June 11). Retrieved from https://www.cdc.gov/flu/pandemic-resources/2009-h1n1-pandemic.html
80. "Shipping of CDC 2019 Novel Coronavirus Diagnostic Test Kits Begins." *CDC*, 6 Feb. 2020, https://www.cdc.gov/media/releases/2020/p0206-coronavirus-diagnostic-test-kits.html.
81. "Officials Say C.D.C. Errors Caused Testing Delays." *The New York Times*, The New York Times, 18 Apr. 2020, www.nytimes.com/2020/04/18/us/coronavirus-live-news.html.
82. Shear, Michael. "The Lost Month: How a Failure to Test Blinded the U.S. to Covid-19." *The New York Times*, The New York Times, 28 Mar. 2020, www.nytimes.com/2020/03/28/us/testing-coronavirus-pandemic.html..
83. "Coronavirus (COVIBID-19) Update: FDA Issues New Policy to Help Expedite Availability of Diagnostics." *FDA*, 29 Feb. 2020, https://www.fda.gov/news-events/press-announcements/coronavirus-covIbid-19-update-fda-issues-new-policy-help-expedite-availability-diagnostics.
84. "FDA's Emergency Use Authorization Process for COVID-19 Tests May Alleviate Shortage." *McGuireWoods*, www.mcguirewoods.com/client-resources/Alerts/2020/3/fdas-emergency-use-authorization-process-for-covid-19-tests-may-alleviate-shortage.
85. Shear, Michael. "The Lost Month: How a Failure to Test Blinded the U.S. to Covid-19." *The New York Times*, The New York Times, 28 Mar. 2020, www.nytimes.com/2020/03/28/us/testing-coronavirus-pandemic.html.

CHAPTER 7

1. "Ebola (Ebola Virus Disease)." *Centers for Disease Control and Prevention*, Centers for Disease Control and Prevention, 5 Nov. 2019, www.cdc.gov/vhf/ebola/index.html.
2. "Ebola Virus Disease." *World Health Organization*, World Health Organization, www.who.int/news-room/fact-sheets/detail/ebola-virus-disease.
3. Ibid.
4. Fredericks, Bob. *CDC Admits Droplets from a Sneeze Could Spread Ebola*. 29 Oct. 2014, nypost.com/2014/10/29/cdc-admits-droplets-from-a-sneeze-could-spread-ebola/.Chumley, Cheryl K. *CDC Admits Ebola Can Be Passed to Others by Sneezing*. 29 Oct. 2014, www.washingtontimes.com/news/2014/oct/29/cdc-admits-ebola-can-be-passed-to-others-by-sneezi/.
5. "Ebola Virus Disease." *World Health Organization*, World Health Organization, www.who.int/news-room/fact-sheets/detail/ebola-virus-disease.
6. *CDC and Texas Health Department Confirm First Ebola Case Diagnosed in the U.S.* 1 Oct. 2014, www.cdc.gov/media/releases/2014/s930-ebola-confirmed-case.html./Allen, Nick. "First Ebola Victim in America Was Sent Home with Antibiotics." *The Telegraph*, Telegraph Media Group, 1 Oct. 2014, www.telegraph.co.uk/news/worldnews/ebola/11132475/First-Ebola-victim-in-America-was-sent-home-with-antibiotics.html.
7. Ibid.
8. Botelho, Greg, and Jacque Wilson. *Thomas Eric Duncan: First Ebola Death in U.S.* 8 Oct. 2014, www.cnn.com/2014/10/08/health/thomas-eric-duncan-ebola/index.html.
9. Ibid.

10   Santora, Marc. "Doctor in New York City Is Sick With Ebola." *The New York Times*, The New York Times, 23 Oct. 2014, www.nytimes.com/2014/10/24/nyregion/craig-spencer-is-tested-for-ebola-virus-at-bellevue-hospital-in-new-york-city.html..

11   "New York Doctor Just Back From Africa Has Ebola." *NBCNews.com*, NBCUniversal News Group, 11 June 2015, www.nbcnews.com/storyline/ebola-virus-outbreak/new-york-doctor-just-back-africa-has-ebola-n232561.

12   Hartocollis, Anemona. *Craig Spencer, New York Doctor with Ebola, Will Leave Bellevue Hospital*. 10 Nov. 2014, www.nytimes.com/2014/11/11/nyregion/craig-spencer-new-york-doctor-with-ebola-will-leave-bellevue-hospital.html.

13   *United States Department of Defense*, archive.defense.gov/home/features/2014/1014_ebola/./

14   Greer, Dale. *United States Africa Command*, www.africom.mil/media-room/article/23757/101st-airborne-soldiers-head-to-liberia-in-support-of-usaid.

15   Zoroya, Gregg. *U.S. Military Will Build Fewer Ebola Clinics in Liberia*. 19 Nov. 2014, www.usatoday.com/story/news/world/2014/11/18/ebola-us-military-clinics-usaid/19233583/

16   *US, Liberia Open 1ST Ebola Treatment Unit for Health Workers*. 24 Nov. 2014, www.voanews.com/africa/us-liberia-open-1st-ebola-treatment-unit-health-workers.

17   Montanaro, Domenico. *Obama Names Ebola 'Czar'*. Edited by Associated Press, 17 Oct. 2014, www.pbs.org/newshour/health/obama-open-appoint-czar-oversee-nations-ebola-response.

18   Davis, Julie H. *Before Ebola, New Czar Handled Political Crises*. 17 Oct. 2014, www.nytimes.com/2014/10/18/us/ron-klain-chief-of-staff-to-2-vice-presidents-is-named-ebola-czar.html.

19   Tapper, Jake. *First on Cnn: Obama Will Name Ron Klain as Ebola Czar*. 19 Oct. 2014, www.cnn.com/2014/10/17/politics/ebola-czar-ron-klain/index.html; "Texas Health Worker Isolated on Cruise Ship over Possible Ebola Contact." *Reuters*, Thomson Reuters, 17 Oct. 2014, www.reuters.com/article/us-health-ebola-usa-cruiseship-idUSKCN0I60F520141017.

20   *Barack Obama 'Not at All Concerned' about Hugging CURED Ebola Patient–Video*. Edited by Reuters, 25 Oct. 2014, www.theguardian.com/us-news/video/2014/oct/25/barack-obama-hugging-cured-ebola-patient-dallas-nurse-nina-pham-video.

21   Rhodes, Rosamond. *Trusted Doctor: Medical Ethics And Professionalism*. Oxford Univ Press, 2020. p. 250.

22   "Obama Tells CDC He Wants Ebola 'SWAT Team' Ready to Go Anywhere." *Los Angeles Times*, 16 Oct. 2014, www.latimes.com/nation/la-na-obama-ebola-20141015-story.html..

23   Stobbe, M. (2014, October 24). CDC details new Ebola response and PREP TEAMS. Retrieved from https://apnews.com/35a896603c4545c0afaa78a12c565d03

24   Ibid.

25   Tavernise, Sabrina, and Michael D Shear. *U.S. to Begin Ebola Screenings at 5 Airports*. 8 Oct. 2014, www.nytimes.com/2014/10/09/us/us-to-begin-ebola-screenings-at-5-airports.html. Miller, Zeke J, and Alexandra Sifferlin. *Ebola Outbreak: U.S. to Screen Passengers from West Africa at Airports*. 8 Oct. 2014, time.com/3482094/ebola-us-west-africa-airports/; Matthews, Karen. "Stepped-up Ebola Screening Starts at NYC Airport." *KSL.com*, www.ksl.com/article/31911466/stepped-up-ebola-screening-starts-at-nyc-airport.t

26   Ibid.

27   McNeil, Donald G. "U.S. Plans 21-Day Watch of Travelers From Ebola-Hit Nations." *The New York Times*, The New York Times, 22 Oct. 2014, www.nytimes.com/2014/10/23/health/us-to-monitor-travelers-from-ebola-hit-nations-for-21-days.html.

28 "Connecticut Declares Preemptive Ebola Health Emergency, Allows Quarantines." *RT International*, www.rt.com/usa/194032-connecticut-health-emergency-prevent-ebola/.

29 Kovner, Josh, and Nicholas Rondinone. "State Orders 9 Quarantined Amid Ebola Concerns." *Courant.com*, Hartford Courant, 12 Dec. 2018, www.courant.com/breaking-news/hc-west-haven-quarantine-1023-20141022-story.html.

30 Karni, A., Lovett, K., & Otis, G. A. (2019, January 09). Travelers in contact with Ebola patients, including returning nurse with Fever, now face MANDATORY 21-DAY quarantine in New York, New Jersey. Retrieved from https://www.nydailynews.com/new-york/mandatory-21-day-quarantine-travelers-risk-ebola-n-y-n-article-1.1986460. Karni, Annie, et al. "Travelers in Contact with Ebola Patients, Including Returning Nurse with Fever, Now Face Mandatory 21-Day Quarantine in New York, New Jersey." *Nydailynews.com*, New York Daily News, 9 Jan. 2019, www.nydailynews.com/new-york/mandatory-21-day-quarantine-travelers-risk-ebola-n-y-n-article-1.1986460.

31 Fisher, Marc. *Perspective | From Ebola to Coronavirus, Trump Always Sees Disease as a Foreign Threat*. 20 Mar. 2020, www.washingtonpost.com/outlook/trump-ebola-coronavirus-xenophobia/2020/03/19/21dff870-694f-11ea-abef-020f086a3fab_story.html.

32 Liptak, Kevin. *Trump Announces New Face Mask Recommendations After Heated Internal Debate*. 4 Apr. 2020, www.cnn.com/2020/04/03/politics/trump-white-house-face-masks/index.html.

33 Fisher, Marc. *Perspective | From Ebola to Coronavirus, Trump Always Sees Disease as a Foreign Threat*. 20 Mar. 2020, www.washingtonpost.com/outlook/trump-ebola-coronavirus-xenophobia/2020/03/19/21dff870-694f-11ea-abef-020f086a3fab_story.html.l

34 Rupar, Aaron. "Trump Is Facing a Coronavirus Threat. Let's Look Back at How He Talked about Ebola." *Vox*, Vox, 26 Feb. 2020, www.vox.com/2020/2/26/21154253/trump-ebola-tweets-coronavirus..

35 Ibid.

CHAPTER 8

1 Blake, Aaron. *Analysis | Trump Keeps Saying 'Nobody' Could Have Foreseen Coronavirus. We Keep Finding out about New Warning Signs*. 19 Mar. 2020, www.washingtonpost.com/politics/2020/03/19/trump-keeps-saying-nobody-could-have-foreseen-coronavirus-we-keep-finding-out-about-new-warning-signs/

2 Ibid.

3 Ibid.

4 *ABC News*, ABC News Network, abcnews.go.com/Politics/intelligence-report-warned-coronavirus-crisis-early-november-sources/story?id=70031273.

5 Treverton, Gregory F., and Molly Jahn. "COVID-19: We Had the Warning but We Lacked the Leadership." *TheHill*, The Hill, 11 Apr. 2020, thehill.com/opinion/white-house/490404-covid-19-we-had-the-warning-but-we-lacked-the-leadership.

6 Ibid.

7 Klippenstein, Ken. *Exclusive: The Military Knew Years Ago That a Coronavirus Was Coming*. 7 Apr. 2020, www.thenation.com/article/politics/covid-military-shortage-pandemic/

8 Ibid.

9 Ibid.

10 Ibid.

11 Ibid.

12 Walcott, John. "Stalled Intelligence Report Warns of Pandemic Dangers." *Time*, Time, 9 Mar. 2020, time.com/5799765/intelligence-report-pandemic-dangers/.

13 Ibid.
14 Ibid.
15 Coleman, Justine. *US Intelligence Warned in November That Coronavirus Spreading in China Could Be 'Cataclysmic Event': Report.* 8 Apr. 2020, thehill.com/policy/national-security/intelligence/491712-us-intelligence-warned-in-november-that-virus-spreading.
16 Ibid.
17 Ibid.
18 Stieb, Matt. "U.S. Intel Warned Trump of Coronavirus Threat as Early as November: Report." *Intelligencer*, Intelligencer, 8 Apr. 2020, nymag.com/intelligencer/2020/04/u-s-intel-warned-of-coronavirus-threat-in-november-report.html.
19 Ibid.
20 Davidson, Helen. "First Covid-19 Case Happened in November, China Government Records Show–Report." *The Guardian*, Guardian News and Media, 13 Mar. 2020, www.theguardian.com/world/2020/mar/13/first-covid-19-case-happened-in-november-china-government-records-show-report.
21 Greg Miller, Ellen Nakashima. "President's Intelligence Briefing Book Repeatedly Cited Virus Threat." *The Washington Post*, WP Company, 27 Apr. 2020, www.washingtonpost.com/national-security/presidents-intelligence-briefing-book-repeatedly-cited-virus-threat/2020/04/27/ca66949a-8885-11ea-ac8a-fe9b8088e101_story.html.
22 Ibid
23 Ibid
24 Ibid.
25 Ibid.
26 Ibid.
27 "It's Going to Disappear': Trump's Changing Tone on Coronavirus." *POLITICO*, www.politico.com/news/2020/03/17/how-trump-shifted-his-tone-on-coronavirus-134246..
28 Ibid.
29 TJacobs, Jennifer, and Jordan Fabian. *"Trump Says Coronavirus Was Expected to Blow Over in February." Bloomberg.com*, Bloomberg, 28 Apr. 2020, www.bloomberg.com/news/articles/2020-04-28/trump-says-coronavirus-was-expected-to-blow-over-in-february.
30 Ibid.
31 Ibid.
32 Ibid.
33 Brannen, Samuel, and Kathleen Hicks. "We Predicted a Coronavirus Pandemic. Here's What Policymakers Could Have Seen Coming." *POLITICO*, POLITICO, 7 Mar. 2020, www.politico.com/news/magazine/2020/03/07/coronavirus-epidemic-prediction-policy-advice-121172.
34 Ibid.
35 Ibid.
36 Ibid.
37 Sanger, David E, et al. "Before Virus Outbreak, a Cascade of Warnings Went Unheeded." *The New York Times*, The New York Times, 19 Mar. 2020, www.nytimes.com/2020/03/19/us/politics/trump-coronavirus-outbreak.html.
38 Ibid.

39 Ibid.

40 Ibid.

41 Brannen, Samuel, and Kathleen Hicks. "We Predicted a Coronavirus Pandemic. Here's What Policymakers Could Have Seen Coming." *POLITICO*, 7 Mar. 2020, www.politico.com/news/magazine/2020/03/07/coronavirus-epidemic-prediction-policy-advice-121172.

42 Sanger, David E, et al. "Before Virus Outbreak, a Cascade of Warnings Went Unheeded." *The New York Times*, The New York Times, 19 Mar. 2020, www.nytimes.com/2020/03/19/us/politics/trump-coronavirus-outbreak.html.

43 Ibid.

44 Ibid.

45 Ibid.

46 Cameron, Beth. "Perspective | I Ran the White House Pandemic Office. Trump Closed It." *The Washington Post*, WP Company, 13 Mar. 2020, www.washingtonpost.com/outlook/nsc-pandemic-office-trump-closed/2020/03/13/a70de09c-6491-11ea-acca-80c22bbee96f_story.html.

47 Ibid.

48 Ibid.

49 Murphy, Chris. "The U.S. Government Must Prepare Now for the Next Pandemic." *Foreign Policy*, 30 Mar. 2020, foreignpolicy.com/2020/03/30/coronavirus-trump-us-government-must-prepare-now-for-the-next-pandemic/./

50 Schmidt, Charles. "Why the Coronavirus Slipped Past Disease Detectives." *Scientific American*, Scientific American, 3 Apr. 2020, www.scientificamerican.com/article/why-the-coronavirus-slipped-past-disease-detectives/.

51 Murphy, Chris. "The U.S. Government Must Prepare Now for the Next Pandemic." *Foreign Policy*, 30 Mar. 2020, foreignpolicy.com/2020/03/30/coronavirus-trump-us-government-must-prepare-now-for-the-next-pandemic/.

52 Ibid.

53 Ibid.

54 "Trump Administration Ended Pandemic Early-Warning Program to Detect Coronaviruses." *Los Angeles Times*, Los Angeles Times, 2 Apr. 2020, www.latimes.com/science/story/2020-04-02/coronavirus-trump-pandemic-program-viruses-detection..

55 "Pandemic Prevention Program Ending after 10 Years." *American Veterinary Medical Association*, www.avma.org/javma-news/2020-01-15/pandemic-prevention-program-ending-after-10-years.

56 Ibid.

57 Ibid.

58 Schmidt, Charles. "Why the Coronavirus Slipped Past Disease Detectives." *Scientific American*, Scientific American, 3 Apr. 2020, www.scientificamerican.com/article/why-the-coronavirus-slipped-past-disease-detectives.

59 Ibid.

60 Ibid.

61 *Sars*. 6 Dec. 2017, www.cdc.gov/sars/about/fs-sars.html.

62 Cheng, Vincent C.C., et al. "Severe Acute Respiratory Syndrome Coronavirus as an Agent of Emerging and Reemerging Infection." *Clinical Microbiology Reviews*, American Society for Microbiology Journals, 1 Oct. 2007, cmr.asm.org/content/20/4/660.

63 Ibid.

64 Schmidt, Charles. "Why the Coronavirus Slipped Past Disease Detectives." *Scientific American*, Scientific American, 3 Apr. 2020, www.scientificamerican.com/article/why-the-coronavirus-slipped-past-disease-detectives.

65 Crews, Clyde Wayne. "Phase 4 Coronavirus Infrastructure Spending To Start At $2 Trillion." *Forbes*, Forbes Magazine, 3 Apr. 2020, www.forbes.com/sites/waynecrews/2020/03/31/phase-4-coronavirus-infrastructure-spending-to-start-at-2-trillion/.

66 Schmidt, Charles. "Why the Coronavirus Slipped Past Disease Detectives." *Scientific American*, Scientific American, 3 Apr. 2020, www.scientificamerican.com/article/why-the-coronavirus-slipped-past-disease-detectives..

67 Ibid.

68 Ibid.

69 Ibid.

70 "Senators Warren, King Question USAID on Decision to Shutter Global Infectious Disease Prevention Program: U.S. Senator Elizabeth Warren of Massachusetts." Senators Warren, King Question USAID on Decision to Shutter Global Infectious Disease Prevention Program | U.S. Senator Elizabeth Warren of Massachusetts, Elizabeth Warren, 31 Jan. 2020, www.warren.senate.gov/oversight/letters/senators-warren-king-question-usaid-on-decision-to-shutter-global-infectious-disease-prevention-program.

71 Ibid.

CHAPTER 9

1 "Coronavirus." *Merriam-Webster*, Merriam-Webster, www.merriam-webster.com/dictionary/coronavirus

2 Tyrrell, D. A. J, and Michael Fielder. *Cold Wars: the Fight against the Common Cold*. Oxford University Press, 2002

3 Ibid.

4 Almelida, J D, et al. "Virology: Coronaviruses." *Nature News*, Nature Publishing Group, Nov. 1968, www.nature.com/articles/22065ob0.

5 Sturman LS, Holmes KV (1983-01-01). Lauffer MA, Maramorosch K (eds.). "The molecular biology of coronaviruses". *Advances in Virus Research*. 28: 35–112. doi:10.1016/s0065-3527(08)60721-6. ISBN 9780120398287. PMC 7131312. PMIB 6362367. [T]hese viruses displayed a characteristic fringe of large, distinctive, petal-shaped peplomers or spikes which resembled a crown, like the corona spinarum in religious art; hence the name coronaviruses.

6 "Chapter 24–Coronavirus." *Fenner's Veterinary Virology*, by Nigel James Maclachlan et al., Fifth Ed ed., Academic Press Is an Imprint of Elsevier, 2017, pp. 435–461.

7 Fehr A.R., Perlman S. (2015) *Coronaviruses: An Overview of Their Replication and Pathogenesis*. In: Maier H., Bickerton E., Britton P. (eds) Coronaviruses. Methods in Molecular Biology, vol 1282. Humana Press, New York, NY

8 Neuman, Benjamin W, et al. "A Structural Analysis of M Protein in Coronavirus Assembly and Morphology." *Journal of Structural Biology*, Academic Press, 3 Dec. 2010, www.sciencedirect.com/science/article/pii/S1047847710003588.

9   Almea, June D. JD, Tyrrell DA (April 1967). "The morphology of three previously uncharacterized human respiratory viruses that grow in organ culture". *The Journal of General Virology*. 1 (2): 175–8. doi:10.1099/0022-1317-1-2-175. PMIB 4293939.

10 McIntosh, K, et al. "Growth in Suckling-Mouse Brain of 'IBV-like' Viruses from Patients with Upper Respiratory Tract Disease." *Proceedings of the National Academy of Sciences of the United States of America*, U.S. National Library of Medicine, Dec. 1967, www.ncbi.nlm.nih.gov/pmc/articles/PMC223830/.

11 Myint, S H. "Human Coronavirus Infections."*Neurotropic Viral Infections*, by S G Sell, Springer, 2016, pp. 389–401; Geller, Chloé, et al. "Human Coronaviruses: Insights into Environmental Resistance and Its Influence on the Development of New Antiseptic Strategies."*Viruses*, MDPI, 12 Nov. 2012, www.ncbi.nlm.nih.gov/pmc/articles/PMC3509683/.

12 Crossley, Beate M, et al. "Identification and Characterization of a Novel Alpaca Respiratory Coronavirus Most Closely Related to the Human Coronavirus 229E." *Viruses*, MDPI, 12 Dec. 2012, www.ncbi.nlm.nih.gov/pmc/articles/PMC3528286/.

13 Su, Shuo, et al. "Epemiology, Genetic Recombination, and Pathogenesis of Coronaviruses." *Trends in Microbiology*, Elsevier Current Trends, 21 Mar. 2016, www.sciencedirect.com/science/article/pii/S0966842X16000718.; Zhu, Na, et al. "A Novel Coronavirus from Patients with Pneumonia in China, 2019." *The New England Journal of Medicine*, Massachusetts Medical Society, 20 Feb. 2020, www.ncbi.nlm.nih.gov/pubmed/31978945/

14 DeGroot, R J, et al. "'Family Coronavirus.'" *Virus Taxonomy: Classification and Nomenclature of Viruses: Ninth Report of the International Committee on Taxonomy of Viruses*, by Andrew M. Q. King, 9th ed., Elsevier/Academic Press, 2012, pp. 806–828.

15 Ibid.

16 Fehr AR, Perlman S (2015). "Coronaviruses: an overview of their replication and pathogenesis". In Maier HJ, Bickerton E, Britton P (eds.). *Coronaviruses. Methods in Molecular Biology*. 1282. Springer. pp. 1–23. doi:10.1007/978-1-4939-2438-7_1. ISBN 978-1-4939-2438-7. PMC 4369385. PMIBIBID 25720466

17 DeGroot, R J, et al. "'Family Coronavirus.'" Virus Taxonomy: *Classification and Nomenclature of Viruses: Ninth Report of the International Committee on Taxonomy of Viruses*, by Andrew M. Q. King, 9th ed., Elsevier/Academic Press, 2012, pp. 806–828.

18 Cui, Jie, et al. "Origin and Evolution of Pathogenic Coronaviruses." *Nature News*, Nature Publishing Group, 10 Dec. 2018, www.nature.com/articles/s41579-018-0118-9.

19 DeGroot, R J, et al. "'Family Coronavirus.'" *Virus Taxonomy: Classification and Nomenclature of Viruses: Ninth Report of the International Committee on Taxonomy of Viruses*, by Andrew M. Q. King, 9th ed., Elsevier/Academic Press, 2012, pp. 806–828..doi:10.1016/B978-0-12-384684-6.00068-9. ISBN 978-0-12-384684-6.

20 Decaro, N. "Alphacoronavirus." *The Springer Index of Viruses*, by Christian A. TIbidona and Gholamreza Darai, Springer, 2011, pp. 371–383. doi:10.1007/978-0-387-95919-1_56. ISBN 978-0-387-95919-1. PMC 7176201.

21 Li, Fang, et al. "Structure of SARS Coronavirus Spike Receptor-Binding Domain Complexed with Receptor." *Science*, American Association for the Advancement of Science, 16 Sept. 2005, science.sciencemag.org/content/309/5742/1864.full.

22 Tang, Xiaolu, et al. "On the Origin and Continuing Evolution of SARS-CoV-2." OUP Academic, Oxford University Press, 3 Mar. 2020, academic.oup.com/nsr/article/7/6/1012/5775463.

23. "Coronavirus Has Two Strains: L-Type More Aggressive and Contagious than S-Type, Says Study." *Latest News by Times Now News*, www.timesnownews.com/health/article/coronavirus-has-two-strains-l-type-more-aggressive-and-contagious-than-s-type-says-study/561144

24. Roblin, Sebastien. "How Deadly Are The Two (Yes, Two) Coronavirus Strains?" *The National Interest*, The Center for the National Interest, 11 May 2020, nationalinterest.org/blog/buzz/how-deadly-are-two-yes-two-coronavirus-strains-152181.

25. Ibid.

26. London, Matt. "How to Tell If It's Allergies or Coronavirus: Dr. Saphier Weighs In." *Fox News*, FOX News Network, 17 Mar. 2020, www.foxnews.com/media/allergies-or-coronavirus-dr-nicole-saphier.

27. "COVID-19: What's RNA Research Got to Do with It?" *NewsCenter*, 12 May 2020, www.rochester.edu/newscenter/covIbid-19-rna-coronavirus-research-428952/.

28. Roblin, Sebastien. "How Deadly Are The Two (Yes, Two) Coronavirus Strains?" *The National Interest*, The Center for the National Interest, 11 May 2020, nationalinterest.org/blog/buzz/how-deadly-are-two-yes-two-coronavirus-strains-152181

29. Sanche, Steven, et al. "The Novel Coronavirus, 2019-NCoV, Is Highly Contagious and More Infectious Than Initially Estimated." *MedRxiv*, Cold Spring Harbor Laboratory Press, 1 Jan. 2020, www.medrxiv.org/content/10.1101/2020.02.07.20021154v1.

30. Ibid.

31. Lovelace, Berkeley. "The Coronavirus May Be Deadlier than the 1918 Flu: Here's How It Stacks up to Other Pandemics." *CNBC*, CNBC, 27 Mar. 2020, www.cnbc.com/2020/03/26/coronavirus-may-be-deadlier-than-1918-flu-heres-how-it-stacks-up-to-other-pandemics.html.

32. Evans, Zachary. "Scientists Claim Newly Dominant Strain of Coronavirus Is More Contagious Than Original." Yahoo! News, Yahoo!, 5 May 2020, news.yahoo.com/scientists-claim-newly-dominant-strain-163608496.html.

33. Ibid.

34. Ibid.

35. Ibid.

36. https://abcnews.go.com/Health/risks-coronavirus/story?Ibid=70624608&cIbid=clicksource_4380645_4_three_posts_card_hed*ABC News*, ABC News Network, abcnews.go.com/Health/risks-coronavirus/story?Ibid=70624608.

37. Ibid.

38. Ibid.

39. Mundell, EJ. "New China Report Sets COVID-19 Death Rate at 1.4%." WebMD, WebMD, 19 Mar. 2020, www.webmd.com/lung/news/20200319/new-china-report-sets-covid-19-death-rate-at-1437

40. McDonald, Scott. "Dr. Deborah Birx Calls China's Extraordinarily Low Coronavirus Death Rate 'Unrealistic.'" *Newsweek*, Newsweek, 19 Apr. 2020, www.newsweek.com/dr-deborah-birx-calls-chinas-low-coronavirus-death-rate-unrealistic-1498778.

41. Rettner, Rachael. "How Does the New Coronavirus Compare with the Flu?" *LiveScience*, Purch, 14 May 2020, www.livescience.com/new-coronavirus-compare-with-flu.html.

42. Secon, Holly. "The Coronavirus Death Rate in the US Is Far Higher than That of the Flu–Here's How the 2 Compare across Age Ranges." *Business Insider*, Business Insider, 30 Mar. 2020, www.businessinsider.com/coronavirus-compared-seasonal-flu-in-the-us-death-rates-2020-3.

43. Ibid.

44 Ibid.
45 Ibid.
46 Ibid.
47 Bendix, Aria. "Coronavirus Deaths in Italy and US Could Be up to Double the Official Counts, New Research Shows." *Business Insider*, Business Insider, 16 May 2020, www.businessinsider.com/actual-coronavirus-deaths-in-italy-us-higher-than-official-count-2020-5.
48 Ibid.
49 Colombo, Asher D., and Roberto Impicciatore. "The Growth in Deaths in Italy in Time of Covid-19." Istituto Cattaneo, 1 Apr. 2020, www.cattaneo.org/wp-content/uploads/2018/03/Colombo-Impicciatore-Covid-09_eng.pdf.
50 Bendix, Aria. "Coronavirus Deaths in Italy and US Could Be up to Double the Official Counts, New Research Shows." *Business Insider*, Business Insider, 16 May 2020, www.businessinsider.com/actual-coronavirus-deaths-in-italy-us-higher-than-official-count-2020-5
51 Coleman, Kali. *The One Symptom That Predicts How Bad Your Coronavirus Case Will Be*, 10 May 2020, www.msn.com/en-us/health/medical/the-one-symptom-that-predicts-how-bad-your-coronavirus-case-will-be/ar-BB13QeKi.
52 Boodman, Eric, et al. "Doctors Lambaste Process for Distributing Covid-19 Drug Remdesivir." STAT, 7 May 2020, www.statnews.com/2020/05/06/doctors-lambaste-federal-process-for-distributing-covid-19-drug-remdesivir/.
53 "Coronavirus Disease 2019 (COVID-19)." *Centers for Disease Control and Prevention*, Centers for Disease Control and Prevention, www.cdc.gov/coronavirus/2019-ncov/index.html.
54 "Cassoobhoy, Arefa. "High Blood Pressure & Coronavirus (Higher-Risk People): Symptoms, Complications, Treatments." *WebMD*, WebMD, 20 Mar. 2020, www.webmd.com/lung/coronavirus-high-blood-pressure.
55 Ibid.
56 https://www.cdc.gov/nchs/products/databriefs/db289.htm
57 Nazario, Brunilda. "High Blood Pressure & Coronavirus (Higher-Risk People): Symptoms, Complications, Treatments." *WebMD*, WebMD, 2 July 2020, www.webmd.com/lung/coronavirus-high-blood-pressure.
58 Bernstein, Lenny, and Ariana Eunjung Cha. "Doctors Keep Discovering New Ways the Coronavirus Attacks the Body." *The Washington Post*, WP Company, 10 May 2020, www.washingtonpost.com/health/2020/05/10/coronavirus-attacks-body-symptoms/?arc404=true.
59 Ibid.
60 Ibid.
61 Yeager, Ashley. "Lost Smell and Taste Hint COVID-19 Can Target the Nervous System." *The Scientist Magazine®*, www.the-scientist.com/news-opinion/lost-smell-and-taste-hint-covIbid-19-can-target-the-nervous-system-67312.
62 Bernstein, Lenny, and Ariana Eunjung Cha. "Doctors Keep Discovering New Ways the Coronavirus Attacks the Body." *The Washington Post*, WP Company, 10 May 2020, www.washingtonpost.com/health/2020/05/10/coronavirus-attacks-body-symptoms/?arc404=true.
63 Ibid.
64 Ibid.
65 Ibid.

66 Ibid.

67 Wan, William, and Saarah Kaplan. "The Coronavirus Isn't Alive. That's Why It's so Hard to Kill." *The Washington Post*, WP Company, 23 Mar. 2020, www.washingtonpost.com/health/2020/03/23/coronavirus-isnt-alive-thats-why-its-so-hard-kill/.

68 Alltucker, Ken. "FDA Tightens Oversight of Blood Tests Used to Detect Coronavirus Antibodies." *USA Today*, Gannett Satellite Information Network, 4 May 2020, www.usatoday.com/story/news/health/2020/05/04/coronavirus-fda-tightens-oversight-antibody-tests-after-fraud/3077512001/.

CHAPTER 10

1 Huang, Chaolin, et. al Clinical features of patients infected with 2019 novel coronavirus in Wuhan, China. *The Lancet Journal*, 395(10233) (2020)., 497-506. doi:https://doi.org/10.1016/S0140-6736(20)30183-5

2 Ibid

3 Page, Jeremy, et al. "How It All Started: China's Early Coronavirus Missteps." *The Wall Street Journal*, Dow Jones & Company, 6 Mar. 2020, www.wsj.com/articles/how-it-all-started-chinas-early-coronavirus-missteps-11583508932.

4 Huang, Chaolin, et. al Clinical features of patients infected with 2019 novel coronavirus in Wuhan, China. *The Lancet Journal*, 395(10233) (2020)., 497-506. doi:https://doi.org/10.1016/S0140-6736(20)30183-5

5 Ibid.

6 Ibid.

7 Page, Jeremy, et al. "How It All Started: China's Early Coronavirus Missteps." *The Wall Street Journal*, Dow Jones & Company, 6 Mar. 2020, www.wsj.com/articles/how-it-all-started-chinas-early-coronavirus-missteps-11583508932.

8 Ignatius, DavIbid. "Opinion | How Did Covid-19 Begin? Its Initial Origin Story Is Shaky." *The Washington Post*, WP Company, 2 Apr. 2020, www.washingtonpost.com/opinions/global-opinions/how-dIbid-covIbid-19-begin-its-initial-origin-story-is-shaky/2020/04/02/1475d488-7521-11ea-87da-77a8136c1a6d_story.html.

9 Ibid.

10 Ibid.

11 Ibid.

12 Ibid.

13 Rogin, Josh. "Opinion | State Department Cables Warned of Safety Issues at Wuhan Lab Studying Bat Coronaviruses." *The Washington Post*, WP Company, 14 Apr. 2020, www.washingtonpost.com/opinions/2020/04/14/state-department-cables-warned-safety-issues-wuhan-lab-studying-bat-coronaviruses/

14 Ibid.

15 Ibid.

16 Ibid.

17 Ibid.

18 Ibid.

19 Ibid

20 Ibid.
21 Ibid.
22 Ibid.
23 Ibid.
24 Ibid.
25 "Lab That First Shared Coronavirus Sequence Closed for 'Rectification'." *South China Morning Post*, 28 Feb. 2020, www.scmp.com/news/china/society/article/3052966/chinese-laboratory-first-shared-coronavirus-genome-world-ordered.
26 Ibid.
27 Ibid.
28 Ibid.
29 Ibid.
30 Ibid.
31 Lew, Linda. "Coronavirus: Whistle-Blower's Mother Demands Answers from Police." *South China Morning Post*, 14 Feb. 2020, www.scmp.com/news/china/society/article/3049706/coronavirus-mother-whistle-blower-li-wenliang-demands-answers.
32 Ibid.
33 Pinqui, Zhuang. "Who Was Li Wenliang and How Did He Become a Coronavirus 'Hero'." *South China Morning Post*, 7 Feb. 2020, www.scmp.com/news/china/society/article/3049561/dr-li-wenliang-who-was-he-and-how-did-he-become-coronavirus-hero.
34 Ibid.
35 Ibid.
36 Woodward, Aylin, and Ryan Pickrell. "Whistleblower Doctor Li Wenliang, Who Was Censored after Sounding the Alarm about the Coronavirus, Has Died in Wuhan." Business Insider, *Business Insider*, 6 Feb. 2020, www.businessinsider.com/coronavirus-whistleblower-doctor-li-wenliang-in-critical-condition-2020-2.
37 Ma, Josephine, and Jun Mai. "Coronavirus Doctor's Death a Catalyst for 'Freedom of Speech' Demands." *South China Morning Post*, 7 Feb. 2020, www.scmp.com/news/china/politics/article/3049606/coronavirus-doctors-death-becomes-catalyst-freedom-speech.
38 Deng, Chao, and Josh Chin. "Chinese Doctor Who Issued Early Warning on Virus Dies." *The Wall Street Journal*, Dow Jones & Company, 7 Feb. 2020, www.wsj.com/articles/chinese-doctor-who-issued-early-warning-on-virus-dies-11581019816.
39 Austin, Henry. "Chinese Doctor Who Raised Alarm over Coronavirus Dies from Disease, Hospital Confirms." *NBCNews.com*, NBCUniversal News Group, 7 Feb. 2020, www.nbcnews.com/news/world/doctor-punished-coronavirus-warnings-dies-disease-who-confirms-n1131556.
40 Ibid.
41 Deng, Chao, and Josh Chin. "Chinese Doctor Who Issued Early Warning on Virus Dies." *The Wall Street Journal*, Dow Jones & Company, 7 Feb. 2020, www.wsj.com/articles/chinese-doctor-who-issued-early-warning-on-virus-dies-11581019816. 6
42 Page, Jeremy, et al. "How It All Started: China's Early Coronavirus Missteps." *The Wall Street Journal*, Dow Jones & Company, 6 Mar. 2020, www.wsj.com/articles/how-it-all-started-chinas-early-coronavirus-missteps-11583508932.
43 Ibid.

44 Ibid.

45 Ibid.

46 Ibid.

47 Abutaleb, Y., Dawsey, J., Nakashima, E., & Miller, G. (2020, April 04). The U.S. was beset by denial and dysfunction as the coronavirus raged. Retrieved from https://www.washingtonpost.com/national-security/2020/04/04/coronavirus-government-dysfunction/?arc404=true

48 Abutaleb, Yasmeen, et al. "The U.S. Was Beset by Denial and Dysfunction as the Coronavirus Raged." *The Washington Post*, WP Company, 4 Apr. 2020, www.washingtonpost.com/national-security/2020/04/04/coronavirus-government-dysfunction/?arc404=true.

49 "Pneumonia of Unknown Cause – China." *World Health Organization*, World Health Organization, 30 Jan. 2020, www.who.int/csr/don/05-january-2020-pneumonia-of-unkown-cause-china/en/.

50 Taylor, Marisa. "Exclusive: U.S. Axed CDC Expert Job in China Months before Virus Outbreak." *Reuters*, Thomson Reuters, 24 Mar. 2020, www.reuters.com/article/us-health-coronavirus-china-cdc-exclusiv-idUSKBN21910S.

51 Abutaleb, Yasmeen, et al. "The U.S. Was Beset by Denial and Dysfunction as the Coronavirus Raged." *The Washington Post*, WP Company, 4 Apr. 2020, www.washingtonpost.com/national-security/2020/04/04/coronavirus-government-dysfunction/?arc404=true.

52 Page, Jeremy, et al. "How It All Started: China's Early Coronavirus Missteps." *The Wall Street Journal*, Dow Jones & Company, 6 Mar. 2020, www.wsj.com/articles/how-it-all-started-chinas-early-coronavirus-missteps-11583508932..

53 Abutaleb, Yasmeen, et al. "The U.S. Was Beset by Denial and Dysfunction as the Coronavirus Raged." *The Washington Post*, WP Company, 4 Apr. 2020, www.washingtonpost.com/national-security/2020/04/04/coronavirus-government-dysfunction/?arc404=true.

54 Ibid.

55 Mason, Jeff. "Trump Ratchets up Criticism of China over Coronavirus." *Reuters*, Thomson Reuters, 18 Mar. 2020, www.reuters.com/article/us-health-coronavirus-trump-china-idUSKBN2153N5.-

56 Ibid.

57 "China_Flu–Intelligence Dossier Lays out Case against China Bat Virus Program." *Reddit*, www.reddit.com/r/China_Flu/comments/gc6r6x/intelligence_dossier_lays_out_case_against_china/.

58 *Leaked Western Intel Dossier Reveals How China Deceived the World about Coronavirus*, www.msn.com/en-us/news/world/leaked-western-intel-dossier-reveals-how-china-deceived-the-world-about-coronavirus/ar-BB13ux3F.

59 Ibid.

60 Ibid.

61 Ibid

62 Ibid.

63 Ibid.

64 Shaw, Adam, et al. "Leaked 'Five Eyes' Dossier on Alleged Chinese Coronavirus Coverup Consistent with US Findings, Officials Say." *Fox News*, FOX News Network, 2 May 2020, www.foxnews.com/politics/five-eyes-dossier-chinese-coronavirus-coverup-u-s-findings.

65 Ibid.

66 Ibid.

67 Ibid.

68   Ibid.

69   Ibid.

70   Miller, Zeke. "Trump Harshly Blames China for Pandemic; a Lab 'Mistake'?" *WBMA*, WBMA, 1 May 2020, abc3340.com/news/nation-world/trump-harshly-blames-china-for-pandemic-a-lab-mistake.

71   Press, The Associated. "Trump Speculates That China Released Virus in Lab 'Mistake'." *Daily Journal*, 30 Apr. 2020, www.dailyjournal.net/2020/04/30/us-virus-outbreak-intelligence/

72   Ibid.; see also Macias, Amanda "Top US Spy Agency Says Coronavirus Was 'Not Manmade or Genetically Modified'." *CNBC*, CNBC, 30 Apr. 2020, www.cnbc.com/2020/04/30/dni-says-coronavirus-was-not-manmade-or-genetically-modified.html.

CHAPTER 11

1   "China Investigates Respiratory Illness Outbreak Sickening 27." *AP NEWS*, Associated Press, 31 Dec. 2019, apnews.com/00c78d1974410d96fe031f67edbd86ec..

2   "HAN Archive–00424." *Centers for Disease Control and Prevention*, Centers for Disease Control and Prevention, 8 Jan. 2020, emergency.cdc.gov/han/han00424.asp.; *see also* "First Travel-Related Case of 2019 Novel Coronavirus Detected in United States." *Centers for Disease Control and Prevention*, Centers for Disease Control and Prevention, 21 Jan. 2020, www.cdc.gov/media/releases/2020/p0121-novel-coronavirus-travel-case.html.

3   Lipton, Eric, et al. "He Could Have Seen What Was Coming: Behind Trump's Failure on the Virus." *The New York Times*, The New York Times, 11 Apr. 2020, www.nytimes.com/2020/04/11/us/politics/coronavirus-trump-response.html.

4   Ibid.

5   Holshue, Michelle L., et al. "First Case of 2019 Novel Coronavirus in the United States: NEJM." *New England Journal of Medicine*, 7 May 2020, www.nejm.org/doi/full/10.1056/NEJMoa2001191.

6   "A Timeline of What Trump Has Said on Coronavirus." *CBS News*, CBS Interactive, www.cbsnews.com/news/timeline-president-donald-trump-changing-statements-on-coronavirus/.

7   Lipton, Eric, et al. "He Could Have Seen What Was Coming: Behind Trump's Failure on the Virus." *The New York Times*, The New York Times, 11 Apr. 2020, www.nytimes.com/2020/04/11/us/politics/coronavirus-trump-response.html

8   Abutaleb, Yasmeen, et al. "The U.S. Was Beset by Denial and Dysfunction as the Coronavirus Raged." *The Washington Post*, WP Company, 4 Apr. 2020, www.washingtonpost.com/national-security/2020/04/04/coronavirus-government-dysfunction/?arc404=true.

9   "CDC Confirms Additional Cases of 2019 Novel Coronavirus in United States." *Centers for Disease Control and Prevention*, Centers for Disease Control and Prevention, 26 Jan. 2020, www.cdc.gov/media/releases/2020/s0126-coronavirus-new-cases.html.

10   Ibid.

11   Neergaard, Lauren, and Ricardo-Alonzo Zaldivar. "US Beefs up Screening of Travelers for New Virus from China." *ABC News*, ABC News Network, 29 Jan. 2020, abcnews.go.com/US/wireStory/us-beefs-screening-travelers-virus-china-68589211.

12   Ibid.

13   "Abutaleb, Yasmeen, et al. "The U.S. Was Beset by Denial and Dysfunction as the Coronavirus Raged." *The Washington Post*, WP Company, 4 Apr. 2020, www.washingtonpost.com/national-security/2020/04/04/coronavirus-government-dysfunction/?arc404=true

14 Ibid.
15 Chappell, Bill. "Coronavirus: Americans Evacuated From Wuhan Will Remain At U.S. Air Base For 3 Days." *NPR*, NPR, 29 Jan. 2020, www.npr.org/sections/goatsandsoda/2020/01/29/800761987/coronavirus-americans-cheer-as-evacuation-flight-from-wuhan-reaches-u-s.
16 Roston, Aram. "Special Report: Former Labradoodle Breeder Was Tapped to Lead U.S. Pandemic Task Force." *Reuters*, Thomson Reuters, 24 Apr. 2020, www.reuters.com/article/us-health-coronavirus-usa-hhschief-speci-idUSKCN2243CE
17 Ibid.
18 Ibid.
19 Ibid.
20 Ibid
21 Ibid.
22 Ibid.
23 (2005, September 3). Retrieved from https://georgewbush-whitehouse.archives.gov/news/releases/2005/09/20050902-2.html
24 NewsHour, PBS. "FEMA Faces Intense Scrutiny." *PBS*, Public Broadcasting Service, 9 Sept. 2005, www.pbs.org/newshour/politics/government_programs-july-dec05-fema_09-09.
25 Roston, Aram. "Special Report: Former Labradoodle Breeder Was Tapped to Lead U.S. Pandemic Task Force." *Reuters*, Thomson Reuters, 24 Apr. 2020, www.reuters.com/article/us-health-coronavirus-usa-hhschief-speci-idUSKCN2243CE
26 Ibid.
27 Ibid.
28 Ibid.
29 Ibid.
30 Ibid.
31 Ibid.
32 Ibid.
33 Haberman, Maggie. "Trade Adviser Warned White House in January of Risks of a Pandemic." *The New York Times*, The New York Times, 7 Apr. 2020, www.nytimes.com/2020/04/06/us/politics/navarro-warning-trump-coronavirus.html.
34 Ibid.
35 Ibid.
36 "Trump: Coronavirus Will Have 'a Very Good Ending for Us'." *POLITICO*, www.politico.com/news/2020/01/30/trump-close-cooperation-china-coronavirus-109701.
37 Watson, Kathryn. "A Timeline of What Trump Has Said on Coronavirus." *CBS News*, CBS Interactive, 3 Apr. 2020, www.cbsnews.com/news/timeline-president-donald-trump-changing-statements-on-coronavirus/.
38 Aubrey, Allison. "Trump Declares Coronavirus A Public Health Emergency And Restricts Travel From China." *NPR*, NPR, 31 Jan. 2020, www.npr.org/sections/health-shots/2020/01/31/801686524/trump-declares-coronavirus-a-public-health-emergency-and-restricts-travel-from-c.
39 Proclamation on suspension of entry as immigrants And Nonimmigrants of persons who pose a risk of transmitting 2019 novel coronavirus. (n.d.). Retrieved from https://www.whitehouse.gov/presi-

40. Eder, Steve, et al. "430,000 People Have Traveled From China to U.S. Since Coronavirus Surfaced." *The New York Times*, The New York Times, 4 Apr. 2020, www.nytimes.com/2020/04/04/us/coronavirus-china-travel-restrictions.html.
41. Ibid.
42. Ibid.

CHAPTER 12

1. Blake, Aaron. *Analysis | Trump Keeps Saying 'Nobody' Could Have Foreseen Coronavirus. We Keep Finding out about New Warning Signs.* 19 Mar. 2020, www.washingtonpost.com/politics/2020/03/19/trump-keeps-saying-nobody-could-have-foreseen-coronavirus-we-keep-finding-out-about-new-warning-signs/.
2. Ibid.
3. Wigglesworth, Alex, et al. "California Sees Third Case of 'Community Spread' Coronavirus as First U.S. Death Is Reported near Seattle." *Los Angeles Times*, Los Angeles Times, 29 Feb. 2020, www.latimes.com/california/story/2020-02-29/coronavirus-california-spread-health-officials.
4. Selsky, Andrew. "Wash. State Sees 1st Virus Death in US, Declares Emergency." *AP NEWS*, Associated Press, 1 Mar. 2020, apnews.com/f175d89567a26d59cab27725c9e8a0d7..
5. Leins, Casey. "Washington, Florida Governors Declare State of Emergency for Coronavirus." *U.S. News & World Report*, U.S. News & World Report, 2 Mar. 2020, www.usnews.com/news/best-states/articles/2020-03-02/washington-florida-governors-declare-state-of-emergency-for-coronavirus.
6. Ortiz, Erik. "More Schools Are Closing Because of Coronavirus. Will That Be the Norm?" *Yahoo! News*, Yahoo!, 2 Mar. 2020, news.yahoo.com/more-schools-closing-because-coronavirus-213600529.html..
7. Altavena, Lily, et al. "After Coronavirus School Closings, Will States Need to Hold Kids Back, Institute Summer School?" *After Coronavirus School Closings, Will States Need to Hold Kids Back, Institute Summer School?*, 19 Mar. 2020, www.msn.com/en-us/news/us/after-coronavirus-school-closings-will-states-need-to-hold-kids-back-institute-summer-school/ar-BB11m3wZ.
8. Qiu, Linda. "Analyzing the Patterns in Trump's Falsehoods About Coronavirus." *The New York Times*, The New York Times, 28 Mar. 2020, www.nytimes.com/2020/03/27/us/politics/trump-coronavirus-factcheck.html.
9. Heeb, Gina. "Trump Signs Emergency Coronavirus Package, Injecting $8.3 Billion into Efforts to Fight the Outbreak | Markets Insider." *Business Insider*, Business Insider, 6 Mar. 2020, markets.businessinsider.com/news/stocks/trump-signs-billion-emergency-funding-package-fight-coronavirus-legislation-covid19-020-3-1028972206.
10. Qiu, Linda. "Analyzing the Patterns in Trump's Falsehoods About Coronavirus." *The New York Times*, The New York Times, 28 Mar. 2020, www.nytimes.com/2020/03/27/us/politics/trump-coronavirus-factcheck.html..
11. Yong, Ed. "Why the Coronavirus Is So Confusing." *The Atlantic*, Atlantic Media Company, 6 May 2020, www.theatlantic.com/health/archive/2020/04/pandemic-confusing-uncertainty/610819/.
12. Qiu, Linda. "Analyzing the Patterns in Trump's Falsehoods About Coronavirus." *The New York Times*, The New York Times, 28 Mar. 2020, www.nytimes.com/2020/03/27/us/politics/trump-coronavirus-factcheck.html...
13. Ibid.
14. Ibid.

15 Ibid.
16 Romano, Benjamin. "Amazon Employee in Seattle Has Tested Positive for Illness Caused by Coronavirus." *The Seattle Times*, The Seattle Times Company, 3 Mar. 2020, www.seattletimes.com/business/amazon/amazon-employee-in-seattle-has-tested-positive-for-illness-caused-by-coronavirus/.
17 Li, Roland. "Coronavirus: Microsoft, Square, Twitter Encourage Employees to Work from Home." *SFChronicle.com*, San Francisco Chronicle, 5 Mar. 2020, www.sfchronicle.com/business/article/Coronavirus-pushes-big-Bay-Area-companies-towards-15105962.php..
18 "A List of What's Been Canceled Because of the Coronavirus." *The New York Times*, The New York Times, 9 Mar. 2020, www.nytimes.com/article/cancelled-events-coronavirus.html.
19 Dowd, Katie. "These Stores Are Closing or Changing Hours Due to Coronavirus." *SFGate*, San Francisco Chronicle, 19 Mar. 2020, www.sfgate.com/news/article/retail-chainsclosing-hours-coronavirus-15132524.php.
20 Alvarez, Priscilla. "Here's What Trump's Coronavirus Emergency Declaration Does." *CNN*, Cable News Network, 13 Mar. 2020, www.cnn.com/2020/03/13/politics/states-coronavirus-fema/index.html.
21 Wilkie, Christina. "Trump Blames Obama for Lack of Coronavirus Tests: 'I Don't Take Responsibility at All'." *CNBC*, CNBC, 14 Mar. 2020, www.cnbc.com/2020/03/13/coronavirus-trump-says-i-dont-take-responsibility-at-all-for-lack-of-tests.html.
22 "Coronavirus: Trump Slams Reporter for 'Nasty Question' over Pandemic Response Team – Video." *The Guardian*, Guardian News and Media, 14 Mar. 2020, www.theguardian.com/us-news/video/2020/mar/13/coronavirus-trump-slams-reporter-for-nasty-question-over-pandemic-response-team-video.
23 "Coronavirus in the U.S.: Latest Map and Case Count." *The New York Times*, The New York Times, 3 Mar. 2020, www.nytimes.com/interactive/2020/us/coronavirus-us-cases.html.
24 Qiu, Linda. "Analyzing the Patterns in Trump's Falsehoods About Coronavirus." *The New York Times*, The New York Times, 28 Mar. 2020, www.nytimes.com/2020/03/27/us/politics/trump-coronavirus-factcheck.html.
25 "Interview: Sean Hannity Interviews Donald Trump ." *Factbase*, 25 Mar. 2020, factba.se/transcript/donald-trump-interview-hannity-fox-news-march-26-2020.
26 Qiu, Linda. "Analyzing the Patterns in Trump's Falsehoods About Coronavirus." *The New York Times*, The New York Times, 28 Mar. 2020, www.nytimes.com/2020/03/27/us/politics/trump-coronavirus-factcheck.html.
27 Ibid.
28 Ibid.

CHAPTER 13

1 Kliff, Sarah, and Julie Bosman. "Official Counts Understate the U.S. Coronavirus Death Toll." *The New York Times*, The New York Times, 5 Apr. 2020, www.nytimes.com/2020/04/05/us/coronavirus-deaths-undercount.htmll
2 Ibid.
3 Ibid.
4 Wigglesworth, Alex. "A Widow Believed Coronavirus Killed Her Husband. It Took Weeks to Learn the Truth. ." 16 Apr. 2020, www.msn.com/en-us/news/us/a-widow-believed-coronavirus-killed-her-husband-it-took-weeks-to-learn-the-truth/ar-BB12JdGZ.
5 Ibid.

6 Ibid.

7 Goodman, J. David, and William K. Rashbaum. "N.Y.C. Death Toll Soars Past 10,000 in Revised Virus Count." *The New York Times*, The New York Times, 14 Apr. 2020, www.nytimes.com/2020/04/14/nyregion/new-york-coronavirus-deaths.html.

8 Ibid.

9 Kliff, Sarah, and Julie Bosman. "Official Counts Understate the U.S. Coronavirus Death Toll." *The New York Times*, The New York Times, 5 Apr. 2020, www.nytimes.com/2020/04/05/us/coronavirus-deaths-undercount.htmll

10 Dewan, Angela, et al. "As Governments Fumbled Their Coronavirus Response, These Four Got It Right. Here's How." *CNN*, Cable News Network, 16 Apr. 2020, www.cnn.com/2020/04/16/world/coronavirus-response-lessons-learned-intl/index.html.

11 Ibid.

12 "How Reuters Journalists Reported South Korea's Swift Action to Test for Coronavirus." *Reuters*, Thomson Reuters, 20 Mar. 2020, www.reuters.com/article/rpb-coronavirustestingsr/how-reuters-journalists-reported-south-koreas-swift-action-to-test-for-coronavirus-idUSKBN2173GH.

13 Ibid.

14 Ibid.

15 Ibid.

16 Ibid.

17 Ibid.

18 Ibid.

19 Ibid.

20 Ibid.

21 Ibid.

22 Ibid.

23 Ibid.

24 Ibid.

25 Ibid.

26 Ibid.

27 Ibid.

28 "Fauci Testifies Coronavirus Testing System 'Not Really Geared to What We Need Right Now.'" *House Committee on Oversight and Reform*, 12 Mar. 2020, oversight.house.gov/news/press-releases/fauci-testifies-coronavirus-testing-system-not-really-geared-to-what-we-need.

29 Shear, Michael D., and Abby Goodnough. "The Lost Month: How a Failure to Test Blinded the U.S. to Covid-19." *The New York Times*, The New York Times, 28 Mar. 2020, www.nytimes.com/2020/03/28/us/testing-coronavirus-pandemic.html.

30 Cohen, Jon, et al. *'I'm Going to Keep Pushing.' Anthony Fauci Tries to Make the White House Listen to Facts of the Pandemic*. 26 Mar. 2020, www.sciencemag.org/news/2020/03/i-m-going-keep-pushing-anthony-fauci-tries-make-white-house-listen-facts-pandemic.

31 Shear, Michael D., and Abby Goodnough. "The Lost Month: How a Failure to Test Blinded the U.S. to Covid-19." *The New York Times*, The New York Times, 28 Mar. 2020, www.nytimes.com/2020/03/28/us/testing-coronavirus-pandemic.html.

32 "Officials Say C.D.C. Errors Caused Testing Delays." *The New York Times*, The New York Times, 18 Apr. 2020, www.nytimes.com/2020/04/18/us/coronavirus-live-news.html.

33 Kaplan, Sheila. "C.D.C. Labs Were Contaminated, Delaying Coronavirus Testing, Officials Say." *The New York Times*, The New York Times, 18 Apr. 2020, www.nytimes.com/2020/04/18/health/cdc-coronavirus-lab-contamination-testing.html.

34 "Officials Say C.D.C. Errors Caused Testing Delays." *The New York Times*, The New York Times, 18 Apr. 2020, www.nytimes.com/2020/04/18/us/coronavirus-live-news.html

35 Kaplan, Sheila. "C.D.C. Labs Were Contaminated, Delaying Coronavirus Testing, Officials Say." *The New York Times*, The New York Times, 18 Apr. 2020, www.nytimes.com/2020/04/18/health/cdc-coronavirus-lab-contamination-testing.html

36 Ibid.

37 "Officials Say C.D.C. Errors Caused Testing Delays." *The New York Times*, The New York Times, 18 Apr. 2020, www.nytimes.com/2020/04/18/us/coronavirus-live-news.html

38 Shear, Michael D., and Abby Goodnough. "The Lost Month: How a Failure to Test Blinded the U.S. to Covid-19." *The New York Times*, The New York Times, 28 Mar. 2020, www.nytimes.com/2020/03/28/us/testing-coronavirus-pandemic.html.

39 Ibid.

40 Weiland, Noah, and Maggie Haberman. "Coronavirus Casts Unwelcome Spotlight on Trump's Health Secretary." *The New York Times*, The New York Times, 29 Apr. 2020, www.nytimes.com/2020/04/29/us/politics/coronavirus-trump-azar.html.

41 Goldberg, Dan. "'It's Going to Disappear': Trump's Changing Tone on Coronavirus." *POLITICO*, POLITICO, 17 Mar. 2020, www.politico.com/news/2020/03/17/how-trump-shifted-his-tone-on-coronavirus-134246.

42 Shear, Michael D., and Abby Goodnough. "The Lost Month: How a Failure to Test Blinded the U.S. to Covid-19." *The New York Times*, The New York Times, 28 Mar. 2020, www.nytimes.com/2020/03/28/us/testing-coronavirus-pandemic.html.

43 Ibid.

44 Ibid.

45 Ibid.

46 Ibid.

47 Ibid.

48 Ibid.

49 Ibid.

50 Grady, Denise. "Coronavirus Test Kits Sent to States Are Flawed, C.D.C. Says." *The New York Times*, The New York Times, 12 Feb. 2020, www.nytimes.com/2020/02/12/health/coronavirus-test-kits-cdc.html.

51 Shear, Michael. "Inside Trump Administration, Debate Raged Over What to Tell Public." *The New York Times*, The New York Times, 7 Mar. 2020, www.nytimes.com/2020/03/07/us/politics/trump-coronavirus.html.

52 Shear, Michael D., and Abby Goodnough. "The Lost Month: How a Failure to Test Blinded the U.S. to Covid-19." *The New York Times*, The New York Times, 28 Mar. 2020, www.nytimes.com/2020/03/28/us/testing-coronavirus-pandemic.html.

53 Ibid.

54 Ibid.

55 "Emergency Use Authorization." *U.S. Food and Drug Administration*, FDA, www.fda.gov/emergency-preparedness-and-response/mcm-legal-regulatory-and-policy-framework/emergency-use-authorization.

56 Shear, Michael D., and Abby Goodnough. "The Lost Month: How a Failure to Test Blinded the U.S. to Covid-19." *The New York Times*, The New York Times, 28 Mar. 2020, www.nytimes.com/2020/03/28/us/testing-coronavirus-pandemic.html.

57 "Meet the Stanford Researchers Mobilizing to Understand, Fight COVID-19." *Stanford News*, 8 May 2020, news.stanford.edu/2020/04/14/covid-19-research-roundup/.

58 Shear, Michael D., and Abby Goodnough. "The Lost Month: How a Failure to Test Blinded the U.S. to Covid-19." *The New York Times*, The New York Times, 28 Mar. 2020, www.nytimes.com/2020/03/28/us/testing-coronavirus-pandemic.html.

59 Ibid.

60 Ibid.

61 Ibid.

62 Ibid.

63 Ibid.

64 Ibid.

65 Ibid.

66 Gates, Bill. *The First Modern Pandemic*. www.gatesnotes.com/Health/Innovation-for-COVID.

Economy amid pandemic. Retrieved from https://observer.com/2020/04/bill-gates-interview-covid19-pandemic-reopen-economy/

67 Hohmann, James. "The Daily 202: Barr Memo Threatening Lawsuits against Coronavirus Restrictions Is a Warning Shot." *The Washington Post*, WP Company, 28 Apr. 2020, www.washingtonpost.com/news/powerpost/paloma/daily-202/2020/04/28/daily-202-barr-memo-threatening-lawsuits-against-coronavirus-restrictions-is-a-warning-shot/5ea7a78e88e0fa3dea9c4414/.

68 Ibid.

69 Ibid.

70 Ibid.

71 Hennigan, W.J. "Testing Czar Says U.S. Can't Run 5 Million Tests a Day." *Time*, Time, 29 Apr. 2020, time.com/5828843/trump-coronavirus-testing-giroir/.

72 'Shabad, Rebecca. "'Pathetic': Schumer Slams Trump's Coronavirus Testing Blueprint." *'Pathetic': Schumer Slams Trump's Coronavirus Testing Blueprint*, 28 Apr. 2020, www.msn.com/en-us/news/politics/pathetic-schumer-slams-trumps-coronavirus-testing-blueprint/ar-BB13jJZw.

73 Ibid.

74 Ibid.

75 Ward, Myah. "Trump: Coronavirus Testing May Be 'Overrated' and Reason for High U.S. Case Count." *POLITICO*, POLITICO, 14 May 2020, www.politico.com/news/2020/05/14/trump-coronavirus-testing-high-case-numbers-259524.

76 Ibid.

77 Ibid.

78 Ibid.

79. "The Coronavirus Outbreak." *The New York Times*, The New York Times, www.nytimes.com/news-event/coronavirus.
80. Ibid; see also, Whitcraft, Teri, et al. "'Road Map' to Recovery Report: 20 Million Coronavirus Tests per Day Needed to Fully Open Economy." *ABC News*, ABC News Network, 20 Apr. 2020, abcnews.go.com/US/road-map-recovery-report-20-million-coronavirus-tests/story?id=70230097.

CHAPTER 14

1. McGinley, Laurie. "FDA Steps up Scrutiny of Coronavirus Antibody Tests to Ensure Accuracy." *The Washington Post*, WP Company, 4 May 2020, www.washingtonpost.com/health/2020/05/04/fda-steps-up-scrutiny-coronavirus-antibody-tests-ensure-accuracy/.
2. Lati, Marisa, and Katie Mettler. "Trump Declares That the U.S. Has 'Prevailed' with Testing; White House Officials Will Wear Masks." *The Washington Post*, WP Company, 12 May 2020, www.washingtonpost.com/nation/2020/05/11/coronavirus-update-us/.
3. "Congress Sounds Alarm Over Inaccurate Antibody Tests." *NBC 5 Dallas-Fort Worth*, NBC 5 Dallas-Fort Worth, 29 Apr. 2020, www.nbcdfw.com/news/coronavirus/congress-sounds-alarm-over-inaccurate-antibody-tests/2360288/.
4. Ibid.
5. Ibid.
6. "Coronavirus Testing Basics." *U.S. Food and Drug Administration*, FDA, www.fda.gov/consumers/consumer-updates/coronavirus-testing-basics.
7. Kliff, Sarah, and Julie Bosman. "Official Counts Understate the U.S. Coronavirus Death Toll." *The New York Times*, The New York Times, 5 Apr. 2020, www.nytimes.com/2020/04/05/us/coronavirus-deaths-undercount.html.
8. "Test for Past Infection (Antibody Test)." *Centers for Disease Control and Prevention*, Centers for Disease Control and Prevention, 23 May 2020, www.cdc.gov/coronavirus/2019-ncov/testing/serology-overview.html
9. "Remarks by President Trump, Vice President Pence, and Members of the Coronavirus Task Force in Press Briefing." *The White House*, The United States Government, www.whitehouse.gov/briefings-statements/remarks-president-trump-vice-president-pence-members-coronavirus-task-force-press-briefing-32/.
10. Ibid.
11. Boyle, Annette. "Two Abbott COVID-19 Tests Receive EUA." *BioWorld RSS*, BioWorld, 12 May 2020, www.bioworld.com/articles/435056-two-abbott-covid-19-tests-receive-eua.
12. Nazaryan, Alexander, and Jana Winter. "Documents Reveal Trump Administration Planning to Use New York City for 'Restore America' Coronavirus Antibody Testing Project." *Yahoo! News*, Yahoo!, 28 Apr. 2020, news.yahoo.com/trump-administration-preparing-to-launch-federal-coronavirus-antibody-testing-project-in-new-york-city-100012217.html.
13. Ibid.
14. Johnson, Carolyn Y., and Joel Achenbach. "Coronavirus Immunity Remains Big Question Mark for a Country Eager to Reopen." *The Washington Post*, WP Company, 14 Apr. 2020, www.washingtonpost.com/health/coronavirus-immunity-remains-big-question-mark-for-a-country-eager-to-reopen/2020/04/14/2c8ccbf4-7e49-11ea-a3ee-13e1ae0a3571_story.html.

15 Lovelace, Berkeley. "WHO Warning: No Evidence That Antibody Tests Can Show Coronavirus Immunity." *CNBC*, CNBC, 19 Apr. 2020, www.cnbc.com/2020/04/17/who-issues-warning-on-coronavirus-testing-theres-no-evidence-antibody-tests-show-immunity.html.

16 Ibid

17 "Information for Laboratories about Coronavirus (COVID-19)." *Centers for Disease Control and Prevention*, Centers for Disease Control and Prevention, 10 June 2020, www.cdc.gov/coronavirus/2019-ncov/lab/index.html.

18 Tan, Chee Wah, et al. "A SARS-CoV-2 Surrogate Virus Neutralization Test (SVNT) Based on Antibody-Mediated Blockage of ACE2-Spike (RBD) Protein-Protein Interaction." (23 April, 2020) *Www.researchsquare.com/*, Research Square, www.researchsquare.com/article/rs-24574/v1.

19 *"Neutralising antibody". Biology-Online. 2008.*

20 Ibid.

21 Schmaljohn, Alan L. "Protective Antiviral Antibodies That Lack Neutralizing Activity: Precedents and Evolution of Concepts." *Current HIV Research*, U.S. National Library of Medicine, July 2013, www.ncbi.nlm.nih.gov/pubmed/24191933.

22 Tan, Chee Wah, et al. "A SARS-CoV-2 Surrogate Virus Neutralization Test (SVNT) Based on Antibody-Mediated Blockage of ACE2-Spike (RBD) Protein-Protein Interaction." (23 April, 2020) *Www.researchsquare.com/*, Research Square, www.researchsquare.com/article/rs-24574/v1.

23 McGinley, Laurie. "Dozens of Coronavirus Antibody Tests on the Market Were Never Vetted by the FDA, Leading to Accuracy Concerns." *The Washington Post*, WP Company, 19 Apr. 2020, www.washingtonpost.com/health/2020/04/19/fda-antibody-tests-coronavirus-review/.

24 "FDA Tightens Rules on Antibody Tests after False Claims, Accuracy Problems." *NBCNews.com*, NBCUniversal News Group, 4 May 2020, www.nbcnews.com/health/health-news/fda-tightens-rules-antibody-tests-after-false-claims-accuracy-problems-n1199431.

25 Ibid.

26 Ibid.

27 Woodyatt, Amy, and Adam Renton. "April 13 Coronavirus News." *CNN*, Cable News Network, 14 Apr. 2020, www.cnn.com/world/live-news/coronavirus-pandemic-04-13-20.

28 Ibid.

29 Lee, Stephanie M. "The FDA Said It Will Now Crack Down On Shoddy Coronavirus Antibody Tests." *BuzzFeed News*, BuzzFeed News, 4 May 2020, www.buzzfeednews.com/article/stephaniemlee/coronavirus-fda-antibody-tests-accuracy.

30 Ibid.

31 Sisson, Paul, and Gary Warth. "County Orders Pop-up Testing Center to Stop Offering Antibody Test." *Tribune*, 15 Apr. 2020, www.sandiegouniontribune.com/news/health/story/2020-04-15/county-shuts-down-pop-up-testing-center.

32 Mcginley, Laurie. "Dozens of Coronavirus Antibody Tests on Market Were Never Vetted by FDA, Leading to Accuracy Concerns." *The Seattle Times*, The Seattle Times Company, 19 Apr. 2020, www.seattletimes.com/nation-world/dozens-of-coronavirus-antibody-tests-on-the-market-were-never-vetted-by-the-fda-leading-to-accuracy-concerns/.

33 Ibid.

34 "FDA Tightens Rules on Antibody Tests after False Claims, Accuracy Problems." *NBCNews.com*, NBCUniversal News Group, 4 May 2020, www.nbcnews.com/health/health-news/fda-tightens-rules-antibody-tests-after-false-claims-accuracy-problems-n1199431.

35 Ibid.

36 Ibid.
37 "Kaplan, Sheila. "F.D.A. Orders Companies to Submit Antibody Test Data." *The New York Times*, The New York Times, 4 May 2020, www.nytimes.com/2020/05/04/health/fda-antibody-tests-coronavirus.html.
38 Proctor, Kate, et al. "'Immunity Passports' Could Speed up Return to Work after Covid-19." *The Guardian*, Guardian News and Media, 30 Mar. 2020, www.theguardian.com/world/2020/mar/30/immunity-passports-could-speed-up-return-to-work-after-covid-19.
39 Vartabedian, Ralph. "Scientists Say a Now-Dominant Strain of the Coronavirus Could Be More Contagious than Original." *Los Angeles Times*, Los Angeles Times, 5 May 2020, www.latimes.com/california/story/2020-05-05/mutant-coronavirus-has-emerged-more-contagious-than-original.
40 Ibid.
41 Ibid.
42 Ibid.
43 Ibid.
44 Ibid
45 "Interim Guidelines for COVID-19 Antibody Testing." *CDC*, n.d., https://www.cdc.gov/coronavirus/2019-ncov/lab/resources/antibody-tests-guidelines.html. Accessed 12 June 2020.
46 Hott, Kasey. "UVA Health Trial Testing Convalescent Plasma as Potential COVID-19 Treatment." *Https://Www.nbc12.Com*, 4 May 2020, www.nbc12.com/2020/05/04/uva-health-trial-testing-convalescent-plasma-potential-covid-treatment/.
47 Ibid.

CHAPTER 15

1 "California Takes Population Lead; But New York Is Still Ahead in Number of Civilians, Census Bureau Says; Pennsylvania is Third; National Total 191,334,000, a Gain of 2.7 Million Over 1963 Figure." *The New York Times*, The New York Times, 1 Sept. 1964, www.nytimes.com/1964/09/01/archives/california-takes-population-lead-but-new-york-is-still-ahead-in.html..
2 Garber, Jonathan. "16 Mind-Blowing Facts about California's Economy." *Business Insider*, 26 Apr. 2019, www.businessinsider.in/16-mind-blowing-facts-about-californias-economy/articleshow/69059659.cms.
3 Ibid
4 Dempsey, C. "Geography of Fortune 1000 Companies in 2018." *Geography Realm*, 13 Nov. 2018, www.geographyrealm.com/geography-of-fortune-1000-companies-in-2018/.
5 Editors, The Bold Italic. "5 Times San Francisco Was Almost Destroyed *Medium*, The Bold Italic, 3 June 2016, thebolditalic.com/5-times-san-francisco-was-almost-destroyed-the-bold-italic-san-francisco-697dcf1177b8.
6 Bristow, Nancy. "1918's Warning for Coronavirus Shutdown Protesters." *Time*, Time, 1 May 2020, time.com/5830265/1918-flu-reopening-coronavirus/.
7 Grimes, Katy. "Why Did Gov. Gavin Newsom Make Hurried $1 Billion Deal With China's BYD for Masks?" *California Globe*, 14 Apr. 2020, californiaglobe.com/section-2/why-did-gov-gavin-newsom-make-hasty-1-billion-deal-with-chinas-byd-north-america-for-masks/.
8 Ibid.
9 Ibid.
10 Ibid.

11 Ibid.

12 Ibid.

13 "County of Santa Clara Public Health Department Reports First Case of Novel (New) Coronavirus." *County of Santa Clara Public Health Department Reports First Case of Novel (New) Coronavirus–Public Health Department–County of Santa Clara*, www.sccgov.org/sites/phd/news/Pages/novel-coronavirus-1-31-2020.aspx.

14 Lovelace, Berkeley, and William Feuer. "CDC Officials Confirm 7th US Case of Coronavirus, in California Man Who Traveled to China." *CNBC*, CNBC, 31 Jan. 2020, www.cnbc.com/2020/01/31/california-and-cdc-officials-confirm-7th-case-of-coronavirus-in-the-us.html.

15 Sulek, Julia Prodis. "Meet the Doctor Who Ordered the Bay Area's Coronavirus Lockdown, the First in the U.S." *The Mercury News*, The Mercury News, 29 Mar. 2020, www.mercurynews.com/2020/03/29/she-shut-down-the-bay-area-to-slow-the-deadly-coronavirus-none-of-us-really-believed-we-would-do-it/.

16 Wadsworth, Jennifer. "Santa Clara County Has Tested Just 647 Patients for COVID-19." *San Jose Inside*, 24 Mar. 2020, www.sanjoseinside.com/news/santa-clara-county-has-tested-just-647-patients-for-covid-19/.

17 Sulek, Julia Prodis. "Meet the Doctor Who Ordered the Bay Area's Coronavirus Lockdown, the First in the U.S." *The Mercury News*, The Mercury News, 29 Mar. 2020, www.mercurynews.com/2020/03/29/she-shut-down-the-bay-area-to-slow-the-deadly-coronavirus-none-of-us-really-believed-we-would-do-it/.

18 Ibid.

19 Palo Alto Weekly Staff. "Coronavirus: Uptick in Cases Leads Santa Clara County to Issue First-in-the-Nation Order on Large Events." *News*, The Almanac, 9 Mar. 2020, www.almanacnews.com/news/2020/03/09/coronavirus-uptick-in-cases-leads-santa-clara-county-to-issue-first-in-the-nation-order-on-large-events.

20 Kelly, George, and Maggie Angst. "Coronavirus: 2 New Deaths, 39 New Cases in Santa Clara County for Total of 302 Cases." *The Mercury News*, The Mercury News, 23 Mar. 2020, www.mercurynews.com/2020/03/22/coronavirus-39-new-cases-in-santa-clara-county-for-total-of-302/.

21 Sulek, Julia Prodis. "Meet the Doctor Who Ordered the Bay Area's Coronavirus Lockdown, the First in the U.S." *The Mercury News*, The Mercury News, 29 Mar. 2020, www.mercurynews.com/2020/03/29/she-shut-down-the-bay-area-to-slow-the-deadly-coronavirus-none-of-us-really-believed-we-would-do-it/.

22 Ibid.

23 Ibid.

24 Arango, Tim, and Jill Cowan. "Gov. Gavin Newsom of California Orders Californians to Stay at Home." *The New York Times*, The New York Times, 20 Mar. 2020, www.nytimes.com/2020/03/19/us/California-stay-at-home-order-virus.html.

25 Sulek, Julia Prodis. "Meet the Doctor Who Ordered the Bay Area's Coronavirus Lockdown, the First in the U.S." *The Mercury News*, The Mercury News, 29 Mar. 2020, www.mercurynews.com/2020/03/29/she-shut-down-the-bay-area-to-slow-the-deadly-coronavirus-none-of-us-really-believed-we-would-do-it/.

26 Ibid.

27 Ibid.

28 Ibid.

29 Ibid.

30. Ibid.
31. Ibid.
32. "Governor Newsom Declares State of Emergency to Help State Prepare for Broader Spread of COVID-19." *California Governor*, 5 Mar. 2020, www.gov.ca.gov/2020/03/04/governor-newsom-declares-state-of-emergency-to-help-state-prepare-for-broader-spread-of-covid-19/.
33. Bhattacharjee, Riya. "California Governor Calls for Closure of All Bars and Wineries, Home Isolation of Seniors." *CNBC*, CNBC, 22 Mar. 2020, www.cnbc.com/2020/03/15/california-governor-calls-for-closure-of-all-bars-and-wineries-home-isolation-of-seniors.html.
34. Edwards, Valerie. "California Closes All Bars and Orders Restaurants to Cut Seating Capacity by 50%." *Daily Mail Online*, Associated Newspapers, 16 Mar. 2020, www.dailymail.co.uk/news/article-8115155/California-closes-bars-orders-restaurants-cut-seating-capacity-50.html.
35. Arango, Tim, and Jill Cowan. "Gov. Gavin Newsom of California Orders Californians to Stay at Home." *The New York Times*, The New York Times, 20 Mar. 2020, www.nytimes.com/2020/03/19/us/California-stay-at-home-order-virus.html.
36. Neuman, Scott. "California Issues 'Stay At Home' Order As Coronavirus Infections Rise." *NPR*, NPR, 20 Mar. 2020, www.npr.org/2020/03/20/818764136/california-issues-stay-at-home-order-as-coronavirus-infections-rise.
37. Ibid.
38. Ibid.
39. Ibid.
40. Kelly, Ronan. "Announcement." *FluTrackers News and Information*, 13 Apr. 2020, flutrackers.com/forum/forum/-2019-ncov-new-coronavirus/united-states-2019-ncov/california-covid-19/837803-california-cdph-reports-of-cases-and-deaths-73-143-cases-and-2-974-deaths/page4.
41. Mcdermott, Marie Tae. "Coronavirus Cases in California." *The New York Times*, The New York Times, 28 Feb. 2020, www.nytimes.com/article/california-coronavirus.html.
42. Id.
43. Kennedy, Merrit. "California Governor Outlines How The State Will Decide To Open Again." *NPR*, NPR, 14 Apr. 2020, www.npr.org/sections/coronavirus-live-updates/2020/04/14/834434343/california-governor-outlines-how-the-state-will-decide-to-open-again.
44. Ibid.
45. Ibid.
46. Ibid.
47. Rodriguez, Eddy. "California Governor Warns State Is 'Not out of the Woods Yet' despite Drop in Coronavirus Hospitalizations." *Newsweek*, Newsweek, 23 Apr. 2020, www.newsweek.com/california-governor-warns-state-not-out-woods-yet-despite-drop-coronavirus-hospitalizations-1499909.
48. "U.S. Cases Increase 2.5%, Slowest Pace This Month: Virus Update." *BloombergQuint*, 24 Apr. 2020, www.bloombergquint.com/coronavirus-outbreak/u-s-cases-slow-new-york-plans-tracing-army-virus-update
49. "Great Plates Delivered: Home Meals for Seniors." *Ca.gov*, covid19.ca.gov/restaurants-deliver-home-meals-for-seniors/.
50. Villarreal, Daniel. "Gov. Newsom Announces Plan for Restaurants to Deliver 3 Meals Daily to Seniors at No Charge." *Newsweek*, Newsweek, 24 Apr. 2020, www.newsweek.com/gov-newsom-announces-plan-restaurants-deliver-3-meals-daily-seniors-no-charge-1500174.

51 Luna, Taryn, and Phil Willon. "Newsom Says California Shutdown Must Continue, but Surge in Testing Will Help." *Yahoo! News*, Yahoo!, 22 Apr. 2020, news.yahoo.com/newsom-says-california-shutdown-must-195006315.html.

52 Vaziri, Aidin. "Swab Shortage Holds up Coronavirus Testing in California." *SFChronicle.com*, San Francisco Chronicle, 25 Apr. 2020, www.sfchronicle.com/bayarea/article/Swab-shortage-holds-up-coronavirus-testing-in-15224961.php.

53 Luna, Taryn, and Phil Willon. "Newsom Says California Shutdown Must Continue, but Surge in Testing Will Help." *Los Angeles Times*, Los Angeles Times, 22 Apr. 2020, www.latimes.com/california/story/2020-04-22/california-coronavirus-testing-increase-stay-at-home-order-remains-gavin-newsom.

54 McAllister, T. "1.5 Million Abbott Serology Tests Ordered For CA: Coronavirus." *Patch*, 22 Apr. 2020, https://patch.com/california/temecula/1-5-million-abbott-serology-tests-ordered-ca-coronavirus.

55 Rabin, Roni Caryn. "First Patient With Wuhan Coronavirus Is Identified in the U.S." *The New York Times*, The New York Times, 21 Jan. 2020, www.nytimes.com/2020/01/21/health/cdc-coronavirus.html.

56 Chappell, Bill. "9 Coronavirus Deaths Now Reported In Washington State." *NPR*, NPR, 3 Mar. 2020, www.npr.org/sections/health-shots/2020/03/03/811690163/9-coronavirus-deaths-now-reported-in-washington-state..

57 Baker, Mike, and Karen Weise. "Coronavirus Deaths Tied to Nursing Center Came Earlier Than Anyone Knew." *The New York Times*, The New York Times, 4 Mar. 2020, www.nytimes.com/2020/03/03/us/coronavirus-washington-death.html.

58 Garber, Nick. "Coronavirus Cases Surpass 13,000 In Washington; 738 Deaths." *Seattle, WA Patch*, Patch, 26 Apr. 2020, patch.com/washington/seattle/coronavirus-cases-surpass-13-000-washington-738-deaths..

59 Ibid.

60 Baker, Peter. "Trump Says 'People Have to Remain Calm' Amid Coronavirus Outbreak." *The New York Times*, The New York Times, 6 Mar. 2020, www.nytimes.com/2020/03/06/us/politics/trump-coronavirus-cdc.html.

61 Ibid.

62 Golden, Hallie. "Washington State Begins to Ask: How Does the Coronavirus Crisis End?" *The Guardian*, Guardian News and Media, 11 Apr. 2020, www.theguardian.com/us-news/2020/apr/11/washington-state-coronavirus-crisis.

63 Ibid.

64 Ibid.

65 Baker, Mike. "Coronavirus Slowdown in Seattle Suggests Restrictions Are Working." *The New York Times*, The New York Times, 29 Mar. 2020, www.nytimes.com/2020/03/29/us/seattle-washington-state-coronavirus-transmission-rate.html.

66 Kaste, Martin. "Washington State Builds Coronavirus Contact Tracing 'Fire Brigade'." *NPR*, NPR, 23 Apr. 2020, www.npr.org/sections/coronavirus-live-updates/2020/04/22/842119284/washington-state-builds-coronavirus-contact-tracing-fire-brigade.

67 Brazile, Liz. "Harborview, UW Medical Centers to Test All Incoming Patients for Covid-19." *KUOW*, 14 Apr. 2020, www.kuow.org/stories/harborview-uw-medical-centers-to-test-all-incoming-hospital-patients-for-covid-19.

68 Hamilton, J. "When Coronavirus Struck Seattle, This Lab Was Ready To Start Testing." *NPR*, 5 Mar. 2020, https://www.npr.org/sections/health-shots/2020/03/05/812679331/when-coronavirus-struck-seattle-this-lab-was-ready-to-start-testing.

69 Golden, Hallie. "Washington State Begins to Ask: How Does the Coronavirus Crisis End?" *The Guardian*, Guardian News and Media, 11 Apr. 2020, www.theguardian.com/us-news/2020/apr/11/washington-state-coronavirus-crisis.

70 "Recovery for Washington State Will Be Gradual during Coronavirus, Says Gov. Inslee." *king5.Com*, 22 Apr. 2020, www.king5.com/article/news/health/coronavirus/gov-inslee-coronavirus-washington-state-recovery-update/281-e1611728-6788-4ffb-ab7f-3ad922bed5cd.

71 "Inslee Announces Washington's COVID-19 Recovery Plan." *Governor Jay Inslee*, www.governor.wa.gov/news-media/inslee-announces-washington%E2%80%99s-covid-19-recovery-plan.

72 "Safe Return to Public Life in Washington State." https://www.governor.wa.gov/sites/default/files/Washington%27s%20Recovery%20Plan%20.pdf.

73 Brown, Jordyn. "First Coronavirus Case in Oregon Is of Unknown Origin." *Guard*, The Register-Guard, 29 Feb. 2020, www.registerguard.com/news/20200228/first-coronavirus-case-in-oregon-is-of-unknown-origin..

74 Zarkhin, Fedor. "Coronavirus Case Confirmed in Oregon." *The Bulletin*, 2 Mar. 2020, www.bendbulletin.com/health/coronavirus-case-confirmed-in-oregon/article_415378f8-5a95-11ea-a8a0-f77fd0a5091e.html.

75 "Gov. Kate Brown Prepares Statewide Stay-at-Home Order amid Coronavirus Outbreak, Report Says." *Oregonlive*, 23 Mar. 2020, www.oregonlive.com/coronavirus/2020/03/gov-kate-brown-prepares-statewide-stay-at-home-order-amid-coronavirus-outbreak-report-says.html.

76 "Oregon Coronavirus Death Toll Reaches 91 as Statewide Cases Surpass 2,300." *KATU*, KATU, 27 Apr. 2020, katu.com/news/local/oregon-coronavirus-death-toll-reaches-91-oha-reports-2311-cases-statewide.

77 "Oregon Gets Doses of Good News in Battling Coronavirus." *U.S. News & World Report*, U.S. News & World Report, www.usnews.com/news/best-states/oregon/articles/2020-04-24/oregon-gets-doses-of-good-news-in-battling-coronavirus.

78 Selsky, Andrew. "Oregon Receives 1.19 Million Masks, with More on the Way." *Mail Tribune*, Mail Tribune, 25 Apr. 2020, mailtribune.com/news/coronavirus/oregon-receives-119-million-masks-with-more-on-the-way.

79 Ibid.

80 Ibid.

81 "Battelle CCDS FAQ." *Battelle*, n.d., https://www.battelle.org/inb/battelle-ccds-for-covid19-satellite-locations. Accessed 19 May 2020.

82 Schmidt, Brad. "How Can Oregon Reopen amid Coronavirus? It May Start with 600 New Contact Tracers." *Kgw.com*, KGW, 24 Apr. 2020, www.kgw.com/article/money/business/how-can-oregon-reopen-amid-coronavirus-it-may-start-with-600-new-contact-tracers/283-fdcc6579-5a4b-47aa-809d-558193155b2f.s

83 Ibid.

84 "Govenor Kate Brown Announces First Oregon Walgreens Rapid COVID-19 Testing Location." *Oregon Gov*, 24 Apr. 2020, https://www.oregon.gov/newsroom/Pages/NewsDetail.aspx?newsid=36501.

85 "California, Oregon & Washington Announce Western States Pact." *California Governor*, 13 Apr. 2020, www.gov.ca.gov/2020/04/13/california-oregon-washington-announce-western-states-pact/.

86 Moshtaghian, Artemis, and Paul LeBlanc. "Colorado and Nevada Join Western States Pact as States Work on Unified Coronavirus Strategy." *CNN*, Cable News Network, 27 Apr. 2020, www.cnn.com/2020/04/27/politics/colorado-nevada-western-states/index.html.

87 Ibid.

CHAPTER 16

1 Booker, Brakkton. "*Seattle-Area Nursing HOME Linked to Dozens of Coronavirus Deaths Faces $600,000 Fine.*" 3 Apr. 2020, www.npr.org/sections/coronavirus-live-updates/2020/04/02/826360394/seattle-area-nursing-home-linked-to-dozens-of-coronavirus-deaths-faces-600-000-f.

2 Kwiatkowski, Marisa. "At Least 2,300 Nursing Homes Have Coronavirus Cases–and the Reality Is Likely Much Worse." *Waynesboro Record Herald–Waynesboro, PA*, www.therecordherald.com/zz/news/20200414/at-least-2300-nursing-homes-have-coronavirus-cases—-and-reality-is-likely-much-worse.

3 Richtel, Matt. "Nursing Homes Are Starkly Vulnerable to Coronavirus." *The New York Times*, The New York Times, 4 Mar. 2020, www.nytimes.com/2020/03/04/health/coronavirus-nursing-homes.html.

4 Ibid

5 Yourish, Karen, et al. "One-Third of All U.S. Coronavirus Deaths Are Nursing Home Residents or Workers." *The New York Times*, The New York Times, 9 May 2020, www.nytimes.com/interactive/2020/05/09/us/coronavirus-cases-nursing-homes-us.html.

6 Ibid.

7 Ibid.

8 Ibid.

9 Geller, Pamela. "90% Of the Coronavirus Deaths in Connecticut Last Week Were Nursing Home Patients." *Geller Report News*, 14 May 2020, gellerreport.com/2020/05/90-of-the-coronavirus-deaths-in-connecticut-last-week-were-nursing-home-patients.html/.

10 "Key Strategies to Prepare for COVID-19 in Long-Term Care Facilities (LTCFs)." *Centers for Disease Control and Prevention*, Centers for Disease Control and Prevention, 21 May 2020, www.cdc.gov/coronavirus/2019-ncov/hcp/long-term-care-strategies.html.

11 Leland, John. "At Least 14 N.Y. Nursing Homes Have Had More Than 25 Virus Deaths." *The New York Times*, The New York Times, 17 Apr. 2020, www.nytimes.com/2020/04/17/nyregion/new-york-nursing-homes-coronavirus-deaths.html/.

12 "Key Strategies to Prepare for COVID-19 in Long-Term Care Facilities (LTCFs)." *Centers for Disease Control and Prevention*, Centers for Disease Control and Prevention, 21 May 2020, www.cdc.gov/coronavirus/2019-ncov/hcp/long-term-care-strategies.html.

13 Yourish, Karen, et al. "One-Third of All U.S. Coronavirus Deaths Are Nursing Home Residents or Workers." *The New York Times*, The New York Times, 9 May 2020, www.nytimes.com/interactive/2020/05/09/us/coronavirus-cases-nursing-homes-us.html.

14 Ibid.

15 Ibid.

16 Tully, Tracey. "After Anonymous Tip, 17 Bodies Found at Nursing Home Hit by Virus." *The New York Times*, The New York Times, 15 Apr. 2020, www.nytimes.com/2020/04/15/nyregion/coronavirus-nj-andover-nursing-home-deaths.html.

17 Ibid.

18 Ibid.

19   Ibid.
20   Ibid.
21   Tully, Tracey. '*The Whole Place Is Sick Now*': 72 Deaths at a Home for U.S. Veterans. 10 May 2020, www.nytimes.com/2020/05/10/nyregion/new-jersey-military-veterans-home.html.
22   Ibid.
23   Ibid.
24   Chicago Tribune Staff. "Coronavirus in Illinois Updates: Here's What Happened April 16 with COVID-19 in the Chicago Area." *Chicagotribune.com*, Chicago Tribune, 17 Apr. 2020, www.chicagotribune.com/coronavirus/ct-coronavirus-pandemic-chicago-illinois-news-20200416-yspbx6q2x-5ajvnesqkg3nofvmu-story.html.
25   NBC Chicago. "To Prepare for 'Surge in Deaths' From COVID-19, Cook County Opens Refrigerated Warehouse to Store Thousands of Bodies." *NBC Chicago*, NBC Chicago, 9 Apr. 2020, www.nbcchicago.com/news/local/to-prepare-for-surge-in-deaths-from-covid-19-cook-county-opens-refrigerated-warehouse-to-store-thousands-of-bodies/2253041/.
26   Hellmann, Jessie. "CDC: 80 Percent of US Coronavirus Deaths Are People 65 and Older." *TheHill*, The Hill, 18 Mar. 2020, thehill.com/policy/healthcare/public-global-health/488305-cdc-80-percent-of-us-coronavirus-deaths-are-people-65.
27   Ibid.
28   Perper, Rosie. "Italy, Now under Lockdown, Has Been Hit Hard by the Coronavirus Outbreak. It Also Has One of the World's Oldest Populations with 60% over Age 40." *Business Insider Australia*, Business Insider Australia, 10 Mar. 2020, www.businessinsider.com.au/italy-coronavirus-old-population-cases-death-rate-2020-3.
29   Harris, Amy Julia, et al. *Nearly 2,000 Dead As Coronavirus Ravages Nursing Homes in N.Y. Region*. 11 Apr. 2020, www.nytimes.com/2020/04/11/nyregion/nursing-homes-deaths-coronavirus.html.
30   Ibid.
31   Ibid.
32   Schoch, Deborah. "Families Worried About Loved Ones In Nursing Homes Amid Coronavirus." *AARP*, AARP, 2 Apr. 2020, www.aarp.org/caregiving/health/info-2020/preventing-coronavirus-in-nursing-homes.html.
33   Ibid.
34   Ibid.
35   Aronson, Louise. "'Covid-19 Kills Only Old People.' Only?" *The New York Times*, The New York Times, 22 Mar. 2020, www.nytimes.com/2020/03/22/opinion/coronavirus-elderly.html.
36   Schoch, Deborah. "Families Worried About Loved Ones In Nursing Homes Amid Coronavirus." *AARP*, AARP, 2 Apr. 2020, www.aarp.org/caregiving/health/info-2020/preventing-coronavirus-in-nursing-homes.html.
37   Aronson, Louise. "'Covid-19 Kills Only Old People.' Only?" *The New York Times*, The New York Times, 22 Mar. 2020, www.nytimes.com/2020/03/22/opinion/coronavirus-elderly.html.
38   Ibid
39   Ibid.
40   Ibid.

41 Tully, Tracey. "After Anonymous Tip, 17 Bodies Found at Nursing Home Hit by Virus." *The New York Times*, The New York Times, 15 Apr. 2020, www.nytimes.com/2020/04/15/nyregion/coronavirus-nj-andover-nursing-home-deaths.html.

42 Aronson, Louise. "'Covid-19 Kills Only Old People.' Only?" *The New York Times*, The New York Times, 22 Mar. 2020, www.nytimes.com/2020/03/22/opinion/coronavirus-elderly.html.

43 Carlson, Chris. "Staff No-Shows, Deaths Hit California Nursing Facilities." *AP News*, Associated Press, 9 Apr. 2020, apnews.com/55f8d0158d97de75cf138a6ba8198204.

44 Ibid.

45 Romero, Simon, et al. "Virginia Nursing Home Had Plenty of Coronavirus Patients but Few Tests." *The New York Times*, The New York Times, 16 Apr. 2020, www.nytimes.com/2020/04/15/us/virginia-nursing-home-coronavirus.html.

46 Ibid.

47 Ibid.

48 Eaton, Joe. "Nursing Home Workers Face Danger During Coronavirus." *AARP*, AARP, 29 Apr. 2020, www.aarp.org/caregiving/health/info-2020/nursing-home-workers-during-coronavirus.html./.

49 Ibid.

50 Ibid.

51 Ibid.

52 Bacon, John. "A Bridge between Life and Death: Most COVID-19 Patients Put on Ventilators Will Not Survive." *USA Today*, Gannett Satellite Information Network, 10 Apr. 2020, www.usatoday.com/story/news/health/2020/04/08/coronavirus-cases-ventilators-covid-19/2950167001/./

53 Ibid.

54 Harris, Amy Julia, et al. "Nearly 2,000 Dead as Coronavirus Ravages Nursing Homes in N.Y. Region." *The New York Times*, The New York Times, 11 Apr. 2020, www.nytimes.com/2020/04/11/nyregion/nursing-homes-deaths-coronavirus.html.

55 Ibid.

56 Ibid.

57 Ibid.

58 Ibid.

59 Ibid.

60 Ibid.

61 Ibid.

62 Eaton, Joe. "Nursing Home Workers Face Danger During Coronavirus." *AARP*, AARP, 29 Apr. 2020, www.aarp.org/caregiving/health/info-2020/nursing-home-workers-during-coronavirus.html./.

63 Ibid.

64 Ibid.

65 Altimari, Dave. "Nearly 90 Percent of the Coronavirus Deaths in Connecticut Last Week Were Nursing Home Patients." *Courant.com*, Hartford Courant, 6 May 2020, www.courant.com/coronavirus/hc-news-coronavirus-80percent-deaths-20200506-fuhlhtusajb7dd7p6sf5xekl54-story.html.

66 Campanile, Carl. "Connecticut Gov. Ned Lamont Fires Health Commissioner in Middle of Coronavirus Crisis." *New York Post*, New York Post, 13 May 2020, nypost.com/2020/05/13/connecticut-gov-lamont-fires-health-commissioner-amid-coronavirus/./

67 Ibid.

68 Miller, Shannon. "Nursing Home Residents Return to Homes After Treatment at COVID-19 Recovery Centers." *NBC Connecticut*, NBC Connecticut, 30 Apr. 2020, www.nbcconnecticut.com/news/local/nursing-home-residents-return-to-homes-after-treatment-at-covid-19-recovery-centers/2264088/.

69 Harris, Amy Julia, et al. "Nearly 2,000 Dead as Coronavirus Ravages Nursing Homes in N.Y. Region." *The New York Times*, The New York Times, 11 Apr. 2020, www.nytimes.com/2020/04/11/nyregion/nursing-homes-deaths-coronavirus.html.

70 Knutson, Jacob. *New York Reports 1,700 "PREVIOUSLY Undisclosed" Coronavirus Deaths in Nursing Homes.* 5 May 2020, www.axios.com/new-york-nursing-home-coronavirus-deaths-133f86d2-33c2-41ef-9209-b6b25135a628.html.

71 Ibid

72 Ibid.

73 Ibid.

74 Ibid.

75 Ibid.

76 Ibid.

77 Ibid.

78 Perano, Ursula. "Facing Backlash, Cuomo Announces New Rules to Protect Nursing Homes from Coronavirus." *Axios*, 10 May 2020, www.axios.com/cuomo-coronavirus-nursing-homes-new-york-c368f4d6-e5e2-4bcb-bcd6-a0296bef97d0.html.

79 Ibid.

80 Ibid.

81 Ibid.

82 Ibid.

83 Ibid

84 Harris, Cayla. "Cuomo: Hospitals Cannot Discharge COVID-19 Patients to Nursing Homes." *Times Union*, Times Union, 10 May 2020, www.timesunion.com/news/article/Cuomo-Hospitals-cannot-discharge-COVID-19-15259931.php.

85 Ibid.

86 Harris, Amy Julia, et al. "Nearly 2,000 Dead as Coronavirus Ravages Nursing Homes in N.Y. Region." *The New York Times*, The New York Times, 11 Apr. 2020, www.nytimes.com/2020/04/11/nyregion/nursing-homes-deaths-coronavirus.html.

87 Ibid.

88 Ibid.

89 Ibid.

90 Wentling, Nikki. "Coronavirus Has Now Hit Veterans Homes in 16 States." Stars and Stripes, Stars and Stripes, 15 Apr. 2020, www.stripes.com/news/veterans/coronavirus-has-now-hit-veterans-homes-in-16-states-1.626187.

91 Ibid.

92   Durkin Richer, A. "Nearly 70 Dead in 'Horrific' Outbreak at Holyoke Solider's Home." *NBC Boston*, 28 Apr. 2020, https://www.nbcboston.com/news/coronavirus/nearly-70-dead-in-horrific-outbreak-at-holyoke-soldiers-home/2115282/.

93   Bullock, Mark, et al. "45 Confirmed COVID-19 Cases, 2 Deaths at Ala. Veterans Homes." *Https://Www.wsfa.com*, 14 Apr. 2020, www.wsfa.com/2020/04/14/confirmed-covid-cases-deaths-ala-veterans-homes/./.

94   Tully, Tracey. *'The Whole Place Is Sick Now': 72 Deaths at a Home for U.S. Veterans.* 10 May 2020, www.nytimes.com/2020/05/10/nyregion/new-jersey-military-veterans-home.html.

95   Ibid.

96   Ibid.

97   Ibid.

98   Ibid.

99   Ibid.

100 Ibid.

101 Ibid.

102 Ibid.

103 Ibid.

104 Ibid.

105 Ibid.

106 Ibid.

107 Ibid.

108 Ibid.

109 Booker, Brakkton. "Seattle-Area Nursing Home Linked to Dozens Of Coronavirus Deaths Faces $600,000 Fine." NPR, NPR, 2 Apr. 2020, www.npr.org/sections/coronavirus-live-updates/2020/04/02/826360394/seattle-area-nursing-home-linked-to-dozens-of-coronavirus-deaths-faces-600-000-f.

110 Ibid.

111 Ibid.

112 Eaton, Joe. "Nursing Home Workers Face Danger During Coronavirus." *AARP*, AARP, 29 Apr. 2020, www.aarp.org/caregiving/health/info-2020/nursing-home-workers-during-coronavirus.html./.

113 Ibid.

114 CBS Chicago. "Nursing Home Workers Threaten Strike In Midst Of Pandemic." *CBS Chicago*, CBS Chicago, 28 Apr. 2020, chicago.cbslocal.com/2020/04/28/nursing-home-workers-threaten-strike-in-midst-of-pandemic/.

115 Ibid.

116 Ibid.

117 Ibid.

CHAPTER 17

1   Chiu, Allyson. "Jared Kushner's Coronavirus Briefing Debut Sparks Outcry, Confusion." *The Washington Post*, WP Company, 3 Apr. 2020, www.washingtonpost.com/nation/2020/04/03/jared-kushner-coronavirus-briefing/.

2. Herszenhorn, David M. "US Pursues EU Reset Efforts with 'Javanka' Dinner in New York." *Politico*, Politico, 26 Sept. 2019, www.politico.eu/article/ivanka-trump-jared-kushner-us-pursues-eu-reset-efforts-with-javanka-dinner-in-new-york/.

3. Liptak, Kevin. "Trump's Secretary of Everything: Jared Kushner." *CNN*, Cable News Network, 3 Apr. 2017, www.cnn.com/2017/04/03/politics/jared-kushner-donald-trump-foreign-policy/index.html.l

4. Ibid.

5. Ibid.

6. Levin, Bess, and Erika Harwood. "Kushner: Palestinians Have Never Done Anything Right in Their Sad, Pathetic Lives." *Vanity Fair*, Vanity Fair, 29 Jan. 2020, www.vanityfair.com/news/2020/01/jared-kushner-peace-plan-palestinians.

7. Ibid.

8. "Remarks by President Trump, Vice President Pence, and Members of the Coronavirus Task Force in Press Briefing." *The White House*, The United States Government, www.whitehouse.gov/briefings-statements/remarks-president-trump-vice-president-pence-members-coronavirus-task-force-press-briefing-18/.

9. Ibid.

10. Ibid.

11. Gittleson, Ben. "After Kushner Says 'It's Our Stockpile,' HHS Website Changed to Echo His Comments on Federal Crisis Role." *ABC News*, ABC News Network, 3 Apr. 2020, abcnews.go.com/Politics/kushner-stockpile-hhs-website-changed-echo-comments-federal/story?id=69936411.

12. Ibid.

13. "Remarks by President Trump, Vice President Pence, and Members of the Coronavirus Task Force in Press Briefing." *The White House*, The United States Government, www.whitehouse.gov/briefings-statements/remarks-president-trump-vice-president-pence-members-coronavirus-task-force-press-briefing-18/.

14. Ibid.

15. Cook, Nancy, and Dan Diamond. "'A Darwinian Approach to Federalism': States Confront New Reality under Trump." *POLITICO*, POLITICO, 31 Mar. 2020, www.politico.com/news/2020/03/31/governors-trump-coronavirus-156875.

16. Ibid.

17. Glasser, Susan B., and Steve Coll. "How Did the U.S. End Up with Nurses Wearing Garbage Bags?" *The New Yorker*, The New Yorker, 9 Apr. 2020, www.newyorker.com/news/letter-from-trumps-washington/the-coronavirus-and-how-the-united-states-ended-up-with-nurses-wearing-garbage-bags.

18. Campanile, Carl, and Ebony Bowden. "Nurses at NYC Hospital Receive Gowns after Post Trash Bag Expose." *New York Post*, New York Post, 2 Apr. 2020, nypost.com/2020/04/02/nurses-at-nyc-hospital-receive-gowns-after-post-trash-bag-expose/.

19. Heer, Jeet. "Trump Helps Big Business Profiteer Off Our Misery." *The Nation*, The Nation, 3 Apr. 2020, www.thenation.com/article/politics/trump-business-coronavirus-profiteering/.

20. Cook, Nancy, and Dan Diamond. "'A Darwinian Approach to Federalism': States Confront New Reality under Trump." *POLITICO*, POLITICO, 31 Mar. 2020, www.politico.com/news/2020/03/31/governors-trump-coronavirus-156875.

21. Ibid

22. Ibid.

23. Ibid.

24 Levin, Bess. "So Jared Kushner Is Running a 'Shadow' Coronavirus Task Force." *Vanity Fair*, Vanity Fair, 26 Mar. 2020, www.vanityfair.com/news/2020/03/jared-kushner-shadow-coronavirus-task-force.

25 Glasser, Susan B., and Steve Coll. "How Did the U.S. End Up with Nurses Wearing Garbage Bags?" *The New Yorker*, The New Yorker, 9 Apr. 2020, www.newyorker.com/news/letter-from-trumps-washington/the-coronavirus-and-how-the-united-states-ended-up-with-nurses-wearing-garbage-bags.

26 Ibid.

27 Ibid.

28 Ibid.

29 Ibid.

30 Ibid.

31 Levy, Rachael. "WSJ News Exclusive | Volunteers in Coronavirus Response Ruffle Some at FEMA." *The Wall Street Journal*, Dow Jones & Company, 21 Apr. 2020, www.wsj.com/articles/volunteers-in-coronavirus-response-ruffle-some-at-fema-11587489141.

32 Ibid.

33 Ibid.

34 Ibid

35 Ibid.

36 Ibid.

37 Confessore, Nicholas, et al. "How Kushner's Volunteer Force Led a Fumbling Hunt for Medical Supplies." *The New York Times*, The New York Times, 5 May 2020, www.nytimes.com/2020/05/05/us/jared-kushner-fema-coronavirus.html.

38 Ibid.

39 Ibid.

40 Ibid.

41 Ibid.

42 Cherny, Robert W. "Graft and Oil … How Teapot Dome Became the Greatest Political Scandal of Its Time." History News Network, Gilder Lehrman Institute, 17 June 2009, historynewsnetwork.org/article/92780

43 Ibid.

44 Rosenthal, Brian. "'The Other Option Is Death': New York Starts Sharing of Ventilators." *The New York Times*, The New York Times, 26 Mar. 2020, www.nytimes.com/2020/03/26/health/coronavirus-ventilator-sharing.html.

45 Confessore, Nicholas, et al. "How Kushner's Volunteer Force Led a Fumbling Hunt for Medical Supplies." *The New York Times*, The New York Times, 5 May 2020, www.nytimes.com/2020/05/05/us/jared-kushner-fema-coronavirus.html.

46 Ibid.

47 Ibid.

48 Mendoza, Martha, and Juliet Linderman. "Relief Package Billions Can't Buy Hospitals out of Shortages." *AP NEWS*, Associated Press, 29 Mar. 2020, apnews.com/cea0967cea2593bbe9fb62d8d462424d.

49 Ibid.

50 Ibid.

51 Ibid.

52 Rose, Joel. "A 'War' For Medical Supplies: States Say FEMA Wins By Poaching Orders." *NPR*, NPR, 15 Apr. 2020, www.npr.org/2020/04/15/835308133/governors-say-fema-is-outbidding-redirecting-or-poaching-their-medical-supply-or.

53 Kanno-Youngs, Zolan, and Jack Nicas. "'Swept Up by FEMA': Complicated Medical Supply System Sows Confusion." *The New York Times*, The New York Times, 6 Apr. 2020, www.nytimes.com/2020/04/06/us/politics/coronavirus-fema-medical-supplies.html.

54 Ibid.

55 Johnson, Jake. "'Dry-Rotted' Supplies and Severe Shortages: HHS Inspector General Report Offers Grim Look at US Coronavirus Response." 6 Apr. 2020, www.commondreams.org/news/2020/04/06/dry-rotted-supplies-and-severe-shortages-hhs-inspector-general-report-offers-grim.

56 Ibid.

57 Ibid.

58 Ibid.

59 Ibid.

60 Ibid.

61 Ibid.

62 Ibid.

63 Ibid.

64 Ibid.

65 Chiacu, Doina. "Trump Slams U.S. Watchdog's Report on Shortages at Coronavirus-Hit Hospitals." *Reuters*, Thomson Reuters, 7 Apr. 2020, www.reuters.com/article/us-health-coronavirus-usa-watchdog/trump-slams-u-s-watchdogs-report-on-shortages-at-coronavirus-hit-hospitals-idUSKBN21P2NR..

66 Johnson, Jake. "'Dry-Rotted' Supplies and Severe Shortages: HHS Inspector General Report Offers Grim Look at US Coronavirus Response." 6 Apr. 2020, www.commondreams.org/news/2020/04/06/dry-rotted-supplies-and-severe-shortages-hhs-inspector-general-report-offers-grim.

67 Lerner, Sharon. *"Trump Fires Inspector General Ahead of Damning Whistleblower Complaint about Bogus Coronavirus Cures."* 4 May 2020, theintercept.com/2020/05/04/rick-bright-hhs-whistleblower-coronavirus/.

68 "Expert Recommendations for US and Global Preparedness for COVID-19." *Center For Global Development*, 13 Feb. 2020, www.cgdev.org/publication/expert-recommendations-us-and-global-preparedness-covid-19.

69 Ibid.

70 Melvin, Craig. "Fmr. Head of U.S. Foreign Disaster Assistance on the Coronavirus: 'The Risk Is Real.'." *MSNBC*, NBCUniversal News Group, 26 Feb. 2020, www.msnbc.com/craig-melvin/watch/fmr-head-of-u-s-foreign-disaster-assistance-on-the-coronavirus-the-risk-is-real-79481925522.

71 Knight, Victoria. "Obama Team Left Pandemic Playbook for Trump Administration, Officials Confirm." *PBS*, Public Broadcasting Service, 15 May 2020, www.pbs.org/newshour/nation/obama-team-left-pandemic-playbook-for-trump-administration-officials-confirm.

72 Ibid.

73 Lippman, Daniel. "Trump Team Failed to Follow NSC's Pandemic Playbook." *POLITICO*, www.politico.com/news/2020/03/25/trump-coronavirus-national-security-council-149285.

74 Ibid.

75 Knight, Victoria. "Obama Team Left Pandemic Playbook for Trump Administration, Officials Confirm." *PBS*, Public Broadcasting Service, 15 May 2020, www.pbs.org/newshour/nation/obama-team-left-pandemic-playbook-for-trump-administration-officials-confirm.

76 Ibid.

77 Marinucci, Carla. "*California to Spend Nearly $1B for 200 MILLION MASKS per Month.*" 8 Apr. 2020, www.politico.com/states/california/story/2020/04/08/california-inks-nearly-1b-deal-to-buy-200-million-masks-each-month-1273702.

78 Klebnikov, Sergei. *Cuomo Calls for National 'BUYING Consortium,' Says He Hasn't Discussed Quarantine With Trump.* 29 Mar. 2020, www.forbes.com/sites/sergeiklebnikov/2020/03/28/cuomo-calls-for-national-buying-consortium-says-he-hasnt-discussed-quarantine-with-trump/.

79 Ibid.

80 Gronewold, Anna. "'Just Madness': Governors Mull Consortium to End Chaos over Medical Supplies." *Politico PRO*, 8 Apr. 2020, www.politico.com/states/new-york/albany/story/2020/04/08/just-madness-governors-mull-consortium-to-end-chaos-over-medical-supplies-1273929.

81 Heer, Jeet. *Trump Helps Big Business Profiteer off Our Misery.* 3 Apr. 2020, www.thenation.com/article/politics/trump-business-coronavirus-profiteering/./

82 "Arizona's Reopening: Salons, Barbershops and Some Retailers Can Welcome Customers Today after Weeks of Closures." *Azcentral*, Arizona Republic, 9 May 2020, www.azcentral.com/story/money/business/consumers/2020/05/08/arizona-reopening-live-updates-salons-barbershops-open/3092697001/.

83 Taylor, Janelle. "Does Ron DeSantis' Stay-at-Home Order Allow Megachurches to Continue Meeting? Looks like It." *Florida Politics–Campaigns & Elections. Lobbying & Government.*, 2 Apr. 2020, floridapolitics.com/archives/326292-does-ron-desantis-safer-at-home-order-allow-megachurches-to-continue-meeting-looks-like-it.

84 Southern California Public Radio. "Market And Business Ties Often Determine Where COVID-19 Supplies Go." *Southern California Public Radio*, 11 Apr. 2020, www.scpr.org/news/2020/04/11/91856/market-and-business-ties-often-determine-where-cov/.

85 Ibid.

86 Heer, Jeet. *Trump Helps Big Business Profiteer off Our Misery.* 3 Apr. 2020, www.thenation.com/article/politics/trump-business-coronavirus-profiteering/.

87 Ibid.

CHAPTER 18

1 Berman, Russell. "The City That Has Flattened the Coronavirus Curve." *The Atlantic*, Atlantic Media Company, 23 Apr. 2020, www.theatlantic.com/politics/archive/2020/04/coronavirus-san-francisco-london-breed/609808/.

2 Lovelace, Berkeley. "NYC Declares State of Emergency, De Blasio Says Coronavirus 'Could Easily Be a 6-Month Crisis'." *CNBC*, CNBC, 12 Mar. 2020, www.cnbc.com/2020/03/12/new-york-city-declares-state-of-emergency.html.

3 Arango, Tim, and Jill Cowan. "Gov. Gavin Newsom of California Orders Californians to Stay at Home." *The New York Times*, The New York Times, 20 Mar. 2020, www.nytimes.com/2020/03/19/us/California-stay-at-home-order-virus.html.

4 Graff, Amy. "Tweets Show SF and NYC Mayors' Drastically Different Approaches to Outbreak." *SFGate*, San Francisco Chronicle, 9 Apr. 2020, www.sfgate.com/bayarea/article/de-Blasio-London-Breed-tweets-coronavirus-March-2-15189898.php.

5   Feuer, William, and Noah Higgins-Dunn. "Cuomo Orders Most New Yorkers to Stay inside–'We're All under Quarantine Now'." *CNBC*, CNBC, 20 Mar. 2020, www.cnbc.com/2020/03/20/new-york-gov-cuomo-orders-100percent-of-non-essential-businesses-to-work-from-home.html..

6   Wojcik, Nik. "Covid-19 Update: May Day Strikes to Take on Renewed Meaning, Some Beaches Close, Bay Area Stays the Course." *SFBay*, SFBay, 1 May 2020, sfbayca.com/2020/04/30/covid-19-update-may-day-strikes-to-take-on-renewed-meaning-some-beaches-close-bay-area-stays-the-course/.

7   PIX11 Web Team. "Latest Coronavirus Updates in New York: Thursday, April 30, 2020." *WPIX*, 30 Apr. 2020, www.pix11.com/news/coronavirus/latest-coronavirus-updates-in-new-york-thursday-april-30-2020.

8   Money, Luke. "Coronavirus-Related Death Toll Passes 2,000 in California, More than Half in L.A. County." *Los Angeles Times*, Los Angeles Times, 30 Apr. 2020, www.latimes.com/california/story/2020-04-30/coronavirus-death-toll-nears-2-000-in-california-more-than-half-are-in-l-a-county.

9   Harris, Connor. "San Francisco's Mayor Did Everything De Blasio Didn't to Fight Coronavirus." *New York Post*, New York Post, 9 Apr. 2020, nypost.com/2020/04/09/san-franciscos-mayor-did-everything-de-blasio-didnt-to-fight-coronavirus/.

10 Ibid.

11 West, Melanie Grayce. "First Case of Coronavirus Confirmed in New York State." *The Wall Street Journal*, Dow Jones & Company, 2 Mar. 2020, www.wsj.com/articles/first-case-of-coronavirus-confirmed-in-new-york-state-11583111692

12 Yan, Holly; Sgueglia, Kristina (March 2, 2020). "New York's first case of coronavirus is a health care worker, and officials say more cases are 'inevitable'". *CNN*. Archived from the original on March 4, 2020..

13 Bendix, Aria. "At Least 28 Coronavirus Cases in New York Are Linked to One Man–a 50-Year-Old Attorney Who Works near Grand Central Terminal. Here's What We Know." *Business Insider*, Business Insider, 6 Mar. 2020, www.businessinsider.com/new-york-second-coronavirus-case-attorney-law-firm-grand-central-2020-3.

14 Goldstein, Joseph, and Jesse Mckinley. "Second Case of Coronavirus in N.Y. Sets Off Search for Others Exposed." *The New York Times*, The New York Times, 3 Mar. 2020, www.nytimes.com/2020/03/03/nyregion/coronavirus-new-york-state.html. *see also* Algar, Selim, et al. "New York Confirms Second Coronavirus Case as Jewish Schools Close over Virus Fears." *New York Post*, New York Post, 3 Mar. 2020, nypost.com/2020/03/03/bronx-jewish-day-school-closes-for-suspected-coronavirus-case/

15 Goldenberg, Sally, and Dana Rubinstein. "De Blasio Was 'Furious' as Library Heads Planned to Close for Coronavirus." *Politico*, 18 Mar. 2020, www.politico.com/states/new-york/albany/story/2020/03/17/de-blasio-was-furious-as-library-heads-planned-to-close-for-coronavirus-1267580.

16 Diaz, Luis. "NYC Mayor De Blasio: No Plans to Cancel the St. Patrick's Day Parade :: March 9, 2020." *New Yorkled Magazine*, 19 Mar. 2020, www.newyorkled.com/nyc-mayor-de-blasio-no-plans-to-cancel-the-st-patricks-day-parade-march-9-2020/.

17 Idliby, Leia. "NYC's St. Patrick's Day Parade Canceled Over Coronavirus." *Mediaite*, 11 Mar. 2020, www.mediaite.com/news/new-york-citys-st-patricks-day-parade-canceled-over-coronavirus-concerns/

18 Harris, Connor. "San Francisco's Mayor Did Everything De Blasio Didn't to Fight Coronavirus." *New York Post*, New York Post, 9 Apr. 2020, nypost.com/2020/04/09/san-franciscos-mayor-did-everything-de-blasio-didnt-to-fight-coronavirus/.

19. Hogan, Bernadette, et al. "Five More New York Coronavirus Cases Confirmed, Bringing State Total to 11." *New York Post*, New York Post, 5 Mar. 2020, nypost.com/2020/03/04/five-more-new-york-coronavirus-cases-confirmed-bringing-state-total-to-11/

20. Parnell, Wes, and Shant Shahrigian. "Mayor De Blasio Says Coronavirus Fears Shouldn't Keep New Yorkers off Subways." *Nydailynews.com*, New York Daily News, 5 Mar. 2020, www.nydailynews.com/coronavirus/ny-coronavirus-bill-de-blasio-coronavirus-subway-20200305-vmjdxjudbndlrjekash-qs3hfou-story.html.

21. "COVID-19 Pandemic in Orange County, New York." *Wikipedia*, Wikimedia Foundation, 6 May 2020, en.wikipedia.org/wiki/COVID-19_pandemic_in_Orange_County,_New_York.

22. Millman, Jennifer. "New York COVID-19 Cases Surge to 45; Dozens Under Mandatory Quarantine Order." *NBC New York*, NBC New York, 7 Mar. 2020, www.nbcnewyork.com/news/local/more-cases-of-coronavirus-expected-as-ny-plans-to-expand-testing-ability/2314911/.

23. Cuomo, Andrew. "UPDATE: We Have Learned of 11 New Confirmed Cases of #Coronavirus in NYS– Bringing the Total Number of Cases to 44. -8 of the New New Cases Are in Westchester County-3 of the New Cases Are in Nassau County[.] We Have Expected the Number of Positive Cases to Go up as We Test." *Twitter*, Twitter, 6 Mar. 2020, twitter.com/NYGovCuomo/status/1236046668220567553.

24. Marsh, Julia. "City Hall Didn't Secure 1st Order of COVID-19 Supplies for NYC until March 6." *New York Post*, New York Post, 20 Mar. 2020, nypost.com/2020/03/20/city-hall-didnt-order-covid-19-supplies-for-nyc-until-march-6/.

25. McGhee, Kaylee. "New York City's Coronavirus Outbreak Has Exposed Bill De Blasio's Ineptitude." *Washington Examiner*, Washington Examiner, 30 Mar. 2020, www.washingtonexaminer.com/opinion/new-york-citys-coronavirus-outbreak-has-exposed-bill-de-blasios-ineptitude.

26. Ford, James. "NYC Leaders Try to Quell Coronavirus Concerns after 1st Confirmed Case." *WPIX*, 2 Mar. 2020, www.pix11.com/news/coronavirus/nyc-leaders-try-to-quell-coronavirus-concerns-after-1st-confirmed-case.

27. Lawson, Kyle. "Coronavirus Risk 'Remains Low' in NYC; Same-Day Testing Now Available, Officials Say." *Silive*, 3 Mar. 2020, www.silive.com/news/2020/03/coronavirus-risk-remains-low-in-nyc-same-day-testing-now-available-officials-say.html.

28. Edelman, Susan. "Two Pols Urge De Blasio to Oust Health Commissioner Barbot over Coronavirus Response." *New York Post*, New York Post, 4 Apr. 2020, nypost.com/2020/04/04/nyc-pols-urge-de-blasio-to-oust-health-commissioner-over-coronavirus-response/.

29. Ibid.

30. Brodner, Curtis. "No Mask, No Gloves, No Service: Southern Brooklyn Businesses Start to Turn Away Customers Without Masks." *BKLYNER*, 24 Mar. 2020, bklyner.com/no-mask-no-gloves-no-service-brooklyn-businesses-start-to-turn-away-customers-without-masks/.

31. Edelman, Susan. "Two Pols Urge De Blasio to Oust Health Commissioner Barbot over Coronavirus Response." *New York Post*, New York Post, 4 Apr. 2020, nypost.com/2020/04/04/nyc-pols-urge-de-blasio-to-oust-health-commissioner-over-coronavirus-response/.

32. Ferré-Sadurní, Luis, et al. "N.Y. Creates 'Containment Zone' Limiting Large Gatherings in New Rochelle." *The New York Times*, The New York Times, 10 Mar. 2020, www.nytimes.com/2020/03/10/nyregion/coronavirus-new-york-update.html.

33. "During Novel Coronavirus Briefing, Governor Cuomo Announces New Mass Gatherings Regulations." Governor Andrew M. Cuomo, 17 Mar. 2020, www.governor.ny.gov/news/during-novel-coronavirus-briefing-governor-cuomo-announces-new-mass-gatherings-regulations.

34. "During Novel Coronavirus Briefing, Governor Cuomo Announces New Mass Gatherings Regulations." Governor Andrew M. Cuomo, 17 Mar. 2020, www.governor.ny.gov/news/during-novel-coronavirus-briefing-governor-cuomo-announces-new-mass-gatherings-regulations.
35. Gartenberg, Chaim. "NYC Just Shut down Broadway for at Least a Month." *The Verge*, The Verge, 12 Mar. 2020, www.theverge.com/2020/3/12/21177162/new-york-coronavirus-ban-public-gathering-broadway-concerts-museums.
36. Croft, Jay. "First Coronavirus-Related Death Reported in New York." *CNN*, Cable News Network, 14 Mar. 2020, www.cnn.com/2020/03/14/us/nyc-coronavirus-related-death/index.html.
37. NBC. "Four COVID-19 Deaths in NY, NJ as Tri-State Cases Surpass 700; New U.S. Travel Limits in Place." *NBC New York*, NBC New York, 14 Mar. 2020, www.nbcnewyork.com/news/local/tri-state-braces-for-further-covid-19-spread-after-house-house-emergency-bill/2326406/.
38. Winter, Tom. "Coronavirus Outbreak: NYC Teachers 'Furious' over De Blasio's Policy to Keep Schools Open." *NBCNews*, NBCUniversal News Group, 15 Mar. 2020, www.nbcnews.com/news/us-news/coronavirus-outbreak-nyc-teachers-furious-over-de-blasio-s-policy-n1159491.
39. Shapiro, Eliza. "New York City Public Schools to Close to Slow Spread of Coronavirus." The New York Times, The New York Times, 15 Mar. 2020, www.nytimes.com/2020/03/15/nyregion/nyc-schools-closed.html.see also: Berger, Paul, et al. "New York City Schools to Close Over Coronavirus." The Wall Street Journal, Dow Jones & Company, 15 Mar. 2020, www.wsj.com/articles/new-york-city-schools-to-close-over-coronavirus-11584307280.
40. "Governor Cuomo Announces All New York City, Westchester, Suffolk and Nassau Public Schools Will Close This Week to Limit Spread of COVID-19." Governor Andrew M. Cuomo, 19 Mar. 2020, www.governor.ny.gov/news/governor-cuomo-announces-all-new-york-city-westchester-suffolk-and-nassau-public-schools-will.
41. Ibid.
42. Mays, Jeffery C., and Joseph Goldstein. "Mayor Resisted Drastic Steps on Virus. Then Came a Backlash From His Aides." *The New York Times*, The New York Times, 16 Mar. 2020, www.nytimes.com/2020/03/16/nyregion/coronavirus-bill-de-blasio.html.
43. Fink, Zack, et al. "Cuomo: There Will Be No Shelter-in-Place Order for New York City." Cuomo: There Will Be No Shelter-in-Place Order for NYC, 17 Mar. 2020, www.ny1.com/nyc/all-boroughs/politics/2020/03/17/new-york-coronavirus-latest-will-new-york-city-have-to-shelter-in-place-be-on-lockdown.
44. Lahut, Jake. "New York City Mayor Bill De Blasio Again Calls for 'Shelter in Place,' Even Though He Can't Make the Order." *Business Insider*, Business Insider, 20 Mar. 2020, www.businessinsider.com/nyc-de-blasio-we-have-to-shelter-in-place-model-2020-3.
45. Duster, Chandelis, and Paul LeBlanc. "New York Governor Dismisses Possibility of Shelter in Place Order after Mayor Urged New Yorkers to Prepare for It." CNN, Cable News Network, 18 Mar. 2020, edition.cnn.com/2020/03/17/politics/bill-de-blasio-andrew-cuomo-new-york-shelter-in-place-coronavirus-cnntv/index.html.
46. Ibid.
47. Feuer, William. "Gov. Cuomo Says He Won't Approve Coronavirus 'Shelter-in-Place' Order for New York City after Mayor Tells Residents to Prepare." *CNBC*, CNBC, 18 Mar. 2020, www.cnbc.com/2020/03/18/cuomo-says-he-wont-approve-coronavirus-shelter-in-place-order-for-new-york-city.html.
48. Lahut, Jake. "New York City Mayor Bill De Blasio Again Calls for 'Shelter in Place,' Even Though He Can't Make the Order." *Business Insider*, Business Insider, 20 Mar. 2020, www.businessinsider.com/nyc-de-blasio-we-have-to-shelter-in-place-model-2020-3.

CHAPTER 18 • ENDNOTES • 611

49. "Governor Cuomo Signs the 'New York State on PAUSE' Executive Order." *Governor Andrew M. Cuomo*, 23 Mar. 2020, www.governor.ny.gov/news/governor-cuomo-signs-new-york-state-pause-executive-order.

50. "Coronavirus Spreading in New York like 'a Bullet Train'." BBC News, BBC, 24 Mar. 2020, www.bbc.com/news/world-us-canada-52012048.

51. Rosenthal, Brian M., et al. "'The Other Option Is Death': New York Starts Sharing of Ventilators." The New York Times, The New York Times, 26 Mar. 2020, www.nytimes.com/2020/03/26/health/coronavirus-ventilator-sharing.html.

52. Andone, Dakin. "New York Will Allow Two Patients to Share a Single Ventilator." CNN, Cable News Network, 26 Mar. 2020, www.cnn.com/2020/03/26/health/splitting-ventilators-coronavirus/index.html.

53. Ibid. see also: Bromwich, Jonah Engel, et al. "N.Y.C. Death Toll Hits 365 as Case Count Tops 23,000." The New York Times, The New York Times, 26 Mar. 2020, www.nytimes.com/2020/03/26/nyregion/coronavirus-new-york-update.html. ??

54. Marsh, Julia. "City Hall Didn't Secure 1st Order of COVID-19 Supplies for NYC until March 6." *New York Post*, New York Post, 20 Mar. 2020, nypost.com/2020/03/20/city-hall-didnt-order-covid-19-supplies-for-nyc-until-march-6/.

55. Edelman, Susan, and Tina Moore. "NYC First Responders Resent Lack of Coronavirus Equipment." *New York Post*, New York Post, 22 Mar. 2020, 9:38 pm, nypost.com/2020/03/21/nyc-first-responders-resent-lack-of-coronavirus-equipment/.

56. Rothfeld, Michael, et al. "13 Deaths in a Day: An 'Apocalyptic' Coronavirus Surge at an N.Y.C. Hospital." *The New York Times*, The New York Times, 25 Mar. 2020, www.nytimes.com/2020/03/25/nyregion/nyc-coronavirus-hospitals.html.

57. Rothfeld, Michael. "Inside a NYC Hospital in an 'Apocalyptic' Situation." *MSNBC*, NBCUniversal News Group, 26 Mar. 2020, www.msnbc.com/the-last-word/watch/inside-a-nyc-hospital-in-an-apocalyptic-situation-81222213672.

58. Fenton, Reuven, and Tamar Lapin. "NYC's Elmhurst Hospital at Coronavirus Breaking Point as 13 Patients Die in 24-Hour Span." *New York Post*, New York Post, 25 Mar. 2020, 10:11 pm, nypost.com/2020/03/25/nycs-elmhurst-hospital-at-breaking-point-as-13-patients-die-in-24-hour-span/. See also:⁵⁸ Russell, David. "Elmhurst Hospital Sees 13 Deaths in 24-Hour Span." *Queens Chronicle*, 26 Mar. 2020, www.qchron.com/editions/central/elmhurst-hospital-sees-deaths-in—hour-span/article_73ddfbea-6f8a-11ea-a763-6371991a6bb1.html.

59. Baker, Mike, et al. "Trump Attacks W.H.O. and Ousts Watchdog for Pandemic Fund." *The New York Times*, The New York Times, 7 Apr. 2020, www.nytimes.com/2020/04/07/world/coronavirus-updates-news-live.html#link-5e549a4e.

60. Krisel, Brendan. "Mt Sinai To Use Lobbies For Coronavirus Patient Rooms: Report." *Upper East Side, NY Patch*, Patch, 26 Mar. 2020, 4:41 pm, patch.com/new-york/upper-east-side-nyc/mt-sinai-use-lobbies-coronavirus-patient-rooms-report. *See also:* Gorenstein, Dan. "Coronavirus Conversations: David Reich." *Tradeoffs*, 31 Mar. 2020, tradeoffs.org/2020/03/31/cc-reich/.

61. Peltz, Jennifer. "Central Park Houses Hospital Ward as NY Races to Add Beds." *WHEC News10NBC*, Associated Press, 2 Apr. 2020, www.whec.com/national/central-park-houses-hospital-ward-as-ny-races-to-add-beds/5690659/.see also:²² Stribling, Dees. "The Scramble Is On To Build Temporary Healthcare Space." *Bisnow*, 30 Mar. 2020, www.bisnow.com/national/news/healthcare/the-scramble-is-on-to-build-temporary-healthcare-space-103661.See also:³ Holcombe, Madeline, et al. "New York's Central Park and Harbor Are Now Home to Makeshift Hospitals." *CNN*, Cable News Network, 30 Mar. 2020, 3:43 pm, www.cnn.com/2020/03/30/us/new-york-coronavirus-cases-deaths/index.html.

62 Sisak, Michael R., and Robert Bumsted. "Surge in Deaths Overwhelms New York's Morgues, Hospitals." *PBS*, Public Broadcasting Service, 31 Mar. 2020, www.pbs.org/newshour/health/surge-in-deaths-overwhelms-new-yorks-morgues-hospitals.

63 Watkins, Ali. "N.Y.C.'s 911 System Is Overwhelmed. 'I'm Terrified,' a Paramedic Says." *The New York Times*, The New York Times, 28 Mar. 2020, www.nytimes.com/2020/03/28/nyregion/nyc-coronavirus-ems.html.

64 Ibid.

65 Ibid.

66 Moreno, J. Edward. "Cuomo Threatens to Sue RI over New Policy to Find New Yorkers in the State." *TheHill*, The Hill, 28 Mar. 2020, thehill.com/homenews/state-watch/490019-cuomo-threatens-to-sue-ri-over-new-coronavirus-policy-targeting-ny.

67 Machado, Steph. "RI Reports 3rd COVID-19 Death; Expanded Travel Order to out-of-State Drivers." *WPRI.com*, WPRI.com, 29 Mar. 2020, www.wpri.com/health/coronavirus/march-29-ri-coronavirus-update/.

68 Myers, Meghann. "The Army Corps of Engineers Has Two or Three Weeks to Get Thousands of New Hospital Beds up and Running." *Military Times*, Military Times, 27 Mar. 2020, www.militarytimes.com/news/your-military/2020/03/27/the-army-corps-of-engineers-has-two-or-three-weeks-to-get-thousands-of-new-hospital-beds-up-and-running/.

69 Tsioulcas, Anastasia. "Central Park And Home Of Tennis' U.S. Open To House Hospital Beds For New York." *NPR*, NPR, 30 Mar. 2020, www.npr.org/sections/coronavirus-live-updates/2020/03/30/824300407/central-park-and-home-of-tennis-us-open-to-house-hospital-beds-for-new-york.

70 Sisak, Michael R., and Michael Hill. "COVID-19 Deaths Climb in NY; Chris Cuomo Tests Positive." *AP NEWS*, Associated Press, 31 Mar. 2020, apnews.com/e80a98f37714622c5b34d27d94bea8ff. *See also:* Stelter, Brian. "CNN Anchor Chris Cuomo Diagnosed with Coronavirus; He Will Continue Working from Home." *CNN*, Cable News Network, 31 Mar. 2020, www.cnn.com/2020/03/31/media/chris-cuomo-coronavirus/index.html.

71 Singman, Brooke. "Cuomo Signs Executive Order Requiring All New Yorkers to Wear Face Coverings in Public amid Coronavirus." *Fox News*, FOX News Network, 15 Apr. 2020, www.foxnews.com/politics/cuomo-signs-executive-order-requiring-all-new-yorkers-wear-face-masks-coverings-in-public-amid-coronavirus.

72 Engel Bromwich, Jonah, et al. "Cuomo Extends Coronavirus Shutdown Order to May 15." *The New York Times*, The New York Times, 16 Apr. 2020, www.nytimes.com/2020/04/16/nyregion/coronavirus-new-york-update.html.

73 Johnson, Ted. "New York To Extend Stay-At-Home Order Through May 15." *Yahoo!*, Yahoo!, 16 Apr. 2020, www.yahoo.com/entertainment/york-extend-stay-home-order-163616750.html.

74 Treisman, Rachel. "Northeast: Coronavirus-Related Restrictions By State." *NPR*, NPR, 4 June 2020, www.npr.org/2020/05/01/847331283/northeast-coronavirus-related-restrictions-by-state.

75 Spector, Joseph. "New York Will Start Regional Contact Tracing to Fight Coronavirus. Here's What That Means." *Lohud.com*, New York State Team, 22 Apr. 2020, www.lohud.com/story/news/politics/2020/04/22/ny-starts-contact-tracing-fight-coronavirus-heres-what-means/3004907001/.

76 Spector, Joseph. "New York Will Start Regional Contact Tracing to Fight Coronavirus. Here's What That Means." *Recordonline.com*, Recordonline.com, 22 Apr. 2020, www.recordonline.com/news/20200422/new-york-will-start-regional-contact-tracing-to-fight-coronavirus-heres-what-that-means.

77 Graff, Amy. "San Francisco Reports First Coronavirus Cases." *SFGate*, San Francisco Chronicle, 5 Mar. 2020, www.sfgate.com/bayarea/article/San-Francisco-first-coronavirus-cases-15108332.php.

78 Campanile, Carl, and Bernadette Hogan. "First Case of Coronavirus Confirmed in New York City." *New York Post*, New York Post, 1 Mar. 2020, nypost.com/2020/03/01/first-case-of-coronavirus-confirmed-in-manhattan/.

79 Allday, Erin. "Bay Area Orders 'Shelter in Place,' Only Essential Businesses Open in 6 Counties." *SFChronicle.com*, San Francisco Chronicle, 16 Mar. 2020, www.sfchronicle.com/local-politics/article/Bay-Area-must-shelter-in-place-Only-15135014.php

80 Harris, Connor. "San Francisco's Mayor Did Everything De Blasio Didn't to Fight Coronavirus." *New York Post*, New York Post, 9 Apr. 2020, nypost.com/2020/04/09/san-franciscos-mayor-did-everything-de-blasio-didnt-to-fight-coronavirus/.

81 Allday, Erin. "N.Y. Facing 10 Times the Cases Seen in California–but Why?" *PressReader.com–Your Favorite Newspapers and Magazines.*, San Francisco Chronicle, 25 Mar. 2020, www.pressreader.com/usa/san-francisco-chronicle/20200325/281487868439968.

82 Graff, Amy. "Tweets Show SF and NYC Mayors' Drastically Different Approaches to Outbreak." *SFGate*, San Francisco Chronicle, 9 Apr. 2020, www.sfgate.com/bayarea/article/de-Blasio-London-Breed-tweets-coronavirus-March-2-15189898.phpId.

83 Ibid.

84 Ibid.

85 Milligan, Susan. "How Coronavirus Made Andrew Cuomo America's Governor." *U.S. News & World Report*, U.S. News & World Report, 23 Mar. 2020, www.usnews.com/news/health-news/articles/2020-03-23/how-coronavirus-made-andrew-cuomo-americas-governor.

86 Robb, Greg. "New York Gov. Cuomo Calls His State 'Canary in Coalmine' as He Pleads with Trump Administration for Ventilators." *MarketWatch*, MarketWatch, 24 Mar. 2020, www.marketwatch.com/story/new-york-governor-cuomo-makes-impassioned-plea-to-trump-administration-for-ventilators-in-next-14-days-2020-03-24.

87 Ibid

88 Platsky, Jeff. "Coronavirus: Andrew Cuomo Urges Federal Government to Take Control of Medical Supply Market." *Pressconnects*, New York State Team, 22 Mar. 2020, www.pressconnects.com/story/news/local/2020/03/22/coronavirus-andrew-cuomo-urges-feds-take-control-medical-supply-market/2894348001/.

89 Rothfeld, Michael, et al. "13 Deaths in a Day: An 'Apocalyptic' Coronavirus Surge at an N.Y.C. Hospital." *The New York Times*, The New York Times, 25 Mar. 2020, www.nytimes.com/2020/03/25/nyregion/nyc-coronavirus-hospitals.html.

90 Dowd, Maureen. "Let's 'Kick Coronavirus's Ass'." *The New York Times*, The New York Times, 27 Mar. 2020, www.nytimes.com/2020/03/27/opinion/sunday/cuomo-new-york-coronavirus.html.

91 Ibid.

92 Hains, Tim. "Cuomo: 'My Mother Is Not Expendable,' Won't Accept 'Premise That Human Life Is Disposable.'" *RealClearPolitics*, 24 Mar. 2020, www.realclearpolitics.com/video/2020/03/24/cuomo_my_mother_is_not_expendable_wont_accept_premise_that_human_life_is_disposable.html.

93 Dowd, Maureen. "Let's 'Kick Coronavirus's Ass'." *The New York Times*, The New York Times, 27 Mar. 2020, www.nytimes.com/2020/03/27/opinion/sunday/cuomo-new-york-coronavirus.html.

94 Ibid.

95 During Trump's April 13, 2020 press conference, he stated: "I have the ultimate authority," later clarifying his position as follows: "When somebody is the president of the United States, the authority is total and that's the way it's got to be. ... It's total. The governors know that." The local leaders, Trump said, "can't do anything without the approval of the president of the United States."

96 Arango, Tim, et al. "Coronavirus Updates: Trump Halts U.S. Funding of World Health Organization." *The New York Times*, The New York Times, 14 Apr. 2020, www.nytimes.com/2020/04/14/us/coronavirus-updates.html.

97 Ibid.

98 Ibid.

99 Marsh, Julia, and Natalie Musumeci. "De Blasio Announces NYC Will Produce Its Own Coronavirus Test Kits." *New York Post*, New York Post, 14 Apr. 2020, nypost.com/2020/04/14/de-blasio-announces-nyc-will-produce-its-own-coronavirus-tests/.

100 Ibid.

101 Ibid.

102 Ibid.

103 Merica, Dan. "Cuomo and De Blasio Can't Put Their Feud aside — Even for Coronavirus." *CNN*, Cable News Network, 13 Apr. 2020, www.cnn.com/2020/04/13/politics/cuomo-vs-de-blasio-feud/index.html.

104 Ibid.

105 Ibid.

106 Gronewold, Anna, and Marie J. French. "Northeast Governors Planning Regional Economic Restart." *Politico PRO*, 13 Apr. 2020, www.politico.com/states/new-york/albany/story/2020/04/13/northeast-governors-planning-regional-economic-restart-1275385.

107 Ibid.

108 Press, Associated. "Democratic Governors Form Multi-State Compacts to Coordinate Loosening of Coronavirus Restrictions." *MarketWatch*, MarketWatch, 13 Apr. 2020, www.marketwatch.com/story/democratic-governors-form-multi-state-compacts-to-coordinate-loosening-of-coronavirus-restrictions-2020-04-13?mod=article_inline.

109 Ibid.

110 Arango, Tim, et al. "Coronavirus Updates: Trump Halts U.S. Funding of World Health Organization." *The New York Times*, The New York Times, 14 Apr. 2020, ww.nytimes.com/2020/04/14/us/coronavirus-updates.html.; see also Schroeder, Robert. "Trump Accuses Governors of 'Mutiny' as Tensions Mount over Reopening." *MarketWatch*, MarketWatch, 14 Apr. 2020, www.marketwatch.com/story/trump-accuses-governors-of-mutiny-as-tensions-mount-over-reopening-2020-04-14.

CHAPTER 19

1 Chappell, Bill. "1st Person-To-Person Spread Of Coronavirus Has Occurred In U.S., CDC Says." *NPR*, NPR, 30 Jan. 2020, www.npr.org/sections/health-shots/2020/01/30/801235064/1st-person-to-person-spread-of-coronavirus-has-occurred-in-u-s-cdc-says.

2 Ibid.

3 Ibid.

4 "Transcript for CDC Media Telebriefing: Update on 2019 Novel Coronavirus (2019-nCoV)." *CDC*, 31 Jan. 2020, https://www.cdc.gov/media/releases/2020/t0131-2019-novel-coronavirus.html.

5   "CDC Confirms Person-to-Person Spread of New Coronavirus in the United States." *Centers for Disease Control and Prevention*, Centers for Disease Control and Prevention, 30 Jan. 2020, www.cdc.gov/media/releases/2020/p0130-coronavirus-spread.html.

6   Ibid.

7   Ibid.

8   Ibid.

9   Ibid.

10 Ibid.

11 Ibid.

12 "Mask Mystery: Why Are U.S. Officials Dismissive of Protective Covering?" *POLITICO*, 30 Mar. 2020, www.politico.com/news/2020/03/30/coronavirus-masks-trump-administration-156327.

13 Ibid.

14 Frias, Lauren. "A Top US Health Official Says the US Needs 300 Million Face Masks for Healthcare Workers." *Business Insider*, Business Insider, 26 Feb. 2020, www.businessinsider.com/us-needs-millions-face-masks-not-very-effective-preventing-coronavirus-2020-2.

15 "March 2020: Dr. Anthony Fauci Talks with Dr Jon LaPook about COVID-19." *CBS News*, CBS Interactive, 18 May 2020, www.cbsnews.com/news/preventing-coronavirus-facemask-60-minutes-2020-03-08/

16 Ibid.

17 "Mask Mystery: Why Are U.S. Officials Dismissive of Protective Covering?" *POLITICO*, 30 Mar. 2020, www.politico.com/news/2020/03/30/coronavirus-masks-trump-administration-156327

18 Ibid.

19 Cerullo, Megan. "Face Mask Prices Surge as Coronavirus Fears Grow." *CBS News*, CBS Interactive, 27 Feb. 2020, www.cbsnews.com/news/amazon-coronavirus-face-mask-price-gouging-shortages//.

20 Mask Mystery: Why Are U.S. Officials Dismissive of Protective Covering?" *POLITICO*, 30 Mar. 2020, www.politico.com/news/2020/03/30/coronavirus-masks-trump-administration-156327.

21 Ibid.

22 Ibid.

23 Ibid.

24 Martuzzi, Marco. "The Precautionary Principle: in Action for Public Health." *Occupational and Environmental Medicine*, BMJ Group, Sept. 2007, www.ncbi.nlm.nih.gov/pmc/articles/PMC2092570/; see also American Journal of Public Health September 2001, Vol 91, No.9 ttps://ajph.aphapublications.org/doi/pdf/10.2105/AJPH.91.9.1358.

25 Blanchard, Ben. "Taiwan to Spend $35 Billion Fighting Virus, to Donate 10 Million Masks." *Reuters*, Thomson Reuters, 1 Apr. 2020, www.reuters.com/article/us-health-coronavirus-taiwan-economy-idUSKBN21J41C.

26 Tucker, Emma. "White House Scrambled to Secure Masks for Staffers as U.S. Discouraged Using Them: Report." *The Daily Beast*, The Daily Beast Company, 15 Apr. 2020, www.thedailybeast.com/white-house-scrambled-to-secure-masks-for-staffers-as-us-discouraged-using-them-report-says.

27 Ibid.

28 Ibid.

29 Dwyer, Colin, and Allison Aubrey. "CDC Now Recommends Americans Consider Wearing Cloth Face Coverings In Public." *NPR*, NPR, 3 Apr. 2020, www.npr.org/sections/coronavirus-live-updates/2020/04/03/826219824/president-trump-says-cdc-now-recommends-americans-wear-cloth-masks-in-public?orgid=123.

30 Ibid.

31 Ibid.

32 Fritze, John. "Trump: Won't Wear a Coronavirus Mask Because It Would Interfere with Foreign Leader Meetings." *Trump: Won't Wear a Coronavirus Mask Because It Would Interfere with Foreign Leader Meetings*, 4 Apr. 2020, www.usatoday.com/story/news/politics/2020/04/03/coronavirus-trump-wont-wear-mask-because-foreign-leader-meetings/2945378001/

33 Ibid.

34 Watson, Kathryn. "Pence Forgoes a Face Mask at Mayo Clinic, Appearing to Violate Policy." *CBS News*, CBS Interactive, 29 Apr. 2020, www.cbsnews.com/news/mike-pence-face-mask-mayo-clinic-visit/.

35 Ibid.

36 Fieldstadt, Elisha. "Ohio Lawmaker Refuses to Wear Mask Because He Says It Dishonors God." *NBCNews.com*, NBCUniversal News Group, 7 May 2020, www.nbcnews.com/news/us-news/ohio-lawmaker-refuses-wear-mask-because-he-says-it-dishonors-n1201106.

37 Ibid.

38 Covid19 impact survey. (n.d.). Retrieved from https://covid19impactsurvey.org/

39 "US & Canada." *BBC News*, BBC, 2020, www.bbc.com/news/world/us_and_canada

40 Ibid.

41 Wingrove, Josh. "Trump Tells Three Democratic States to Liberate Themselves." *Bloomberg.com*, Bloomberg, 18 Apr. 2020, www.bloomberg.com/news/articles/2020-04-17/trump-tells-three-democratic-states-to-liberate-themselves.

42 "Coronavirus: Boris Johnson 'Responding to Treatment' in Intensive Care." *BBC News*, BBC, 8 Apr. 2020, www.bbc.com/news/uk-52208156.

43 "Masks Become a Flash Point for Protests and Fights as Businesses Beaches and Parks Reopen." *Masks Become a Flash Point for Protests and Fights as Businesses, Beaches, and Parks Reopen*, 5 May 2020, www.msn.com/en-us/news/us/masks-become-a-flash-point-for-protests-and-fights-as-businesses-beaches-and-parks-reopen/ar-BB13C7VU.

44 Ibid.

45 Ibid.

46 Ibid.

47 Ibid.

48 Ibid.

49 Ibid.

50 *Proclamation on Suspension of Entry as Immigrants And Nonimmigrants of Persons Who Pose a Risk of Transmitting 2019 Novel Coronavirus*. www.whitehouse.gov/presidential-actions/proclamation-suspension-entry-immigrants-nonimmigrants-persons-pose-risk-transmitting-2019-novel-coronavirus/.

51 Riess, Rebekah. "Protesters Pour into Michigan Capitol Calling for End of State of Emergency." *CNN*, Cable News Network, 1 May 2020, www.cnn.com/2020/04/30/us/michigan-stay-at-home-protest/index.html.

52. "Whitmer Says This Week's Protests Depicted Racism–CNN Video." *CNN*, Cable News Network, 3 May 2020, www.cnn.com/videos/politics/2020/05/03/sotu-whitmer-full.cnn.
53. "Andrew Cuomo New York COVID-19 Briefing Transcript May 4." *Rev*, 6 May 2020,
54. "Mike Pence's Press Secretary Is Second White House Staffer to Test Positive for Covid-19 This Week." *The Guardian*, Guardian News and Media, 9 May 2020, www.theguardian.com/world/2020/may/08/coronavirus-outbreak-us-trump-pence-press-secretary.
55. Collins, Kaitlan. "One of Trump's Personal Valets Has Tested Positive for Coronavirus." *CNN*, Cable News Network, 7 May 2020, www.cnn.com/2020/05/07/politics/trump-valet-tests-positive-covid-19/index.html..
56. "Mike Pence's Press Secretary Is Second White House Staffer to Test Positive for Covid-19 This Week." *The Guardian*, Guardian News and Media, 9 May 2020, www.theguardian.com/world/2020/may/08/coronavirus-outbreak-us-trump-pence-press-secretary.
57. Ibid.
58. Mettler, Katie, et al. "Trump Declares That the U.S. Has 'Prevailed' with Testing; White House Officials Will Wear Masks." *The Washington Post*, WP Company, 12 May 2020, www.washingtonpost.com/nation/2020/05/11/coronavirus-update-us/.
59. Ibid.
60. Ibid.
61. Walters, Joanna. "Donald Trump Goes without Mask at Michigan Ford Plant despite Company Request." *The Guardian*, Guardian News and Media, 22 May 2020, www.theguardian.com/us-news/2020/may/21/trump-ford-factory-mask-michigan.
62. Ibid.
63. Gregorian, Dareh. "Trump Wears Mask with Presidential Seal during Part of Ford Plant Tour." *NBCNews.com*, NBCUniversal News Group, 22 May 2020, www.nbcnews.com/politics/donald-trump/trump-refuses-wear-mask-front-cameras-during-ford-tour-n1212466.
64. Ibid.
65. Guzman, Joseph. "Michigan AG Could 'Take Action' against Companies That Let Trump Visit without Mask." *TheHill*, 21 May 2020, thehill.com/changing-america/well-being/prevention-cures/499029-michigan-ag-could-take-action-against-companies.

CHAPTER 20

1. Coaston, Jane. "Why Coronavirus Conspiracy Theories Have Spread so Quickly." *Vox*, Vox, 13 Apr. 2020, www.vox.com/2020/4/13/21205833/coronavirus-pandemic-conspiracy-theories.
2. Ibid.
3. Ibid.
4. Ibid.
5. "Fake News Is Fooling More Conservatives than Liberals. Why?" *The Economist*, The Economist Newspaper, 3 June 2020, www.economist.com/international/2020/06/03/fake-news-is-fooling-more-conservatives-than-liberals-why?utm_campaign=coronavirus-special-edition&utm_medium=newsletter&utm_source=salesforce-marketing-cloud&utm_term=2020-06-06&utm_content=article-link-6.
6. Id.

7   Id.
8   Id.
9   Id.
10 Id.
11 "Trump: Coronavirus Will Have 'a Very Good Ending for Us'." *POLITICO*, 30 Jan. 2020, www.politico.com/news/2020/01/30/trump-close-cooperation-china-coronavirus-109701.
12 Levin, Bess. "Trump Claims Coronavirus Will 'Miraculously' Go Away by April." *Vanity Fair*, Vanity Fair, 11 Feb. 2020, www.vanityfair.com/news/2020/02/donald-trump-coronavirus-warm-weather..
13 Bump, Philip. "Analysis | Trump Again Downplays Coronavirus by Comparing It to the Seasonal Flu. It's Not a Fair Comparison." *The Washington Post*, WP Company, 24 Mar. 2020, www.washingtonpost.com/politics/2020/03/24/trump-again-downplays-coronavirus-by-comparing-it-seasonal-flu-its-not-fair-comparison/.
14 Ibid.
15 Ibid.
16 Krugman, Paul. "The Right Sends In the Quacks." *The New York Times*, The New York Times, 21 Apr. 2020, www.nytimes.com/2020/04/20/opinion/coronavirus-conservatives.html.
17 Johnson, Timothy. "Alex Jones Won't Stop Suggesting the Supplements He Sells Provide a Benefit against the Novel Coronavirus." *Media Matters for America*, www.mediamatters.org/coronavirus-covid-19/alex-jones-wont-stop-suggesting-supplements-he-sells-provide-benefit-against.
18 Ibid.
19 Ibid.
20 Bump, Philip. "Analysis | Trump and Fox Went All-in on a Coronavirus Silver Bullet. But Maybe the Wrong One." *The Washington Post*, WP Company, 19 Apr. 2020, www.washingtonpost.com/politics/2020/04/19/trump-fox-went-all-in-coronavirus-cure-what-if-they-picked-wrong-one/.
21 Ibid.
22 Ibid.
23 Kaplan, Talia. "Pence: FDA Approving 'off-Label' Use for Hydroxychloroquine to Help Coronavirus Patients." *Fox News*, FOX News Network, 24 Mar. 2020, www.foxnews.com/media/pence-fda-hydroxychloroquine-off-label-coronavirus.
24 Eban, Katherine. "'Really Want to Flood NY and NJ': Internal Documents Reveal Team Trump's Chloroquine Master Plan." *Vanity Fair*, Apr. 2020, www.vanityfair.com/news/2020/04/internal-documents-reveal-team-trumps-chloroquine-master-plan/
25 Ibid.
26 Ibid.
27 Ibid.
28 Ibid.
29 Ibid.
30 Kaplan, Talia. "Pence: FDA Approving 'off-Label' Use for Hydroxychloroquine to Help Coronavirus Patients." *Fox News*, FOX News Network, 24 Mar. 2020, www.foxnews.com/media/pence-fda-hydroxychloroquine-off-label-coronavirus.
31 Ibid.
32 Ibid.

33. Tucker, Emma. "Laura Ingraham, Fox Guests Met With Trump at White House to Tout Unproven COVID-19 Drug: WaPo." *The Daily Beast*, The Daily Beast Company, 7 Apr. 2020, www.thedailybeast.com/laura-ingraham-fox-guests-met-with-trump-to-tout-unproven-covid-19-drug-hydroxychloroquine-report-says.

34. Ibid.

35. Ibid.

36. "Why Trump Silenced Fauci on Hydroxychloroquine." *CCN.com*, 8 May 2020, www.ccn.com/why-trump-silenced-fauci-on-hydroxychloroquine/.

37. Baker, Peter, et al. "Trump's Aggressive Advocacy of Malaria Drug for Treating Coronavirus Divides Medical Community." *The New York Times*, The New York Times, 6 Apr. 2020, www.nytimes.com/2020/04/06/us/politics/coronavirus-trump-malaria-drug.html.

38. Servick, Kelly, and Amanda Heidt. "Antimalarials Widely Used against COVID-19 Heighten Risk of Cardiac Arrest. How Can Doctors Minimize the Danger?" *Science*, 21 Apr. 2020, www.sciencemag.org/news/2020/04/antimalarials-widely-used-against-covid-19-heighten-risk-cardiac-arrest-how-can-doctors.

39. Ibid.

40. Rowland, Christopher. "Anti-Malarial Drug Trump Touted Is Linked to Higher Rates of Death in VA Coronavirus Patients, Study Says." *The Washington Post*, WP Company, 21 Apr. 2020, www.washingtonpost.com/business/2020/04/21/anti-malarial-drug-trump-touted-is-linked-higher-rates-death-va-coronavirus-patients-study-says/.

41. Servick, Kelly, and Amanda Heidt. "Antimalarials Widely Used against COVID-19 Heighten Risk of Cardiac Arrest. How Can Doctors Minimize the Danger?" *Science*, 21 Apr. 2020, www.sciencemag.org/news/2020/04/antimalarials-widely-used-against-covid-19-heighten-risk-cardiac-arrest-how-can-doctors.

42. Kreiter, Marcy. "The Latest On Hydroxychloroquine Treatment For Coronavirus: Lancet Study Concludes It's Dangerous, Not Effective." *International Business Times*, 22 May 2020, www.ibtimes.com/latest-hydroxychloroquine-treatment-coronavirus-lancet-study-concludes-its-dangerous-2980958.

43. Ibid.

44. Ibid.

45. "Authors Retract Hydroxychloroquine Study, Citing Concern Over Data." *Nevada Public Radio*, knpr.org/npr/2020-06/authors-retract-hydroxychloroquine-study-citing-concern-over-data.

46. Nadi, Aliza. "'Lifesaving' Lupus Drug in Short Supply after Trump Touts Possible Coronavirus Treatment." *NBCNews.com*, NBCUniversal News Group, 24 Mar. 2020, www.nbcnews.com/news/us-news/lifesaving-lupus-drug-short-supply-after-trump-touts-possible-coronavirus-n1166981.

47. Grynbaum, Michael M. "Fox News Stars Trumpeted a Malaria Drug, Until They Didn't." *The New York Times*, The New York Times, 22 Apr. 2020, www.nytimes.com/2020/04/22/business/media/virus-fox-news-hydroxychloroquine.html.

48. Ibid.

49. Ibid.

50. Ibid.

51. Ibid.

52. Ibid.

53 Grynbaum, Michael M. "Health Dept. Official Says Doubts on Hydroxychloroquine Led to His Ouster." *The New York Times*, The New York Times, 23 Apr. 2020, www.nytimes.com/2020/04/22/us/politics/rick-bright-trump-hydroxychloroquine-coronavirus.html.

54 Ibid.

55 Ibid.

56 Broad, William J, and Dan Levin. "Trump Muses About Light as Remedy, but Also Disinfectant, Which Is Dangerous." *The New York Times*, The New York Times, 24 Apr. 2020, www.nytimes.com/2020/04/24/health/sunlight-coronavirus-trump.html.

57 Ibid.

58 Ibid.

59 Ibid.

60 Ibid.

61 Ibid.

62 Ibid.

63 Neuman, Scott. "Man Dies, Woman Hospitalized After Taking Form Of Chloroquine To Prevent COVID-19." *NPR*, NPR, 24 Mar. 2020, www.npr.org/sections/coronavirus-live-updates/2020/03/24/820512107/man-dies-woman-hospitalized-after-taking-form-of-chloroquine-to-prevent-covid-19.

64 Ibid

CHAPTER 21

1 Owoseje, Toyin. "Coronavirus Is 'the Great Equalizer,' Madonna Tells Fans from Her Bathtub." *CNN*, Cable News Network, 23 Mar. 2020, https://www.cnn.com/2020/03/23/entertainment/madonna-coronavirus-video-intl-scli/index.html

2 "COVID-19 Deaths Analyzed by Race and Ethnicity." *APM Research Lab*, https://www.apmresearchlab.org/covid/deaths-by-race

3 Ibid.

4 Ibid.

5 Reid, Kaydian. "Why the Coronavirus Hits Harder in Communities of Color." *Courant.com*, Hartford Courant, 1 May 2020, https://www.courant.com/opinion/op-ed/hc-op-reid-coronavirus-race-0503-20200502-ysyomu6r2fevvdu23ou5jcw7ty-story.html

6 Fears, Darryl. "Kizzmekia Corbett Spent Her Life Preparing for This Moment. Can She Create the Vaccine to End a Pandemic?" *The Washington Post*, WP Company, 6 May 2020, www.washingtonpost.com/climate-environment/2020/05/06/kizzmekia-corbett-vaccine-coronavirus/

7 Levenson, Eric. "Why Black Americans Are at Higher Risk for Coronavirus." *CNN*, Cable News Network, 8 Apr. 2020, www.cnn.com/2020/04/07/us/coronavirus-black-americans-race/index.html.

8 "It's No Surprise the Coronavirus Is Hitting African Americans Harder." *U.S. News & World Report*, U.S. News & World Report, www.usnews.com/news/healthiest-communities/articles/2020-04-20/its-no-surprise-coronavirus-is-hitting-african-americans-harder.

9 "Milwaukee County Circuit Court." *Milwaukee County Courts | Milwaukee County Circuit Court System*, county.milwaukee.gov/EN/Courts..

10. Williams, J. "Black People Are Disproportionately Getting and Dying from COVID-19." *US News*, 7 Apr. 2020, https://www.usnews.com/news/healthiest-communities/articles/2020-04-07/black-people-are-disproportionately-dying-from-coronavirus.
11. Ibid.
12. Aguilar, Louis, et al. "Black Communities Hit Harder by Coronavirus in Michigan, Not Just Detroit." *Bridge Magazine*, 1 May 2020, www.bridgemi.com/michigan-health-watch/black-communities-hit-harder-coronavirus-michigan-not-just-detroit.
13. Dwyer, Colin. "New York City's Latinx Residents Hit Hardest By Coronavirus Deaths." *NPR*, NPR, 8 Apr. 2020, www.npr.org/2020/04/08/829726964/new-york-citys-latinx-residents-hit-hardest-by-coronavirus-deaths.
14. "As Experts Feared, Black People Are Disproportionately Getting and Dying From COVID-19." *U.S. News & World Report*, U.S. News & World Report, 2020, www.usnews.com/news/healthiest-communities/articles/2020-04-07/black-people-are-disproportionately-dying-from-coronavirus.
15. Nagle, Rebecca. "Native Americans Being Left out of US Coronavirus Data and Labelled as 'Other'." *The Guardian*, Guardian News and Media, 24 Apr. 2020, www.theguardian.com/us-news/2020/apr/24/us-native-americans-left-out-coronavirus-data.
16. Ibid.
17. Ibid.
18. Ibid.
19. *Covid-19 Deaths by Race/Ethnicity Group*. NYC Health, 6 Apr. 2020, www1.nyc.gov/assets/doh/downloads/pdf/imm/covid-19-deaths-race-ethnicity-04082020-1.pdf.
20. Picheta, Rob. "Black People Four Times More Likely to Die from Covid-19 than White People, New UK Data Shows." *CNN*, Cable News Network, 7 May 2020, www.cnn.com/2020/05/07/uk/uk-coronavirus-ethnicity-deaths-ons-scli-gbr-intl/index.html.
21. http://ldh.la.gov/assets/media/AccesstoCareReport20132018final.pdf
22. Picheta, Rob. "Black People Four Times More Likely to Die from Covid-19 than White People, New UK Data Shows." *CNN*, Cable News Network, 7 May 2020, www.cnn.com/2020/05/07/uk/uk-coronavirus-ethnicity-deaths-ons-scli-gbr-intl/index.html.
23. "Office of Minority Health." *Home Page–Office of Minority Health (OMH)*, www.minorityhealth.hhs.gov/omh/browse.aspx.
24. Kolata, Gina. "Black Americans Are Living Longer, C.D.C. Reports." *The New York Times*, The New York Times, 2 May 2017, www.nytimes.com/2017/05/02/health/black-americans-death-rate-cdc-study.html.
25. Ibid.
26. Ibid.
27. Nagle, Rebecca. "Native Americans Being Left out of US Coronavirus Data and Labelled as 'Other'." *The Guardian*, Guardian News and Media, 24 Apr. 2020, www.theguardian.com/us-news/2020/apr/24/us-native-americans-left-out-coronavirus-data.
28. Ibid.
29. Cineas, Fabiola. "Covid-19 Is Disproportionately Taking Black Lives." *Vox*, Vox, 7 Apr. 2020, www.vox.com/identities/2020/4/7/21211849/coronavirus-black-americans.
30. Ibid.

31 Farmer, B. "The Coronavirus Doesn't Discriminate, But U.S. Health Care Showing Familiar Biases." *NPR*, 2 Apr. 2020, https://www.npr.org/sections/health-shots/2020/04/02/825730141/the-coronavirus-doesnt-discriminate-but-u-s-health-care-showing-familiar-biases.

32 Eligon, John, et al. "Black Americans Face Alarming Rates of Coronavirus Infection in Some States." *The New York Times*, The New York Times, 7 Apr. 2020, www.nytimes.com/2020/04/07/us/coronavirus-race.html. *See also*; Farmer, Blake. "Long-Standing Racial and Income Disparities Seen Creeping into COVID-19 Care." *Modern Healthcare*, Nashville Public Radio, 6 Apr. 2020, www.modernhealthcare.com/safety-quality/long-standing-racial-and-income-disparities-seen-creeping-covid-19-care?utm_source=modern-healthcare-covid-19-coverage&utm_medium=email&utm_campaign=20200406&utm_content=article3-headline.

33 Kertscher, Tom. "PolitiFact–Melanin Doesn't Protect against Coronavirus." *@Politifact*, 10 Mar. 2020, www.politifact.com/factchecks/2020/mar/10/facebook-posts/melanin-doesnt-protect-against-coronavirus/.

34 "Africans in America/Part 3/The Yellow Fever Epidemic." *PBS*, Public Broadcasting Service, www.pbs.org/wgbh/aia/part3/3p1590.html.

35 Ibid.

36 Eligon, John, et al. "Black Americans Face Alarming Rates of Coronavirus Infection in Some States." *The New York Times*, The New York Times, 7 Apr. 2020, www.nytimes.com/2020/04/07/us/coronavirus-race.html.

37 Eligon, John, et al. "Black Americans Face Alarming Rates of Coronavirus Infection in Some States." *The New York Times*, The New York Times, 7 Apr. 2020, www.nytimes.com/2020/04/07/us/coronavirus-race.html.

38 Ibid.

39 Ibid.

40 Ibid.

41 Ibid.

42 Ibid.

43 McMinn, Sean, et al. "In Large Texas Cities, Access To Coronavirus Testing May Depend On Where You Live." *NPR*, NPR, 27 May 2020, www.npr.org/sections/health-shots/2020/05/27/862215848/across-texas-black-and-hispanic-neighborhoods-have-fewer-coronavirus-testing-sit.

44 Ibid.

45 Ibid

46 "COVID-19 in Racial and Ethnic Minority Groups." *Centers for Disease Control and Prevention*, Centers for Disease Control and Prevention, 4 June 2020, www.cdc.gov/coronavirus/2019-ncov/need-extra-precautions/racial-ethnic-minorities.html.

47 Dwyer, Colin. "New York City's Latinx Residents Hit Hardest By Coronavirus Deaths." *NPR*, NPR, 8 Apr. 2020, www.npr.org/2020/04/08/829726964/new-york-citys-latinx-residents-hit-hardest-by-coronavirus-deaths.

48 Holmes, Kristen, and Kevin Bohn. *Azar Lays Part of Blame for Covid-19 Death Toll on State of Americans' Health*, 18 May 2020, www.msn.com/en-us/news/us/azar-lays-part-of-blame-for-covid-19-death-toll-on-state-of-americans-health/ar-BB14dsjU?ocid=spartandhp.

49 Ibid.

50 Ibid.

51. Fears, Darryl. "Kizzmekia Corbett Spent Her Life Preparing for This Moment. Can She Create the Vaccine to End a Pandemic?" *The Washington Post*, WP Company, 6 May 2020, www.washingtonpost.com/climate-environment/2020/05/06/kizzmekia-corbett-vaccine-coronavirus/.
52. Ibid.
53. Ibid.
54. Saxena, Vivek. "Scientist Spearheading Coronavirus Vaccine Has Been Launching Some Troubling Racially Charged Tweets." *Conservative News Today*, 18 Apr. 2020, www.bizpacreview.com/2020/04/18/scientist-spearheading-coronavirus-vaccine-has-been-launching-some-troubling-racially-charged-tweets-909959.
55. Ibid.
56. Ibid.
57. Fears, Darryl. "Kizzmekia Corbett Spent Her Life Preparing for This Moment. Can She Create the Vaccine to End a Pandemic?" *The Washington Post*, WP Company, 6 May 2020, www.washingtonpost.com/climate-environment/2020/05/06/kizzmekia-corbett-vaccine-coronavirus/.
58. Cineas, Fabiola. "Covid-19 Is Disproportionately Taking Black Lives." *Vox*, Vox, 7 Apr. 2020, www.vox.com/identities/2020/4/7/21211849/coronavirus-black-americans.

CHAPTER 22

1. "Text Of Bush Speech." *CBS News*, CBS Interactive, 5 Jan. 2003, www.cbsnews.com/news/text-of-bush-speech-01-05-2003/.
2. "White House Pressed on 'Mission Accomplished' Sign." *CNN*, Cable News Network, 28 Oct. 2003, us.cnn.com/2003/ALLPOLITICS/10/28/mission.accomplished/.
3. Bergen, Peter. "Time to Fire Jared and Ivanka." *CNN*, Cable News Network, 17 Apr. 2020, www.cnn.com/2020/04/16/opinions/fire-ivanka-and-jared-passover-travel-bergen/index.html.
4. Cahill, Petra. "Trump Pushes Country to Reopen despite Risks as Coronavirus Task Force Winds Down." *NBCNews.com*, NBCUniversal News Group, 6 May 2020, www.nbcnews.com/news/morning-briefing/trump-pushes-country-reopen-despite-risks-coronavirus-task-force-winds-n1201096.
5. "Trump Says 'We Have Prevailed,' as Memo Tells White House Staffers to Wear Masks." *NBCNews.com*, NBCUniversal News Group, 12 May 2020, www.nbcnews.com/health/health-news/blog/2020-05-11-coronavirus-news-n1204156.
6. *At Senate Hearing, Government Experts Paint Bleak Picture of the Pandemic*, 12 May 2020, www.msn.com/en-us/news/politics/at-senate-hearing-government-experts-paint-bleak-picture-of-the-pandemic/ar-BB13ZkwI.
7. Haberman, Maggie, and Michael D. Shear. "White House Races to Contain Virus in Its Ranks: 'It Is Scary to Go to Work'." *The New York Times*, The New York Times, 10 May 2020, www.nytimes.com/2020/05/10/us/politics/white-house-coronavirus-trump.html?action=click&module=Top%2BStories&pgtype=Homepage.
8. Baker, Peter, and Michael Crowley. "Two White House Coronavirus Cases Raise Question of If Anyone Is Really Safe." *The New York Times*, The New York Times, 8 May 2020, www.nytimes.com/2020/05/08/us/politics/white-house-coronavirus-safety.html.
9. Ibid.

CHAPTER 23

1. McMahon, Jeff. "New Data Show Air Pollution Drop Around 50 Percent In Some Cities During Coronavirus Lockdown." *Forbes*, Forbes Magazine, 17 Apr. 2020, www.forbes.com/sites/jeffmcmahon/2020/04/16/air-pollution-drop-surpasses-50-percent-in-some-cities-during-coronavirus-lockdown/.

2. "Paris Climate Deal: US and China Formally Join Pact." *BBC News*, BBC, 3 Sept. 2016, www.bbc.com/news/world-asia-china-37265541.

3. Ibid.

4. Ibid.

5. Deverian, Joe. "President Obama Bypasses Congress By Formally Committing U.S. to Paris Climate Agreement." *American Legislative Exchange Council*, American Legislative Exchange Council, 22 Sept. 2016, www.alec.org/article/president-obama-bypasses-congress-by-formally-committing-u-s-to-paris-climate-agreement/.

6. "MEPs call for Trump to dump the Paris climate deal". Roger Helmer. April 20, 2017..

7. Samuelsohn, Darren. "Fact: Trump Claimed Climate Change Is a Hoax Created by China." *POLITICO*, 27 Sept. 2016, www.politico.com/blogs/2016-presidential-debate-fact-check/2016/09/fact-trump-claimed-climate-change-is-a-hoax-created-by-china-228711.

8. Guskin, Emily. "Analysis | By the Numbers, Trump's Big Environmental Regulation Rollback Is All Kinds of Unpopular." *The Washington Post*, WP Company, 29 Mar. 2017, www.washingtonpost.com/news/the-fix/wp/2017/03/29/trumps-rollback-of-obamas-environmental-legacy-is-all-kinds-of-unpopular/.

9. Schupak, Amanda. "A Doctor Explains Why The Solutions To Coronavirus And Climate Change Are The Same." *HuffPost*, HuffPost, 28 May 2020, www.huffpost.com/entry/why-solutions-coronavirus-climate-change-same_n_5e908f19c5b6260471e0d840.

10. Ibid.

11. "Link between Air Pollution and Coronavirus Deaths in England, Study Suggests." *The National*, The National, 21 Apr. 2020, www.thenational.scot/news/uk-news/18394027.link-air-pollution-coronavirus-deaths-england-study-suggests/.

12. Ibid.

13. Ibid.

14. Friedman, Lisa. "New Research Links Air Pollution to Higher Coronavirus Death Rates." *The New York Times*, The New York Times, 7 Apr. 2020, www.nytimes.com/2020/04/07/climate/air-pollution-coronavirus-covid.html.

15. Ibid.

16. McGrath, Matt. "Coronavirus: Air Pollution and CO2 Fall Rapidly as Virus Spreads." *BBC News*, BBC, 19 Mar. 2020, www.bbc.com/news/science-environment-51944780.

17. Davidson, Jordan. "Amazon Deforestation Is Causing 20% of Forests to Release More Carbon Than They Absorb." *EcoWatch*, EcoWatch, 12 Feb. 2020, www.ecowatch.com/amazon-deforestation-carbon-emissions-2645127492.html.see also Newberger, Emma. "Habitat Destruction, Deforestation, Pandemics: CNBC." *Habitat Destruction, Deforestation, Pandemics: CNBC | YaleGlobal Online*, 12 May 2020, yaleglobal.yale.edu/content/habitat-destruction-deforestation-pandemics-cnbc.

18. Zee, Renate van der. "How Amsterdam Became the Bicycle Capital of the World." *The Guardian*, Guardian News and Media, 5 May 2015, www.theguardian.com/cities/2015/may/05/amsterdam-bicycle-capital-world-transport-cycling-kindermoord.

19. Simon, Matt. "How Is the Coronavirus Pandemic Affecting Climate Change?" *Wired*, Conde Nast, www.wired.com/story/coronavirus-pandemic-climate-change/.
20. Ibid.
21. Ibid.

CHAPTER 24

1. Lakhani, Nina. "US Coronavirus Hotspots Linked to Meat Processing Plants." *The Guardian*, Guardian News and Media, 15 May 2020, www.theguardian.com/world/2020/may/15/us-coronavirus-meat-packing-plants-food.
2. Ibid.
3. Ibid.
4. "Coronavirus in the U.S.: Latest Map and Case Count." *The New York Times*, The New York Times, 3 Mar. 2020, www.nytimes.com/interactive/2020/us/coronavirus-us-cases.html.
5. Lakhani, Nina. "US Coronavirus Hotspots Linked to Meat Processing Plants." *The Guardian*, Guardian News and Media, 15 May 2020, www.theguardian.com/world/2020/may/15/us-coronavirus-meat-packing-plants-food.
6. Friedman, Scott, and Jack Douglas. "Official Confirms More Than 200 COVID-19 Cases at North Texas Meat Plant." *NBC 5 Dallas-Fort Worth*, NBC 5 Dallas-Fort Worth, 27 May 2020, www.nbcdfw.com/investigations/official-confirms-more-than-200-covid-19-cases-at-north-texas-meat-plant/2377391/.
7. Lakhani, Nina. "US Coronavirus Hotspots Linked to Meat Processing Plants." *The Guardian*, Guardian News and Media, 15 May 2020, www.theguardian.com/world/2020/may/15/us-coronavirus-meat-packing-plants-food.
8. Ibid.
9. Ibid.
10. Douglas, Leah. "Mapping Covid-19 Outbreaks in the Food System." *Food and Environment Reporting Network*, 19 June 2020, thefern.org/2020/04/mapping-covid-19-in-meat-and-food-processing-plants/.
11. Ibid.
12. Ibid.
13. Ibid.
14. Dorning, Mike. "Thirty Workers, Four USDA Inspectors Dead Amid Meat Plant Coronavirus Outbreaks." *Time*, 14 May 2020, https://time.com/5836973/usda-inspector-meat-workers-dead-coronavirus/.
15. Otter, Chris. "The Vital City: Public Analysis, Dairies and Slaughterhouses in Nineteenth-Century Britain." *Cultural Geographies*, vol. 13, no. 4, 2006, pp. 517–537. JSTOR, www.jstor.org/stable/44251124. Accessed 25 June 2020.
16. Ibid.
17. "Humane Methods of Slaughter Act." *Animal Welfare Institute*, https://awionline.org/content/humane-methods-slaughter-act. Accessed 29 May 2020.
18. "Part I: The 1906 Food and Drugs Act and Its Enforcement." *U.S. Food and Drug Administration*, FDA, www.fda.gov/about-fda/fdas-evolving-regulatory-powers/part-i-1906-food-and-drugs-act-and-its-enforcement.

19 "United States Department of Labor." *Home | Occupational Safety and Health Administration*, www.osha.gov/.
20 Lowe, Peggy. "Working 'The Chain,' Slaughterhouse Workers Face Lifelong Injuries." *NPR*, NPR, 11 Aug. 2016, www.npr.org/sections/thesalt/2016/08/11/489468205/working-the-chain-slaughterhouse-workers-face-lifelong-injuries.
21 Wasley, Andrew. "Two Amputations a Week: the Cost of Working in a US Meat Plant." *The Guardian*, 5 July 2018, www.theguardian.com/environment/2018/jul/05/amputations-serious-injuries-us-meat-industry-plant.
22 Lewis, Cora. "America's Largest Meat Producer Averages One Amputation Per Month." *Buzzfeed News*, 18 Feb. 2018, https://www.buzzfeednews.com/article/coralewis/americas-largest-meat-producer-one-amputation-per-month#.pxxm3zY5Z.
23 Lakhani, Nina. "US Coronavirus Hotspots Linked to Meat Processing Plants." *The Guardian*, 15 May 2020, https://www.theguardian.com/world/2020/may/15/us-coronavirus-meat-packing-plants-food.
24 Wasley, Andrew, and Alexandra Heal. "Revealed: Shocking Safety Record of UK Meat Plants." *The Bureau of Investigative Journalism*, The Bureau of Investigative Journalism, 30 July 2018, www.thebureauinvestigates.com/stories/2018-07-29/uk-meat-plant-injuries.
25 Nagesh, Ashitha. "The Harrowing Psychological Toll of Slaughterhouse Work." *Metro*, 22 Jan. 2018, metro.co.uk/2017/12/31/how-killing-animals-everyday-leaves-slaughterhouse-workers-traumatised-7175087/; see also Lebwohl, Michael. "A Call to Action: Psychological Harm in Slaughterhouse Workers." *Yale Global Health Review*, 25 Jan. 2016, yaleglobalhealthreview.com/2016/01/25/a-call-to-action-psychological-harm-in-slaughterhouse-workers/.
26 Iulietto, Maria Francesca, et al. "Noise Assessment in Slaughterhouses by Means of a Smartphone App." *Italian Journal on Food Safety*, vol. 7, no. 2, 2018, doi:10.4081/ijfs.2018.7053.
27 Baran, Benjamin E., et al. "Routinized Killing of Animals: Going beyond Dirty Work and Prestige to Understand the Well-Being of Slaughterhouse Workers." *Organization*, vol. 23, no. 3, May 2016, pp. 351–369, doi:10.1177/1350508416629456.
28 Dorovskikh, Anna. "Killing for a Living: Psychological and Physiological Effects of Alienation of Food Production On Slaughterhouse Workers." *Undergraduate Honors Thesis, University of Colorado Boulder*, 2015, scholar.colorado.edu/concern/undergraduate_honors_theses/mp48sd395.
29 Fitzgerald, Amy J., et al. "Slaughterhouses and Increased Crime Rates: An Empirical Analysis of the Spillover From 'The Jungle' Into the Surrounding Community." *Organization & Environment*, vol. 22, no. 2, June 2009, pp. 158–184, doi:10.1177/1086026609338164.
30 Waldman, Peter. "America's Worst Graveyard Shift Is Grinding Up Workers." *Bloomberg Businessweek*, 29 Dec. 2017, https://www.bloomberg.com/news/features/2017-12-29/america-s-worst-graveyard-shift-is-grinding-up-workers.
31 Grabell, Michael. "Exploitation and Abuse at the Chicken Plant." *The New Yorker*, 1 May 2017, https://www.newyorker.com/magazine/2017/05/08/exploitation-and-abuse-at-the-chicken-plant.
32 Human Rights Watch, 2010, *Human Rights Watch Work on Abuses against Migrants in 2010*, www.hrw.org/report/2010/12/11/rights-line/human-rights-watch-work-abuses-against-migrants-2010#.
33 "Lives on the Line: The High Human Cost of Chicken." *Oxfam America*, 23 May 2018, www.oxfamamerica.org/livesontheline/.
34 Nabhan-Warren, Kristy. "Coronavirus Pandemic Shines a Light on the Risks Meatpackers Are Facing." *USA Today*, Gannett Satellite Information Network, 24 Apr. 2020, www.usatoday.com/story/opin-

ion/2020/04/24/coronavirus-pandemic-makes-meatpacking-more-dangerous-than-we-thought-column/3006430001/.

35 Ibid.

36 Fremstad, S. et al. "Meatpacking Workers are a Diverse Group Who Need Better Protections." *CEPR*, 29 Apr. 2020, https://cepr.net/meatpacking-workers-are-a-diverse-group-who-need-better-protections/.

37 Ibid.

38 Nabhan-Warren, Kristy. "Coronavirus Pandemic Shines a Light on the Risks Meatpackers Are Facing." *USA Today*, Gannett Satellite Information Network, 24 Apr. 2020, www.usatoday.com/story/opinion/2020/04/24/coronavirus-pandemic-makes-meatpacking-more-dangerous-than-we-thought-column/3006430001/.

39 Honig, Esther, and Ted Genoways. "'The Workers Are Being Sacrificed': As Cases Mounted, Meatpacker JBS Kept People on Crowded Factory Floors." *Mother Jones*, 1 May 2020, www.motherjones.com/food/2020/05/meatpacking-coronavirus-workers-factory-jbs-tyson-smithfield-covid-crisis-sacrifice-outbreaks-beef/.

40 "51-3023 Slaughterers and Meat Packers." *U.S. Bureau of Labor Statistics*, U.S. Bureau of Labor Statistics, 31 Mar. 2020, www.bls.gov/Oes/current/oes513023.htm.

41 Honig, Esther, and Ted Genoways. "'The Workers Are Being Sacrificed': As Cases Mounted, Meatpacker JBS Kept People on Crowded Factory Floors." *Mother Jones*, 1 May 2020, www.motherjones.com/food/2020/05/meatpacking-coronavirus-workers-factory-jbs-tyson-smithfield-covid-crisis-sacrifice-outbreaks-beef/.

42 Ibid.

43 Feuer, William. "CDC Says 3% of Workers in Surveyed Meat Processing Plants Tested Positive for Coronavirus." *CNBC*, CNBC, 1 May 2020, www.cnbc.com/2020/05/01/coronavirus-cdc-says-3-percent-of-workers-in-surveyed-meat-processing-plants-infected.html.

44 Ibid.

45 Ibid.

46 Ibid.

47 Ibid.

48 Faulkner, Abby. "Pilgrim's Pride Workers Hold Walkout Over Coronavirus Fears." *AM 1240 and FM 95.3 WJON*, 29 Apr. 2020, wjon.com/pilgrims-pride-workers-hold-walkout-over-coronavirus-fears/.

49 Hughlett, M. "Jennie-O temporarily closes Melrose turkey processing plant." *StarTribune*, 29 Apr. 2020, https://www.startribune.com/jennie-o-temporarily-closes-melrose-turkey-processing-plant/570059752/.

50 Swanson, A. & Yaffe-Bellany, D. "Trump Declares Meat Supply 'Critical,' Aiming to Reopen Plants." *The New York Times*, 28 Apr. 2020, https://nyti.ms/2YaymWS.

51 Hartman, Mitchell. "COVID-19 Exposes U.S. Meat Supply's Dependence on a Few Large Plants." *Marketplace*, 7 May 2020, www.marketplace.org/2020/05/06/covid-19-meat-shortages-processing-plants-grocery-stores/.

52 Ibid.

53 Corkery, Michael. "Powerful Meat Industry Holds More Sway After Trump's Order." *The New York Times*, 29 Apr. 2020, nyti.ms/3bOtJWh.

54 Colwell, A. "Workers, officials say too little too late after Tyson closes Waterloo pork plant: 'All they talked about was production'." *CNN*, 23 Apr. 2020, https://www.cnn.com/2020/04/22/us/tyson-waterloo-iowa-plant-employees-coronavirus/index.html.

55 Ibid.

56 Ibid.

57 Ibid.

58 Ibid.

59 Dickerson, Caitlin & Jordan, Miriam. "South Dakota Meat Plant Is Now Country's Biggest Coronavirus Hot Spot." *The New York Times*, 15 Apr. 2020, https://nyti.ms/2VxCNYL.

60 Ibid.

61 Ibid.

62 Swanson, A. & Yaffe-Bellany, D. "Trump Declares Meat Supply 'Critical,' Aiming to Reopen Plants." *The New York Times*, 28 Apr. 2020, https://nyti.ms/2YaymWS.

63 Ordonez, F. "Trump Signs Order To Beef Up Meat Production After Coronavirus Hits Plants." *NPR*, 28 Apr. 2020, https://www.npr.org/sections/coronavirus-live-updates/2020/04/28/847432897/trump-plans-to-beef-up-meat-production-after-coronavirus-hits-plants.

64 Jackson, David. "Trump Orders Meat and Poultry Processing Plants to Stay Open during Coronavirus." *USA Today*, Gannett Satellite Information Network, 29 Apr. 2020, www.usatoday.com/story/news/politics/2020/04/28/coronavirus-trump-plans-order-meat-processing-plants-stay-open/3038300001/.

65 "Trump Will Order U.S. Meat Processing Plants to Stay Open amid Coronavirus Fears." *MSN*, 28 Apr. 2020, www.msn.com/en-us/news/politics/trump-will-order-us-meat-processing-plants-to-stay-open-amid-coronavirus-fears/ar-BB12WKus?ocid=spartandhp.

66 Chalfant, M. "Trump to sign order compelling meat plants to stay open during pandemic." *The Hill*, 28 Apr. 2020, https://thehill.com/homenews/administration/495055-trump-order-compelling-meat-plants-stay-open-coronavirus-outbreak.

67 "Trump Will Order U.S. Meat Processing Plants to Stay Open amid Coronavirus Fears." *MSN*, 28 Apr. 2020, www.msn.com/en-us/news/politics/trump-will-order-us-meat-processing-plants-to-stay-open-amid-coronavirus-fears/ar-BB12WKus?ocid=spartandhp.

68 Ibid.

69 Munshi, Millie. "CDC Cites Limited Distancing at Meat Plants With Thousands Sick." *Bloomberg.com*, Bloomberg, 1 May 2020, www.bloomberg.com/news/articles/2020-05-01/thousands-of-u-s-meat-workers-got-sick-with-deaths-reaching-20.

70 Applebaum -, Michael. "Plant-Based Meats Report: Retailers Invest in Private Brands." *Store Brands*, 23 Apr. 2020, storebrands.com/plant-based-meats-report-retailers-invest-private-brands..

71 Samuel, Sigal. "Demand for Meatless Meat Is Skyrocketing during the Pandemic." *Vox*, Vox, 5 May 2020, www.vox.com/future-perfect/2020/5/5/21247286/plant-based-meat-coronavirus-pandemic-impossible-burger-beyond.

72 Yilek, Caitlin. "Demand for Plant-Based Meat Surges amid Coronavirus Pandemic." *Washington Examiner*, 6 May 2020, www.washingtonexaminer.com/news/demand-for-plant-based-meat-surges-amid-coronavirus-pandemic.

73 "Beyond Meat Reports First Quarter 2020 Financial Results." *Beyond Meat*, 5 May 2020, https://investors.beyondmeat.com/news-releases/news-release-details/beyond-meatr-reports-first-quarter-2020-financial-results.

74 "Impossible Foods' Flagship Product Debuts in Over 750 Grocery Stores." *Impossible Foods*, 16 Apr. 2020, https://impossiblefoods.com/announcements/impossible-burger-debuts-in-additional-750-grocery-stores/.

CHAPTER 25

1 Holt, Donald Van. "The Unofficial Home Page of FDNY." THE UNOFFICIAL HOME PAGE OF FDNY *New York City Fire Department*, www.nyfd.com/..
2 "Police Back on Day-to-Day Beat after 9/11 Nightmare." *CNN*, Cable News Network, edition.cnn.com/2002/US/07/20/wtc.police/.
3 "Post-9/11 Report Recommends Police, Fire Response Changes." *USA Today*, Gannett Satellite Information Network, 19 Aug. 2002, usatoday30.usatoday.com/news/nation/2002-08-19-nypd-nyfd-report_x.htm. .
4 Messinger, Brus. "Medic Tribute." *EMT & Paramedics*, 2017, web.archive.org/web/20170203041213/http:/www.world-memorial.org/Tribute/EMS/medics.html.
5 Chang, Dean. "'Father's Wait Ends; Fire Patrol Vet Pulls Son's Remains from WTC'. ." *New York Daily News.*, 29 Dec. 2001, www.nydailynews.com/search/Chang,+Dean+(29+December+2001).+-Fathers+Wait+Ends;+Fire+Patrol+vet+pulls+sons+remains+from+WTC.+New+York+Daily+News./100-y/ALL/score/1/?
6 "911-Safety-and-Health-Lessons-Learned." *StackPath*, www.ehstoday.com/emergency-management/article/21907239/911-safety-and-health-lessons-learned.
7 Ibid.
8 Ibid.
9 Yip, Jennifer, et al. "World Trade Center-Related Physical and Mental Health Burden among New York City Fire Department Emergency Medical Service Workers." *Occupational and Environmental Medicine*, vol. 73, no. 1, 2015, pp. 13–20., oem.bmj.com/content/73/1/13.info; *see also* "9/11 Emergency Workers Suffer Chronic Health Issues: Study." *Safety+Health Magazine*, Safety+Health Magazine, 22 Apr. 2015, www.safetyandhealthmagazine.com/articles/12206-11-emergency-workers-suffer-chronic-health-issues-study.
10 Putman, Barbara, et al. "Low Serum IgA and Airway Injury in World Trade Center-Exposed Firefighters: a 17-Year Longitudinal Study." *Thorax*, vol. 74, no. 12, 2019, pp. 1182–1184., doi:10.1136/thoraxjnl-2019-213715.
11 Reinberg, Steven. "More Evidence of Long-Term Illness in 9/11 Responders." *MedicineNet*, MedicineNet, 17 Apr. 2015, www.medicinenet.com/script/main/art.asp?articlekey=188017.
12 Edwards, Erika. "COVID-19 Cases among Health Care Workers Top 62,000, CDC Reports." *NBCNews.com*, NBCUniversal News Group, 26 May 2020, www.nbcnews.com/health/health-news/covid-19-cases-among-health-care-workers-top-62-000-n1215056. .
13 Ibid.
14 Stelloh, Tim. "Thousands of Health Care Workers Demand Investigation of Hospitals' Coronavirus Response." *NBCNews.com*, NBCUniversal News Group, 29 Apr. 2020, www.nbcnews.com/news/us-news/thousands-health-care-workers-demand-investigation-hospitals-coronavirus-response-n1194711.
15 Ibid.
16 Ibid.

17 Griffith, Janelle. "Nurses in Multiple States to Protest over 'Lack of Preparedness'." *NBCNews.com*, NBCUniversal News Group, 2 Apr. 2020, www.nbcnews.com/news/us-news/nurses-multiple-states-protest-over-lack-preparedness-n1174971.

18 Edwards, Erika. "COVID-19 Cases among *NBCNews.com*, NBCUniversal News Group, 26 May 2020, www.nbcnews.com/health/health-Health Care Workers Top 62,000, CDC Reports." news/covid-19-cases-among-health-care-workers-top-62-000-n1215056.

19 Ramos, Manny. "Nursing Home Worker Claim They Were Fired Over Demands For More PPE." *The Chicago Suntimes*, 14 Apr. 2020, https://chicago.suntimes.com/2020/4/14/21221311/nursing-home-workers-claim-they-were-fired-over-demands-for-more-ppe-seiu-chicago.

20 Ibid.

21 "Democrats Introduce Legislation to Protect Health Care Workers Against COVID-19." *Congressman Bobby Scott*, 11 Mar. 2020, bobbyscott.house.gov/media-center/press-releases/democrats-introduce-legislation-to-protect-health-care-workers-against.

22 Saez, Emmanuel, et al. "Economic Growth in the United States: A Tale of Two Countries." *Equitable Growth*, 14 May 2019, equitablegrowth.org/economic-growth-in-the-united-states-a-tale-of-two-countries/.

23 Shierholz, Heidi. "Weakened Labor Movement Leads To Rising Economic Inequality." *Economic Policy Institute*, 27 Jan. 2020, https://www.epi.org/blog/weakened-labor-movement-leads-to-rising-economic-inequality/.

24 United States, Congress, Congress, and Bobby Scott. *Protecting the Right to Organize: Fact Sheet*, 2 May 2019. edlabor.house.gov/imo/media/doc/2019-05-02%20PRO%20Act%20Fact%20Sheet.pdf.

25 Hammonds, Clare and Kerrissey, Jasmine. "'We Are Not Heroes Because It Is Not a Choice': A Survey of Essential Workers' Safety and Security During COVID-19." *UMass Amherst Labor Center*, 1 May 2020, www.umass.edu/lrrc/sites/default/files/Western%20Mass%20Essential%20Worker%20Survey%20-%20May%202020.pdf.

26 Ibid.

27 Ibid.

28 Ibid.

29 Lapin, Tamar. "Amazon Fires Workers Who Organized Strike Over Coronavirus Response." *The New Yorker*, 30 Mar. 2020, https://nypost.com/2020/03/30/amazon-fires-worker-who-organized-strike-over-coronavirus-response/.

30 Ibid.

31 Ibid.

32 Ibid.

33 Bond, Shannon. "'We're Out There' So Protect Us, Protesting Workers Tell Amazon, Target, Instacart." *NPR*, 1 May 2020, https://www.npr.org/2020/05/01/849218750/workers-walk-off-jobs-demand-safer-working-conditions.

34 Ibid.

35 Ibid.

36 Ibid.

37 Hetrick, Christian and Park, Katie. "Whole Foods and Other Retailers Have Ended Hazard Pay For Workers Even As Coronavirus Remains A Threat." *The Philadelphia Inquirer*, 4 June 2020, https://www.inquirer.com/news/coronavirus-whole-foods-hazard-pay-20200604.html.

38. Ibid.
39. Maniscalco, Joe. "Fired For Demanding Protective Equipment." *D.C. Report*, 16 Apr. 2020, https://www.dcreport.org/2020/04/16/fired-for-demanding-protective-equipment/.
40. Ibid.
41. Ibid.
42. Ibid.
43. Ibid.
44. Ibid.
45. "Stevens, Pappas Introduce the Essential Worker Protection Act." *Haley Stevens House Congresswoman*, 29 Apr. 2020, https://stevens.house.gov/media/press-releases/stevens-pappas-introduce-essential-worker-protection-act.
46. Ibid.
47. H.R. Res 6139, 116th Cong. (2020) (enacted).
48. David Madland, Sarah Jane Glynn. "How the Federal Government Can Protect Essential Workers in the Fight Against Coronavirus." *Center for American Progress*, 8 Apr. 2020, www.americanprogress.org/issues/economy/news/2020/04/08/482881/federal-government-can-protect-essential-workers-fight-coronavirus/.
49. Ibid.
50. Ibid.
51. Rosenberg, Eli. "Congress's Most Ambitious Attempt to Strengthen Unions in Years Is Set for a House Vote next Week." *The Washington Post*, WP Company, 29 Jan. 2020, www.washingtonpost.com/business/2020/01/29/most-ambitious-attempt-strengthen-unions-years-will-be-voted-next-week/.
52. Ibid.
53. Ibid.

CHAPTER 26

1. Doyle, Elaine. "Why Is Coronavirus Killing So Many More People in the UK Than in Ireland?" The Guardian, The Guardian, 14 Apr. 2020, www.theguardian.com/commentisfree/2020/apr/14/coronavirus-uk-ireland-delay.
2. Cottle, Michelle. "Boris Johnson Should Have Taken His Own Medicine." *The New York Times*, The New York Times, 27 Mar. 2020, https://nyti.ms/2wFnLHW.
3. Doyle, Elaine. "Why Is Coronavirus Killing So Many More People in the UK Than in Ireland?" *The Guardian*, The Guardian, 14 Apr. 2020, www.theguardian.com/commentisfree/2020/apr/14/coronavirus-uk-ireland-delay
4. "Coronavirus: UK Schools, Colleges and Nurseries to Close from Friday." *BBC News*, BBC, 18 Mar. 2020, www.bbc.co.uk/news/uk-51952314.
5. *"The Health Protection (Coronavirus, Business Closure) (England) Regulations 2020"* (PDF). Archived from the original (PDF) on 23 March 2020.
6. "Coronavirus: Strict New Curbs on Life in UK Announced by PM." BBC News, BBC, 24 Mar. 2020, www.bbc.co.uk/news/uk-52012432.
7. Rayner, Christopher Hope; Gordon. "What Is in the Coronavirus Bill? Key Areas of the New Legislation." The Telegraph, Telegraph Media Group, 25 Mar. 2020, www.telegraph.co.uk/politics/2020/03/25/coronavirus-bill-summary/.

8   Triggle, Nick. "Coronavirus: We Can Cope with Peak, Hospital Bosses Say." BBC News, BBC, 15 Apr. 2020, www.bbc.co.uk/news/health-52293762.

9   "UK's Social Distancing Has Flattened COVID-19 Curve–Science Official." Reuters, Thomson Reuters, 15 Apr. 2020, uk.reuters.com/article/uk-health-coronavirus-britain-curve/uks-social-distancing-has-flattened-covid-19-curve-science-official-idUKKCN21X2LD.

10 "Coronavirus: Boris Johnson Says UK Is Past the Peak of Outbreak." BBC News, BBC, 30 Apr. 2020, www.bbc.com/news/uk-52493500.

11 Triggle, Nick. "Coronavirus: Nine in 10 Dying Have Existing Illness." BBC News, BBC, 16 Apr. 2020, www.bbc.co.uk/news/health-52308783.

12 "Coronavirus UK Map: How Many Confirmed Cases Are There in Your Area?" BBC News, BBC, 30 June 2020, www.bbc.co.uk/news/uk-51768274.

13 Ibid.

14 Ibid.

15 "Coronavirus in NI on 3 May." BBC News, BBC, 3 May 2020, https://www.bbc.com/news/live/uk-northern-ireland-52435093.

16 Doyle, Elaine. "Why Is Coronavirus Killing so Many More People in the UK than in Ireland? | Elaine Doyle." The Guardian, Guardian News and Media, 14 Apr. 2020, www.theguardian.com/commentisfree/2020/apr/14/coronavirus-uk-ireland-delay.

17 Ibid.

18 Ibid.

19 Moriarty, Gerry. "Covid-19 Death Toll in NI Set to be 'less severe' Than 3,000 Predicted." The Irish Times, The Irish Times, 15 Apr. 2020, https://www.irishtimes.com/news/ireland/irish-news/covid-19-death-toll-in-ni-set-to-be-less-severe-than-3-000-predicted-1.4229579.

20 Ng, Kate. "Coronavirus Daily Tests Fall to 76,496 Just Two Days After 100,000 Target Met." Independent, Independent, 3 May 2020, https://www.independent.co.uk/news/uk/home-news/coronavirus-uk-testing-rate-daily-target-falls-hancock-a9496656.html.

21 David. "U.K. Paid $20 Million for New Coronavirus Tests. They Didn't Work." The New York Times, The New York Times, 16 Apr. 2020, www.nytimes.com/2020/04/16/world/europe/coronavirus-antibody-test-uk.html.

22 Ibid.

23 Ibid.

24 Ibid.

25 Aderoju, Darlene. "U2 Donates $10.9 Million to Ireland to Help Fight Against the Coronavirus." PEOPLE.com, 10 Apr. 2020, people.com/music/u2-donates-ireland-coronavirus-relief/.

26 Carswell, Simon. "Third Flight of U2-Bought PPE for Health Workers Lands in Dublin." The Irish Times, The Irish Times, 3 May 2020, www.irishtimes.com/news/health/third-flight-of-u2-bought-ppe-for-health-workers-lands-in-dublin-1.4243887.

27 Ibid.

28 Kemeny, Richard. "Bolsonaro's Denial of Coronavirus Puts the Country at Risk." The World from PRX, 2020, www.pri.org/stories/2020-04-14/bolsonaro-s-denial-coronavirus-puts-country-risk.

29 Lopes, Marina. "Brazil's Bolsonaro Fires Health Minister Mandetta after Differences over Coronavirus Response." The Washington Post, 16 Apr. 2020, www.washingtonpost.com/world/the_americas/

coronavirus-brazil-bolsonaro-luiz-henrique-mandetta-health-minister/2020/04/16/c143a8b0-7fe0-11ea-84c2-0792d8591911_story.html.

30 Phillips, Tom. "'So What?': Bolsonaro Shrugs Off Brazil's Rising Coronavirus Death Toll." The Guardian, The Guardian, 29 Apr. 2020, https://www.theguardian.com/world/2020/apr/29/so-what-bolsonaro-shrugs-off-brazil-rising-coronavirus-death-toll.

31 "Casos De Coronavírus e Número De Mortes No Brasil Em 11 De Maio." G1, 11 May 2020, g1.globo.com/bemestar/coronavirus/noticia/2020/05/11/casos-de-coronavirus-e-numero-de-mortes-no-brasil-em-11-de-maio.ghtml.

32 "Brazil Health Minister Teich Resigns Just Weeks into the Job." Brazil News | Al Jazeera, Al Jazeera, 15 May 2020, www.aljazeera.com/news/2020/05/brazil-health-minister-resigns-weeks-job-200515152054715.html.

33 Paraguassu, Lisandra, and Ricardo Brito. "Bolsonaro Threatens WHO Exit as COVID-19 Kills 'a Brazilian per Minute'." The Star Online, 6 June 2020, www.thestar.com.my/news/world/2020/06/06/brazil039s-covid-19-deaths-surpass-italy039s-daily-toll-hits-record-high.

34 Barbara, Vanessa. "Brazil Is in Coronavirus Free Fall." The New York Times, The New York Times, 8 June 2020, www.nytimes.com/2020/06/08/opinion/brazil-coronavirus-bolsonaro.html.

35 "Coronavirus: Hard-Hit Brazil Removes Data amid Rising Death Toll." Yahoo! News, Yahoo!, 7 June 2020, news.yahoo.com/coronavirus-hard-hit-brazil-removes-035152059.html.

36 Ibid.

37 https://apnews.com/8ceb44235a63dfb59da10f2ceffb9160

CHAPTER 27

1 Dewan, Angela, et al. "As Governments Fumbled Their Coronavirus Response, These Four Got It Right. Here's How." CNN, Cable News Network, 16 Apr. 2020, www.cnn.com/2020/04/16/world/coronavirus-response-lessons-learned-intl/index.html.

2 Ibid.

3 "News." Pandemic, pandemic.internationalsos.com/reports/covid-19-in-taiwan-apr-17-2020.

4 Dewan, Angela, et al. "As Governments Fumbled Their Coronavirus Response, These Four Got It Right. Here's How." CNN, Cable News Network, 16 Apr. 2020, www.cnn.com/2020/04/16/world/coronavirus-response-lessons-learned-intl/index.html.

5 Ibid.

6 Ibid.

7 Ibid.

8 Ibid.

9 "Taiwan Is Using Humor to Quash Coronavirus Fake News." MSN Money, 5 June 2020, www.msn.com/en-us/finance/other/taiwan-is-using-humor-to-quash-coronavirus-fake-news/ar-BB154CgL.

10 "Economic Chaos Fuels Hunger and Strongmen." The New York Times, The New York Times, 22 Apr. 2020, www.nytimes.com/2020/04/22/world/coronavirus-cases-world.html.

11 Ibid.

12 Dewan, Angela, et al. "As Governments Fumbled Their Coronavirus Response, These Four Got It Right. Here's How." CNN, Cable News Network, 16 Apr. 2020, www.cnn.com/2020/04/16/world/coronavirus-response-lessons-learned-intl/index.html.

13. Ibid.
14. Ibid.
15. Ibid.
16. Ibid.
17. Kolbert, Elizabeth, et al. "How Iceland Beat the Coronavirus." *The New Yorker*, 8 June 2020, www.newyorker.com/magazine/2020/06/08/how-iceland-beat-the-coronavirus.
18. Dewan, Angela, et al. "As Governments Fumbled Their Coronavirus Response, These Four Got It Right. Here's How." *CNN*, Cable News Network, 16 Apr. 2020, www.cnn.com/2020/04/16/world/coronavirus-response-lessons-learned-intl/index.html.
19. Ibid.
20. Ibid.
21. Ibid.
22. Steinhauer, Jennifer. "Frustrated by Lack of Coronavirus Tests, Maryland Got 500,000 From South Korea." *The New York Times*, The New York Times, 20 Apr. 2020, www.nytimes.com/2020/04/20/us/larry-hogan-wife-yumi-korea-coronavirus-tests.html.
23. Ibid.
24. "Testing the Waters: South Korea's Waterparks Open Under New Anti-Virus Measures." *U.S. News & World Report*, U.S. News & World Report, 5 June 2020, www.usnews.com/news/world/articles/2020-06-05/testing-the-waters-south-koreas-waterparks-open-under-new-anti-virus-measures.
25. O'Hare, Ryan. "Crunching the Numbers for Coronavirus: Imperial News: Imperial College London." *Imperial News*, 13 Mar. 2020, www.imperial.ac.uk/news/196137/crunching-numbers-coronavirus/.
26. Cullen, Paul. "Coronavirus Cases Now Confirmed in Every County in Ireland." *The Irish Times*, The Irish Times, 22 Mar. 2020, www.irishtimes.com/news/health/coronavirus-cases-now-confirmed-in-every-county-in-ireland-1.4209389..
27. Kelly, Brendan, and . "Varadkar Addresses Nation…from Washington, D.C." *Irish Echo*, 12 Mar. 2020, www.irishecho.com/2020/03/varadkar-addresses-nationfrom-washington-d-c/.
28. Leahy, Pat, et al. "Coronavirus: Schools, Colleges and Childcare Facilities in Ireland to Shut." *The Irish Times*, The Irish Times, 12 Mar. 2020, www.irishtimes.com/news/health/coronavirus-schools-colleges-and-childcare-facilities-in-ireland-to-shut-1.4200977.
29. Ibid.
30. McGowran, Leigh. "Coronavirus: St Patrick's parade cancelled in Stepaside Dublin for Public Health". *Dublin Live.ie*, Dublin Live, 6 Mar. 2020, https://www.dublinlive.ie/news/dublin-news/coronavirus-st-patricks-day-parade-17879218.
31. Murray, Sean. "Taoiseach announces all non-essential shops to close, restrictions on gatherings of more than four people". *TheJournal.ie*, The Journal, 24 Mar. 2020, https://www.thejournal.ie/coronavirus-new-measures-5055686-Mar2020/.
32. "Simon Harris to Extend Emergency Garda Powers Until 18 May." *The Journal.ie*, The Journal, 2 May 2020, https://www.thejournal.ie/garda-powers-covid-189-extended-5090055-May2020/.
33. Spread of Covid-19 infection has reached a 'plateau' with growth rate 'close to zero'". *Irish Examiner*, 16 April 2020.
34. "Holohan: 'Important to Continue Measures until 5 May." *RTE.ie*, RTÉ, 18 Apr. 2020, www.rte.ie/news/coronavirus/2020/0418/1132249-coronavirus-ireland/.

35 "Coronavirus: 19 More Deaths and 330 Additional Cases." *RTE.ie*, RTÉ, 3 May 2020, www.rte.ie/news/2020/0503/1136346-covid-update-ireland/.

36 Power, Jack. "Over-65s Account for 90% of Coronavirus Deaths Recorded in Ireland.'" *The Irish Times*, 13 Apr. 2020, www.msn.com/en-gb/news/uknews/over-65s-account-for-90percent-of-coronavirus-deaths-recorded-in-ireland/ar-BB14sAUm.

37 Cullen, Paul. "Nursing Homes Account for 50 per Cent of Coronavirus Deaths in Ireland." *The Irish Times*, The Irish Times, 30 Apr. 2020, www.irishtimes.com/news/health/nursing-homes-account-for-50-per-cent-of-coronavirus-deaths-in-ireland-1.4241723.

38 Ibid.

39 Ibid.

40 Osborne Samuel "Irish Honour 173-Year-Old Great Famine Debt to Native American Tribe Hit by Coronavirus." *The Independent*, Independent Digital News and Media, 5 May 2020, www.independent.co.uk/news/world/europe/coronavirus-naive-american-ireland-great-famine-donation-gofundme-a9499251.html.

41 O'Loughlin, Ed and Zaveri, Mihir. "Irish Return an Old Favor, Helping Native Amercians Battling the Virus." *The New York* Times, The New York Times, 5 May 2020, https://nyti.ms/2zcM7d4.

42 Kaur, Harmeet. "The Irish Are Sending Relief to Native Americans, Inspired By A Donation From a Tribe During the Great Famine." *CNN*, CNN, 6 May 2020, https://www.cnn.com/2020/05/06/world/ireland-native-americans-choctaw-gift-trnd/index.html.

43 Bennhold, Katrin. "A German Exception? Why the Country's Coronavirus Death Rate Is Low." *The New York Times*, The New York Times, 4 Apr. 2020, www.nytimes.com/2020/04/04/world/europe/germany-coronavirus-death-rate.html.

44 Dewan, Angela, et al. "As Governments Fumbled Their Coronavirus Response, These Four Got It Right. Here's How." *CNN*, Cable News Network, 16 Apr. 2020, www.cnn.com/2020/04/16/world/coronavirus-response-lessons-learned-intl/index.html.

45 Ellyatt, Holly. "What's the Best Way to Lift a Coronavirus Lockdown? Germany Could Have the Answers." *CNBC*, CNBC, 5 May 2020, www.cnbc.com/2020/04/21/lifting-coronavirus-lockdowns-germany-could-be-the-example-to-follow.html.

46 Ibid.

47 Ibid.

48 Ibid.

49 Ibid.

50 Ibid.

51 "Germany and U.S. on Divergent Paths to Reopen." *The New York Times*, The New York Times, 6 May 2020, www.nytimes.com/2020/05/06/us/coronavirus-live-updates.html.

52 Ibid.

53 "Economic Chaos Fuels Hunger and Strongmen." *The New York Times*, The New York Times, 22 Apr. 2020, www.nytimes.com/2020/04/22/world/coronavirus-cases-world.html.

54 Ibid.

55 "Germany and U.S. on Divergent Paths To Reopen." *The New York Times*, The New York Times, 6 May 2020, https://nyti.ms/3b7TVtN.

56 Evans, Zachary. "New Zealand Appears to Have Completely Eradicated Coronavirus." *Yahoo! News*, Yahoo!, 8 June 2020, news.yahoo.com/zealand-appears-completely-eradicated-coronavirus-122845924.html.

57 Ibid.
58 Ibid.
59 Taylor, Chloe. "How New Zealand's 'eliminate' Strategy Brought New Coroanvirus Cases Down to Zero." *CNBC*, CNBC, 5 May 2020, https://www.cnbc.com/2020/05/05/how-new-zealand-brought-new-coronavirus-cases-down-to-zero.html.
60 Ibid.
61 Ibid.
62 Ibid.
63 Ibid.

CHAPTER 28

1   "What the Numbers Say about Sweden's Coronavirus Strategy." *The Mercury News*, The Mercury News, 29 Apr. 2020, www.mercurynews.com/2020/04/28/what-the-numbers-say-about-swedens-coronavirus-strategy/.
2   Ibid.
3   Ibid.
4   Ibid.
5   Anderson, Christina, and Henrik Pryser Libell. "In the Coronavirus Fight in Scandinavia, Sweden Stands Apart." *The New York Times*, The New York Times, 28 Mar. 2020, www.nytimes.com/2020/03/28/world/europe/sweden-coronavirus.html.
6   Ibid.
7   Ibid.
8   Ibid.
9   Ibid.
10 Ibid.
11 Ibid.
12 "What the Numbers Say about Sweden's Coronavirus Strategy." *The Mercury News*, The Mercury News, 29 Apr. 2020, www.mercurynews.com/2020/04/28/what-the-numbers-say-about-swedens-coronavirus-strategy/.
13 Ibid.
14 Ibid.
15 Ibid.
16 Nikel, David. "Sweden: 600,000 Coronavirus Infections In Stockholm By May 1, Model Estimates." *Forbes*, Forbes Magazine, 22 Apr. 2020, www.forbes.com/sites/davidnikel/2020/04/21/sweden-600000-coronavirus-infections-in-stockholm-by-may-1-model-estimates/#5f8a520978d6.
17 "What the Numbers Say about Sweden's Coronavirus Strategy." *The Mercury News*, The Mercury News, 29 Apr. 2020, www.mercurynews.com/2020/04/28/what-the-numbers-say-about-swedens-coronavirus-strategy/.
18 Anderson, Christina, and Henrik Pryser Libell. "In the Coronavirus Fight in Scandinavia, Sweden Stands Apart." *The New York Times*, The New York Times, 28 Mar. 2020, www.nytimes.com/2020/03/28/world/europe/sweden-coronavirus.html.
19 Ibid.

20. "Scandinavia: The Surprising Coronavirus Hot Spot." *OZY*, 25 Mar. 2020, www.ozy.com/the-new-and-the-next/scandinavia-the-surprising-coronavirus-hot-spot/290256/.

21. "Countries With the Most Well-Developed Public Health Care Systems." *U.S. News & World Report*, U.S. News & World Report, www.usnews.com/news/best-countries/slideshows/countries-with-the-most-well-developed-public-health-care-system.

22. Ibid.

23. "At Least 11 Percent of Swedes May Have Contracted Covid-19, Antibody Study Suggests." *RT International*, www.rt.com/news/486471-sweden-contracted-coronavirus-antibody-study/.

24. "Inside Daily Brief: COVID-19 By the Numbers." *Inside Daily Brief*, Inside, 9 June 2020, https://inside.com/campaigns/inside-daily-brief-2020-06-09-23400.

25. Karlsson, Carl-Johan. "Sweden's Coronavirus Failure Started Long Before the Pandemic." *Foreign Policy*, 23 June 2020, foreignpolicy.com/2020/06/23/sweden-coronavirus-failure-anders-tegnell-started-long-before-the-pandemic/.

26. "Coronavirus in Norway: The Latest News on the COVID-19 Outbreak." *Life in Norway*, 3 July 2020, www.lifeinnorway.net/coronavirus-in-norway/.

27. "Norway Launches 'Smittestopp' App to Track Coronavirus Cases." *The Local.co*, The Local, 16 Apr. 2020, https://www.thelocal.no/20200416/norway-launches-smittestop-app-to-track-coronavirus-cases.

28. Pohjanpalo, Kati. "Finland Registers Sharp Slowdown In Spread of Coronavirus." *Bloomberg World*, Bloomberg, 27 Apr. 2020, https://www.bloomberg.com/news/articles/2020-04-27/finland-registers-sharp-slowdown-in-spread-of-coronavirus.

29. Weiland, Noah, and Maggie Haberman. "Coronavirus Casts Unwelcome Spotlight on Trump's Health Secretary." *The New York Times*, The New York Times, 29 Apr. 2020, www.nytimes.com/2020/04/29/us/politics/coronavirus-trump-azar.html.

30. Whelan, Corey. "These 10 Secrets of Scandinavians Are Why They're So Health." *Reader's Digest*, Reader's Digest, 31 Jan. 2018, https://www.rd.com/article/health-secrets-of-scandinavians/.

31. "Scientists Uncover Why Sauna Bathing Is Good for Your Health." *ScienceDaily*, ScienceDaily, 5 Jan. 2018, www.sciencedaily.com/releases/2018/01/180105124005.htm.

32. Whelan, Corey. "These 10 Secrets of Scandinavians Are Why They're So Health." *Reader's Digest*, Reader's Digest, 31 Jan. 2018, https://www.rd.com/article/health-secrets-of-scandinavians/.

CHAPTER 29

1. Jansen, Bart. "'Draconian'? 'House Arrest'? Coronavirus Lockdown Prompt Raft of Lawsuits against States.' ." *USA Today*, 25 May 2020, www.usatoday.com/story/news/politics/2020/05/25/coronavirus-lockdowns-prompt-raft-lawsuits-against-states/5231533002/.

2. Villa, Virginia. "Most States Have Religious Exemptions to COVID-19 Social Distancing Rules." *Pew Research Center*, Pew Research Center, 31 May 2020, www.pewresearch.org/fact-tank/2020/04/27/most-states-have-religious-exemptions-to-covid-19-social-distancing-rules/.

3. Baker, Peter. "Firing a Salvo in Culture Wars, Trump Pushes for Churches to Reopen." *The New York Times*, The New York Times, 22 May 2020, www.nytimes.com/2020/05/22/us/politics/trump-churches-coronavirus.html.

4. Frum, David. "Trump Brings Religion Into the Coronavirus Culture War." *The Atlantic*, Atlantic Media Company, 1 May 2020, www.theatlantic.com/ideas/archive/2020/05/trump-brings-religion-coronavirus-culture-war/611044/.

5   Bremer, Francis J., et al. *Puritans and Puritanism in Europe and America: a Comprehensive Encyclopedia.* ABC-Clio, 2006.

6   Carroll, Rory. "America's Dark and Not-Very-Distant History of Hating Catholics." *The Guardian*, Guardian News and Media, 12 Sept. 2015, www.theguardian.com/world/2015/sep/12/america-history-of-hating-catholics.

7   Pat, Perrin (1 January 1970). *Crime and Punishment: The Colonial Period to the New Frontier.* Discovery Enterprises. p. 24.

8   *Catholic Higher Education in Protestant America: the Jesuits and Harvard in the Age of the University*, by Kathleen A. Mahoney, Johns Hopkins University Press, 2003, pp. 47–47.

9   Zimmerman, Mark. "Symbol of Enduring Freedom." *Columbia Magazine*, Knights of Columbus, 4 Mar. 2010, issuu.com/columbia-magazine/docs/columbiamar10en.

10   Finkelman, Paul. "Maryland Toleration Act." *Encyclopedia of American Civil Rights*, Routledge, 2006, pp. 975-976..

11   The Religious Freedom Restoration Act of 1993, Pub. L. No. 103-141, 107 Stat. 1488, codified at 42 U.S.C. § 2000bb through 42 U.S.C. § 2000bb-4,

12   "Two Centuries of Law Guide Legal Approach to Modern Pandemic." *American Bar Association*, 29 Mar. 2020, www.americanbar.org/news/abanews/aba-news-archives/2020/03/legal-pandemic-approach/.

13   186 U.S. 380 (1902).

14   Ibid. at 397.

15   197 U.S. 11 (1905).

16   See e.g. *Hickox v. Christie*, 205 F. Supp. 3d 579, 591 (D.N.J. 2016).

17   In *Jew Ho v. Williamson*, 103 F. 10 (C.C.D.Cal.1900),

18   Ibid. at 26.

19   Ibid. at 23.

20   In re Smith, 101 Sickels 68, 76, 146 N.Y. 68, 40 N.E. 497 (1895).

21   Wendy Parmet. Quarantining the Law of Quarantine: Why Quarantine Law Does Not Reflect Contemporary Constitutional Law, 9 WAKE FOREST J. OF L. & POL'Y, No. 1, 7 (2018).

22   Ibid. at 9.

23   Jacobson v. Massachusetts, 197 U.S. 11, 27 (1905).

24   "Kentucky Coronavirus Patient Resisted Quarantine." *U.S. News & World Report*, U.S. News & World Report, 14 Mar. 2020, www.usnews.com/news/best-states/kentucky/articles/2020-03-14/kentucky-coronavirus-patient-resisted-quarantine.

25   Hohmann, James. "The Daily 202: Barr Memo Threatening Lawsuits against Coronavirus Restrictions Is a Warning Shot." *The Washington Post*, WP Company, 28 Apr. 2020, www.washingtonpost.com/news/powerpost/paloma/daily-202/2020/04/28/daily-202-barr-memo-threatening-lawsuits-against-coronavirus-restrictions-is-a-warning-shot/5ea7a78e88e0fa3dea9c4414/.

26   Ibid.

27   Ibid.

28   Singman, Brooke, and Jake Gibson. "DOJ Intervenes in Mississippi Drive-in Church Case, Says City's Actions 'Target Religious Conduct'." *Fox News*, FOX News Network, 14 Apr. 2020, www.foxnews.com/politics/doj-mississippi-church.

29 http://cdn.cnn.com/cnn/2020/images/04/14/ecf_us_statement_of_interest_in_support_of_plaintiffs_0

30 In re Abbott, —- F.3d —-, 2020 WL 1685929, at *6 (5th Cir. Apr. 7, 2020).

31 Ibid.

32 Ibid.

33 Ibid.

34 Ibid.

35 First Pentecostal Church of Holly Springs v. City of Holly Springs, 2020 U.S. Dist. LEXIS 72533 (N.D. Miss. Apr. 24, 2020)

36 Givas, Nick. "Devastating Mississippi Church Fire Investigated as Arson." *Fox News*, FOX News Network, 23 May 2020, www.foxnews.com/faith-values/mississippi-church-fire-investigated-arson.

37 Kelly v. Legislative Coordinating Council, 460 P.3d 832 (Kan. 2020); see also Gjelten, Tom. "Opposing Church Closures Becomes New Religious Freedom Cause." *NPR*, NPR, 17 Apr. 2020, www.npr.org/sections/coronavirus-live-updates/2020/04/17/837698597/opposing-forced-church-closures-becomes-new-religious-freedom-cause.

38 Ibid.; see also, Kansas Pltf's Verified Complaint: http://www.adfmedia.org/files/FirstBaptistComplaint.pdf

39 Kansas (J. Broomes) US Dist. Court Decision: First Baptist Church v. Kelly, No. 20-1102-JWB, 2020 U.S. Dist. LEXIS 68267 (D. Kan. Apr. 18, 2020)

40 Kelly v. Legislative Coordinating Council, 460 P.3d 832 (Kan. 2020)

41 Grimmett, Brian. "Kansas Gov. Kelly Strikes Court Deal With Churches, Hints At Easing Coronavirus Shutdown." *KCUR 89.3–NPR in Kansas City. Local News, Entertainment and Podcasts.*, 26 Apr. 2020, www.kcur.org/news/2020-04-26/kansas-gov-kelly-strikes-court-deal-with-churches-hints-at-easing-coronavirus-shutdown. Motion: https://sunflowerstatejournal.com/wp-content/uploads/2020/04/settlechurches.pdf

42 US Dist. Court Decision: Legacy Church, Inc. v. Kunkel, 2020 U.S. Dist. LEXIS 68415 (D.N.M. Apr. 17, 2020).

43 Ibid.

44 Ibid.

45 Pell, Samantha. "Judge Allows Drive-in Louisville Church Services, Says Mayor 'Criminalized the Communal Celebration of Easter'." *The Washington Post*, WP Company, 12 Apr. 2020, www.washingtonpost.com/nation/2020/04/11/louisville-church-coronavirus/.

46 *On Fire Christian Ctr. v. Fischer*, No. 3:20-CV-264-JRW, 2020 U.S. Dist. LEXIS 65924 (W.D. Ky. Apr. 11, 2020)

47 Ibid.

48 Mcconnell, Michael W., and Max Raskin. "If Liquor Stores Are Essential, Why Isn't Church?" *The New York Times*, The New York Times, 21 Apr. 2020, www.nytimes.com/2020/04/21/opinion/first-amendment-church-coronavirus.html.

49 "Pell, Samantha. "Judge Allows Drive-in Louisville Church Services, Says Mayor 'Criminalized the Communal Celebration of Easter'." *The Washington Post*, WP Company, 12 Apr. 2020, www.washingtonpost.com/nation/2020/04/11/louisville-church-coronavirus/./.

50 *Wis. Legislature v. Palm*, 2020 WI 42, ¶56 (2020); *see also* Mahbubani, Rhea. "'We're the Wild West': Unmasked Wisconsinites Crowd Bars after the State Supreme Court Struck down the Governor's

Stay-at-Home Order." *Business Insider*, Business Insider, 14 May 2020, www.businessinsider.com/wisconsin-supreme-court-overturns-coronavirus-tony-evers-shutdown-packed-bars-2020-5..

51 *Palm*, 2020 WI 42, ¶7.

52 *Palm*, 2020 WI 42, ¶132.

53 Ibid.

54 "Judge Tosses Out Oregon's Coronavirus Restrictions." *U.S. News & World Report*, U.S. News & World Report, 18 May 2020, www.usnews.com/news/best-states/oregon/articles/2020-05-18/judge-tosses-out-oregons-coronavirus-restrictions. see also, Oregon Pltf's Verified Complaint: file:///Users/damaracarousis/Downloads/OR_CIR_BAK_20CV17482_Complaint_Amended_CMAM_with_optional_services%20(1).pdf

55 "Oregon Supreme Court Halts Judge's Order Rescinding Kate Brown's Stay-at-Home Restrictions." *The Washington Times*, The Washington Times, 18 May 2020, www.washingtontimes.com/news/2020/may/18/oregon-supreme-court-halts-ruling-rescinding-kate-/..

56 Ibid.; Or. Cir. Court Opinion: https://www.westlaw.com/Document/I328100c09a1411eab2c3c7d85ec85a54/View/FullText.html?transitionType=Default&contextData=(sc.Default)&VR=3.0&RS=cblt1.0

57 Flaccus, G. & Selsky, A. "Oregon Supreme Court halts order nixing virus restrictions." MSN, 18 May 2020, www.msn.com/en-us/news/us/judge-tosses-out-oregons-coronavirus-restrictions/ar-BB14gvfo?ocid=spartandhp.

58 Ibid.; Oregon Supreme Court Order: https://www.courthousenews.com/wp-content/uploads/2020/05/OregonOrderStay.pdf

59 Ibid.

60 Johnson, Kevin. "DOJ Sides with Church in Challenge to Coronavirus State Order Limiting Gatherings in Virginia." *USA Today*, Gannett Satellite Information Network, 5 May 2020, www.usatoday.com/story/news/politics/2020/05/04/coronavirus-church-gets-backing-feds-challenge-state-order/3077991001/.

61 Hedgpeth, Dana, and Peter Jamison. "White House Coronavirus Task Force Leader Says D.C. Region Has Highest Rate of Positive Test Results in U.S." *The Washington Post*, WP Company, 22 May 2020, www.washingtonpost.com/dc-md-va/2020/05/22/coronavirus-dc-maryland-virginia-live-updates/. *See also* Complaint: http://lc.org/042420LighthouseFellowshipChurchVerifiedComplaint.pdf

62 DOJ's Statement of Interest: https://www.justice.gov/opa/press-release/file/1273211/download?utm_medium=email&utm_source=govdelivery

63 *Lighthouse Fellowship Church v. Northam*, No. 2:20cv204, 2020 U.S. Dist. LEXIS 91508, *1 (E.D. Va. May 21, 2020).

64 Ibid.

65 Ibid.

66 Ibid.

67 Ibid.

68 "Governor Northam Announces Phase One Guidelines to Slowly Ease Public Health Restrictions." 9 May 2020, https://www.governor.virginia.gov/newsroom/all-releases/2020/may/headline-856681-en.html.

69 Smith, Gregory A. "White Evangelicals among Groups with Slipping Confidence in Trump's Handling of COVID-19." *Pew Research Center*, Pew Research Center, 31 May 2020, www.pewresearch.org/fact-

tank/2020/05/14/white-evangelicals-among-groups-with-slipping-confidence-in-trumps-handling-of-covid-19/.

70. Bowden, Ebony, and Bob Fredericks. "Trump Orders All Places of Worship to Open, Declaring Them Essential." *New York Post*, New York Post, 23 May 2020, nypost.com/2020/05/22/trump-orders-all-places-of-worship-to-open-declaring-them-essential/.

71. Liptak, Adam. "Supreme Court, in 5-4 Decision, Rejects Church's Challenge to Shutdown Order." *The New York Times*, The New York Times, 30 May 2020, www.nytimes.com/2020/05/30/us/supreme-court-churches-coronavirus.html..

72. Haberman, Clyde. "Religion and Right-Wing Politics: How Evangelicals Reshaped Elections." *The New York Times*, The New York Times, 28 Oct. 2018, www.nytimes.com/2018/10/28/us/religion-politics-evangelicals.html.

73. Baker, Peter. "Firing a Salvo in Culture Wars, Trump Pushes for Churches to Reopen." *The New York Times*, The New York Times, 22 May 2020, www.nytimes.com/2020/05/22/us/politics/trump-churches-coronavirus.html..

74. Ibid.

75. Ibid.

76. Ibid.

77. Ibid.

78. Ibid.

79. Ibid.

80. Ibid.

81. Ibid.

82. Ibid.

83. Ibid

84. Ibid.

85. *S. Bay United Pentecostal Church v. Newsom*, No. 19A1044, 590 U.S. __ (2020); *see also* Liptak, Adam. "Supreme Court, in 5-4 Decision, Rejects Church's Challenge to Shutdown Order." *The New York Times*, The New York Times, 30 May 2020, www.nytimes.com/2020/05/30/us/supreme-court-churches-coronavirus.htm

86. *S. Bay United Pentecostal Church v. Newsom*, No. 20-55533, 2020 U.S. App. LEXIS 16464 (9th Cir. May 22, 2020).

87. This "highly deferential" standard the 9th Circuit wound up using limited the court to determine 'whether the [Governor's] actions were taken in good faith and whether there is some factual basis for [the] decision'. *See United States v. Chalk*, 441 F.2d 1277, 1281 (4th Cir. 1971).

88. *Newsom*, 2020 U.S. App. LEXIS 16464 at *3.

89. Ibid.

90. Ibid. at *20-21. (Collins, J., dissenting).

91. Supplemental Brief in Support of Emergency Application for Writ of Injunction Relief Requested by Sunday, May 31, 2020 at 2, S. Bay United Pentecostal Church v. Newsom, 590 U.S. __ (2020) (No. 19A1044).

92. *Newsom*, No. 19A1044, 590 U.S. __ (2020) (Roberts, C.J., concurring).

93. Ibid.

94 *Newsom*, No. 19A1044, 590 U.S. __ (2020) (Kavanaugh, J. dissenting).

95 Ibid.

96 Ibid.

97 Ibid.

98 Ibid.

99 *Elim Romanian Pentecostal Church v. Pritzker*, No. 20 C 2782, 2020 U.S. Dist. LEXIS 84348,*1, *11 (N.D. Ill. May 13, 2020).

100 *Elim Romanian Pentecostal Church v. Pritzker*, No. 20 C 2782, 2020 U.S. Dist. LEXIS 84348,*1, *11 (N.D. Ill. May 13, 2020).

101 Seventh Circuit Unsigned Order: https://www.westlaw.com/Document/I93886f50993511ea8cb395d-22c142a61/View/FullText.html?transitionType=Default&contextData=(sc.Default)&VR=3.0&RS=cblt1.0; see also Liptak, Adam. "Supreme Court, in 5-4 Decision, Rejects Church's Challenge to Shutdown Order." *The New York Times*, The New York Times, 30 May 2020, www.nytimes.com/2020/05/30/us/supreme-court-churches-coronavirus.html.

102 Ibid.

103 Ibid.

104 *Calvary Chapel Dayton Valley v. Steve Sisolak, Governor of Nevada, et al.*, 591 U. S. ____, No. 19A1070 (July 24, 2020)

105 Ibid.

CHAPTER 30

1 Shear, Michael, and Donald McNeil. "Criticized for Pandemic Response, Trump Tries Shifting Blame to the W.H.O." *The New York Times*, The New York Times, 14 Apr. 2020, www.nytimes.com/2020/04/14/us/politics/coronavirus-trump-who-funding.html

2 Wilkie, Christina, and Dan Managan. "Trump Blames Obama for Lack of Coronavirus Tests: 'I Don't Take Responsibility at All'." *CNBC*, CNBC, 14 Mar. 2020, www.cnbc.com/2020/03/13/coronavirus-trump-says-i-dont-take-responsibility-at-all-for-lack-of-tests.html.

3 "Remarks." *The White House*, The United States Government, 14 Apr. 2020, www.whitehouse.gov/remarks/..

4 Ibid.

5 Ibid.

6 Ibid.

7 Kristof, Nicholas. "Trump's Deadly Search for a Scapegoat." *The New York Times*, The New York Times, 15 Apr. 2020, www.nytimes.com/2020/04/15/opinion/coronavirus-trump-world-health-organization-who.html.

8 @realDonaldTrump (Donald J. Trump). "China has been working very hard to contain the Coronavirus. The United States greatly appreciates their efforts and transparency. It will all work out well. In particular, on behalf of the American People, I want to thank President Xi!" *Twitter*, 24 Jan. 2020, 4:18 PM, https://twitter.com/realDonaldTrump/status/1220818115354923009.

9 DeMarche, Edmund. "Trump Says US Working Closely with China on Coronavirus after Call with Xi." *Fox News*, FOX News Network, 27 Mar. 2020, www.foxnews.com/politics/trump-says-us-china-working-closely-together-on-coronavirus-outbreak-after-call-with-xi..

10. @realDonaldTrump (Donald J. Trump). "Just had a long and very good conversation by phone with President Xi of China. He is strong, sharp and powerfully focused on leading the counterattack on the Coronavirus. He feels they are doing very well, even building hospitals in a matter of only days … Great discipline is taking place in China, as President Xi strongly leads what will be a very successful operation. We are working closely with China to help!" *Twitter*, 7 Feb. 2020, 5:31 AM, https://twitter.com/realDonaldTrump/status/1225728755248828416.

11. Bump, Philip. "Analysis | What Trump Did about Coronavirus in February." *The Washington Post*, WP Company, 20 Apr. 2020, www.washingtonpost.com/politics/2020/04/20/what-trump-did-about-coronavirus-february/.

12. Ibid.

13. Ibid.

14. Wang, Vivian. "China's Coronavirus Battle Is Waning. Its Propaganda Fight Is Not." *The New York Times*, The New York Times, 8 Apr. 2020, www.nytimes.com/2020/04/08/world/asia/coronavirus-china-narrative.html

15. Ibid.

16. Ibid.

17. "Statement on the Second Meeting of the International Health Regulations (2005) Emergency Committee Regarding the Outbreak of Novel Coronavirus (2019-nCoV)." *WHO*, World Health Organization, 30 Jan. 2020, https://www.who.int/news-room/detail/30-01-2020-statement-on-the-second-meeting-of-the-international-health-regulations-(2005)-emergency-committee-regarding-the-outbreak-of-novel-coronavirus-(2019-ncov).

18. Shear, Michael, and Donald McNeil. "Criticized for Pandemic Response, Trump Tries Shifting Blame to the W.H.O." *The New York Times*, The New York Times, 14 Apr. 2020, www.nytimes.com/2020/04/14/us/politics/coronavirus-trump-who-funding.html

19. Ibid.

20. Shaw, Adam. "Trump Announces US 'Terminating' Relationship with WHO." *Fox News*, FOX News Network, 29 May 2020, www.foxnews.com/politics/trump-us-terminating-relationship-with-who.

21. Ibid.

22. Wang, Vivian. "China's Coronavirus Battle Is Waning. Its Propaganda Fight Is Not." *The New York Times*, The New York Times, 8 Apr. 2020, www.nytimes.com/2020/04/08/world/asia/coronavirus-china-narrative.html.

23. Ibid.

24. Ibid.

25. Ibid.

26. Weissert, Will. "DHS Report: China Hid Virus' Severity to Hoard Supplies." *AP NEWS*, Associated Press, 4 May 2020, apnews.com/bf685dcf52125be54e030834ab7062a8.

27. Ibid.

28. Ibid.

29. Ibid.

30. "US Intelligence Report Accuses China of Hiding Coronavirus Severity to Hoard Supplies." *ABC News*, 4 May 2020, www.abc.net.au/news/2020-05-04/china-hid-coronavirus-severity-to-hoard-supplies-says-us-intel/12213868.

31. Wang, Vivian. "China's Coronavirus Battle Is Waning. Its Propaganda Fight Is Not." *The New York Times*, The New York Times, 8 Apr. 2020, www.nytimes.com/2020/04/08/world/asia/coronavirus-china-narrative.html.

32 Ibid.

33 Ibid.

34 Ibid.

35 Ibid.

36 Ibid.

37 Ibid.

38 Ibid.

CHAPTER 31

1 "CDC Telebriefing: Report Shows 20-Year U.S. Immunization Program Spares Millions of Children from Diseases." *Centers for Disease Control and Prevention*, Centers for Disease Control and Prevention, 24 Apr. 2014, www.cdc.gov/media/releases/2014/t0424-immunization-program.html.

2 Cohen, Jon. "Speed Coronavirus Vaccine Testing by Deliberately Infecting Volunteers? Not so Fast, Some Scientists Warn." *Science*, 31 Mar. 2020, www.sciencemag.org/news/2020/03/speed-coronavirus-vaccine-testing-deliberately-infecting-volunteers-not-so-fast-some. Cohen, Jon, et al. "Speed Coronavirus Vaccine Testing by Deliberately Infecting Volunteers? Not so Fast, Some Scientists Warn." Science, 1 Apr. 2020, www.sciencemag.org/news/2020/03/speed-coronavirus-vaccine-testing-deliberately-infecting-volunteers-not-so-fast-some.

3 Ibid.

4 Eyal, Nir, et al. "Human Challenge Studies to Accelerate Coronavirus Vaccine Licensure." *The Journal of Infectious Diseases*, vol. 221, no. 11, 2020, pp. 1752–1756., doi:10.1093/infdis/jiaa152.

5 Cohen, Jon, et al. "United States Should Allow Volunteers to Be Infected with Coronavirus to Test Vaccines, Lawmakers Argue." *Science*, 21 Apr. 2020, www.sciencemag.org/news/2020/04/united-states-should-allow-volunteers-be-infected-coronavirus-test-vaccines-lawmakers.

6 Grady, Denise. "Researchers Debate infecting People on Purpose to Test Coronavirus Vaccines." *The New York Times*, The New York Times, 1 July 2020, https://nyti.ms/2AkLYFo. Grady, Denise. "'Researchers Debate Infecting People on Purpose to Test Coronavirus Vaccines.' ." The New York Times, The New York Times, 1 July 2020, www.nytimes.com/by/denise-grady.

7 Sanger, David, et al. "Profits and Pride at Stake, the Race for a Vaccine Intensifies." *The New York Times*, The New York Times, 2 May 2020, https://nyti.ms/2KUHyqw.

8 Corum, Jonathan, et al. "Coronavirus Vaccine Tracker." *The New York Times*, The New York Times, updated 8 July 2020, https://www.nytimes.com/interactive/2020/science/coronavirus-vaccine-tracker.html.

9 Corum Jonathan, et al. "Different Approaches to a Coronavirus Vaccine." *The New York Times*, The New York Times, 20 May 2020, https://www.nytimes.com/interactive/2020/05/20/science/coronavirus-vaccine-development.html.

10 Corum, Jonathan, et al. "Coronavirus Vaccine Tracker." *The New York Times*, The New York Times, updated 8 July 2020, https://www.nytimes.com/interactive/2020/science/coronavirus-vaccine-tracker.html.

11 Ibid.

12 Corum Jonathan, et al. "Different Approaches to a Coronavirus Vaccine." *The New York Times*, The New York Times, 20 May 2020, https://www.nytimes.com/interactive/2020/05/20/science/coronavirus-vaccine-development.html.

13 Ibid.

14. Ibid.
15. See Chapter 12 (Know Thy Enemy).
16. "Get the Facts about a COVID-19 (Coronavirus) Vaccine." *Mayo Clinic*, Mayo Foundation for Medical Education and Research, 10 June 2020, www.mayoclinic.org/diseases-conditions/coronavirus/in-depth/coronavirus-vaccine/art-20484859.
17. Corum, Jonathan and Zimmer, Carl. "Bad News Wrapped in Protein: Inside the Coronavirus Genome." *The New York Times*, The New York Times, 3 Apr. 2020, https://www.nytimes.com/interactive/2020/04/03/science/coronavirus-genome-bad-news-wrapped-in-protein.html.
18. Corum Jonathan, et al. "Different Approaches to a Coronavirus Vaccine." *The New York Times*, The New York Times, 20 May 2020, https://www.nytimes.com/interactive/2020/05/20/science/coronavirus-vaccine-development.html.
19. Ibid.
20. Ibid.
21. Ibid.
22. Wee, Sui-Lee. "China's Coronavirus Vaccine Drive Empowers a Troubled Industry." *The New York Times*, The New York Times, 4 May 2020, https://nyti.ms/3dbWgFv
23. Corum Jonathan, et al. "Different Approaches to a Coronavirus Vaccine." *The New York Times*, The New York Times, 20 May 2020, https://www.nytimes.com/interactive/2020/05/20/science/coronavirus-vaccine-development.html.
24. Ibid.
25. Wee, Sui-Lee. "China's Coronavirus Vaccine Drive Empowers a Troubled Industry." *The New York Times*, The New York Times, 4 May 2020, https://nyti.ms/3dbWgFv.
26. Sanger, David, et al. "Profits and Pride at Stake, the Race for a Vaccine Intensifies." *The New York Times*, The New York Times, 2 May 2020, https://nyti.ms/2KUHyqw.
27. Ibid.
28. Maron, Dina Fine. "Fact or Fiction?: Vaccines Are Dangerous." *Scientific American*, Scientific American, 6 Mar. 2015, www.scientificamerican.com/article/fact-or-fiction-vaccines-are-dangerous/
29. Ibid.
30. "Older Adults." *Centers for Disease Control and Prevention*, Centers for Disease Control and Prevention, 25 June 2020, www.cdc.gov/coronavirus/2019-ncov/need-extra-precautions/older-adults.html.
31. "Opinion | Speed Is Essential in Developing This Vaccine. But so Is Safety." *The Washington Post*, WP Company, 5 May 2020, www.washingtonpost.com/opinions/global-opinions/speed-is-essential-in-developing-this-vaccine-but-so-is-safety/2020/05/05/55a9ec68-8e36-11ea-a9c0-73b93422d691_story.html.
32. Ibid.
33. Ibid.
34. Smith, Chris. "Dr. Fauci Delivered More Good News about Coronavirus Vaccines." *BGR*, BGR, 11 June 2020, bgr.com/2020/06/11/coronavirus-vaccine-trials-update-fauci-confirms-phase-3-usa/.
35. Ibid.
36. Ibid.
37. Chico Harlan, Stefano Pitrelli. "From Oxford to an Italian Lab, One Race for Coronavirus Vaccine Is Gaining Backers." *The Washington Post*, WP Company, 20 June 2020, www.washingtonpost.com/world/

europe/vaccine-coronavirus-oxford-italy-trials/2020/06/20/4b8f5e0a-af1c-11ea-98b5-279a6479a1e4_story.html.

38 Ibid.
39 Ibid.
40 Ibid.
41 Ibid.
42 "AstraZeneca to Supply Europe with up to 400 Million Doses of Oxford University's Vaccine at No Profit." *AstraZeneca Press Release*, 2020, www.astrazeneca.com/media-centre/press-releases/2020/astrazeneca-to-supply-europe-with-up-to-400-million-doses-of-oxford-universitys-vaccine-at-no-profit.html.
43 Chico Harlan, Stefano Pitrelli. "From Oxford to an Italian Lab, One Race for Coronavirus Vaccine Is Gaining Backers." *The Washington Post*, WP Company, 20 June 2020, www.washingtonpost.com/world/europe/vaccine-coronavirus-oxford-italy-trials/2020/06/20/4b8f5e0a- af1c-11ea-98b5-279a6479a1e4_story.html.
44 Kirkpatrick, David. D. "$1.2 Billion From U.S. to Drugmaker to Pursue Coronavirus Vaccine." *The New York Times*, The New York Times, 21 May 2020, https://nyti.ms/2ARyAsn.
45 Ibid.
46 Ibid.
47 Ibid.
47 Ibid.
48 Ibid.
49 Ibid.
50 Paton, James, et al. "U.S. Likely to Get Sanofi Vaccine First If It Succeeds, CEO Says." *Bloomberg.com*, Bloomberg, 13 May 2020, www.bloomberg.com/news/articles/2020-05-13/u-s-to-get-sanofi-covid-vaccine-first-if-it-succeeds-ceo-says.
51 Coleman, Justine. "French Official: 'Unacceptable' That US Might Get Sanofi Coronavirus Vaccine First." *TheHill*, The Hill, 14 May 2020, thehill.com/policy/international/europe/497718-french-official-unacceptable-that-us-might-get-sanofi-coronavirus.
52 Paton, James, et al. "U.S. Likely to Get Sanofi Vaccine First If It Succeeds, CEO Says." *Bloomberg.com*, Bloomberg, 13 May 2020, www.bloomberg.com/news/articles/2020-05-13/u-s-to-get-sanofi-covid-vaccine-first-if-it-succeeds-ceo-says.
53 Ibid.
54 "Coronavirus Lockdown May Spur Surge in Mental Illness, U.N. Warns." *The New York Times*, The New York Times, 14 May 2020, https://nyti.ms/2Au64Ng.
55 Sanger, David, et al. "Profits and Pride at Stake, the Race for a Vaccine Intensifies." *The New York Times*, The New York Times, 2 May 2020, https://nyti.ms/2KUHyqw.
56 Ibid.
57 Ibid.
58 Gardy, Denise. "Moderna Coronavirus Vaccine Trial Shows Promising Early Results." *The New York Times*, The New York Times, 18 May 2020, https://nyti.ms/2X69NIz.
59 Ibid.
60 Ibid.

61 Diamond, Dan. "Ousted Vaccine Expert Battles with Trump Team Over His Abrupt Dismissal." *Politico*, Politico, 22 Apr. 2020, https://www.politico.com/news/2020/04/22/hhs-ousts-vaccine-expert-as-covid-19-threat-grows-201642.

62 Hopkins, Jared. "Coronavirus Vaccine Enters Humans Testing U.S.." *The Wall Street Journal*, 5 May 2020, www.wsj.com/articles/coronavirus-vaccine-enters-human-testing-in-u-s-11588675501?mod=cx-recs_join#cxrecs_s\.

63 Kirkpatrick, David. D. "$1.2 Billion From U.S. to Drugmaker to Pursue Coronavirus Vaccine." *The New York Times*, The New York Times, 21 May 2020, https://nyti.ms/2ARyAsn.

64 Thomas, Katie. "U.S. Will Pay $1.6 Billion to Novavax for Coronavirus Vaccine." *The New York Times*, The New York Times, 7 July 2020, https://nyti.ms/3e6sRNd

65 Welna, David. "General Tapped To Lead 'Operation Warp Speed' Vaccine Drive Faces Skeptical Senators." *NPR*, National Public Radio, 18 June 2020, https://www.npr.org/2020/06/18/880592090/general-tapped-to-lead-operation-warp-speed-vaccine-drive-faces-skeptical-senators.

66 Ibid.

67 Ibid.

68 Knowles, Hannah and Shaban, Hamza. "Californians Required to Cover Their Faces in Most Settings Outside the Home." *The Washington Post*, WP Company, 19 June 2020, www.washingtonpost.com/nation/2020/06/18/coronavirus-live-updates-us/.

69 Stevis-Gridness, Matina and Jakes, Lara. "World Leaders Join to Pledge $8 Billion for Vaccines as U.S. Goes It Alone." *The New York Times*, The New York Times, 4 May 2020, https://nyti.ms/2WuQRTt.

70 Ibid.

71 Ibid.

72 Ibid.

73 Sanger, David, et al. "Profits and Pride at Stake, the Race for a Vaccine Intensifies." *The New York Times*, The New York Times, 2 May 2020, https://nyti.ms/2KUHyqw.

74 Ibid.

75 Ibid.

76 Twohey, Megan. "Who Gets a Vaccine First? U.S. Considers Race in Coronavirus Plans." *The New York Times*, The New York Times, 9 July 2020, https://nyti.ms/2BSb3IC.

77 Ibid.

78 Ibid.

79 Ibid.

80 Ibid.

81 Ibid.

82 Ibid.

83 Ibid.

84 Marchione, Marilynn. "Desperation Science Slows the Hunt for Coronavirus Drugs." *AP NEWS*, Associated Press, 8 July 2020, apnews.com/db08697f6260038f196b1106fe574228?utm_source=piano&utm_medium=email&utm_campaign=morningwire&pnespid=1vR.suQB-BQKNprYy7yDfU9.

85 Ibid.

86 Ibid.

87   Ibid.
88   Ibid.
89   Ibid.
90   Ibid.
91   Ibid.

CHAPTER 32

1   Scott, Dylan. "Coronavirus Is Exposing All of the Weaknesses in the US Health System." *Vox*, Vox, 16 Mar. 2020, www.vox.com/policy-and-politics/2020/3/16/21173766/coronavirus-covid-19-us-cases-health-care-system.
2   Ibid.
3   Ibid.
4   Ibid.
5   Ibid.
6   Ibid.
7   Ibid.
8   Ibid.
9   Ibid.
10 Ibid.
11 Kliff, Sarah. "Hospitals Knew How to Make Money. Then Coronavirus Happened." *The New York Times*, The New York Times, 15 May 2020, https://nyti.ms/3cBp2PZ.
12 Ibid.
13 Ibid.
14 Carbone, Christopher. "Mayo Clinic to Furlough or Cut Pay of 30,000 Employees." *Fox News*, FOX News Network, 27 Apr. 2020, www.foxnews.com/science/mayo-clinic-furlough-or-cut-pay-employees.
15 Kliff, Sarah. "Hospitals Knew How to Make Money. Then Coronavirus Happened." *The New York Times*, The New York Times, 15 May 2020, https://nyti.ms/3cBp2PZ.
16 Ibid.
17 Ibid.
18 Ibid.
19 Ibid.
20 Ibid.
21 "New AHA Report Finds Financial Impact of COVID-19 on Hospitals & Health Systems to Be over $200 Billion through June." *American Hospital Association*, 2020, www.aha.org/press-releases/2020-05-05-new-aha-report-finds-financial-impact-covid-19-hospitals-health-systems.
22 Kliff, Sarah. "Hospitals Knew How to Make Money. Then Coronavirus Happened." *The New York Times*, The New York Times, 15 May 2020, https://nyti.ms/3cBp2PZ.
23 Ibid.
24 Ibid.
25 Ibid.
26 Ibid.

27 Ibid.

28 Ibid.

29 "Governor Cuomo Announces New Directive Requiring New York Insurers to Waive Cost-Sharing for Coronavirus Testing." *Governor Andrew M. Cuomo*, 6 Mar. 2020, www.governor.ny.gov/news/governor-cuomo-announces-new-directive-requiring-new-york-insurers-waive-cost-sharing.

30 Perlberg, Heather. "How Private Equity Is Ruining American Health Care." *Bloomberg Law*, 2020, news.bloomberglaw.com/health-law-and-business/how-private-equity-is-ruining-american-health-care; *see also* Morgenson, Gretchen, and Emmanuelle Saliba. "Private Equity Firms Now Control Many Hospitals, ERs and Nursing Homes. Is It Good for Health Care?" *NBCNews.com*, NBCUniversal News Group, 14 May 2020, www.nbcnews.com/health/health-care/private-equity-firms-now-control-many-hospitals-ers-nursing-homes-n1203161.

31 Morgenson, Gretchen, and Emmanuelle Saliba. "Private Equity Firms Now Control Many Hospitals, ERs and Nursing Homes. Is It Good for Health Care?" *NBCNews.com*, NBCUniversal News Group, 14 May 2020, www.nbcnews.com/health/health-care/private-equity-firms-now-control-many-hospitals-ers-nursing-homes-n1203161.

32 Perlberg, Heather. "How Private Equity Is Ruining American Health Care." *Bloomberg Law*, 2020, news.bloomberglaw.com/health-law-and-business/how-private-equity-is-ruining-american-health-care.

33 Ibid.

34 Morgenson, Gretchen, and Emmanuelle Saliba. "Private Equity Firms Now Control Many Hospitals, ERs and Nursing Homes. Is It Good for Health Care?" *NBCNews.com*, NBCUniversal News Group, 14 May 2020, www.nbcnews.com/health/health-care/private-equity-firms-now-control-many-hospitals-ers-nursing-homes-n1203161.

35 Ibid.

36 Perlberg, Heather. "How Private Equity Is Ruining American Health Care." *Bloomberg Law*, 2020, news.bloomberglaw.com/health-law-and-business/how-private-equity-is-ruining-american-health-care.

37 Ibid.

38 Kocieniewski, David, and Caleb Melby. "Private Equity Lands Billion-Dollar Backdoor Hospital Bailout." *Bloomberg.com*, Bloomberg, 2 June 2020, www.bloomberg.com/news/features/2020-06-02/private-equity-lands-billion-dollar-backdoor-hospital-bailout.

39 Ibid.

40 "HHS to Begin Immediate Delivery of Initial $30 Billion of CARES Act Provider Relief Funding." *HHS.gov*, Apr. 2020, www.hhs.gov/about/news/2020/04/10/hhs-to-begin-immediate-delivery-of-initial-30-billion-of-cares-act-provider-relief-funding.html.

41 Kocieniewski, David, and Caleb Melby. "Private Equity Lands Billion-Dollar Backdoor Hospital Bailout." *Bloomberg.com*, Bloomberg, 2 June 2020, www.bloomberg.com/news/features/2020-06-02/private-equity-lands-billion-dollar-backdoor-hospital-bailout.

42 Ibid.

43 Ibid.

44 Morgenson, Gretchen, and Emmanuelle Saliba. "Private Equity Firms Now Control Many Hospitals, ERs and Nursing Homes. Is It Good for Health Care?" *NBCNews.com*, NBCUniversal News Group, 14 May 2020, www.nbcnews.com/health/health-care/private-equity-firms-now-control-many-hospitals-ers-nursing-homes-n1203161.

45 Ibid.

46 Ibid.

47   Ibid.

48   Ibid.

49   Magee, Mike. "COVID-19 Makes the Case for a National Health Care System." *The Health Care Blog*, 13 Apr. 2020, thehealthcareblog.com/blog/2020/04/13/covid-19-makes-the-case-for-a-national-health-care-system/.

CHAPTER 33

1   "Cases in the U.S." *Centers for Disease Control and Prevention*, Centers for Disease Control and Prevention, 9 July 2020, www.cdc.gov/coronavirus/2019-ncov/cases-updates/cases-in-us.html.

2   Wu, Jiachuan, and Nigel Chiwaya. "Coronavirus Map: Confirmed COVID-19 Cases, per Country." *NBCNews.com*, NBCUniversal News Group, 13 July 2020, www.nbcnews.com/health/health-news/coronavirus-map-confirmed-cases-2020-n1120686.

3   Maer, Thoka. "'An Anvil Sitting on My Chest': What It's Like to Have Covid-19." *The New York Times*, The New York Times, 6 May 2020, www.nytimes.com/article/coronavirus-symptoms.html.

4   Behr, Zachary. "Recovery for COVID-19 Survivors Begins in the ICU: Johns Hopkins Medicine." *Recovery for COVID-19 Survivors Begins in the ICU | Johns Hopkins Medicine*, 5 May 2020, www.hopkinsmedicine.org/coronavirus/articles/icu-recovery.html.

5   Rana, Preetika. "Coronavirus Patients Lose Senses of Taste, Smell-and Haven't Gotten Them Back." *The Wall Street Journal*, Dow Jones & Company, 1 June 2020, www.wsj.com/articles/coronavirus-patients-lose-senses-of-taste-smelland-havent-gotten-them-back-11591007522.

6   Belluck, Pam. "'They Want to Kill Me': Many Covid Patients Have Terrifying Delirium." *The New York Times*, The New York Times, 28 June 2020, https://nyti.ms/2YFYvfZ.

7   Ibid.

8   Ibid.

9   Ibid.

10   Ibid.

11   Wan, William. "The Coronavirus Pandemic is Pushing America into a Mental Health Crisis." *The Washington Post*, 4 May 2020, https://www.washingtonpost.com/health/2020/05/04/mental-health-coronavirus/.

12   Ibid.

13   Ibid.

14   Ibid.

15   Edelman, Susan, et al. "EMT John Mondello Kills Himself after Less than Three Months on the Job." *New York Post*, 25 Apr. 2020, nypost.com/2020/04/25/nyc-emt-commits-suicide-with-gun-belonging-to-his-dad/.

16   Ibid.

17   Ibid.

18   Wan, William. "The Coronavirus Pandemic is Pushing America into a Mental Health Crisis." *The Washington Post*, 4 May 2020, https://www.washingtonpost.com/health/2020/05/04/mental-health-coronavirus/.

19   Ibid.

20 Long, Heather, and William Wan. "'Cries for Help': Drug Overdoses Are Soaring during the Coronavirus Pandemic." The Washington Post, WP Company, 1 July 2020, www.washingtonpost.com/health/2020/07/01/coronavirus-drug-overdose/.

21 Alter, Aliese, and Christopher Yeager. Overdose Detection Mapping Application Program, 2020, The Consequences Of Covid-19 On The Overdose Epidemic: Overdoses Are Increasing, www.odmap.org/Content/docs/news/2020/ODMAP-Report-May-2020.pdf.

22 Kilmer, Graham. "EMS Calls Show 54% Spike in Drug Overdoses, 80% Increase in Suicide Attempts." Urban Milwaukee, 7 May 2020, https://urbanmilwaukee.com/2020/05/07/ems-calls-show-54-spike-in-drug-overdoses-80-increase-in-suicide-attempts/.

23 Long, Heather, and William Wan. "'Cries for Help': Drug Overdoses Are Soaring during the Coronavirus Pandemic." The Washington Post, WP Company, 1 July 2020, www.washingtonpost.com/health/2020/07/01/coronavirus-drug-overdose/.

24 Phillips, Julie A., and Colleen N. Nugent. "Suicide and the Great Recession of 2007–2009: The Role of Economic Factors in the 50 U.S. States." *Social Science & Medicine*, vol. 116, 2014, pp. 22–31., doi:10.1016/j.socscimed.2014.06.015.

25 Meadows Mental Health Policy Institute, 2020, Projected COVID-19 MHSUD Impacts, www.texasstateofmind.org/uploads/whitepapers/COVID-MHSUDImpacts.pdf.

26 Ibid.

27 Wan, William. "The Coronavirus Pandemic is Pushing America into a Mental Health Crisis." *The Washington Post*, 4 May 2020, https://www.washingtonpost.com/health/2020/05/04/mental-health-coronavirus/.

28 National Action Alliance, 2020, National Response to COVID-19, theactionalliance.org/covid19.

29 Mock, Jillian. "Frontline Trauma." *Scientific American*, vol. 322, 2020, pp. 36-37, doi:10.1038/scientificamerican0620-36.

30 Richardson, Safiya, et al. "Presenting Characteristics, Comorbidities, and Outcomes Among 5700 Patients Hospitalized With COVID-19 in the New York City Area." JAMA, vol. 323, no. 20, 26 May 2020, pp. 2052–2059., doi:10.1001/jama.2020.6775.

31 Wan, William. "The Coronavirus Pandemic is Pushing America into a Mental Health Crisis." *The Washington Post*, 4 May 2020, https://www.washingtonpost.com/health/2020/05/04/mental-health-coronavirus/.

32 Ibid.

33 Ibid.

34 Ibid.

35 "Mental Health By the Numbers." *NAMI*, Last updated Sep. 2019, https://www.nami.org/mhstats.

36 Ibid.

37 Weir, Kirsten. "Worrying Trends in U. S. Suicide Rates." Monitor on Psychology, vol. 50, no. 3, Mar. 2019, p. 24, http://www.apa.org/monitor/2019/03/trends-suicide.

38 Wan, William. "The Coronavirus Pandemic is Pushing America into a Mental Health Crisis." *The Washington Post*, 4 May 2020, https://www.washingtonpost.com/health/2020/05/04/mental-health-coronavirus/.

39 "NAMI Calls on Congress To Respond To The Mental Health And Addiction Crisis Caused By The COVID-19 Pandemic." *NAMI*, 8 Apr. 2020, https://www.nami.org/About-NAMI/NAMI-News/2020/NAMI-Calls-on-Congress-to-Respond-to-the-Mental-Health-and-Addiction-Crisis-Caused-By-the-COVID-19-P.

40. *See* Coronavirus Aid, Relief, and Economic Security Act [CARES], 116 P.L. 136, 2020 Enacted H.R. 748, 116 Enacted H.R. 748, 134 Stat. 281; "SAMHSA Releases $15 Million in Supplemental Grant Awards for Tribal COVID-19 Behavioral Health Response." SAMHSA Newsroom, SAMHSA, 1 May 2020, www.samhsa.gov/newsroom/press-announcements/202005011645.
41. "Public Health and Social Services Emergency Fund." Received by Secretary Alex Azar, Psychiatry, 2020, Public-Health-Social-Services-Emergency-Fund-04272020.pdf.
42. Ibid.
43. Wan, William. "The Coronavirus Pandemic is Pushing America into a Mental Health Crisis." *The Washington Post*, 4 May 2020, https://www.washingtonpost.com/health/2020/05/04/mental-health-coronavirus/.

CHAPTER 34

1. Cohan, William D. "'People Will Die. People Do Die.' Wall Street Has Had Enough of the Lockdown." *Vanity Fair*, 2020, www.vanityfair.com/news/2020/05/wall-street-has-had-enough-of-the-lockdown.
2. https://www.reuters.com/article/health-coronavirus-usa/us-coronavirus-deaths-top-150000-toll-ranks-6th-in-deaths-per-capita-
3. Id.
4. Berger, Miriam, and Mark Berman. "Experts Warn of Second Coronavirus Wave in Dallas, Houston, Alabama and Parts of Florida." *The Washington Post*, WP Company, 21 May 2020, www.washingtonpost.com/nation/2020/05/20/coronavirus-update-us/.
5. Mervosh, S. & Harmon, A. "All 50 States Are Now Reopening. But at What Cost?" *The New York Times*, The New York Times, 20 May 2020, https://nyti.ms/36flRva.
6. Ibid.
7. Witte, Griff, and Toluse Olorunnipa. "Trump Cheers on Governors Even as They Ignore White House Coronavirus Guidelines in Race to Reopen." *The Washington Post*, WP Company, 5 May 2020, www.washingtonpost.com/politics/trump-cheers-on-governors-as-they-ignore-white-house-coronovirus-guidelines-in-race-to-reopen/2020/05/04/bedc6116-8e18-11ea-a0bc-4e9ad4866d21_story.html.
8. "Opening Up American Again." *White House*, n.d., https://www.whitehouse.gov/openingamerica/.
9. Collins, K. "Coronavirus Testing Needs to Triple Before the U.S. Can Reopen, Experts Say." *The New York Times*, The New York Times, 17 Apr. 2020, https://www.nytimes.com/interactive/2020/04/17/us/coronavirus-testing-states.html.
10. Ibid.
11. Brewster, Jack. "These 41 States Aren't Testing Enough For Coronavirus To Safely Reopen, Experts Say." *Forbes*, Forbes Magazine, 7 May 2020, www.forbes.com/sites/jackbrewster/2020/05/07/these-41-states-arent-testing-enough-for-coronavirus-to-safely-reopen-experts-say/#4526624c2b2c.
12. Shabad, Rebecca. "Fauci Warns Reopening States: 'You Can't Just Leap over Things'." *NBCNews.com*, NBCUniversal News Group, 30 Apr. 2020, www.nbcnews.com/politics/congress/fauci-warns-reopening-states-you-can-t-just-leap-over-n1196306.
13. Brewster, Jack. "These 41 States Aren't Testing Enough For Coronavirus To Safely Reopen, Experts Say." *Forbes*, Forbes Magazine, 7 May 2020, www.forbes.com/sites/jackbrewster/2020/05/07/these-41-states-arent-testing-enough-for-coronavirus-to-safely-reopen-experts-say/#4526624c2b2c.
14. Witte, Griff, and Toluse Olorunnipa. "Trump Cheers on Governors Even as They Ignore White House Coronavirus Guidelines in Race to Reopen." *The Washington Post*, WP Company, 5 May 2020, www.

washingtonpost.com/politics/trump-cheers-on-governors-as-they-ignore-white-house-coronovirus-guidelines-in-race-to-reopen/2020/05/04/bedc6116-8e18-11ea-a0bc-4e9ad4866d21_story.html.

15 Ibid.
16 Ibid.
17 Ibid.
18 Ibid.
19 Wagner, John, and Marisa Iati. "U.S. Daily Coronavirus Death Rate Will More than Double by June 1, Draft Government Report Projects." *The Washington Post*, WP Company, 5 May 2020, www.washingtonpost.com/nation/2020/05/04/coronavirus-update-us/.
20 Sternlicht, Alexandra. "New Cases Spike In Reopened States, Though Some Say That's Due To Increased Testing." *Forbes*, Forbes Magazine, 18 May 2020, www.forbes.com/sites/alexandrasternlicht/2020/05/17/new-cases-spike-in-reopened-states-though-some-say-its-due-to-increased-testing/#5235cc286bc9.
21 Ibid.
22 Weiner, Rachel, and Joel Achenbach. "Study Estimates 24 States Still Have Uncontrolled Coronavirus Spread." *The Washington Post*, WP Company, 22 May 2020, www.washingtonpost.com/health/study-estimates-24-states-still-have-uncontrolled-coronavirus-spread/2020/05/22/d3032470-9c43-11ea-ac72-3841fcc9b35f_story.html.
23 Sternlicht, Alexandra. "New Cases Spike In Reopened States, Though Some Say That's Due To Increased Testing." *Forbes*, Forbes Magazine, 18 May 2020, www.forbes.com/sites/alexandrasternlicht/2020/05/17/new-cases-spike-in-reopened-states-though-some-say-its-due-to-increased-testing/#5235cc286bc9.
24 Ibid.
25 Ibid.
26 Weiner, Rachel, and Joel Achenbach. "Study Estimates 24 States Still Have Uncontrolled Coronavirus Spread." *The Washington Post*, WP Company, 22 May 2020, www.washingtonpost.com/health/study-estimates-24-states-still-have-uncontrolled-coronavirus-spread/2020/05/22/d3032470-9c43-11ea-ac72-3841fcc9b35f_story.html.
27 Ibid.
28 Ibid.
29 Ibid.
30 Ibid.
31 Ibid.
32 Ibid.
33 Ibid.
34 Ibid.
35 Tahir, D. & Cancryn, A. "Bad state data hides coronavirus threat as Trump pushes reopening." *Politico*, Politico, 27 May 2020, https://www.politico.com/news/2020/05/27/bad-state-coronavirus-data-trump-reopening-286143.
36 Ibid.
37 Ibid.
38 Ibid.

39 Ibid.
40 Ibid.
41 Ibid.
42 Ibid.
43 Ibid.
44 Ibid.
45 Ibid.
46 Ibid.
47 Ibid.
48 Ibid.
49 "Top Health Experts Paint Bleak Picture of Pandemic." *The New York Times*, The New York Times, 12 May 2020, https://nyti.ms/3bqd4aJ.
50 Ibid.
51 Ibid.
52 Hogberg, David. "White House Reportedly Shelved Detailed CDC Report on Reopening." *Washington Examiner*, 7 May 2020, www.washingtonexaminer.com/news/white-house-reportedly-shelved-detailed-cdc-report-on-reopening.
53 Bernstein, Lenny, and William Wan. "Draft Report Predicts Covid-19 Cases Will Reach 200,000 a Day by June 1." *The Washington Post*, WP Company, 4 May 2020, www.washingtonpost.com/health/government-report-predicts-covid-19-cases-will-reach-200000-a-day-by-june-1/2020/05/04/02fe743e-8e27-11ea-a9c0-73b93422d691_story.html.
54 Axelrod, Tal. "CDC Director Says Guidance Shelved by White House Was 'in Draft Form'." *The Hill*, The Hill, 9 May 2020, thehill.com/homenews/administration/496937-cdc-director-says-guidance-shelved-by-white-house-was-in-draft-form.
55 Ibid.
56 Klein, Charlotte. "CDC Replaces In-Depth Reopening Report With 6 Pages of Trump-Friendly Graphics." *Vanity Fair*, Vanity Fair, 18 May 2020, www.vanityfair.com/news/2020/05/cdc-replaces-in-depth-reopening-report-with-6-pages-of-trump-friendly-graphics.
57 Ibid.
58 Slavitt, Andy, et al. "Health Leaders: We stuck together to #StayHome, now we can start together to #OpenSafely." *USA Today*, Gannett Satellite Information Network, 20 May 2020, https://www.usatoday.com/story/opinion/2020/05/20/coronavirus-still-spreading-america-must-open-safely-column/5216824002/.
59 Center for Disease Control, 2020, *CDC Activities and Initiatives Supporting the COVID-19 Response and the President's Plan for Opening America Up Again*, www.cdc.gov/coronavirus/2019-ncov/downloads/php/CDC-Activities-Initiatives-for-COVID-19-Response.pdf.
60 Berkeley, Lovelace Jr. "CDC Quietly Releases Detailed Guidelines for Reopening America." *CNBC*, CNBC, 20 May 2020, www.cnbc.com/2020/05/20/coronavirus-cdc-quietly-releases-detailed-guidelines-for-reopening-us.html.
61 "As Pandemic Wrecks Budgets, States Cut and Borrow to Balance Books." *The New York Times*, The New York Times, 14 May 2020, https://nyti.ms/2yWs5nr.
62 Ibid.
63 Ibid.

64 Ibid.

65 Gabriel, Trip. "G.O.P. Defiance of Pennsylvania's Lockdown Has 2020 Implications." *The New York Times*, The New York Times, 14 May 2020, www.nytimes.com/2020/05/14/us/politics/pennsylvania-tom-wolf-coronavirus.html.

66 Bendix, Trish. "Late Night Laughs Off Trump's Saying Hosts Have Zero Talent." *The New York Times*, The New York Times, 6 May 2020, https://nyti.ms/3b7wa5a.

67 Phelps, Jordyn, and Ben Gittleson. "Trump to ABC's Muir: 'It's Possible There Will Be Some' Deaths as Country Reopens." *ABC News*, ABC, 2020, abcnews.go.com/Politics/trump-abcs-david-muir-covid-19-deaths-country/story?id=70515537.

68 "Models Project Sharp Rise in Deaths as States Reopen." *The New York Times*, The New York Times, 4 May 2020, https://nyti.ms/2SQWDOn.

69 Ibid.

70 Ibid.

71 Baker, P. "Trump's New Coronavirus Message: Time to Move On to the Economic Recovery." *The New York Times*, The New York Times, 6 May 2020, https://nyti.ms/2L68SST.

72 Ibid.

73 Ibid.

74 Ibid.

75 Ibid.

76 Ibid.

77 Orecchio-Egresitz, H. "Texas Gov. Greg Abbot acknowledged in a private call that reports indicate ending lockdown is dangerous." *Business Insider*, Business Insider, 6 May 2020, https://www.businessinsider.com/texas-governor-admits-in-call-ending-lockdown-dangerous-2020-5.

78 Sternlicht, Alexandra. "New Cases Spike In Reopened States, Though Some Say That's Due To Increased Testing." *Forbes*, Forbes Magazine, 18 May 2020, www.forbes.com/sites/alexandrasternlicht/2020/05/17/new-cases-spike-in-reopened-states-though-some-say-its-due-to-increased-testing/#5235cc286bc9.

79 Ibid.

80 Ibid.

81 Board, Editorial. "Opinion | Three Weeks after Memorial Day, the Coronavirus Is Surging Dangerously in States That Opened Quickly." *The Washington Post*, WP Company, 12 June 2020, www.washingtonpost.com/opinions/the-surges-of-the-coronavirus-across-the-nation-could-force-more-shutdowns/2020/06/12/e6985b94-acd9-11ea-a9d9-a81c1a491c52_story.html.

82 "COVIDView: A Weekly Surveillance Summary of U.S. COVID-19 Activity." *Centers for Disease Control and Prevention*, Centers for Disease Control and Prevention, 10 July 2020, www.cdc.gov/coronavirus/2019-ncov/covid-data/covidview/index.html.

83 Board, Editorial. "Opinion | Three Weeks after Memorial Day, the Coronavirus Is Surging Dangerously in States That Opened Quickly." *The Washington Post*, WP Company, 12 June 2020, www.washingtonpost.com/opinions/the-surges-of-the-coronavirus-across-the-nation-could-force-more-shutdowns/2020/06/12/e6985b94-acd9-11ea-a9d9-a81c1a491c52_story.html.

84 Birnbaum, Michael, and Derek Hawkins. "Arizona, Florida, Texas Are Latest Coronavirus Epicenters." *The Washington Post*, WP Company, 29 June 2020, www.washingtonpost.com/nation/2020/06/28/coronavirus-live-updates-us/.

85 Berger, Miriam, and Hannah Knowles. "Texas Announces Record Number of Hospitalizations as Its Daily Death Toll Rises." *The Washington Post*, WP Company, 18 June 2020, www.washingtonpost.com/nation/2020/06/17/coronavirus-live-updates-us/.

86 "U.S. States Backtrack on Reopening as Coronavirus Cases Climb." *The New York Times*, The New York Times, 27 June 2020, https://nyti.ms/2B7qj49.

87 Ibid.

88 Ibid.

89 Ibid.

90 Ibid.

91 Hassan, Jennifer. "Disney World Set to Reopen despite Severe Outbreak Unfolding in Florida." *The Washington Post*, WP Company, 10 July 2020, www.washingtonpost.com/travel/2020/07/10/disney-world-set-reopen-despite-severe-outbreak-unfolding-florida/.

92 Associated Press. "Florida Reports Largest, Single-Day Increase in Covid Cases." *The New York Times*, The New York Times, 12 July 2020, https://nyti.ms/3o3oqot.

93 Barry, John. "The Pandemic Could Get Much, Much Worse. We Must Act Now." *The New York Times*, The New York Times, 14 July 2020, https://nyti.ms/38YdA06.

94 Ibid.

95 Rodriquez, Adrianna. Can kids spread the coronavirus? 'Conclusively, without a doubt – yes,' experts say." *USA Today*, Gannett, 20 July 2020 https://www.usatoday.com/story/news/health/2020/07/17/coronavirus-can-kids-spread-covid-19-spreadquestions-answered/5450062002/

96 Associated Press. "Florida Reports Largest, Single-Day Increase in Covid Cases." *The New York Times*, The New York Times, 12 July 2020, https://nyti.ms/3o3oqot.

97 Elliott, Christopher. "'This Is Not the Summer for a Spontaneous Road Trip': The Case for Canceling Your Vacation." *USA Today*, Gannett Satellite Information Network, 10 July 2020, www.usatoday.com/story/travel/advice/2020/07/10/coronavirus-why-you-should-cancel-your-summer-vacation/5399403002/.

98 Joseph, Andrew, et al. "As Covid-19 Cases Surge, Pence Touts Progress Made from Earlier Peaks." *STAT*, 26 June 2020, www.statnews.com/2020/06/26/as-covid-19-cases-surge-pence-touts-progress-made-from-earlier-peaks/.

CHAPTER 35

1 Tappe, Anneken. "1 In 4 American Workers Have Filed for Unemployment Benefits during the Pandemic." *CNN*, Cable News Network, 28 May 2020, www.cnn.com/2020/05/28/economy/unemployment-benefits-coronavirus/index.html.

2 Ibid.

3 Jacobs, Emily. "Federal Reserve Predicts 32% Unemployment Rate Thanks to Coronavirus." *New York Post*, New York Post, 31 Mar. 2020, nypost.com/2020/03/31/federal-reserve-predicts-32-unemployment-rate-thanks-to-coronavirus/.

4 Branigin, Anne. "Florida Police Release Video of Massive Block Party After Allegations of Racial Profiling." *The Root*, The Root, 20 May 2020, www.theroot.com/florida-police-release-video-of-massive-block-party-aft-1843564387.

5 Burke, Minyvonne. "Video Appears to Show Georgia Man Shot While Jogging; Lawyers Call for Arrests." *NBCNews.com*, NBCUniversal News Group, 12 May 2020, www.nbcnews.com/news/nbcblk/video-appears-show-georgia-man-shot-while-jogging-lawyers-call-n1201301.

6   Fausseset, Richard. "What We Know About the Shooting Death of Ahmaud Arbery." *The New York Times*, The New York Times, 10 Sept 2020, www.nytimes.com/article/ahmaud-arbery-shooting-georgia.html.

7   Ibid.

8   Rojas, Rick. "Man Who Filmed Ahmaud Arbery's Death Is Charged With Murder." *The New York Times*, The New York Times, 21 May 2020, www.nytimes.com/2020/05/21/us/william-bryan-arrest-ahmaud-arbery.html.

9   Hill, Evan, et al. "How George Floyd Was Killed in Police Custody." *The New York Times*, The New York Times, 31 May 2020, www.nytimes.com/2020/05/31/us/george-floyd-investigation.html.

10 Hanna, Jason. "3 Recordings. 3 Cries of 'I Can't Breathe.' 3 Black Men Dead after Interactions with Police." *CNN*, Cable News Network, 10 June 2020, www.cnn.com/2020/06/10/us/cant-breathe-deaths-javier-ambler-george-floyd-manuel-ellis/index.html.

11 Hill, Evan, et al. "How George Floyd Was Killed in Police Custody." *The New York Times*, The New York Times, 31 May 2020, www.nytimes.com/2020/05/31/us/george-floyd-investigation.html.

12 "After Widespread Looting, Curfew Is Moved Up to 8 P.M." *The New York Times*, The New York Times, 2 June 2020, https://nyti.ms/2BoHs99.

13 "Fiery Clashes Erupt Between Police and Protestors Over George Floyd Death." *The New York Times*, The New York Times, 30 May 2020, https://nyti.ms/3diIamn.

14 Ibid.

15 Sprunt, Barbara. "The History Behind 'When The Looting Starts, The Shooting Starts'." *NPR*, NPR, 29 May 2020, www.npr.org/2020/05/29/864818368/the-history-behind-when-the-looting-starts-the-shooting-starts.

16 Ibid.

17 Collins, Kaitlan, and Noah Gray. "Trump Briefly Taken to Underground Bunker during Friday's White House Protests." *CNN*, Cable News Network, 1 June 2020, www.cnn.com/2020/05/31/politics/trump-underground-bunker-white-house-protests/index.html.

18 Rogers, Katie, et al. "As Trump Calls Protesters 'Terrorists,' Tear Gas Clears a Path for His Walk to a Church." *The New York Times*, The New York Times, 1 June 2020, https://nyti.ms/2XRgoqE.

19 Ibid.

20 Ibid.

21 Ibid.

22 Waller, John. "Here's What Charlie Baker Said after Boston's George Floyd Protests Turned Violent." *Boston.com*, The Boston Globe, 1 June 2020, www.boston.com/news/local-news/2020/06/01/charlie-baker-boston-george-floyd-protests-violence.

23 386 U.S. 547 (1967).

24 Harlow v. Fitzgerald, 457 U.S. 800, 102 S. Ct. 2727 (1982)

25 136 S.Ct. 305, 316 (2015) (Sotomayor, J., dissenting).

26 929 F.3d 1304 (2019).

27 931 F.3d 978 (2019).

28 George, Alice. "The 1968 Kerner Commission Got It Right, But Nobody Listened." *Smithsonian.com*, Smithsonian Institution, 1 Mar. 2018, www.smithsonianmag.com/smithsonian-institution/1968-kerner-commission-got-it-right-nobody-listened-180968318/.

29 Buchanan, Larry, et al. "Black Lives Matter May Be the Largest Movement in U.S. History." *The New York Times*, The New York Times, 3 July 2020, https://www.nytimes.com/interactive/2020/07/03/us/george-floyd-protests-crowd-size.html?action=click&module=RelatedLinks&pgtype=Article.
30 Ibid.
31 Ibid.
32 Ibid.
33 Ibid.
34 Ibid.
35 Kristof, Nicholas. "We Interrupt This Gloom to Offer . . . Hope." *The New York Times*, The New York Times, 16 July 2020, https://www.nytimes.com/2020/07/16/opinion/sunday/coronavirus-blm-america-hope.html?action=click&module=Opinion&pgtype=Homepage.
36 Goldberg, Michelle. "America Is a Tinderbox." *The New York Times*, The New York Times, 29 May 2020, www.nytimes.com/2020/05/29/opinion/george-floyd-protests-minneapolis.html.
37 Ibid.
38 Ibid.
39 Meyer, Robinson. "The Protests Will Spread the Coronavirus." *The Atlantic*, Atlantic Media Company, 1 June 2020, www.theatlantic.com/health/archive/2020/06/protests-pandemic/612460/.
40 Obama, Barack. "How to Make This Moment the Turning Point for Real Change." *Medium*, Medium, 1 June 2020, medium.com/@BarackObama/how-to-make-this-moment-the-turning-point-for-real-change-9fa209806067.
41 Ibid.
42 Smith, Kyle. "No, Martin Luther King Was Not Pro-Riot." *National Review*, National Review, 2 June 2020, www.nationalreview.com/2020/06/no-martin-luther-king-was-not-pro-riot/.
43 Ibid.
44 Buchanan, Larry, et al. "Black Lives Matter May Be the Largest Movement in U.S. History." *The New York Times*, The New York Times, 3 July 2020, https://www.nytimes.com/interactive/2020/07/03/us/george-floyd-protests-crowd-size.html?action=click&module=RelatedLinks&pgtype=Article.

CHAPTER 36

1 Stracqualursi, Veronica and Enten, Harry. "Trump Campaign Demands CNN Apologize for Poll That Shows Biden Leading." *CNN*, Cable News Network, 10 June 2020, www.cnn.com/2020/06/10/politics/trump-campaign-cnn-poll/index.html.
2 Ibid.
3 Dawsey, Josh. "Trump Asked China's Xi to Help Him Win Reelection, According to Bolton Book." *The Washington Post*, WP Company, 18 June 2020, www.washingtonpost.com/politics/trump-asked-chinas-xi-to-help-him-win-reelection-according-to-bolton-book/2020/06/17/d4ea601c-ad7a-11ea-868b-93d63cd833b2_story.html.
4 Taylor, Derrick Bryson. "So You Want to Learn About Juneteenth?" *The New York Times*, The New York Times, 19 June 2020, www.nytimes.com/article/juneteenth-day-celebration.html.
5 Ibid.
6 Reports, From Staff. "Pickup Rolls through Protesters Gathered on Interstate 244; State Troopers Questioning Driver." *Tulsa World*, 1 June 2020, tulsaworld.com/news/local/pickup-rolls-through-

protesters-gathered-on-interstate-244-state-troopers-questioning-driver/article_f6703c70-2c6d-5455-85cb-ea41373fc7e8.html.

7   Waldman, Paul. "Opinion | The Whole World Is Watching America's Failure." *The Washington Post*, WP Company, 19 June 2020, www.washingtonpost.com/opinions/2020/06/19/whole-world-is-watching-americas-failure/.

8   Madrigal, Alexis C. "How to Misinform Yourself About the Coronavirus." *The Atlantic*, Atlantic Media Company, 6 Mar. 2020, www.theatlantic.com/technology/archive/2020/01/china-coronavirus-twitter/605644/.

9   Brown, DeNeen L., and Bret J. Schulte. "Tense Mood Grips Tulsa as Trump Fans and Protesters Gather Ahead of Campaign Rally." *The Washington Post*, WP Company, 19 June 2020, www.washingtonpost.com/politics/tulsa-imposes-curfew-ahead-of-trump-rally-to-prevent-violent-protesting/2020/06/19/56d31058-b21f-11ea-8f56-63f38c990077_story.html.

10 Egan, Lauren. "Outside Trump's Tulsa Rally Site, Few Face Masks and No Social Distancing." *NBCNews.com*, NBCUniversal News Group, 20 June 2020, www.nbcnews.com/politics/donald-trump/outside-trump-s-tulsa-rally-few-face-masks-no-social-n1231610.

11 Ibid.

12 Ibid.

13 Ibid.

14 Ibid.

15 Ibid.

16 Shear, Michael D., et al. "Trump Rally Fizzles as Attendance Falls Short of Campaign's Expectations." *The New York Times*, The New York Times, 20 June 2020, www.nytimes.com/2020/06/20/us/politics/tulsa-trump-rally.html.

17 Williams, Pete and Gregorian, Dareh. "Oklahoma Supreme Court Denies Legal Challenge to Trump Rally." *NBCNews.com*, NBCUniversal News Group, 19 June 2020, www.nbcnews.com/politics/2020-election/oklahoma-supreme-court-denies-legal-challenge-trump-rally-n1231564.

18 Musto, Julia. "Oklahoma Gov on Trump Rally, Reopening during COVID-19: 'We Are Going to Be Very Safe'." *Fox News*, FOX News Network, 19 June 2020, www.foxnews.com/media/ok-gov-on-tulsa-trump-rally-reopening-during-covid-19-pandemic.

19 Parker, Mario and Egkolfopoulou, Misyrlena. "Trump Spokeswoman McEnany Says She Won't Wear Mask at Rally." *Bloomberg.com*, Bloomberg, 19 June 2020, www.bloomberg.com/news/articles/2020-06-19/trump-spokeswoman-mcenany-says-she-won-t-wear-mask-at-rally.

20 Brown, DeNeen L. "Black Leaders in Tulsa Rush to Cover up Black Wall Street Memorials before Planned Tour by Pence." *The Washington Post*, WP Company, 21 June 2020, www.washingtonpost.com/politics/2020/06/20/black-leaders-tulsa-rush-cover-up-black-wall-street-memorials-before-planned-tour-by-pence/.

21 Itkowitz, Colby and Weigel, David. "After Campaign Boasting, a Smaller-than-Expected Crowd Shows up for Trump's Tulsa Rally." *The Washington Post*, WP Company, 21 June 2020, www.washingtonpost.com/politics/after-days-of-camapaign-bombast-a-smaller-than-expected-crowd-shows-up-for-trumps-tulsa-rally/2020/06/20/5b2652de-b353-11ea-8758-bfd1d045525a_story.html.

22 Macaya, Melissa. "Trump Criticizes Removal of Confederate Monuments." *CNN*, Cable News Network, 21 June 2020, www.cnn.com/politics/live-news/trump-rally-tulsa-oklahoma/h_6775cd-83fe672059d304a5c21e23cbdd.

23 Lozano, Alicia Victoria. "Trump Tells Tulsa Crowd He Wanted to 'Slow down' COVID-19 Testing; White House Says He Was Joking." *NBCNews.com*, NBCUniversal News Group, 22 June 2020, www.nbcnews.com/politics/2020-election/trump-tells-tulsa-crowd-he-wanted-slow-down-covid-19-n1231658.

24 Klemko, Robert and Hernández, Arelis. "Trump Gives Grievance-Filled Speech to Unfilled Arena as Protests Stay Mostly Peaceful." *The Washington Post*, WP Company, 21 June 2020, www.washingtonpost.com/politics/2020/06/20/tulsa-trump-rally/.

25 Ibid.

26 Dowd, Maureen. "Double, Double, Trump's Toil, Our Trouble." *The New York Times*, The New York Times, 1 Aug. 2020, www.nytimes.com/2020/08/01/opinion/sunday/trump-coronavirus-herman-cain.html.

27 Ibid.

28 Breuninger, Kevin Breuninger. "Former GOP Presidential Candidate Herman Cain Hospitalized with Covid-19." *CNBC*, CNBC, 2 July 2020, www.cnbc.com/2020/07/02/herman-cain-hospitalized-with-covid-19.html.

29 O'Sullivan, Donne. "TikTok Users Troll the Trump Campaign over Tulsa rally21." *TikTok Users Troll the Trump Campaign over Tulsa Rally*, 21 June 2020, www.msn.com/en-us/news/politics/tiktok-users-troll-the-trump-cam-paign-over-tulsa-rally/ar-BB15N5ic.

30 Ibid.

31 Allyn, Bobby. "Microsoft In Talks To Buy TikTok As Trump Threatens A Ban." *NPR*, NPR, 31 July 2020, www.npr.org/2020/07/31/897752390/microsoft-in-talks-to-buy-teen-fav-tiktok-as-trump-ramps-up-pressure.

CHAPTER 37

1 Belvedere, Matt. "Trump Says He Trusts China's Xi on Coronavirus and the US Has It 'Totally under Control.'" *CNBC*, CNBC, 22 Jan. 2020, www.cnbc.com/2020/01/22/trump-on-coronavirus-from-china-we-have-it-totally-under-control.html.

2 Lahut, Jake. "Jared Kushner Said the US Would Be 'Really Rocking Again' by July. 7 States Are Shutting Back down, and New COVID-19 Cases Have Set Records 6 Times in July's First 10 Days." *Business Insider*, Business Insider, 10 July 2020, www.businessinsider.com/kusher-rocking-again-by-july-quote-coronavirus-states-reopening-2020-7.

3 Rupar, Aaron. "Trump's Dangerous 'LIBERATE' Tweets Represent the Views of a Small Minority." *Vox*, Vox, 17 Apr. 2020, www.vox.com/2020/4/17/21225134/trump-liberate-tweets-minnesota-virginia-michigan-coronavirus-fox-news.

4 Smith, Allan. "Trump Backs down after Cuomo, Other Governors Unite on Coronavirus Response." *NBCNews.com*, NBCUniversal News Group, 15 Apr. 2020, www.nbcnews.com/politics/donald-trump/trump-backs-down-after-cuomo-governors-unite-coronavirusk-response-n11183471.

5 Bellware, Kim. "U.S. Sets Record for New Coronavirus Cases, Surpassing 55,000." *The Washington Post*, WP Company, 3 July 2020, www.washingtonpost.com/nation/2020/07/02/coronavirus-live-updates-us/.

6 Stolberg, Sheryl Gay and Weiland, Noah. "Fauci Says U.S. Could Reach 100,000 Virus Cases a Day as Warnings Grow Darker." *The New York Times*, The New York Times, 13 July 2020, https://nyti.ms/2AjhRhJ.

7. Schladebeck, Jessica. "Dr. Fauci Says Coronavirus Surge 'Way beyond Worst Spikes We've Seen' as U.S. Sets New Single-Day High." *Nydailynews.com*, New York Daily News, 2 July 2020, www.nydailynews.com/coronavirus/ny-coronavirus-united-states-new-record-50k-cases-24-hours-20200702-chqjewknonbdhbsfav7aodbyt4-story.html.
8. Lee, Carol E., et al. "'We Need to Live with It': White House Readies New Message for the Nation on Coronavirus." *NBCNews.com*, NBCUniversal News Group, 6 July 2020, www.nbcnews.com/politics/politics-news/we-need-live-it-white-house-readies-new-message-nation-n1232884.
9. "U.S. Coronavirus Cases Soar as 18 States Set Single-Day Records This Week." *The New York Times*, The New York Times, 25 July 2020, https://nyti.ms/2BzKWpO.
10. Lee, Carol E., et al. "'We Need to Live with It': White House Readies New Message for the Nation on Coronavirus." *NBCNews.com*, NBCUniversal News Group, 6 July 2020, www.nbcnews.com/politics/politics-news/we-need-live-it-white-house-readies-new-message-nation-n1232884.
11. Karni, Annie. "Trump Uses Mount Rushmore Speech to Deliver Divisive Culture War Message." *The New York Times*, The New York Times, 3 July 2020, www.nytimes.com/2020/07/03/us/politics/trump-coronavirus-mount-rushmore.html.
12. "Remarks by President Trump on the Jobs Numbers Report." *The White House*, The United States Government, 2020, https://www.whitehouse.gov/briefings-statements/remarks-president-trump-jobs-numbers-report-2/.
13. Birenbaum, Gabby. "Trump Administration Extends Support for Texas COVID-19 Testing Sites." *TheHill*, The Hill, 13 July 2020, thehill.com/homenews/state-watch/507049-trump-administration-extends-support-for-texas-covid-19-testing-sites.
14. Samuels, Brett. "Arizona Asks for 500 Additional Medical Personnel amid Spike in Virus Cases." *TheHill*, The Hill, 1 July 2020, thehill.com/homenews/state-watch/505517-arizona-asks-for-500-additional-medical-personnel-amid-spike-in-virus.
15. "Trump Must Respect Sovereignty When He Visits Mt. Rushmore on July 3." *Native American Rights Fund*, 2 July 2020, www.narf.org/south-dakota-tribes-covid/.
16. Groves, Stephen, and Associated Press. "Trump Pushes Racial Division, Flouts Virus Rules at Rushmore." *WSLS*, WSLS 10, 4 July 2020, www.wsls.com/news/politics/2020/07/03/trumps-rushmore-trip-draws-real-and-figurative-fireworks/.
17. Karni, Annie. "Trump Uses Mount Rushmore Speech to Deliver Divisive Culture War Message." *The New York Times*, The New York Times, 7 July 2020, https://nyti.ms/2ZxySNL.
18. "Remarks by President Trump at South Dakota's 2020 Mount Rushmore Fireworks Celebration." *The White House*, The United States Government, 2020, www.whitehouse.gov/briefings-statements/remarks-president-trump-south-dakotas-2020-mount-rushmore-fireworks-celebration-keystone-south-dakota/.
19. Karni, Annie. "Trump Uses Mount Rushmore Speech to Deliver Divisive Culture War Message." *The New York Times*, The New York Times, 7 July 2020, https://nyti.ms/2ZxySNL.
20. "Remarks by President Trump at the 2020 Salute to America." *The White House*, The United States Government, 2020, www.whitehouse.gov/briefings-statements/remarks-president-trump-2020-salute-america/.
21. Dowdy, David, and D'Souza, Gypsyamber. "Early Herd Immunity against COVID-19: A Dangerous Misconception." *Johns Hopkins Coronavirus Resource Center*, Johns Hopkins University, 2020, coronavirus.jhu.edu/from-our-experts/early-herd-immunity-against-covid-19-a-dangerous-misconception.
22. "Donald Trump Blames China's 'Secrecy, Deception and Cover-up' for COVID-19, Says Country Must Be Held Accountable–World News , Firstpost." *Firstpost*, 6 July 2020, www.firstpost.com/

world/donald-trump-blames-chinas-secrecy-deception-and-cover-up-for-covid-19-says-country-must-be-held-accountable-8561271.html.

CHAPTER 38

1. Goldstein, Dana. "Research Shows Students Falling Months Behind During Virus Disruptions." *The New York Times*, The New York Times, 5 June 2020, www.nytimes.com/2020/06/05/us/coronavirus-education-lost-learning.html.
2. Ibid.
3. Ibid.
4. Ibid.
5. Ibid.
6. Adams-Heard, Rachel, et al. "Trump Insists Schools Must Open, but Teachers Aren't so Sure." *StamfordAdvocate*, Washington Post, 23 July 2020, www.stamfordadvocate.com/news/article/Trump-insists-schools-must-open-but-teachers-15391420.php.
7. Ibid.
8. Stein, Jeff, and Erica Werner. "McConnell Calls for Five-Year Lawsuit Shield for Businesses as Part of next Coronavirus Bill." *The Washington Post*, WP Company, 6 July 2020, www.washingtonpost.com/us-policy/2020/07/06/congress-departed-two-week-recess-without-addressing-coronavirus-spikes-economic-strains/.
9. Burke, Michael. "Schools in Los Angeles, San Diego Won't Reopen for in-Person Learning next Month." *EdSource*, EdSource, 14 July 2020, edsource.org/2020/schools-in-los-angeles-san-diego-wont-reopen-for-in-person-learning-next-month/635924.
10. Goldstein, Dana. "Research Shows Students Falling Months Behind During Virus Disruptions." *The New York Times*, The New York Times, 5 June 2020, www.nytimes.com/2020/06/05/us/coronavirus-education-lost-learning.html.
11. Ibid.
12. Baker, Peter, and Erica L. Green. "Trump Leans on Schools to Reopen as Virus Continues Its Spread." *The New York Times*, The New York Times, 7 July 2020, www.nytimes.com/2020/07/07/us/politics/trump-schools-coronavirus.html.
13. Diallo, Ayshatu. "Trump Insists That Schools Open, But Teachers Aren't So Sure." *BloombergQuint*, Bloomberg Quint, 8 July 2020, www.bloombergquint.com/politics/trump-insists-schools-must-open-but-teachers-aren-t-so-sure.
14. Adams-Heard, Rachel, et al. "Trump Insists Schools Must Open, but Teachers Aren't so Sure." *StamfordAdvocate*, Washington Post, 23 July 2020, www.stamfordadvocate.com/news/article/Trump-insists-schools-must-open-but-teachers-15391420.php.
15. Ibid.
16. Holmes, Kristen. "CDC Director Says No Revised School Guidelines despite Trump's Push." *CNN*, Cable News Network, 9 July 2020, www.cnn.com/2020/07/09/politics/cdc-guidelines-school-reopenings/index.html.
17. Ibid.
18. Ibid.
19. "73,400 New Coronavirus Cases in U.S., Nearing Single-Day Record." *The New York Times*, The New York Times, 24 July 2020, https://nyti.ms/390aGln.

20 Ibid.

21 Ibid.

22 Mandavilli, Apoorva. "Older Children Spread the Coronavirus Just as Much as Adults Large Study Finds." *The New York times*, The New York Times, 18 July 2020, https://nyti.ms/3jpd7cb.

23 73,400 New Coronavirus Cases in U.S., Nearing Single-Day Record." *The New York Times*, The New York Times, 24 July 2020, https://nyti.ms/390aGln.

24 Bellagante, Ginia. "Schools Bear Earlier Plagues With Outdoor Classes. We Should, Too." *The New York Times*, The New York Times, 17 July 2020, https://nyti.ms/3haaZ64.

25 Ibid.

26 Ibid.

27 Ibid.

28 Ibid.

29 Stank, Kevin. "New York City Public Schools Won't Fully Reopen for Its 1.1 Million Students This Fall, Mayor De Blasio Says." *CNBC*, CNBC, 8 July 2020, www.cnbc.com/2020/07/08/coronavirus-new-york-city-public-schools-wont-fully-reopen-for-its-1point1-million-students-this-fall-mayor-de-blasio-says.html.

30 Bellagante, Ginia. "Schools Bear Earlier Plagues With Outdoor Classes. We Should, Too." *The New York Times*, The New York Times, 17 July 2020, https://nyti.ms/3haaZ64.

31 Ibid.

32 Ibid.

33 Pearson, Catherine. "America's Pediatricians Say Schools Should Reopen This Fall." *HuffPost*, HuffPost, 30 June 2020, www.huffpost.com/entry/americas-pediatricians-say-schools-should-reopen-this-fall_l_5efb5931c5b6ca9709157324.

34 Ibid.

35 Ibid.

36 Sparks, Sarah D. "Nation's Pediatricians: Get Kids Back in Class This Fall." *Education Week*, 29 June 2020, blogs.edweek.org/edweek/inside-school-research/2020/06/nations_pediatricians_mitigate.html.

37 Pearson, Catherine. "America's Pediatricians Say Schools Should Reopen This Fall." *HuffPost*, HuffPost, 30 June 2020, www.huffpost.com/entry/americas-pediatricians-say-schools-should-reopen-this-fall_l_5efb5931c5b6ca9709157324.

38 Strauss, Valerie. "Analysis | Trump Administration Cites the American Academy of Pediatrics to Make Its Case for School Reopening. Here's What the AAP Really Said." *The Washington Post*, WP Company, 13 July 2020, www.washingtonpost.com/education/2020/07/13/trump-administration-cites-american-academy-pediatrics-make-its-case-school-reopening-heres-what-aap-really-said/.

39 "Pediatricians, Educators and Superintendents Urge a Safe Return to School This Fall." *American Academy of Pediatrics*, 2020, services.aap.org/en/news-room/news-releases/aap/2020/pediatricians-educators-and-superintendents-urge-a-safe-return-to-school-this-fall/.

40 Ibid.

41 Ibid.

42 Baker, Peter, et. al. "Trump Threatens to Cut Funding if Schools Do Not Fully Reopen." *The New York Times*, The New York Times, 8 July 2020, https://nyti.ms/2W1wo11.

43 Goldstein, Dana and Shapiro, Eliza. "Many Students Will Be in Classrooms Only Part of the Week This Fall." *The New York Times*, The New York Times, 26 June 2020, https://nyti.ms/2NxYQLp.

44. Britt, Robert Roy. "What It Would Take to Safely Reopen Schools." *Medium*, GEN, 6 July 2020, gen.medium.com/huge-risks-loom-whether-schools-reopen-or-not-41fe7f25f40f.
45. Calarco, Jessica. "What Is Betsy DeVos Thinking?" *The New York Times*, The New York Times, 15 July 2020, https://nyti.ms/3fv703F.
46. Ibid.
47. Hartocollis, Anemona. "Colleges Plan to Reopen Campuses, But For Just Some Students at a Time." *The New York Times*, The New York Times, 6 July 2020, https://nyti.ms/38xTpFN.
48. Ibid.
49. Ibid.

CHAPTER 39

1. Feuer, Alan, et al. "N.Y.'s Legal Limbo: Pandemic Creates Backlog of 39,200 Criminal Cases." *The New York Times*, The New York Times, 22 June 2020, https://nyti.ms/3140T1K.
2. Williams, P. "Supreme court makes history with oral arguments by phone. But its business as usual for justices." *NBC News*, 4 May 2020, https://www.nbcnews.com/politics/supreme-court/supreme-court-makes-history-oral-arguments-phone-it-s-business-n1199446.
3. Ibid.
4. Ibid.
5. De Vogue, A. & Stracqualursi, V. "Ruth Bader Ginsburg participate in Supreme Court arguments from hospital." *CNN*, 6 May 2020, https://www.cnn.com/2020/05/06/politics/ruth-bader-ginsburg-supreme-court-coronavirus/index.html/.
6. Liptak, Adam. "Supreme Court Hints at Split Decision in Two Cases on Obtaining Trump's Financial Records." *The New York Times*, The New York Times, 12 May 2020, https://nyti.ms/2Ws5UOV.
7. Ibid.
8. *See* Trump v. Mazars USA, LLP, 591 U.S. ___ (2020) (slip op.); Trump v. Vance, 591 U.S. ___ (2020) (slip op.).
9. Ibid.
10. Trump v. Vance, 591 U.S. ___ (2020) (slip op. at 1).
11. Ibid./ *see also* Totenberg, Nina. "Supreme Court Says Trump Not 'Immune' From Records Release, But Hedges On House Case." *NPR*, NPR, 9 July 2020, www.npr.org/2020/07/09/884447882/supreme-court-says-trump-not-immune-from-records-release-pushes-back-on-congress.
12. Totenberg, Nina. "Supreme Court Says Trump Not 'Immune' From Records Release, But Hedges On House Case." *NPR*, NPR, 9 July 2020, www.npr.org/2020/07/09/884447882/supreme-court-says-trump-not-immune-from-records-release-pushes-back-on-congress.
13. Trump v. Vance, 591 U.S. ___ (2020) (slip op. at 22).
14. Second Amended Complaint, Trump v. Vance, No. 1:19-cv-08694-VM (S.D.N.Y. July 27, 2020).
15. *See* United States v. Nixon, 418 U.S. 683 (1974).
16. *See* Clinton v. Jones, 520 U.S. 681 (1997).
17. Ibid.
18. Trump v. Mazars USA, LLP, 591 U.S. ___ (slip op. at 4).
19. Ibid.
20. Ibid.

21. Rashbaum, William K. and Weiser, Benjamin. "D.A. Is Investigating Trump and His Company Over Fraud, Filing Suggests." *The New York Times*, The New York Times, 3 Aug. 2020, https://nyti.ms/3k4sBlX.
22. Ibid.
23. U.S. Const. amend. VI.
24. *See* Klopfer v. North Carolina, 386 U.S. 213, 226 (1967) (Identifying right to speedy trial as fundamental liberty applicable to states through Due Process Clause of the Fourteenth Amendment).
25. Feuer, Alan, et al. "N.Y.'s Legal Limbo: Pandemic Creates Backlog of 39,200 Criminal Cases." *The New York Times*, The New York Times, 22 June 2020, https://nyti.ms/3I40T1K.
26. Ibid.
27. Ibid.
28. Ibid.
29. Ibid.
30. Ibid.
31. Ibid.
32. Ibid.
33. Ibid.
34. Dewan, Shaila. "Jurors, Please Remove Your Masks: Courtrooms Confront the Pandemic." *The New York Times*, The New York Times, 10 June 2020, https://nyti.ms/37ih7W1.
35. Ibid.
36. Ibid.
37. Ibid.
38. Ibid.
39. Ibid.
40. Ibid.
41. Ibid.

CHAPTER 40

1. Zarroli, Jim, and Avie Schneider. "3.3 Million File Unemployment Claims, Shattering Records." *NPR*, NPR, 26 Mar. 2020, www.npr.org/2020/03/26/821580191/unemployment-claims-expected-to-shatter-records.
2. Ibid.
3. Ibid.
4. "'Jaw-Dropping' Fraud Reported as Jobless Claims Reach 38.6 Million." *The New York Times*, The New York Times, 21 May 2020, https://nyti.ms/3cU7leH.
5. LaBrecque, Leon. "The CARES Act Has Passed: Here Are The Highlights." *Forbes*, Forbes Magazine, 29 Mar. 2020, www.forbes.com/sites/leonlabrecque/2020/03/29/the-cares-act-has-passed-here-are-the-highlights/.
6. Ibid.
7. Taibbi, Matt. "How Wall Street Is Using the Bailout to Stage a Revolution." *Rolling Stone*, Rolling Stone, 25 June 2018, www.rollingstone.com/politics/politics-news/how-wall-street-is-using-the-bailout-to-stage-a-revolution-177251/.

8. Emergency Economic Stabilization Act of 2008, Pub. L. No. 110-343, 122 Stat. 3765.
9. Judge, Kathryn. "The Truth About The COVID-19 Bailouts." *Forbes*, Forbes Magazine, 15 Apr. 2020, www.forbes.com/sites/kathrynjudge/2020/04/15/the-covid-19-bailouts/.
10. Ibid.
11. Werner, Erica. "As White House Pushes Firms to Reopen, New Report Says Much of Bailout Stimulus Money Remains Unspent." *The Washington Post*, WP Company, 18 May 2020, www.washingtonpost.com/us-policy/2020/05/18/treasury-coronavirus-bailout-fund-cares-act/.
12. Ibid.
13. Ibid.
14. Ibid.
15. Ibid.
16. "TRANSCRIPT: Warren Takes Questions on Coronavirus Bailout and Stimulus Negotiations: U.S. Senator Elizabeth Warren of Massachusetts." *TRANSCRIPT: Warren Takes Questions on Coronavirus Bailout and Stimulus Negotiations | U.S. Senator Elizabeth Warren of Massachusetts*, 22 Mar. 2020, www.warren.senate.gov/newsroom/press-releases/transcript-warren-takes-questions-on-coronavirus-bailout-and-stimulus-negotiations.
17. Bresnahan, John, and Marianne LeVine. "Dems Seize on 'Slush Fund' to Oppose Republican Rescue Package." *POLITICO*, POLITICO, 23 Mar. 2020, www.politico.com/news/2020/03/23/democrats-slush-fund-republican-rescue-package-143565.
18. Drucker, Jesse. "The Tax-Break Bonanza Inside the Economic Rescue Package." *The New York Times*, The New York Times, 24 Apr. 2020, https://nyti.ms/2VzfL4X.
19. Ibid.
20. Ibid.
21. O'Connell, Jonathan. "AutoNation, a Retailer Worth Billions, Says It Received Nearly $80 Million in SBA Funds." *The Washington Post*, WP Company, 24 Apr. 2020, www.washingtonpost.com/business/2020/04/24/autonation-an-auto-retailer-worth-billions-received-nearly-95-million-sba-funds/.
22. "The CARES Act's Changes to Section 163(j): Partnership, International, and US State Tax Implications." *McDermott Will & Emery*, 10 Apr. 2020, www.mwe.com/insights/cares-acts-changes-section-163j-partnership-international-us-state-tax-implications/.
23. "The Corrupt Tax Provision in the CARES Act: Rep. Doggett & Sen. Whitehouse: U.S. Senator Sheldon Whitehouse of Rhode Island." *Home*, 23 Apr. 2020, www.whitehouse.senate.gov/news/op-eds/the-corrupt-tax-provision-in-the-cares-act-rep-doggett-and-sen-whitehouse.
24. Osborne, James. "Oil Firms See Relief from Stimulus Tax Provision." *HoustonChronicle.com*, Houston Chronicle, 20 May 2020, www.houstonchronicle.com/business/energy/article/Oil-firms-see-relief-from-stimulus-tax-provision-15286484.php.
25. Frank, Robert. "American Billionaires Got $434 Billion Richer during the Pandemic." *CNBC*, CNBC, 21 May 2020, www.cnbc.com/2020/05/21/american-billionaires-got-434-billion-richer-during-the-pandemic.html.
26. Bauer, Lauren. "The COVID-19 Crisis Has Already Left Too Many Children Hungry in America." *Brookings*, Brookings, 12 May 2020, www.brookings.edu/blog/up-front/2020/05/06/the-covid-19-crisis-has-already-left-too-many-children-hungry-in-america/.
27. Claxton, Gary, et al. "Eligibility for ACA Health Coverage Following Job Loss." *KFF*, 14 May 2020, www.kff.org/coronavirus-covid-19/issue-brief/eligibility-for-aca-health-coverage-following-job-loss/.

28. Clifford, Tyler. "Jim Cramer: The Pandemic Led to 'One of the Greatest Wealth Transfers in History'." *CNBC*, CNBC, 4 June 2020, www.cnbc.com/2020/06/04/cramer-the-pandemic-led-to-a-great-wealth-transfer.html?__twitter_impression=true.

29. Wu, Tim. "Opinion | How to Avoid a 'Rich Man's Recovery'." *The New York Times*, The New York Times, 18 July 2020, www.nytimes.com/2020/06/18/opinion/covid-economic-recovery-inequality.html?action=click.

30. Iacurci, Greg. "4 Ways the Coronavirus Law Pays Small Businesses to Keep Workers." *CNBC*, CNBC, 1 Apr. 2020, www.cnbc.com/2020/03/31/the-coronavirus-relief-law-gives-businesses-a-motive-to-keep-workers.html.

31. Health and Economic Recovery Omnibus Emergency Solutions Act, H.R. 6800, 116th Cong. (2020).

32. "Health and Economic Recovery Omnibus Emergency Solutions Act (Heroes Act)." *The Washington Post*, WP Company, 2020, www.washingtonpost.com/context/health-and-economic-recovery-omnibus-emergency-solutions-act-heros-act/5dd94d3e-6e59-431d-b757-c36a7ae0a2f5/?itid=lk_inline_manual_6.

33. Ibid.

34. "Judge Blocks Green Card Wealth Tests, Citing Pandemic Hardships." *The New York Times*, The New York Times, 4 Aug. 2020, https://www.nytimes.com/2020/07/29/world/coronavirus-covid-19.html?action=click&module=Top%20Stories&pgtype=Homepage#link-54ae3ccf.

35. Stein, Jeff, and Erica Werner. "Economic Relief Talks Ramp up as GOP Releases Bill; Democrats, White House Officials Meet." *The Washington Post*, WP Company, 28 July 2020, www.washingtonpost.com/us-policy/2020/07/27/senate-stimulus-coronavirus/.

36. "Opinion: Mitch McConnell Could Rescue Millions. What Is He Waiting For?" *The New York Times*, The New York Times, 30 July 2020, https://nyti.ms/30e0qJz.

37. Ibid.

38. Ibid.

39. Dionne, E.J. "Opinion | This Republican Implosion Has Been a Long Time Coming." *The Washington Post*, WP Company, 29 July 2020, www.washingtonpost.com/opinions/the-gop-has-earned-itself-a-multi-year-expulsion-from-politics/2020/07/29/724d13ac-d1d1-11ea-8d32-1ebf4e9d8e0d_story.html.

40. Thehill.com/homenews/senate/509459-gop...

41. Dionne, E.J. "Opinion | This Republican Implosion Has Been a Long Time Coming." *The Washington Post*, WP Company, 29 July 2020, www.washingtonpost.com/opinions/the-gop-has-earned-itself-a-multi-year-expulsion-from-politics/2020/07/29/724d13ac-d1d1-11ea-8d32-1ebf4e9d8e0d_story.html.

42. "U.S. Surpasses 5 Million Cases." *The New York Times*, The New York Times, 8 Aug. 2020, https://nyti.ms/30EIgRt.

43. Holmes, Kristen, et al. "Breaking down the Executive Actions Trump Signed on Coronavirus Relief." *CNN*, Cable News Network, 10 Aug. 2020, edition.cnn.com/2020/08/09/politics/trump-executive-actions-coronavirus-explainer/index.html.

44. News, WINK. "Breaking down the Executive Actions Trump Signed on Coronavirus Relief." *WINK NEWS*, 9 Aug. 2020, www.winknews.com/2020/08/09/breaking-down-the-executive-actions-trump-signed-on-coronavirus-relief/.

CHAPTER 41

1. Banks, Ralph Richard. "An End to the Class vs. Race Debate." *The New York Times*, The New York Times, 21 Mar. 2018, www.nytimes.com/2018/03/21/opinion/class-race-social-mobility.html.
2. Ibid.
3. Van Dam, Andrew. "Analysis | The Unluckiest Generation in U.S. History." *The Washington Post*, WP Company, 5 June 2020, www.washingtonpost.com/business/2020/05/27/millennial-recession-covid/.
4. Ibid
5. United States, Congress, Consumer and Community Research Section of the Federal Reserve Board's Division of Consumer and Community Affairs, et al. *Report on the Economic Well-Being of U.S. Households in 2018*, Board of Governors of The Federal Reserve System, 2019.
6. Van Dam, Andrew. "Analysis | The Unluckiest Generation in U.S. History." *The Washington Post*, WP Company, 5 June 2020, www.washingtonpost.com/business/2020/05/27/millennial-recession-covid/.
7. Ibid.
8. Kelley, Lora. "'I Am the Portrait of Downward Mobility'." *The New York Times*, The New York Times, 17 Apr. 2020, www.nytimes.com/interactive/2020/04/17/opinion/inequality-economy-1980.html.
9. Ibid
10. Ibid
11. Ibid
12. Ibid
13. Ibid
14. Ibid
15. Ibid
16. Ibid
17. Ibid
18. Ibid
19. Ibid
20. Deparle, Jason. "Harder for Americans to Rise From Lower Rungs." *The New York Times*, The New York Times, 5 Jan. 2012, www.nytimes.com/2012/01/05/us/harder-for-americans-to-rise-from-lower-rungs.html.
21. "Understanding Mobility in America." *Center for American Progress*, 27 Mar. 2007, www.americanprogress.org/issues/economy/news/2006/04/26/1917/understanding-mobility-in-america/.
22. Ibid.
23. "'Scandinavian Dream' Is True Fix for America's Income Inequality." *CNNMoney*, Cable News Network, money.cnn.com/2015/06/03/news/economy/stiglitz-income-inequality/index.html.
24. Luthar, Suniya. "The Problem With Rich Kids." *Psychology Today*, Sussex Publishers, 5 Nov. 2013, www.psychologytoday.com/us/articles/201311/the-problem-rich-kids.
25. Rosenfeld, Jake. "Union Decline Lowers Wages of Nonunion Workers: The Overlooked Reason Why Wages Are Stuck and Inequality Is Growing." *Economic Policy Institute*, 30 Aug. 2016, www.epi.org/publication/union-decline-lowers-wages-of-nonunion-workers-the-overlooked-reason-why-wages-are-stuck-and-inequality-is-growing/.
26. Krugman, Paul. "Millionaire For A Day." *The New York Times*, The New York Times, 3 Nov. 2011, krugman.blogs.nytimes.com/2011/11/03/millionaire-for-a-day/.

27. See also: Mitnik, Pablo A., and David B. Grusky. "Pursuing the American Dream: Economic Mobility in the United States.'" *Economicmobility.org*, The Pew Charitable Trust and The Russel Sage Foundation, July 2015.
28. Ibid.
29. Haskins, Ron, et al. "Promoting Economic Mobility by Increasing Postsecondary Education." The Pew Charitable Trusts, May 2009, www.pewtrusts.org/en/research-and-analysis/reports/0001/01/01/promoting-economic-mobility-by-increasing-postsecondary-education.
30. "2009 HHS Poverty Guidelines." ASPE, 23 Nov. 2015, aspe.hhs.gov/2009-hhs-poverty-guidelines.
31. Haskins, Ron, et al. "Promoting Economic Mobility by Increasing Postsecondary Education." *The Pew Charitable Trusts*, May 2009, www.pewtrusts.org/en/research-and-analysis/reports/0001/01/01/promoting-economic-mobility-by-increasing-postsecondary-education.
32. Vedder, Richard. "For Many, A College Degree Is A Bad Investment." *Forbes*, Forbes Magazine, 27 Jan. 2020, www.forbes.com/sites/richardvedder/2020/01/27/for-many-a-college-degree-is-a-bad-investment/.

CHAPTER 42

1. Berman, Russell. "The Night Socialism Went Mainstream." *The Atlantic*, Atlantic Media Company, 13 Feb. 2020, www.theatlantic.com/politics/archive/2020/02/bernie-sanders-wins-new-hampshire/606022/.
2. Goldberg, Michelle. "Opinion: The New Great Depression Is Comping. Will There Be a New New Deal?" *The New York* Times, The New York Times, 2 May 2020, https://nyti.ms/2SrnWhM.
3. Wilkie, Christina. "Pelosi Says Guaranteed Income Could Be 'Worthy of Attention Now' as Coronavirus Stifles Economy." *CNBC*, CNBC, 28 Apr. 2020, www.cnbc.com/2020/04/27/coronavirus-update-universal-basic-income-could-be-worthy-of-attention-pelosi-says.html.
4. Clifford, Cat. "Pope Francis: 'This May Be the Time to Consider a Universal Basic Wage'." *CNBC*, CNBC, 13 Apr. 2020, www.cnbc.com/2020/04/13/pope-francis-it-may-be-the-time-to-consider-a-universal-basic-wage.html.
5. Ibid.
6. Ibid.
7. Goldberg, Michelle. "Opinion: The New Great Depression Is Comping. Will There Be a New New Deal?" *The New York* Times, The New York Times, 2 May 2020, https://nyti.ms/2SrnWhM.
8. Goldberg, Michelle. "Opinion: The New Great Depression Is Comping. Will There Be a New New Deal?" *The New York* Times, The New York Times, 2 May 2020, https://nyti.ms/2SrnWhM.
9. Ibid.
10. Ibid.
11. "Elizabeth Warren and Ro Khanna Unveil Essential Workers Bill of Rights: U.S. Senator Elizabeth Warren of Massachusetts." *And Ro Khanna Unveil Essential Workers Bill of Rights | U.S. Senator Elizabeth Warren of Massachusetts*, 13 Apr. 2020, www.warren.senate.gov/newsroom/press-releases/elizabeth-warren-and-ro-khanna-unveil-essential-workers-bill-of-rights.
12. "Franklin Roosevelt's Re-Nomination Acceptance Speech (1936)." *The American Yawp Reader*, www.americanyawp.com/reader/23-the-great-depression/franklin-roosevelts-re-nomination-acceptance-speech-1936/.
13. "Opinion: The America We Need." *The New York Times*, The New York Times, 9 Apr. 2020, https://nyti.ms/34Xm7OV.

14 Bailey, Peggy. "Housing and Health Partners Can Work Together to Close the Housing Affordability Gap." *Center on Budget and Policy Priorities*, 17 Jan. 2020, www.cbpp.org/research/housing/housing-and-health-partners-can-work-together-to-close-the-housing-affordability.

15 Stelloh, Tim. "Las Vegas Officials Invited Homeless to Parking Lot after Coronavirus Closed Shelter." *NBCNews.com*, NBCUniversal News Group, 31 Mar. 2020, www.nbcnews.com/news/us-news/las-vegas-officials-invited-homeless-parking-lot-after-coronavirus-closed-n1172636.

16 Leonhardt, David and Serkez, Yarna. "Opinion: America Will Struggle After Coronavirus. These Charts Show Why." *The New York Times*, The New York Times, 10 Apr. 2020, https://www.nytimes.com/interactive/2020/04/10/opinion/coronavirus-us-economy-inequality.html.

17 "Covid-19: We Are Not 'All in It Together'-Less Privileged in Society Are Suffering the Brunt of the Damage." *The BMJ*, 1 June 2020, blogs.bmj.com/bmj/2020/05/22/covid-19-we-are-not-all-in-it-together-less-privileged-in-society-are-suffering-the-brunt-of-the-damage/.

18 "The Economic Bill of Rights." *Ushistory.org*, Independence Hall Association, www.ushistory.org/documents/economic_bill_of_rights.htm.

19 *San Antonio Independent School District v. Rodriguez*, 411 U.S. 1 (1973).

20 "History and Culture." *National Parks Service*, U.S. Department of the Interior, www.nps.gov/home/learn/historyculture/index.htm.

CHAPTER 43

1 Aleksander, Irina. "Sweatpants Forever." The New York Times, The New York Times, 6 Aug. 2020, https://www.nytimes.com/interactive/2020/08/06/magazine/fashion-sweatpants.html?action=click&algo=top_con.

2 Smalls, C. Isaiah. "Broward Judge Tells Lawyers to Get out of Bed and Wear a Shirt for Zoom Hearings." *Miamiherald*, Miami Herald, 13 Apr. 2020, www.miamiherald.com/news/local/community/broward/article241976371.html.

3 Ibid.

4 Ibid.

5 Feeley, Jef, and Leonard, Michael. "Simon Countersues Gap Over $107 Million in Lease Payments." *Bloomberg.com*, Bloomberg, 5 Aug. 2020, www.bloomberg.com/news/articles/2020-08-05/simon-countersues-gap-over-107-million-in-lease-payments.

6 Aleksander, Irina. "Sweatpants Forever." *The New York Times*, The New York Times, 6 Aug. 2020, https://www.nytimes.com/interactive/2020/08/06/magazine/fashion-sweatpants.html?action=click&algo=top_con.

7 Ibid.

8 Ibid.

9 Ibid.

10 Ibid.

11 Ibid.

12 Ibid.

13 Ibid.

14 Ibid.

CHAPTER 44

1. Fisher, Helen. "How Coronavirus Is Changing the Dating Game for the Better." *The New York Times*, The New York Times, 7 May 2020, www.nytimes.com/2020/05/07/well/mind/dating-coronavirus-love-relationships.html.
2. Ibid.
3. "Kinsey Institute COVID-19 Research." *Research Impact*, research.impact.iu.edu/coronavirus/kinsey-institute-covid19.html.
4. Wilkins, Tyler. "Researchers Study COVID's Effect on Relationships." *UGA Today*, 22 May 2020, news.uga.edu/research-covid19-effect-on-relationships/.
5. Ibid.
6. Ibid.
7. Ibid.
8. Ibid.
9. Ibid.
10. "Kinsey Institute COVID-19 Research." *Research Impact*, research.impact.iu.edu/coronavirus/kinsey-institute-covid19.html.
11. Harrison, Marissa A., and Susan M. Hughes. "Sex Differences in Romantic Kissing among College Students: An Evolutionary Perspective–Susan M. Hughes, Marissa A. Harrison, Gordon G. Gallup, 2007." *SAGE Journals*, journals.sagepub.com/doi/full/10.1177/147470490700500310.
12. Hassan, Jennifer, and Miriam Berger. "Governments Urge Singles to Find a 'Cuddle Buddy' or 'Support Bubble' during Pandemic." *The Washington Post*, WP Company, 11 June 2020, www.washingtonpost.com/world/2020/06/11/governments-urge-singles-find-cuddle-buddy-or-support-bubble-during-pandemic/.

CHAPTER 45

1. "What World Post-COVID-19? Three Scenarios." *Atlantic Council*, 17 July 2020, www.atlanticcouncil.org/content-series/shaping-post-covid-world-together/what-world-post-covid-19-three-scenarios/.
2. Crawford, Alan. "A New World Order for the Coronavirus Era Is Emerging." *BloombergQuint*, 11 July 2020, www.bloombergquint.com/politics/a-new-world-order-for-the-coronavirus-era-is-emerging.
3. Fink, Sheri and Baker, Mike. "'It's Just Everywhere Already': How Delays in Testing Set Back the U.S. Coronavirus Response." *The New York Times*, The New York Times, 10 Mar. 2020, https://nyti.ms/39SdV3K.
4. Robert Muggah. "5 Facts You Need to Understand the New Global Order." *World Economic Forum*, Jan. 2018, www.weforum.org/agenda/2018/01/five-facts-you-need-to-understand-the-new-global-order/.
5. Amighini, Alessia. *China: Champion of (Which) Globalisation?* Ledizioni, 2018.
6. Singh, Manish. "Alibaba's Singles' Day Sales Top $38 Billion." *TechCrunch*, TechCrunch, 11 Nov. 2019, techcrunch.com/2019/11/11/alibaba-singles-day-record/.
7. "Are You Ready to Go Back to the Office?" *The New York Times*, The New York Times, 21 May 2020, www.nytimes.com/2020/05/21/business/dealbook/office-reopening-coronavirus.html.
8. Reinhart, Carmen M., et al. "This Time Truly Is Different by Carmen M. Reinhart." *Project Syndicate*, 23 Mar. 2020, www.project-syndicate.org/commentary/covid19-crisis-has-no-economic-precedent-by-carmen-reinhart-2020-03.

9   Ibid.
10 Pazzanese, Christina. "Carmen Reinhart Named Chief Economist at the World Bank." *Harvard Gazette*, Harvard Gazette, 20 May 2020, news.harvard.edu/gazette/story/2020/05/carmen-reinhart-named-chief-economist-at-the-world-bank/.
11 Bildt, Carl. "Opinion | The Post-American World Is Now on Full Display." *The Washington Post*, WP Company, 19 May 2020, www.washingtonpost.com/opinions/2020/05/19/post-american-world-is-now-full-display/.
12 "Remarks by President Trump at the White House Business Session with Our Nation's Governors." *The White House*, The United States Government, 2020, www.whitehouse.gov/briefings-statements/remarks-president-trump-white-house-business-session-nations-governors/.

CHAPTER 46

1   "Pope's Easter Urbi Et Orbi Message: 'The Contagion of Hope.'" *Vatican News*, 12 Apr. 2020, www.vaticannews.va/en/pope/news/2020-04/pope-easter-urbi-et-orbi-blessing.html.
2   Ibid
3   Ibid
4   Ibid
5   Berardelli, Jeff. "Italian Priest Dies of Coronavirus after Giving up His Ventilator to Help Others." *CBS News*, CBS Interactive, 25 Mar. 2020, www.cbsnews.com/news/italian-priest-coronavirus-ventilator-don-giuseppe-berardelli/.
6   Buckley, Pat "Mar 2020." *BISHOP PAT BUCKLEY*, Mar. 2020, bishoppatbuckley.blog/2020/03/. See also: "Italian Priest Who Gave up Respirator Dies from Coronavirus." *Catholic Outlook*, 24 Mar. 2020, www.catholicoutlook.org/italian-priest-who-gave-up-respirator-dies-from-coronavirus/.
7   "Coronavirus: At Least 50 Priests Killed by Coronavirus." *BBC News*, BBC, 25 Mar. 2020, www.bbc.com/news/world-europe-52015969.
8   Casey, Nicholas. "The Walls of the Church Couldn't Keep the Trump Era Out." *The New York Times*, The New York Times, 20 June 2020, www.nytimes.com/2020/06/20/us/politics/evangelical-church-trump-alabama.html.
9   Ibid
10 Ibid
11 Ibid.
12 Ibid.
13 Ibid.
14 Ibid
15 "'11 A. M. Sunday Is Our Most Segregated Hour'; In the Light of the Racial Crisis, a Christian Leader Assays 'the Structure and Spirit' of the Nation's Churches, and Asks Some Probing Questions." *The New York Times*, The New York Times, 2 Aug. 1964, www.nytimes.com/1964/08/02/archives/11-a-m-sunday-is-our-most-segregated-hour-in-the-light-of-the.html.
16 Merritt, John W. "The Betrayal: the Hostile Takeover of the Southern Baptist Convention an a Missionary's Fight for Freedom in Christ." *Amazon*, R. Brent and Co., 2005, www.amazon.com/Betrayal-takeover-Southern-Convention-Missionarys/dp/096780616X.
17 "Forming Together." *Cooperative Baptist Fellowship*, cbf.net/.

18 Casey, Nicholas. "The Walls of the Church Couldn't Keep the Trump Era Out." *The New York Times*, The New York Times, 20 June 2020, www.nytimes.com/2020/06/20/us/politics/evangelical-church-trump-alabama.html.

19 Halaschak Zachary. "'Faith Is a Good Thing': Fauci Says Religion Plays 'Important Role' during Coronavirus Pandemic." *Washington Examiner*, 12 Apr. 2020, www.washingtonexaminer.com/news/faith-is-a-good-thing-fauci-says-religion-plays-important-role-during-coronavirus-pandemic.

20 "State of the Union." *CNN*, Cable News Network, 2020, transcripts.cnn.com/TRANSCRIPTS/2004/12/sotu.01.html.

21 Schjonberg, Mary Frances. "Remembering Jonathan Daniels 50 Years after His Martyrdom." *Episcopal News Service*, 13 Aug. 2015, www.episcopalnewsservice.org/2015/08/13/remembering-jonathan-daniels-50-years-after-his-martyrdom/. See Also: Troy, Gil. "Jonathan Daniels: The Forgotten Civil Rights Preacher Killed by a Cop in Alabama." *The Daily Beast*, The Daily Beast Company, 21 Aug. 2016, www.thedailybeast.com/jonathan-daniels-the-forgotten-civil-rights-preacher-killed-by-a-cop-in-alabama.

22 "Responding to Racist Violence." *Episcopal Church*, 4 Aug. 2020, episcopalchurch.org/responding-to-racist-violence.

23 Becker | June 07, Carlin. "Mitt Romney Joins Hundreds of Evangelical Protesters in March to White House." *Washington Examiner*, 7 June 2020, www.washingtonexaminer.com/news/mitt-romney-joins-hundreds-of-evangelical-protesters-in-march-to-white-house.

EPILOGUE

1 Bouie, Jamelle. "Opinion | John Lewis Was the Anti-Trump." *The New York Times*, The New York Times, 31 July 2020, www.nytimes.com/2020/07/31/opinion/john-lewis-trump-election-2020.html?action=click.

2 Leonhardt, David. "It's 2022. What Does Life Look Like?" *The New York Times*, The New York Times, 10 July 2020, www.nytimes.com/2020/07/10/opinion/sunday/coronavirus-economy-two-years.html?action=click.

3 Ibid.

www.ingramcontent.com/pod-product-compliance
Lightning Source LLC
Chambersburg PA
CBHW070516010526
44118CB00012B/1024